PSYCHOLOGY

ADDISON-WESLEY PUBLISHING COMPANY, INC., Reading, Massachusetts • ADDISON-WESLEY (CANADA) LIMITED, Don Mills, Ontario

Wilbert James McKeachie, UNIVERSITY OF MICHIGAN

Charlotte Lackner Doyle, CORNELL UNIVERSITY

PSYCHOLOGY

ADDISON-WESLEY
PUBLISHING COMPANY, INC.
READING, MASSACHUSETTS
Palo Alto • London
NEW YORK • DALLAS • ATLANTA • BARRINGTON, ILLINOIS

ADDISON-WESLEY (CANADA) LIMITED
DON MILLS, ONTARIO

*To the Psychology Department
of the University of Michigan
we gratefully dedicate this book*

preface

In the last decade the field of psychology has made tremendous advances in the integration of its many diverse areas. Motivation, learning, perception, personality, and physiological and social psychology no longer need be unrelated topics in an eclectic approach to human behavior. In this book we hope to bring integrative theoretical thinking in psychology to the beginning student. This does not mean that there is a bias toward behavioristic, gestalt, Freudian, or any other theory; rather we are attempting to present a consistent contemporary formulation.

While we include the standard content, our organization is different from that of most texts. For example, we emphasize "learning," not only in a separate chapter, but throughout the book. New developments in physiological psychology are included in a number of chapters even though they are introduced in Chapter 3. Similarly, the developmental-dynamic approach to personality is not treated in a single section on Freudian psychology, but is treated in a number of chapters. In each chapter relevant materials on individual differences, development, and applications are included. We hope that this uniformity of treatment will contribute to ease of learning.

This book is written with a view to aiding student understanding through consistency. Once a concept is introduced, it will ordinarily be used later. We have tried to clarify concepts which often have several different labels and to be consistent in our vocabulary. The concepts of psychology are complex and their understanding is complicated by the student's previous experiences in describing human behavior in common-sense terms. Where this previous experience can be helpful, we have tried to build upon it; where common-sense notions interfere with learning the psychological approach, we have tried to make the distinction clear.

The book is not abstract or esoteric, but, through selection of concepts, attempts to achieve an integrated simplicity rooted in the concrete experiences of students, and leading to the theoretical thinking of contemporary psychology.

Acknowledgements

Many people helped us in the preparation of this book and we would like to thank all of them. We are especially grateful to Donald G. Marquis, whose ideas were the original impetus for this book.

We would like to acknowledge the help of the many people who read portions of the manuscript and who made valuable suggestions and criticisms. Among these people are: Theodore Newcomb; Justin Aaronfreed, Joseph Adelson, James Allison, John W. Atkinson, David Beardslee, Edward Bordin, Carl Brown, Angus Campbell, Crawford Clark, Clyde Coombs, Richard Cutler, Russell DeValois, Raphael Ezekiel, Shelia Feld, Paul Fitts, Stewart Fliege, P. James Geiwitz, Stephen Glickman, Lewis Goldberg, William Hays, Roger Heyns, Max Hutt, Robert Isaacson, E. Lowell Kelly, Charles Kepner, Samuel Komarita, Leonard Lansky, Marvin Lickey, John Liebeskind, Richard Mann, Robert McCleary, Elton McNeil, David McNeill, Arthur Melton, Warren Norman, Patricia O'Connor, James Olds, Richard Pew, Howard Pollio, Michael Posner, Barbara Cook Pottharst, Milton Rosenburg, C. Robert Schuster, Richard Teevan, Roland Tharp, Edward Walker, Daniel Weintraub, Norman Weissburg, Marian Winterbottom, Martha Sturm White; Abram Amsel, Donald Dulany, Wayne Holtzman, Lloyd Humphreys, Harold Johnson, R. A. Kinchla, A. A. Lumsdaine, Brendan Maher, David Marlowe, Albert Rabin, Alberta Siegel, Sheldon White, Dael Wolfle; James J. Doyle, John Pickering; Claude Buxton, Charles Cofer, John Gustad, Robert MacLeod; L. E. Cole, William Hunt, Robert Leeper, James McConnell, John Milholland, Wilbert Ray. We are grateful to each of them.

Louis Berman was a consultant on graphics; he gave us very creative suggestions for illustrations during the development of the manuscript, and we would like to thank him very much. Eastman Kodak was very helpful to us in planning the color plate section. We appreciate this help.

Our colleagues in the preparation of associated materials also gave us many helpful suggestions on content and organization. We thank Jay Caldwell, Neil Carrier, L. A. Seibert, and Carol Slater for their devotion and help.

We would like to thank the secretaries who typed portions of the manuscript. They include: June Crockett, Barbara Davis, Karen Farr, Miriam Lamb, Sue Maine, Virginia McKeachie, Ann Naymik, Mary Lee Pierce, Wilma Schmadtke, Jan Wasser, Mary Jo Winer, and Shelia Wright. Ruth Surrell and Patricia Yonas helped us in arranging references and illustrations; Rosamond Valentine helped us in putting together the index; Clyde and Harriet Gray were also very helpful. Our thanks to them.

Finally we would like to acknowledge the very special help of James J. Doyle and Virginia McKeachie, whose inspiration and support made this work possible.

Ann Arbor, Michigan   W. J. McK.
Ithaca, New York   C. L. D.
February, 1966

table of contents

Chapter 1   What Is Psychology?   1

How is scientific explanation different from common sense?   3
What does a psychologist observe?   4
How does the psychologist handle "mental processes"?   6
How are theoretical explanations useful to science?   10
How does a psychologist observe behavior?   11
How is psychological knowledge used?   17

PART I   THE BACKGROUND OF BEHAVIOR

Chapter 2   The Cultural Background of Behavior   22

The meaning of culture   24
Roles of men and women in three primitive cultures   24
What aspects of human functioning are affected by culture?   26
How do people learn to behave in accordance with their
culture?   29
From whom does a child learn his culture?   31
What are the sources of variability of behavior within a
society?   33

Chapter 3   The Biological Background of Behavior   44

On what levels can we study the organism?   46
What are the basic structures and functions of the nervous
system?   47
What determines which circuits of the CNS will be active?   57
How is CNS activity modulated by external factors?   60

Color Plates .... opp. 64
Plate 1. Medial aspect of the brain
Plate 2. The autonomic nervous system
Plate 3. The hypothalamic-pituitary system
Plate 4. The circle of hues
Plate 5. Variations in brightness and saturation

Plate 6. The three-dimensional model of color
Plate 7. Additive mixture
Plate 8. Subtractive mixture (1)
Plate 9. Subtractive mixture (2)
Plate 10. A test of color-blindness
Plate 11. Simultaneous contrast
Plate 12. Successive contrast
Plate 13. The Land effect
Plate 14. *Current* by Bridget Riley

Chapter 4 **Heredity and Maturation**   70
What is inherited?   72
How does the genetic blueprint develop into an organism?   74
To what extent is behavior dependent on heredity and
maturation alone?   75
Which stable characteristics of the individual are dependent
on heredity?   85

PART II   THE DETERMINANTS OF BEHAVIOR

Chapter 5 **An Introduction to Learning**   98
How can we study the learning process?   100
What is conditioning?   102
What occurs inside the organism during conditioning?   115
How is conditioning related to learning in general?   128
On what basis are acts selected?   133

Chapter 6 **Perception**   138
The phenomena of perception: Part 1   140
The phenomena of perception: Part 2   171
The dynamics of perception   179
The development of perception   188
Individual differences   193
Practical applications   196

Chapter 7   **Motivation** 204
The phenomena of motivation 208
The dynamics of motivation 236
The development of motives 245
Individual differences 250
Practical applications 254

Chapter 8   **Action: Learning and Performance** 258
The phenomena of action 260
The dynamics of action 266
The development of action 285
Individual differences 293
Practical applications 295

Chapter 9   **Cognition: Memory, Language, and Meaning** 302
PART 1. MEMORY 304
The phenomena of memory 305
The dynamics of memory 308
The development of memory 318
Individual differences 319
Practical applications 321
PART 2. LANGUAGE AND MEANING 324
The phenomena of language 324
The dynamics of language: the analysis of meaning 325
The development of language 328
Individual differences in language 335
Implications 338

Chapter 10   **Cognition: Reasoning, Problem Solving,
Decision Making, and Intelligence** 342
The phenomena of problem solving 344
The dynamics of problem solving 347
Individual differences in problem solving 353

The development of thinking 364
Practical applications 369

Chapter 11   Frustrations and the Mechanisms of Defense 374
What are the sources of frustration? 376
What are the reactions of frustrating situations? 380
The development of reactions to frustrating situations 396
Individual differences 400
Practical applications 402

PART III   THE PERSON

**Chapter 12   The Person: Personality Characteristics
and Their Assessment** 408
How can personality traits be identified? 412
How can personality traits be assessed? 419
How are personality traits used to predict behavior? 439
Can personality traits help us provide a description of a total
personality? 443

Chapter 13   The Development of the Person 448
Early infancy 450
The second year 458
Early childhood 465
Later childhood 468
Adolescence 470
Adulthood 477
Old age 480

Chapter 14   Maladjustment 484
Neuroses 488
Psychomatic disorders 501

Psychoses 505
Conduct disorders 512

Chapter 15 **Interpersonal Relations** 520
Social perception and judgment 522
Motivation and group membership 530
Group action 536
The individual in the group: the problem of leadership 549

Chapter 16 **The Person and Society** 558
What is an attitude? 560
How are attitudes measured? 562
Are the various components of attitudes consistent with one
another? 566
How are attitudes formed? 569
How are attitudes organized? 572
How do attitudes change? 574
What factors contribute to compliance? 587

Appendix I. A short guide to statistics 596
Why do we need statistics? 598
Which descriptive statistics accomplish what objectives? .. 598
How statistics are used to help make inference and decisions 611

Appendix II. Psychology in today's world 616
Man–machine systems: automation 618
Teaching machines and instructional technology 622
Utilization of human resources 624
The psychological effects of drugs 626
Mental health as a social problem 628
Changing patterns of family organization 631

Bibliography 637

Index 673

what is psychology?

chapter 1

HOW IS SCIENTIFIC EXPLANATION DIFFERENT
FROM COMMON SENSE?

WHAT DOES A PSYCHOLOGIST OBSERVE?

HOW DOES THE PSYCHOLOGIST HANDLE
"MENTAL PROCESSES"?

HOW ARE THEORETICAL EXPLANATIONS USEFUL
TO SCIENCE?

HOW DOES A PSYCHOLOGIST OBSERVE BEHAVIOR?

HOW IS PSYCHOLOGICAL KNOWLEDGE USED?

Man has always been challenged by himself. He has continually asked himself such questions as, "Why do I act as I do?" "What do my dreams mean?" "Why are people different from one another?"

Ancient astrologers looked to the sky for answers. To them, the positions of the stars at the moment of birth determined the character of the newborn baby. For example, an infant born under the constellation of the Lion was destined to become strong and lordly like a lion.

Some ancient people looked for predictors of human character in man's outward appearance, his physiognomy. One method related the similarity of appearance between man and animals to similar psychological characteristics. Thus a man who looked like a fox would be sly, and one who resembled a wolf was thought to be a predator.

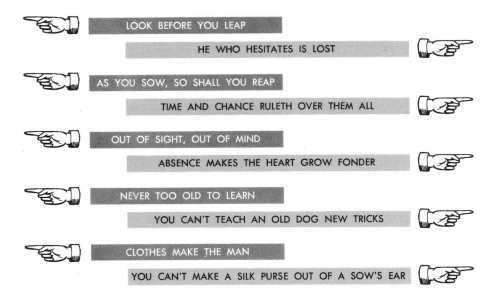

LOOK BEFORE YOU LEAP

HE WHO HESITATES IS LOST

AS YOU SOW, SO SHALL YOU REAP

TIME AND CHANCE RULETH OVER THEM ALL

OUT OF SIGHT, OUT OF MIND

ABSENCE MAKES THE HEART GROW FONDER

NEVER TOO OLD TO LEARN

YOU CAN'T TEACH AN OLD DOG NEW TRICKS

CLOTHES MAKE THE MAN

YOU CAN'T MAKE A SILK PURSE OUT OF A SOW'S EAR

FIG. 1–1. The trouble with folk wisdom is that it gives no guide for determining which of two contradictory sayings is appropriate in a particular situation. Thus the usefulness of such sayings is quite limited.

Astrology and physiognomy are only two of the many ways man has tried to explain human behavior. Over the years, common-sense answers to everyday problems of human relations have been passed on from generation to generation in the form of proverbs, fables, and folk wisdom, such as: "You can't teach an old dog new tricks." "Experience is the best teacher." "Absence makes the heart grow fonder." "Out of sight, out of mind." Others are listed in Fig. 1–1.

At the same time, great thinkers have speculated on the nature of human beings. Jeremy Bentham (1748–1832) decribed man as a rational being, making choices and decisions is terms of enlightened self-interest. Le Bon (1841–1931) stressed the irrationality and impulsiveness of men in crowds. Hobbes (1588–1679) viewed man as selfish and aggressive, one whose strivings had to be restrained by a powerful government. Rousseau (1712–1778) saw the restraints of civilization as the force that was destroying the nobility of natural man, the noble savage. These men were brilliant thinkers, and each of their conceptions seems to contain some truth. A major weakness of all these prescientific modes of explanation—superstition, common sense, and intuitive philosophy—is that contradictory predictions and explanations are offered without any means for resolving the differences.

How Is Scientific Explanation Different from Common Sense?

Within the last few hundred years, man has developed *scientific* methods for answering some of the questions that have troubled him over the centuries. For about three centuries, science has been of increasing importance in the study of the biological world. During the past hundred years, science has been applied to the study of man and society, and, since the latter part of the last century, psychology, bridging the biological and social sciences, has been carried forward by the use of scientific methods.

Just as Copernicus refused to accept the earth-centered conception of the solar system, so did social scientists begin to challenge the folklore about man. Freud listened to his patients' memories and dreams. Thorndike watched animals as they learned to open cages to get at food. Ebbinghaus constructed lists of nonsense syllables and carefully recorded his recall of them.

These scientific approaches are unique, not because they deal with new problems or because tradition, common sense, and philosophy have been discredited. Scientific explanations are different because the basis upon which they are accepted or rejected is different. The force of tradition, the appeal to analogy, the erudition and creativity of the author are not sufficient. *In science, authority comes only from factual evidence derived from systematic, repeatable observation.* Ideas that have been accepted for centuries, that have been supported by brilliant and eminent men, must be discarded or revised as new facts emerge. Concepts that seem strange and implausible but which can explain and predict previously unpredictable phenomena are examined and accepted. Science is active, always testing, revising, reformulating, always changing.

Accurate observations of one set of events become the basis for predicting future events. If the predictions are confirmed, a general law may be suggested. The basic assumption on which science is built is that this is a lawful universe in which there is *consistency of events*. Science deals with *consistent rela-*

tionships; the psychological scientist deals with consistencies in behavior. He attempts to find general laws that will enable him to understand and predict behavior. Of course, this task is impossible unless there *are* consistencies in behavior. The psychologist assumes that by careful study he can find the factors that will enable him to improve his predictions. As your knowledge of psychology grows, you will be able to judge for yourself how well the psychologist has succeeded in his effort to find order in the apparent chaos of behavior.

Perhaps aspects of behavior such as which thumb is on top when one clasps his hands, or which foot one moves first in walking from a standing position seem completely unpredictable. While these behaviors have not been studied much, we suspect that even such inconsequential acts occur in a fairly consistent fashion and can be predicted with a certain degree of success. Moreover, we can develop a science of behavior without being able to predict perfectly what a person will do. Any generalization is useful if it can help us improve our understanding and increase the accuracy of our predictions. For example, we cannot predict perfectly which students will do well in college, but even a moderately accurate prediction is useful both to the student and to the college admissions officer. Similarly, we may not be able to predict perfectly the degree to which prompt reward for correct answers will speed up learning, but even a general prediction that it will result in some improvement is useful to the teacher.

Even partial knowledge of the consistency of events enables us to make better predictions than we could make on the basis of intuition or guesswork. Furthermore, scientists are able to estimate the limitations of their predictions by observing the variability of events. It is just as important to know that high school grades are not perfect predictors of college success as to discover that there is some relationship between the two events.

You have probably noted that we have been talking about "predictors" rather than "causes." In doing so we are anticipating one of the major themes of this book. In common usage the word "cause" implies a relationship in which one event invariably precedes another (the "effect"). Our theme will be that most psychological events are effected by several "causes." Thus we will more often talk about "predictors," "variables," and "factors" than about "causes" in the sense of a single cause and effect.

What Does a Psychologist Observe?

Psychology looks at behavior. The psychologist looks for determinants of behavior in hereditary characteristics; he looks for the influences of parental training and other past experiences; he looks for factors in the present situation.

You may be wondering why psychologists emphasize the study of behavior instead of the study of the "mind." A review of the history of psychology reveals that in its early days psychology *was* the study of the mind.

Around 1875 a group of scientists and philosophers led by Wilhelm Wundt became interested in the possibility of applying scientific methods to the study of the human mind. By observing and analyzing the "contents of the mind," they felt that they could develop a new science of psychology. They searched for basic elements of consciousness, for the way the elements were connected, and for the laws of connection. For example, one of Wundt's students, Titchener, divided consciousness into the elements of sensations, images, and feelings.

The basic approach of these pioneers was introspection, which is the systematic observation of one's own mental processes. The young science soon ran into difficulty with this new method. Different investigators, each using observations of himself as evidence, reported different characteristics of mind. For example, an intense controversy developed over the possibility of having thoughts without any images. Disagreement usually is a stimulant for new experimentation in science, but in this case, where observations were private, there was no method for resolving differences. Furthermore, the work of Sigmund Freud and other students of abnormal psychology suggested that significant areas of mental life were "unconscious," that is, unavailable for study by introspection. In addition, introspection was obviously not applicable in some areas. Early workers in child psychology, for instance, could not use subjects' reports of mental processes. Students influenced by Darwinian theories of evolution wanted to develop a comparative psychology of animals and had to devise new methods. All these trends converged into a growing dissatisfaction with introspection and mentalistic psychology.

One of the leaders of the movement to focus psychology on the study of behavior was J. B. Watson. Watson felt that the essence of science was that its material be publicly observable and measurable. According to Watson, the domain of psychology should be the relations between *responses* (measurable muscle movements of an organism) and *stimuli* (changes in the physical energy of some aspect of the environment). For Watson, consciousness, feelings, images, and all the mental processes that were necessarily private and unobservable could not be part of a science of psychology. Only when a private event could be reinterpreted as an aspect of behavior could it be considered for investigation. For example, Watson admitted the word "thinking" to his vocabulary only after he defined thinking as subvocal movements of the larynx, tongue, and other muscles.

Redefining terms in words that refer to external, observable events is known as *operationalizing* or as giving *operational definitions*. You can think of an operational definition as a set of directions for observing. If you want to observe thinking, said Watson, observe a person's muscle movements. Thinking as a mental process cannot be observed or measured; muscle movement can.

Watson's approach to psychology, with its emphasis on *observable* behavior, became known as *behaviorism*. The major problem with this approach was that it excluded from psychology some of its major concerns. No one can directly observe the motives, feelings, perceptions, thoughts, and memories of others.

Redefining thought in terms of muscle movements made thought a measurable event, but ignored some of the properties of thought that make it psychologically interesting. The behaviorists became committed to the study of muscle movements in place of an analysis of thought.

How Does the Psychologist Handle "Mental Processes"?

Most modern psychologists agree with Watson that the evidence on which psychological theories are based must be publicly observable. However, they also agree with the introspectionists that the processes of mind are of psychological interest and that a person's report of his private experiences may be of scientific value. And they recognize, as Freud did, that a person is not aware of all the factors that are affecting his thinking and his behavior. How can these apparently conflicting points of view be reconciled?

The key to resolving the problem is the distinction modern psychologists make between *data* and *inference*. Let us first discuss data, which are the results of an experiment. Data can be reported in terms of the procedures of the experimenter and the behavior of the subject. Data are public. All those who observe the experiment will report the same results.

Suppose we observe a classroom and collect the following hypothetical data: Most of the students are yawning, looking out of the window, and doodling in their notebooks as the instructor lectures. Then the instructor announces an examination for the following week. Most of the students straighten up in their seats, stop doodling, and begin to copy into their notebooks the words that the instructor writes on the board. In the examination the following week, most of the students answer correctly those questions dealing with material covered after the announcement, but do not give correct answers to those dealing with material covered in the lecture prior to the announcement.

Let us collect data in another hypothetical situation. As people leave a motion picture theater, an interviewer asks, "How did you like the picture?" Many people report, "I did not like it very much. I was bored." Then the interviewer asks the people to describe the plot. Those people who say they were bored do not report the major incidents of the movie accurately.

So far the descriptions have been in terms of the observable situation—the stimuli, and the observable behavior—the responses. Note that the responses may be either verbal or nonverbal. If you were present in the classroom or at the interviews, you would probably report the same data.

Now suppose that we wish to interpret the data in terms of mental processes occurring inside the student and the movie-goer. From the behavior of yawning, doodling, and staring, we can *infer* a mental state which we label boredom. From the behavior of stating "I'm bored," we may *infer* the same mental state. From the behavior of straightening up in a chair, focusing eyes on the black-

FIG. 1–2. Scene in the balcony of the Opera House in San Francisco during the proceedings of the Japanese Peace Treaty Conference. From the behavior of these people, it is certainly possible to infer that some are interested and some are bored. (Wide World Photos)

board, and writing, and also from the later behavior of answering certain test questions correctly, we can *infer* that the students had begun to attend to the words of the instructor. From the behavior of the people pictured in Fig. 1–2, we can *infer* that some people were interested, others were bored with the proceedings. These inferences, or *constructs*, are assumptions about structures and processes that occur where they cannot be directly observed.

Note that the modern psychologist does not equate the mental process with the observable nonverbal behavior as Watson did, nor does the modern psychologist equate the verbal report with direct observation of the mental process as the introspectionists did. Today's psychologist would be more likely to go through the following steps: (1) observe behavior in a situation; (2) infer a construct with certain properties; (3) make guesses about the effects of such a construct on behavior in new situations; (4) observe behavior in the new situation and see whether it corresponds with the guesses made on the basis of the inferred construct.

"Staring out of a window" is not a definition of boredom. It is possible for a person to stare out of a window while listening attentively. Similarly, the statement, "I was bored," may be made for a variety of reasons, such as annoyance at being questioned. But suppose we infer from the variety of the students' behavior before the examination announcement that they were bored, and that the movie-goers' verbal reports did indicate their mental processes.* And suppose that on the basis of steps 1 and 2 we make the guess that boredom leads to poor retention (3). Then our two sets of data—the examination results and the movie reports—support our inferences: that there is a state of the organism, boredom, which affects a person's recall of the events.

A construct is an abstraction that helps us to summarize a number of observations and to make predictions in new situations. On the basis of our interpretation of the events in the classroom, we could have predicted that the incidents in a movie considered boring would not be recalled very well (Fig. 1–3).

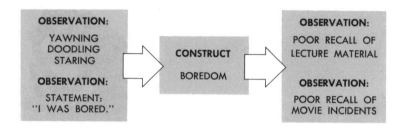

FIG. 1–3.   A construct, such as boredom, helps us to relate various observations to one another, and to make predictions.

Inferences are made in all sciences and in everyday life as well. Whenever you say "He's hungry," "She is intelligent," "That man is unhappy," you are referring to characteristics you cannot observe directly. You are using the constructs, hunger, intelligence, and unhappiness. Your constructs, like those of the psychologists, are inferences you made from your observation of people's behavior in various situations. Like the psychologist, you may be correct or mistaken in your inferences, and you discover your errors when your predictions are wrong.

After many observations, an investigator may infer a number of constructs. He may suggest how the constructs are related to one another and how their interaction affects behavior. When he does all this, he has constructed a *theory*.

Freud saw neurotic patients over a number of years. One of his earliest discoveries was that patients who could not recall the sources of their problems in an ordinary interview were able to do so when questioned under hypnosis. This observation led to one of the central constructs of Freud's theory, the *uncon-*

---

* In effect, we are operationalizing boredom by these observations. However, we realize that the correspondence between the construct *boredom* and our behavior indicators—our operational definitions of boredom—is not perfect.

scious. Freud went on to suggest differences between conscious and unconscious processes, and their relationships to behavior. One such relationship, according to Freud's theory, was that unpleasant memories were pushed from the conscious into the unconscious portions of the mind.

A theory consists of general laws. These general laws suggest *hypotheses*, which are predictions that particular events should occur in particular situations. One psychologist, Meltzer, hypothesized on the basis of Freudian theory that pleasant experiences would be recalled for a longer period than unpleasant ones. He then collected data.

■ He asked college students who had just returned from a Christmas vacation to record their memories of their holiday and to rate each memory as either pleasant or unpleasant. Six weeks later, he asked the students once again to record their memories of the vacation. During the second testing, the students listed fewer memories than they had recorded six weeks earlier, but they recalled a larger percentage of the memories that had been rated pleasant than of those that had been rated unpleasant. (Meltzer, 1930) ■

Meltzer's data consisted of the reports of students. He inferred that a student's rating of an event as pleasant indicated the private feeling of the student during the event. Thus the construct, *pleasantness,* was operationalized (made observable) by the use of verbal report. The results confirmed Meltzer's original hypothesis and thus supported Freudian theory.

Note that this one result does not prove that Freudian theory is the best explanation for the dynamics of forgetting; other theories could predict the same result. Verification (or disproof) usually grows out of a number of different observations, each of which logically follows from the theory, but no single observation by itself provides conclusive proof of the theory. In psychology, there is no one all-embracing theory that provides adequate explanations of all phenomena. Theorists tend to limit their speculations to particular aspects of mind and behavior. Psychology includes theories in varying stages of verification; some well established, others for which we have not been able to provide critical tests. This means that in an area where no theory is well established, psychologists can observe identical results and still interpret the meaning of the results differently, each according to his own theory.

However, science provides us with a rule for choosing between alternative theories and explanations. The *law of parsimony* states that the best theory is the one that covers the most facts with the fewest assumptions and inferences. If a theory assumes a new construct for each phenomenon it explains, it is not very useful. Instinct theories were criticized on this basis. Aggressive behavior was explained by the existence of an inferred aggressiveness instinct; the fact that people often seek the company of others was explained by the existence of a gregarious instinct; toe-tapping was explained by a toe-tapping instinct. With each new unexplained behavior, the instinct theorist added a new instinct. Such explanations are rejected in favor of theories that can explain and predict a variety of behaviors with only a few explanatory constructs. Later on in this chapter we shall see how the construct *anxiety* is useful in explaining many phenomena.

How Are Theoretical Explanations Useful to Science?

You may have noticed that theoretical explanations of experimental results are not necessary for prediction. We can use the data from Meltzer's experiment to predict that events that are labeled "pleasant" will probably be recalled for a longer period than events labeled "unpleasant" without any references to the internal mental states and unconscious processes hypothesized by Freud. Of what value is the theoretical explanation? The answer depends, in part, on how a scientist conceptualizes the goal of science. Some scientists would list prediction as the goal of science; others would say that the real goal of science is understanding and that prediction is important only because it is a test of understanding. But even the investigator who feels that prediction is his primary goal often finds that constructs and theories facilitate his experimentation.

Obviously, the scientist is more interested in some types of prediction than in others and theory helps to focus research on significant problems. For example, we might be able to predict that Mr. Allison will put his left thumb on top the next time he clasps his hands just by observing that he had done this the last five times he clasped his hands. Such a prediction (whether of trivial or important behavior) based solely on the observation of past behavior is not as interesting to the scientist as a prediction that tells him something about the factors influencing Mr. Allison's hand-clasping behavior or that relates it to other characteristics of Mr. Allison. Furthermore, an explanation relating behavior to constructs and inferred processes suggests new areas for investigation. Freud's theory suggests that not only pleasant events, but also many, many other diverse phenomena will be recalled. To support or discredit Freud's theory, psychologists have asked: "Can events that are not recalled still have an effect on behavior?" "In what ways do early feeding and toilet training affect later adult behavior?" "Can motives and conflicts lead to a distortion of reality?" In evaluating the results of experiments stimulated by these questions, psychologists have rejected some aspects of Freud's theory and accepted others. Whether or not the theoretical explanations are eventually verified is not the only test of their value; they also stimulate the working scientist to new ideas and further research.

If there were no theories to relate the diverse phenomena that scientists observe, science would be a mere catalog of facts. Little generalization or prediction would be possible. Theories organize the knowledge of the past and integrate it with newer discoveries. Theoretical statements point to common relationships in seemingly unrelated phenomena.

Sometimes the student of psychology feels that psychology fails to capture the richness of human experience. But this is the difference between biography or literature and science. The very nature of science is abstraction—abstracting consistencies out of many individual events. Just as the laws of gravity fail to differentiate between bombs and snowflakes, so do the laws of learning apply to both criminals and saints. The more phenomena an explanation can encompass, the better the explanation. The more general an explanation, the greater the potential number of derived hypotheses and predictions, and the more likely that it will stimulate further research.

How Does a Psychologist Observe Behavior?

The means of confirming hypotheses the test of a theory's generality and parsimony, the method that systematizes observation—is the empirical study. A study is an arrangement of conditions such that the relationship between events can be observed. A psychological study is an arrangement of conditions such that the effects of various conditions on a particular aspect of behavior can be observed systematically. A classic study in educational psychology will serve as an example.

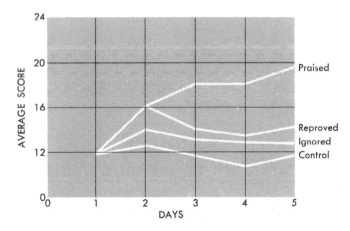

FIG. 1-4. The effect of praise and reproof on the performance of grade-school girls doing arithmetic problems. (After Hurlock, 1925)

■ An experimenter wondered: What is the difference between the effects of praise and reproof on test performance? She decided to answer this question by observing the effects of praise and reproof on the performance of fourth- and sixth-grade girls on arithmetic problems. The girls were divided into four groups of equal age and equal ability. For five successive days, the girls were given 30 problems to solve in 15 minutes. After each day's test, the girls in group I were asked to come to the front of the class and were complimented on their fine work *regardless of their actual performance*. The girls in group II were singled out and chided for careless, inaccurate work. The girls in group III listened to the praise and reproof of their classmates but received no comments on their own work. Those in group IV worked in a separate room each day, heard no comments on their own work, and did not observe the treatments of the others. The results of the arithmetic tests on the five successive days are presented in Fig. 1—4. The average score was the same for the four groups on the first day; then the effects of the treatment began to appear. On the second day, both the praised and the reproved groups improved considerably. The praised group continued to improve, but the reproved group dropped steadily in performance. The other two groups showed no consistent improvement. (Hurlock, 1925) ∎

The behavior selected for observation by the experimenter in this case is performance on a series of arithmetic problems. In general, the behavior selected for observation in an experiment is known as the *dependent variable*. The condition whose effect on the dependent variable is studied is known as the *independent variable*. In this study the independent variable was the kind of comment the pupil received for her performance: praise, reproof, or silence. Note that the fourth group worked under ordinary circumstances and heard none of the comments. Such a group, one which receives no special experimental treatment, is known as a *control group*. The four groups contained girls of equal age and ability. If the experimenter had not been careful to match her groups in this manner, the observed difference between them might not have been the effect of the independent variable, but rather a result of the differences between the girls in the groups. Hurlock tried to keep all the relevant conditions other than the independent variable the same for all of the groups.

The factors influencing human behavior are extremely complex, and experimenters often look at the effects of a number of independent variables simultaneously. During the 1960 election campaigns, the Survey Research Center of the University of Michigan conducted national surveys, not so much to predict the outcome of the election as to understand the many factors influencing voting.

∎ Their procedure was to ask a variety of questions about the issues, the candidates, and the respondent. One question, "For which candidate will you vote?" assessed the dependent variable, voting behavior. Four categories of questions revealed some of the relevant factors:

(1) *Strength of party affiliation.* Those who identify themselves as strong Republicans and strong Democrats are less likely to cross party lines than those who identify themselves as moderate or weak party members. In 1960, when the religious issue overrode some other considerations, only 3 percent of the strong Republicans voted for Kennedy and fewer than 10 percent of the strong Democrats voted for Nixon.

(2) *Opinion on campaign issues.* As you might expect, people who express opinions on domestic and foreign policy issues that are similar to those of a particular political party tend to vote for that party's candidate. In 1952, 73 percent of those favoring the Republican position voted for Eisenhower; 64 percent of those favoring the Democratic position on major issues voted for Stevenson. Note that opinion on issues is not a perfect predictor of voting.

(3) *Attitude toward the candidate's personal characteristics.* Those who make favorable comments about a candidate, like "He's wonderful" and "He's a great leader" tend to vote for him.

(4) *Religious identification.* In 1956 the survey found no relationship between church attendance and voting. However, in 1960 this was one of the most important variables influencing voting. One out of every nine votes reflected a change from normal voting patterns. The more regularly a Protestant Democrat attended church, the more likely he was to vote for Nixon (see Fig. 1–5). Almost half the Catholic Republicans voted for Kennedy. (Campbell, *et al.,* 1960; Campbell, *et al.,* 1961) ■

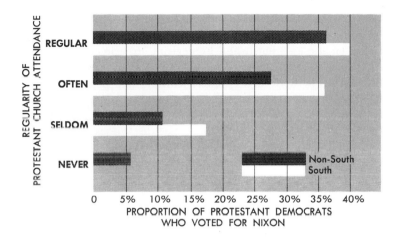

FIG. 1–5.   The relationship between regularity of church attendance by Protestant Democrats and the frequency with which they voted for Nixon in 1960. (After Campbell *et al.,* 1961)

These four dimensions—strength of party affiliation, opinion on major issues, attitude toward the candidates, and religious identification—were the independent variables that were shown to affect the dependent variable, voting behavior. To investigate these factors, the Survey Research Center staff did not interview every voter in the United States. They selected a sample of voters and projected the results from the sample to make generalizations about the population. In 1952, the Survey Research Center accurately predicted which states would go Democratic and which would go Republican, on the basis of interviews with only a fraction of the population. (Campbell, *et al.,* 1960)

These two studies, the one of the effect of praise on test performance and the other of the factors influencing voting, illustrate the two major categories of investigation: those in which the experimenter *manipulates* the independent variable and those in which the experimenter *assesses* the independent variable. When an experimenter uses the manipulation approach, he does something to one or more of the groups that he is studying to produce a change in behavior and then observes the consequences. Hurlock took four approximately equal groups of girls and created variations in them by giving them different comments on their arithmetic performance. The assessment approach studies differences as they already exist in individuals and groups. Here the experimenter does not create the variation; he finds some way of measuring the variation that already exists and relates this variation to other behavior. The Survey Research interviewers were not interested in changing anyone's vote. They wanted to find out which natural differences among people were related to voting behavior.

We sometimes use both methods in examining an hypothesis. The original hypothesis may come from a theory originally derived from unsystematic observations, such as those found in case histories. The hypothesis may then be supported both by systematic assessment and by devising experiments in which variables are manipulated. As an illustration let us see how each method may be applied to the problem, "How does anxiety affect learning and performance?"

■ *Case History.* Frank was a 10-year-old boy brought to a psychologist because his grades were failing despite the fact that he had above-average intelligence. In talking over the background of the case with the psychologist, Frank's mother mentioned that his difficulties seemed to have arisen or at least become noticeable about a year previously. She could think of no reason why this should be so. Later she mentioned that her husband had taken a position involving a great deal of traveling about a year previously, and from her comments it was apparent that she had opposed this plan even to the extent of threatening divorce. With further study the psychologist concluded that Frank's poor learning in school was due to his anxiety about his parents and the possibility that they would be divorced and might leave him. ■

The psychologist's observation here did not involve systematic assessment but was simply derived from the mother's own reports of the situation. Note that the counseling psychologist interpreted Frank's school performance with an inference about an unobservable condition within Frank, anxiety. An experimental psychologist used the same construct, *anxiety*, in a controlled study.

■ *Assessment.* Taylor (1951) hypothesized that anxious individuals would learn more rapidly than nonanxious individuals. She studied a simple form of learning, conditioning. When a puff of air is blown into the eye, the normal person blinks. If some signal, such as a light, regularly precedes a puff of air, the subject soon learns to blink in response to the signal before the air puff appears. Thus, Taylor studied learning by observing how quickly the subject learned to blink as soon as the light appeared. Taylor's major problem was to find an objective way of selecting anxious and nonanxious subjects. This is how she operationalized anxiety: First she administered a test made up of items judged by clinical psychologists to be measures of anxiety. Then she selected two groups of students, those who scored in the upper 12 percent of all scores on the test, and those who scored in the bottom 9 percent. These operations were based on the assumption that subjects having high scores would be characterized by high anxiety; those with low scores by low anxiety. Thus anxiety was measured by an assessment procedure. Taylor observed the rate of learning of these anxious and nonanxious persons in a conditioning situation and found that the anxious subjects learned more rapidly.

Manipulation of variables in an experiment. While Taylor's observations supported her hypothesis that anxiety helps learning, it is possible that there were other differences between her anxious and nonanxious subjects, and that these other differences produced the results. To check this, she experimentally manipulated anxiety by telling half her subjects that the intensity of the puff of air was going to be increased, while the other half of her subjects were told that the intensity would be decreased. Assuming that her subjects would be more anxious if they expected a stronger puff of air, she compared the learning of the two groups, but found no differences. ■

At this point we are therefore left in doubt. The case history suggested that anxiety interferes with learning; Taylor's first study found that anxiety facilitated learning; and her second experiment found no differences. As you might guess, this is the type of situation that leads to further research, and a number of experiments have been carried out to clarify the relationship of anxiety and instructions to learning.

■ Another study (Montague, 1953) tested the hypothesis derived from a theory of learning that high anxiety would facilitate simple learning but hinder complex learning. Comparing the learning of highly anxious and nonanxious individuals on three tasks differing in complexity, he found that his hypothesis was supported. Students high in anxiety were superior to those low in anxiety on a simple task, but were inferior on a complex task. ■

■ The relationship of anxiety to learning is further illuminated by a study carried out by Sarason (1956), who studied the effect of different instructions on individuals assessed as being high and low in anxiety. He found that with instructions designed to produce high motivation, the highly anxious individual did more poorly than the less anxious person, but with low-motivating instructions, the highly anxious person did relatively better. ■

It now appears that anxiety facilitates simple learning and learning under low-motivating instructions, but that high anxiety is detrimental to complex learning and tasks accompanied by high-motivating instructions. Our examples illustrate how generalizations from case histories or observations of selected groups may be tied down and made more precise by further observation and experimentation. You should not, however, conclude that research on anxiety and learning is now ended. As more evidence has been gathered, new problems have appeared, and further experiments are now going on.

The experiments on anxiety and learning again illustrate two major types of approaches to the study of human behavior, i.e., the assessment and the manipulation approaches. Taylor first used tests which assessed the anxiety of her subjects. In her other study, Taylor used the manipulation approach when she tried to arouse anxiety by telling her subjects that the intensity of the air puff would increase.

Today more and more psychologists are using both the assessment and the manipulation methods, as the studies of Montague and Sarason illustrate. In using tests to differentiate between individuals high and low in anxiety, they employed an assessment approach. In Sarason's use of different instructions and in Montague's use of tasks of varying complexity, we see examples of the manipulation approach.

All these studies were designed to determine the effect of anxiety upon learning. In the terminology we introduced earlier, some measure of anxiety is an *independent variable*; change in performance due to learning is a *dependent variable*. In the assessment studies the independent variables were measured by tests of anxiety; in the manipulation studies the independent variables were instructions of the experimenter.

In classic experimental designs, only one independent variable is manipulated and all other variables that might influence the dependent variable are carefully controlled. Newer experimental designs, such as the one used in studying voting, permit the experimenter to study several independent variables in the same experiment, but the experimenter still controls all other variables that might influence his results. With both assessment and manipulation methods the dependent variable is measured as carefully as possible.

FIG. 1–6.   The window in the room through which we see the woman is actually a one-way vision screen. To the woman, the window appears to be a huge mirror. This arrangement permits observation of a subject's behavior without his constant awareness of being watched. (Courtesy of Bernard Tursky, Massachusetts Mental Health Center, Boston, Mass.)

LABORATORY VS. NATURAL SETTINGS FOR RESEARCH. Manipulation or assessment methods may be used either in laboratory or in natural settings. Typically, manipulation studies have been carried out in the laboratory and assessment studies in natural settings, but this is not necessary. Taylor's study, for example, used an assessment procedure in a laboratory study of conditioning; Hurlock studied the effects of giving different comments on performance in a classroom, a manipulation experiment in a natural setting.

In natural settings both the behavior and the factors influencing it are extremely complex. This is both an advantage and a disadvantage. It is often difficult to disentangle the effects of the independent variables being studied from the effects of all the other variables in the situation. On the other hand, the very complexity of the natural situation and the unexpectedness of some of the responses observed may be a source of ideas about relationships not previously suggested by theory. A psychologist may start his investigations of a new problem by simply observing behavior in natural settings relevant to the problem, developing methods of categorizing the stimuli and behaviors observed, and finally, developing hypotheses about situations in which experimental variations are planned or in which systematic assessments are possible.

In both natural and laboratory settings, the researcher must deal with the special problem of the reaction of the subject to the research itself. For example, a number of studies have shown that the results of studies of the effect of anxiety upon learning may depend upon reactions of the subjects to the experimenter (e.g., Axelrod, Cowen, and Helizer, 1956). Similarly, in research in natural settings, the researcher must deal with the possibility that subjects under observation may behave differently from the way they would naturally. Fortunately, psychologists have long been aware of such effects and have developed some methods for controlling them. One of these methods, the observation room shown in Fig. 1–6, allows the psychologist to observe his subjects without their being aware of it.

How Is Psychological Knowledge Used?

As the psychologist learns the factors influencing the behavior of human beings, the results of his research can be applied to the solution of practical problems. Psychological knowledge may be applied to simple questions such as "What is the best color for a traffic sign that people will notice both at night and during the day?" and to complex questions such as "What is the best way to educate our children?"

The unique domain of psychology is the study of the total individual organism. Sociology looks at the behavior of groups. Economics and political science look at particular aspects of the behavior of people in groups. Thus psychological knowledge can make a unique contribution to the solution of social problems. Together with other social scientists, psychologists are trying to understand and solve such problems as juvenile delinquency, racial and religious prejudice, the displacement of workers due to automation, international diplomacy, and world peace. Today's social institutions are extremely complex, and no single approach provides a complete understanding of them. Psychologists are contributing both by revealing general principles about the behavior of human beings, who collectively comprise social institutions, and by studying the behavior of individuals in particular social contexts.

Just as major social decisions may be based on the scientific knowledge of human behavior, so may our personal decisions be based on such knowledge. "How can I learn to study more effectively?" "Why do I argue with my parents so much?" "What shall I choose for my life's work?"—these problems involve psychological questions. Learning the principles of human behavior may help us to understand ourselves and our relationships to other people more fully.

Summary

Concepts

Responses.   Observable movements of an organism

Stimuli.   Measurable changes in the physical environment of an organism

Operational definition.   A definition in terms of observable events

Data.   The observed results of an experiment

Inference.   A guess about unobservable processes that is based on data

Construct.   An inferred structure or process

Theory.   A systematic account of unobservable events usually in terms of *constructs,* the *relationships among constructs,* and the *relationships between constructs and behavior*

Hypothesis.   A prediction often derived from a theory about the relationships between observed events

Empirical study.   An arrangement of conditions so that observations can be made systematically

Dependent variable (in psychology).   The behavior measure selected for observation

Independent variable.   The condition which is assessed or manipulated in order to see how behavior varies as the condition varies

Principles

1. In science, evidence for generalizations is derived from systematic and repeatable observations.

2. Science is built on the assumption that there is consistency in events; psychology is built on the assumption that there is consistency in *behavior.*

3. Most psychological phenomena cannot be explained in terms of single causes.

4. Most modern psychologists study mental processes via inferences from behavior.

5. There is no single all-embracing theory that provides an adequate explanation for all psychological phenomena.

6. In choosing between alternative theories, scientists prefer the theory which covers the greatest number of data with the fewest assumptions.

7. Theories are useful in science because they provide explanations, stimulate research, organize facts, and provide guidelines for generalizing from observations.

8. Two major categories of psychological research are: (1) *manipulation,* in which the experimenter creates the variation in the independent variable he wishes to study, and (2) *assessment,* in which the experimenter measures variations already existing in people.

Suggested Readings *

Voting Behavior

BERELSON, B. R., P. F. LAZARFELD, and W. W. MCPHEE, *Voting,* Chicago: University of Chicago Press, 1954.

CAMPBELL, A., P. E. CONVERSE, W. E. MILLER, and D. E. STOKES, *The American Voter,* New York: Wiley, 1960. Describes in detail the studies of the 1952 and 1956 elections from which we drew the material on voting in this chapter.

Psychology as a Science

KIMBLE, G. A., *Principles of General Psychology,* New York: Ronald Press, 1956. Chapter II of this textbook for beginning students contains a more detailed introduction to scientific method.

CONANT, J. B., *On Understanding Science,* New York: New American Library, 1951. (Mentor Book M68). An excellent introduction to science.

* Throughout this book, listings appear in order of pertinence to material being covered.

THE BACKGROUND OF BEHAVIOR

PART 1

the cultural background of behavior

chapter 2

THE MEANING OF CULTURE

ROLES OF MEN AND WOMEN IN THREE
PRIMITIVE CULTURES

WHAT ASPECTS OF HUMAN FUNCTIONING ARE
AFFECTED BY CULTURE?

HOW DO PEOPLE LEARN TO BEHAVE IN
ACCORDANCE WITH THEIR CULTURE?

FROM WHOM DOES A CHILD LEARN HIS
CULTURE?

WHAT ARE THE SOURCES OF VARIABILITY OF
BEHAVIOR WITHIN A SOCIETY?

The Meaning of Culture

Where should we begin our study of human behavior? A common-sense answer might be "Why not begin at the point of man's beginning—his birth—and trace his development through childhood to maturity?" But even this approach does not take us back to the real beginnings—for the newborn baby is the product of a combination of genes derived from many ancestors, and he arrives in a world that has already prescribed certain patterns of behavior which his mother should use in caring for him. He is born into a *society*, a group of people who are dependent upon one another and who have developed patterns of organization that enable them to live together and survive as a group. Most important to the newborn individual is the fact that certain kinds of behavior are not only available but are required by his society. These prescribed patterns of behavior and the other ways in which society is structured are aspects of *culture*. We can consider culture to be the patterns of behaving and thinking and the products of behavior that are transmitted from generation to generation within any continuing society.

The study of culture is the province of the anthropologist, but to understand the behavior of an individual, the psychologist too must have some understanding of the culture in which the individual lives and was reared. Since so much of a person's behavior is determined by his relation to the society in which he lives, we can understand him as an individual only if we understand how his behavior fits the expectations of his society and know when his behavior is deviating from such expectations. Hence we shall use the concept of culture as our starting point.

Roles of Men and Women in Three Primitive Cultures

How the newborn infant will behave as an adult is influenced by the society into which he is born. One way of demonstrating this is by comparing the behavior of people in different cultures.

Let us, for example, look at the question: To what degree is characteristic behavior of men and women in our culture determined by inherited factors, and to what degree by the culture? In our culture we assume that men are naturally different in temperament from women. If men are inherently more aggressive, more competitive, more dominant, and less emotional than women, we should expect them to display these characteristics in all societies. If men's roles differ from culture to culture, this is strong evidence that they are learned.

Margaret Mead, an anthropologist, visited New Guinea and wrote descriptions of three of the cultures there: the Arapesh, the Mundugumor, and the Tchambuli (Mead, 1935). The following is a summary of her impressions:

■ The mountain *Arapesh* are poor people whose tiny villages cling to the sides of barren mountains. Their gardens perch on hillsides, difficult to fence off from the wild pigs. Hunting is poor and life is difficult. The Arapesh women are gentle, cooperative, loving mothers, much like most women are expected to be in our culture. But the Arapesh men are also gentle, cooperative, and loving. They work together in their gardens, readily forsaking their own work to help a neighbor with his. The Arapesh men cannot conceive of any normal person wanting to be a leader. The ''necessary'' leaders of the tribe reluctantly assume leadership functions and are happy to relinquish them. The Arapesh baby is born into a warm and loving world. Both his mother and father care for him and consider it a tragedy if he cries. The Arapesh believe that both men and women are naturally cooperative and gentle and would think it odd that women and men should be expected to differ in personality.

The *Mundugumor*, who live on the banks of one of the rivers of New Guinea, were headhunters until recent times. Their land is rich and grows much tobacco and coconuts. The Mundugumor men are fierce warriors and hunters and have violent tempers. However, Mundugumor women are neither gentle nor loving. The Mundugumor women continually fight with their husbands and teach their sons at an early age to taunt their fathers with the names and epithets that are most irritating to them. The Mundugumor woman does not enjoy being a mother. She handles her children roughly and leaves them hanging on the wall in their cradleboards until their crying can no longer be endured. Both men and women in the Mundugumor culture are arrogant, violent, individualistic, possessing the sort of personality characteristics we would consider more masculine than feminine.

The *Tchambuli* people are lake dwellers. They have ample food which can be stored so that there is little chance of famine. Like their neighbors, the Tchambuli were headhunters, but for them headhunting was a ceremonial obligation in which they took no great pleasure. Tchambuli men are artists. They enjoy painting, music, and drama. The men spend much of their time in ornamenting themselves [in this they are not unique, as Fig. 2–1 shows] and playing parts in various rituals and dramas. The men gather in groups which change frequently, for as all Tchambuli know, men are sensitive creatures whose feelings are easily hurt, and the gossip of the men's circles may create and magnify petty jealousies. The women of the Tchambuli

FIG. 2–1. A Samburu dancer. In his culture in East Africa, it is considered quite appropriate to the masculine role to wear cosmetics and jewelry. Note, however, that he is an outstanding warrior who can throw a spear one hundred yards with deadly accuracy. (United Press International Photo)

carry on most of the necessary work of life. The men may occasionally organize a fishing party as a lark, but what is important is the social event, not the fish that are caught. Food getting is women's work. The women are tolerant of the men's amusements and enjoy seeing the men's latest artistic productions. Nominally, the man controls the family wealth, but if he wishes something he usually obtains the wife's consent. In short, Tchambuli society almost reverses the sex roles that are considered "natural" for men and women in our culture. ■

These descriptions illustrate the importance of culture in establishing social *roles*, which are prescribed patterns of behavior assigned to particular classes of individuals, such as male or female, young or old, chiefs, priests, or warriors. In our society as well as in Tchambuli society, sex is the basis for assigning important roles; the role assigned to each sex differs in the two societies (see Fig. 2–1).

Roles are a part of culture which may be so pervasive that we fail to recognize that the roles are learned, rather than inherited. Because most of us conform effortlessly to cultural standards of behavior we sometimes lose sight of them as standards and take the prescribed behavior for granted as an inescapable part of human nature. Each of us learns to adjust to a culture that existed when we were born and that will continue to exist after we die.

What Aspects of Human Functioning Are Affected by Culture?

Sex-role variations among cultures provide one example of the many significant ways in which cultures differ. The culture prescribes standards for almost all aspects of behavior. But to understand how culture influences behavior, we must look at how it affects the processes of the organism, perception, motivation, thinking, and preparation for action. Thus we will describe the effect of culture in terms of some constructs that many psychologists use in their explanations of behavior. In each case we shall point out *behavior* that is common to members of a culture but that differs among cultures, for in the behavior we can directly *observe* the impact of culture. From the behavior, we try to infer the effects of culture on the mental processes of human beings. In the following discussion, see whether you can pick out the inferred constructs and processes.

Percepts, Concepts, and Beliefs

In a society where fishing is important, members of the society can discriminate small changes in the weather and in the conditions of the sea which would go unnoticed by most members of our culture. Eskimos can discriminate variations in different kinds of snow that most Americans would simply identify as snow. We can conclude that people in different cultures learn to perceive the world differently.

Differences in the way people perceive the world lead to differences in the way people categorize and interpret events. Let us look at the way different American Indians handle the concept of time.

■ A Navaho Indian can recall precisely the sequence of a series of events, but would have difficulty trying to remember the specific date of any one of these events; conversely the St. Lawrence Eskimo has no difficulty recalling the date of any specific event, but he might have trouble trying to remember what happened first.

Hopi Indians do not understand time as a continuity from the past through the present to the future; nor do they have a noun to express our concept of time. To them something is either "earlier" or "later." The Hopi further divide events into *objective* and *subjective*: the objective include what exists, or has been perceived; the subjective, what is thought, imagined, or expected, which includes what we would call the future. (Whorf, 1940) ■

Differences in ways of perceiving and conceptualizing the world can often be studied by looking at the differences in the words and grammar of the language spoken by different peoples. The Arabic language has 6000 words referring to the camel (Thomas, 1937).

When we talk about beliefs we are referring to organizations of percepts and concepts stored in the minds of individuals. Many beliefs are common to almost all members of a particular culture. The myths and religions, the rites and cere- monies, the literature and the paintings of cultures reveal to us their beliefs about their world. Beliefs have profound effects on behavior. In some cultures, the people believe certain acts are prohibited by the gods, who will punish by death the person who performs these acts. Fear of violating such a taboo* is so strongly learned that when someone does so, even accidentally, he sometimes stops eating and dies. (Cannon, 1942; Barber, 1961)

Motives and Values

We can infer that a person has a motive for a goal when we observe that this person's behavior is persistently directed toward that goal. A man who has not eaten for five hours and who searches the streets until he finds a restaurant is demonstrating his motive for food. A general category of goals sought by many members of a society is called a value. And one of the major differences between cultures is in their hierarchies of values. In the Navaho culture, esthetic experiences, such as singing, are sought and considered holy. In other cultures, such as our own, utilitarian values are more important: "Handsome is as hand- some does." The Navaho value skill and excellence in work, but do not value success as we do (Kluckhohn and Leighton, 1947).

---

* A serious social prohibition on behavior.

Values integrate many specific motives. The Navaho, who value beauty, learn motives for creating and enjoying beauty in many specific forms.

Habits, Customs, and Norms

When we say that a man has a habit, we mean that he has the tendency to act in specific ways under specific circumstances. A man may have a habit of lighting a cigarette every time he sits down to drink coffee. This is an idiosyncratic habit, but many habits are learned by all the members of a particular culture. Let us look at gestures as an example:

■ Efron (1941) made a careful study of gestures used by three groups: Italian immigrants living in an Italian district of New York, Polish and Lithuanian Jews living in a Jewish section of New York, and Americanized Italians and Jews living in an Americanized environment. He found that the Italian gestures with his arms, while the Jew employs his head as well as his arms, hands, and fingers. Jewish gestures change direction more frequently than Italian gestures. Italian gestures tend to be made symmetrically by both hands while Jewish gestures are asymmetrical. Jewish gestures tend to be directed toward the body while the Italian gestures tend to be away from the body. Many other significant differences appeared. All of these differences tended to disappear among the acculturated group, and gesturing was generally less frequent in this group. ■

Patterns of behavior—habits—that are typical of the members of a society are known as *customs*. Different cultures have different customs for many ordinary tasks. For example, customs surrounding eating determine not only the type of food eaten but the manner in which it is eaten. If an individual fails to carry out a custom, there are no serious consequences—except in the case of one kind of custom, a *norm*. The defining characteristic of a norm is that if an individual deviates from it, he is punished by the rest of society. There are serious prohibitions against deviating from accepted patterns of behavior with regard to powerful motives like sex and aggression in most societies. We saw earlier how different the norms about aggressive behavior are in the Arapesh and Mundugumor cultures.

Values, the general goals of a society, help to integrate norms into a consistent system. There are clusters of norms surrounding the major values of a culture. For example, we have a whole group of norms surrounding the value of cleanliness in our culture: our patterns of cleaning our houses, our clothes, and ourselves regularly.

Imagine a person who grew up outside of a culture. What would he be lacking? Obviously, he would lack many of the goals we have, such as becoming a success or being popular, but in addition he would lack the skills we learn to achieve our goals. Not only would he be unable to read or speak, but he would also be unable to perceive and structure the environment as we do. Probably the most striking illustration of this are the children who are alleged to have

FIG. 2-2. Bound so that he will not run away, this culturally deprived boy feasts on a diet that appears to be more antelopian than human. The "Gazelle Boy" was found in 1946 running wild in the Syrian Desert. There he had grown up without any influence of culture whatsoever. (United Press International Photo)

grown up in the forest living with animals. Anecdotal accounts of these children describe them as if they resembled animals more than human beings (see Fig. 2-2)

Constructs and Culture

Were you able to pick out the constructs that help us to summarize and explain the effect of culture on the individual? We spoke in terms of percepts, concepts, beliefs, motives, values, habits, and patterns of habits. They are part of our own experiences, but we cannot observe them directly in others. You cannot see someone else's perceptions and beliefs; you cannot touch concepts and motives. However, after observing people in a variety of cultures we can summarize the effect of culture on the individual by saying: the culture not only influences the perception and interpretation of the world but also sets up goals (values) for which individuals learn to strive and provides typical patterns of behavior (customs and norms) which people may use to attain them (see Fig. 2-3).

How Do People Learn to Behave in Accordance with Their Culture?

The most impressive thing about a culture is its continuity. This continuity results from the techniques developed in all cultures for strengthening the tendency to behave in the desired manner and for weakening the tendencies to

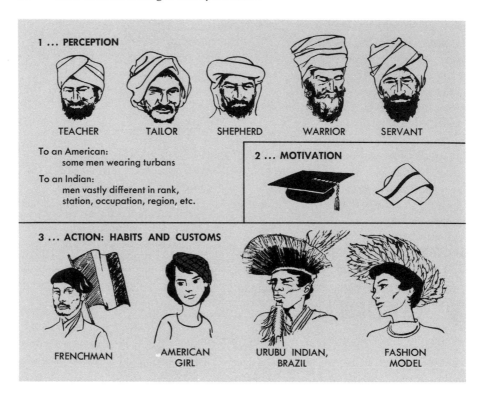

FIG. 2–3. The effect of culture on the mental processes of its members can be seen via the meanings and uses of head coverings. (1) An Indian would perceive vast differences among these men in turbans, whereas an American would not. (2) In our culture, hats may be used to indicate that a person has achieved a valued goal such as graduation from college or nurse's training. (3) Cultures prescribe the customary head coverings for men and women.

behave deviantly. Each individual who enters the culture by birth or by immigration learns to act in accordance with the basic beliefs, values, and norms of his culture.

Much of this training occurs in childhood. As the child experiments with his own behavior, other members of the culture respond to him. Very early in life, the boys hear such phrases as, "Young men don't act like that." "Only little girls play with dolls." "See how your father does it." When the boy acts as people in his culture are expected to act, he is praised. When he deviates, he is punished. In our culture physical punishment, threat of withdrawal of love, or ridicule may be used as punishments for nonconformity. Love, acceptance, and praise are rewards for fulfilling cultural expectations. The patterns of punishments and rewards guide the behavior of the young child toward habits typical of the culture.

Children learn their culture not only via punishment and reward of specific habits, but also via general habits* such as obedience and imitation. If you have ever observed young children, you have probably noticed the striking resemblance between the gestures, accents, and words of a child and his parent. A little girl, playing with her dolls, scolds and praises them with the same words and intonations her mother used with her. When a child imitates people who reflect the culture, his behavior and his thinking also begin to show cultural features.

In addition to teaching children certain patterns of behavior, each culture has devices for instilling motives to want to conform. Once this motivation is strong, a person will be more likely to act in accordance with the norms of his culture as soon as he discovers what these norms are, and no other specific punishment or reward is necessary. An example is the familiar desire to "keep up with the Joneses" for its own sake.

This motive is also very important in maintaining the continuity of a culture. The child who has been raised in a culture grows up and becomes a parent. It is partly because of his motivation for conformity that he trains *his* child in the values, norms, and beliefs of the society.

From Whom Does a Child Learn His Culture?

Culture is not a passive, impersonal force. A child learns about his culture from people and from the creations of people. We have already mentioned the parents as important agents for transmitting the culture. Parents in different societies solve the problems of infant care in different ways. For example, in all societies babies must be fed. Typically, the baby is fed at the mother's breast, but sooner or later the baby must be weaned to drink from a cup and eat solid food. There are at least 52 societies for which reports are available concerning the age weaning is begun. In most societies weaning is begun sometime between 2 and 3 years of age, but one tribe in India does not begin weaning until age 5 or 6; well toward the other extreme is our society, where weaning typically begins much earlier (Whiting and Child, 1953).

Parents in different societies handle the problems of restriction and discipline of the child differently. Many Americans have tended to think of the child as subject to dangerous impulses that must be checked if the child is to attain satisfactory adult adjustment. Thus American parents in general feel a heavy responsibility for training their children properly so that they will be good law-abiding citizens. In contrast, many Samoans think of socialization as a process of unfolding or development. They believe that children have simply not yet developed the ability to behave according to the cultural standards, and hence do not need special training. Since children may be nuisances because of their

----

* Specific and general habits are discussed more fully in Chapters 5 and 7.

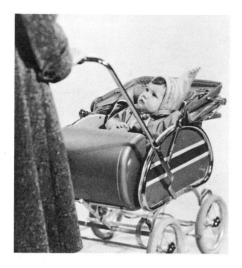

FIG. 2–4. In all cultures mothers transport their babies as they carry out other chores. The American mother is likely to use a baby carriage, whereas this French Moroccan mother carries her baby on her back. In addition to the mother's veiled face, another cultural facet can be seen in the child's partially shaved head. (Left photo: Wide World Photos; right photo: United Press International Photo)

inability to conform to the cultural norms, Samoan babies are watched by young girls, and if a baby does misbehave, he is dragged out of earshot of the group. Thus Samoan children do not learn, "If I am to receive reward and escape being spanked, I must do what my parents ask," but "If I am to be let alone and allowed to stay where I like, I must keep quiet, sit still, and obey the rule."

Samoan children are ignored, but the Hopi child is lord of the manor. While he is a young child, adults and older sisters seem almost subservient to him. What he wants, he takes. But suddenly the situation changes, and his parents, his uncles, and other adults begin to exert pressure toward cooperative, unselfish behavior. One of the chief factors used in Hopi socialization is fear of supernatural beings that will hurt or eat children. (Thompson and Joseph, 1944; Mead, 1928)

All these differences in the ways parents care for their children contribute to making an American child peculiarly American; a Samoan child peculiarly Samoan; a Hopi child, a Hopi. (See Fig. 2–4.)

As a child grows older, he comes in contact with many different people and things that familiarize him with the beliefs, values, and norms of the culture, and that reward him for acting in accordance with them. Classmates and playmates, judges, teachers, and ministers, books, films, and television all serve as communicators and enforcers of culture in a modern society.

In a well-integrated culture the motives and patterns of behavior that the child learns in early childhood are reinforced by his experiences throughout life. Sometimes, however, the pattern taught in the home differs greatly from that in the rest of society. In some cases the home is part of a subculture differing from the general culture; in other cases the individual home offers deviant training.

■ Johnny's mother had wanted a daughter. When Johnny was born, she was so disappointed that she refused to treat him as a boy. She let his hair grow long and kept him in baby dresses for an unusually long time. The pressure of the culture made itself felt through friends and relatives so that she eventually had Johnny's hair cut and dressed him in shorts. But even when Johnny was beginning school she insisted that Johnny avoid rough, dirty games, and started him studying ballet and tap dancing. The other boys wouldn't play with Johnny and called him "sissy." Johnny was unhappy; he became disobedient and ill-tempered. The behavior he had been rewarded for learning at home was not the behavior expected of boys in our American culture, and he was being punished for deviation. Fortunately, Johnny's mother sought professional help, and the problem was eventually solved as the mother learned what was at the root of Johnny's unhappiness and her own behavior. ■

In cases like these there may be conflicting pressures and strain. Note that our society has a technique, psychological counseling, for dealing with this strain.

What Are the Sources of Variability of Behavior Within a Society?

Thus far we have emphasized the uniformity and stability of behavior in a given culture. However, we have already hinted at the fact that no culture achieves complete conformity. Not only do immigrants enter societies, but the culture itself is continually in a process of change. Individuals are inherently different and consequently perceive and conform to the cultural norms differently. Families differ in the way in which they teach the values and customs of the culture. These and other factors produce variability within a culture.

We have statistical techniques for describing both the average behavior and the degree to which it varies. If we were to compare Arapesh, Mundugumor, and American people on a scale of cooperativeness as measured by time spent working together toward a common goal, we would first be interested in how the average times differed. The arithmetical average, or *mean,* is a concept you undoubtedly learned in high school. If we added up scores for cooperativeness for a group of Arapesh and divided the sum by the number in the group we would probably find a mean higher than that for groups of Mundugumors or of Americans.

But in addition we would probably find that Americans were much more variable than Arapesh or Mundugumors. One statistic for describing variability is called the *standard deviation* (see Fig. 2–5). In this case we say that the

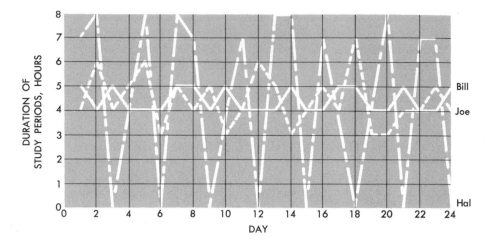

FIG. 2–5. The number of hours spent in study by three students on 24 successive days. All three boys studied 4½ hours a day on the average, but there was considerable difference in the variability of their study times. Joe's study periods were quite regular every day, Bill's hours were slightly more variable, and Hal's study times were very variable, ranging from no studying at all on some days to 8 hours of study on others. If we were to compute the standard deviations of the study hours per day of each boy, we would find that the standard deviation of Hal's hours was much higher than Bill's, which in turn was slightly higher than Joe's—even though the mean of their study periods was identical.

standard deviation of the American distribution is greater than that of the Arapesh.

The *mean* and *standard deviation** are statistical concepts useful in describing many kinds of distributions of psychological characteristics. It is important to realize that both concepts are relevant when one speaks about a social custom. When we speak about a custom, we are usually describing something approximating the mean in a distribution of behavior. But ordinarily there is some variability in behavior, which can be represented by larger or smaller standard deviations. Cultures differ not only in the average behavior, but also in the amount of variability that results from the interaction of the individual and his cultural training.

Variability within a culture can be partitioned into three categories—variability due to differences among individuals, variability due to differences among roles, and variability due to differences among subgroups of the society. We shall now look at each in turn.

---

* A more complete discussion of mean, standard deviation, and other statistical concepts introduced in the text may be found in Appendix I.

Individual Differences in Behavior

In the following chapters we shall discuss at more length some of the biologically determined sources of individual differences. Here we need only point out that even at birth individuals differ from one another. Hereditary factors inevitably result in variability of behavior among people in the same culture. Big, strong men are likely to act differently from smaller, weaker men; hereditary factors influencing intelligence will affect the ease with which different children learn and the roles they adopt.

In addition to his inherited individuality, each person is born to and raised by parents whose perceptions and applications of the cultural norms differ. Families differ in the way they train their children; in fact, even in the same family the training of children born at different times may differ. An oldest son obviously has an environment quite different from that of his baby brother. Brothers and sisters may form alliances, compete against one another, or one may follow where another leads. Homes may be broken by death or separation of the parents, so that the emotional balance of the family shifts. Children may rebel against parental authority and adopt forms of behavior different from that of their parents. As a result of these factors, plus other environmental differences, we have a great range of individual differences in a given culture even though behavior is clustered around certain characteristic patterns of behavior.

Differences in Behavior Resulting from Roles

Although some of the demands of a given culture are the same for all members, many of the patterns of behavior that are expected of an individual depend upon his sex, age, occupation, and many other factors. Patterns of behavior that are typical of people in particular positions in society are called *roles*. We have already seen how sex roles differ, but in addition to sex, other positions of an individual will determine how he is expected to behave. A man's behavior is expected to differ from a boy's and a banker is expected to dress and act differently from a factory worker. Each individual has a number of roles that he is expected to play (see Fig. 2–6), and these differences in role prescriptions account for some of the variability of behavior in a society. A person learns his roles as he discovers that different patterns of behavior are rewarded and punished under different circumstances.

Individuals learn to conform to the expectations of society in a number of roles, such as the role of the oldest son in the family, the role of an adolescent boy in age-sex grouping, and the role of captain of the high school football team. These roles may be in harmony, or they may demand patterns of behavior that are mutually incompatible. For example, while the pattern of behavior expected of an adolescent by his parents is one of obedience, he is expected by his friends to assert his independence from his parents. It has been suggested that an in-

FIG. 2–6. In the course of a day, the same person has a number of different roles: (a) at home, this man is a parent relaxing with his daughter; (b) at the office, he is a businessman, interviewing an applicant for a loan; (c) in the evening, he is a teacher, giving a course in finance in a community college; (d) he is also a civic leader, accepting the president's gavel from the retiring president.

dividual in a given situation usually behaves in terms of only one or a few of his roles, shifting roles as he enters a situation where he has a different position or status. When roles conflict, however, he must work out some system of priority or compromise. If he finds this impossible, he will have to deal with the resulting frustration.

Thus we see that some of the differences in behavior result from combinations of roles individuals play. However, we must also remember our first source of variance—differences among individuals. Two individuals may differ greatly in the manner in which they carry out the functions of the same role. Presidents Kennedy and Johnson obviously behaved quite differently in the role of President of the United States.

Subcultural Differences

A third source of cultural variability is the variation among groups within a culture. Norms of behavior differ for different groups within a society. For example, it is commonly assumed that there are differences in customs between people living in rural areas and those living in the city. This common assumption is supported in some respects by studies of the population of the United States. The average educational level of the urban population is higher than that of rural areas. City dwellers tend to vote Democratic while rural dwellers tend to vote Republican. In a national survey of adjustments, people living in metropolitan areas expressed more general worry and less happiness than people in smaller towns or rural areas. However, those in rural areas reported less marital happiness than city dwellers. (Gurin, Veroff, and Feld, 1960) Such differences may be important. Nevertheless, social scientists suggest that the differences between country and city people seem to be much less marked in the United States than in most other countries.

Within our culture, nationality and racial groups also form subcultures with differing beliefs, values, and norms. In many cities groups with certain ethnic backgrounds tend to live together partly because of choice but sometimes as a result of pressure from dominant groups. Such minority groups naturally develop their own group norms, some of which may differ from those of the society as a whole.

Subcultures may also form on the basis of religious groupings. The difference between Roman Catholic and Protestant norms of church attendance and permanence of marriage is evident, but it may be surprising to learn that the differences between religious groups extend to child rearing. Protestants are less likely to use physical punishment than are Catholics (Miller and Swanson, 1958). Jews are characterized by higher achievement motivation and more liberal social and political attitudes than other people in our society (e.g., Gurin, Veroff, and Feld, 1960).

SOCIAL CLASS DIFFERENCES. Even more important than religious or ethnic differences are subcultural differences in social class. Most people are aware of some distinctions among people of different education, wealth, and occupation. While most Americans feel that such class distinctions are not so important in the United States as in Europe, they do recognize that the patterns of behavior differ for members of different social classes. The social class structure of several American communities has been studied, and although different authors use different criteria for dividing social classes, their results agree with some common ideas about social distinctions. That the results from research on social classes should agree with popular conceptions is not surprising, since one of the factors bringing about convergence into a social class is the fact that people within the group regard the group as having certain homogeneous characteristics.

Although one might classify people into as many social classes as he wished, at least three major categories are typically used: lower, middle, and upper class. Additional distinctions such as upper-middle, lower-middle, and working class are sometimes made. People may be ranked in terms of several dimensions. Typically one thinks of wealth, family background, education, occupation, nationality, and race as being dimensions relevant to one's status in society. If he thinks of social class at all, the average person thinks of social class as an all-or-nothing category. Either one is a member of the upper class, or one is not. However, societies differ in the degree to which different dimensions of status are related. For example, in medieval society, one's family, his wealth, and his education were highly related. It is clear, however, that in America one may rank high or low on one dimension without having corresponding status in the other dimensions, even though we would expect a positive overall relationship.

One way of studying social classes is in terms of individual perceptions. If people are asked, they can usually identify certain families as members of the "upper crust" and others as "no-goods." Another method of studying social class is to determine who associates with whom. In a society where class lines are very clear most of a person's associations are with others of similar status. Studies indicate that even in public high schools, cliques tend to be made up of members of the same social class (Hollingshead, 1949).

After having developed social-class categories on the basis of criteria such as those we have discussed, the social scientist is interested in finding out what other characteristics are associated with social class membership. Some data, such as membership in clubs, offices held, and private or public education, are objective and can be obtained by observation or by study of official records. However, other differences between social classes can be obtained only by talking to the individuals themselves.

Since it is not possible to talk to everyone, the social scientist draws a random sample* of members of each social class, interviewing those families drawn in his sample. By carefully designing an interview which does not contain ques-

---

* A random sample is a number of individuals or items chosen from a group in such a way that every member of the group has the same chance to be chosen as has each of the other members.

tions biased toward certain answers, by choosing and training interviewers in such a way that the interviewer's own attitudes will not affect his interviews, and by using trained coders to classify the responses reported by the interviewer, it is possible to obtain quite reliable data even on such unobservable constructs as values and attitudes. There are, of course, special problems in knowing how much of what people say corresponds with what they really feel and do, but the results may be valid enough to be useful.

■ A team of social scientists (Useem, Tangent and Useem, 1942) conducted a study of social classes in a Midwestern town. As an example of their findings, let us look at what their study revealed about the class at the top of the social structure, the "uppers," and the class at the bottom, the "lowers." The uppers were those who had been in the upper class for years. They were mostly college graduates who owned their own homes and were considered wealthy. They customarily associated with one another, both socially and in business, prided themselves on their culture, and frequently visited larger cities. The upper women belonged to clubs and were often mentioned on the society pages of the local papers. The men owned or operated their own businesses, sat on boards of directors at banks and were consulted about community decisions. The norms rewarded among the uppers were urbanity, success, both business and social, and fashionable dress. They avoided ostentation, tended to be conservative, had a strong sense of the past and of the traditional way of doing things.

Contrasted with these, the lowers at the very bottom of the social structure were unskilled or semiskilled laborers whose work was irregular and who constantly faced economic disaster. They did not mind getting help from each other in time of trouble. They were poorly educated— grammar school at best—and lived in cheap housing. Although the family was the most important social group among the lowers, their marriages lacked stability, the women usually worked, in spite of their many children. The lowers felt no ambition to try to "get ahead," since they could see no hope of improving their lot and they resented the uppers. They placed no value on reading or on cultural activity. Their behavior was often aggressive, their speech and sexual activity frequently uninhibited. ■

Cultural Change and Conflict

Within the variability of a culture lie the seeds of cultural change. Individuals discover and create new ideas, new ways of behaving, and new products. These may spread to other members of society. A single change in a cultural practice often sets off a chain reaction that leads to modification in a number of cultural practices. Yet because so many people have learned the old ways so well, dramatic changes in one area may cause little immediate change in other aspects of the culture.

This delay in change of some aspects of a culture is called *cultural lag.* Such lags are found in almost all aspects of a changing culture (see Fig. 2–7). For example, the construction of adequate highways lags behind the manufacture of more and faster automobiles; similarly, everyone is aware of the critical lag between the development of nuclear bombs and the development and acceptance of adequate controls. Another example of cultural lag in human behavior is the change in America from the authoritarian farm family of the 19th century to the greater freedom of the family in the 20th century. In the 19th century the wife and children worked in producing the necessities for the family's existence, and the father was the boss of the family production unit. Economic conditions changed, releasing wife and child from their work. Modern women are likely to work in positions independent of their husbands. However, the family pattern was much slower to change than the economy and in many families, the father still exerts the old-style authority. (Ogburn and Nimkoff, 1955)

FIG. 2–7. In this street scene from Saigon we see evidence of cultural lag. Although automobiles, paved streets, and many other modernizations are evident in this city, man is still used as a beast of burden. (United Press International Photo)

As the new African and Asian nations adopt some of the political and technical aspects of Western culture, there will be many examples of strain brought about by cultural lag. Surely the stabilizing influences to which we have pointed will make rapid change difficult.

During periods of cultural change, there may be a difference between the norms, values, and beliefs held by the older generation and those held by the younger. The individual is caught among the expectations of his parents, the desire of his parents to comprehend the change, and the pressures of his peer group. This phenomenon is illustrated in the difficulties of the children of immigrants to the United States.

■ Child (1943) studied the conflicts between first- and second-generation Italian Americans. The children in these immigrant families are exposed to one set of customs at home and another set of customs among their peers—customs related to food, gesture, recreation, family organization, selection of a marriage partner, etc. The children find greater social and economic success if they drop the Italian customs and follow American ones. Yet they feel the pull of the ways they have learned at home. They cannot, however, turn to their parents for help. The parents want their children to become Americanized, yet they feel a sense of loss, distance, and resentment as they see the "old country" ways being shed. ■

Faced with such conflict, the youth may be unable to use their set of customs with security. However, such pressures can also lead to a constructive search for order that results in a unique synthesis of old and new.

Culture and Psychology

In our brief survey of the cultural background of behavior, many questions have been raised: What are the dynamics of learning habits and motives? How can differences in cultural training lead to differences in perception? What determines how a person will respond to conflict and frustration? How do individuals modify and change the continuous stream of culture?

These are psychological questions, and to answer them we must look at the psychological processes of individuals in greater detail. Just as an understanding of the individual requires a consideration of culture, so we cannot fully understand the impact of culture without an understanding of individual psychological processes.

Summary

Concepts

Society. A group of people living in one area who have developed methods of getting along with one another and surviving as a group longer than the individuals within the group

Culture. The total set of values, expectations, attitudes, beliefs, and customs shared by the members of a group, nation, or religion

Role. A prescribed pattern of behavior assigned to particular categories of individuals in a society

Norm. A custom so important in a society that conformity is rewarded and deviation punished

Mean.   The arithmetic average of a group of numbers

Standard deviation.   A statistic describing the variability of a set of numbers

Social class.   A group of people differentiated from other members of society in terms of income, housing, values, and prestige, who associate with other members of the group socially and are perceived by themselves and others as belonging to a distinctive social level

Principles

1. Different cultures have different standards of behavior.

2. From observing consistencies in the behavior of people from the same society and differences in the behavior of people from different societies, we can infer that culture affects perception, motivation, thinking, and action.

3. People learn to live in accordance with their culture from their interactions with other people, especially their parents, and from their contacts with cultural products such as literature and art.

4. There is a range of behavior within a culture even though most behavior centers around characteristic customs.

5. Differences in behavior within a society result from individual differences in heredity, from differences in families, from differences in roles, and from differences in subcultures.

6. Because so many social institutions reinforce cultural norms, cultures are stable and change slowly. Because societies are systematically organized, acceptance of change in one sort of behavior initiates changes away from other traditional patterns of behavior.

7. Cultural lag occurs when older practices persist despite modern developments which render the older practices obsolete.

Suggested Readings

MEAD, MARGARET, *Sex and Temperament in Three Primitive Societies.* Mentor Book MD133. Contains more about the Arapesh *et al.*

FORTUNE, R., "Arapesh Warfare," *American Anthropologist,* 41 (1939), 22–41.

KATZ, D., "Field Studies," in Festinger, L., and D. Katz (eds.), *Research Methods in the Behavioral Sciences.* New York: Holt, Rinehart, and Winston, 1953. Compares the methods of anthropological studies with other types of field studies.

MEAD, MARGARET, *Coming of Age in Samoa.* Mentor MD153. Describes the socialization practices in Samoa. You'll find particularly interesting the difference between Samoan culture and ours in the stresses of adolescence and sexual adjustment.

BENEDICT, RUTH, *Patterns of Culture*. Mentor MD89. A classic account of the common behavior patterns in different societies.

KLUCKHOHN, C., *Mirror for Man*. Premier D58. A more comprehensive popular account of cultural anthropology.

KAHL, J. A., *The American Class Structure*. New York: Holt, Rinehart, and Winston, 1957. A survey of studies of social class.

the biological background of behavior

chapter 3

ON WHAT LEVELS CAN WE STUDY THE
ORGANISM?

WHAT ARE THE BASIC STRUCTURES AND
FUNCTIONS OF THE NERVOUS SYSTEM?

WHAT DETERMINES WHICH CIRCUITS OF
THE CNS WILL BE ACTIVE?

HOW IS CNS ACTIVITY MODULATED BY
EXTERNAL FACTORS?

On What Levels Can We Study the Organism?

The problem of understanding the functioning of the human organism is similar to the problem of understanding the working of an unknown highly complex machine. If someone showed us a computer in operation, we could learn something about it by observing the input to it (the punched paper tape) and the output from it (printed-out letters, words, and numbers and punched paper tape). If we could understand the paper-tape code, we would see that the message going into the computer consists both of material to be processed and instructions on how to process it; for example, a series of numbers with an instruction to add them. We might notice that some of the instructions refer to inputs that were presented to the machine at an earlier time, and from this we could infer that the machine has the capacity to store information in a "memory." From the fact that certain material is selected and transformed to produce the output, we could infer that there was an active processing unit. By observing inputs and outputs, we could construct a fairly accurate picture of the overall functions of the computer. This method of study is similar to the one we described for studying human beings. The psychologist can observe the inputs to the organism (*stimuli* from the environment) and outputs from the organism (the *behavior*). By observing both the situation and the behavior, the psychologist makes inferences about the kinds of functions that occur inside the organism. In the last chapter, we inferred that many of our habits, concepts, beliefs, and motives were learned from the cultural environment, stored inside the person, and activated to influence behavior under certain conditions (see Fig. 3–1).

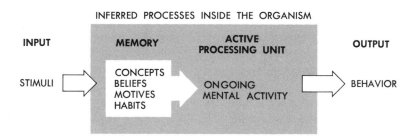

FIG. 3–1. One level on which we can study the organism is the *behavioral* level. Observations of the situation and behavior lead to inferences about processes occurring inside the organism.

However, there is another way to study the computer, and that is by taking the machine apart, looking at its components, and trying to understand the function of each component in its relation to the other components and in its relation to the whole machine. Similarly, we can look at the machinery that is responsible for mental processes and behavior: the sense organs, the muscles, the glands, and the nervous system. So, before we begin our discussion of psychological processes, let us examine the biological background of behavior.

What Are the Basic Structures and Functions of the Nervous System?

While characteristics of the muscles, skin, and other physiological aspects of the organism may influence a person's behavior, the nervous system is the chief coordinating system and the major focus of our interest. Its importance was dimly understood over 2000 years ago as is indicated by the following passage written about 400 B.C.:

■ And men should know that from nothing else but from the brain come joys, delights, laughters, and jests, and sorrows, griefs, despondency and lamentations. And by this, in an especial manner, we acquire wisdom and knowledge, and see and hear and know what are foul and what are fair, what sweet and what unsavory . . . And by the same organ we become mad and delirious and fears and terrors assail us, some by night and some by day—and dreams and untimely wanderings, and cares that are not suitable and ignorance of present circumstances, destitute and unskillfulness. All these things we endure from the brain . . . (Hippocrates, trans. 1886) ■

As we shall see, modern physiologists and physiological psychologists have discovered the nature of many of the relationships, which Hippocrates hypothesized, between the brain and experience.

Whenever we adjust to a change in our environment, our behavior involves three kinds of structures: (1) *receptors*, which are the structures that are sensitive to stimulation in our eyes, ears, and other sense organs; (2) *effectors*, which are our muscles and glands, our bodily equipment for doing things; and (3) *the nervous system*, which connects the receptors and the effectors. The nervous system extends throughout the body; at each point on the body where one can feel pressure, pain, heat, or cold the *sensory* or *afferent* nerves transmit the message sent by the receptor. *Motor* or *efferent* nerves run to each muscle and gland transmitting the message to contract or relax or to secrete.

One of the most remarkable things about the nervous system is that messages can be routed from almost any receptor to any effector. This is possible because most messages are routed through a central coordinating center—the central nervous system, or CNS.

THE NEURON. The basic unit of the nervous system is the neuron, a single nerve cell. Usually when we think of a cell, we think of a small compact unit. Neurons, however, have treelike *dendrites* extending from one end of their cell bodies and long strandlike *axons* extending from the other end. The neuron and its relationship to the nervous system is depicted in Fig. 3–2.

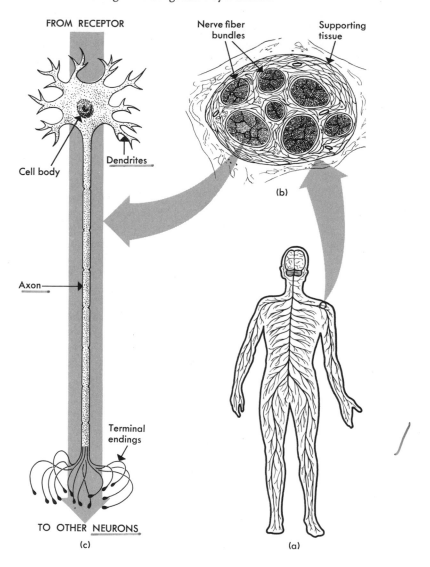

FIG. 3–2. The nervous system (a), with a cross section of a nerve
shown in (b), consists of billions of nerve cells called *neurons* (c).

The function of the neuron is to transmit messages from one point in the
nervous system to another. The different structures of the neuron are specialized for different aspects of the task. The dendrites and the cell body are the
areas that receive and integrate messages from other neurons, the axon is the
structure that transmits the message over long distances, and the terminal endings of the axon relay it to the next neuron.

The "message" to which we have been referring is actually a pattern of electrical and chemical changes in various portions of the neuron. The resting cell —one which is neither sending nor receiving messages—has a polarized cell membrane; that is, throughout the cell the inside of the cell is electrically negative with respect to the outside.

When the initial segment of the axon is sufficiently excited, an electrochemical disturbance is propagated from this point to the end of the axon. This electrochemical disturbance, which is called the *nerve impulse* (see Fig. 3–3), consists of a reversal of polarity in segments of the axon. It is a chain reaction; the reversal of polarity in the initial segment sets off changes in the polarity of the adjacent segment which in turn sets off changes in the next segment, and so on, to the end of the axon. The nerve impulse is an *all-or-none* reaction; that is, the strength of the nerve impulse is equal in each segment of the axon. The fact that the nerve impulse is conducted without decrement means that it can be transmitted over long distances without weakening.

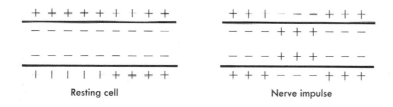

Resting cell   Nerve impulse

FIG. 3–3. In the resting cell, the inside of the cell is negatively charged in relation to the outside. As the nerve impulse travels along the cell, successive portions of the cell reverse their electrical charges.

The speed at which the nerve impulse travels varies with the size and the type of axon. In the largest fibers the impulse travels at a rate of 200 to 300 feet per second. In fibers of smaller diameter, the rate may be as low as two feet per second. For example, it takes only about $\frac{1}{30}$ of a second for an impulse to travel from a person's toe to the top of his spine.

The endings of an axon contain sacs called *synaptic vesicles* which contain chemicals known as transmitter substances. Physiologists have identified several compounds as transmitter substances (e.g., acetylcholine and epinephrin), and have suggested several others as possible transmitter substances (see Fig. 3–4). When the nerve impulse reaches the terminal endings of the axon, it causes the vesicles to secrete the transmitter substance into the tiny space between the axon and the dendrites or the cell body of the adjacent neuron. Note that two neurons do not actually touch each other, but are separated by extremely small spaces. This space between the axon endings of one neuron and the dendrites or cell body of another neuron is called a *synapse*.

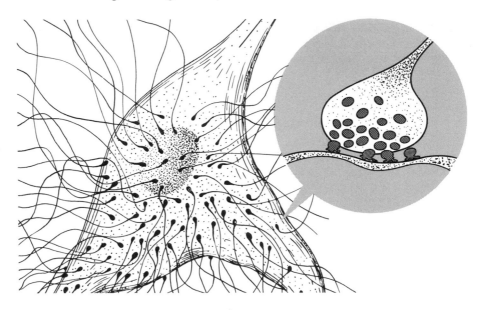

FIG. 3–4. This enlargement of a small portion of the receiving area of a neuron reveals that the end foot of a sending neuron contains sacs filled with transmitter substances.

The transmitter substance travels across the synapse and produces changes in the *postsynaptic* membrane, that is, the membrane of the cell body or the dendrite of the receiving neuron.

The postsynaptic membrane is chemically sensitive and it responds to the transmitter substance in one of two ways: (1) Some transmitters cause the postsynaptic membrane to reverse its polarity. As we shall see, this increases the probability that the nerve impulse will be initiated, and the postsynaptic cell is said to be *facilitated*. (2) Some transmitters cause the postsynaptic membrane to become even more polarized (hyperpolarized), that is, to become even more negative inside the axon with respect to the outside. This decreases the probability that the nerve impulse will be initiated, and the postsynaptic cell is said to be *inhibited*.

These electrochemical changes in the postsynaptic membrane differ from the nerve impulse in several ways: (1) Rather than being all-or-none, the size of the postsynaptic disturbance varies with the amount of transmitter substance. (2) The postsynaptic disturbance becomes weaker as it travels toward the axon; it is conducted with a decrement (see Fig. 3–5).

The dendrites and the cell body of a neuron may have synapses with as many as 10,000 other neurons. Thus at any given time, various areas of the postsynaptic membrane are initiating hyperpolarizing reactions and reactions which reverse polarity. All these reactions are combined at the initial segment of the axon. If the electrochemical disturbance at this point is sufficient, the all-or-none nerve impulse will travel the length of the axon. If the electrochemical disturbance at the initial segment is not sufficiently strong, there will be no nerve impulse. Each neuron has a *threshold,* an amount of electrochemical disturbance at the initial segment of the axon, which is sufficient to set off the all-or-none nerve impulse. Whether or not the electrochemical disturbance reaches the threshold depends on the pattern of facilitation and inhibition produced at the cell's various synapses.

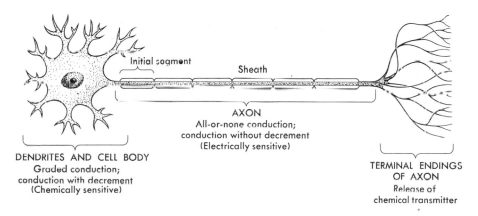

Initial segment

Sheath

AXON
All-or-none conduction;
conduction without decrement
(Electrically sensitive)

DENDRITES AND CELL BODY
Graded conduction;
conduction with decrement
(Chemically sensitive)

TERMINAL ENDINGS
OF AXON
Release of
chemical transmitter

FIG. 3–5.   Different portions of a neuron vary in the stimuli to which they are sensitive and the manner in which they transmit the "message."

Another nerve impulse cannot be initiated immediately after the nerve impulse traverses an axon. During this period, called the *absolute refractory* period, no amount of electrochemical disturbance at the initial segment is sufficient to initiate the nerve impulse. This is followed by a *relative refractory* period, during which the threshold of the cell is higher than normal. Thus during the relative refractory period, a greater electrochemical disturbance than usual is necessary in order to "fire the neuron"; that is, to initiate the nerve impulse. We can see that whether or not a particular cell conducts a nerve impulse depends on the interaction of a number of factors: the threshold of the individual cell, the pattern of facilitation and inhibition, and the time elapsed since the most recent previous nerve impulse. When we consider that physiologists have estimated that there are approximately ten billion (10^{10}) neurons in a mammalian nervous system, and $10^{2,000,000}$ synapses, we can appreciate the tremendous complexity of the "machinery" which is responsible for mental experience and behavior.

Gross Structure and Function

From each of the major sense organs there are many neurons arranged in parallel; for example, a million neurons connect the eye to the brain. Similarly, bundles of parallel neurons go from the spinal cord to muscles and glands. The distance between the brain, spinal cord, and the other structures, (receptors and effectors) is spanned by bundles of axons called *nerves,*

Neurons originating from the sense organs scattered throughout the body synapse with the central nervous system at the spinal cord,* a series of neurons in the center of the spinal column. At the nape of the neck the central nervous system widens to become the brain.

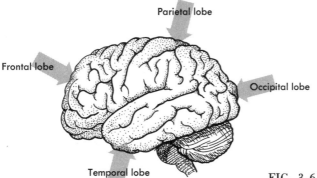

Parietal lobe

Frontal lobe

Occipital lobe

Temporal lobe

FIG. 3–6. The lobes of the cortex.

The human brain can be divided into several major parts, as indicated in Plate 1.† The lower portion, which is continuous with the spinal cord, is the brain stem. The upper portion is the cerebral cortex, a complex structure folded in upon itself (see Fig. 3–6). The cortex itself is divided into four lobes: frontal, parietal, occipital, and temporal. Like most body systems, the nervous system is bilaterally symmetrical; the right half and the left half are mirror images of each other.

How can the functioning of a complex mass of 10 billion neurons be studied? Psychologists, physiologists, and physicians have developed a number of methods that provide a way to begin to find the answer.

One method is to study the effects of damage to the nervous system. In the course of treating their patients, physicians have noted changes in behavior accompanying injuries, tremors, and diseases. For example, damage to an area in the frontal lobe has been associated with a patient's inability to speak. The effects of damage to various portions of the brain can be studied more systemati-

---

* Sense organs located in the head are connected by a series of neurons directly to the brain.

† Color plates are inserted between pp. 64 and 65.

cally in animals. A small portion of the animal's brain can be surgically removed. Then, after the animal recovers, his behavior can be observed through a variety of observations and tests. One series of such studies shows that adult rats, cats, and monkeys have no pattern vision after areas in the occipital lobe are destroyed, although they can still discriminate between different levels of brightness.

Another method of studying nervous system functioning is by recording the electrical activity of the nervous system in various ways. The summated electrical activity of the neurons in the brain is so great that it can be recorded through electrodes attached on the outer surface of the head. Such recordings are known as electroencephalograms (EEG's). One finding using this technique is that different patterns of electrical activity accompany different levels of alertness in human beings. Figure 3–7 shows the EEG's of persons who are sleeping, a person relaxing with his eyes shut, and a person who is excited.

Since the initial segments of axons respond to electrical stimulation, another technique for studying brain function involves stimulating various areas and observing the results. For example, in 1870 Fritsch and Hitzig (cited by Ferrier, 1886) applied electric currents to the back of the frontal areas of the cortex. They found that stimulating particular areas in this region elicited a particular movement.

Stimulation techniques have also been used as part of the procedure in brain surgery. In order to discover what particular areas of the brain do, prior to

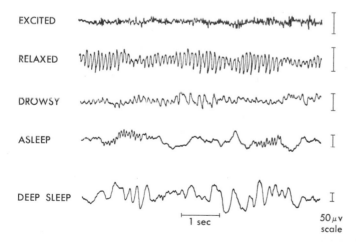

EXCITED

RELAXED

DROWSY

ASLEEP

DEEP SLEEP

1 sec   50 μv
scale

FIG. 3–7. These EEG's were taken from people in different states of alertness. The vertical lines at the right show the scale used or the deflection represented by 50 Mv. The scale of the recording of a person in deep sleep is reduced more than the others. If it were not reduced, the waves would appear much larger. (Penfield, W. and H. Jasper, *Epilepsy and Functional Anatomy of the Brain*. Boston: Little, Brown, 1954. Reprinted by permission.)

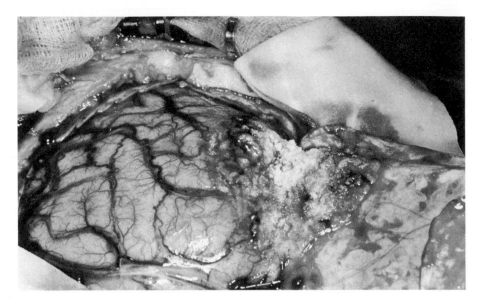

FIG. 3–8. A human brain, surgically exposed, during a brain tumor operation. To determine how much tissue to remove, the surgeon might electrically stimulate areas surrounding the tumor and thus find out what their functions are and whether the areas are essential. (Photo courtesy of Dr. Joseph F. Dorsey, Director, Neurosurgical Foundation, Brighton, Mass.)

possible removal due to tumor or disease (see Fig. 3–8), a weak electric current has been applied to specific parts of the cortex of human beings. The brain itself is insensitive, and the awake patient feels no pain during this procedure. In conjunction with such exploration, Penfield and Rasmussan (1950) have found specific functions for specific areas: an area in the frontal lobe, whose stimulation produces movement; an area in the parietal lobe, whose stimulation yields sensations of being touched in various parts of the body; an area in the occipital lobe, whose stimulation yields visions of splotches of light; and an area in the temporal lobe, whose stimulation produces sensations of sound. Stimulation in another area of the temporal lobe causes the patients to recall very vividly, almost to relive, events from their past (Penfield and Roberts, 1959).

These studies, and others using animal subjects, show that different areas of the cortex do have specialized functions (see Fig. 3–9). However, we should not conclude from this discussion that the only brain area concerned with vision is the occipital lobe; or that the only area concerned with sound is the temporal lobe. The brain is a highly complex structure. Each brain area has interconnections with many, many other parts of the brain. Thus when a study shows that the temporal lobe has some auditory (hearing) functions, this means that *one* of the important links in the nervous system chain which results in hearing has been located.

For many years, physiologists and psychologists have known that the cortex has much to do with the way we move and the way we receive and interpret information from the world around us. But until recently we knew little about the psychological significance of the portion of the brain lying between the cortex and the lower brain stem. It was almost impossible to investigate these areas without widespread damage to the cortex and other areas. Within the last thirty years, techniques have been developed which permit psychologists and physiologists to investigate these areas with the recording, stimulation, and ablation techniques. Basically, these techniques involve insertion of very small needlelike electrodes deep into the brain. The electrodes are so small that there is very little cortical damage. They range from $\frac{1}{100}$ in. in diameter for stimulating, recording from and destroying groups of neurons to $\frac{1}{100000}$ for recording from and stimulating single neurons. These techniques have opened up a new world to the psychologist interested in the neural mechanisms of behavior.

A structure in the upper brain stem known as the *hypothalamus* has been investigated both by stimulation and by surgery in animals. Electrical stimulation of different regions of the hypothalamus produces fearlike and ragelike reactions and changes in eating, drinking, and sexual behaviors. Removal of

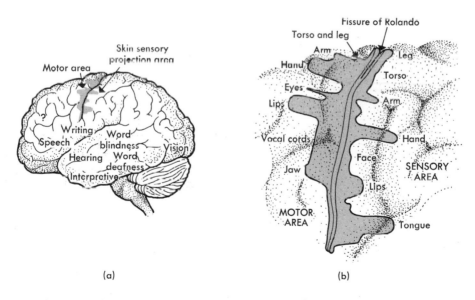

(a)   (b)

FIG. 3–9.   (a) Some of the psychological functions of different areas of the cortex. (b) An enlargement of the motor and sensory areas shaded in (a). Note the identification of specific areas where various portions of the body are represented. Note also that the amount of brain devoted to each part of the body depends not on the size but on the sensitivity of that part (in the sensory area) and the fineness of movement of that part (in the motor area). Thus in the sensory area, the tongue has a much larger representation than does a region of the torso of comparable size, and in the motor area the lips have a much larger representation in the brain than does a comparable region of leg.

particular areas produces animals that overeat, that stop eating, that never sleep, and that manifest other abnormalities. These hypothalamic areas are apparently associated with the positive and negative motivations that are so important in directing behavior.* (Hess, 1957)

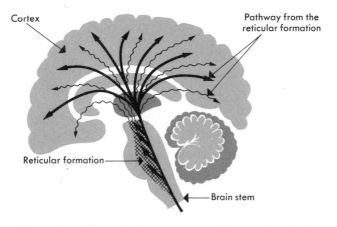

Cortex

Pathway from the reticular formation

Reticular formation

Brain stem

FIG. 3–10. The reticular formation (the crosshatched region) has synapses with neurons throughout the cortex. (The arrows indicate pathways from the reticular formation.) One of the functions of the reticular formation is believed to be the regulation of amount of activity in the cortex.

Another structure of special psychological interest is the reticular formation, a network of neurons in the center of the lower brainstem (see Fig. 3–10). The reticular formation receives branches from all sensory nerves on their way to the cortex and from particular areas in the cortex. The formation sends axons to all parts of the cortex. Injury to the reticular formation produces sleep or coma. Stimulation of the upper-area formation in monkeys awakens them from sleep, increases the amount of neuron activity in their cortices, and produces general alertness. Stimulation of lower areas has opposite effects, inducing sleep and inhibiting movement. These results suggest that one of the functions of the reticular formation is to act like a volume control, regulating the amount of activity in the nervous system.

We do not know the functions of all the parts of the brain, nor do we know how all the different areas relate to one another. But physiologists and psychologists have been discovering many pieces of the puzzle. We know that the brain has areas that receive and interpret sensory information (such as the sensory cortex), areas that send messages to muscles and glands (such as the motor cortex), areas that regulate the general alertness of the brain (such as the reticular formation), and areas that relate the needs and

* More studies on the relationship between the hypothalamus and motivation are presented in Chapter 7.

motions of the organism with behavior (such as the hypothalamus). Note that no area was singled out as a thinking area or as a problem-solving area. Complex psychological functions such as these have not been localized, even partially, to any one region. These functions require integrated activity in many areas of the brain.

What Determines Which Circuits of the CNS Will Be Active?

The nervous system is always active. Waves of electrochemical activity are continuously sweeping across the brain. A change in the on-going activity of the nervous system can occur as a result of new stimuli from the environment, as a result of metabolic conditions inside the body, or as a result of spontaneous central activity.

External Stimuli

When a stimulus, such as a light, activates a sense organ, such as the eye, it sets up activity in sensory neurons. The sensory nerves trigger activity in the spinal cord and in the brain. Sometimes the specific path taken by the activity is determined by one specific arrangement of neurons (see Fig. 3–11).

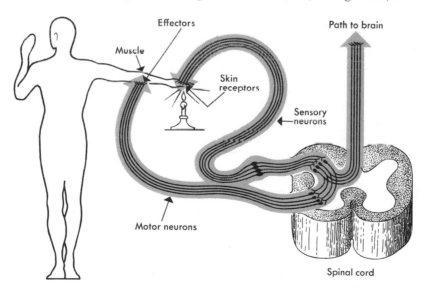

FIG. 3–11. A diagrammatic sketch of a reflex arc, which shows how some responses are dependent on the built-in circuitry of the nervous system. When the sensory neurons are stimulated, they fire neurons in the spinal cord, which in turn fire motor neurons which cause a muscle to contract. Thus a stimulus, such as the flame, almost inevitably results in the response of retraction.

In this case activity in sensory neurons reliably produces activity in motor neurons, and a particular stimulus reliably produces a particular response. A response that is dependent on such built-in sensory-motor circuitry is called a *reflex*. Reflexes often involve only sensory neurons, neurons in the spinal cord, and motor neurons; the response occurs before the activity reaches the brain. The immediate reaction of removing your hand when you inadvertently touch a hot stove is an example of a reflex. Have you ever noticed that you remove your hand *before you feel the pain?* This is because the paths from the sensory neurons through the spinal cord to the motor neurons are more direct than the paths up the spinal cord to the cortex, the area whose activity is probably responsible for your sensation of pain.

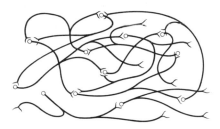

FIG. 3–12. A diagramatic representation of the arrangement of neurons in the cortex.

In lower animals, there are built-in circuits activated by complex patterns of internal and external stimuli that lead to a complex series of responses (instinctive behaviors). For example, migratory flight in birds is a reaction to changes in hormone balance and in the amount of light per day.

The pathways activated in human beings by most stimuli are not this rigidly fixed. The neurons in the brain are not arranged in neat tracts of axons laid out in parallel; they are arranged more like a pan of spaghetti, *each axon leading*

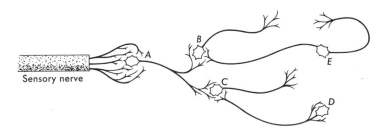

Sensory nerve

FIG. 3–13. This diagram shows how the effect of an incoming impulse from a sensory nerve depends on the on-going activity of the brain. An incoming sensory nerve triggers activity in neuron *A*. If the thresholds of *B* and *C* require facilitation from two neurons in order to fire, there are four possible outcomes: If neither *D* nor *E* is conducting nerve impulses, neither *B* nor *C* will fire. If both *D* and *E* are active, both *B* and *C* will fire. If *E* alone is firing when *A* is firing, then *B* alone will fire.

to a different, perhaps remote, portion of the brain (see Fig. 3–12). There are a number of potential pathways over which the activity can travel. The pathway taken by a series of nerve impulses depends not only on the activity started by the stimulus but also on the other activity going on in the brain. Earlier we mentioned that each individual neuron has a threshold, an amount of electrochemical disturbance which is sufficient to trigger the nerve impulse in the axon. Usually, facilitation from at least two neurons is necessary to reach the threshold of a third. In the brain, where pathways diverge and on-going activity interacts with the activity coming in from stimuli, there are many possible patterns of facilitation and inhibition (see Fig. 3–13); thus the effects of a stimulus depend upon other neural activity. For example, what does the word "beat" mean? Did it make you think of pounding on a drum? winning a game? an accent in music? whipping a dog? or a certain subculture? The effect of this word on your mental processes depended on the kinds of activity already going on in your brain. Because the pattern of nerve activity evoked by the word was not rigidly set down at birth and because there were a number of possible paths of neural activity, the response depended not only on the stimulus, but also on your other brain activity.

Metabolic Activity

The nervous system receives information not only about the environment external to the person but also about the physiological state of the "internal environment of the body." In order for an organism to survive, the physiological balance of the body must be kept within certain limits. The processes by which the internal environment is kept within these limits are called *homeostatic processes*. Many of these processes are automatic. If, for example, blood sugar is low, the liver secretes sugar into the blood until the concentration of blood sugar is restored to the normal level. If body temperature falls, the person shivers, producing heat. If he becomes too warm, sweating occurs, reducing the temperature. Similar mechanisms maintain equilibrium in blood pressure, heart rate, salt and water balance, calcium and phosphorous balance, and so on. These processes do not affect the higher portions of the nervous system, and often we do not experience them when they occur.

However, some aspects of the balance of the internal environment are maintained by the intervention of behavior. When the concentration of salt in the blood increases, there are cells in the hypothalamus which become active. These cells set off nerve impulses in many specific areas, including the reticular formation, which increases the general activity of the nervous system. As this activity occurs in a person's brain, he becomes restless and uncomfortable, and he feels thirsty. When he gets a drink of water, he feels better. One of the mechanisms that helps to maintain the balance of the internal environment is this arousal of feeling that accompanies some physiological imbalances.

Autonomous Central Activity

Not all the integrated activity of the nervous system can be traced to an origin in external or internal stimulation. The brain, particularly the human brain, is capable of maintaining long chains of integrated activity without each phase being initiated by a source external to the brain. Autonomous changes in brain activity are set off as we think, solve problems, and create.

The Brain and Learning

One of the most remarkable features of the "machinery of behavior" is that it is set up to change itself. On a behavioral level, we see this process in learning. A situation in which a person once made many uncoordinated responses after a period of learning elicits a smooth coordinated set of movements, in learning how to play golf, for example. On a physiological level, we noted earlier that an individual is born with a brain that has many potential pathways. One way of conceptualizing the effects of a person's experiences on the brain is to think of learning as a process by which specific pathways in the brain become more and more probable in specific situations.

No one knows exactly how experiences change brain structure. The relation between brain and learning is the subject of much current experimentation and theorizing. To illustrate current thinking on the subject, we shall mention two theories: Hebb's theory of synaptic growth and the RNA hypothesis.

Hebb (1949) assumed that when one neuron A frequently facilitates another neuron B, the terminal endings of neuron A actually grow, so that the space between A and B is smaller. This according to Hebb, would increase the probability that A would facilitate B. Thus if sets of neurons have "fired" each other several times in the past, they will tend even more strongly to fire each other in the future.

Another theory assumes that the structural change in learning is a change in the structure of the giant protein molecule, ribonucleic acid (RNA). Ribonucleic acid normally controls the formation of new proteins in the cell. Hyden (1962) hypothesized that the altered RNA causes protein changes which modify the secretion of the transmitter. This change in the pattern of transmitting secretion will in turn modify the pathway over which the nerve impulse will be conducted.

How Is CNS Activity Modulated by External Factors?

The central nervous system does not function in isolation. It is affected by events occurring elsewhere in the body, by substances taken into the body, and by injury. We cite the four following case histories to illustrate the effects of these factors.

■ Charles C. is depressed. His face shows his anxiety and worry. He has difficulty sleeping and has a poor appetite. He realizes that his memory is poor and fears that he is losing his mind and will become seriously ill. He feels that Communists are persecuting him and is fearful that they will kill him. He complains of sensations of ants crawling over his body, and has had visions of Christ and angels speaking to him. (Mr. C. is suffering from pellagra, a disease in which nerve fibers degenerate, resulting in symptoms of which those above are fairly typical.) ■

■ Donald D. was in a serious automobile accident. He was unconscious when taken from the automobile, but after some hours regained consciousness in the hospital. After being released from the hospital some weeks later, he complained of headaches and dizziness. He reported that he no longer was able to concentrate and that he seemed to lack endurance even on relatively simple tasks. These symptoms worried him. (Donald D. shows symptoms of brain injury, probably in the front part of the brain.) ■

■ Elmer E. has lost his pep. He does not want to bother to do anything at all. He pays little attention to what is going on around him. Elmer notices that he is gaining weight and that his skin is getting dry and coarse, but it seems like too much trouble to do anything about it. (Elmer's thyroid gland is underactive.) ■

■ Fred F. is excited. He is engaged in boisterous horse play with a group of friends. When one of his friends fails to appreciate the humor of having his chair yanked from under him, Fred becomes angry and invites the friend outside to fight. On the way outside he walks unsteadily and when the fight begins sees double images of his opponent. (Fred shows symptoms of alcoholic intoxication.) ■

The Effects of Other Body Systems: the Endocrine Glands

The nervous system depends on other body systems for its life processes. It must be supplied with nutrients, and its waste must be carried away. Malfunction anywhere in the body can affect the CNS.

The endocrine glands are particularly closely associated with the central nervous system. These glands secrete hormones chemical substances which, when carried through the body by the blood stream, affect cells in the CNS. Since the rate of flow of the blood is slower than the speed of a nerve impulse, this system of communication is slower than the nervous system, but recent research indicates that it is faster than was previously thought; endocrine secretions may be effective within a period of a few minutes and perhaps even within seconds. Glands can influence the nervous system in two ways. One of these ways is through neural centers which are sensitive to particular hormones. The second way in which endocrine glands affect behavior is through their effect on metabolism, which may alter the functioning of all neurons and thus have very general effects on the nervous system.

Figure 3–14 illustrates the location of the endocrine glands. Of particular importance to us are the thyroid glands, the adrenal glands, the gonads or sex glands, and the pituitary gland. Each of these glands controls certain functions.

THE THYROID GLAND. The thyroid gland influences metabolism. If the thyroid gland is overactive, an individual is likely to be overactive, anxious, and unstable. These symptoms may be related to the fact that thyroid secretions affect the activity of the reticular system. A deficiency in thyroid secretion continuing from early childhood may result in sluggishness, body deformation, and low intelligence. Such a deficiency in adulthood leads to the kinds of symptoms shown by Elmer E.

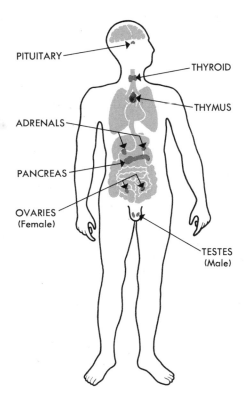

FIG. 3–14. The endocrine glands.

THE ADRENAL GLANDS. The adrenal glands are divided into two sections: an inner adrenal medulla and an outer adrenal cortex. One of the secretions of the adrenal medulla, epinephrin, is a stimulant that prepares the body for action. When the individual perceives a threat, the part of the nervous system (the sympathetic nervous system) controlling the adrenal gland is activated and epinephrin is secreted. Increased epinephrin in the bloodstream leads to faster heartbeat, release of sugar from the liver, diversion of the blood to the muscles, and other changes which prepare the body for emergency action.

Recent research also suggests that the type of reaction to stress, fear, or anger may be related to the adrenal secretions. The adrenal medulla, which secretes epinephin, also secretes another similar hormone called norepinephrin. Mental patients who are generally angry at other people secrete more norepinephrin than patients whose general emotional reaction is fear or depression. The depressed, fearful patients, on the other hand, secrete more epinephrin. This finding checks with the findings that aggressive animals, such as the lion, have a relatively high amount of norepinephrin while rabbits and domestic animals have a relatively high amount of epinephrin (Funkenstein, 1955).

A secretion of the adrenal cortex, *cortin,* is necessary to maintain the proper level of sodium in the body. Since sodium is necessary for nerve excitability, undersecretion of cortin results in inactivity. Cortin is essential for life; if the adrenal cortex is removed from an animal, it will die.

THE GONADS. Sex hormones are secreted by the *gonads.* During the early years of life the gonads are relatively inactive, but during adolescence the gonads increase in size and their secretions regulate the secondary sex characteristics, such as growth of a beard and change of voice in the male and development of breasts in the female. In addition to the importance of these characteristics for fulfillment of one's sex role, the male sex hormone, testosterone, heightens aggressiveness and sexual motivation in men. The female sex hormones, such as estrogen and progestin, regulate the monthly cycle as well as the course of pregnancy.

THE PITUITARY GLAND. In some ways the pituitary gland is analogous to the brain, for just as the brain is the chief controlling center of the nervous system, so the pituitary regulates the activity of the other endocrine glands. The pituitary sends hormonal messengers through the blood which increase or diminish the amount of secretion of the other glands.

NERVOUS CONTROL OF THE ENDOCRINE SYSTEM. The nervous system and the endocrine system interact. The endocrine glands secrete hormones that have profound effects on nervous system function; at the same time, the nervous system itself coordinates endocrine activity.

The autonomic nervous system (ANS) is a series of neurons running from the spinal cord to various effectors, including the endocrine glands. (See Plate 2.) The ANS has two divisions: the sympathetic nervous system, which is most active during times of stress, and the parasympathetic nervous system, which is more active in times of quiescence.

The coordinator of the autonomic nervous system is the hypothalamus, the structure that has centers for body needs and emotions. The hypothalamus also exerts direct influence over the endocrine system. In Plate 3, you can see that there is a blood system connecting the hypothalamus and the pituitary gland. The hypothalamus contains cells which secrete substances into this blood system, which goes directly to the pituitary gland. Thus the hypothalamus affects the endocrine system through two media: (1) via the autonomic nervous system, which ennervates the individual endocrine glands and (2) via its effect on the pituitary gland, which is the chief coordinator of endocrine activity.

The Effects of Substances Taken into the Body

NUTRITION. While fish is commonly referred to as "brain food," there seems to be no way in which the efficiency of the nervous system of the average person can be improved by nutrition. Like the rest of the body, the CNS has nutritional requirements, but the chief one is glucose, which the body can derive from almost any diet. In fact, most deficiencies damage other parts of the organism before affecting the CNS. Certain extreme nutritional lacks, however, do affect the nervous system and thus affect behavior. For example, the behavior of Mr. C., the man who feared Communists, was due to pellagra, a disease primarily caused by lack of nicotinic acid (niacin), a B-vitamin, in the diet. Without niacin, nerve fibers, particularly those in the peripheral nervous system, degenerate. These effects on the nervous system may account for some of the unusual psychological symptoms in pellagra, such as bizarre beliefs or delusions.

Certain cases of feeble-mindedness have been shown to be caused by a deficiency of glutamic acid. When this substance was given to children whose diet has been deficient in it, their intelligence test scores rose. Glutamic acid does not, however, affect the intelligence of children not suffering from a deficiency.

■ Twenty-five children selected by Smith and Field (1926) as markedly underweight were given school lunches over a six-month period, together with health lessons and various motivational devices designed to bring about physical improvement. As compared with normal controls, striking gains were shown in weight, but mental development appeared to be unaffected. ■

Every so often, popular magazines tell of miraculous changes in intelligence brought about by giving feeble-minded children a drug or vitamin. While lack of certain vitamins or other nutritional substances may result in mental deficiency that can be corrected by administering the missing substance, no substance has been found which will improve the intelligence of children who have had an adequate diet.

DRUGS. The blood that brings nourishment to the brain may also carry substances, such as drugs, that change its functions. Any student who has seen an intoxicated person could guess that certain drugs affect the nervous system. A great many studies of the effects of alcohol have been made, and we now can relate some of the observable changes in behavior to changes alcohol produces in the nervous system. For example, the exhilaration and excitement characteristic of the mildly intoxicated individual is not the result of stimulation but is due to the removal of the inhibitory effect of the higher brain center.

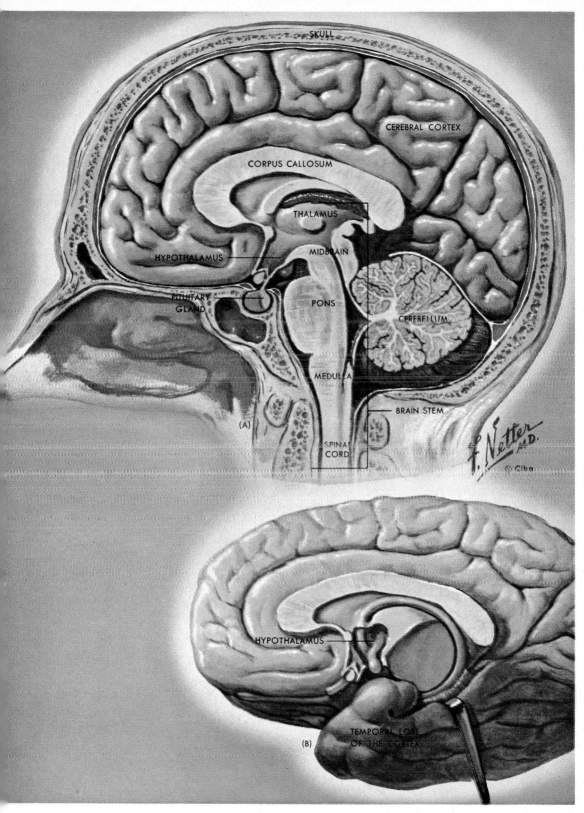

PLATE 1. Medial aspect of the brain (as though a cut were made from the nose, to the forehead, to the back of the head). B shows structures hidden by lower brainstem in A. (Adapted from THE CIBA COLLECTION OF MEDICAL ILLUSTRATIONS by Frank H. Netter, M.D. Copyright CIBA.)

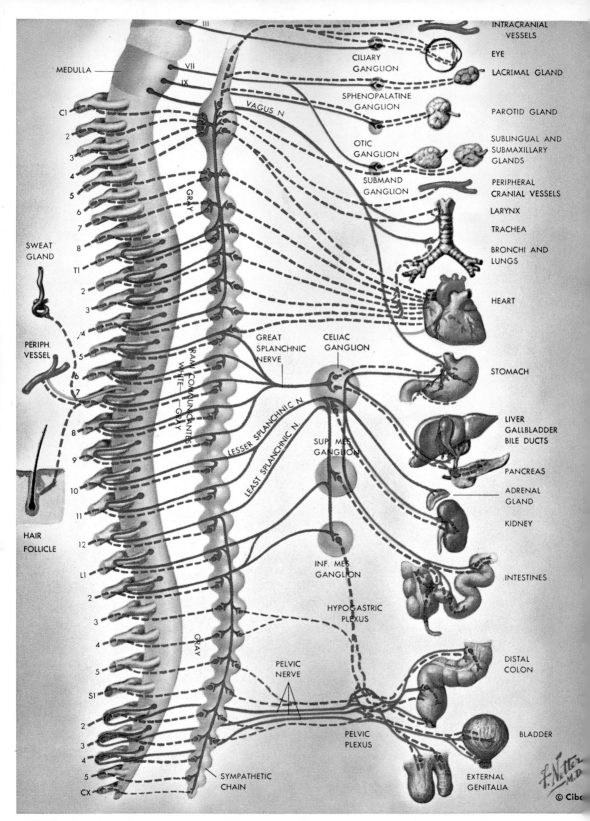

PLATE 2. The autonomic nervous system and the organs it affects. The sympathetic nervous system is shown in red and the parasympathetic in blue. (From THE CIBA COLLECTION OF MEDICAL ILLUSTRATIONS by Frank H. Netter, M.D. Copyright CIBA.)

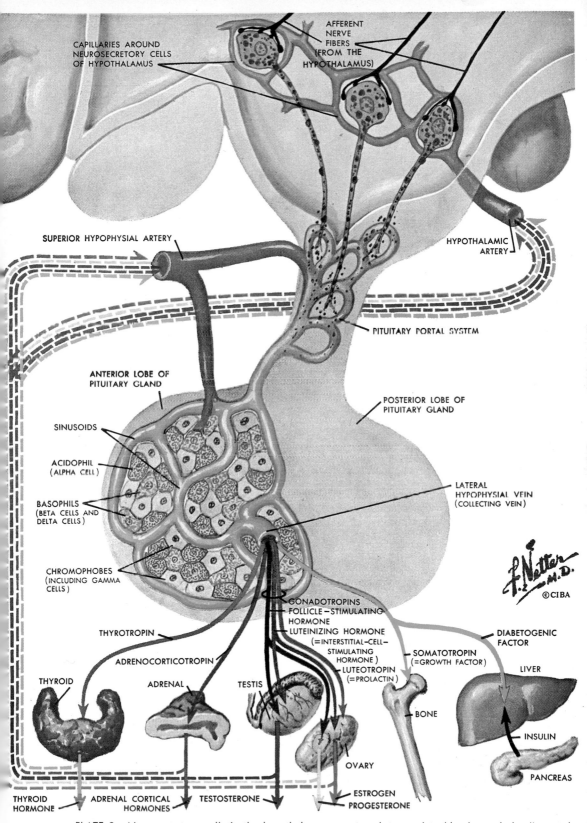

CAPILLARIES AROUND NEUROSECRETORY CELLS OF HYPOTHALAMUS

AFFERENT NERVE FIBERS (FROM THE HYPOTHALAMUS)

SUPERIOR HYPOPHYSIAL ARTERY

HYPOTHALAMIC ARTERY

PITUITARY PORTAL SYSTEM

ANTERIOR LOBE OF PITUITARY GLAND

POSTERIOR LOBE OF PITUITARY GLAND

SINUSOIDS

ACIDOPHIL (ALPHA CELL)

BASOPHILS (BETA CELLS AND DELTA CELLS)

LATERAL HYPOPHYSIAL VEIN (COLLECTING VEIN)

CHROMOPHOBES (INCLUDING GAMMA CELLS)

GONADOTROPINS
FOLLICLE-STIMULATING HORMONE
LUTEINIZING HORMONE (=INTERSTITIAL-CELL-STIMULATING HORMONE)
LUTEOTROPIN (=PROLACTIN)

THYROTROPIN

ADRENOCORTICOTROPIN

SOMATOTROPIN (=GROWTH FACTOR)

DIABETOGENIC FACTOR

LIVER

THYROID

ADRENAL

TESTIS

BONE

INSULIN

OVARY

PANCREAS

THYROID HORMONE

ADRENAL CORTICAL HORMONES

TESTOSTERONE

ESTROGEN PROGESTERONE

F. Netter M.D.
©CIBA

PLATE 3. Neurosecretory cells in the hypothalamus secrete substances into blood vessels leading to the pituitary gland, which controls other endocrine glands via its hormones. (Adapted from THE CIBA COLLECTION OF MEDICAL ILLUSTRATIONS by Frank H. Netter, M.D. Copyright CIBA.)

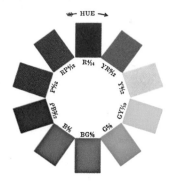

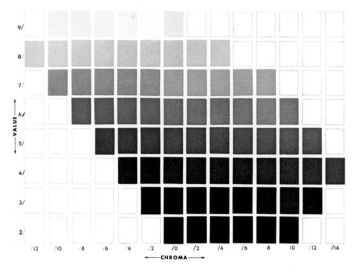

PLATE 4. Some hues at maximum saturation. Complementary hues are directly opposite each other.

(Materials for the illustrations on this page were furnished by Munsell Color Company, Inc., Baltimore, Maryland.)

PLATE 5. Variations in brightness (↑) and saturation (→) within a single hue.

PLATE 6. Variations in the experience of color can be summarized in this three-dimensional model in which the vertical represents brightness, the horizontal represents saturation, and the circumference represents hue.

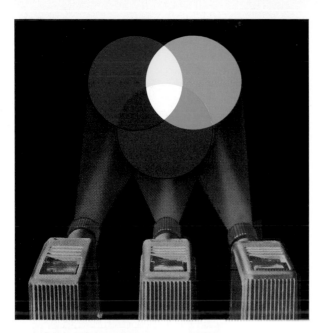

PLATE 7. Additive mixture of lights. Projectors using red, blue, and green filters produce the hues.

PLATE 8. Subtractive mixture. (a) The yellow filter absorbs blue but transmits red and green light. (b) The magenta filter absorbs green but transmits blue and red light. (c) The Cyan filter absorbs red but transmits blue and green light.

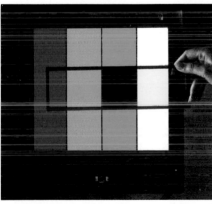

a

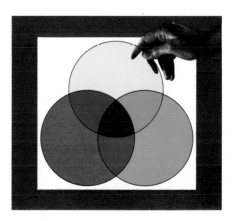

b

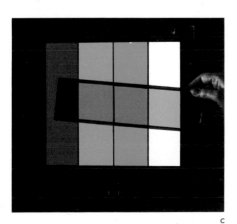

c

PLATE 9. Subtractive mixture produced by superimposing cyan, magenta, and yellow filters.

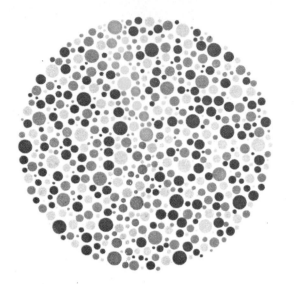

PLATE 10. Because of variations in both hue and saturation, normal people see one bar, color-blind people see two bars, at ten feet. (Used by special arrangement with Dr. Milton B. Jensen.)

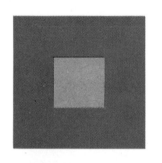 

◀ PLATE 11. The four gray patches are identical. Variations in your perception of them are due to simultaneous contrast.

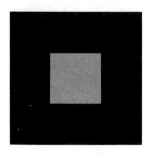 

▼ PLATE 12. Stare at the center of each circle for 30 seconds, then look at a white surface. An after-image in the complementary color should appear. Other interesting after-images can be obtained by shifting your gaze from one circle to another.

PLATE 13. The Land effect. A scene is photographed simultaneously on black-and-white film with two cameras, one whose lens is covered with a red filter, the other with a green filter. The processed slides are then projected by two projectors: the slide taken through the red filter is projected by a red-filtered light; the other, taken through the green filter, by ordinary white light. When the two images are superimposed, the viewer perceives a full color image, such as that shown in the lower photograph. (From Land, E. H., "Experiments in color vision," *Sci. Amer.*, May, 1959. Reproduced by permission. Transparencies by William Vandivert.)

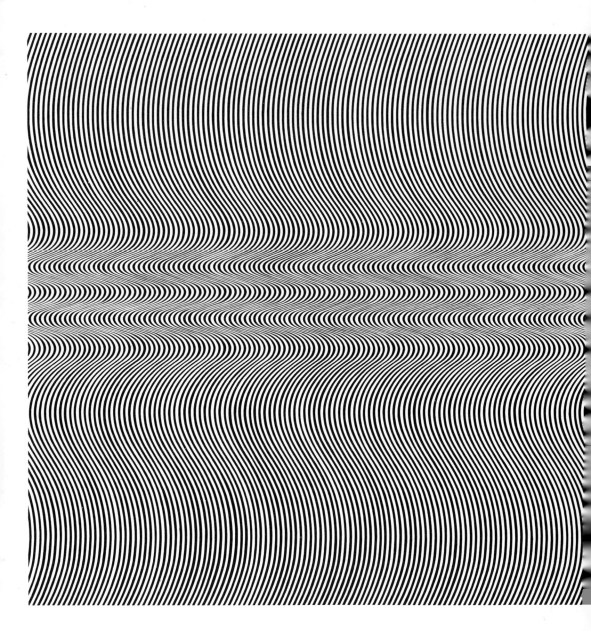

PLATE 14. This "op art" painting by Bridget Riley shows how the experience of hue and movement can be produced by stationary black and white lines. Move and tilt the page for maximum effect. (*Current*, by Bridget Riley, 1964. Collection, The Museum of Modern Art, New York. Philip C. Johnson Fund.)

It is generally believed that alcohol impairs ability to think clearly. One of the best experimental studies of this problem indicated that approximately 4 oz of whisky administered to a 165-lb man produced 11 to 25 percent loss in efficiency on such tasks as coding words and substituting digits for symbols (McFarland and Barach, 1936). The researchers believe that alcohol has these effects because it impairs oxidation, especially in the brain. When alcohol was administered while the subject was breathing air enriched with oxygen, the bad effects were reduced.

Caffeine, benzedrine, and other stimulants increase the individual's general alertness when he is fatigued and thus may indirectly affect decision making. Barbiturates, on the other hand, tend to reduce alertness.

Other drugs also affect behavior through their effect upon the brain.* Two classes of these drugs are of particular interest to psychologists: (1) the tranquilizers, which are used extensively in the treatment of mental illness and (2) psychotomimetic drugs, which produce some of the symptoms of severe mental illness. Tranquilizers are drugs which have the effect of calming a person, although they do not make him sleepy or interfere in other ways with normal mental processes. There are many substances which have tranquilizing effects, and research suggests that different types of tranquilizers reduce anxiety and excitability by affecting different parts of the brain. One, chlorpromazine, depresses the reticular formation, while another, reserpine, does not (Morgan, 1965).

The psychotomimetic drugs produce symptoms such as feelings of unreality, visual hallucination in the absence of external stimulation, and distortions of time and space. One of these drugs, mescaline, was used by the Southwestern American Indians as part of their religious ritual. Another, d-lysergic acid diethylamide (LSD-25), is similar in chemical structure to a substance which occurs naturally in the brain and which has been suggested as a central transmitter substance. This similarity has led to hypotheses and research on biochemical factors in mental illness.

Injury to the Nervous System

The effect of a brain injury on personality and behavior depends on its extent and its location. Injury to the hindmost area in the frontal lobes of the cortex often results in paralysis. Injuries to other cortical areas lead to loss of speech, blindness, and other disabilities. There is some disagreement about the effect of damages to the forward areas of the frontal lobe. Some reports state that damage here leads to loss of anxiety, loss of ability to plan ahead, and lowered concern for ethical values. Other reports describe widespread damage to this area with little or no psychological damage.

---

* The story of these drugs is told in Appendix II.

The lower brainstem has centers that regulate functions which are essential to life, such as heartbeat and breathing. Injuries to these vital centers may be fatal.

Data from human subjects can, of course, be obtained only from neurosurgery or cases of brain injury. But, as we saw earlier, extensive and well-controlled research has been carried out with animals. Experimenters have made many careful studies of the effect of cutting certain fibers or of removing certain sections of the brains of animals. Research with animals has given us much of our information about the CNS and its functions, and has increased understanding of the effects and treatment of various human brain injuries and diseases.

Summary

Concepts

Receptors.   The structures that are sensitive to stimulation

Effectors.   The muscles and glands

Sensory nerves.   The bundles of neurons that conduct impulses from the receptors to the central nervous system

Motor nerves.   The bundles of neurons that conduct impulses from the central nervous system to muscles and glands

Central nervous system (CNS).   The spinal cord and the brain

Neurons.   The single cells constituting the nervous system

Nerve impulse.   The temporary electrochemical disturbance in an axon when its initial segment is stimulated above threshold

Threshold of a neuron.   The amount of excitation necessary in a neuron to initiate the nerve impulse

All-or-none law.   The rule that, in an axon, the nerve impulse fires at full strength or not at all

Synapse.   The space between the terminal axon endings of one neuron and the dendrites or the cell body of another

Reflex.   An automatic response to a stimulus, dependent on unlearned neural connections

Homeostasis.   The maintenance of the "internal environment" of the body within certain physiological limits

Endocrine glands.   A group of glands which secrete hormones directly into the bloodstream

Autonomic nervous system (ANS). The part of the nervous system that regulates glands and certain muscles. Its *sympathetic* division is most active in times of stress; its *parasympathetic* division, in times of quiescence

Principles

1. An organism can be studied both on a behavioral and a physiological level.

2. The axon endings of one neuron cause changes in the postsynaptic neuron by the release of a transmitter substance.

3. Whether or not a neuron conducts the nerve impulse depends on its threshold, the pattern of facilitation and inhibition produced by other neurons, and the time since the last nerve impulse was conducted by the neuron.

4. The brain consists of the brain stem (which contains the reticular formation and the hypothalamus) and the cerebral cortex.

5. The functions of the brain have been studied by systematic observations of behavior following injury, surgery, and stimulation in human beings and animals, and by electrical recording.

6. Various areas of the brain have been shown to play an important role in certain psychological functions: The sensory cortex and the interpretive cortex are important in the reception and interpretation of stimuli; the motor cortex is important in initiation of movement; the reticular formation is important in maintaining various states of alertness; and the hypothalamus is involved in biological drives and emotions.

7. The nervous system is always active. The effects of new stimuli on behavior depend on the pattern of neural activity already in progress.

8. The neurons in the brain have vast and complex interconnections with one another.

9. The endocrine glands affect and are affected by the nervous system.

10. CNS activity may be influenced by dietary deficiencies, injuries, and drugs.

Suggested Readings

The following readings supply more information about the brain.

GERARD, R. W., "Your brain and behavior," *Saturday Evening Post*, **231** (1959), 22, 79–82.

PFEIFFER, JOHN, *The Human Brain*, New York: Harper, 1955.

CUSHING, HARVEY, "Faradic stimulation of the post-central gyrus," *Brain*, **32** (1909), 44–53. A classic account of earlier studies of localization.

WIENER, NORBERT, *Cybernetics*, New York: Wiley, 1948. This recent classic has greatly influenced thinking about human-computer similarities. Wiener also wrote a book for laymen: *The Human Use of Human Beings*, Boston: Houghton-Mifflin, 1950.

VON NEUMANN, JOHN, *The Computer and the Brain*, New Haven: Yale University Press, 1958. A nonmathematical, fascinating book, which was planned by Prof. von Neumann to be delivered as the Sillman lectures at Yale University.

If you are interested in the broader philosophic implications of our study of the biological nature of man, you will be stimulated by reading the following: HERRICK, C. J., *The Evolution of Human Nature*, Austin: University of Texas Press, 1956. Herrick was one of the great men in biology. He wrote this book when past the age of 80.

chapter 4

heredity and maturation

chapter 4

WHAT IS INHERITED?

HOW DOES THE GENETIC BLUEPRINT DEVELOP
INTO AN ORGANISM?

TO WHAT EXTENT IS BEHAVIOR DEPENDENT
ON HEREDITY AND MATURATION ALONE?

WHICH STABLE CHARACTERISTICS OF THE
INDIVIDUAL ARE DEPENDENT ON HEREDITY?

Much of the biological structure of an organism is inherited. The capacity to learn from a cultural environment is also inherited. In this chapter, we shall look at the mechanism of heredity, the unfolding of the hereditary blueprint through maturation, and the effects of hereditary factors on various aspects of behavior.

What Is Inherited?

Each human being begins life as a single cell, which was formed by the union of a spermatozoon from the father and an egg cell from the mother. The nucleus of this composite cell, like all other cells, contains rodlike structures called chromosomes (see Fig. 4–1). Each chromosome is made up of strands of deoxyribonucleic acid (DNA), complex protein molecules that are elementary transmitters of hereditary influences. These protein molecules provide the chemical blueprint for the developing organism.

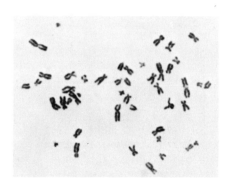

FIG. 4–1. A photomicrograph of human chromosomes. (Courtesy of Drs. T. T. Puck and J. H. Tjio)

Modern biochemists are beginning to unravel the code by which DNA transmits information. Before the discovery of DNA as the biochemical transmitter of inheritance, geneticists discussed the passing on of specific hereditary traits in terms of *genes*. Thus a gene is a construct, a hypothetical structure, which was used to account for the fact that specific traits are inherited. Now scientists are discovering that the properties hypothesized for genes can be accounted for by the activity of DNA.

The chromosomes in the fertilized egg (and in all body cells) occur in pairs; one of each pair came from the sperm cell of the father, the other came from the egg cell of the mother. What is the relation between the chromosomes in the body cells of the parents and the chromosomes in the fertilized egg? The nucleus of every body cell in a human being contains 23 pairs of chromosomes. Each of the sex cells, sperm and egg, is formed from the division of such a body cell. However, the sex cells have only 23 single chromosomes. The reduction of the number of chromosomes occurs when two sex cells are formed from one body cell. Each chromosome pair in the body cell splits, and one of each pair goes to each newly forming cell. Which member of each chromosome pair goes to each cell is a matter of chance, and there are many possible combinations of 23 single chromosomes. The chance combinations of chromosomes in the formation of sex cells and in the formation of the fertilized egg can be compared to dividing and combining decks of cards. Suppose that we have two decks of 46 cards each. The black deck has two suits, spades and clubs, and the red deck has two suits, hearts and diamonds. The cards in all four suits are numbered from 1 to 23. If we take each deck and arrange the cards in pairs according to number, we will have 23 red piles of two cards each and 23 black piles of two cards each. Now we choose one card from each of the red piles. Some of the cards we have chosen will be hearts and some will be diamonds, but we will have one card for each number. Similarly, the body cell divides its 23 pairs of chromosomes and randomly sends one of each pair to each forming sex cell. If we rearrange the cards into the original 23 red pairs, and choose one from each pile again, we will probably come up with a different assortment of hearts and diamonds. In the same way, different sex cells have different assortments of chromosomes.

Suppose that we now choose one card from each of the red pairs and one card from each of the black pairs. We now have 46 cards, 23 pairs numbered 1 through 23. One of each pair will be red; one will be black. The red one in a given pair can be either hearts or diamonds; the black one, spades or clubs. This is similar to the 46 chromosomes in the fertilized egg.

Our two decks, red and black, correspond to the two parents, mother and father. The hearts and diamonds correspond to the chromosomes the mother inherited from her father and mother, respectively, and the spades and clubs correspond to the chromosomes the father inherited from his father and mother. (See Fig. 4–2.)

It is very improbable that we would choose an identical set of 46 cards on successive occasions, though some "runs" of the same cards might occur. Similarly, brothers and sisters do not inherit identical characteristics, although they do inherit some common characteristics. Only in the case of identical twins, when two new organisms develop from a single fertilized egg, will the chromosome inheritance be identical.

The structure of the sex cells of the parent is not influenced by ordinary events that take place in his lifetime. Most of the characteristics that a man acquires in the course of interacting with his environment do not affect the characteristics of the chromosomes he passes on to the next generation. A parent may have acquired a well-tanned skin, work-gnarled hands, a fear of black cats, or a skill in playing five different instruments. His son will not inherit these traits.

The fact that children do not inherit their parents' acquired characteristics has interesting implications. Man today is biologically little different from primitive *homo sapiens*. Although some characteristics may have selectively survived, so that there are some biological differences, the major differences

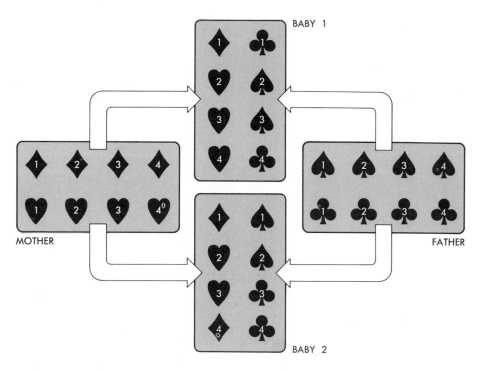

FIG. 4–2. We can diagram hereditary transmission from parents to babies by using the card analogy described in the text. For simplicity, we are diagraming only four of the 23 pairs of chromosomes in human beings.

between primitive man and modern man are due to culture, which enables the experience of one generation to be passed on to the next.

There is one major exception to the rule that acquired characteristics will not affect the offspring. An event which alters the biochemical structure of the sex cells during the lifetime of either parent may influence the inheritance of later children. One example comes from the effects of radiation, either natural or man-made. If radioactive particles bombard the gonial cells, which are the cells that produce the sex cells of the parents, then the chromosome structure of the sex cells can be altered drastically, changing the chemical blueprint that will be inherited by the child at conception.

How Does the Genetic Blueprint Develop into an Organism?

All that is inherited is DNA. These protein molecules are the chemical patterns which guide the growth of the new organism, both before birth and after. The single fertilized cell divides and divides again. The descendants of the original fertilized egg differentiate; some become skin cells, some become muscle cells, some become neurons. Cells develop into functional organs and systems. This growth process, which is dependent on heredity, is called *maturation.**

Maturation cannot proceed unless the environment in which it is taking place provides the proper materials. In the uterus there is a close association between the blood system of the mother and that of the baby. At this point, oxygen, nutrients, and other substances can leave the mother's system and enter that of the baby. Usually the intrauterine environment provides a consistent environment for the normal development of the new organism. However, unusual chemical conditions in the mother can affect the development of the baby at particular stages. For example, if the mother takes the drug thalidomide in her seventh week of pregnancy, the baby's limbs may not grow properly.

After the baby is born, he continues to develop in accordance with the hereditary blueprint. He still depends on his environment to provide the surroundings required for growth. Now he needs not only nutrients and oxygen to keep him alive, but also certain kinds of experiences in order to develop normally.

To What Extent Is Behavior Dependent on Heredity and Maturation Alone?

Reflexes

Some behavior depends chiefly on neural maturation. This behavior results from the activation of built-in circuits in the nervous system. A *reflex* is an automatic unlearned response that takes place in the presence of the appropriate stimulus as soon as the neurons involved are functional. When a bright light shines on the eye, the pupil contracts reflexively.

Instincts

As we pointed out earlier, in lower animals, unlearned connections mediate complex responses to a complex series of stimuli. Such complex patterns of behavior, which are dependent to a large extent on built-in circuitry, are called *instincts.* The state of present knowledge of the nervous system does not permit us to identify most instincts on the basis of their neural patterning. Rather,

---

* The words "growth," "development," and "maturation" are often used almost synonymously. We shall use "growth" to refer to physical development and "maturation" to refer to developmental changes due to heredity (assuming a normal environment). Maturation can refer to physical or behavioral changes. "Development" will be used as the broadest of these terms, referring to the sequence of change in the organism from conception to death.

FIRST STAGE. The male stickleback (left) swims in a zigzag motion toward the female. The female then swims toward him with her head elevated. The abdomen of the female is extended, containing from 50 to 100 eggs.

SECOND STAGE. The male stickleback swims toward the nest he has built and pushes his snout into it several times. He then turns on his side and raises his dorsal spines toward the female.

FIG. 4–3. Courtship of the stickleback. (Drawings reproduced by permission of *Scientific American*)

investigators identify a pattern of behavior as an instinct by these criteria: (1) the particular stereotyped sequence of behavior is typical of every member of the species in the appropriate situation; (2) the behavior is performed adequately the first time; (3) the behavior differs from a reflex in that the instinct involves more complex interrelations between stimuli and responses over a period of time.

We can see the complicated sequences involved in instincts in the following description of mating behavior in the three-spined stickleback.

THIRD STAGE. The female swims into the nest, and the male prods the base of her tail, causing her to lay eggs. When the female leaves the nest, the male enters and fertilizes the eggs.

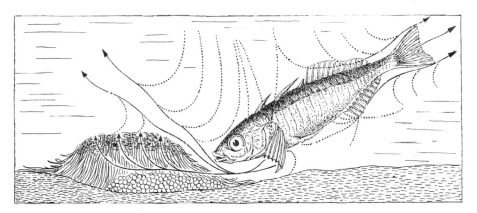

FOURTH STAGE. Using his fins, the male circulates the water through the nest to enrich the oxygen supply of the eggs. The dotted lines show the movement of a colored solution placed in the tank; the solid lines, the direction of the water currents.

■ First, each male leaves the school of fish and stakes out a territory for itself from which it will drive any intruder, male or female. Then it builds a nest. It digs a shallow pit in the sand bottom, carrying the sand away mouthful by mouthful. When this depression is about two inches square, it piles in a heap of weeds, preferably algae, coats the materials with a sticky substance from its kidneys, and shapes the weedy mass into a mound with its snout. It then bores a tunnel in the mound by wriggling through it. The tunnel, which is slightly shorter than an adult fish, is the nest.

Having finished the nest, the male suddenly changes color. Its normally inconspicuous gray coloring had already begun to show a faint pink blush on the chin and a greenish gloss on the back and in the eyes. Now the pink becomes a bright red and the back turns a bluish white. In this colorful, conspicuous dress the male at once begins to court females.

Whenever the female enters the male's territory, he swims toward her in a series of zigzags, with first a sideways turn away from her. After each advance the male stops for an instant and then performs another zigzag. This dance continues until the female takes notice and swims toward the male in a curious head-up posture. He then turns and swims rapidly toward the nest, and she follows. At the nest the male makes a series of rapid thrusts with his snout into the entrance. He turns on his side. As he does so, he raises his dorsal spines toward his mate. Thereupon, with a few strong tail beats, she enters the nest and rests there, her head sticking out from one end and her tail from the other. The male now prods her tail base with rhythmic thrusts and this causes her to lay her eggs. The whole courtship and egg-laying ritual takes only about one minute. See Fig. 4–3. (Tinbergen, 1952) ■*

Each phase of the instinctive behavior is elicited by specific cues. The stimulus that elicits each portion of the instinctive behavior is called a *sign stimulus,* and investigators have isolated the properties that make some sign stimuli effective. Tinbergen, for example, found that the male stickleback would court cardboard models as long as the model had a swollen abdomen. In this case, the swollen abdomen is a sign stimulus.

Mating rituals and maternal behavior are common examples of behavior that is labeled instinctive. In predicting the occurrence of such behavior we need not investigate the previous experience of the organism but need know only that it is a member of a particular species in its ordinary environment. But whereas earlier psychologists treated instinctive behavior and learning as two quite distinct things, present-day psychologists think of an instinct-learning continuum on which behaviors fall at various points. One of the phenomena that caused psychologists to reevaluate their thinking on the nature of instinct was imprinting.

Imprinting

Why does a gander choose a goose for a mate? An obvious answer is instinct; the gander's neural circuitry is set up so that at sexual maturity, the gander will respond to a goose with his courting ritual. This answer may be obvious, but it is inaccurate. Why do baby geese follow the mother goose? Because it is instinct? Again, this answer is inaccurate.

■ Lorenz hatched goslings in an incubator. The first moving thing the goslings saw was Lorenz. The goslings followed Lorenz (see Fig. 4–4) and reacted to his call as if he were their mother. Furthermore, at sexual maturity, the goslings had no interest in other geese, but chose Lorenz as the object of their mating ritual (Lorenz, 1937). ■

---

* N. Tinbergen, "The Curious Behavior of the Stickleback," *Sci. Amer.*, December, 1952. Reprinted by permission.

Controlled laboratory studies have shown that a number of birds will show a following response to whatever moving object they see during a critical period shortly after birth. The strength of the response (the degree to which the bird will continue to follow the object of the initial exposure) depends on several factors. Stimuli of certain sizes and shape tend to be more effective for certain species. Also, the greater the amount of effort exerted by the baby bird the first time he follows the object, the more persistent are his later following responses (Hess, 1959).

FIG. 4–4. Konrad Lorenz, the imprinted "mother" to these goslings, leads his charges on a morning stroll. Dr. Lorenz was the first moving object observed by the goslings upon hatching. (Thomas D. McAvoy, *Life* Magazine © Time, Inc.)

The "following" responses belong to a category called *imprinted* behavior. Imprinted behavior depends both on inheritance and an event early in the life of the organism that has lasting effects. In purely instinctive behavior neural connections are built in by heredity and maturation in such a way that only a specific stimulus is needed to elicit the behavior. In the case of imprinted behavior, the built-in circuit has a missing part that is filled in by the first experiences of the young animal.

The major reason it took so long for scientists to realize the importance of the early experiences for the goslings' "mother-following" responses and later mating behavior was that the same behavior was typical of every member of the species. The mating of a gander with a goose is species-specific behavior. But if some behavior is characteristic of a species, the reason may be either that it is entirely dependent on inherited connections or more probably that it is partially shaped by some characteristic of the environment that is the same for every member of the species. Almost every gosling born in a natural habitat will be hatched by a mother goose. Under normal conditions the first moving object the gosling sees is its mother, and it will follow her. Only when the gosling is taken out of its natural habitat and subjected to laboratory manipulation can we see the manner in which the following response will vary as early experiences varied.

Other studies of instinctive behavior also suggest the importance of a normal environment for the development of species-specific behavior. Nest-building and the cleaning and nursing of babies are behaviors that are considered maternal instincts. All normal female rats display them at the appropriate time, although the females have never practiced them or seen them performed. However, if a female rat is reared without any experience with nest-building materials, without any objects that she can carry from one part of the cage to another, she will not build a nest when the materials are available at the appropriate time. A female rat who is raised with a rubber collar around her neck that prevents her from licking her own genital area will not clean and nurse her babies. (Jaynes and Beach, 1954)

These studies suggest that behavior that has previously been classified as completely unlearned may be affected by early experience. Thus there may be species-specific behavior that appears with no previous practice but is still shaped by environmental events. According to our three criteria for instinct, such behavior should be called instinctive. This means we have to modify our concept of instinct to include the possible dependence of the instinct on early experience. Thus even in the case of stereotyped species-specific behavior we see an interaction between the effects of the genetic blueprint and the environment in which it develops.

What about human behavior? To what extent is human behavior dependent on the genetic blueprint? Human beings exhibit reflexes and they do show some species-specific responses, though perhaps none as complex and so stereotyped as the instinctive behavior we described in lower animals. For example, most children at three months respond to a smiling face with a smile. Certainly, sexual behavior has some species-specific components, although even the basic sexual pattern varies as a result of learned cultural and individual differences. Growing children exhibit the same sequence of development as they attain sensory and motor integration, but here again, this development does not depend on heredity alone; it also depends on the opportunities provided by normal surroundings.

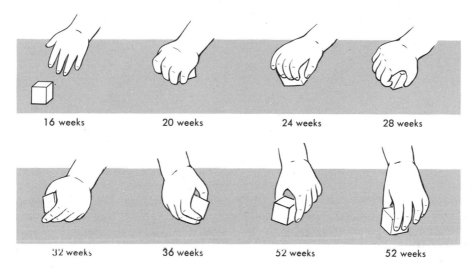

16 weeks   20 weeks   24 weeks   28 weeks

32 weeks   36 weeks   52 weeks   52 weeks

FIG. 4–5. As a baby matures, his movements related to grasping a cube become finer and finer. At 20 weeks, he grabs the cube with his whole hand (without special use of his thumb). At 52 weeks he can grasp the cube with only his thumb and forefinger. (After Halverson, 1931)

Neural Maturation

Growth occurs in ordered sequences; a child can reach an advanced stage only after he has passed through earlier stages. Neural maturation proceeds from the *center to the periphery* of the body. Thus, in reaching for objects the infant is able to control his shoulder and arm movements before he gets good control of his fingers (see Fig. 4–5). Maturation also tends to proceed from *head to foot.* A baby first raises his head from his bed, then his shoulders, and finally uses both arms and legs to crawl and walk. Maturation of voluntary behavior tends to proceed in a sequence from *mass, undifferentiated* activity to *differentiated, integrated* behavior. The infant tends to use his whole body in doing everything; the older child makes precise movements of hands and fingers coordinating his movements with his eyes. Such sequences are essentially based on the sequence of development of connections in the nervous system.

Individual Differences in Rate of Maturation

Although the sequences of maturation are the same (see Fig. 4–6), individuals and species differ in rate of maturation and in the limits of maturation. Such differences are most apparent when we compare men with other animals; they are especially noticeable when we compare man to his closest evolutionary relatives, the apes.

Students at primate laboratories have observed the developmental sequences of their animals. Several chimpanzees have been brought up in human environments and their rates of development have been compared to those of human children.

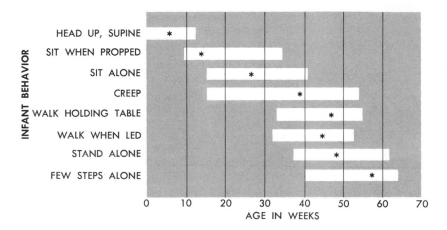

FIG. 4–6.   The range of ages at which forty babies showed various skills. The asterisk indicates the median age. (After Munn, 1955)

■ Dr. and Mrs. W. N. Kellogg (1933) adopted a seven and one-half month old female chimpanzee, Gua, whom they reared with their ten-month-old son for nine months. Dr. and Mrs. Keith Hayes (1951) adopted a three-day-old female chimpanzee, whom they reared in their home for six years. All these investigators found that both human and chimpanzee infants showed similar sequences of development. During the first year of life the chimpanzee was generally ahead of the child in behavioral development. At the age of nine months the dexterity of the chimpanzee, Gua, in pulling a cap off her head was equal to the performance of the boy, Donald, at an age of eighteen and one-half months. Not only did Gua mature more rapidly than Donald, but she also learned such simple acts more rapidly. Nevertheless, in spite of human environment, the limitations placed upon development by heredity became evident. Although Gua learned more quickly than Donald to respond to verbal commands like "Come here," she didn't learn to speak, and even at the age of three, Viki, the Hayes' chimpanzee, understood only about 50 words, whereas the average three-year-old child understands almost 900. ■

While the limits of learning defined by heredity and maturational level can be most clearly observed in such comparisons between species, they operate within the species as well. For example, school teachers observe that some children learn more slowly than others. Parents continually compare their children with others, and rejoice when the baby walks or talks earlier than other infants. Such individual differences are evident in the development of many human skills, and are primarily determined by differences in the rate of maturation, given a normal human environment.

Maturation and Practice

While heredity determines to a large extent the rate of maturation and the limits of abilities, most behavior is affected not only by maturation but also by practice. This has important practical consequences. If certain kinds of behavior depend upon maturation, attempts by parents to teach the child this behavior before the appropriate maturational level is attained are likely to be frustrating both to the parent and the child. On the other hand, if practice is required, failure to provide the child with opportunity to practice may retard his development.

The type of study carried out to investigate such problems is well illustrated by the experiment of Gesell and Thompson (1929), who separated a pair of one-year-old identical twins.

■ One twin was given daily practice in playing with blocks and climbing stairs, while for six weeks the second twin was kept away from these experiences. At the end of six weeks the practiced twin was no better than her sister playing with blocks but was clearly superior in climbing stairs. With two weeks practice, however, the unpracticed sister caught up to her. Maturation is a major factor in development of such early skills; early practice does not lead to greater skill. ■

■ Dennis (1940) observed the age of walking in Hopi Indian children. In some Hopi villages the babies are bound to a cradle board for the first six months of life and have little chance to move around except for one hour of freedom each day. In Americanized villages such restraints are not used. In spite of their lack of practice, however, Hopi infants who had been bound to cradle boards began walking at the same age as the children who were not bound to cradle boards. ■

An opportunity to practice an hour a day was sufficient for maturation to proceed normally. If, however, the environment provides no opportunity for practice *at all* during the critical period of maturation, growth may not proceed normally. Children who are hospitalized by illness or injury and who have no opportunity for practice at the appropriate time, are retarded in the development of their ability to walk. For normal maturational development a child needs certain kinds of experiences.

In skills like reading, maturation may play an important role. Special remedial programs for slow-developing children frequently produce only temporary improvement in reading skill, and the student may drop back to his maturational level soon after the program is ended. Recent research suggests that the techniques of teaching reading must be adapted to the child's maturational level. Just as reading would be impossible without some practice, so practice is necessary for the development of most abilities. Maturation determines the potential at each age level, but only practice can bring most potential ability into actuality.

Early experience seems to be particularly important in determining development of perception and intelligence. As we shall see in later chapters, an infant reared in an environment with little stimulation is likely to be retarded in intellectual development. An organism deprived of pattern vision in early infancy may be permanently retarded in pattern vision.

Maturation and Culture

In human beings, the maturation process takes place in a cultural environment. This environment determines the kinds of opportunities for practice that will be provided and the kinds of demands that will be made on the children.

In some cases cultural demands and maturation are not synchronized. Cultures differ in the degree to which they try to push the child to the limits of his maturation level. While cultures generally gear their demands to biological maturation, they do not always take account of individual differences in rate of maturation. For example, Sparta, in classical Greece, put great emphasis on physical development for young men. The demands of Sparta were so close to the limits of biological maturation that many individuals had to be sacrificed.

Cultures often make heavy demands upon one aspect of man's biological nature. For example, a culture may strictly control expression of aggression. In a culture like that of the Arapesh, which stresses benevolence and non-aggression, an individual who has stronger inherent tendencies toward aggression would have much greater difficulty than he would have in a culture like that of the Mundugumor, which encourages aggressive activity.

In a culture where children are hurried to maturity, slow-maturing children may be made anxious and unhappy by their inability to do what is demanded of them. Because anxiety interferes with complex learning, we often do not know how much of a retarded child's difficulty with school subjects is due to his anxiety and his feeling that it is useless to try.

The Dependence of Behavior on Heredity: a Summary

We have seen that the organism which develops normally is born with built-in circuits for reflexive behavior. Lower animals show complex, stereotyped, species-specific instincts. These instincts may be partially dependent on the environment to fill in some of the blanks in the built-in circuits, as we saw in the case of imprinting. The development of human behavior follows an orderly sequence, though the rate of development may vary. As a child's physical equipment matures, he develops simple motor skills, given some opportunity to practice at the appropriate time.

The nervous system is partially organized at birth. The individual's experiences will determine the details of organization, but they affect a nervous system that is already structured to some degree. Thus we have a continuum of acts on a dimension that varies according to the dependence of the specific

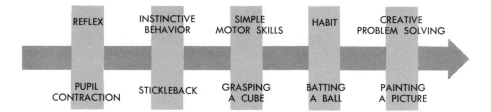

FIG. 4–7. Acts can be considered to be on a continuum that is based on the degree to which they are primarily dependent on heredity and maturation.

act on the genetic blueprint (see Fig. 4–7). In this chapter, we have discussed the part of the continuum that describes behavior typical of every member of a species. Yet even this species-specific behavior depends on an environment that provides the kinds of experiences necessary for normal growth.

Which Stable Characteristics of the Individual Are Dependent on Heredity?

We have discussed individual acts that are chiefly dependent on the unfolding of the genetic blueprint. Now we shall discuss stable characteristics of the organism to which hereditary factors make a contribution.

Hereditary Differences in Organisms

The genes a dog passes on to his offspring produce characteristics in the puppy which make him a dog. The genes a human being passes on to the infant make him a human baby. What does this difference mean to a human being in terms of psychological characteristics? How has the evolutionary development of man made him different from other living creatures?

Several human characteristics are related to the great development of the nervous system, particularly in the brain (see Fig. 4–8). The upper brainstem and the cortex of man contain more potential pathways than do the nervous systems of lower species. As a result, fewer of man's responses to stimuli are shaped by his inherited structure and more are determined by his experience. As we go up the evolutionary scale, we find more and more complex nervous systems (see Fig. 4–9), accompanied by the ability to learn more and more complex relationships. The one-celled paramecium makes few adjustments in its behavior as a result of experience; man has the ability to use his past experience in solving new problems. The difference between man and other animals is not that man can learn simple tasks faster. Cockroaches, rats, and people learn to traverse comparable mazes with about equal facility. Man is different in that

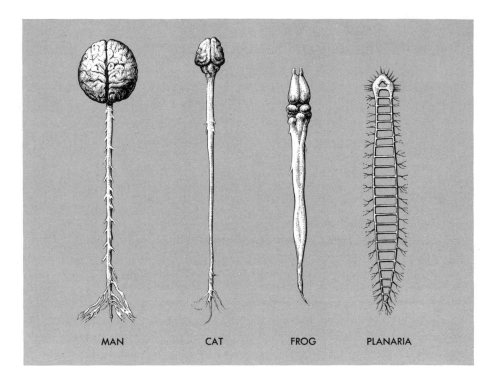

FIG. 4-8. The nervous systems of four organisms. Note the increase in the size and complexity of the brain relative to the rest of the nervous system as the organism becomes more complex.

he can abstract and manipulate more complex relationships. Science and art are unique products of man that exemplify his ability to abstract and organize from the elements of his experience.

Human beings inherit a structure that gives them the potentiality to symbolize their experience in a language. This permits an individual to benefit not only from his personal experience, but also from the experience of other people and from other generations of people.

The sensory equipment people inherit differs from that of other animals. Vision and hearing predominate over touch and smell as channels of information about the world.

Men inherit a skeletal and muscular structure that enables them to walk upright. Their arms and hands are thus free to carry and manipulate objects. This, coupled with a nervous system permitting visual and kinesthetic coordination of the fingers and hands, allows man to construct and use tools that enormously increase his power to deal with his environment.

Another important characteristic of man is his relatively long period of immaturity and dependence. In our culture children are dependent on the parents and live with them until the late "teens." The adults have many years in which to teach their children, both at home and in the schools. The length of human infancy and childhood permits one generation to pass its experience on to the next and thus to preserve the continuity of culture. And in addition, human beings are born with characteristics that enable them to profit from their cultural environment. The comparisons between human baby and chimpanzee have shown that chimpanzees are born with characteristics that influence their response to cultural training. For example, Gua, the chimpanzee, was much more active than Donald Kellogg. Donald could sit still and watch a house painter at work; Gua was continually running, climbing, and pulling. The chimpanzee and human infant also differed in emotional responses. When Gua was angry, she would defecate, urinate, or run blindly into a hedge or the street, Donald's emotional responses were less violent and more manageable.

At the same time that we marvel at man's capacities we should remember that in many ways he is similar to other animals and in some ways inferior to them. Man is very similar to the great apes in bone structure, muscles, and digestive and other physiological systems. Like other animals, man's awareness of his environment depends upon his senses, and while he has relatively good

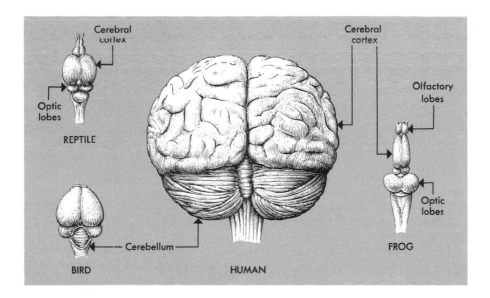

FIG. 4–9. The brains of four vertebrates. Note the increase in the amount of cortex and in the number of convolutions in the cortex as one advances on the evolutionary scale from frog to man.

vision and hearing, it is inferior to that of some other animals. Many birds can see much farther than humans, dogs can hear sounds inaudible to us; and moths and dogs are much more sensitive to odors than we.* Like other animals, man has basic physiological needs like hunger, thirst, and sex, but he lacks many of the inherited built-in response mechanisms by which other animals satisfy their needs. Obviously, he also lacks some of the response capabilities of other animals. He cannot fly; he cannot run as fast as many other animals. Thus we see that man's biological nature sets his limitations as well as his potentialities.

Comparative psychologists specialize in comparisons of the behavior of different species of animals. The study of animal behavior is interesting for its own sake, but the results from such study also have relevance to human behavior. Because so many important characteristics of man are shared by other animals, we can learn much about psychological processes by studying other organisms. Working with animals, psychologists can more easily manipulate and control the variables they are studying; in fact, in some cases researchers with animals can manipulate variables (such as breeding) that they cannot manipulate in studies of humans. Knowledge of the similarities and differences between different species helps us appreciate the unique capabilities of man or of other species in which we are interested.

Hereditary Variation in Human Beings

THE CENTRAL NERVOUS SYSTEM. What is the role of heredity in determining differences in the nervous system? We know that the structure of the nervous system is inherited, but, except for gross abnormalities, the effect of the structure on behavior cannot be seen. Certain types of feeble-mindedness are caused by inherited defects. Similarly, cretinism may be caused by an inherited thyroid difficulty which in turn affects the CNS. Despite the importance of heredity in such extreme states, we know little about the manner in which inherited characteristics of the brain, endocrine glands, or other physiological characteristics are related to variations in the behavior of people within the normal range. One study with rats is a beginning toward understanding the relation between biochemical variations and psychological characteristics.

■ Three decades ago Tryon (1940) bred fast-learning male rats with fast-learning females and slow-learning males with slow-learning females for 18 generations. Generation after generation the offspring showed more and more differences in their maze-learning ability until by the ninth generation, the very best of the "dull" offspring were no better than the very worst of the "bright" offspring. Twenty-five years later, Krech hypothesized that the descendants of these two strains

---

* Note that with man's better vision and intelligence and dog's superior hearing and smell, a man and dog together are more efficient at hunting than either alone.

of rats would differ in the level of cholinesterase activity in the CNS. Cholinesterase is an enzyme which breaks down acetylcholine, a chemical transmitter of neural impulses. The more neural activity, the more cholinesterase is necessary to break down the accumulated transmitter substance. Although a biochemical analysis of parts of the cerebral cortex supported the hypothesis, further research has indicated that the differences are not this simple. One of the things to watch for in reports of current research will be further tests of the hypothesis that the differences in mental ability are related to inherited differences in enzyme activity. (Krech, Rosenzweig, Bennett, and Krueckel, 1954; Rosenzweig, Krech, and Bennett, 1960) ■

RACIAL DIFFERENCES. All living men belong to a single species, *homo sapiens*. Men in different regions of the world tend to differ from other groups of people in some inherited physical characteristics such as skin color, hair, height, body hair, eye color, and shape. But the races of man are not so distinct that anthropologists have been able to agree on a clear classification. The same hereditary characteristics tend to be found in all races, even though there may be some differences in frequency. While people of different races tend to differ from one another in some biological characteristics, the psychologist has found no striking differences in psychological capacities. Most characteristics are distributed in about the same manner in all of the races. Where apparent differences exist, they are likely to be due to cultural factors rather than to inherited racial characteristics.

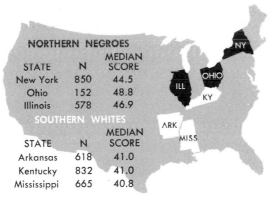

FIG. 4–10. Median scores on the Army intelligence tests for Negroes from three northern states and for whites from two southern and one border state. (Yerkes, 1921)

■ For example, the first large-scale intelligence* testing was done during the first World War. After the war, statistics were released showing that the *mean* score of the white men tested was higher than the mean score of the Negroes tested. This difference between the means was hailed by advocates of white supremacy (although the distribution of scores included thousands of Negroes who had scored higher than thousands of whites).

---

* A discussion of intelligence test score and its relation to inherited potentiality appears in Chapter 10.

Another statistical analysis of the data was made separating those tested into four categories: Northern whites, Northern Negroes, Southern whites, Southern Negroes. It was now revealed that Northern Negroes had higher mean scores than Southern whites, as Fig. 4–10 indicates (Yerkes, 1921).

Did this mean that more intelligent Negroes migrate to the north, or was this difference in test scores due to differences in education? A study by Klineberg (1935) attempted to answer this question. Klineberg compared the grades made in Southern schools by those who subsequently migrated north and by those who remained in the south. He found no significant difference. Furthermore, he found that intelligence tests of children in the public schools of New York demonstrated that the longer the residence of Negro children in New York, the higher their average intelligence test scores (see Fig. 4–11). The original interpretations of the difference in intelligence between Negroes and whites had forgotten to take into account differences in experience with the sort of problems involved in the test. ■

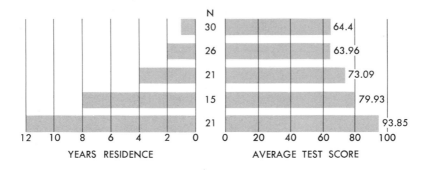

FIG. 4–11. The relationship between Negro intelligence test scores and number of years of residence in New York City. The numbers in the N-column indicate the number of cases in each residence category. (Klineberg, 1935)

The psychological similarities between people of all races are so great that we must look to individuals rather than races if we are to find hereditary factors related to differences in behavior.

SEX DIFFERENCES. In Chapter 2 we saw that many of the differences between men and women which we assume to be inherited are actually influenced by culture. This should not, however, lead you to conclude that all sex differences are culturally determined. At almost all age levels boys are stronger, more active, more aggressive, and less reactive to physiological stress. Girls learn to talk before boys and are less likely to stutter. It seems quite possible that there is an inherited physiological basis for such differences; however, within each sex there is still much variability in individual characteristics. How can we assess the importance of heredity in effecting these differences?

Heredity, Environment, and Individual Differences

We have seen that characteristics of the nervous system and glands are affected by hereditary factors and also by such environmental factors as nutrition, drugs, and injury. Biological differences between people can be produced by hereditary factors, by environmental factors, or by a combination of both. In most cases individual differences are the result of the interaction of both heredity and environment. Heredity can determine tendencies to develop in a certain way or can set limits upon development, but these tendencies cannot develop without an adequate environment. Thus, two persons may have the same ability despite the fact that one has inherited a greater potential than the other if the one with greater potential has had a dietary deficiency, or has lacked learning experiences for developing his potential. Similarly, a potential hereditary defect can often be remedied or compensated for if it is recognized and treated.

To determine the relative contributions of hereditary and environment to normal variations in some characteristic, we need to control one while varying the other. Since we can seldom completely control environments of human beings, much of our knowledge of the relative importance of heredity and environment depends on the use of identical twins, who have the same heredity. If heredity is an important determinant of a psychological characteristic, we would expect identical twins to be more similar than other brothers and sisters, even when the identical twins have been reared in differing environments. However, since most identical twins are reared together, we cannot be so sure of the relative contribution of heredity and environment, because identical twins may be treated more nearly alike than other brothers and sisters.

INTELLIGENCE. What can such studies of identical twins tell us? As an example, let us again take up the problem of whether or not environment affects intelligence test scores. One way of determining this is to see whether or not identical twins differ.

Newman, Freeman, and Holzinger (1937) found that for nineteen pairs of twins reared apart, the average difference in intelligence test scores was 8.2 points. Thus the answer would seem to be that environment does affect intelligence scores. But since no test is perfect, we would expect some differences just by chance. If we find such results for only nineteen pairs of identical twins, how can we be sure that we would get the same results if we had more twins? Could it be that Newman happened to get twins who *chanced* to score differently?

■ Mathematicians have worked out statistical techniques for telling us the probability that there really is not a difference between two groups whenever we have data from a random sample of each group. A statistical technique for determining the *significance of a difference* is described in Appendix II, Statistical Tools. When such a test is applied to these data we find that a difference of 8.2 points is very unlikely to occur between two such groups chosen randomly from the same population. In fact, it would occur less than one time in a hundred if there were not really differences between identical twins reared apart. Since each pair of twins had identical heredity, we thus know that environment affects intelligence test performance. Nevertheless, the identical twins do show a great deal of resemblance in intelligence and the difference between them is much less than the difference between other sisters and brothers reared apart. Although we do not know how different their environments really were, it seems safe to conclude that heredity is also important in determining intelligence. ■

PERSONALITY. Among lower animals, characteristics analogous to human personality characteristics are inherited. For example, in a classic experiment, Stone (1932) demonstrated that rats could be bred for wildness, establishing strains with clear-cut differences in this characteristic. Everyone is familiar with the temperamental differences between different kinds of dogs, such as the differences between collies and terriers. Well-controlled studies show that these inherited differences affect dog behavior in a variety of ways (Scott, 1958).

The degree to which temperamental differences in man are influenced by heredity is still unknown. One of the major problems in studying such differences is obtaining adequate measures of personality characteristics.* Eysenck (1952), Cattell (1957), Vandenberg (1962), and Gottesman (1963), carried out twin studies using questionnaires and other measures to assess personality characteristics. The similarity between identical twins was greater than that between fraternal twins on questionnaire measures of extraversion and activity. Even though the environment of identical twins may be more similar than that of fraternal twins, it is probable that this greater similarity of identical twins is partially the result of their hereditary identity.

■ While we can convey the general meaning of the results of these studies by such phrases as "greater similarity" or "more alike," we obviously need more precise terminology for statements about degrees of similarity. Statistics is again able to help us. A statistic called the *correlation coefficient* enables us to state the degree of similarity between pairs of scores. Correlation coefficients are numbers like 0.4, 0.1, or −0.3, ranging from 0 to ±1. As Fig. 4–12 indicates, correlation coefficients close to zero indicate that there is little relationship between two sets of scores; correlations of 0.8 or 0.9, approaching +1.0, indicate that a high score in one of a pair of scores is very likely to go with a high score for the other member of the pair; and correlations of −0.8 or −0.9, approaching −1.0, indicated that a high score in one member of a pair is very likely to go with a low score in the other member of the pair. Note that correlations of +0.8 and −0.8 both indicate a high degree of relationship. The sign indicates only the direction of the relationship. ■

When we compare correlations between identical twins on a number of characteristics, we find that to the degree that high twin correlations can be attributed to heredity, differences in biological structure are strongly influenced by heredity, differences in abilities are somewhat less hereditarily determined, differences in temperamental characteristics still less, and attitudes and opinions are least influenced.

---

* This problem is discussed in Chapter 12.

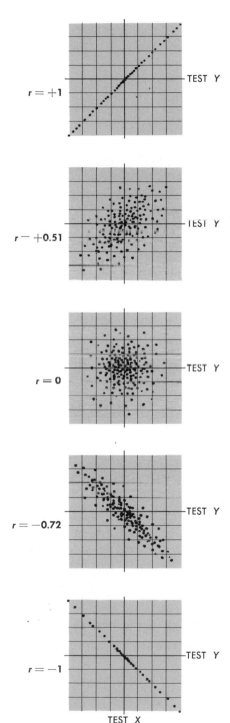

How then can we resolve the age-old problem of heredity versus environment? Each characteristic of the individual is the result of an interaction between hereditary and environmental factors. Heredity provides the over-all blueprint that makes us human beings. From the environment come the materials (nutrition, oxygen, etc.) and the detailed construction plans (the effects of learning). Is the blueprint more important than the material? Are the detailed plans more important than the over-all design in determining individual differences? These are questions that do not really have any meaning. Without a hereditary structure, environment could have no effect. Without an environment, the general plan set down by heredity could never be brought to fruition in a living organism. In every person, it is the continual interplay of hereditary and environmental factors that results in the development of a unique human being.

FIG. 4–12. Graphic plottings of correlation coefficient. The correlation coefficient shows the degree of relationship between two sets of scores. For example, suppose that a group of people took two tests, X and Y. If each person performed at the same level on the two tests, relative to the group, and if we represent each person's score on the two tests by a single dot, then the plot would be similar to the top graph. If a person who scored high on one test tended to score low on the other, the plot would look something like the graph marked $r = -0.72$. If there were no relationship between a person's score on Test X and his score on Test Y, the plot would look like the graph marked $r = 0$.

Summary

Concepts

Chromosomes. The structures in the nucleus of any cell which contains desoxyribonucleic acid

Desoxyribonucleic acid (DNA). The complex protein molecules responsible for transmission of hereditary characteristics

Gene. A construct postulated to account for the transmission of hereditary characteristics

Maturation. The sequence of developmental changes due primarily to heredity

Instinct. A complex species-specific behavior which an organism performs correctly the first time it is appropriate

Sign stimulus. A stimulus which triggers off one phase of an instinct

Imprinting. A relatively irreversible learning process in very young birds which results in their following the first moving object they see as though it were their mother

Significant difference. A difference between two statistics which is so great that it is quite unlikely that it could have occurred by chance

Correlation coefficient. A statistic representing the degree of relationship between pairs of scores

Principles

1. All that is inherited is DNA.

2. Development from the genetic blueprint provided by DNA depends on a relatively normal environment both before and after birth.

3. Some instinctive behaviors have been shown to require normal early experiences.

4. An infant's sensory and motor development follows orderly sequences.

5. The development of certain human skills requires opportunities for practice at the appropriate time. Premature practice will not accelerate development.

6. Individuals differ in rates and limits of maturation.

7. The brain and the cortex increase in size and complexity as organisms progress up the evolutionary scale. This is related to the greater capacity for complex learning in higher species.

8. Psychological characteristics do not differ from race to race; cultural factors are more important determiners of psychological differences between groups.

9. Identical twins, who share the same heredity, are most alike in physical characteristics, somewhat less alike in abilities, still less in personality, and least of all in opinions and attitudes.

10. Development involves a constant intermingling of hereditary and environmental factors.

Suggested Readings

ANASTASI, ANNE, *Differential Psychology*, New York: Macmillan, 1958.

FULLER, J. L., and W. R. THOMPSON, *Behavior Genetics*, New York: Wiley, 1960.

SINNOTT, E. D., L. C. DUNN, and T. DOBZHANSKY, *Principles of Genetics*, New York: McGraw-Hill, 1958.

THE DETERMINANTS OF BEHAVIOR

PART 2

an introduction to learning

chapter 5

HOW CAN WE STUDY THE LEARNING PROCESS?

WHAT IS CONDITIONING?

WHAT OCCURS INSIDE THE ORGANISM DURING CONDITIONING?

HOW IS CONDITIONING RELATED TO LEARNING IN GENERAL?

ON WHAT BASIS ARE ACTS SELECTED?

Chapters 2, 3, and 4 presented an overall view of the sources of similarities and differences among human beings. Each person develops according to a genetic blueprint, which guides the growth of the individual. At birth his nervous system is partly structured with built-in circuits, partly modifiable to incorporate his experience. A major contribution to the experience of the individual is the cultural environment, which communicates its norms, beliefs, values, and role prescriptions.

In the present chapter, we shall look more closely at the process by which the organism changes through experience, the process of learning.

How Can We Study the Learning Process?

We tend to associate learning with formal education, but actually learning takes place in every context. We learn how to play the piano, how to make a friend smile, how to find an address in a strange city. Even in the classroom, the student learns more than subject matter. He may be learning the speech habits of his professor, where the pretty girls in the class are seated, how to appear attentive while daydreaming. In all these situations, there has been a relatively permanent change in the individual as a result of his experience. This change is reflected in his behavior. The child whose fingers moved clumsily over the piano keys now moves those same fingers in an integrated pattern that produces music. The man who spent several hours locating a street in a strange city, finds the same house in ten minutes the second time he visits.

What has actually changed? There has been some modification in the machinery that shapes behavior—the nervous system. No one knows precisely how the experience of the individual changes the functioning of his brain. As we saw earlier, most theories assume that there is a physiological change in the neurons that are active during an event. This structural change serves as a permanent trace of the experience.

We do know that no single portion of the brain alone is responsible for learning. Recordings of the electrical activity of the brains of cats, as they learned to press a bar for a reward of milk, showed widespread electrical changes throughout the brain (John and Killam, 1959). Surgical studies in rats showed that the more cortical tissue removed, the poorer the performance in learning the maze. Which area of the cortex was removed was much less important than the amount removed (Lashley, 1926). These results suggest that an individual's experience with his environment gives rise to changes in activity in many areas of the brain.

Although we cannot observe the changes in the central nervous system that are the basis of learning, we can observe the effects of learning—the changes in an individual's behavior. From the changes in behavior we can infer that learning has taken place. A teacher infers that his students have learned the appropriate material if they can answer questions at the end of the course that they could not have answered at the beginning. The same stimuli, test questions, are presented on two occasions. Between the two presentations, the students are exposed to certain materials. The differences in the students' performance on the two occasions are attributed to the effects of the intervening experience, learning.

Psychologists interested in the learning process study the kinds of conditions that will lead to changes in behavior. Analyses of the effects of various conditions suggest ways of conceptualizing what is taking place inside the organism during learning. Of course, the "events" inside the organism are in the realm of inference and theory, and psychologists sometimes disagree. Later in the chapter we shall look at some of the issues psychologists have pondered and the kinds of experiments they have devised to clarify them.

In conjunction with their observations of behavior and the changes in behavior from which learning is inferred, psychologists have developed a special vocabulary which enables them to describe their observations precisely. We have already introduced some of these words, and we shall introduce more of them throughout the chapter and the book. In the following sections we shall consider the description of the two major components of any experimental observation: the situation and the behavior.

Describing Behavior

The human being seldom waits passively for special situations to appear to which he can respond. Even when a person is sitting on a porch in a rocking chair, his eyes move to look at moving objects, he cocks his head to listen to a strange noise, and he moves the muscles of his legs and trunk to maintain his rocking motion. Recordings of the electrical activity of the brain show changes in the brain waves with progressive degrees of relaxation, but there is always some electrical activity. The neurons are never completely at rest; a person is always active to some degree, even during sleep. An *act* is a modification of activity—a unit in the constantly flowing stream of behavior. An act is not the onset of activity in a passive organism, but a change in on-going activity. Each act is a pattern of muscular movements that occur together. The muscles are coordinated by the nervous system. Eating a meal, walking across the campus, answering a question, saying "Yes," whistling at a girl, blushing in embarrassment, reporting what you have seen, trembling—these are common acts in everyday life. An act is often called a *response* when it can be traced to the effects of a stimulus.

The flow of behavior can be divided into acts in many ways. We can describe acts in very narrow or very general terms. Let us suppose a student is writing a term paper. We can describe his behavior in terms of individual muscle movements, in terms of the words and sentences written on each day, or as the one act that has taken place over the course of the semester. The detail of our description depends on the purpose of our observation. If we were interested in muscle fatigue, we would choose to describe the acts in terms of individual muscle movements. If we were interested in his rate of progress, we would use a level of description that would enable us to compare his behavior on different days. If we were interested in comparing his work with that of others, we might use the overall product, the term paper, as a unit.

Describing the Environment

All acts take place within the context of a situation. The external situation, too, can be described on a number of levels. It may be described in terms of physical energy or in terms of light, sound, or heat energy. However, some of the energy surrounding us cannot be perceived; for example, our eyes are not sensitive to ultraviolet rays. The term *stimulus* refers to a change in the physical energy of the environment which affects a receptor. Not all the aspects of the situation are in the external environment. Our senses give us information about conditions inside the body, and the situation includes these stimuli, too.

The term *object* refers to a relatively stable aspect of the environment with relatively consistent meanings for the individual. For example, we can describe an aspect of the environment as being about 6 inches long, cold, silver in color, etc. This is a description in terms of the physical attributes of the stimulus. We can also describe the same aspect of the environment as an object, a spoon.

Depending upon the level of behavior which we are trying to understand, our descriptions of the environment may be very broad or very narrow. When we are interested in understanding an individual's decision to go to college, we may describe his situation in terms of his family, teachers, friends, geographical distance from college, and savings. When we try to predict his answer to a test question, we may need to describe the situation only in terms of the question. Because we are trying to understand behavior in context, we describe the environment in terms of the unit that is appropriate for the acts we are studying.

Psychologists often study very simple situations, simple stimuli, and simple movements. If we can understand how variations in simple conditions lead to variations in behavior, we have a basis for analyzing more complex processes. Therefore we shall begin our study of learning with two kinds of conditioning; these are simple forms of learning which have been studied extensively.

What Is Conditioning?

Classical Conditioning

We see conditioning illustrated in one of the earliest experiences of learning in the life of the newborn infant.

A baby who has not been fed for four hours becomes increasingly active—squirming, kicking, and finally crying lustily. He continues to move and cry until the nipple is placed in his mouth. Then he quiets down and begins to suck. In the same situation a few weeks later, the baby again becomes active and cries. Now, as soon as he hears his mother's footsteps, he stops thrashing around and crying.

Psychologists call this type of learning *classical conditioning*. It involves the presentation of two stimuli: a *neutral stimulus* (NS) and an *unconditioned stimulus* (UCS). The unconditioned stimulus elicits an automatic reflex response, the unconditioned response (UCR). Prior to conditioning, the neutral stimulus does not lead to performance of the unconditioned response. In the case of our baby described above, the unconditioned stimulus was the touching of the infant's lips with a nipple. Reflexively, the baby stopped crying, shut his mouth, and sucked. The neutral stimulus was the sound of footsteps, which originally had little effect on the baby's crying.

The conditioning procedure consists of many pairings of the two stimuli— the neutral stimulus immediately followed by the unconditioned stimulus. The change in behavior as a result of the procedure is that portions of the unconditioned response now appear in response to the formerly neutral stimulus. The formerly neutral stimulus is now called the *conditioned stimulus* (CS) and the response made to the conditioned stimulus is called the *conditioned response* (CR). As a result of the baby's exposure to the footsteps (NS), immediately followed by the nipple (UCS), the baby stopped crying and made sucking movements (CR) as soon as he heard the footsteps (CS). The classical conditioning procedures in general and in the example of the baby are diagrammed in Fig. 5–1.

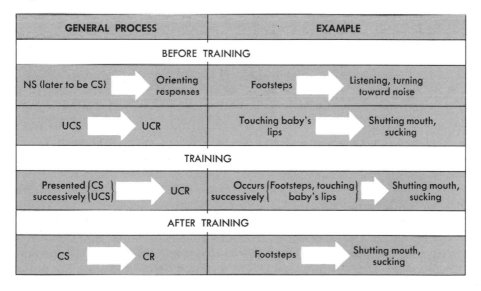

GENERAL PROCESS		EXAMPLE	
BEFORE TRAINING			
NS (later to be CS) →	Orienting responses	Footsteps →	Listening, turning toward noise
UCS →	UCR	Touching baby's lips →	Shutting mouth, sucking
TRAINING			
Presented {CS / UCS} successively →	UCR	Occurs {Footsteps, touching baby's lips} successively →	Shutting mouth, sucking
AFTER TRAINING			
CS →	CR	Footsteps →	Shutting mouth, sucking

FIG. 5–1. Classical conditioning.

The man who first described and studied classical conditioning was the Russian physiologist, Ivan P. Pavlov (1849–1936). Pavlov, who had done outstanding work on the physiology of the digestive system in dogs, became interested in the conditions under which digestive juices were secreted. He noticed that such secretions appeared not only when there was food in the dog's stomach, but also at other times, such as when it heard its keeper's footsteps. These observations led to a series of systematic studies of the salivary response. Pavlov knew that food in the dog's mouth produced reflexive salivation. (Food was a UCS for the UCR, salivation). He also knew that the sound of a tuning fork was a neutral stimulus so far as salivation was concerned. For a series of trials, Pavlov sounded the tuning fork and immediately thereafter placed food in the dog's mouth. In the beginning, the dog salivated only when the food was placed in his mouth. But after a few paired presentations of tuning fork and food, the dog began to salivate as soon as the tuning fork sounded, *before* the food was placed in its mouth. The formerly neutral stimulus, the tuning fork, had become a CS and salivation, a CR.

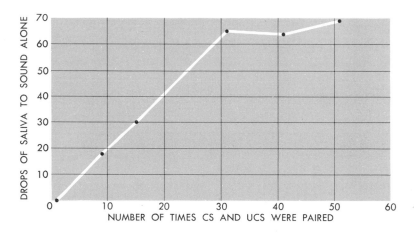

FIG. 5–2. The relationship between the number of times CS and UCS were presented and the magnitude of the animal's response to the CS.

In this experiment the dependent variable, salivation, was measured very precisely. Pavlov surgically diverted the duct of the dog's salivary gland to the outside of his mouth, and collected saliva secreted. Thus the amount of saliva served as a measure of the effectiveness of the conditioning procedure. Pavlov found that the greater the number of pairings of tuning fork and food, the more saliva the dog secreted. Using a procedure similar to Pavlov's, Anrep (1920) found that after 9 pairings of tone and food, the dog secreted 18 drops of saliva; after 15 pairings, the dog secreted 30 drops of saliva. The relationship Anrep found is illustrated in Fig. 5–2. We can conclude that one variable that affects the strength of conditioning is the *frequency* of pairing CS and UCS.

Since Pavlov's original work, classical conditioning has been demonstrated in many organisms, from the flatworm to the college freshman, using a variety of unconditioned stimuli and responses. The flatworm, whose body reflexively contracts when he receives an electric shock, has been conditioned to contract in the presence of light (Thompson and McConnell, 1955). Electric shock has also been used to condition heart rate in fish. (McCleary, 1961). A very commonly used procedure which has been employed frequently to study conditioning in human beings is eyelid conditioning, in which a puff of air on the cornea is the UCS, a weak light is the CS, and the closing of the eyelid is the CR.

One of the most famous demonstrations of classical conditioning was carried out by the behaviorist, John B. Watson, and his associate. Watson was interested in showing that emotional responses could be put under the control of a conditioned stimulus.

■ Watson first showed that his subject, a nine-month-old infant named Albert, had no original fear of a tame white rat; his response to it was mild curiosity. Watson had previously shown that loud noises do elicit fear responses, such as trembling and crying in young children. This background enabled Watson to test conditioning, using the white rat as CS and a loud noise as the UCS. Just after the white rat was presented to Albert, someone produced a loud, unpleasant sound behind Albert's head by striking a steel bar. After several such repetitions Albert began to cry and to show other manifestations of fear as soon as he saw the white rat (Watson and Raynor, 1920). ■

Instrumental Conditioning

To illustrate instrumental conditioning, let us return to the learning experiences of a young child. When he is about nine months old, he begins to babble meaningless sounds. One day in the midst of many other sounds, he utters the syllables "ma-ma." Suddenly his mother puts down her broom, picks up the child, and cuddles and kisses him. Perhaps the child repeats the syllables that preceded the change in his mother—"ma-ma-ma-ma-ma-ma"—to Mama's delight. That night mother reports to father that Gerry has said his first words.

This type of learning, *instrumental conditioning*, differs from classical conditioning in several ways. In classical conditioning, the response to the CS that is learned is elicited reflexively by a stimulus, the UCS. In instrumental conditioning, or learning, the response occurs spontaneously as a result of maturation (as in the case of Gerry's babbling) or as a result of previous learning.

In classical conditioning, the stimuli are presented in the same way regardless of what the organism does. Pavlov gave the dog powdered meat whether or not he salivated when the fork sounded. In instrumental learning, what the organism does has an effect on what happens to him. When little Gerry was babbling, he was rewarded *only when* he said the magic syllables.

FIG. 5–3. The Skinner box. Left: Diagram showing the box, consisting of a lever, lights above it to provide stimuli, and a slot to the rat's left where food may appear. Right: Photograph of a rat pressing a lever in such a box.

The Skinner box, a box containing a lever and a food cup, is an apparatus that experimenters frequently use to investigate the effects of various conditions on instrumental conditioning (see Fig. 5–3). The apparatus is so arranged that every time the animal presses the lever he receives some reward, such as food. The appearance of food thus depends on the response of the animal. Under these conditions, the more times he receives food upon lever-pressing, the more likely it is that he will continue to press the lever when hungry.* Instrumental learning in mice, rats, cats, and pigeons has been studied extensively in the Skinner box.

Another apparatus that experimental psychologists frequently use to study instrumental learning is the maze. Mazes, which have been adapted for both human and animal subjects, range from very simple to rather complex. Figure 5–4 shows some examples. The simple T-maze is the maze used most frequently in animal learning studies. This maze consists of a start box, a short runway, a choice point at which the animal must make a 90° turn either to the left or to the right, and goal boxes at the end of the left and right alleys. Normally one goal box will contain a reward, such as food or water, and the other will be empty. Animals who initially show no preference for either the left or the right at the choice point will, after a series of rewarded trials, go always to the rewarded side.

----

* If the animal is not hungry, food is no longer a reward to him.

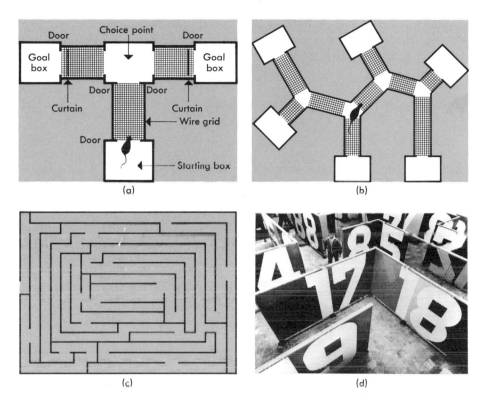

FIG. 5-4. Mazes which have been used to study instrumental learning in rats and humans: (a) simple T-maze for rats, (b) a more complex maze for rats; (c) a maze through which a person traces a path with a pencil; (d) a "walk-through" maze for children, which was exhibited at the Seattle World's Fair.

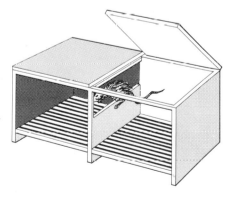

FIG. 5-5. The shuttle box. The opening in the center wall allows the animal a chance to avoid the shock.

Both Skinner boxes and mazes usually make use of a positive reward such as food. However, there are also instrumental learning paradigms that use the cessation or prevention of an unpleasant stimulus, such as electric shock, for a reward. For such experiments an apparatus known as the shuttle box is frequently used (see Fig. 5-5). The shuttle box is divided into two sections, each of which has a grid floor and can be electrified independently of the other. If an animal is placed in one side of the shuttle box and the shock is turned on, he soon learns to escape to the other side. Furthermore, if the shock is always preceded by a buzzer, the animal learns to escape to avoid the shock by jumping to the other side before the shock comes on. The difference between this type of avoidance learning and classical conditioning using shock as a UCS is that in the former the animal can make a response to avoid the shock, whereas in the latter he cannot.

■ Brogden, Lipman, and Cruller (1938) compared the classical and instrumental procedures, both employing shock, in an experiment on two groups of guinea pigs. Each guinea pig was placed in a revolving drum. Since electric shock causes these animals to run, it was chosen to serve as a UCS. In the classical conditioning group, a tone was always followed by an electric shock which the guinea pig could not escape or avoid. In the instrumental conditioning group, once the tone sounded, the guinea pig could avoid the shock by running and making the drum rotate. The experimenters were interested in differences in the behavior of the two groups of guinea pigs when the tone sounded. There were distinct differences after training. The instrumental group soon learned to avoid the shock as soon as the tone was presented. The classical conditioning group never learned to run at the sound of the tone; rather, they showed signs of fear such as trembling, cowering, and stiffening. Although running was a UCR, it never became a CR. The emotional responses, which were also part of the UCR to shock, became the CR in the classical conditioning group. ■

Both groups of guinea pigs learned something as a result of their experiences. One group, the instrumental group, learned to perform a response. The other group learned only to be afraid when the buzzer sounded. This study and many others suggest that different kinds of responses are most easily learned as a result of classical and instrumental conditioning. With classical conditioning, involuntary responses, such as salivation and emotional reactions, are most easily learned. With instrumental conditioning, voluntary responses, such as lever pressing and running in new situations, are learned.

Thus we find three differences between classical and instrumental conditioning.

● (1) The origin of the response: In classical conditioning the response is reflexively elicited by the UCS; in instrumental conditioning it occurs spontaneously.

● (2) The organism's control over the situation: In classical conditioning the animal's behavior has no effect on the training procedure; in instrumental conditioning the animal's responses determine what happens to him—whether or not the food appears or the shock is turned off.

● (3) The kinds of responses that can be most easily modified: Involuntary responses seem to be most easily trained via classical conditioning, and voluntary responses are most easily trained by instrumental methods.

Extinction and Spontaneous Recovery

What happens, after a period of classical conditioning, if the sound of the tuning fork is no longer followed by food in the dog's mouth; if, in instrumental conditioning, pressing the bar in the Skinner box is no longer followed by food dropping into the food cup? This procedure of removing the UCS or the reward from the training situation is called *extinction.* As you might expect, the result of such a procedure is a gradual reduction of the learned response in both classical and instrumental conditioning (see Fig. 5–6).

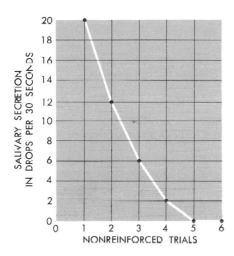

FIG. 5–6. Extinction of a classically conditioned salivary response in a dog. (Data from Pavlov, 1927.)

Although after conditioning and extinction the animal no longer makes the previously trained response, you should not conclude that the learning has somehow been erased and that the animal is now like a completely untrained animal. Pavlov demonstrated this in the following way:

■ After he conditioned the salivary responses, he extinguished the response by presenting the sound of the tuning fork without the UCS, food. Soon the dog stopped salivating to the sound. When the response disappeared, Pavlov returned the dog to his home cage. The next day, when the dog was once again exposed to the CS, the tuning fork, the salivary response returned in almost full strength. ■

This phenomenon, extinction followed by rest, followed by the recovery of the CR is called *spontaneous recovery.* The term "spontaneous" is appropriate since there is no retraining between extinction and the recovery.

If, during the training session after spontaneous recovery, the CS is still presented without the UCS, the animal's response will gradually extinguish once again. The following day, he may again show some spontaneous recovery, but

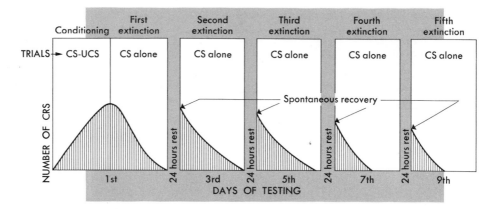

FIG. 5–7.   The course of extinction and spontaneous recovery.

it will not be as great as that of the day before. Eventually, the response will disappear completely. See Fig. 5–7. However, the animal is still different from an untrained one. If the conditioning procedure were instigated again following complete extinction, it would not take the organism as long to show the conditioned response as it did in the original conditioning.

The Problem of Reinforcement

The result of classical and instrumental conditioning training is that after conditioning the organism makes a response in a situation which he did not formerly make. After training, babies stop crying as soon as they hear footsteps, dogs salivate at sounds, rats press bars more frequently in Skinner boxes. These changes occur when formerly neutral stimuli, bells, boxes, and footsteps, are paired with a special event—the UCS in classical conditioning and a reward in instrumental conditioning. Furthermore, omission of the UCS or the reward makes the learned response disappear, as we just saw in our description of extinction.

Any event which increases the frequency of a response in a particular situation is called a *reinforcer*. Stimuli whose presence increase the frequency of the response are called *positive reinforcers*; those whose termination increase the frequency of the response are called *negative reinforcers*. Thus food is a positive reinforcer and shock is usually a negative reinforcer.

In the course of their experimentation, psychologists have discovered and used a variety of reinforcers. They have also pondered the questions: What makes a particular stimulus reinforcing? What effects do reinforcers have on the organism that make them effective? There is no conclusive answer to either of these questions. Several psychologists have suggested theories. One of the most influential theorists, Clark Hull (1943), hypothesized that every organism is born with a number of basic biological drives—hunger, thirst, sex, and pain. A reinforcer, according to Hull, is any stimulus which reduces a drive. Food and shock certainly fit this description of a reinforcer.

Another theory states that certain stimuli are innately pleasant or unpleasant and that the reinforcing properties depend on the degree of pleasantness or unpleasantness produced (McClelland, 1951). This is the position we will take throughout this text. There are several reasons why we chose it over the drive-reduction theory. First, saccharine, which is a nonnutritive substance and therefore cannot reduce the biological hunger drive at all, serves as an extremely effective reinforcer in learning experience (Sheffield and Roby, 1951). In another series of studies Young and his associates (Young, 1961) have shown that animals who are completely satiated so far as food is concerned will still respond when sugar or saccharine is the reward. Young concludes that the reinforcing power results not from the sugar's ability to reduce hunger, but simply from its good taste. We find a similar phenomenon on the human level. Have you ever gone into a room not feeling hungry at all and seen a dish of salted nuts? In an offhand way, have you eaten one and then found that you could not stop eating them? Your behavior of reaching for the nuts was reinforced not because the nuts reduced a hunger drive, but because you enjoyed the flavor of the nuts. Finally, a pleasantness-unpleasantness interpretation fits in well with our own private experience. Subjectively, we seek positive goals and also try to reduce our biological drives. Of course, drive reducers are included among reinforcers even with our interpretation because drive reduction is one of many pleasant experiences.

Secondary Reinforcement

Some stimuli, such as food and shock, seem to be natural reinforcers. These are called *primary reinforcers*. One of the most important phenomena uncovered in the study of conditioning is that stimuli that are associated with primary reinforcement themselves take on some reinforcing properties.

■ Pavlov first demonstrated this phenomenon for classical conditioning. A dog was trained to salivate in response to the sound of a metronome, with food used as a UCS. When the salivary response to the metronome became very consistent, Pavlov instituted what he called *second-order conditioning*. He now presented a black square to the dog and immediately followed it with the sound of the metronome for a series of trials. As a result of the dog's earlier training, he responded to the sound with salivation. After many pairings of square and metronome, the black square began to lead to salivation before the sound was heard. In effect, the metronome, which had been the CS in the original training, served as the UCS in the *second-order conditioning*. ■

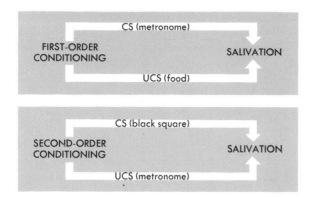

FIG. 5–8.   In second-order conditioning the stimulus
which was a CS in earlier conditioning, now serves
as a UCS.

We can diagram the process as shown in Fig. 5–8. The metronome has become
a *secondary reinforcer* as a result of its presentation at about the same time
as food.

Secondary reinforcement has been demonstrated in instrumental conditioning
with an experiment using the Skinner box. Two groups of rats learned to press
a bar for a food reward. The food-delivery mechanism made a clicking noise
so that the food was always preceded by a click. The extinction procedure
began by eliminating the food reward from the situation. For one group of
rats, pressing the bar had no consequences at all; for the second group, pressing
the bar led to the sound of the click. The experimenter now observed how long
it took the two groups to stop pressing the bar. He found that the group whose
pressing led to the click continued to press for a longer period than the other
group. He concluded that the sound had acquired some reinforcing properties
through its earlier association with food (Bugelski, 1938).

Another interesting demonstration of secondary reinforcement comes from
a study involving chimpanzees. Chimps were trained to lift a heavy lever to
obtain a grape as reward. Along with the grape, the chimp received a poker
chip as a bonus. After this training, the chimps continued to lift the lever for
the poker chip alone (Wolfe, 1936).

Clicks, chips, and squares have become secondary reinforcers for laboratory
animals. We can only speculate on the wide range of stimuli that have become
secondary reinforcers for human beings. Money is certainly an object which
is associated with many primary reinforcers and acquires powerful reinforcing
properties. Praises, smiles, even grades in school may be other examples. We
shall consider further implications of secondary reinforcement for human behavior in Chapter 7. For now, let us see how this concept helped to explain
a puzzling result.

Time Relations in Classical and Instrumental Conditioning

Conditioning, both classical and instrumental, depends on *temporal contiguity* —on events occurring close to one another in time. In classical conditioning the CS and the UCS must be in temporal contiguity; in instrumental conditioning the response must be closely followed by the reward. A logical experimental question was: What are the optimum time intervals involved?

Many studies have tested the effectiveness of various time intervals between the CS and the UCS. Most of the studies showed that conditioning is most effective when the conditioned stimulus precedes the unconditioned stimulus by about half a second. Longer delays lead to less effective training. Some experimenters wondered whether any conditioning would occur if the unconditioned stimulus *preceded* the conditioned stimulus (this procedure is called *backward conditioning*). Most attempts at backward conditioning have failed. Kimble (1956) took the data from many studies and drew a composite curve (see Fig. 5–9) to show the relative effectiveness of various time intervals.

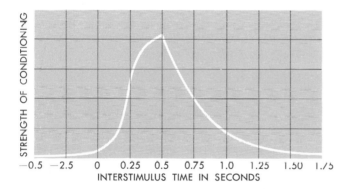

FIG. 5–9. The effect of the time interval between CS and UCS on the strength of conditioning. (Gregory A. Kimble and Norman Garmezy, *Principles of General Psychology*, second edition. Copyright © 1963 The Ronald Press Company.)

In instrumental conditioning the time interval that seemed as though it should be crucial was the interval between the response and the reinforcement. But early results were conflicting. In an early study, Watson (1917) found that rats trained to dig through sawdust to a food cup performed equally well whether they were permitted to eat immediately or whether they had to wait 30 seconds. Skinner (1938) found no differences in rats who after bar-pressing had to wait 1, 2, 3, or 4 seconds for their reinforcement. Perin (1943), using the Skinner box situation also, found that a delay of 5 and 10 seconds cut learning efficiency in half. Wolfe (1934) got similar results in a T-maze. How can these results be explained?

Perkins (1948) hypothesized that secondary reinforcement could explain the differences. If, during the delay, the organism is in the presence of stimuli that have been associated with primary reinforcement, the time delay between response and reinforcement need not impair learning significantly. The more secondary reinforcers are eliminated during the delay, the smaller the time interval that will still produce learning. Perkins tested his ideas in a T-maze study on rats. The rats were rewarded if they turned toward one side and not toward the other. Just before they reached a goal box they were delayed in a delay chamber (whether they turned right or left at the choice point; see Fig. 5–10). Perkins predicted that the effects of delay would depend in part on how different the delay chambers used in the right and left alleys of the maze were. He reasoned that if the delay chamber always associated with reward was distinctive, the stimuli in it would become secondary reinforcers. If the delay chambers were alike, the stimuli would be associated equally with reward and nonreward and would not become secondary reinforcers. Perkins' results supported his hypothesis. In cases where the delay boxes were alike, even a delay of 5 seconds impaired learning. When they were very dissimilar, much longer periods had little effect.

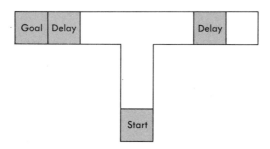

FIG. 5–10.   Perkins used this type of maze to test the effects of different delays on learning.

Perkins' results help to explain why Watson's rats showed no deficit in learning with a delay of 30 seconds. Although the delayed rats could not eat, they were permitted to see the food cup and smell the food during the delay. The sights and smells, which had been so closely associated with eating previously, had become powerful secondary reinforcers.

The fact that cues associated with primary reinforcement help to bridge a time gap between response and reinforcement is extremely important in understanding human behavior, where the time elapsed between performance and reward is often quite long. We work and are paid once a week or once a month, for example. Very often words are the cues that help to bridge this gap. If all these cues were removed, a delay of more than 5 seconds would make our performance poorer.

What Occurs Inside the Organism During Conditioning?

Thus far we have done little more than to summarize the relationships observed during conditioning. Now let us go beyond observable events and analyze conditioning in terms of what is happening inside the organism. In doing so, we shall infer three major constructs. Many psychologists agree that these particular constructs are useful for understanding learning, although others offer alternative interpretations. What follows, then, is one way of interpreting conditioning and learning.

Perceptual Learning

We have described classical conditioning as a procedure in which two stimuli are paired. Each stimulus (S) triggers some neural activity (s). When the organism makes the conditioned response to the previously neutral stimulus, we can infer that some kind of s_{CS}–s_{UCS} linkage has been formed, so that s_{CS} triggers off neural and behavioral preparations for the coming of the UCS. Stored in the brain is an *if . . . then* expectancy: If the CS appears, then the UCS will soon appear. If baby hears Mama's footsteps, then his tummy will soon stop hurting. If the bell sounds, then the dog will soon feel meat in his mouth. We shall call the storage of such s_{CS}–s_{UCS} relationships *perceptual expectancies* or *percepts*.

If the appearance of the conditioned stimulus does trigger off an expectancy of the unconditioned stimulus, we hypothesize that the organism's response to the conditioned stimulus would be a preparation for the coming of the unconditioned stimulus. This interpretation helps explain why the CR and the UCR are not always alike and helps predict which aspects of the UCR will appear as the CR. In Pavlov's experiment, the unconditioned response to food in the mouth is salivation, vigorous chewing, and swallowing. The conditioned response is only salivation. Salivation is an appropriate preparation for expected food; chewing and swallowing are not.

Our theory states that an s-s expectancy is stored in the brain after two stimuli have appeared together frequently. This implies that an animal should be able to learn relationships between stimuli without making any observable response to either stimulus. Some psychologists who believed that all learning consisted of associations between stimuli and responses questioned this possibility. In a very ingenious study, Brogden (1939) demonstrated that stimulus relationships can be learned without an overt response.

■ There were three stages in Brogden's experiment. In the first stage, a light and a bell were presented in rapid succession for 200 trials to a group of dogs. In the second stage, the dogs were classically conditioned to lift their paws to the bell by pairing the bell with a mild electric shock. In the third stage, the light was presented alone. The light had never been paired with

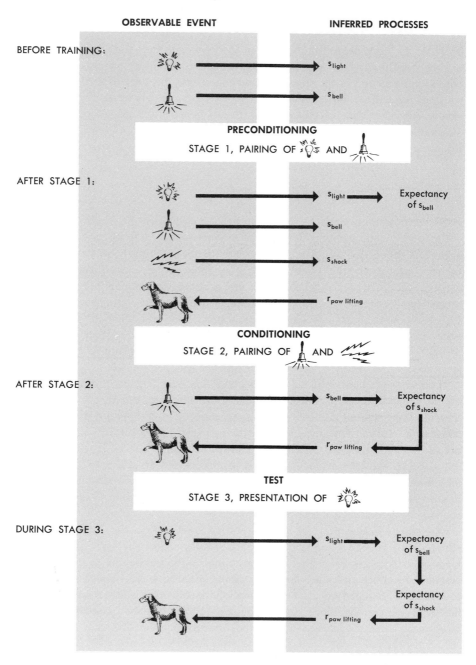

FIG. 5–11. The procedures and results of Brogden's experiment, in terms of both observable events and inferred processes.

shock. Nevertheless, the dogs showed a significant tendency to lift their paws when the light was presented. We can summarize the relationships as shown in Fig. 5–11. ■

Brogden's experiment is consonant with the interpretation that in classical conditioning the organism stores in its brain, expectancies about relationships between stimuli. Another study which supports the theory in favor of an all-encompassing stimulus-response interpretation is one done on cats, using the drug bulbocapnine. Bulbocapnine, although leaving the sensory system intact, immobilizes the organism so that it can make no responses at all. Cats under the influence of the drug were presented with a tone followed by a shock to the foot. During training, they could not, of course, avoid the shock. As soon as the drug wore off, however, the cats, with no further training, made the appropriate flexion response as soon as they heard the tone. They had learned to expect shock even though they could make no responses during training (Beck and Doty, 1957).

Motivational and Act Learning

We shall analyze instrumental conditioning in terms of two kinds of learning. A classic experiment by Blodgett (1929) will help us to separate the two kinds of learning in a maze study.

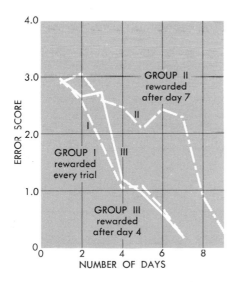

FIG. 5–12. The results of Blodgett's latent learning experiment. (After Blodgett, 1929)

■ Blodgett used three groups of rats: The rats in group I ran the maze once a day for 7 days and always found food in the goal box. The rats in group II ran the maze for 9 days. For the first 6 days, they found an empty goal box. On day 7 and the 2 succeeding days, food was in the goal box. The rats in group III were handled in the same way as group II except that food was first introduced on day 3. Figure 5–12 shows the mean number of errors made by the rats in each group each day. As you can see, group I gradually reduced their errors each day. Group II showed little improvement until day 8, the day after food had been introduced. Then there was a sudden drop in the number of errors. For group III the sudden drop occurred on day 4, the day after food was introduced for that group. ■

What were the rats learning in the maze? What accounts for the gradual reduction in errors for the group that was fed every day in the maze and the sudden drop in errors when food was introduced for groups II and III? In order to explain the results, we have to assume that the animals were learning something, although the learning was not reflected immediately in the error score. As each rat was running through the maze, he was receiving information about the spatial relationships in the maze; he was learning that if he made particular turns at a given choice point, he would see (hear and smell) particular alleys. As a result of this informational feedback from the environment, the rat stored in his brain a series of *stimulus-response-stimulus* (s-r-s) relationships (also called *act expectancies* or habits). However, the rat in group II or III had no reason to prefer any one of the paths with which he was familiar. When the food was introduced on the seventh day, the rat learned something new—the goal box contained something which was pleasant* to him. From this affective feedback, he learned to associate the stimuli of the goal box with a pleasant event. He learned a *stimulus-affect* (s-a) relationship (also called a *motivational expectancy* or motive). If we make the simple assumption that organisms seek pleasant situations and avoid unpleasant ones, the results of the experiment become clear. When the animals in group II and III learned the goal-box-food expectancy, they made use of the s-r-s expectancies they had previously learned in the maze. This was reflected in the sudden error drop. The animals in group I, who received food on every trial, learned s-r-s and s-a expectancies simultaneously; they were thus motivated to use their knowledge as soon as they learned it. This study has been called a *latent-learning* study because the rats in groups II and III learned something without immediately reflecting their learning through their behavior.

Note that in instrumental conditioning the organism changes its behavior as a result of the consequences of its previous behavior. We have distinguished two kinds of consequences: <u>*Informational feedback*, by which the organism learns the effect of his response on the environment and *affective feedback*, by which the organism learns whether this changed situation will be pleasant or unpleasant.</u> Informational feedback leads to the buildup of s-r-s expectancies; affective feedback to the buildup of s-a expectancies. It may be recalled that

---

* The feelings of affect, pleasantness, and unpleasantness, are unobservable private feelings. We use them as constructs and infer them from behavior. The operations by which we infer them are discussed in Chapter 7.

earlier we defined reinforcement as any event which leads to an increase in frequency of response in a situation. When the effects of feedback are reflected in an immediate increase in the frequency of responses, the term feedback is synonymous with reinforcement. Sometimes, however, these effects of feedback are not reflected in behavior, as we saw in Blodgett's latent learning experiment.

We saw earlier that frequency and temporal contiguity are important factors in conditioning. The laws of frequency and contiguity can be applied to both informational and affective feedback. In Army marksmanship training, recruits traditionally have seen the results of their efforts only after they have fired a number of shots. It was found that training proceeded more rapidly if the recruit was made aware of the results immediately after *each* shot. Here we have contiguity between act and informational feedback which strengthens s-r-s expectancies. If members of the recruit's squad could cheer each bull's-eye, the learner's motivation would also benefit from closely contiguous *affective* feedback, building up s-r-s-a expectancies.

Kinds of Affective Feedback: Punishment and Reward

Affective feedback implies a change in the feeling of an organism along the dimension of pleasantness or unpleasantness. There are four ways in which this change could occur: reward (or in the terms we used earlier, reinforcement) is obtaining a pleasing stimulus or having an unpleasant one removed; punishment is being subjected to a painful stimulus or having a pleasant one removed. We are familiar with examples in each of these categories: receiving an unexpected gift, changing to lighter clothing when it is very hot, being spanked for misbehavior, getting a reduction in pay for being late.

An analysis of the two kinds of feedback shows that the effects of punishment and reward on behavior are not identical. When an organism learns a stimulus-pleasantness relationship, he acts so as to obtain the stimulus; reward increases the probability that he will *do* something. On the other hand, after punishment he avoids stimuli associated with the expectancy of unpleasantness; he learns what *not to do* (Solomon, 1964).

How effective is punishment in suppressing undesired behavior? Several studies have shown that the intensity of the unpleasant stimulus is a crucial variable. Very mild stimuli have no effect, fairly unpleasant stimuli temporarily reduce the rate of responding, with the response returning as soon as punishment is omitted, and extremely intense punishment eliminates the behavior completely and permanently (Estes, 1949; Karsh, 1962; Azrin, 1959, 1960, 1961). However, intense punishment for undesired behavior may also lead to long-lasting emotional side effects.

This discussion does not imply that the use of extremely painful stimuli is essential if punishment is to be used to modify behavior permanently. We noted that intermediate intensity punishments reduce or eliminate the undesired behavior temporarily. If this period of temporary suppression is coupled with opportunity and reward for new behavior, low-intensity punishments can make significant changes in behavior. Whiting and Mowrer (1943) demonstrated this principle with a study on rats.

■ The rats were trained to take one route in a maze with a food reward in the goal-box. Then they were punished with a low-intensity electric shock for taking this route. This mild punishment temporarily stopped the rats from traversing the old route. Now Whiting and Mowrer opened up a new route which also led to food. The rats quickly learned the new route and never again used the old one. ■

If an alternate rewarded route had not been provided, the temporary avoidance of the punished route probably would have been overcome. The coupling of mild punishment for undesired behavior with reward for alternative behavior is a powerful training device.

Just as the time between response and reward is a significant factor in their effectiveness, so is the time interval between response and punishment. Animal studies have shown that the sooner the punishment follows the response, the greater its effect (Kamin, 1959). In Kamin's study a delay of 10 seconds made punishment rather ineffective. In human beings, for whom language can span much larger time gaps, we would not expect so drastic an effect.

Punishment: a Summary with Practical Implications

What guidance can these concepts and principles give to parents and teachers who are faced with the practical problem of training children?

Punishment may teach a child to avoid a particular kind of undesirable behavior. However, it does not give the child guidance in selecting acceptable behavior. Thus we would expect that punishment is most effective when it is important to teach a child to avoid something, and when the parent does not care what else he does instead, e.g., punishment should be more effective than reward alone in teaching a child not to play in the street. Unless the punishment is extremely intense, it will have longer-lasting effects if it is coupled with reward for alternative behavior.

The effectiveness of both reward and punishment depends upon their contiguity with the behavior being rewarded or punished. In fact, punishment is more effective if applied at the beginning of the response than if used after the response is over, since effective prevention of the response depends upon the association of unpleasantness with the stimuli that initiate the undesirable response. Thus (continuing our example of a child playing in the street), punishment will be more effective if the child is punished as he goes into the street than if he is punished after playing there for some time.

Conditioning and Expectancy: Summary

We can summarize what is learned during conditioning with three theoretical constructs (see Fig. 5–13): (1) perceptual expectancies (percepts or s-s relationships), (2) motivational expectancies (motives or s-a relationships), and (3) act expectancies (habit or s-r-s relationships). These expectancies are learned when there is consistent informational and affective feedback from the environment. The two kinds of affective feedback, reward and punishment, affect behavior in different ways: one identifies positive goals and how to attain them; the other indicates negative goals and how to avoid them. Classical conditioning can be interpreted as an example of stimulus-stimulus learning. Instrumental conditioning may be analyzed in terms of learning affective expectancies and habits.

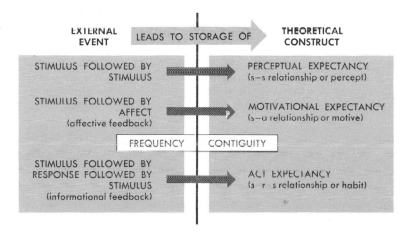

FIG. 5–13. From the data of conditioning experiments, we hypothesize three major constructs: perceptual, motivational, and act expectancies. All three are learned as a result of frequency and contiguity of certain events.

Some Additional Conditioning Phenomena: Partial Reinforcement

In most real-life instrumental learning we do not get either consistent reinforcement or consistent nonreinforcement. Sometimes the baby sees his mother, and she ignores him; sometimes you study for an examination and still do poorly; sometimes you expect an interesting lecture, and it turns out to be 42 minutes of dullness and 7 minutes of lively stimulation. Most everyday learning involves a mixture of experiences of rewards, punishments, and absence of rewards or punishments. Consequently, psychologists have been particularly interested in experiments in which reward is not presented on every trial— experiments in *partial reinforcement*.

Learning occurs more slowly when partial reinforcement is used than when every response is reinforced. The failure to reinforce on every trial is particularly detrimental to classical conditioning. Pavlov (1927) found that regularly omitting the food on more than two or three consecutive trials during training made conditioning almost impossible.

Partial reinforcement also makes instrumental conditioning more difficult, but the procedure is not nearly so detrimental as it is in classical conditioning. Furthermore, the use of partial reinforcement—especially in Skinner box experiments—has led to some very intriguing demonstrations. One major finding is that the pattern of responding depends on the pattern of reinforcement.

There are two ways of scheduling partial reinforcement: (1) an interval schedule in which the organism receives reinforcement after a set interval of time (such as every two minutes) regardless of how many responses he has made during the interval and (2) a ratio schedule in which the organism receives reinforcement after he has made a certain number of responses. (For example, if the ratio is 10 : 1, the organism will be rewarded after every 10 responses.) Each of these schedules may be presented in either a *fixed* or a *variable* manner. A fixed-interval schedule is one in which the reinforcement occurs after a fixed interval of time, such as every two minutes. A variable-interval schedule is one in which reinforcement occurs on the average every two minutes, but sometimes the interval is much longer, sometimes quite a bit shorter. Similarly, in a variable ratio schedule of 10 : 1, the organism is rewarded on the average about every 10 responses, but sometimes he is rewarded after a smaller number, sometimes he has to make more than ten responses before he receives a reward. These schedules of reinforcement are analogous to different ways of paying employees. Most people are on a "fixed"-interval schedule; that is, they are paid after one week or one month of work. However, "piece-rate" workers are on a fixed-ratio schedule; that is, they are paid according to the number of products they complete.

Skinner developed a very easy way of recording and comparing the response patterns of organisms under different schedules of reinforcement in a Skinner box. The lever which the organism presses in order to get food is attached to a recording pen. The pen makes contact with a strip of paper which moves under the pen at a constant speed. Thus the pen makes a horizontal line across the paper. Whenever the animal depresses the lever, the pen makes a small vertical movement. Hence the height of the curve drawn by the pen tells us how many total responses the organism has made up to that time. The steepness of the curve tells us about the rate of responding. See Fig. 5–14.

Figure 5–15 shows some typical cumulative response curves produced by individual animals under different schedules of reinforcement. As you can see, under a fixed-interval schedule (see Fig. 5–15a), the cumulative response curve looks like a series of scallops. The curve takes this form because, following reinforcement, the organism's response rate is slow at the beginning of each new

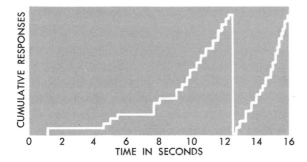

FIG. 5–14. This is the kind of record produced by a rat pressing a bar in a Skinner box. Each vertical jump represents one bar press. Thus the rat pressed once during the first second and three times in the fourth and fifth seconds. His rate accelerated after the ninth second. The pen of the cumulative recorder reached the top of the paper in the twelfth second and so it dropped to the baseline. The slope (the slant) of the line made by the pen during its climb tells us the rate at which the organism is responding.

interval. The closer the animal gets to the end of the interval (and reinforcement) the greater response rate. This response pattern can be interpreted as a reflection of the organism's expectancies; immediately after reinforcement, he has learned that his responses will not lead to a pleasant reward, and thus his rate is low.

The highest and most stable rates of responding occur with ratio reinforcement schedules, as shown in Fig. 5–15c. Typically, an animal is gradually introduced to a ratio schedule. First, he is rewarded on every trial, a little later every third trial, and so on. With such a procedure, the behavior of rats and pigeons has been sustained at very high levels with very little reward.

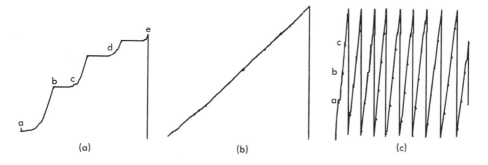

FIG. 5–15. The response rates of pigeons under different schedules of partial reinforcement. (a) A cumulative response curve produced under a fixed-interval schedule. (b) A cumulative response curve produced under a variable-interval schedule. (c) A cumulative response curve produced under a fixed-ratio schedule.

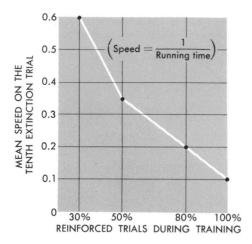

FIG. 5–16. The relationship between speed during extinction and reinforcement schedule during training. Four groups of rats were trained to run down a runway each under a different reinforcement schedule. The smaller the percentage of rewarded trials during the training, the faster they ran down the runway during extinction (Kimble and Garmezy, 1963, after Weinstock, 1954).

Skinner reports that rats have been trained to respond quickly and consistently when they were rewarded with food only once every 192 responses (Skinner, 1938)! We find human beings with equally stable rates of responding with high reinforcement ratios in Reno, Nevada, using a modified Skinner box called a slot machine.

We noted earlier that the acquisition of a response, even an instrumental response like lever-pressing, occurs more slowly under partial reinforcement than under 100-percent reinforcement. But what about resistance to extinction? When an instrumental act is learned under partial reinforcement, it persists much longer after removal of all reinforcement than an act learned under 100-percent reinforcement (see Fig. 5–16). We can theorize that under partial reinforcement, one learns to expect instances of nonreinforcement. Thus the extinction procedure is not radically different from the training procedure, and the organism continues to respond as before. A 100-percent reinforcement schedule produces expectancies of reward after every response. Thus when extinction begins, one perceives a radical change in the situation, and the rate of responding falls off sharply.

This same type of reasoning has been applied to another puzzling result. You would expect that the more training an organism has had (under 100-percent reinforcement), the more resistant he would be to extinctions; the better the learning, the more persistent the behavior when reward is omitted. However, we frequently find that "overlearning," additional training after the organism has learned the correct response, leads to less rather than more persistent behavior under extinction. We could interpret this result in the following way: The more training an organism has had, the stronger his expectancy of reward. When he finds no reward in spite of his strong expectancy, he learns more quickly that reward is not forthcoming. In a sense, the more unexpected the lack of reward, the bigger the news.

Some writers have also pointed out that the lack of reward when an organism strongly expects it is a frustrating experience. They hypothesize that the first reaction to a frustrating situation is increased persistence of responding (Amsel, 1958). This hypothesis also explains the partial reinforcement and overlearning phenomena. Thus these phenomena continue to stimulate theory and research.

Generalization and Discrimination

After a person or an animal has received conditioning training, his response to the stimulus to which he has been trained changes. The baby now stops crying when he hears the footsteps of his mother. The rat now presses a bar in a Skinner box. Albert cries when he sees a white rat. However, the training stimuli are not the only ones which now produce the new behavior. Baby not only stops crying when he hears Mother's footsteps, but also when his sister Sally's light steps are heard. The rat will press a white bar as well as the black bar on which he was trained. And Albert will cry and shudder at the sight of a white rabbit, a furry white glove, and a ball of cotton. This phenomenon of responding to similar stimuli in the same way as to the training stimulus is called *stimulus generalization*.

In general, the more similar the test stimulus is to the stimulus on which training took place, the greater the generalization (see Fig. 5–17). Guttman and Kalish (1956) illustrated these phenomena in an instrumental learning experiment with pigeons.

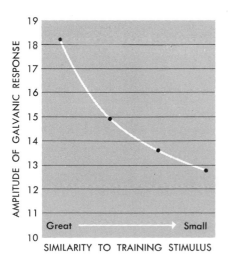

SIMILARITY TO TRAINING STIMULUS

FIG. 5–17. Generalization from classical conditioning. The CS was a tone and the UCS a mild electric shock. The CR was the change in skin resistance (called galvanic skin response) which is a physiological response to emotion. After conditioning training, the experimenter measured his subjects' galvanic response to tones which differed in pitch from the CS. He found that the less similar in pitch the test tone was to the CS, the smaller the subject's response to it. (After Hovland, 1937)

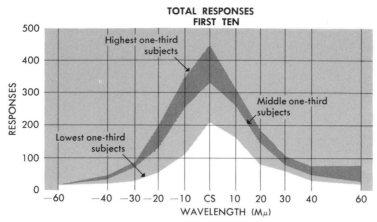

FIG. 5–18.   Generalization from Operant Conditioning. The experiment is described in the text. The three curves show the generalization gradients of pigeons divided into three categories: the third of the group that achieved the highest response rate during training, the third that achieved the lowest rate, and the middle third. Note that the shape of the generalization gradient is about the same for each of the three groups. (After Guttman and Kalish, 1956)

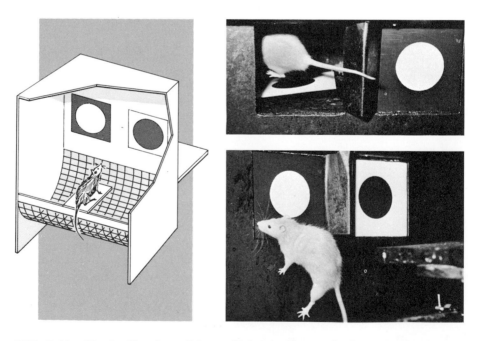

FIG. 5–19.   The Lashley "jump" box, which is used to study discrimination in rats. If the rat jumps to the correct card, the card falls and he finds food behind it. If he makes an incorrect choice, the card stays in place and the rat falls into a net. (Photographs courtesy *Life* Magazine © 1965, Time, Inc. All rights reserved.)

■ Pigeons learned to peck at a yellow-green light for a food reward on a partial reinforcement schedule. When the pecking response became very consistent, the effects of other colors were tested: sometimes the test light was orange, sometimes blue, etc. The different colors were presented in random order. The number of pecks the pigeon made to each wavelength* (color) is illustrated in Fig. 5–18. As you can see, the closer the wavelength to that of the training color, the more times the pigeon pecked at it. ■

Stimulus generalization occurs spontaneously, with no training other than the conditioning. However, organisms can learn to respond differently to similar stimuli. Such learning is called *discrimination learning*.

Most discrimination learning experiments involve two choices. A rat, for example, is trained to jump to a black card rather than a white card. In training the rat to make this discrimination, the experimenter constructs a situation in which the rat receives food when he jumps to the correct card, but fails to receive food when he jumps to the wrong one. See Fig. 5–19. You might think that the information from a wrong jump should be as great as that from a "correct" jump. However, discrimination learning is not quite that simple. Because being fed provides affective as well as informational feedback, the correct choice increases the rat's tendency to respond in this situation, while the effects of the incorrect choice decrease any tendency to respond. A series of wrong choices may then not only weaken the tendency to go to the white circle but also weaken the tendency to jump at all.

Discrimination learning is thus likely to be most efficient if the correct responses occur early in the sequence of responses. If incorrect interfering responses are dominant, learning is slow. As we would expect from this principle, experimental evidence shows that guidance or an example is especially helpful in the early stages of learning.

A closely related principle is that a discrimination is learned most rapidly if the two stimuli to be discriminated are markedly different. This has a practical implication for situations in which an experimenter wants to train discriminations along certain dimensions.

■ Lashley demonstrated that whereas rats require 150 trials to learn to discriminate two shades of grey, they can learn a black-white discrimination in 10 trials, which they are then able to transfer to the grey discrimination without further training. Similarly, chicks trained to discriminate red from green continue to discriminate yellow from grey or yellow from red (Lashley, 1916). ■

We can interpret generalization and discrimination according to the organism's expectancies: the more similar the test stimulus to the training stimulus, the more he expects it to have the same consequences. Discrimination learning sets clear limits on the stimulus ranges within which the consequences are expected.

---

* Different colors differ physically in wavelengths.

How Is Conditioning Related to Learning in General?

The examples of conditioning we have discussed represent the simplest form of learning in perception, motivation, and action. In each case, the organism learns a simple temporal relationship between events. By studying learning in such well-controlled situations, psychologists have discovered and described precisely the effects of variables, such as frequency, pattern, and delay of reinforcement, on behavior. These laws provide a basis for understanding more complex forms of learning.

Percept and Concept Learning

In classical conditioning, the organism learns that the expectancy, S_1, will be followed by S_2. Another simple form of perceptual learning involves storing the information that combinations of stimuli consistently appear together. We learn to organize such patterns of stimuli into unitary objects. Once this learning has taken place, occurrence of part of the stimulus pattern sets off an expectancy for perception of the entire object. Even a glimpse of a friend's face enables us to recognize him.

When we have formed a perceptual expectancy on the basis of such stimuli (expecting to see a friend from a glimpse), we usually gain more information if we remain in the situation. For example, we may approach our friend and begin to talk with him. The additional information received from approaching him and his response to our greeting acts as feedback. If it confirms our original percept, it increases the likelihood that we will recognize the friend from the same cues the next time we meet. On the other hand, if we find that our original percept was mistaken, we will be less likely to form that friend perception when next the cues occur. As in learning temporal sequences, confirming informational feedback increases the probability that certain cues will elicit a percept; nonconfirming feedback decreases the probability.

Organisms, especially human beings, not only have the ability to store spatial and temporal relationships between stimuli; they can also abstract certain properties from the stimuli and make this abstraction the basis of their behavior. Let us look at an example of this type of learning in monkeys.

■ A monkey is presented with three objects over a series of trials. The three objects are different on every trial, but with every given set of three, two of the objects are alike and one is different. On every trial, a raisin is placed under the object that is different. At first, the monkey makes many errors, often having to lift all three objects before finding the raisin. After being exposed to a series of such tasks, the monkey learns always to pick out the odd object, regardless of the size, shape, color, and arrangement of the three objects (see Fig. 5–20). ■

What has the monkey learned? He has learned some s-r-s expectancies, that if he picks up one of the objects presented, he may or may not find a raisin.

But he has also learned an s-s relationship, which enables him to discriminate objects which cover raisins from those that do not. The monkey has learned the relationships: s_1 is the same as s_2; s_1 and s_2 are different from s_3. He has learned to abstract the properties of *similarity* and *difference* from all the other properties of the sets of three objects, which are different on each trial. We can infer that this abstraction has taken place because we observe the animal responding in a way that can be explained only on the basis of such an abstraction. When he was confronted with the oddity problem, other more simple stimulus relationships failed to provide a consistent solution. Then he learned to use the oddity property as the basis for his response.

FIG. 5–20. A monkey making a correct choice in the "oddity problem." (Photo courtesy of Dr. H. Harlow)

When an organism abstracts a property of a stimulus and can now classify objects or events on the basis of this property, he has learned a *concept*. The monkey, by his behavior, demonstrated that he had stored in his brain the concept of oddity. As we look at the behavior of animals from simple to complex organisms, we find a greater and greater ability to abstract concepts from their experience and to respond on the basis of them.

Concepts and Generalization

One can demonstrate that an organism has a concept stored in his brain and that the concept provides an important basis for responding, by showing that he generalizes along the conceptual dimension. Almost all animals in whom conditioning has been studied show generalization along simple physical dimensions (such as pitch and loudness for auditory stimuli). Animals also show some tendency to abstract and to generalize on the basis of pattern or form. Here we find species differences.

■ Two two-year-old children and two young chimpanzees were seated so that each faced two small boxes. In each trial one of the boxes had a white triangle on the front, while the other had a different marker. The figure was moved from box to box on successive trials, and the children and chimps learned that they could get food from the box bearing the triangle. Even though the stimulus was changed from box to box, the subjects continued to select the box with the triangle. Once this had been learned, the experimenter tried changing the size of the triangle. No matter what size the triangle was, the subjects continued to choose it. The experimenter now tried re-orienting the triangle so that the base was not horizontal. The subjects now crooked their heads to the side before choosing, but still they made the right response. Finally, the experimenter tried turning the triangle upside down. The children still made the right choice, but now the chimpanzees had great difficulty. (Gellerman, 1933) ■

Human beings are unique, not in their ability to respond on the basis of concepts, but in their ability to label them and manipulate them symbolically in a language. Experiments show that human beings have a strong tendency to generalize from words which serve as a conditioned stimulus to words whose meaning is related to the CS.

■ Lacey and Smith (1954, 1955) carried out a series of conditioning experiments with college students. The subjects were seated in an armchair with eyes closed. Over a loudspeaker the subject would hear a stimulus word (e.g., copper) and would begin responding with any words that he associated with the signal word. Some of the stimulus words were repeated. Each time the subject finished responding to the word "cow," he received an electric shock on his upper arm.

During the hour of the experiment, skin resistance, digital blood flow, and heart rate were continually recorded. Lacey and Smith found that the heart rate changed not only to the word "cow" but also to other rural words on the list. Thus the subjects' heart rates also changed when they heard the word "barn." Nonrural words did not produce the reaction. Generalization apparently was along a meaning dimension connecting rural words. ■

Thus we see that organisms can store (learn) a number of kinds of stimulus relationships: simple temporal relationships between stimuli, as in conditioning; spatial relationships, as in the organization of stimuli into objects; and abstracted relationships derived from stimulus properties, that is, concepts.

Motive Learning and Inconsistent Affect

One aspect of the organism's learning in instrumental conditioning is storing the expected relationships between a pattern of stimuli and affect (either pleasantness or unpleasantness). In most real-life situations and in many laboratory experiments, the stimulus-affect relationship is more complex. Even a simple reward like food does not always lead to the same affect. Food is a pleasant reward if you are hungry; but it may also be unpleasant, as when a hostess urges you to try her newest dessert after you've already overeaten. This is why many animal experimenters put animals on a feeding schedule, ensuring that food will be rewarding when the animal is being trained and tested. In the case of food we soon learn to discriminate between the conditions when the stimulus will lead to pleasantness and when it will not. We learn when to expect the positive (pleasant) affect.

In some cases this discrimination is very difficult, for the same object may unpredictably lead to either a positive or a negative affect. A baby's mother is the source of many pleasant feelings, but she is also the agent of discipline and punishment. If baby cannot learn the conditions under which to expect each type of behavior, Mother will become an object of ambivalence and conflict. We shall return to these problems in Chapter 11.

General Motives

Just as human beings learn to abstract relationships among stimuli to form concepts, so they abstract from many situations that produce affect and identify general classes of goals. For example, a child who is rewarded for high achievement in school work, in athletics, and in performing for his parents' friends may seek *any* situation in which achievement may be rewarded. Achievement itself has become a general motive for him. We shall consider the kinds of general motives that people acquire and how these motives develop in Chapter 7.

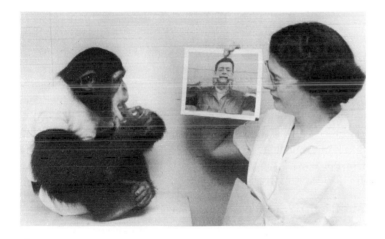

FIG. 5–21. The chimp Vicki, at the age of four, imitating a photograph to the command "Do this." (Photo courtesy of Dr. Keith J. Hayes)

Act Learning and General Habits

In simple instrumental learning, the organism learns that making a specific response (i.e. pressing a bar, turning right, etc.) in a situation will lead to a goal; this is a simple temporal s-r-s expectancy. However, much of our learning does not consist of learning specific responses in a situation, but rather learning to vary our responses in some constant relationship to the stimulus situation. Imitation is a common example. Here what seems to be stored in the organism's brain is the general expectancy "doing whatever you observe will have certain consequences." There have been a number of experiments which show that animals can vary their responses in this way. Miller and Dollard (1941) trained a group of rats to "follow the leader" in a maze problem. Heron (1942) reported that cats who observe a fellow cat solve a problem, themselves solve it more easily. Talking birds learn to mimic the sounds of their trainer. Perhaps the most striking examples of learned imitation in animals comes from the recorded exploits of Vicki, the chimpanzee who was raised in the home of Keith and Catherine Hayes. Vicki spontaneously imitated a number of household tasks she observed Mrs. Hayes performing. She was later trained to imitate a response on the command "Do this." Figure 5–21 shows a picture of Vicki imitating a photograph.

Such learning is quite common in people. Learning the general relationship "imitating what you hear will have certain consequences" is probably a very important element in a baby's learning to speak. People learn the general habit of responding appropriately to verbal directions in a new situatiton. Mrs. J. G. opens a new package of cereal correctly the first time she buys it by following the directions "press here." Earlier she had learned that following package directions will result in a neatly opened box.

In all these cases, the people are not learning to make a specific response to obtain a result but to respond to a new situation with a response that bears the same relationship to the new situation as a previous response bore to an old situation. We shall call learning such a mode of responding a *general habit*. The response in the second situation may look entirely different from the one in the first situation. The direction "cut along the dotted line" produces a response which is entirely different from that given to the instruction "press here." Yet both are the result of the same general habit.

Learning and Conditioning: a Synthesis

If we interpret learning as the storage of relationships, we can classify learning into three types with some form of conditioning providing a simple model of each. This classification is depicted in Fig. 5–22.

Even the more complex forms of learning depend on frequency, contiguity, and reinforcement. Ambivalence is learned when two opposite kinds of reinforcement are frequently associated with the same stimulus. Object and concept learning depend on informational feedback from the environment. ("Mommy, is that a dog?" "No, Howie, it's a horse.") General habits are learned when the same mode of responding leads to the same informational and affective consequences.

We shall look at the process and the results of these forms of learning in greater detail in the following chapters; Chapter 6 deals with perception, Chapter 7 with motives, Chapter 8 with action, Chapters 9 and 10 with concepts.

TYPE OF LEARNING	STORED RELATIONSHIP	EXAMPLE OF A STORED RELATIONSHIP
PERCEPTUAL LEARNING		
Classical conditioning	s—s	Light will be followed by a shock
Object learning	s—s—s | | | s—s—s	All the stimuli appear together and are given the label "Mama"
Concept learning	s s ——→ Common s property	All the objects are red
MOTIVE LEARNING		
Goal learning in instrumental conditioning	s—a(+) or s—a(−)	Goal box will contain food Shuttle box floor is electrified
Ambivalence	s—a(±)	Mother sometimes rewards, sometimes punishes
General motive	s—a(+) s—a(+) → Common s—a(+) → property (+) s—a(+)	Achievement in all situations is pleasant
HABIT LEARNING		
Simple instrumental habit	s—r—s	In the Skinner box, bar-pressing leads to food
General habit	s_1 s_2 — Common — r_2 s_3 — relationship — r_3 s_4 r_1 r_4	Following whatever directions are printed on the package leads to the easy opening of it

FIG. 5–22. A theoretical classification of types of learning.

On What Basis Are Acts Selected?

We have constructed a picture of the kinds of relationships that are stored by the organism. Now we may ask, how do these stored relationships become translated into action?

There are three major categories of action that we can distinguish. First, we are born with the tendency to respond to certain stimuli with inborn reflexes. Second, we learn some very reliable relationships from the environment, and we almost automatically respond appropriately to them; e.g., we learn to stop at a red light in crowded traffic. This involves well-established, unambiguous

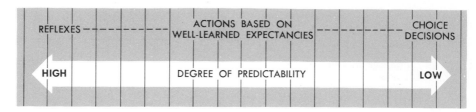

FIG. 5–23. The predictability of acts based on knowledge of the species of the organism and the stimulus situation alone varies from high in reflexes to low in complex choice decisions.

percepts, motives, and habits. Finally, we are faced with choice decisions, where there are a number of possible actions leading to different goals. Here the actions depend on the perceived goals in the situation (s-s relationships), the affective values of the goals (s-a relationships), and the expected probability that given acts will lead to the goals (s-r-s relationships). We can put these three categories of action on a continuum that varies in the degree to which we can predict action on the basis of our knowledge of the stimulus situation (see Fig. 5–23). We can almost perfectly predict responses to unconditioned stimuli. Actions based on very well-learned expectancies are less predictable and choice decisions still less.

One of the outstanding characteristics of human behavior is variability. People act differently in the same situation, and the same person acts differently in different situations. Some major sources of this variability are the learning experiences of the individual, which give him a basis with which to perceive, evaluate, and choose among many possible actions.

Summary

Concepts

Act. A pattern of muscular movements which constitute a unit in the continuous stream of behavior.

*Response.** An act that can be traced to the effects of a stimulus

*Stimulus.** A change in the physical energy of an organism's environment which affects a receptor

Object. A relatively stable aspect of the environment with relatively consistent meanings

---

* These definitions of stimulus and response are more precise than the ones given in Chapter 1.

Classical conditioning. A simple form of learning in which a formerly neutral stimulus consistently precedes an unconditioned stimulus (UCS); the result is that the formerly neutral stimulus, now called the *conditioned stimulus* (CS), elicits a conditioned response (CR) which is some portion of the unconditioned response (UCR) to the UCS

Instrumental conditioning or *instrumental learning.* A simple form of learning in which the frequency of a spontaneously occurring response increases after the response is reinforced consistently

Extinction. The procedure of eliminating reinforcement in classical and instrumental conditioning, which results in disappearance of the learned response

Spontaneous recovery. The reappearance of the conditioned response without further training following extinction and rest

Reinforcer. An event which increases the frequency of a response in a situation

Secondary reinforcer. A stimulus which acquires reinforcing properties by being paired with a reinforcer

Informational feedback. The stimuli which follow an organism's responses which show him the effect of his responses

Affective feedback. The feelings of pleasantness or unpleasantness following an organism's responses

Punishment. Presentation of a painful stimulus or the removal of a pleasant stimulus

Partial reinforcement. The procedure of presenting reinforcement on only a fraction of the conditioning trials

Stimulus generalization. Responding to stimuli which are similar to a stimulus to which the response has been learned

Discrimination learning. Learning to make different responses to similar stimuli

Principles

1. Although we do not know the precise neurophysiological events involved in learning, we can study learning by observing behavior changes and making inferences.

2. Classical and instrumental conditioning differ in the origin of learned responses, the organism's control over the situation, and in the types of responses most easily modified.

3. The nature of reinforcement is a theoretical controversy in psychology. One theory interprets reinforcement as drive reduction; another as a change in affect.

4. Conditioning depends on temporal contiguity between events, the frequency of their occurrence, and reinforcement.

5. If cues (stimuli) which have been associated with a reinforcer are present, an organism can learn even if there is a time gap between his response and reinforcement.

6. Classical conditioning may be understood in terms of perceptual expectancies. Instrumental conditioning may be understood in terms of affective expectancies (s-a relationships) and act expectancies (s-r-s relationships).

7. The effects of reward and punishment on behavior differ. Reward increases the probability of one of several alternative acts. Punishment reduces the probability of a particular act.

8. Each time an individual's expectancies are promptly confirmed by feedback, the expectancies are strengthened and acts based on the expectancies become more probable.

9. Partial reinforcement in instrumental conditioning leads to greater resistance to extinction than 100 percent reinforcement.

10. The laws of conditioning provide a basis for understanding more complex forms of perceptual, motivational, and act learning.

Suggested Readings

BIRNEY, R. C., and R. C. TEEVAN (eds.), *Reinforcement*. Princeton, N.J.: Van Nostrand, 1961.

MEDNICK, S. A., *Learning*. Englewood Cliffs, N. J.: Prentice-Hall, 1964. This paperback and the one listed above give readable extensions of the material in this chapter.

HILGARD, ERNEST R., and DONALD MARQUIS, *Conditioning and Learning*, G. A. KIMBLE (ed.). New York: Appleton-Century-Crofts, 1961. Contains a complete presentation of the facts of learning.

chapter 6

perception

THE PHENOMENA OF PERCEPTION: PART 1

THE PHENOMENA OF PERCEPTION: PART 2

THE DYNAMICS OF PERCEPTION

chapter 6   THE DEVELOPMENT OF PERCEPTION

INDIVIDUAL DIFFERENCES

PRACTICAL APPLICATIONS

Throughout the first five chapters, we have referred to the effects of the environment on the individual. We noted that people in different cultures interpret the world differently. We saw that the environment provides energy which activates receptors and triggers off chains of activity in the central nervous system. We also saw evidence of the relatively permanent effects of some of this activity, the products of learning. In this chapter, we shall look more closely at the immediate effects of stimuli on the organism, at how we organize and interpret information from the environment—the process of perception.

As we pointed out earlier, perception refers to a mental process which we cannot observe directly in others. Our scientific knowledge of perception comes from two sources: from the behavior of people and animals, especially the verbal reports of human beings, and from physiological studies of the receptors and sensory pathways.

Historically, the subject matter we are considering under perception was separated into two areas. The introspectionists divided their experiences of the world into the receiving of stimuli (sensation) and the interpretation of stimuli as meaningful objects (perception). The modern view of perception rejects this separation. People do not report a two-step process when they identify something. We do not first see a confusion of shapes and objects which we then consciously interpret as an object. As you look around the room, your immediate experience—the first you can report—is the perception of objects: a desk, a chair, a telephone, not a mass of meaningless stimuli. Physiologically, we can separate receptor processes from CNS processes, but it is the indivisible interaction of the two that gives rise to our experience of the world. Some psychologists still use the word *sensation* to refer to simple perceptual processes or to that area of perception that emphasizes the relationship between the physical stimulus, the receptor, and the experience. In that sense, the first part of the phenomena section would be considered *sensation* and the remaining sections *perception*.

The Phenomena of Perception: Part 1

How Does the Nervous System Code Stimuli?

In general, our picture of the world is so consistent that we assume our perceptions are of the world as it "is." As we move about the environment, we see, hear, smell, and touch objects out in the world. Nevertheless, the immediate events that give rise to our perceptions are not outside us but in our nervous systems.

Prescientific thinkers hypothesized that an object emitted copies of itself which traveled to the mind. Today, we know from physics that objects do not emit copies. Rather, what we see is triggered off by light waves reflected by an object. The energy of the light strikes our eyes, causing chemical changes in the retina; these changes activate neurons, and nerve impulses travel to the brain. Between the eye and the brain there is no train of images; there is nothing but a stream of nerve impulses passing over a large number of neurons. It is only at the end of this chain that perception occurs. While the perception depends upon neural activity in the brain, we *experience* objects as being in the environment outside us.

The process of perception thus involves a series of coding operations in which information from one form or pattern of energy is translated into another. Despite these changes in energy, certain information is present all the way from the object to the perception of the observer. We take for granted many examples of such coding in our daily lives. For example, a secretary may take down in shorthand a telegram dictated by her employer. She then calls the telegraph company and repeats the message to them. The operator writes down the message and sends it by telegraph to another operator. The message has now changed from sound waves to a written code (shorthand), to sound waves (speech), to electrical waves (telephone), to writing, to telegraph, to writing, all the while retaining the same information. In addition to these observable transformations, each time a person was involved, the message was coded into nerve impulses entering the brain via sensory neurons and leaving via neurons leading to voluntary muscles.

Just as the telegraph operator translates written words into a Morse code of dots and dashes, so the receptors translate a variety of types of physical energy into patterns of nerve impulses. You see this book because light waves are reflected from it to your eyes; you hear a violin because the vibration of the strings sets in motion waves of air which reach your ears; you feel that the radiator is warm because heat energy has stimulated nerve endings in your skin.

What kind of code does the nervous system employ to transmit information about the environment? First, the nervous system encodes the *kind* of energy. The psychological experiences produced by light, heat, and sound energy are different because their effects on the nervous system are different. Each form of energy to which we are sensitive stimulates a different sense organ. Our ears are not affected by light, nor are our eyes sensitive to sound waves. Each receptor transforms the energy to which it is sensitive into nerve impulses which travel along a particular path to a particular area in the brain. Thus the retina of the eye sends nerve impulses along the optic nerve to the visual cortex; the hair cells in the cochlea of the ear originate impulses which travel along the auditory nerve to the temporal lobe of the cortex. The *difference* between brain activity which results in the experience of sight and that which results in the experience of sound is *where* the activity occurs—the nerve impulses involved are physiologically identical. If, for some reason, the optic nerve is

TABLE 6-1

Sense modality	Physical stimulus	Receptor	Cortical projection area	Dimensions of the psychological experience
Vision	Electro-magnetic waves	Rods and cones in the retina of the eyes	Occipital lobe	Hue Intensity Saturation
Hearing (audition)	Compression and expansion in a medium such as air	Hair cells in the cochlea of the inner ear	Temporal lobe	Pitch Loudness Timbre
Smell (olfaction)	Molecules in the air	Hair cells in the olfactory epithelium in the nose	None. The olfactory nerve terminates in lower centers	? (No simple dimensions)
Taste (gustation)	Molecules in solution	Hair cells in the tastebuds on the tongue	Parietal lobe	Sweet Salty Sour Bitter
Pressure	Mechanical deformation of the skin	Nerve endings in the skin	Parietal lobe	Extent Duration Intensity
Temperature	Temperature changes from "physiological zero"	Nerve endings in the skin	Parietal lobe	Cold to warm to hot
Pain	Intense stimuli; tissue injury	Nerve endings in the skin	Parietal lobe	Sharp Dull Throbbing
Kinesthesia	Stretching of muscles and joints	Nerve endings in muscles and tendons	Parietal lobe	Position Load
Equilibrium	Body movement and acceleration	Hair cells in the semicircular canals and vestibular sacs of the inner ear	?	Movement in three planes; body position

stimulated by energy other than light, the resultant experience will still be visual. A boxer who takes a left hook near his eye "sees stars" because the mechanical stimulation was so strong that it activated the optic nerve. If you press your own eyeball, you too may experience light from mechanical stimulation.

A category of psychological experience which depends on a particular kind of energy affecting a particular receptor is known as a sense modality. Traditionally, five sense modalities are attributed to man—sight, sound, smell, taste, and touch. Actually, according to our definition of sense modality, we have several more. The sense of touch can be broken down into three separate modalities—pressure, pain, and temperature—each a separate experience dependent on a different type of receptor, which is sensitive to a particular form of energy. Furthermore, we have receptors that tell us the position of our bodies, whether or not we are moving, and where our muscles are. Table 6–1 lists the sense modalities.

Of course, the nervous system code is more complex than a simple separation of experience into different sense modalities. Within each modality we are able to detect a wide range of differences. We do not only detect the presence of light; we also experience its brightness, its color, its duration, its distance from us. We do not simply detect sound; we experience sound of a particular pitch, duration, and loudness. These psychological experiences of quality, intensity, duration, and distance are based on certain properties of the physical event which the nervous system is capable of translating into nerve impulses. Not all changes in energy are perceived. The minimum intensity difference consistently reacted to is called the *threshold*. As we examine each sense modality, we shall look at the kinds of physical variation to which the receptors are sensitive, the resultant variations in experience, and the nervous-system link between them.

Vision

The physical stimulus for vision is electromagnetic energy. Its characteristics may be conceptualized in terms of waves. If the lengths of the waves fall between 400 millimicrons (0.0000156 inch) and about 700 millimicrons (0.0000273 inch), we experience light (see Fig. 6–1). Electromagnetic energy varies in wavelength, amplitude, and range of wavelength. As these physical dimensions vary, so does the psychological experience reported by an observer. When the light wave increases in intensity or amplitude, an observer will report an increase in *brightness*. As the *wavelength* of the wave changes from 400 to 500 to 600 to 700 millimicrons, an observer will see changes in hue from blue to green to yellow to red. The major portion of visible light consists of not a single wavelength but a mixture of many. Moreover, just as the range of the wavelengths varies from narrow range to wide, with one wavelength dominant, so does the psychological experience of saturation change from a pure color to a "dirty" color (see Plates 4, 5, and 6).

THE ELECTROMAGNETIC SPECTRUM

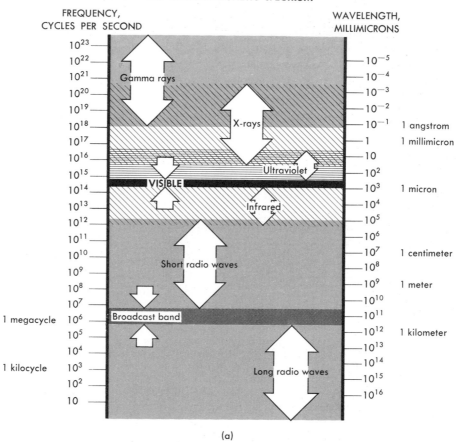

(a)

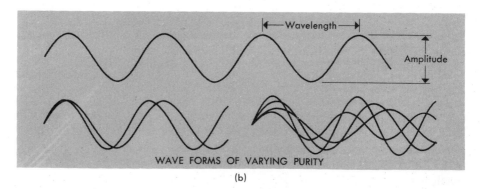

WAVE FORMS OF VARYING PURITY

(b)

FIG. 6–1. (a) The electromagnetic spectrum. Only a small range of wavelengths in the spectrum result in visible light. (b) A diagrammatic representation of the physical characteristics that produce variations in visual experience.

If there is no one dominant wavelength, the psychological experience of color depends on the particular mixture of wavelengths. Some pairs of wavelengths, such as 575 millimicrons (seen as yellow) and 460 (seen as blue), result in the perception of white when they are superimposed. Such pairs of colors are called complementaries. Mixtures of noncomplementary wavelengths result in the perception of a color intermediate between the two. For example, when wavelengths of 650 (seen as red) and 570 (seen as yellow) are mixed, the resulting perception is orange. With appropriate mixtures of three distant non-complementary wavelengths, all the hues of the spectrum can be induced (see Plate 7).

■ You may be wondering why the laws of color mixture that we just described are so different from the ones you are familiar with when mixing pigments in a paintbox. When we superimpose yellow and blue lights, the result is white light; when we mix yellow and blue paint, the result is green. The difference between mixing lights and pigments is the difference between additive and subtractive mixtures. When lights are superimposed on a screen, the wavelengths of the two lights are added, and the perception is the resultant of the two wavelengths. Pigments give color to paint by *absorbing* most of the wavelengths in the white light that strike its surface and by reflecting only a limited band of wavelengths to the eye. Blue pigments usually reflect a band of wavelengths around 470 millimicrons, including the wavelengths that usually give a perception of blue, green, and violet. Yellow pigments absorb most of the wavelengths except those which we see as yellow, green, and orange. When the two pigments are mixed, the yellow pigment absorbs most of the wavelengths from the blue end of the spectrum and the blue pigment absorbs most of the wavelengths from the yellow end of the spectrum. The majority of the wavelengths that are reflected are the "green" wavelengths, which give rise to the perception of green. Subtractive mixtures are depicted in Plates 8 and 9. ■

THE EYE. Light waves are reflected from an object to our eyes. The eye has been compared to a camera. It contains a *lens* that can focus, an *iris* that controls the amount of light that enters, and a light-sensitive layer of cells, the *retina*, which contains chemically active substances that convert electromagnetic energy into nerve impulses. As in a camera picture, the more distant an object, the smaller its image on the retina. The parts of the eye are illustrated in Fig. 6–2.

So far, the relationships seem simple. Physical variation is accompanied by psychological variation with a camera-like organ in between. But a look at a few other visual phenomena will show the tremendous complexity of visual functioning.

First of all, the analogy between the eye and the camera is a crude one. The eye is a very poor camera. Between the lens and the photosensitive retina is a chamber filled with liquid which blurs the sharp light rays. Blood vessels lie on the retina itself, blocking light from certain portions. The retina even has a hole in it, a section where there are no photosensitive elements. Here the nerve fibers converge, form the optic nerve, and lead back to the central nervous

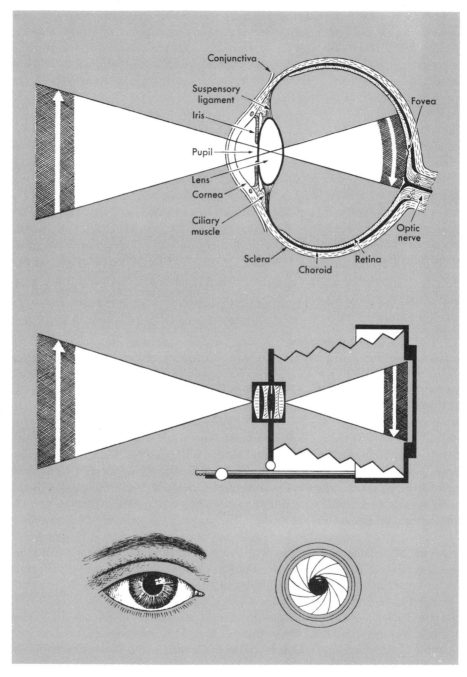

FIG. 6–2. The parts of the eye and their counterparts in a camera. (From Wald, G., "Eye and Camera," *Sci. Amer.*, August, 1950. Reproduced by permission.)

FIG. 6–3. To find your own blind spot, close your left eye and fixate your right eye on the dot in the center of the lines on the left. Move the book back and forth between 5 and 15 inches from your right eye. At about 10 inches the face in the circle should disappear. The circle is now falling on the part of your retina where there are no light-sensitive cells, that is, on your blind spot.

system. If the eye were a camera, every picture would have a gap in it. See Fig. 6–3 to locate your blind spot.

Furthermore, there are at least two different kinds of cells in the retina: rods and cones. These cells have different anatomical connections—*many* rods converge on a single nerve fiber, whereas *each* cone connects with one nerve fiber (see Fig. 6–4). Cones are most dense in the *fovea*, a small depression at the center of the retina, and are less dense in the periphery. Rods are most dense in the periphery.

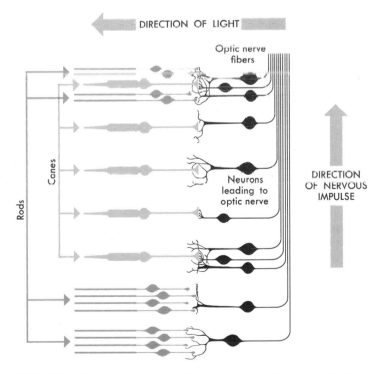

FIG. 6–4. The neuron connections of rods and cones. Each cone synapses with a single neuron. A number of rods converge on a single neuron. (After Polyak, 1941)

This anatomical differentiation helps to explain some psychological phenomena. In normal daylight, we see colors and patterns clearly, and our vision is best when we look directly at an object. Cone vision is precise enough to detect the presence of an object the size of a grapefruit at a distance of a quarter of a mile. At night, color and pattern vision is poorer, and detection is best when we use the periphery (where the rods are) to spot a light.

These functional differences between daylight (light-adapted) vision and night (dark-adapted) vision can be tied to the different characteristics of cones and rods. Biochemically associated with rods is a protein substance called *rhodopsin*. Rhodopsin bleaches when exposed to light. In bright light, the rhodopsin is constantly bleached, the message sent to the brain by the rods does not vary much, and hence the *cones* are responsible for most of the variations in visual perception. At night, the cones are not functional, and the rods in the periphery of the retina send most of the visual information. Rods are insensitive to color, and their multiple connections with the next neuron do not permit precise pattern vision. The cones, on the other hand, have higher thresholds (that is, it takes more light to stimulate them) and, with their one-to-one connections with the next neuron, permit more precise pattern vision. Theorists have guessed that there are several types of cones, each maximally sensitive to different wavelengths, which are responsible for color vision. Presumably, color-blind people lack one or more types of cones and are consequently unable to distinguish certain colors. Color blindness can be detected through the use of special tests, such as that seen in Plate 10.

Already our picture of the simple relationships between stimulus and experience has broken down. The brightness of a light depends not only on the intensity of the stimulus, but also on the intensity of its background and the state of the eye. When you first walk into a darkened room, you can see nothing until your eye becomes accustomed to the dark, that is, until rhodopsin has built up. Once your eye is dark-adapted, you can detect lights you would be unable to see in daylight.

The psychological experience of brightness also depends on the wavelength of the stimulus light. Yellow of a particular intensity seems brighter than red or green at the same intensity.

The relationship between hue and wavelength is also not perfect. The perceived color of an object is affected by the color of the objects or background next to it. For example, if we put a gray patch of paper on a blue background, the gray takes on a yellowish tinge, and similarly, if we place a yellow patch on a red background, the yellow will appear to be greener. This phenomenon is called *simultaneous contrast*. A similar phenomenon occurs when the eye is first stimulated by one color and then by another. The resulting experience of color is called an after-image or *successive contrast*. Thus, if we left a room illuminated with blue light, ordinary light would seem yellowish. In both simultaneous and successive contrast the color induced in the figure observed is the complementary color of that in the original background. These phenomena are illustrated in Plates 11 and 12.

■ Recently, E. H. Land, the inventor of the Polaroid Land Camera, has shown that the taking and projecting of black and white slides with appropriate filters can produce the experience of a wide range of colors (Land, 1959). This is his procedure: First he photographs the same scene on black-and-white film twice; once with a green filter over the camera lens, once with a red filter over it. Then the film is made into two slides which are placed in two projectors in such a way that the slides can be focused simultaneously on the same screen. The slide taken with the red filter is projected with red light. Thus, if the red light projector alone is turned on, the scene appears in varying shades of red. The slide taken with the green filter is projected with ordinary white light. If this projector alone is turned on, the scene appears in ordinary black, white, and gray. However, when the two projectors are turned on simultaneously and their projections are superimposed, the scene suddenly appears in full color! See Plate 13. It has been suggested that simultaneous contrast is responsible for the appearance of color, though this is still a point of theoretical controversy. ■

One of the most hotly debated theoretical controversies in psychology centers about the nature of color vision. Many psychologists accepted a theory proposed by Young in 1801 and rediscovered by Helmholtz in 1852 which accounted for the phenomena of color vision by hypothesizing three types of color receptors in the eye: one most sensitive to red wavelengths, one to green, and one most sensitive to blue. Since appropriate combinations of those three wavelengths will produce any color of the spectrum, this theory accounts for the facts of color mixture with a very small number of assumptions. However, it does not explain the facts of simultaneous and successive contrast. Hering's theory (1874) postulated that there were three substances in the eye, each of which responded to a different pair of complementary hues: one which was sensitive to red and green, one which was sensitive to yellow and blue, and one which was sensitive to black and white. Perception of one of each of the complementaries—red, yellow, and white—caused a chemical breakdown of its representative substance in the eye. Light from the remaining hues—green, blue, and black—caused a chemical build-up of their respective substances. The theory explains why mixture of complementaries yields gray (the two processes neutralize each other) and why exposure to one color is followed by induction of the other (building-up processes automatically follow breaking-down processes).

Although a great deal of research and further theorizing attempted to prove or disprove which of these two basic theories was correct, the question was never fully resolved. New techniques using microelectrodes to record the impulses both in the eye and in the brain are now unraveling some of the complexities of the visual system. Recording from optic nerve fibers, the Swedish neurophysiologist, Granit (1955), and other vision researchers, found some fibers which discharged when a light came on; some which fired when a light was turned off, and others which discharged both at the time a light was turned on and at the time it was turned off. There were fibers which responded to a wide band of visual stimuli and others which responded to relatively limited ranges of color. Moreover, the narrow-band fibers tended to be of three types of much the same sensitivity as suggested by the Young-Helmholtz theory.

But recordings further back in the visual system gave some inklings why neither of the two theories has ever been able to displace the other. Studies of the cells in the thalamus, which are excited by colored lights, indicated that certain layers of cells do, as the Helmholtz theory would predict, contain cells which are sensitive to certain wavelengths. However, other layers of cells responded more nearly as Hering theorists would expect (DeValois, Smith, and Kitai, 1959). Additional information comes from studies of pigments (like rhodopsin) in the retina. While studies of cones have found red-absorbing, green-absorbing, and blue-absorbing pigments supporting the Young-Helmholtz theory (Marks, Dobelle, and MacNichol, 1964), it now seems that the distribution of these pigments in the retina and the interactions in the visual pathways into the brain result in a more complex system than was envisioned by either theorist. Because (according to most theories), we have three (or more) kinds of cones, we are able to code information about color. Because we have rods, we are able to detect and code some information from very dim light. By a combination of cells varying in their sensitivity to brightness and to different colors, we can get a great deal of information from light patterns.

There is still another dimension of our visual experience that the preceding description does not account for, that is, our ability to see in three dimensions. Light coming from a three-dimensional object strikes the retina, a relatively flat surface, yet our perception is of a solid object, a certain distance away. Some of our distance cues are contained in the visual image itself, and we can illustrate these cues in a photograph or a painting. We learn to judge the dis-

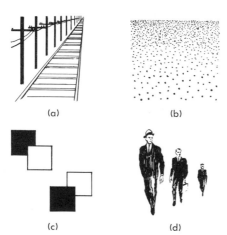

(a)

(b)

(c)

(d)

FIG. 6–5. Some perceptual cues of distance. (a) Linear perspective: parallel lines appear to converge at a distance. (b) Texture gradients: the texture becomes more dense as the scene becomes more distant. (c) Interposition: objects that partially cover others appear to be closer. (d) Relative size: the smaller figures appear to be more distant.

FIG. 6–6. This photograph provides an impression of depth and distance as a result of a number of depth cues. Note the differences in relative size and texture, the interposition of buildings, the linear perspective. Note also how hazy the distant portions are, and how the shadows contribute to the impression of fullness and depth. (Wide World Photos)

tance of an object from its relative size, the shadows cast by it, its position in front of and behind objects, the relative distinctness of detail (see Figs. 6–5, 6–6, 6–7, and 6–8). However, other cues depend on the fact that we have two eyes. If you look at an object with one eye closed, then open that eye and close the other, you will note that the image of the object is slightly different as seen by each eye. These differing patterns of light striking the retina are coded into nerve impulses which are transmitted to the brain. There the disparity between the two neural patterns helps give us our depth perception. If the object is close (within 15 feet) the eyes have had to turn in slightly to focus on the object, and the nerve impulses from the muscles controlling this *convergence* are also sent to the brain. In order to focus the light rays on the retina, the lens of the eye (see Fig. 6–2) has also had to become more or less flattened, and the muscles accomplishing this accommodation also cause neural impulses to be transmitted to the brain. Still another cue comes from the fact that our eyes perceive movement; a close object moves faster in relation to its background than a more distant one.

You can see from the preceding discussion that there is no one simple physical event which results in our experience of distance and depth. Space perception depends on the integration of cues from a variety of sources.

Thus far we have talked about the eye as a motionless organ, responding to the physical energies that impinge upon it. Actually our eyes are always moving. When we perceive an object, our eyes move from one part of it to another for several seconds. When we perceive something moving in the periphery of

FIG. 6–7. The same depth cues that give a three-dimensional quality to a photograph were used by artist Benjamin Cunningham to create the impression of depth in an abstract work. Note the use of perspective, interposition, and shadow. (*Equivocation*, by Benjamin Cunningham, 1964. Collection, The Museum of Modern Art, New York. Larry Aldrich Foundation Fund.)

FIG. 6–8. The importance of shadows for perceiving depth is illustrated by turning this picture of a crater upside down. It now appears to be a mound. This change occurs because we always see the light as coming from above. (From Anders, E., "Diamonds in meteorites," *Sci. Amer.*, October, 1965. Photo by K. C. Publications.)

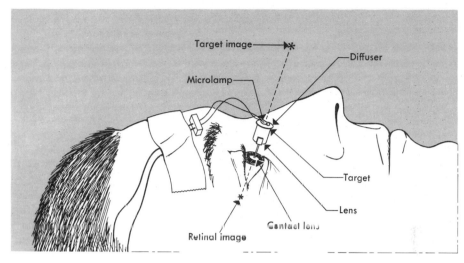

FIG. 6–9. A device used to produce a stabilized retinal image. A tiny projector mounted on a contact lens projects an image which always falls on the same portion of the retina; this is because the projected image moves whenever the eye moves. (After Pritchard, 1961)

our field of vision, our eyes center on the moving object and follow it. In addition to these obvious movements, there is a constant tremor in our eyes all the time.

What effect does this tremor have on our vision? What would happen if the effects of this tremor were eliminated?

■ Riggs, Ratliff, and Cornsweet (1953) sought the answer to this question with a very ingenious apparatus. Since it is impossible to stop the eye from moving without injuring its normal functioning, these three investigators devised a way of moving an image at exactly the same rate as the eye so that the image would always fall on the same part of the retina. They did this by attaching a tiny projector to a contact lens. The lens, hence the projector, moved whenever the eye did. The eye and the retina were not moving relative to the images. See Fig. 6–9. The results under these conditions were quite striking. After a very short period, the person could no longer see the image projected. The constant image on the retina did not produce a constant perception, but the disappearance of perception. Only if the image projected was flashed on intermittently did perception of the constant image return. ■

All these phenomena have forced psychologists to revise their notions about the functioning of the eye in perception. The eye is an active organ, changing its sensitivity with changing conditions (as in dark-adaptation), producing the experience of color in the absence of the normal physical stimulus (as in successive contrast and the Land phenomenon), and unlike a camera, constantly moving in order to produce the experience of a stable object. (See Plate 14.)

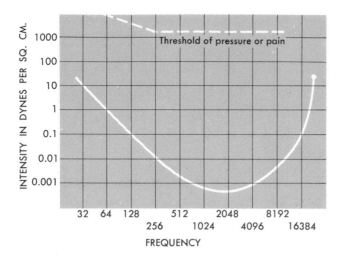

FIG. 6–10. The minimum amount of energy that different frequencies must have for a person to report that sound is present. If a tone of 2000 cycles per second were played at the minimum intensity needed for hearing 100 cycles, it would sound louder than the 100-cycle-per-second tone at that amplitude. (After Boring, Langfeld, and Weld, 1948)

Audition

When we hear a sound, our experience is the result of *sound waves* striking the ears. Sound waves are alternate compressions and expansions of pressure in the air or other media. They vary in *frequency* (the number of compressions and expansions in a period of time) and *amplitude* (the degree of compression and expansion). A given sound may consist of a wave of one frequency or of a mixture of frequencies; thus another physical dimension is *complexity*.

If the frequency of compression and expansion is between 20 and 20,000 cycles per second, human beings perceive sounds. Dog whistles produce sounds of higher frequencies that are inaudible to humans, but are audible to dogs. The largest organ pipes produce some sounds below the range of human hearing. When these are played, we feel the basic pressure waves through skin or body tissue instead of hearing them. Nevertheless, our hearing is so acute that were the threshold slightly lower, we could hear the collision of air molecules in random Brownian movement. With aging, women show a greater loss for low frequency tones than men, while men exhibit a greater loss for tones of higher frequency.

As a sound wave varies in frequency, a listener will report variations in *pitch*. As the wave varies in amplitude, a listener will report variations in *loudness*. As in vision, the relationship between the physical stimulus and the psychological experience is not perfect. Faint tones can be detected more easily around

2000–4000 cycles per second (three or four octaves above middle C) than at very high or very low frequencies. Even with the same amplitude of energy, a frequency of 2000 cycles per second will usually be heard as louder than a frequency of 100 cycles per second (see Fig. 6–10). The amplitude or intensity also influences perception of pitch. When the intensity of a low tone is increased it not only seems louder but also lower; high tones, on the other hand, seem higher when intensity is increased; tones in the area of maximal sensitivity change very little in pitch with increases in intensity.

The standard pitch produced by 440 cycles per second is A above middle C. This same pitch sounds different when it is played on a piano, a violin, or a clarinet. The reason is that a single note played on a musical instrument does not produce a single frequency but a complex wave consisting of a *fundamental* tone and a number of *overtones* which are multiples of the frequency of the fundamental. For example, the fundamental of standard A is 440 cycles per second, and the overtones are at 880, 1320, 1760, etc. The difference in quality between the tone produced by a clarinet and that by a piano comes from a difference in the number and intensity of overtones. We call such a difference in quality of tone a difference in timbre. The wave forms of some simple and complex tones are diagrammed in Fig. 6–11.

When two wavelengths of light are superimposed, the resultant perception is a single color. When two tones are sounded together, we can still distinguish the two tones. However, when a number of unrelated frequencies are combined, the resultant perception has no distinct pitch; we hear it as noise.

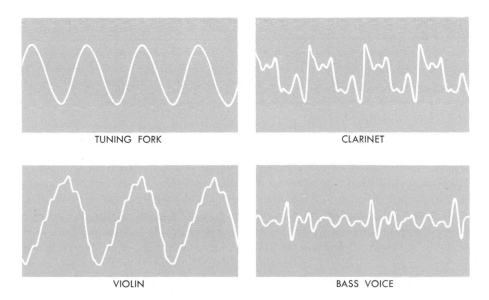

FIG. 6–11.   The differences in wave form that result in differences in timbre.

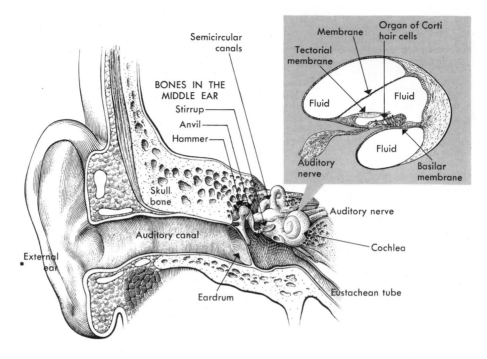

FIG. 6–12.   A diagram of the ear with a cross section of the cochlea.

How do air vibrations become translated into nerve impulses? Figure 6–12 shows the basic chain of transmission of sound vibrations through the ear. Sound waves cause the eardrum to vibrate. Its vibrations cause vibration in the chain of bones in the middle ear, which, in turn, acts as a wave-making device to cause vibrations in the cochlea. The cochlea is divided in half lengthwise by a bony shelf and the *basilar membrane,* upon which lie hair cells and the endings of the auditory nerve.

Physiologists and psychologists have puzzled over how the nervous system codes pitch. There are two major classical theories. One theory, the "place theory" (proposed by the same Helmholtz whose theory of vision we described), suggests that different frequencies stimulate different places on the basilar membrane, which trigger off different neurons in the auditory nerve and cortex. This theory is sometimes called the "harp theory," because Helmholtz based it on the fact that different fibers in different places on the basilar membrane respond to different pitches just as different strings on a harp produce different sounds. The place theory finds support in data from injury to the basilar membrane. When certain areas of the membrane are damaged, hearing of a certain band of pitches is lost.

The "telephone" or "frequency theory" of hearing, first proposed by Rutherford in 1886, suggests that the basilar membrane vibrates as a whole, as does the diaphragm of a telephone. Its basic principle is that the auditory nerve transmits impulses with the same frequency as the frequency of vibration of the basilar membrane. Since neurons cannot fire nearly as fast as 20,000 times per second (the frequency of the upper limit of audible sounds), Wever and Bray extended the frequency theory with the "volley principle." According to the volley principle (Wever, 1949), at tones of low frequencies, neurons can keep up as required by the telephone theory; with higher frequencies, however, some neurons respond to one vibration, others to the next, still others to the next, and so on. Each movement of the membrane therefore fires some neurons and the whole bundle of neurons thus carries nerve impulses corresponding to the frequency of the sound even though a single neuron may be firing only every fourth, fifth, or tenth wave. The frequency volley theory finds support in data obtained from the auditory nerve by electrical recording. Up to about 5000 cycles per second, the auditory nerve does seem to fire at the frequency of the stimulus.

Nobel prize winner Georg von Békésy has suggested that a complete theory of hearing requires a combination of the place and frequency mechanisms in the light of recent data. Recordings of basilar membrane activity show that at frequencies below 60 cycles per second, the basilar membrane vibrates as a whole. Above this frequency, vibration begins to be unequal in different parts for different pitches. Above 4000 cycles per second, there is one small area of the basilar membrane at which vibration is at a clear maximum and activity in areas adjacent to the maximum is inhibited. We noted earlier that recordings from the auditory nerve show that nerve firing follows the frequency of the stimulus up to about 5000 cycles per second. Von Békésy (1953, 1959) takes account of all these data by postulating different kinds of neural coding for different stimulus frequencies. At very low frequencies, the frequency of firing alone accounts for the perception of pitch. In an intermediate range, from about 400 to 5000 cycles per second, both frequency and place mechanisms seem to be operating in complementary fashion. Above 5000 cycles per second, the area of the membrane stimulated alone can account for the coding of pitch.

The Chemical Senses

SMELL.* We sense odors from substances in the air which has entered the nose. We have no simple classification of these substances, nor have we isolated physical dimensions of the substances which can be tied to dimensions of psychological experience.

---

* A technical term for the sense of smell is *olfaction*.

The receptors for smell are embedded in the mucous membrane of the upper part of the nose. Our sensitivity to smell is remarkable, though inferior to that of some other species. For example, we can smell mercapton (an unpleasant-smelling sulfur compound) in a concentration of one part in 30 billion parts of air. We are able to distinguish among a wide variety of different odors; one investigator estimates that a person can discriminate 17,000 different odors. However, there are also many substances which we are unable to smell at all. Carbon monoxide is one of the most common and dangerous examples.

Individuals differ in sensitivity, and sensitivity also varies from time to time. Appetite may be one factor related to this variation. For example, sensitivity increases from breakfast until lunchtime, then decreases after lunch. Some people cannot detect certain floral odors at all. Musk has a strong odor for most women, but men, boys, and young girls are relatively insensitive to it. In mature women, sensitivity to musk varies with the menstrual cycle. During ovulation women can detect a concentration of musk only $\frac{1}{1000}$ of that required for detection at the high point of the cycle. This suggests that smell sensitivity is dependent upon the internal chemical state of the organism.

TASTE. The normal stimulus for taste is a chemical solution on the taste buds of the tongue. The word "normal" in the foregoing sentence is placed there purposely because both smells and tastes seem also to be affected by chemicals in the blood. Sometimes a patient receiving an intravenous injection will report tasting the substance injected a few seconds after the injection. It may be, then, that our sense of taste (and of smell) depends upon the relationship between the chemical state of the taste (and smell) receptors and the chemical state of the blood supply which nourishes them. In any event, taste receptors are sensitive to ions and molecules in solution.

We usually identify taste with the many varying flavors we can differentiate in food. Actually, taste alone is not as important as one might think. Many of the perceptions we call "taste" are a combination of taste, smell, and pain experiences. There are four elementary qualities of taste: sweet, salt, sour, and bitter. Our taste experiences are the result of combinations of these four. The exotic flavor nuances that we usually associate with taste are actually the result of smell. For example, maple syrup and honey taste the same; they are both predominantly sweet. The differences in their flavors are the result of different smells. Have you ever noticed that food appears to lose its "taste" when you have a head cold? Actually, your cold has little effect on your taste buds; rather it results in blocked nasal passages which affect your smell receptors.

Different regions of the tongue are differentially sensitive to the four basic tastes. The sweet receptors are located mostly along the tip of the tongue; sour receptors are along the sides of the tongue; bitter at the base of the tongue; and salt on the tip and the sides. Thus, if you want to minimize the bitterness of a pill, you should keep it away from the base of the tongue. But this does not mean that there are just four types of taste receptors—one for each taste quality. Rather, electrical recordings of nerve impulses from taste buds indicate that some taste receptors respond to more than one kind of stimulus. (Pfaffman, 1941)

Current research is concerned with the chemical nature of the stimuli for taste and the neural code for taste. Not all substances can be tasted, and we do not yet know the chemical limits of the taste receptors.

We do, however, have data on the sensitivity of taste. Although the results differ somewhat depending on the method used, the following indicates the order of sensitivity. Sweetness can be detected in a dilution of one part in 50, saltiness in a dilution of one part in 30, sourness in one part in 500, and bitterness in one part in 2,000,000!

Sensitivity of taste varies from individual to individual and from time to time. For example, the sensitivity to salt and acid is reduced during pregnancy, as is sensitivity to smells. This again suggests that there is a close relationship between the chemical state of the blood and sensitivity to tastes and smells.

An interesting similarity to color blindness is the inability of some individuals to taste phenylthiocarbamide, a substance which tastes bitter to other people. This "taste blindness" is inherited.

OTHER CHEMICAL SENSATIONS. In addition to taste and smell receptors, a third type of chemical receptor is found in the nose and mouth. These receptors are sensitive to irritating smells and tastes such as ammonia and strong acids. They are functional even in a newborn baby, and are the receptors which set off such violent reactions as sneezing. Probably they belong to the same group as the touch receptors discussed below.

The Skin Senses

We said earlier that the "sense" of touch was actually a composite of at least three sense modalities. If someone takes a blunt wire and probes an area of your skin lightly, you will not report a feeling of pressure every place the wire contacts your skin, but only at certain points. Similarly, if the wire is cooled and your skin is tested again, you will report a feeling of cold at different specific points. Probing of the skin with a warm wire will yield reports of warm points, and probing with a pin point will yield reports of pain spots. This suggests that different points on the skin are serviced by receptors sensitive to different energies.

PRESSURE. The physical stimulus for pressure is mechanical deformation of the skin. Different areas of the skin are differentially sensitive to such stimulation. Some indication of the sensitivity of different regions of the skin comes from the *two-point threshold*. When someone touches your skin at two points very close together, you will report that you feel pressure at only one point. As the points of contact are moved farther apart, a distance is reached at which you can feel two separate points of contact. The minimum distance between points of contact at which *two* points of pressure are perceived is the two-point threshold. The two-point threshold is 2.68 inches on the back; 0.039 inch on the tip of the tongue. Another indication of sensitivity to pressure comes from the number of pressure-sensitive spots revealed by the probe of the skin. There are about 13 times as many pressure-sensitive spots on the ball of the thumb as in the same area of the upper arm. Although the amount of energy required to arouse perception of pressure is very small (as little as 0.03 erg), the minimum is at least 100 million times the minimum energy required for vision and hearing.

TEMPERATURE. We saw earlier that a probe of the skin reveals some spots which yield a perception of cold, others that yield a perception of warm, indicating two separate receptor systems. The number of cold-sensitive spots is greater than the number of warm-sensitive spots—another indication that there are separate receptors mediating the two experiences. On the average, a square centimeter of skin surface will contain 13 cold spots and two warm spots. Sensitivities of both warmth and cold are much greater along the trunk than in the hands and other extremities. This is probably why we can endure cold or warmth with our bare hands more easily than we can with a bare back.

The stimulus for perception of cold is a *drop* in skin temperature; the stimulus for perception of warm is a *rise* in skin temperature. Note that the temperature receptors, like other receptors we have discussed, do not respond to the absolute level of stimulation, but to changes from a neutral point.

■ You can demonstrate this by placing one hand in a pan of cold water and the other hand in a pan of warm water. Within a short time you will note that the sensation of warmth comes only from a ring around the hand where there is a change from the warm water to the air, and similarly, the sensation of cold comes only from the area where the cold water meets the air. Now, if you place both hands in a pan of lukewarm water, you will find that it feels warm to the hand which was in cold water and cold to the hand which was in warm water. The experience of temperature on the skin covered by the lukewarm water depends on the temperature to which the skin has adapted. ■

The perception of warmth and the perception of heat depend on different patterns of receptor activity. Stimuli which produce a large increase in body temperature stimulate not only warm spots, but also cold spots. The cold receptors are thus stimulated by two kinds of temperature changes: a *drop* and a large *increase*. Evidence for this interpretation of heat coding comes from the following experiment.

■ Two intertwining pipes were presented to a subject (see Fig. 6–13). Warm water was circulated through one pipe; cold water through the other. When the subject touched each pipe separately, he reported warmth and cold, respectively. However, when he grasped both pipes with one hand, he reported the perception of heat. ■

FIG. 6–13. A perception of heat results from grasping intertwining pipes, one of which contains warm water, the other, cold water.

PAIN. The receptors for pain are also located in the skin and internal organs. Pain receptors seem to be more generally dispersed throughout the skin than the other skin receptors and, unlike the others, can be stimulated by several forms of stimuli, such as pressure, heat, chemical solutions, and electricity. To activate the pain receptors, the stimuli must be of high intensity.

The study of pain perception has been perplexing to sensory psychologists and physiologists. For the other senses, definite receptors and nerve tracts carrying the information have been identified. Pain, however, seems to be received by a variety of nerve endings and to be transmitted by a number of different pathways. Moreover, these pathways lead to wide areas of the brain rather than to a specific center. One type of pain seems to be related to the firing of neurons which transmit impulses more slowly than other sensory impulses are transmitted. This is the throbbing, dull pain which often follows the sharp, quick pain which is the immediate result of a painful injury. It thus appears that painful stimuli may activate two neural pathways—one which has a normal speed of neural transmission and the other which transmits at a slower speed.

Occasionally an individual is discovered who is unable to sense pain. Such individuals may be unaware that they have cut themselves until they see blood. For these people, frostbite and sunburn are frequent because heat and cold are not painful.

■ A study of one such person reported: "At no time had she ever reported any form of ache or pain such as headache, earache, toothache, or stomachache ... The hands, legs, and feet showed multiple scars which had been produced by cuts, bites, and scratches, many of which were unnoticed. After a day on the beach she had to inspect her feet carefully for cuts." It is also interesting that she reported never having felt the sensation of itch. (McMurray, 1950) ■

Kinesthesis

If you close your eyes and raise your hand, you still know the location of your hand. You can touch your nose with your index finger even when you are blindfolded. The sense modality that informs us of the positions and movements of our muscles and joints is called kinesthesia. There are several kinds of kinesthetic receptors: some are embedded in the muscles and send information about the load on the muscle and its state of contraction; others are embedded in tendons and joints. Discrimination of movements is remarkably good, but varies with the different joints. In the shoulder and wrist a movement of one-third of a degree can be detected. In the ankle the movement required is over a degree, and the joint of the big toe is least sensitive of all.

The kinesthetic input information does not always give rise to perception of which we are ordinarily conscious. Yet it provides extremely important information about the effects of our movements without which normal movement would be impossible. In the disease *locomotor ataxia*, the neurons carrying kinesthetic impulses are destroyed. Without this feedback, the patient cannot walk without watching his feet.

The Equilibrium Senses

When you whirl around in a circle, you stimulate receptors located in the region of the inner ear (see Fig. 6–12). In this region there are three fluid-filled semicircular canals perpendicular to one another. Body movements in any direction will cause displacement of fluid in one or more canals. The movement of the fluid stimulates hair cells. These cells are the receptors that send the messages which give rise to our perceptions of movement.

Another set of receptors tell us whether we are in a vertical or horizontal position. Between the semicircular canals and the cochlea are the *vestibular sacs*, which contain granules (otoliths or ear stones) and hair cells. The normal pressure of gravity on the granules stimulate the hair cells which give rise to the perception of uprightness. When you tilt your head, the pressure on the otoliths changes, changing the message of the vestibular receptors and your perception of body position.

Adaptation and Perception of Stimulus Change

In this brief survey of the senses, you may have noticed some principles that are common to many receptors. We shall review and extend some of those principles here.

In several sense modalities, we noted that continuous reception of the same stimulus results in a reduction of perception of that stimulus. This phenomenon is known as *adaptation*. We mentioned the adaptation to temperature in the two-pan experiment and the adaptation to the visual stimulus when the portion of the retina stimulated remains constant. Such adaptation is familiar to all of us. If we enter a room which at first smells musty, we are soon unable to smell the mustiness. We ordinarily do not feel the pressure of our clothes on our bodies, and we ordinarily do not notice the temperature of the room in which we are working.

There is some evidence that adaptation takes place with a change in the neural message sent by the incoming afferent fibers. Repeating a click results in a gradual reduction of activity in the cochlear nucleus, the first auditory sub-station. This change is induced by inhibitory fibers descending from the reticular formation and other brain centers.

A process analogous to adaptation occurs in the perception of forms. If we look at a figure for a period of time, perception of another figure will be distorted. This phenomenon is called *figural aftereffect* (see Fig. 6–14).

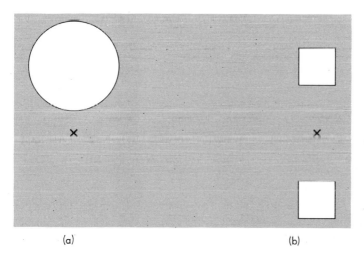

(a)   (b)

FIG. 6–14. The figural after-effect. Close one eye. Stare at the X in part (a) for about 60 seconds. Now very quickly focus on X in part (b). The top square should appear smaller than the bottom square. (After Köhler and Wallach, 1944)

The level of stimulation to which we adapt now becomes the reference point for our judgments of other stimuli. This reference point is called the *adaptation level*. For example, the light from a single candle in a darkened room would appear brighter than in daylight. The individual becomes more sensitive to differences in stimuli near the adaptation level than to changes at a distance from it. The adaptation level can not only be produced by continued stimulation at a given level, but also by a series of different stimuli. The adaptation level in such a case is based on the geometric mean of the series. Thus every judgment a person makes is a function not only of the stimuli from the attribute being judged but also of the individual's adaptation level. Since our adaptation level changes as the context changes, our judgments vary from time to time. A girl who looks homely at one time may be judged beautiful at a different time or place.

THE DIFFERENCE THRESHOLD. One of the oldest series of studies in psychology asked this question: Given a certain level of stimulation, what is the minimum amount of added stimulation which will be detected as a change by an observer? This minimum amount is called the *difference threshold* or *just-noticeable difference.*

In the middle of the nineteenth century, E. H. Weber, a German physiologist, studied the ability of individuals to detect differences in lifted weights. On the basis of his results, he formulated a law which, in modified form, has held up for over 125 years: The change in the stimulus which will be a just-noticeable difference (ΔS) is a constant ratio of the original stimulus (S),

$$\Delta S/S = K.$$

Weber's law states that the amount of change that will be noticed depends on the level of stimulation to which it is compared; the more you have of something, the more it takes to make a difference.

■ Suppose, for example, we find that a person can just barely distinguish between a 50-ounce weight and a 51-ounce weight. Then the 50-ounce weight is the original stimulus (S) and the change in the stimulus (ΔS) is 1 ounce. What predictions could we make about the difference threshold at 100 ounces, or at 25 pounds? According to our original data $\Delta S/S$ is $\frac{1}{50}$. Thus $\frac{1}{50}$ is the constant-weight ratio that will be just noticed. If the original stimulus is now 100 ounces, Weber's law would predict that 1 ounce would not be a sufficient difference to be noticed; at least 2 additional ounces or a 102-ounce weight would be necessary. Similarly, if the original stimulus is 25 pounds, $25\frac{1}{2}$ pounds would be necessary before a difference would be noticed between the two weights. The Weber fraction varies for different sense modalities; it is about $\frac{1}{60}$ for vision, $\frac{1}{10}$ for hearing, and $\frac{1}{50}$ for lifted weights. ■

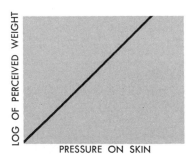

FIG. 6–15.   The logarithmic relationship between pressure and perceived weight.

Although Weber's law proved useful in stimulating decades of research, it is not completely accurate, especially for extremes of stimulation. At very high or very low energies, the amount of change required for detection is greater than that in the central range of normal stimulation. Thus it takes more change in the intensity of very dim or very bright lights to be detected than we would expect from Weber's law.

Soon after publication of Weber's results, G. Fechner extended Weber's results with additional experiments and mathematical calculations. He said that as the physical stimulus increases in geometric progression, the perception will increase in arithmetic progression; the perception will bear a logarithmic relationship to the stimulus. This type of relationship is illustrated in Fig. 6–15.

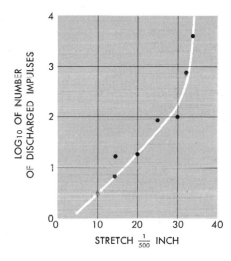

FIG. 6–16. The logarithmic relationship between the amount of stretch of a frog's skin and the number of nerve impulses discharged. (After Lowenstein, 1956)

Recent physiological experiments have shown that a similar logarithmic relationship occurs in the transformation of physical energy into nerve impulses. When the frequency of firing of a single neuron on the skin of a frog was plotted against the stretch of the skin, frequency of firing was proportional to the logarithm of the amount of stretch (see Fig. 6–16). Later recordings of the frequency of firing in visual and auditory neurons show similar results, although the curves have a tendency toward an S-shape, indicating again that the law does not hold for extremes. These results suggest that there is a neurophysiological basis for the Weber-Fechner law.

ABSOLUTE THRESHOLD. Another category of perception of change that has been carefully studied is the absolute threshold. The absolute threshold is the minimum amount of energy whose presence an observer can detect. For example, what is the minimum amount of light energy in a darkened room which an observer will report seeing? As we discussed each sense modality, in many cases we named a number which represented the lower limit of sensitivity. Actually, the absolute thresholds vary from person to person and in the same person at different times, even though conditions are kept as constant as possible. The figure cited as an absolute threshold represents a statistical average of many measurements.

Some recent studies have shown that absolute thresholds measured by verbal reports do not establish the limits of information received by the nervous system. Even when a person says he cannot detect a very faint stimulus, when asked to guess his guesses are better than chance. Very small changes in stimulus energy are still coded by the receptors and reflected by changes in the brain. Since the neural activity in the brain varies from moment to moment even when no stimulus is affecting receptors, the individual may not be conscious of a very faint stimulus which arouses activity little different from that occurring when there is no stimulus. But though his errors become greater, as the stimulus grows fainter, he can still respond to the stimulus even when he thinks he is guessing.

Thus verbal reports are not a perfect index of one's reception of information. A person may obtain information from the environment of which he is only partially aware. Thus students of perception must sometimes use methods other than verbal reports to measure perception, and the word "perception," which once referred only to a conscious process, is now used to include input processes of which the perceiver is unaware.

SUBLIMINAL PERCEPTION. Perception below the conscious threshold is called *subliminal*. For example, Miller (1942) asked subjects which of three figures was being projected on a screen in light so dim that the subjects reported that they saw nothing. He found that even when the subjects thought they were only randomly guessing which figure was shown, their guesses were correct much more often than would be expected by chance. This indicates that the correctness of the guesses depended not on "extrasensory perception," but on visual stimuli which were below the lower conscious threshold.

Similarly, we are seldom consciously aware of the kinesthetic sensations which guide our movements. One does not need to be aware of a stimulus for it to affect his behavior. On the other hand, it should also be pointed out that a stimulus does not gain any mystical power over behavior simply because it is subliminal. So-called subliminal advertising has not been demonstrated to be more effective than conventional advertising.

Threshold Measurement and Type of Task

We have seen that the determination of absolute threshold depends on the *way* in which the measurement is made, on what the observer is asked to do. If a person is asked to guess whether a stimulus is present, the results will show a lower absolute threshold than if he is asked simply to state when he first detects the presence of a stimulus. Making a verbal report describing a stimulus (identification) requires more information and thus has a higher threshold than reporting simply that something is there (detection); thus a lookout, before he can describe what he sees, can report that there is an object on the horizon. A verbal report that something is there may require more information than still other types of responses to the stimulus; e.g., a stimulus may arouse an emotional reaction when presented so faintly that the individual says that he cannot see it.

SENSORY INTERACTIONS. An individual's threshold for one sense may be affected by what is happening to the other senses. In the CNS, parts of the sensory systems come together in regions of the reticular formation and thalamus. Interactions can take place here, and direct stimulation of these areas has shown that some connections are inhibitory. One of the most interesting and practically useful interactions is that between pain and sound. Loud sounds will suppress pain. Consequently, some dentists now provide headphones and a control box to their patients. The patient listens to stereophonic music until he begins to feel pain. He then turns up the intensity of a random noise stimulus, sounding like a waterfall, and the pain is drowned out. Bright lights have been demonstrated to have a similar effect. Other sensory interactions seem to increase sensitivity. The presence of sound lowers the threshold for light. There is no simple rule which tells us the conditions under which certain combinations of stimuli will increase sensitivity and those which tend to decrease it.

Other Energies

Despite our complex array of receptors, there are many kinds of energy to which we are not sensitive. For example, we cannot sense magnetic fields, atomic radiation, radio waves, etc. To detect such energies man has devised instruments which change the energy into a form which can be perceived. Thus a compass transforms a magnetic field into movement of a needle which one can see, and a Geiger counter emits sounds when it is affected by radioactivity. Even changes in energy which do affect our sense organs may be more accurately measured by instruments which change the energy into a form which we can detect more easily. For example, a thermometer translates temperature changes into movements of a liquid which we can see. As a result, we can detect changes of temperature too small to be felt. By creating such instruments, man has tremendously increased his ability to detect changes of energy in the world around him.

Perception Without Stimulation

Does all perception depend upon stimulation of sense organs? Since perception is an activity of the brain, the individual can experience sensations when no physical energy is stimulating a receptor. For example, during brain operations, a patient may report images when the temporal lobe is stimulated electrically. Sometimes these images are simple flashes of light or sound; at other times, these images evoke in the person the sensation that he is reliving an earlier experience or dreaming.

Neural cells in the brain are constantly firing. While most neurons are fired as a result of chains of neural activity set in motion by energy striking the sense organs, some firing occurs randomly simply as a result of metabolism. If energy builds up long enough in a nerve cell, it will eventually fire itself. While the individual is ordinarily unaware of this random activity, it could be that some "imaginary" flashes of light or sounds are actually the result of such random firing.

When an individual reports that he sees, hears, or otherwise experiences things which do not correspond to reality as perceived by other people, his perception is called a *hallucination*. Some hallucinations are simply flashes of light or sounds, but most are organized perceptions of objects. Hallucinations can be most easily understood in terms of the effects of motivation and learning rather than simply by the sort of random activity we have just described. For example, in one experiment, a light flash was always followed by a tone. When the light was flashed without the tone, subjects still reported hearing the tone (Ellson, 1941). Drugs like mescaline or LSD also cause individuals to experience hallucinations. These drugs apparently affect the biochemical balance in the CNS so that certain normal connections between neurons are blocked, but the details of the mechanisms by which they cause hallucinations are not known.

Extrasensory Perception

One of the age-old questions has been, "Can man know things in ways other than through his senses?" History has given a number of different answers to this question. At one time or other, men have believed that one could "know" things through memories inherited from ancestors, through supernatural revelations, or through mind reading. Scientific psychology has not established the existence of such phenomena.

Within recent years there has been great interest in demonstrating, under laboratory conditions, knowledge not based on known sense organs. Is it possible to read another person's mind (telepathy)? Is it possible to perceive what is happening elsewhere, such as in another country (clairvoyance)? Is it possible to know what is going to happen before it occurs (precognition)? These questions, and others, have been grouped under the heading of *extrasensory perception* (ESP).

■ A typical experiment on extrasensory perception was one performed by Coover (1917). In this experiment, the experimenter shuffled a deck of playing cards, cut the pack, and, holding the cards concealed, looked at the bottom card. The image of the card was held in his mind, and he willed that it be projected into the mind of a subject who was seated with his back to the experimenter. The subject recorded the card which he believed to have been in the mind of the experimenter. Coover found that neither normal subjects nor spiritualist mediums were correct more than would be expected by chance. ■

Despite many experiments on telepathy and clairvoyance, there is no clear agreement on the interpretation of the results of this experimental work. In a number of the experiments the results originally seemed to indicate the existence of ESP, but it later became apparent that there were difficulties in carrying out this research. For example, clerical errors in recording the data seemed to be consistently in one direction so that the subjects' guesses were reported to have been better than they actually were (Kennedy, 1939). In other research there was evidence that the experimenter was unintentionally whispering the correct response to the subject. When a sound reflector was placed behind the experimenter's head, the subject's score improved. If the experimenter was simply asked to think of a number which the subject was to guess, the experimenter tended to choose certain numbers such as 3 or 7 more often than others so that the subject had a better chance of guessing correctly. In addition, the cards which were used in the early mind-reading experiments were defective in that the printing on the cards actually showed through the back of the cards. As a result, without knowing, many subjects who thought they were reading minds may have been reading the backs of the cards. In a sense, these early experiments were actually forerunners to later research on subliminal perception.

With all these possible errors removed, some experimenters' studies on ESP still show results that are somewhat better than chance, although other researchers are not always able to secure this result. The effects, when found, seem to be small. Some scientists believe that the positive results can be accounted for by the tendency for a researcher to publish positive results but not to publish negative results. Experimenters decide whether to accept or reject their hypotheses on the basis of how different the results are from those one would expect by chance. One commonly used criterion is that the results should be at least so different from those expected by chance that they would occur no more than five percent of the time if only chance factors were operating. This means that if 100 experiments were run in different places, about five of them would be expected to have results which the experimenter would believe to be significant support for his hypothesis even though only chance were operative. If these five experimenters publish their results and the other 95 do not, our conceptions may be greatly distorted. Such a criticism may be applied to almost any field of research; it has probably been used in evaluating ESP research because scientists prefer theories which fit in with or encompass what we already know. Such theories lead to further research instead of simply describing phenomena. Theories on extrasensory perception are sufficiently disturbing to our knowledge of energy and information transmission to create doubts about their validity on the part of most scientists. Few psychologists accept the other extreme of believing ESP to be absolutely impossible, but the majority are unconvinced by the data (for example, see Gerden, 1962).

The Coding of Stimuli: a Summary

We have seen that the nervous system is capable of transmitting information about many energy variations in the environment to the brain. The differentiation into different sense modalities depends on where the neural activity occurs. A specific band of electromagnetic waves stimulates the retina of the eye and results in optic nerve activity. All other things being equal, changes in the amplitude of light waves result in changes in the brightness perceived; changes in wavelength result in perception of different hues; changes in range of wavelengths, in perception of different saturations. However, the brightness and hue perceived depend not only on these stimulus characteristics, but also on the state of the eye and the context in which the stimulus appears. Three-dimensional vision depends on the integration of a variety of cues.

Hearing depends on the transmission of vibrations to the basilar membrane in the inner ear. Physical variations in amplitude, frequency, and complexity generally result in variations in the psychological experiences of loudness, pitch, and timbre, respectively. Modern theories, which are syntheses of apparently conflicting earlier notions, suggest how the nervous system codes hue in vision and pitch in hearing.

Chemical interactions between substances and the membranes of the nose and the tastebuds on the tongue give rise to the perceptions of taste and smell. We do not know the relevant physical dimensions. There are four elementary tastes, but we have no adequate classification of smell.

The skin senses consist of pressure, temperature, and pain. We have evidence that there are separate receptors sensitive to a different kind or range of energy for each modality.

In addition to these senses that give us information about the world outside us, we receive information about the state of our body from the kinesthetic impulses, from our muscles, tendons, and joints, from the semicircular canals that tell us whether we are in motion, from the vestibular sacs that give us our orientation to gravity, and from the pressure, pain, and temperature receptors in our internal organs.

Our nervous systems are built to respond to change. Continued constant stimulation results in adaptation. The level of adaptation provides a reference point for perception of change.

The change in stimulation which constitutes a just-noticeable difference (difference threshold) depends on the level of stimulation to which it is being compared. The larger the original stimulus, the larger the minimum change necessary to be noticed. The minimum energy that will be noticed in a modality is called the *absolute threshold*. The absolute threshold arrived at depends on the method used to determine it. People may respond to a stimulus whose presence they cannot report definitely.

Since perception is a function of CNS activity, it may occur in the absence of receptor stimulation. However, studies of ESP have failed to convince most psychologists of the validity of extrasensory knowledge.

The Phenomena of Perception:　Part 2

What Do We Perceive?

In the preceding section we dealt with the phenomena of perception by looking at the effects of known stimuli on the sense organs and perception. This survey described the limits of perception and the possible variations in stimuli to which we are sensitive. But within the range of stimuli to which we potentially may respond, only a few are perceived. Furthermore, understanding the range of sensitivity is only the first step toward understanding such complex perceptual processes as the recognition of a friend in a crowd, the appreciation of a symphony, the attraction of a perfume. Let us now consider the selection and organization of sights, sounds, and smells into the world of perception we experience. Since visual and auditory perception are both the most complex and the most studied senses, we shall emphasize data from these modalities.

Attention

Many, many energy changes occur in the environment of an individual at any moment. Information from about 260 million visual cells comes into the CNS. Over 48,000 cells are available for auditory information. The other senses have at least 78,000 receptor cells. While the potential amount of information a person receives is tremendous, the human brain cannot process all of it. One psychologist suggested it would take a brain the size of a cubic light year to process just the information received by the two eyes.

Note the many potential stimuli in your immediate environment vying for your perception at this moment.

Let us begin with the sensations from your skin and muscles. Note the pressure of your clothing on your body: the muscle tensions in your feet, legs, arms, and back. Feel the contact of your chair against your body, the weight of this book in your hands. Note the sensations from your digestive tract, the slight itchiness in your nose.

If you move your tongue around your mouth, you will find differences in taste, even though you are not eating. Sniff the air, and note the odors which are perceptible. Now listen and note the multitude of sounds which are audible. Even when your eyes are focusing on this page, note all the objects that are within your field of vision.

Of all the stimuli impinging on your sense organs, you are ordinarily aware of only a few. Your perception is quite selective. Those aspects of the environment of which you are aware at a given moment are said to have your *attention*. All the other stimuli provide a rather diffuse background.

How many aspects of the environment can you attend to at once? If we present a number of cards of brightly illuminated dots and ask observers how many dots they perceive, their reports will usually be correct if the actual number of dots is fewer than nine. When the cards contain more than nine dots, an observer cannot perceive the correct number in a single glance. If the stimulus cards consist of figures with shapes and colors, and if the observer must correctly report both shape and color, he can usually be accurate only if the number of figures on a card is fewer than four. The mean is 3.3. Again, the observer is unable to perceive more than ten separate elements at a glance, considering the shape of a figure and the color of a figure as separate elements.

The number of elements that can be perceived in an instant is called the *span of attention*. While individuals differ in their attention spans, no one can grasp more than a small portion of the information available at any moment.

Attention Shifts and the Determiners of Attention

In any new situation, we scan the environment, shifting our attention from one aspect of the environment to another. Part of this scanning involves active changes in our receptors. Our eyes jump from one point of fixation to another. Our hands move over the surface of the object we are examining. But essentially these shifts of attention involve changes in activity in the central nervous system, rather than only receptor adjustments. We can listen first for the flute, then for the violin in a symphony without moving at all. Similarly, your eye may be fixed on a single spot and you still can vary what you see.

What determines which features of the environment will be noticed in scanning? Sometimes we can predict which aspects of the environment will be noticed just by examining the stimulus situation. Listed below are the external determiners of attention.

In general, the largest and brightest object, the loudest sound, the strongest smell will be noticed, suggesting *intensity* as a determiner of attention.

We notice a page of color in a black and white magazine, the occasional dissonance in a harmonious musical composition, the 5′8″ basketball player on a team of six-footers. These are examples of the effectiveness of *contrast* in capturing attention. A primary principle of camouflage is to avoid such contrast.

A visitor to Broadway attends almost immediately to the advertising signs in which figures move, liquid fills a glass, or a message flashes on and off. These advertisements use the fact that we tend to notice stimuli that *change*. The security of the bird who sits on her nest while hunters tramp the underbrush is partially maintained by the fact that we often fail to notice unchanging objects.

The advertiser who repeats his message again and again is applying the principle of *repetition*. If a listener failed to attend the first time, perhaps he will notice the second or third message. However, overly frequent repetition leads to adaptation, and the stimuli merge into the unnoticed background.

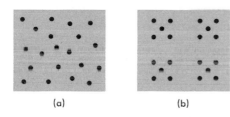

(a)   (b)

FIG. 6–17. At a glance, can you tell how many dots are in part (a)? Can you tell how many are in part (b)?

Figure-Ground Organization

Earlier we said that the attention span is limited to fewer than a dozen elements. But is it? Observe Fig. 6–17(b). There are many stimuli, yet you can attend to all of them at once. You probably grouped the dots into four squares of five dots each. This illustrates another basic phenomenon in perception: economy through organization.

The most basic organization in perception is the separation of the perceptual field into two parts—one dominant and unified, which is the focus of attention, the other more homogeneous and diffuse. This phenomenon is called figure-ground organization.

The factors which make a particular group of stimuli stand out from their background as a unified figure are illustrated in Fig. 6–18. These principles

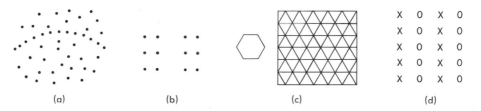

(a)   (b)   (c)   (d)

FIG. 6–18. Some determiners of figure-ground organization: (a) continuity, (b) proximity, (c) inclusiveness, and (d) similarity.

of grouping are often called gestalt principles, from the German word for figure or configuration, *gestalt*.

In Fig. 6–18(a), why do we see some of the dots grouped into an arc? In part (b) of this figure, why do we see two groups of dots, rather than twelve separate dots? In part (c), why is it difficult to see the hexagon in the second sketch? In part (d), why do we see vertical columns of X's and O's rather than horizontal rows? Each of the above configurations illustrates one of the factors influencing figure-ground organization, and we shall discuss them in turn.

CONTINUITY. In part (a) the arc is seen because of its *continuity*. Other things being equal, those stimuli which have continuity will stand out from the background and be organized together. Following the melody in a symphony is an example of the principle of continuity.

PROXIMITY. Part (b) illustrates the effect of *proximity*. When stimuli are close together, they tend to be grouped together.

INCLUSIVENESS. In part (c), we see a simple example of camouflage based upon the factor of *inclusiveness*. Generally speaking, the figure we are most likely to see is that figure which includes the greatest number of stimuli. In part (c) the hexagon is included in a more complex figure. This principle is often used in military camouflage. Camouflage often attempts to keep something from being perceived by destroying its configuration through incorporating it in a more inclusive figure.

SIMILARITY. In part (d) we see columns of X's and O's because *similar* things tend to be grouped together. If we switch the arrangement, we see a figure of rows rather than columns:

X X X X X
O O O O O
X X X X X
O O O O O

COMMON FATE. Stimuli which change together in the same direction tend to be organized together. For example, when we see a group of lights moving together down a river, we organize them into a unit just as we do the lights of an airplane against the stars. This principle of organization is called *common fate*.

CONTRAST. In Fig. 6–19(a) we see the circle as a figure; in (b) we see the cross as a figure. This is because stimuli which are different from their surroundings are organized together and are seen as a configuration. In this case, the contrast is in terms of form.

If we look back at our first figure of twenty dots we can see that proximity, similarity, and inclusiveness were factors in the stimulus situation that permitted an organization into a few figures which ostensibly increased the span of attention.

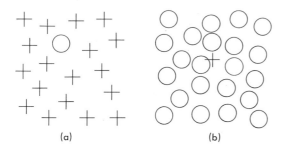

FIG. 6–19. Contrast as a determiner of figure-ground organization. In part (a), the circle is a figure and the crosses serve as ground. In part (b) the cross is a figure against a ground of circles.

ILLUSIONS. However, the organization of figures into wholes may lead us to misjudge the properties of the parts. Many illusions are based on this principle. In the Mueller-Lyer illusion, for example, when we judge the lengths of the lines, we tend to include the arrowhead in our judgment. Figure 6–20 illustrates several common illusions.

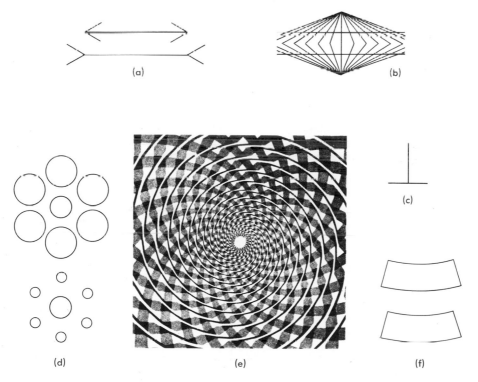

FIG. 6–20. Some optical illusions. (a) The Mueller-Lyer illusion. Which line looks longer? Actually they are the same size. (b) Do the horizontal lines look curved? A ruler will show you that they are straight. (c) Does the horizontal or the vertical line look longer? They are the same size. (d) Which central circle looks larger? Both central circles are the same size. (e) Does this look like a spiral? It is a group of concentric circles. (f) Which figure looks larger? Both are identical.

FIG. 6–21. What are these three figures? Your response may have been affected by your sex. See the text. These items come from a series of sketches, each of which tends to evoke different percepts in men and women. (From *Sex and Personality* by L. Terman and C. Miles, Copyright 1936, McGraw-Hill Book Co. Used by permission.)

Individual Differences

Although these determiners of attention and principles of gestalt permit us to predict to some extent which aspects of the environment will be noticed and how they will be organized, it is important to realize that different people select and organize stimuli differently. For example, a man and a woman looking at the same hardware store window will probably notice different objects. At first glance, a man is more likely to notice the guns and fishing rods, whereas a woman would probably notice the kitchen appliances. Figure 6–21 shows some examples of figures which tend to evoke different responses in men and women. Men tend to see the left figure as a brush or a centipede; women are more likely to report that it is a comb or a set of teeth. Men tend to see the middle figure as a target, women are more likely to see it as a dish. Other responses, such as a ring and tire, are given equally by both sexes. Men are more likely to report that the figure on the right is a head; women are more likely to see it as a cup or bowl. Both men and women are equally likely to say that it looks like a man. In addition to sex differences in percepts, the same person organizes the same situation differently at different times. Figure 6–22 includes some simple examples of this phenomenon. We shall return to this problem later in this chapter.

(a)

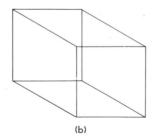

(b)

FIG. 6–22. Reversible figures. Can you see both the vase and the two profiles in (a)? Can you see the box in (b) with both the higher section and the lower section closest to you?

Constancy

You may be wondering what grouping dots into figures has to do with your perceptual experience. You normally see objects, not groups of dots. The principles of grouping are more understandable if, for experimental purposes, they are divorced from objects. But now let us return to one of the peculiar problems involved in the perception of objects: the phenomenon of constancy.

Try this simple demonstration. Hold a pencil about a foot from your eyes. Place your thumb on the point of the pencil and your index finger on the other end. Now hold your thumb and forefinger in this position and, with the other hand, move the pencil farther away. What happens to the image of the pencil? Compare the new image of the pencil with the space which it formerly occupied between your thumb and forefinger. You will see that the image of the pencil is now smaller. Yet despite differences in the stimulation, you have no difficulty in recognizing the same pencil. The two different sensory inputs give rise to the same percept, the same meaningful organization of stimuli in the central nervous system. This tendency to perceive an object as being the same under different conditions when the sensory input produced by it differs is called *constancy*.

The fact that objects do not seem to change their shapes although we view them from different angles is called *form constancy*. As you walk around a table, the projection from the table to your retina varies from a rectangle to a trapezoid. Yet you do not perceive it as an elastic table, changing its shape as you change your angle of vision.

Constancy applies to size, color, brightness, shape, and other characteristics of the object; e.g., we see a person walking toward us as being the same size even though the image on our eyes becomes larger and larger as he comes closer. This tendency to see an object as being the same size despite the changing of the image in the eye is known as *size constancy*.

A similar phenomenon is *brightness constancy*. We know that in general those things which reflect a great deal of light are seen as white or black. However, the amount of light reflected by snow in sunlight is obviously much greater than that reflected by snow in the shade. If we were to use a light meter, we would find that a piece of coal in bright sunlight reflects more light than a spot of snow in deep shade. Nevertheless, we see the snow, whether in sunlight or shade, as white, and the coal, even in bright sunlight, as black. By viewing objects through a peep-hole, we can destroy constancy because we are unable to identify the object and to take its context into account.

Color pictures taken in the morning are bluish; those taken in the afternoon have an orange cast. The fact that our perception of the color of an object remains the same despite such difference in the light reflected to our eyes is called *color constancy*.

Constancy depends on integration of several factors in the situation. In size constancy, for example, the perceiver integrates the size of the retinal image (and other cues to size) with the perceived distance of the object. Thus if he misjudges the distance, constancy is impaired. Often the perceived size of an object is a compromise between the actual size and the size of the retinal image. Similarly, in brightness constancy the perceiver integrates the amount of light reflected from the object to the eye and the perceived illumination. If the illuminating conditions are misjudged, brightness constancy suffers. Other constancies also depend upon an integration of the stimulation from the stimulus object with characteristics of the total situation. Such integration may be built into the nervous system through heredity (Hubel, 1963; Hubel and Wiesel, 1963) or may be easily learned from moving about in the environment (Hebb, 1949). Studies of lower animals indicate that their constancy is at least as great as man's.

Probably the most dramatic example of constancy comes from experiments in which people wear lenses that systematically distort the visual field. In one series of studies people wore lenses which completely inverted the visual field; up and down were visually reversed.

■ In another study, half of the lens for each eye was tinted yellow, the other half blue. At first, the wearers of the glasses reported the expected distortions, but after a period of days, the distortions lessened and the world appeared normal again. After the glasses were removed, the opposite distortion appeared, and it took some time before vision without any lenses became normal. For example, the wearer of the tinted lenses in which the left half of each lens was yellow and the right half was blue reported that at first the world appeared to be tinged with yellow when he turned his eyes to the left, and with blue when he turned his eyes to the right. This effect disappeared after a few days. After the glasses were removed the world appeared to be tinged with blue when his eyes turned to the left, and with yellow when his eyes turned to the right, although the subject wore no lenses at all. (Kohler, 1961) ■

Again we see the tremendous flexibility of the visual system. The variations in the sensory messages caused by the distorted lenses were somehow compensated for, and after a period of adaptation, the world appeared to be almost as constant and stable as always.

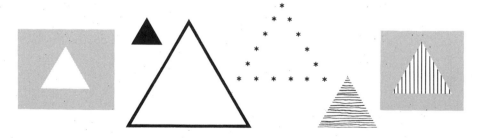

FIG. 6–23. You identify all these shapes as triangles even though the stimuli making up the elements are quite different.

TRANSPOSITION. Constancy is closely related to the phenomenon of *transposition*. Transposition is the recognition of common patterns, although the elements that make up the pattern are different. Just as we recognize a visual pattern as being the same object whether it is close or far away, so in music we recognize the same tune whether it is played in the key of C or of G, on a piano or on a violin. Our perceptions of melody are based upon relationships between the stimuli, rather than upon the absolute stimulus characteristics. Our response to the words on these pages is much the same whether the type is large or small, capital letters or lower case, in printing or in script. See Fig. 6–23 for examples of spatial transposition.

This figure illustrates a perceptual principle of great importance. In studying constancy we were concerned about how a particular object could be perceived as the same under different conditions. The phenomenon of transposition again illustrates that different stimuli may elicit the same perception even though they come from different sources, i.e., stimuli may be responded to as though they were equivalent.

The Dynamics of Perception

What Factors Determine How the Sensory Input Will Be Perceived?

We have seen that different sensory inputs will give rise to the perception of the same object, as in the phenomena of constancy. Also, we have seen that the same sensory input can give rise to different perceptions, as in the case of ambiguous figures. If the sensory input alone does not determine what we perceive, what else does?

Let us look at Fig. 6–24. When people are asked what they see in this figure, most of them say "a dog." Yet everyone realizes that there is no dog there, that the sketch is incomplete. Our ability to reinstate whole objects even though only part of the stimuli are present is called *redintegration*. Obviously, a person who has never had any experience with a dog or with pictures of dogs would be unable to get a meaningful perception from Fig. 6–24. This suggests that what we see is determined in part by our past experience.

FIG. 6–24. Do these black blotches produce a meaningful percept for you? If they do, it is because you are using partial cues to reinstate a whole figure. (After Street, 1931)

Our perception depends on a relationship between the present stimulation and our past experience with similar stimulation. We may infer that the past experience has left in the brain some kind of trace, which, when activated by external stimuli, will give rise to the perception of a dog. A number of different sets of stimuli can trigger off the "dog" activity, such as Fig. 6–24, a photograph of a dog, the letters d-o-g, or the sound of barking.

What must be stored in the brain is not simply an image of one specific dog but rather an abstraction of the properties that many specific dogs have in common. As we said in Chapter 5, when the properties of stimuli are abstracted and stored by an individual so that he can classify objects and events on the basis of these properties, the set of abstracted properties is called a *concept* or a *category*. When sensory input triggers off the activity associated with a concept, we call the stimuli involved *cues*, and the resultant experience, a *percept*. The process by which input is identified with a concept is called *categorization*.

For example, all of us have a conceptual category which includes the following properties: animal, four-legged, makes mooing noises, cud chewer, gives milk, etc. This is your concept of cow. You can manipulate this concept in your mind without seeing or hearing a cow. When you see a picture of an animal and the properties of the animal match your concept, you will experience a percept of a cow. This means that you categorize the sensory input as falling within the boundaries of the concept and you will assign many of the properties associated with your "cow" concept to the animal you see.

Some Experimental Evidence

This analysis of perception is theoretical; concepts and percepts are constructs. What experimental evidence do we have that a categorization process affects the perception of object characteristics?

■ Postman, Bruner, and Rodrigues (1951) asked subjects to match the colors of various pictures with standard colors. All the pictures were the same color, gray. The stimuli were presented on a blue-green background. As a result of simultaneous contrast, the figures appeared orange-colored. The objects included a tomato, a carrot, and a banana. Even though the subjects said that the drawings were all the same color, the color they matched with the tomato was redder, and the color matched with the banana was yellower, than the color matched with the carrot. ■

Such errors illustrate the tendency to assign properties included in a concept to a stimulus pattern which has been categorized as an example of the concept.

Features of the Categorization Process

The categorization process does not imply that you fail to observe the unique characteristics of the particular object in front of you. Each percept consists of concepts plus some of the unique characteristics of the object relayed via the sense organs.

Categories vary in their breadth, i.e., the number of elements they include. The concept "fruit" is broader than and includes the concept "peach." Also, the same object can potentially be categorized into several categories: a fruit, a ball, an ornament, or many others.

When a set of stimuli from an object is associated with several mutually exclusive concepts, the individual strives to get more information with which to establish a correct categorization. As in the case of identical twins, the differences may in some cases be very small.

As we categorize, we learn that certain cues are less reliable than others. As we have seen, such cues as the shape on the retina, the size of the retinal image, and the absolute brightness change as an object moves. Consequently, they are rather unreliable guides to categorization. Spatial relations, relative size, and relative brightness are, however, much more reliable cues. Thus a whole range of stimuli are reacted to as equivalents. In some cases we recognize that there are differences even though we react the same way. In the case of constancy, however, we are likely to be unaware of the actual differences in stimulation when we perceive the object under different viewing conditions.

Discrimination

Our discrimination of differences is finest in the areas representing boundaries between two concepts. For example, in speech perception the words "doe" and "toe" both begin with a sound wave of rising frequency followed by the vowel sound "o" of lower frequency. The difference between them is the time between onset of the consonant sound and the vowel. Using a sound synthesizer,* one can vary this time period within the range usually identified as "doe," within the "toe" range, and in the area of the boundary. College students tested on this could detect much finer differences in the boundary region than within either category. Similarly, one would expect color discriminations to be best in the boundary area between colors called by one name and the colors called by another.

Factors Determining Which Concepts Will Be Activated

CONCEPT STRENGTH. A given cue may be associated with several concepts. On different occasions you may have perceived a book as "a source of information," "a paperweight," "a weapon to be thrown." Each time the appropriateness of your categorization was probably revealed by events following the categorization.

---

* An instrument which can produce any desired pattern of sound waves.

The book did or did not provide information; it did or did not hold down the papers; it was or was not a useful weapon. Thus the environment either *confirmed* or *disconfirmed* the appropriateness of the categorization. We hypothesize that the greater the number of times cues have been categorized as belonging within a concept without disconfirmation, the greater the *concept strength*. Probably the categorization of a particular set of cues depends not on the absolute number of times the categorization was made without disconfirmation, but on this absolute number compared to the number of times other categorizations of this same set of cues have occurred.

We can illustrate concept strength by asking you to look at the following:

$$H \: {}^{O}_{A} \: U S E$$

You probably first perceived the word HOUSE if English is your native language. If German is your native language, you probably perceived HAUSE. If you are bilingual, your perception probably corresponded to the language with which you have had the most experience.

The greater the concept strength, the fewer cues necessary for recognition. For example, if you know a person well, you can recognize him even if his back is turned or his face is dirty. Experimental evidence for this principle comes from this study:

■ Solomon and Howes (1951) flashed words on a screen very rapidly with a tachistoscope (see Fig. 6–25). The words were chosen because they differ in the frequency with which they are used in English. Those words which are used most frequently were recognized at an exposure time shorter than the minimum exposure time for less familiar words. For example, "automobile" was first identified at a shorter exposure time than "limousine." ■

The cues associated with categories involved in familiar words have higher concept strength, hence require fewer cues to activate the category.

SET. The concept activated depends not only on the concept strength of the cues in the stimulus being categorized, but also on what concepts are simultaneously aroused by other stimuli in the situation.

The effects of other stimuli on the categorization of a particular stimulus pattern are called *set*. Sometimes the set is induced by stimulus events occurring just prior to the pattern being categorized. Here is an example by which you can demonstrate "set" for yourself. As you come into your room carrying some books, say to your roommate "Is it all right if I bump my books here?" Then ask him what you said. Probably he will have heard "bump" as "dump." The other words in the sentence have given him a set which has influenced his perception.

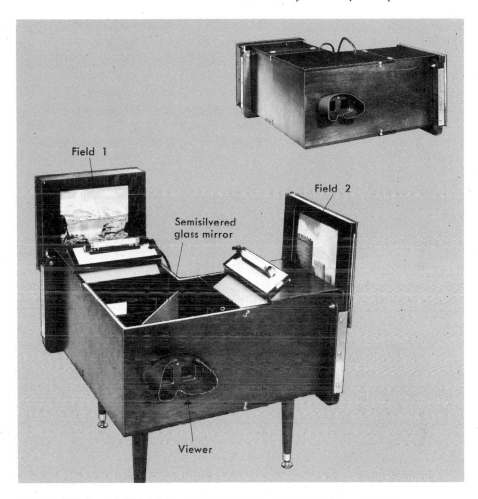

FIG. 6–25. The tachistoscope, an instrument which permits rapid exposure of stimulus material. When an observer looks through the viewer at the semisilvered glass mirror, he sees the stimulus material for the field that is lighted. By rapidly changing the lighting, one can present different stimuli for very short intervals.

Different stimuli have different probabilities of inducing a set. Leeper showed picture (a) in Fig. 6–26 to a group of subjects who were asked to write down what they saw. A second group first saw picture (b) before being asked to describe picture (a). A third group first saw picture (c), and a fourth group was given only verbal preparation beforehand, being told "You will be shown a drawing of a young woman's head" (or "an old woman's head"). The results are shown in Fig. 6–27. Differences in set made clear differences in what was perceived (Leeper, 1935). The pictures had a higher probability of inducing the desired set than did the verbal preparations.

FIG. 6–26. The stimuli used in Leeper's experiment. See the text for explanation. (After Leeper, 1935)

SETS AND THRESHOLDS. We can think of absolute threshold measurements as a process of categorization. The subject assigns an experience as belonging either to the category "a stimulus was present" or to the category "a stimulus was absent."

This kind of categorization is also affected by set. Experiments by Tanner and Norman (1954) have shown that the absolute threshold is lower when the subject is told that a tone to be detected will have a particular pitch than if he is told that the tone might have either of two pitches. Activating the category associated with one particular pitch facilitates the perception of that

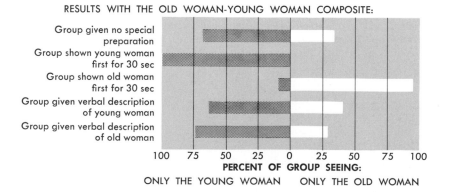

FIG. 6–27. Leeper's results. See the text for explanation. (After Leeper, 1935)

pitch at low energy levels. The greater the number of mutually exclusive categories active at a given time, the longer and more difficult is the categorization process.

ON-GOING BRAIN ACTIVITY. Some of the activity in the brain cannot be attributed to stimuli in the present situation. However, such activity can include concepts which affect perception. For example, if you are thinking about buying a plane ticket and you see a flying object not quite clearly enough to identify it, you will probably perceive it as a plane. Other on-going brain activity might have facilitated perception of a bird.

Motivation

The presence of certain expectancies of affect influences how we perceive. Here is an example:

■ McClelland and Atkinson (1948) studied the perceptions of men who had had no food for one hour, four hours, and sixteen hours. The subjects were asked to write down the impressions they had of pictures which were to be projected on the screen very dimly. The projection operator went through all the motions of inserting pictures, but actually no pictures were projected. The men did report meaningful perceptions anyway; the longer the men had been without food, the more food-related perceptions were reported. ■

Hunger increases the expectancy that food will be present and activates concepts related to eating. The increased motivation thus increases the probability of activating food-related concepts. The men interpreted very ambiguous sensory input in terms of concepts which were activated by motivational rather than sensory factors.

VIGILANCE AND DEFENSE. Motivation does not always increase the probability that a particular percept will be experienced. In the case of expectancies of unpleasantness, the motive may serve to decrease the probability of a percept despite the presence of the appropriate cues.

■ Blum (1954) exposed four pictures (see Fig. 6–28), very briefly in a tachistoscope so briefly that the subjects could not identify what the pictures were. He asked subjects to report which of the stimuli seemed clearest—top, bottom, left, or right. Following 54 trials of this sort to determine the subjects' usual way of responding, the subjects were shown two of the four pictures, one of which was described in anxiety-arousing terms, the other in neutral terms. Then Blum repeated the very brief flashing of the four pictures. In the next 54 trials (during which the position of the stimuli was varied randomly) subjects tended to select the anxiety-arousing picture as clearest, even though they could not recognize it. The exposure time was then lengthened so that the pictures were almost identifiable. The subjects were then asked the location of the neutral and anxiety-arousing stimuli. Blum now found that the subjects had more difficulty locating the "clear" anxiety-arousing stimulus than they had in locating the neutral stimulus. ■

FIG. 6–28. The type of picture Blum (1954) used in his experiment. For a given subject, this picture could be described either in anxiety-arousing terms or neutral terms. (Courtesy of Dr. G. Blum)

The increased sensitivity demonstrated in the first part of the experiment is called *vigilance,* and the slow and inaccurate recognition exhibited in the second part is termed *perceptual defense.*

It appears that the individual has a tendency to notice anxiety-arousing stimuli, but the expectancy of unpleasantness somehow inhibits or interferes with the tendency to be consciously aware of concepts associated with these stimuli. In this case, the factors producing the conscious perception of the anxiety-producing concept must be stronger than normal for conscious recognition.

MOTIVATION AND THRESHOLDS. Motivation has been shown to influence absolute threshold categorization. Suppose the experimenter rewards the subject every time he detects the stimulus and penalizes him very little for making a mistake in reporting that the stimulus has occurred when it hasn't. In this situation the threshold drops and the subject reports even very faint stimuli (although he also makes errors). Let us now reverse the payoff, reducing the reward for reporting a stimulus when there was none. The subject's threshold now moves up so that a much higher intensity is required before he reports it. This again illustrates that thresholds vary with the conditions under which the measurement is made (Tanner and Swets, 1953). One important factor is motivational expectancy, which facilitates or inhibits the tendency toward a particular categorization.

MOTIVATION AND ATTENTION. As we mentioned in our discussion of perceptual vigilance, motivation affects what we will notice as well as how we categorize. A man walking along the street with his wife may notice sporting goods or men's clothing but will probably not notice at once the hat or jewelry which attracts his wife's attention. The college man notices the beautiful blonde before he sees the escort at her side. Advertising men make use of this principle. Because sex is an important human need, it is not surprising that one notes many drawings of alluring females in advertisements in men's magazines. The advertisers hope that the pictures of the females will draw attention not only to the girls, but also to the product and the product name which are in close spatial contiguity to the girls.

Ambiguity

We have seen that concept strength, set, on-going activity, and motivation
are four factors that determine which percept will be aroused by a stimulus
pattern. It may be that the combinations of these factors activate several
mutually exclusive concepts. We call this situation *ambiguity*. The more
percepts that are possible, the greater the ambiguity. The first response to ambiguity is an active search for more information. A person looks more closely;
he makes tentative categorizations and seeks confirmation. However, if categorization is still impossible, the person is likely to feel anxious and withdraw
from the situation.

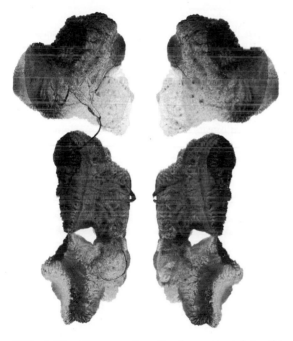

FIG. 6–29. Because the stimulus material in this picture is ambiguous, different
people will perceive it differently. Some see fossilized bones; others see two women
talking to each other. Your perception may be different from either of these.

PERCEPTION AND PERSONALITY. The more ambiguous the stimulus to most people
(i.e., the more concepts with which it can be related), the more the factors unique
to an individual will be dominant in influencing categorization. The projective
personality tests are based on this principle. Ambiguous stimulus patterns are
presented, and the subject is asked to describe what he sees. Since no one
categorization is clear from the sensory input, the factors unique to each
individual, unusual associations of stimuli with concepts, on-going activity, and
strong motivations will be revealed. See Fig. 6–29 for a sample of an ambiguous
stimulus.

We can interpret hallucinations in a similar way. Extremely high levels of concept strength, set, persistent activity, and motivation may activate the concept without the relevant sensory input. The "concept" activity is so persistent that the hallucinating individual fails to distinguish between perception and thought. This explanation is supported by the clinical observation that hallucinations associated with psychological disorders seem to be related to states of strong motivation.

The Development of Perception

The Infant

The sensory equipment of the newborn infant is far from mature. He is sensitive to pressure on his skin, to cold, to differences in taste, to sounds, and to light. However, the optic nerve and related neural structures are not fully developed. He seems to be somewhat insensitive to pain and to warmth. He blinks at bright lights, but probably does not see clear images.

Obviously we cannot ask a baby what he sees the first time he opens his eyes. However, we do have data from an analogous situation. Some patients, blind from birth, have gained their vision as the result of operations. Since they had had no practice in seeing, what they saw when their bandages were removed is of interest.

The case histories of these patients indicate that they did not experience normal perception immediately. When an object was shown to them, they could see that something against a background was in front of them (figure-ground organization), but they could not identify it, its shape, or its distance from them.

Following the removal of the bandages came a long period of learning how to see. Color discriminations were learned immediately. However, learning to identify forms and objects in different contexts was a long and difficult process. For example, one patient learned to identify an egg, a potato, and sugar in normal light on a table after many repetitions. He failed to recognize those same objects in colored light or when they were suspended by a thread with a change of background (Von Senden, 1960).

Although some of the patient's difficulties may be caused by the strength of other systems of categorization he has developed, it is likely that an infant goes through a similar period of learning. In the second or third week, he begins to follow a moving light with his eyes. By the twelfth week he pays attention to people.

The ability of the human child to use his receptors also changes with age. For example, an additional reason that the young baby does not clearly differentiate objects is that he is unable to fixate his eyes accurately, and each eye moves almost independently during the first day or two of life.

During the early weeks of infancy, the infant doesn't know "what goes with what." Although conditioned reflexes can be set up, different sensations from the same object are apparently not easily associated. The young baby, for example, will chew on his toes and cry because it hurts, but may keep on chewing because he fails at first to associate the pleasant sensation from chewing with the pain in the toe. Even when he is pricked with a pin, he seems unable to localize the pain until he is about eight months old, and he probably won't be able to put his hand on the spot until he is over a year old. Thus even perception of one's own body is built up through learning. But some characteristics of perception develop primarily through maturation. Move a light across the infant's field of vision and his eyes jumpily follow. Sound a tone repeatedly and he quiets. These bases of organization are already present.

As soon as he is old enough to crawl, the infant can discriminate depth. This was demonstrated by a series of "visual cliff studies" (Gibson and Walk, 1960).

FIG. 6–30. A baby being tested on the "visual cliff" in one of the Gibson and Walk experiments. The baby refused to crawl to his mother over the "deep" side when she called him, though he crawled to her immediately when she stood on the shallow side. (Photo by William Vandivert)

■ The visual cliff consists of a board laid across a piece of glass which is supported by legs a foot or so above the floor. On one side of the board a sheet of patterned paper is placed up against the glass; on the other side, the paper was placed on the floor, giving the illusion of a large drop (see Fig. 6–30). Children (age 6–14 months) were placed in the center of the board and their mothers called to them from both the "shallow" and the "deep" side of the cliff. Most of the children readily crawled to Mama across the shallow side, but refused to crawl over the apparent drop. ■

This, of course, does not indicate that depth perception is innate in children. The subjects had had at least six months to learn how to perceive depth. However, experiments in lower animals who can walk at birth, such as kids, lambs, and chicks, show that they, at least, perceive depth and avoid drops at birth (Gibson and Walk, 1960).

Because adults are so visually oriented, it is difficult for us to realize that vision is probably not the most important avenue of perception for the infant. In the early months of life, the infant's primary sensations probably come from internal and skin receptors, rather than from vision. From experiments with baby monkeys and observations of human infants, we know that bodily contact and cuddling is extremely important to the infant's contentment and well-being. During the first six months of life everything goes into the mouth, for it is there that the child can feel its shape, taste it, and gain the elements of his perceptions. A little later, touching, handling, and moving seem to become dominant. Through these checks of visual perception against his other senses, the child develops his ability to size up objects with vision alone.

The first objects which have meaning to the baby are probably those which have most to do with pleasant feelings, and which are repeated, as we would expect from our theory of the relation of motivation to perceptual learning. Adults may respond emotionally to words flashed on a screen too rapidly to recognize (Lazarus and McCleary, 1951). Similarly, the baby's first perceptual discriminations may be linked to emotional responses before there is more complete recognition of the particular objects with which these responses are associated. The first person the infant visually recognizes is ordinarily his mother, and this recognition usually develops around the age of four months (Gesell, 1940). At the same time that the infant is developing an awareness of other people, he is learning to discriminate between himself and his environment. Things that happen to him are different from those happening in the rest of his environment. His own "self" begins to become an object of his perception. He investigates his body, putting his hands in his mouth, touching, biting, and even pinching himself until he knows what is "me." The things that happen to his body begin to be perceived as happenings to his own self, and by the second half-year of his life, he learns that it hurts (himself) when he kicks something hard.

As the child grows older, more and more objects are differentiated. Maturation and learning proceed together. By the end of his first year of life the baby's sense organs are completely functional and he continues to develop expectations on the basis of experience.

How Are Perceptual Categories Formed?

The answer to this question is not known. Some categories seem to depend on the structure of the organism and seem to be inherited. The tendency to respond to stimuli that are physically similar—*primary stimulus generalization*—seems to be one example.

But most of our concepts seem to be the result of learning. This learning in-volves abstraction of common properties of stimuli. This tendency to abstract properties of stimuli and to organize new stimulus patterns in accordance with these properties is a basic characteristic of human perception and thinking.

Obviously the first requisite for the occurrence of this process is contact with stimuli. However, attention is another important factor. This is illustrated in studies which compared the ability to use cues other than visual in blind and normal people. Formerly, blind people were thought to use some special sense which enabled them to detect obstacles. Blind people, however, said that they "just felt" that obstacles were near and were unable to indicate how they did it. Some thought it was from air currents, others from sound, others from special senses in the skin. A series of experiments were carried out (Supa, Cotyen, and Dallenbach, 1944) in order to determine the nature of this ability.

■ Comparing blind subjects to normal blindfolded subjects, it was found that the blind subjects could sense objects at a distance while the normal subjects bumped into them. When the subjects approached the obstacle walking with stocking feet on a carpet, they were less efficient than they had been when wearing shoes on a wood floor. When the subjects wore ear plugs, they were completely unable to detect the obstacle. These results, plus those of other experiments, indicated that the subjects were able to avoid obstacles by responding to sound waves reflected from the obstacle, even though they were not initially aware that they were using these cues. People with vision who were blindfolded improved greatly with practice. ■

While everyone has the necessary experience, he is not ordinarily motivated to attend to these sound cues. The blind person must attend to them if he is to avoid bumps. Apparently one learns to use those cues which help avoid pain or increase pleasure.

As children attend to more and more stimulus patterns, they begin to group them along various dimensions. Concepts are formed on the basis of common physical characteristics, spatial or temporal contiguity, common functions (you can hit your baby sister both with a block and a book), or common contexts (things that are put on a plate by mother are all food), and probably many other bases. Words which label different objects in the same way facilitate the formation of concepts.

As the perceptual concepts are formed, new stimuli are tentatively categorized. As we said earlier, if subsequent events confirm the perception, the concept strength is increased. Now let us look at what constitutes confirmation.

In general, we tend to organize our perception in such a way that the per-ceptual world remains stable. We integrate information from many senses to produce a single impression of the world. For example, an infant learns to judge the distance of an object from him by reaching for it, missing, trying again. He checks his perception of the visual form of an object by manipulat-ing it and putting it in his mouth. We learn that people and objects do not expand and shrink as their sizes projected on our retinas change and we learn

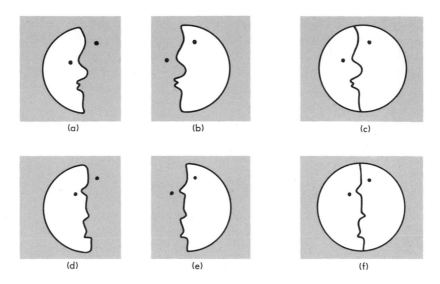

FIG. 6–31. Schafer and Murphy (1934) used these profiles in an experiment. Subjects were shown the profiles in (a), (b), (d), and (e) many times in random order. Some subjects were given money whenever (a) appeared; other groups were rewarded for seeing (b), (d), and (e), respectively. When the subjects were shown the reversible profiles shown in (c) and (f), they tended to see the profiles for which they had been rewarded.

to judge their sizes in relation to their background. Because we cannot check the size of the moon by touching it, because there are few relevant background cues, most of us never learn to perceive it as large. Here we have no feedback to confirm or reject our expectation; hence our perceptions of the moon's size are inaccurate.

Sometimes a particular perception of an object satisfies a particular motive. The reward acts as additional confirmation. If college students are given a monetary reward for perceiving an ambiguous figure consistently the same way, they will tend to identify the figure this way even when there no longer is monetary reward (see Fig. 6–31). If an individual were repeatedly exposed to situations in which he could avoid pain by not perceiving an object, we would expect the concept strength of that object to be greatly weakened, so that other possible perceptions might have greater concept strength. This may be the way that perceptual defense is learned. Thus confirmation of a percept may involve specific punishment or reward.

But we should remember that one of the dominant motives in learning to perceive and conceive is to achieve an impression of the world which is consistent yet flexible enough to encompass the wide range of events which human beings experience.

Individual Differences

Thus far we have described the principles of perception that are common to everyone. Let us now look briefly at the way people differ from one another in perception.

Sensory

It is apparent that individual differences in sensory acuity may be significant in many tasks. See Fig. 6–32. Color blindness was a severe handicap in driving automobiles until the position of the red and green traffic lights was standardized and enough blue was put into the green to make the stop or go lights appear different even for the color blind.

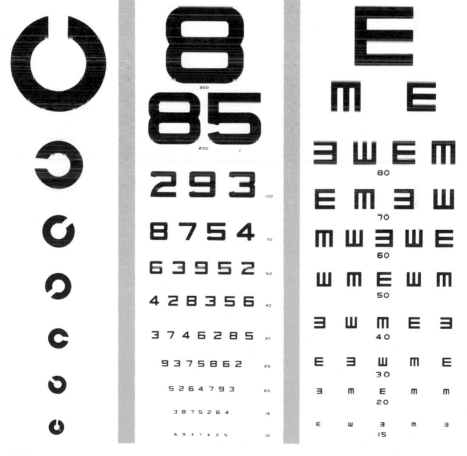

FIG. 6–32. Optometrists and oculists use charts such as these to measure the sensory acuity of their patients.

Individual Differences in Constancy

Individuals differ in their tendency to judge an object's characteristics accurately under varying viewing conditions. If subjects are asked to place two squares of differing sizes at such distances that they look the same size, less intelligent subjects tend to be more influenced by the real size, i.e., they show greater constancy and move the larger square farther away (Thouless, 1932). Women show a greater tendency to constancy than men; i.e., they tend to see objects of the same size as being the same even when one is farther away than the other. Older people show greater constancy than younger people. Patients suffering from the mental illness *paranoid schizophrenia* tend to judge a distant object as being larger than do normal subjects (Raush, 1952). These individual differences have been obtained in experiments comparing responses of different groups to the same instructions. It is worth noting, however, that the task usually is to judge how large an object "looks" and this may be an ambiguous instruction. The same subjects might give different responses if they were then asked, "How large do you think it really *is?*"

Discrimination and Comparison

Individuals differ in the speed with which they compare likenesses and differences. Tests of this ability, *perceptual speed*, have been successfully used in the selection of clerical workers, and scores on the test correlate around 0.5 with the output of bookkeeping machine operators.

Musical Ability

Among the oldest and most widely used aptitude measures are the "Seashore Measures of Musical Talent." This test is based upon the assumption that ability to play various musical instruments depends in differing degrees upon the person's ability to discriminate pitch, loudness, rhythm, tone quality and other attributes of music. Phonograph records are used to produce the tones used in testing for such discrimination. Instructions for the pitch discrimination test are typical. "You will hear two tones which differ in pitch. You are to judge whether the second is higher or lower than the first." Scores on the test seem to be relatively independent of musical training. While the test has been criticized for not measuring more complex aspects of musicianship, it has proved to be a useful aptitude test.

Spatial Abilities

Analysis of intelligence tests reveals that one or more of the abilities measured have to do with the comprehension of object relationships and the visualization of how an object will look after it is moved or rotated. Spatial abilities are useful in predicting success in architecture and engineering. While part of the usefulness of such items in predicting success in various fields lies in the fact that they measure general intelligence, studies of spatial abilities of engineers, dentists, watch repairmen, and of others in similar occupations indicate that in these occupations spatial ability is particularly relevant to success. Individual differences in this factor are influenced by experience, for studies of engineering students show that their scores on spatial ability tests improve during engineering training (Blade and Watson, 1955).

Organization

Individuals differ in their ability to organize an incomplete or vaguely organized group of stimuli. One of the tests of this ability, "The Street Gestalt Completion Test," uses drawings of black blotches barely suggestive of the outlines of objects (see Fig. 6–33). The subject is asked to interpret the drawing within three seconds. Ability to recognize objects with reduced cues is positively correlated with intelligence.

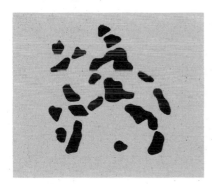

FIG. 6–33. An item from the Street Gestalt Completion Test. (After Street, 1935)

Flexibility

Individuals also differ in their ability to reorganize their perceptions with new information. Frenkel-Brunswick (1949) developed a series of sketches which gradually changed from one object to another. In one series, for example, the first sketch was clearly a cat and the last sketch was clearly a dog. In between, the cats gradually got more doglike. The sketches were shown to people who differed in their attitudes toward minority groups. Those who tended to be intolerant of minorities clung to their original percept longer than people who were more tolerant. Further research (Klein, 1951) showed that people who clung to a percept also had difficulty in finding a simple figure concealed in a complex one, and were described by psychiatrists as being characterized by retreat from objects, avoidance of competition and need for nurture. Thus perceptual differences are again seen to be related to motivational and behavioral differences.

Practical Applications

Detection

The individual's ability to detect a stimulus is of great importance in the designing of methods of presenting information to an airplane pilot or to anyone who must control a complex system. Information on detection is also useful in training. For example, in situations where early detection is vital, such as for lookouts or search-radar operators, we need to recognize the effects of rewards for early recognition versus punishments for false alarms in determining the cut-off level which the operator uses.

Psychologists studying instrument design have discovered that certain methods of presenting information are much more efficient than others. For example, auditory signals are generally more efficient than visual signals for warning devices, since audition is not as directional or selective as vision. Visual signals may, however, be more efficient than auditory ones for continuous presentation of several different kinds of information, for fine discriminations, and for simultaneous comparisons. For visual presentations, direct numerical presentation is interpreted more accurately than pointer reading.

Can Perception Be Improved?

What are the effects of practice upon the accuracy of perception? Practice fails to increase our sensory acuity. However, it may help to make us aware of cues which we formerly ignored. As we saw earlier, a blindfolded person can learn to respond to auditory cues which he would otherwise not notice, and can then detect obstacles by the reflection of the sounds of his footsteps.

A similar problem of recognition was a major concern of the armed forces during World War II. Fliers and gunners had to be able to recognize enemy aircraft and to distinguish them from friendly aircraft. It was obvious that practice would be necessary in training fliers and gunners to do this. A number of problems immediately presented themselves.

For example, one of the early methods of training was to provide practice in identifying numbers flashed on a screen for a very brief period or in estimating the number of dots in a flash presentation. Trainees made remarkable gains in their ability to recognize such stimuli at very short exposures. Would this improve their general recognition efficiency so that they would be better able to spot enemy aircraft?

Another problem involved the method of presenting pictures of planes. One commonly used method was to present a plane's picture together with the model designation of the plane, which the instructor repeated. Another method used the same procedure for the first trial, but on succeeding trials, the students were required to write down or guess at the name of the plane. As soon as they had written down the name, the picture was shown again and identified. Which of these methods was better?

Research showed that students who had practiced recognizing dots and numbers with brief exposure did not develop a general efficiency which helped them in aircraft recognition. Their recognition learning scores were no better than those of students who had not had special training. This suggests that practice is most efficient when carried out in a situation as similar as possible to that in which training is applied. In fact, even training on rapid recognition of pictures of aircraft had little relationship to skill in recognition of real airplanes.

The problem of presentation method was also investigated by research. The method of active participation and confirmed or unconfirmed responses proved to be much superior to the passive learning method. In terms of our theory we would expect that the active participation method not only created greater motivation but also forced subjects to form and to test categorization of the stimulus objects.

Using our knowledge of the factors influencing perception, it is fairly easy to see some other ways which would be conducive to the improvement of perception. For example, one's perception is limited by the number of categories into which he can classify information. By learning new concepts or categories, perception can be improved. When a zoology professor sketches the protozoa his student should be seeing under the lens of a microscope, it becomes easier for the student to perceive them. What the zoology professor has done is to help the student form a new concept by providing a model. Learning this vocabulary of a field of study and the things to which it refers similarly help in providing more categories into which to fit new experiences. Learning vocabulary in a course, therefore, is not just a waste of time but a first step in further learning.

As we learn more categories we can make more accurate discriminations between stimulus patterns, but this practice does not improve our ability to make accurate observations in fields not covered by the concepts we have learned. For example, umpires have a good deal of experience in accurate observation, but one would not expect the umpire's practice in discriminating between balls and strikes to make him a better aircraft spotter.

We have seen that our ability to fit stimuli into the right categories depends upon how motivated we are to make the discrimination between one object and similar objects. The person who cannot tell one symphony from another can learn to do so if he is motivated and has the opportunity to check his guesses against the actual facts.

Improving Concentration

As we have seen, one's attention is not completely at the mercy of the environment. True, it is partly determined by environmental factors, but the past experience, motives, and set of the person are also important in perception, and these internal factors are to some degree under voluntary control.

In concentrating we attempt to do for ourselves the things which the experimenter does in experiments on perception. That is, we try to reduce distracting stimuli and maintain a high degree of motivation.

One of the factors enabling one to work under adverse conditions is adaptation. As we have seen, one ignores distracting stimuli to which he is accustomed. Thus one aid to concentration is studying regularly in the same place under the same conditions.

Distracting thoughts are not only caused by external cues but by internal needs. If one is motivated for study, his mind is less likely to wander. Thus reminding yourself of why you are studying a particular subject may help. Similarly, both asking yourself questions about the material you have just covered and looking for the answers to questions in the material you are covering help improve concentration and learning. Like the soldiers in aircraft recognition classes, you will find that actively forming tentative categorizations which are then tested against the facts will speed your learning.

Conclusion

We have seen that variations in physical stimuli lead to variations in perception, but that our minds are incapable of comprehending every stimulus. We selectively attend to certain aspects of the environment. What we attend to is affected both by characteristics of the stimulus, such as intensity and contrast, and by internal factors, such as motivation. While the number of unrelated elements we can perceive at an instant is limited, we broaden our perception by organizing separate elements into unified wholes. Different people may organize the same stimulus patterns differently on different occasions.

Furthermore, we recognize patterns as being the same although the elements that make up the patterns are quite different (transposition) and we recognize objects as being the same although they project a number of different images on the retina (constancy).

One of the basic processes determining how we perceive a given stimulus is categorization. We relate stimuli to concepts we have formed in the past. The resultant percept will depend on four factors: the various concept strengths associated with the stimulus, the concept associations of other stimuli in the situation or of immediately preceding stimulation (set), on-going brain activity, and current motivation. The interaction of these factors produces definite categorization in some cases, tentative categorization in others, and the discomfort of ambiguity in still others. The categorization is either confirmed or unconfirmed by subsequent experiences. If the categorization is consistent with other perceptions, or if it is specifically rewarded, the tendency toward the categorization is increased; if it does not fit in with our other percepts or if we are punished for perceiving a stimulus in this way, the tendency toward the categorization will be decreased.

The newborn baby's sensory apparatus is not completely functional at birth. He probably can divide the visual field into a figure and a ground, but he does not discriminate forms and objects. His senses of touch and smell probably give him more information than vision.

As he grows older he learns to use some inherited categories and he forms new categories on the basis of his experience. An important feature of category formation is the tendency for the organism to abstract properties from the objects in his experience.

There are widespread individual differences in sensory acuity, constancy, musical and spatial ability, and flexibility in perception. Some of these characteristics are related to differences in occupational selection, general intelligence, and personality. Many of the principles of perception can be applied to the improvement of recognition and concentration.

We emerge with a picture of perception that may be disturbing to you. The old saying "Seeing is believing" has to be modified. Although our own perceptions are immediate and compelling, other people may view the same situation quite differently. But so long as we are not blinded by strong motivations or by persistent preconceptions, we find that our perceptions will give to us a unified, consistent picture of our world, yet one which is flexible enough to integrate its variability and complexity.

Summary

Concepts

Sense modality. A category of perceptual experience which depends on a particular kind of energy affecting a particular receptor

Adaptation. The reduction in the perception of a stimulus resulting from continuous reception of that stimulus

Adaptation level. The level of stimulation to which we are adapted that becomes the reference point for other stimulus judgments

Difference threshold or *just-noticeable difference.* The minimum amount of added stimulation (given an initial level of stimulation) that will be detected by the observer

Absolute threshold. The minimum amount of energy that can be detected by a perceiver on the average

Hallucination. Perception in the absence of stimulation

Attention span. The number of elements that can be perceived in an instant

Constancy. The tendency to see an object as being the same under different conditions of stimulation

Transposition. The tendency to recognize common patterns in stimulus configurations made up of different elements

Concept. A set of abstracted properties

Categorization. The process by which input is identified with a concept

Cue. A stimulus which triggers off activity associated with a concept

Set. The expectancies produced by cues, other than those in the stimulus pattern being perceived, which affect the categorization of the stimulus pattern

Ambiguity. The arousal of mutually exclusive concepts by a stimulus pattern

Principles

1. The nervous system encodes the information provided by physical energy into nerve impulses.

2. The difference between nervous system activity involved in different sense modalities lies in *where* the activity occurs, not in the nature of the nerve impulses.

3. Variation in the intensity, dominant wavelength, and range of wavelengths of light tends to result in variations of perceived brightness, hue, and saturation, respectively.

4. Brightness, hue, and pattern vision depend on the state of the eye as well as the physical stimulus.

5. Variation in the frequency, amplitude, and complexity of sound waves tend to result in variations of pitch, loudness, and timbre, respectively.

6. Taste and smell depend both on the properties of the substances that reach the receptors of the tongue and the nose, and on the chemical state of the body.

7. Pressure, pain, and temperature receptors are dispersed throughout the skin and internal organs.

8. Receptors in the muscles and joints transmit information about the states of muscles and limbs to the brain. Receptors in the inner ear transmit information about the position of the body and its movement.

9. The amount of change that will be noticed (a just-noticeable difference) depends on the level of stimulation to which it is being compared.

10. The absolute-threshold quantity which emerges from an experiment depends on the type of task required of the perceiver.

11. Factors in the environment, such as intensity, contrast, and repetition, and factors inside the organism, such as motivation, determine the aspects of our environment to which we will attend.

12. Our perception of the environment at any given moment is divided into figure and ground. Stimulus characteristics such as continuity, proximity, similarity, inclusiveness, common fate, and contrast determine which stimuli are perceived as figure.

13. The organization of elements into figures increases the number of elements which can be perceived at a glance.

14. How sensory input will be perceived is determined by:

    (a) the input

    (b) the principles of figure-ground organization

    (c) the concepts which have been previously associated with the input

    (d) the set of the perceiver

    (e) on-going brain activity in the perceiver

    (f) the motives of the perceiver

15. Individuals may differ in their perception of a situation and not recognize the inadequacies of their perception.

16. Human development is characterized by improvement in sensory-motor adjustment, and by the development of increasing numbers of categories.

17. Training in perception does not improve general acuity but may improve discrimination of certain stimulus patterns.

Suggested Readings

One of the things that is touched only lightly in this chapter is what we know about the senses. For more information about them, read GELDARD, F. A., *The Human Senses.* New York: Wiley, 1953.

DEMBER, W., *Psychology of Perception.* New York: Holt, 1960. This very readable book picks up where Geldard leaves off and deals with the problems of measurement in perception, perceptual organization, learning and perception, set, motivational effects, and the relationship of stimulus complexity to curiosity.

ALLPORT, F., *Theories of Perception and the Concept of Structure.* New York: Wiley, 1955. One of the classic volumes of the last decade.

LEEPER, R., and P. MADISON, *Toward Understanding Human Personalities.* New York: Appleton-Century-Crofts, 1959. Perception as it relates to understanding personality is discussed in Chapter 6 of this book.

WITTREICH, W. J., "Visual perception and personality," *Sci. Amer.*, **200** (1959), 55–60. A readable account of studies showing that motivational factors influence the amount and sort of distortion experienced in certain perceptual demonstrations.

chapter 7

motivation

THE PHENOMENA OF MOTIVATION

THE DYNAMICS OF MOTIVATION

THE DEVELOPMENT OF MOTIVES

chapter 7   INDIVIDUAL DIFFERENCES

PRACTICAL APPLICATIONS

Each chapter of this book is a partial answer to the question, "Why do people act as they do?" In this chapter we will deal with one of the most important factors determining behavior—motivation.

Psychologists use the concept of motivation in conjunction with three basic characteristics of behavior:

(1) Variations in the *energy* with which an act is performed. Sometimes you walk briskly to your classes; other times you walk slowly and languorously. Sometimes you promptly get out of bed and are on your way in a few minutes, other times you require an hour before you are ready and on your way.

(2) Differences in the *direction* of behavior under the same conditions. Walking down the same street, sometimes you stop in a restaurant, other times in a bookstore, or at a movie, or at the home of a friend.

(3) Different degrees of *persistence.* If there is a magazine article you are interested in reading, sometimes you will check the corner newsstand, and if it is not there, you will forget it. Other times you will try several stores that sell magazines, go to the library and look it up, ask your friends whether they have a copy, or even write to the publisher for a back issue.

To account for the energy, direction, and persistence of behavior, psychologists have assumed that, at different times, our behavior is influenced by different motives. The word "motive" is derived from the Latin word *movere,* to move, and some of its original meaning is retained in the psychological use of the term. We shall define a *motive* as an expectancy of pleasantness or unpleasantness.* It is the activation of these expectancies by the situation which "moves" us into action.

How Can We Operationalize Affect and Motive?

Pleasantness and unpleasantness are aspects of personal feelings which cannot be observed directly in others. You, perhaps, know what the words refer to in your own experience, and one way of assessing affect (feeling) is by a person's report of his own feelings. Other behavioral signs of affect come from facial expressions such as smiling, weeping, and frowning. Finally, we can infer the feelings of affect produced by an object, by observing whether a person approaches or avoids it. Objects that give rise to pleasant feelings will be approached; those that give rise to unpleasant feelings will be avoided. An object that gives rise to pleasant feelings is called an *incentive* or *goal.*

We defined a motive as an expectancy of affect: pleasantness (sometimes called a positive affect) or unpleasantness (sometimes called a negative affect).

---

* All psychologists do not define the construct *motive* in the same way. We are following the definition of motive put forth by McClelland (1951). In addition to this definition, motives have been defined as the tendency to strive for goals (Tolman, 1951) or as any event which arouses the organism (Hebb, 1955). We include the characteristics of the other definitions as consequences of expectancies of affect rather than as definitions of motive.

A motive, of course, cannot be observed directly either. But when a stored motive is activated by a situation we can see its effects on behavior. We then say a person is motivated, or we speak of his *motivation*. Psychologists have developed a number of standard situations which they assume will activate the stored expectancies of affect into energizing and directing behavior. Let us look at some of them.

USE OF LEARNED BEHAVIOR IN A SITUATION. In Chapter 5, we introduced the construct of motive by referring to Blodgett's latent learning experiment. Here, rats made use of learned relationships when the incentive of food was introduced. In general, when a learned skill is used for the achievement of a goal, we can infer an expectancy of pleasantness from the achievement of that goal. The speed or vigor with which the learned response is performed and the frequency of performance are measures of the strength of the motive.

THE DIRECTION OF BEHAVIOR IN A CHOICE SITUATION. A rat can be placed in a simple maze with two goal boxes. In the left goal box there is food; in the right goal box, there is water. After a period of learning, the rat turns left when he is deprived of food and right after having been deprived of water. We infer that the rat chose the goal that was appropriate to his strongest motive, i.e. to his strongest expectancy of pleasantness.

Similarly, the motives of people have been studied by observing the kinds of choices they make. Sometimes they are asked to make real choices. Often people are asked to choose among a group of statements, each statement representing either a motive or a goal. From the pattern of choice, motives can be inferred.

PROJECTIVE TECHNIQUES. In our discussion of perception we mentioned that perception of unstructured stimulus situations will be affected by motivation. To reveal motives, subjects have been asked to interpret ink blots, tell stories about pictures, and add words to incomplete sentences. Themes which recur in the statement of a subject point to strong motives. These techniques for assessing motives are called projective because the respondent "projects" his motives onto the ambiguous stimulus material.

PERSISTENCE IN PURSUING A GOAL. A hungry rat will cross an electrified grid in order to obtain food. He persists despite the fear and the pain. This *obstruction* method is one way of assessing motive strength in animals. Seward and Seward, for example, used this technique to show that the motivation of a mother guinea pig to cross a barrier to reach her babies decreases as the age of her babies increases (Seward and Seward, 1940).

People have been observed as they perform a variety of tasks: puzzles, word games, mechanical repairs and social decisions. One measure of their affective expectancies is the persistence with which they continue despite the difficulty of the task, discouragement by others, distractions, and interruptions.

Using these methods, psychologists have sought to identify motives, assess relative motive strength, and determine how motives develop. First, let us look at the major human motives that have been identified and studied.

The Phenomena of Motivation

What Are the Major Human Motives?

A newborn baby has no motives. Expectancies of affect are built up from a person's experience with his environment. Since everyone's experiences are different, we would expect different people to have different motives. On the other hand, certain experiences will be felt as pleasant or unpleasant by almost everyone from birth. Eating food is pleasant to a hungry baby; drinking water is pleasant to a thirsty baby. A baby enjoys stroking, gentle movement, the taste of sweetness. A baby will show signs of displeasure with pain, with sudden falls, with the taste of bitter substances. These innate sources of affective feeling are the foundations on which motives are built. They set the stage for common learning experiences; for example, all people learn to expect pleasure from drinking water when they are very thirsty. However, learning experiences can be quite different in different cultures. Therefore we would expect greater similarity among the motives of people in the same culture than among the motives of people in different cultures. (The sight of a hissing snake will activate an expectancy of pleasure to hungry people in some cultures.) Finally, the unique experiences of an individual may give rise to unique motives.

Perhaps because some motives are common to all people, some to people within cultures, and some unique to individuals, it is difficult to present an exhaustive list of motives. We can, however, classify the motives psychologists have studied extensively into three categories: motives related to *physiological needs*, motives related to *interactions with other people*, motives related to competence and self.

MOTIVES RELATED TO PHYSIOLOGICAL NEEDS

In Chapter 3, we pointed out that the body must remain within a certain range with regard to concentration of substances in the blood, its temperature, its water content. Many of the processes that maintain the balance are automatic physiological processes. For example, when body temperature goes up, sweating, which is a cooling process, occurs.

Some physiological lacks give rise to physiological and psychological states which arouse the organism to an increase in general activity. A physiological need which leads to this aroused state is called a *drive*. When a newborn baby is aroused in this way, his general activity increases, but he shows no specific directed activity which reduces the drive state. He knows he is uncomfortable, but he does not know what to do about it; he has drives, but no motives.

Through his experience, he learns several things. First, he learns to differentiate between different drives. At different times, baby's aroused state is triggered off by hunger, by thirst, by the discomfort of wetness or coldness, or by pain. Each of these states is accompanied by stimuli peculiar to the particular drive as well as the general arousal common to all drive states.

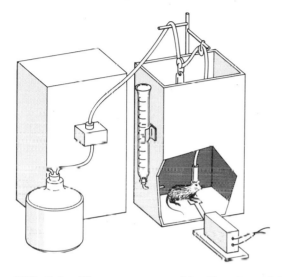

FIG. 7–1. The apparatus used by Epstein and Teitelbaum to investigate the relationship between hunger and stimuli in an organism's stomach. By pressing the lever, the rat injects food directly into his stomach via a tube which enters the skin at his head and goes under his skin to his stomach. He drinks water normally from the water bottle on the side. (After Epstein and Teitelbaum, 1962)

■ Our own experience suggests that the stimuli associated with hunger come from our stomachs. There is some experimental support for this. Shuford (1955) experimented with rats that were permitted to drink one of two equally sweet sugar solutions, sucrose and glucose. The two solutions differ in osmotic pressure, however. The amount that the rats drank depended on the osmotic pressure of the solution in their stomachs. The rats stopped eating (and presumably stopped feeling hungry) earlier when the osmotic pressure of the solution was greater. Another relevant study was done by Epstein and Teitelbaum (1962). They arranged an experiment in which rats could feed themselves by injecting food directly into their stomachs (see Fig. 7–1). In a short time, the rats regulated their feeding just as normal rats do. We assume that stimuli from the stomach were important cues to this regulation. These studies support the notion that stimuli from an organism's stomach affect the feeling of hunger; of course, the studies do not provide conclusive proof.

However, case studies of men whose stomachs have been surgically removed report that these men without stomachs can still feel hunger. Furthermore, animal studies show the importance of the brain in hunger and eating behavior. If an area near the ventromedial nucleus of a rat's hypothalamus is removed, the rat will stop eating. He will die unless he is fed artificially. If the ventromedial nucleus of the hypothalamus itself is removed, the rat will eat much more than normal, growing two to three times his normal size. This indicates that the hypothalamus contains two centers related to eating: a hunger center and a satiation center. It has been suggested that one of the events that influences hypothalamic activity in these two centers is the blood sugar level near the hypothalamus (Mayer, 1955). Another may be sensory information from the stomach.

The physiological studies of thirst and drinking have shown similar results. Feelings of thirst and drinking behavior are partially dependent on the wetness of the mouth and stomach (Adolf, 1940, 1941). However, the integrator of thirst and drinking activity is again in the hypothalamus. Electrical stimulation of the thirst center produces drinking. Moreover, if a salt solution is injected into the brain fluid of a goat, he will begin to drink, although he has just previously drunk until he was satiated. Thus a major source of information to the thirst center of the hypothalamus is the concentration of water in the brain fluid near the hypothalamus (Anderson, 1953). ■

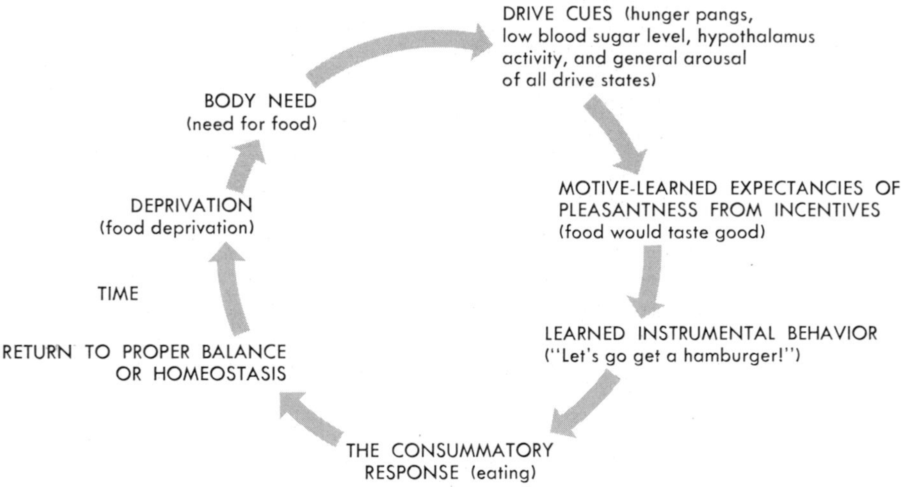

DRIVE CUES (hunger pangs, low blood sugar level, hypothalamus activity, and general arousal of all drive states)

BODY NEED (need for food)

MOTIVE-LEARNED EXPECTANCIES OF PLEASANTNESS FROM INCENTIVES (food would taste good)

DEPRIVATION (food deprivation)

TIME

RETURN TO PROPER BALANCE OR HOMEOSTASIS

LEARNED INSTRUMENTAL BEHAVIOR ("Let's go get a hamburger!")

THE CONSUMMATORY RESPONSE (eating)

FIG. 7–2. How behavior helps to maintain homeostasis. The diagram shows the general process and a specific example (hunger).

In addition to learning the cues peculiar to each drive, a baby learns the incentives which will reduce the drive and which give rise to a feeling of pleasantness. When a hungry baby has learned to expect food to be pleasant, he has learned a hunger motive.* Later, he learns the actions he must perform when he is hungry in order to acquire food. Thus in an adult, we can see the drive-motive cycle that helps to maintain the internal balance of the body (see Fig. 7–2).

Some physiological needs never go through this route because the needs are satisfied automatically. Most of us do not learn a series of actions to be performed whenever we feel suffocation, because we feel this way so rarely. Some

---

* We have been describing hunger as though it were a single motive. Actually, we should note that we have many specific hungers. For example, if salt is eliminated from an organism's diet, then even though he has just eaten, he will still feel hungry until he has received an adequate amount of salt (Richter, 1943).

needs are not provided for at all. We have no way of experiencing the presence of damaging x-rays and radioactivity; hence no drive states and no motives arise from their presence. But several basic human motives derive from learning to satisfy physiological needs: hunger, thirst, avoidance of pain, and extreme temperature.

MOTIVES RELATED TO INTERACTIONS WITH OTHER PEOPLE

From the beginning of our lives, we are social. We live with other people and we depend on them. A baby's first social relationships are with his parents. Then his sphere of acquaintances broadens, and he forms relationships with people of his own age (his peers). At maturity, a dominant aspect of his social life is his relationship to members of the opposite sex. Each of these relationships serves to form and to satisfy powerful social motives.

MATERNAL MOTIVES. The mothers of many species are equipped to take care of their infants. Mother rats build nests at the appropriate time, nurse their young, and retrieve their babies if they are separated from them. Much of this behavior is instinctive and is triggered by hormonal changes in the mother's body. As we look at animals higher on the phylogenetic scale, we see that maternal be havior is less and less stereotyped. While the physiological changes from child-bearing probably set up a drive state, a human mother's affective responses to her baby depend largely on *her* learning experiences as a baby and as a member of a culture.*

INFANT-MOTHER MOTIVES. A human infant cannot satisfy his physiological needs by himself. He needs his mother to feed him, to keep him warm, etc. As she provides all these things that are pleasing to him, her presence itself produces in the baby an expectancy of pleasure.

Recent studies in monkeys show that the affective feelings of the infant toward his mother arise from more than just her part in satisfying physiological needs.

■ Harlow (1958) studied newborn monkeys who were separated from their mothers within six to twelve hours after birth. These babies were then given two substitute mothers, one made of wood and sponge rubber and covered with terry cloth, the other made of wire mesh (see Fig. 7–3). Half the babies were bottle-fed through a nipple inserted in the wire "mother" and half through the cloth "mother," thus testing the importance of nursing versus the "feel" of the mother.

Harlow then observed the amount of time spent in contact with each "mother." The results were clear-cut. Even when the babies were fed from the wire mother, they spent most of their time huddled against the cloth mother.

If the baby monkeys were placed in a strange or frightening situation they first clung to the cloth mother; then they ventured out and explored. If the cloth mother were absent, the same

---

* Different maternal responses in different cultures were considered in Chapter 2.

situation produced frozen crouching, rocking, sucking, or other emotional behavior. The babies showed no constructive investigatory behavior.

The monkey's attachment to its cloth mother is not a temporary phenomenon. It persists. In fact, during the six-month duration of Harlow's observations the babies displayed the same attachment to the cloth mothers as other infant monkeys display to their real mothers. Apparently, then, the infant monkey's attachment to his mother is not just a matter of being fed, but is also related to other satisfactions, such as tactual stimulation. Harlow calls the feel—the warmth and cuddliness—of the cloth-mother surrogate *contact comfort*. As we have seen, contact comfort is not only an important source of pleasure, but also serves to reduce the fear of strange objects for the infant monkeys. ■

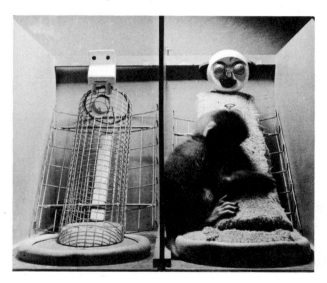

FIG. 7–3. The two artificial mother surrogates—one made of wire, the other of terry cloth—which Harlow used in his study. (Photo courtesy of Dr. H. Harlow)

It is interesting to see the effects of such affective infantile experiences on other social motives. Both the monkeys who were raised with the cloth-mother surrogates and the wire-mother surrogates *failed* to show normal sexual behavior, even when paired with experienced partners. This made it quite difficult to study the effects of a motherless infancy on maternal behavior. However, a few of the formerly motherless infants became pregnant. Those mothers who had known only cloth and wire dolls as "mothers" did not take care of their babies. They avoided them, pushed them away, and beat them savagely—so much so that the infants had to be separated from their mothers. (Harlow, 1961)

SEXUAL MOTIVES. In many ways the sexual motive resembles the motives related to physiological need. Changes in the organism lead to a restless drive state. There are specific cues associated with the drive which are integrated by a center in the hypothalamus (stimulation of this center in male monkeys will produce erection). The incentive is usually a member of the opposite sex; the consummatory act is intercourse; and the drive state is reduced.

The drives and responses associated with sex are partially under hormonal control. If the ovaries of a female rat are removed, she will no longer copulate. If the testes of a male rat are surgically removed, he will continue to mount and copulate for only about six months. Injections of the appropriate hormones in males and females will restore sexual behavior.

The higher an animal on the phylogenetic scale, the smaller the dependence on hormones. Castrated dogs continue to copulate for about two years. Case reports of human males and females show that in some cases castration does not decrease either desire or potency, in other cases there is a gradual decrease. Moreover, the higher an animal on the phylogenetic scale, the more significant the effects of learning on sexual behavior, and the less stereotyped the sex act.

FIG. 7–4. A monkey father taking care of an infant monkey. Such behavior is not uncommon among male primates. (Photo courtesy Dr. H. Harlow)

Although the sexual motive has many features in common with the motives that satisfy physiological needs, there are also several important differences. First of all, sexual satisfaction is not essential to the life of the individual. The continuation of the species, of course, depends on sex and reproduction, but any individual can survive without sexual satisfaction.

Second, the normal goal object for the sexual motive is another person. Among human beings and some of the other primates the sexual relationship between two individuals becomes the basis of an enduring social relationship. The two mates and their offspring become a family unit in which both father and mother care for and protect the child (see Fig. 7–4).

Finally, in most cultures, the expression of the human sexual motive is restricted in some way. There are mores which prohibit certain partners; e.g., most societies have taboos against incest, in many states of the United States

there are laws against homosexuality and sodomy. There are rules which prescribe the appropriate time for the sex act; e.g., premarital intercourse is prohibited by some religions and societies. Such pressures result in motive conflicts.
Considerable speculation surrounds the problem of what the specific effects are.
For example, the conflict between the sexual motive and society is the key factor
in personality development according to Freud's theory.*

PEER GROUP RELATIONS: THE AFFILIATION MOTIVE. As a child grows up his social
relationships broaden and he forms bonds with people of his own age. First, if
he is not an only child, he accepts his brothers and sisters; later on his classmates
and playmates become important. The social motives of an individual also
broaden to include motives for group acceptance, status, and perhaps leadership
and power. These motives may not be universal, and different people show
different motive strengths for them.

Recently there has been considerable experimental interest in the *affiliation*
motive. This term refers to the general expectancy of pleasantness from the
company of other people. A classic experiment by Schachter (1959) shows one
method of assessing the strength of the affiliation motive, one way in which the
affiliation motive may be aroused, and one source of individual differences in
motive strength.

■ College women reporting for the experiment were divided into two groups. One group was
assured that the experiment in which they were to participate was nothing to be afraid of and
involved no pain. The other group was shown some complex electronic apparatus which the
subjects were told would be used to deliver painful but harmless electric shocks. Both groups
were then told that there would be a delay before the experimental procedures would begin.
The subjects were given a choice between waiting alone and waiting in the company of other
subjects in the experiment. The actual experiment was over as soon as the subjects stated their
decision. The stated preference was taken as a measure of motive strength; those with more
strongly aroused affiliation motives would prefer company while waiting.

There was a significant difference in the two groups of women. A larger number of those in
whom an expectation of pain was aroused preferred to wait with other people than of those
who were assured the experiment would not be uncomfortable. ■

Schachter interprets this result as evidence that fear of pain arouses the affiliation
motive and directs behavior toward seeking the company of others.†

Schachter also acquired background data on all his subjects. When he
analyzed the choices of people under threat of pain, he found an interesting
difference in the backgrounds of those who preferred to wait alone from those

---

* We shall examine responses to frustration and conflict in Chapter 11.
† Further studies have shown that one reason anxious subjects choose to wait with
other anxious subjects is in order to compare their reactions.

who preferred to wait with others. First-born children—the oldest in the family or the only child—tended to choose waiting with other people more than later-born children. The reasons for this difference are not clear. Schachter has conjectured that perhaps parents are more sensitive to the fears and discomforts of their oldest children than they are to those of later-born children. This might develop a greater tendency in first-born children to expect relief from such discomfort by being in the presence of other people.

If this relationship between birth order, anxiety, and affiliation is a general one, we would expect that birth order would be related to other activities in which affiliation is an important component. Several studies from outside the laboratory support this relationship.

One way of thinking about an alcoholic is as a person who does not use the company of others to solve his problems. This would suggest that first-born children would be less likely to be alcoholics than later-born children. A study by Bakan (1949) shows that a significantly greater proportion of alcoholics are later-born children than would be expected by chance. On the other hand, we would expect a greater proportion of first-born children to use psychotherapy to handle their problems, since this involves the help of another person. Wiener and Strepner studied veterans who were receiving disability pensions for nervous disorders. They found that first-born veterans were more likely to go into psychotherapy and were likely to stay in treatment for a longer period than later-born veterans (Wiener and Strepner, reported by Schachter, 1959).

MOTIVES RELATED TO COMPETENCE AND SELF

For many years, theorists in psychology have been trying to encompass as much behavior as possible with the smallest number of basic assumptions. One of the most influential theories in experimental psychology (Hull, 1943, 1953) viewed all motivation as stemming from physiologically based drives, with social motives learned by association with physiological drives. Hull's theory was simple, elegant, and rigorous, but experiments in the fifties and sixties have suggested some difficulties in the Hullian conception. In particular, work with mice, rats, monkeys, and people indicates that some behavior can be most easily explained by assuming that stimulus change and opportunities to explore and manipulate objects in the environment themselves may serve as powerful incentives. We group these motives under the title *competence*, because their satisfaction increases an organism's competence to deal with his environment.

PERCEPTUAL INCENTIVES. What evidence do we have that a change in stimulation may serve as an incentive? In one study (McCall, 1965), the circuit of a Skinner box was hooked up so that each time a rat pressed a bar, a light in the box glowed for a few seconds. That was the only effect of pressing the bar. Still, the rate of bar-pressing for a light incentive was significantly greater than it was with no incentive. Similarly, McCall found that rats also press at a high rate to turn *off* continuous illumination. This indicates that the effective incentive is not the presence of light *per se*, but the change in illumination. Another series of studies has shown that monkeys will learn discrimination problems for the reward of opening a window which looks onto the experimental room (Butler, 1953).

If stimulus change is an important reward, what would be the effect of cutting off as much variation in stimulation as possible? This question was answered by a series of studies on sensory deprivation.

■ College students lay alone in rooms on cots with goggles or visors over their eyes which admitted only homogeneous light (see Fig. 7–5). Padding covered their arms and legs preventing change in tactual stimuli. An air conditioner and a fan or, in some experiments, earphones, provided a monotonous noise. These students were paid handsomely to remain in this situation for as long as they could. Yet few of them could tolerate it for more than eight hours. The subjects reported restlessness, inability to think clearly, and in some cases, hallucinations. These disturbances continued for about 24 hours after the students returned to normal conditions. Furthermore, some subjects in sensory deprivation were given the option of hearing an old stock market report as often as they requested. The subjects asked for the report over and over again. Any stimulus change at all was very desirable. (Heron, 1957) ■

All these studies point to the interpretation that the organism needs stimulus change for effective brain functioning, that he will seek stimulus change as he does any other goal, that sensory deprivation is an extremely unpleasant and disruptive experience.

A number of studies show that the incentive value of a stimulus depends not only on its novelty (the degree of change from previous stimulation), but also on stimulus *complexity*, the amount of variety in the pattern itself. Complexity

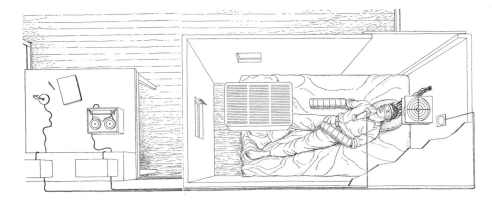

FIG. 7–5. The sensory-deprivation situation used in the experiments described by Heron. (From Heron, W., "The pathology of boredom," *Sci. Amer.*, January, 1957. Reproduced by permission.)

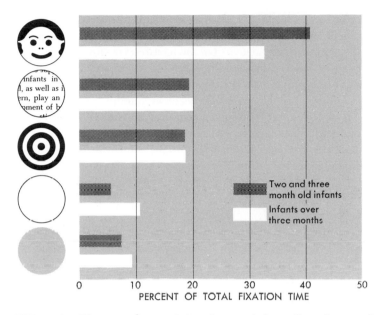

FIG. 7–6. The percentage of time human infants fixated on each of the patterns shown on the left. The striped bars show the results for infants under three months. The white bars show the results for children over three months. (Adapted from Fantz, R. L., "The origin of form perception," *Sci. Amer.*, May, 1961. Reproduced by permission.)

depends on the number of elements in a stimulus pattern as well as their dissimilarity from one another and degree of disorganization. The effect of complexity in attracting attention may be found even in infancy (see Fig. 7–6). Fantz (1958, a and b) found that both human and chimpanzee infants looked at a chessboard pattern rather than a colored square, and Berlyne (1958) similarly found that the first fixations of the eyes of three- to nine-month-old infants were likely to be on the most complex of four stimulus figures. Laboratory rats, too, show a preference for complexity. When part of a maze was painted in vertical black stripes, rats spent more time in it than in comparable sections painted all black, all white, or with horizontal stripes (Dember, Earl, and Paradise, 1957). Note that in none of the experiments cited were the complex figures "very complex."

EXPLORATION AND MANIPULATION. Closely related to the phenomenon of seeking stimulus change is the tendency for an animal to explore his environment and to investigate strange objects in it. If we place a rat in a T-shaped maze at the base of the T and allow him to enter one of the arms of the T, the chances are that if he is put back at the starting point, he will now enter the other arm of the T. This phenomenon is called *spontaneous alternation*. Or let us place a rat in a

box with an alcove and keep track of the time he spends in the alcove. We find
that the rat spends less time there on successive trials. Now, however, we put a
little toy block or other object in the alcove. On the next trial we find that the rat
spends a great deal of time in the alcove sniffing around the block. If we give a
chimpanzee a pair of objects and record the amount he manipulates and observes
them, we find that the time spent drops as he becomes familiar with them but
quickly rises when new objects are presented. Give a monkey a latch puzzle
which he can take apart and put together and he will do this for hours (see Fig.
7–7). Systematic studies (Berlyne, 1960; Harlow, 1950) along the lines we have
just described clearly suggest that animals and men have motives to explore
the environment, to find out "where things are" and "how they work."

FIG. 7–7. A monkey will take apart
and put together this latch puzzle over
and over again. (Courtesy of Myron
Davis and *Scientific American*)

COGNITIVE ORGANIZATION. As organisms seek change and investigate their environment, they learn the consistencies in it. Each organism develops conceptual or
cognitive expectancies of his world. The more complex the brain of the organism,
the more complex the cognitive representation of the environment. There is
some evidence that we have motives to maintain some consistency in our cognitive representation and that events which are inconsistent with our conceptual
expectancies are disturbing unless we can revise the framework to encompass
the new event.

Some animal observations show the effect of disrupting strongly established
expectancies. Hebb observed that monkeys become quite disturbed if they are
shown a monkey's head separated from his body. But the disparity between
expectancy and event need not be nearly this dramatic. One monkey showed
signs of great agitation when one experimenter entered the animal room wearing
another experimenter's coat! (Hebb, 1949).

■ Pavlov (1927) demonstrated a similar phenomenon using the classical conditioning procedure. The unconditioned stimulus was food, the conditioned stimulus was a circle, and the measured conditioned response was salivation. During the conditioning procedure, the dog was presented with ellipses (ovals) as well as circles, but the ellipses were never paired with food, whereas the circles were. The dog soon learned to discriminate between the circle and the ellipse; that is, he salivated only when he saw the circle. During the training, the ratio between the length and width of the ellipse was 2 : 1. Once the dog learned this discrimination, Pavlov tested the dog with a series of circles and ellipses in which the ellipses were made more and more circular. When the ratio between the length and width of the ellipse was 9 : 8, discrimination broke down and the dog salivated indiscriminately when he saw either the circle or the ellipse. But that was not the only change in the dog's behavior. Instead of standing still obediently, the dog growled and struggled to get out of the apparatus. He became unwilling to return to the experimental room. When confronted with a much easier discrimination (circle versus ellipse with a 2 : 1 ratio), he still salivated for both stimuli. The disturbance of the dog was so severe that Pavlov called it an "experimental neurosis." ■

Why was the dog so disturbed? He had never been punished for making an incorrect discrimination. But his conceptual expectancies were no longer applicable to the situation. He had learned to expect different results from the presentations of a circle and an ellipse. When he could no longer distinguish between them—when his cognitive organization broke down—he became quite upset.

Human beings also show evidence of seeking consistency in cognitive organization. For example, Festinger has shown that people cannot tolerate inconsistency between their beliefs and their actions, and may even distort their perception of reality in order to maintain consistent cognitive organization. For example, the evaluation of a report linking smoking and lung cancer differs according to the smoking habits of the reader. The heavier the smoker, the less likely he is to accept the evidence as valid (Festinger, 1957).

All these studies suggest that we seek consistency in our conceptual picture of the world, that a breakdown in this picture is disturbing, and that we will search for ways in which to reestablish cognitive harmony. Perhaps it is the motive for cognitive harmony that draws the scientist to construct a theory to put together many disparate experiments and the novelist to weave many elements of his experience into an organic whole.

ACHIEVEMENT MOTIVATION. Our motives to explore, to manipulate, and to organize enable us to satisfy another important motive, the motive *to do*. This motive has been studied by a number of experimenters under the name *achievement motivation.**

How can a motive as vague and poorly defined as achievement be assessed and studied? One of the most promising techniques for measuring such motives

---

* Some investigators define achievement motivation as "concern over competition with some standard of excellence." We are using achievement in a broader sense which does not necessarily require competition.

is a projective one. It involves the presentation of a number of pictures such as that in Fig. 7–8. Each picture is exposed for 20 seconds, and the subjects are asked to write a story about it. To ensure some uniformity in the stories, the subjects are asked to answer the following questions.

1. What is happening? Who are the persons?
2. What has led up to this situation? That is, what has happened in the past?
3. What is being thought? What is wanted? By whom?
4. What will happen? What will be done?

After four minutes, the next picture is presented and the same procedure is repeated. The test ordinarily consists of four to six pictures.

FIG. 7–8. A sample picture from the Thematic Apperception Test. Similar pictures in the test are used to measure achievement motivation (to maintain the value of the test as a diagnostic instrument, this picture is the only one of the series that can be reproduced). (Reprinted by permission of the publishers. From Henry A. Murray, *Thematic Apperception Test*, Cambridge, Mass.: Harvard University Press, copyright, 1943, by the President and Fellows of Harvard College.)

The scoring of the stories requires training but is highly objective. Trained scorers average better than 90-percent agreement. The score is found by categorizing the content of statements in the story. One category of the scoring is achievement. Content which suggests success, accomplishment, striving for goals would fall into this category. This projective achievement measure correlates with objective measures of achievement. For example, students scoring high in achievement motivation on the projective test do well in competitive tasks like solving anagram puzzles (Lowell, 1959).

There is some evidence that people who score low on the achievement motive do so not because they do not find achievement a pleasant goal, but because of a fear of failure which overrides the achievement motive. In one experiment (McClelland, 1958), students took part in a ring-toss game in which the contestants could choose how far they stood from the target. Those who scored high on the projective achievement measure tended to choose medium distances from the target; success was probable but certainly not a sure thing. Those who scored low on the achievement measure tended to choose distances either very far from or very close to the target. Atkinson interprets the behavior of the low achievers in this way: The low achievers were more concerned about the implications of their acts for themselves than about the task. If they stood very close to the target, they were sure to score well; if they stood very far away, they could not be blamed if they missed (Atkinson, 1957).

THE MOTIVE FOR SELF-ESTEEM. This type of analysis points to another strong motive, the motive for self-esteem. Part of our conceptual picture of the world is our own *self-image*, the way we see ourselves. We want to feel capable, worthy of respect and love. If we do not have this kind of positive image of ourselves, we will seek ways of enhancing our self-images even at the expense of realistic problem solving. As we saw in the ring-toss experiment, some people preferred either certain success or certain failure to a task that would be a challenge. Similarly Mahone (1960) reported that students who are anxious are more likely to choose vocations inappropriate to their interests than those who feel sure of themselves.

How do feelings of self-esteem or anxiety about one's self develop? One theory (Rogers, 1961) states that our self-images develop from the attitudes and behavior of others toward us. If parents respect and love their child unconditionally, the child learns to esteem himself without reservation or fear.

The Major Human Motives: a Summary

In our survey of the motives psychologists have studied, we have covered wide territory. We have gone from physiological motives whose arousal and satisfaction can be stated in precise neurological language to motives whose goals can only be vaguely specified as self-esteem or consistency in cognitive organization. You may be wondering, "Are all these motives equally important, or does one motive supersede all the others?" There is no simple overall answer to such

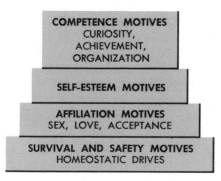

FIG. 7–9. This hierarchy of motives is similar to the hierarchy Maslow hypothesizes. The term *competence* for the highest level on the hierarchy was suggested by the work of White (1959).

a question. Obviously, there are individual differences. However, one theorist (Maslow, 1955) provides an interesting way of interrelating many human motives. He arranges the motives in a hierarchy, which we present in modified form in Fig. 7–9.

Maslow believes that the motives lowest in the hierarchy will be aroused first and must be satisfied or they will be dominant. However, once they are satisfied to a large degree, motives on the next highest level become the primary energizers and directors of behavior. This implies that the hungry man will not philosophize, and similarly, the lonely man will have difficulty respecting himself. However, after all other motives are satisfied, man will engage in activity for its own sake, giving him a comprehension of the world in which he lives and the skill to use his understanding to create something of value to himself.

What Roles Do Feelings Play in Motives?

In our review of the basic human motives, most of the evidence we cited came from observing the behavior of animals and men in relation to goals. But there is another dimension to the motivational experience: The feelings arising from various aspects of the motivational process are significant parts of our personal experience. When a stored motive is activated by the situation, subjects often report characteristic feelings. For example, deprivation of food and water results in feelings of hunger and thirst. Similarly, we suggest that the feeling of loneliness may be associated with the affiliation motive, boredom with the motive for stimulus change, and puzzlement with the motive for cognitive consistency.

As the behavior toward a positive goal or away from a negative goal is successful or unsuccessful, again our feelings may reflect the other events: We feel joy, contentment, and satisfaction or grief, depression, and anger. It is the affective aspect of these feelings, their pleasantness or unpleasantness, that serves to build up and strengthen our motives. For example, pleasantness of receiving a score of 100 on an examination may serve to strengthen the motive for academic achievement.

However, we must realize that our feelings do not always reflect our motives. Sometimes there are expectancies stored and aroused within us of which we are not aware. We many not realize that our behavior is directed toward a particular goal and our own behavior may puzzle us. Other times we have feelings of fear or joy which do not seem appropriate to the situation. All these facts point toward the existence of unconscious motives which nevertheless energize and direct our behavior.*

---

* We shall discuss some unique consequences of unconscious motives in Chapter 11.

EMOTIONS

Our subjective feelings are often accompanied by characteristic actions and physiological changes. For example, fear is characterized by withdrawal behavior and by a typical facial expression. We shall call a feeling which is normally accompanied by characteristic behavioral and physiological events *an emotion*. Fear, anger, and euphoria are three feelings that fall within the category of emotion.

Psychologists have studied fear and anger extensively. We shall look at these two emotions, the conditions that produce them, and the individual's response to them, in greater detail.

FEAR. Fear is the feeling associated with expectancies of unpleasantness. This may involve an expectancy of actual pain or it may involve an expectancy of distress of another sort, like a fear of failure or a fear of loneliness. Sometimes the basis of a fear is not understood by the person. Then we call the fear an *anxiety*.

However, there seem to be several other categories of events which produce the same feeling. Any sudden or great change in stimulation seems to arouse fear; for example, noise, loss of support, or intense flashes of light. Chimpanzees and human beings seem to have an unlearned fear of snakes; that is, they show signs of fear *the first time they see a snake*. This means that the fear cannot be based on an unpleasant experience with a snake. This fear does have some relation to learning, though. An infant chimpanzee who is frequently exposed to snakelike objects from birth will not show this fear. Thus the "unlearned" fear of snakes in adults depends on *not having* certain perceptual experiences.

Any great discrepancy between what an individual expects and what actually occurs seems to produce fear. In children, we see this phenomenon when, at the age of nine months, they show a fear of strange people. This fear gradually subsides as the youngster learns to expect the presence of people other than those of his immediate family. Again, the fear of strangers depends on learning, in this case the learning to recognize familiar people. Perhaps these fears are related to the motive for cognitive consistency.

The most prevalent source of human fear seems to depend on learned expectancies of pain or distress. In Chapter 5, we described Watson's demonstration of how such fears may be learned by classical conditioning. (Albert became afraid of a tame white rat when its presence was always paired with a loud unpleasant noise.)

The feeling of fear itself is exceptionally unpleasant, and the reduction of fear serves as a positive goal. When fear is associated with a particular cue, such as Albert's white rat, avoidance of the cue becomes a goal. Miller (1948) demonstrated this with an experiment on rats in a shuttle box similar to the one illustrated in Chapter 5.

■ The two parts of the shuttle box were painted distinctively; one section black and the other white. The experiment began with each rat being placed in the white compartment and given several brief electric shocks. No further shocks were given to the rats in any part of the experiment. Now a wheel was added to the white compartment. When this wheel was turned, a door opened which permitted entry into the black compartment. Each rat was again placed in the white compartment. Although the rats received no further shocks in the white part of the box, they quickly learned to turn the wheel which opened the door which allowed their escape. The learning and the performance of the rats were motivated by escape, not from pain but from fear-producing cues. ■

Interestingly, the fear—the learned expectancy of pain—is often more unpleasant than the unlearned avoidance of pain itself. When college students are given a choice between taking a shock immediately and postponing it, they prefer to take the shock immediately (D'Amato and Gumenik, 1960).

In general, the greater the pain originally experienced, the greater the fear. A study by Miller (1951) provides some evidence. Using the same shuttle-box technique described above, Miller subjected three different groups of rats to three different shock intensities in the first part of the experiment. He found that the rats who received the strongest shock learned to turn the wheel and escape the fastest. Those who received a weak shock did not learn to escape at all.

Evidence from outside the laboratory on this point is found in fear reactions of civilians who have experienced bombing raids. Those who develop the most fear during future raids are those who have had close calls, such as being knocked down by a blast or barely escaping from a collapsing building.

An important factor in determining the degree of fear experience is one's knowledge of when the painful experience will occur. If a warning signal regularly precedes the pain, general fear is much less. Dentists make good use of this principle by giving the familiar warning, "This is going to hurt a little." The relationship of uncertainty to fear in combat is illustrated in the following excerpt from a book about the U.S. Army in World War II.

■ "In combat, the individual soldier was rarely sure of what had just happened, what was going on at the moment, or what was likely to occur next. He was subject to continual distraction by violent stimuli, and lived always under the tension of expecting the unexpected. This kind of unceasing confusion—the lack of firm constants to which behavior could be oriented—exposed the individual to insidious anxieties. All people need some stability in their environment; it has been repeatedly shown that personality integration and the development of regularized patterns of behavior are strongly conditioned upon the existence of stable referents for activity. One of the prime functions of any sort of social organization is to provide the individual with a dependable set of expectations. Unless one knows, at least within broad limits, what behavior to expect from others, the very concept of adjustment becomes meaningless. So it is that the uncertainties and confusions of combat were themselves an identifiable source of stress." (From Stouffer *et al.*, *The American Soldier*, Vol. 2. Princeton, N. J: Princeton University Press, 1949. Reprinted by permission.) ■

TABLE 7-1

Fear Symptoms Reported by Troops in Combat Divisions*

Symptom	Percent of Men Reporting Occurrence of Symptom
Violent pounding of the heart	84
Sinking feeling in the stomach	69
Shaking or trembling all over	61
Feeling sick at the stomach	55
Cold sweat	56
Feeling of weakness or feeling faint	49
Feeling of stiffness	45
Vomiting	27
Losing control of bowels	21
Urinating in pants	10

* These data are from 2095 men who were in Division A, South Pacific. Data are in response to the following question: "Soldiers who have been under fire report different physical reactions to the dangers of battle. Some of these physical reactions are in the following list. How often have you had these reactions when you were under fire?" (From Stouffer *et al.*, 1949)

RESPONSES TO FEAR. The armed forces have been much concerned with the effect of fear on combat effectiveness. Studies of combat troops during the Second World War showed that men were not blamed by their fellow soldiers for being afraid, and that most men would readily admit that they experienced fear in combat. Despite such symptoms as those listed in Table 7-1, most men did not panic and performed their duties. Not only was this true of soldiers, who had been trained to withstand stress, but it was also true of civilians who were under intensive bombings. In spite of widespread fear reactions, overt behavior was usually well controlled. Most people continued their day-to-day work at their jobs, continued to look after their families, and took appropriate safety measures. Moreover, it seemed that individuals who had jobs to do were better able to withstand the stress of continued bombings than those without jobs. From these observations it appears that engaging in purposeful activity helps in the management of fear.

Another major factor determining reactions to danger is support from a group. Regardless of the degree of danger, reactions to bombing were calmer when a person went through the bombing with his family or some other group in which he felt emotionally secure than when he was alone or with strangers. Combat troops reported that one of the major helps in keeping going was the feeling that they could not let down the other men in their group. A soldier's pride in his group was positively related to his ability to stand combat stress.

Combat units with high morale had fewer noncombatant casualties than those with low morale (Stouffer *et al.*, 1949).

ELIMINATION OF FEAR. But how can the fear itself be eliminated? Since fears may be learned by a classical conditioning process, you might expect that they could be eliminated by extinction. Thus if an organism learned to fear a room in which he had been shocked, you might expect that the fear would dissipate after the shock was discontinued. However, extinction of a learned fear is not so easy to accomplish.

■ Solomon and Wynne (1953) trained dogs to avoid a shock by jumping from one compartment of a shuttle box to another as soon as a light came on. After 10 trials the shock was turned off, so that even if the animal remained in the "shock" compartment, he would feel no more shock. The experimenters expected that the avoidance behavior would eventually extinguish. So they continued to test the dogs for hundreds of trials. There was no *decrease* in avoidance behavior. For as long as the experimenters persisted in testing the dogs, the dogs continued to jump out of the compartment in which they had once been shocked. ■

Not all studies reported have shown that avoidance behavior is completely unextinguishable, but fears tend to be extremely persistent. One reason for this is that the organism's reaction to fear-producing stimuli is avoidance. If the cues associated with fear are avoided, then the organism has no opportunity to find out that the situation is now harmless. Solomon's dogs did not stay in the "shock" compartment long enough to find out that a shock no longer followed the light. If the animals had been forced to stay in the shock compartment for a period of time then, according to this analysis, the extinction procedure would have been more effective. Page and Hall (1953) found that the avoidance behavior of rats in the shuttle box extinguished more quickly when the rats were confined in the "shock" compartment for a few seconds for the first few trials of extinction. Presumably the forced confinement in the shock compartment enabled rats to find out that the fear-producing cues were no longer precursors of shock.

Jones (1924) describes a less drastic way of eliminating fear than forcing close and immediate contact with the fear-producing cues. A case study was brought to her attention that was reminiscent of Albert and the white rat.

■ A two-year-old boy named Peter showed great fear of white rabbits. The origin of the fear was unknown. Jones's procedure was to put the rabbit in the same room with Peter while the boy was happily engaged in some other activity such as playing with other children. The rabbit was caged and was a long distance from Peter. Peter showed few signs of fear in this situation. On succeeding days, Peter was placed in a high chair and fed his favorite foods, while the rabbit was brought closer and closer. After a number of such training periods, Peter not only ceased to show fear of the rabbit, but he even expressed fondness for it. Furthermore, he also showed interest in other strange animals—a phenomenon not seen previously in Peter. ■

Why did the fear disappear? The fear-producing cue was presented while Peter was engaged in a pleasant activity. The rabbit was originally far enough away that the mildness of the fear reaction did not interfere with the on-going activity. Thus fear of the rabbit at a distance was gradually extinguished. As the rabbit was brought closer and closer, it became more and more associated with pleasant rather than unpleasant feelings. This new association superseded the earlier association between the rabbit and fear.

ANGER. Anger seems to be almost universally aroused by frustrating situations, i.e., situations in which a person cannot reach his goals. In addition, there may be certain unlearned cues to anger. The typical reactions of cats and dogs to each other may be an example of this. Similarly, the infant whose arms are held tightly is likely to get red in the face, kick, struggle, and cry. This pattern appears to be a primitive version of the anger response. Observations of chimpanzees indicate that signs of timidity on the part of another chimpanzee evoke the attack response as does the sight of an anesthetized animal at a distance. One should remember, however, that anger in these animal studies has been operationally defined as the attack response, and while this is convenient terminology to apply to animals, it is not completely comparable to the operations used in our definition of anger in human adults.

It has been suggested that the degree of anger evoked in a situation seems to be a function of the strength of the motive whose satisfaction is blocked and of the individual's expectation that the motive will be satisfied (Dollard *et al.*, 1938). In addition, both the degree of anger and the ease with which it is elicited are dependent to some extent on the hormone level of the body. Increasing the level of testosterone (a male sex hormone) increases the tendency to react aggressively.

The feeling of anger is accompanied by a definite behavioral pattern in children. Angry children kick, stamp, jump up and down, throw themselves on the floor, hold their breath, pull, struggle, pout, frown, throw things, grab, bite, hit, scream, and attack the frustrating object. While no one child displays all of these symptoms in a single temper tantrum, they are recognizable as belonging to the same emotional pattern. One of the major tasks of socialization is training in the management of anger and aggression. Parents expend a great deal of time and energy in teaching us not to strike other people when we are angry. We learn to express anger in words rather than actions. Furthermore our culture provides many opportunities for people to "blow off steam" in socially acceptable ways. This is certainly one of the functions of sports. Wit, fantasy, competition, and muscular activities may also act as tension releasers. Everyone meets frustrations, and the expression of anger and aggression is severely limited by the culture. Thus anger and the motives opposing its expression are a major topic of psychological study. More complex methods of dealing with feelings of fear and anger will be discussed in Chapter 11, "Frustration."

The Dimensions of Feeling

Human feelings have many subtle shades and nuances. The number of words in our dictionary referring to different feelings is enormous. Psychologists have wondered whether there is any simple way to classify them. One way of getting public information about private feelings has been to study responses to facial expressions.

We usually think that it is quite easy to judge what emotion is being expressed by a facial expression. However, sometimes it is quite difficult to make accurate judgments when the context of the expression is unknown (see Fig. 7–10). It is interesting that more people can agree on the emotional meaning of a facial expression when it is posed by an actor than on the same emotion portrayed by a candid photograph. This is not surprising since the actor has trained himself to use facial expression and gesture as a means of communication.

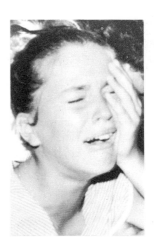

FIG. 7–10. What are the feelings of each of these girls? Turn to page 527 to see the situations in which the girls are expressing their feelings. (Adapted from Wide World Photos)

How have photographs posed by actors been used to study feelings? Several studies have shown that students are able to classify the emotions expressed by photographs with a considerable degree of accuracy (Feleky, 1922; Schlosberg, 1941). In Schlosberg's study there were six categories: (1) happiness, (2) surprise, (3) fear, (4) anger, (5) disgust, and (6) contempt. One of the interesting results was that when errors of classification were made, they were not made randomly, but followed a definite pattern; e.g., surprise was sometimes confused with fear and anger, but never with love or disgust. This suggested that some feelings are more alike than others, that perhaps by arranging feelings according to similarity, the dimensions of feeling could be deduced. Schlosberg studied the patterns of error and sorted out feelings so that they could be arranged along three dimensions: (1) pleasantness-unpleasantness, (2) intensity, (3) the degree of interest or rejection. Then he asked a new group of subjects to judge the same photos. This time they were not supposed to name the feeling expressed but to judge where the photo would fall along the three dimensions. The actual positions selected by the subjects correspond closely to the theoretical positions assigned by Schlosberg which he obtained by studying errors of judgment (see Figs. 7–11 and 7–12). More recent work indicates that only two dimensions are needed to describe underlying differences between judgments of facial expression: pleasantness-unpleasantness and intensity.

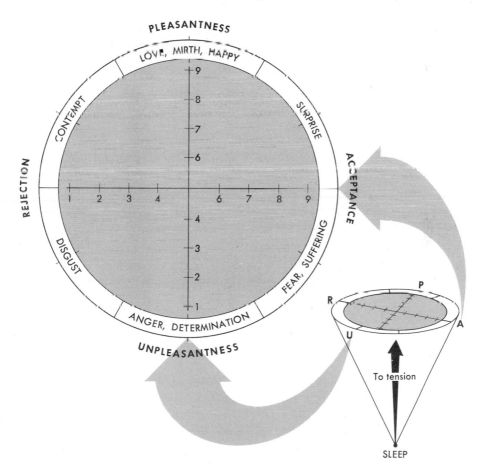

FIG. 7–11. The three-dimensional model of feeling hypothesized by Schlosberg and its relation to names given to feelings, such as surprise and disgust. (After Schlosberg, 1952)

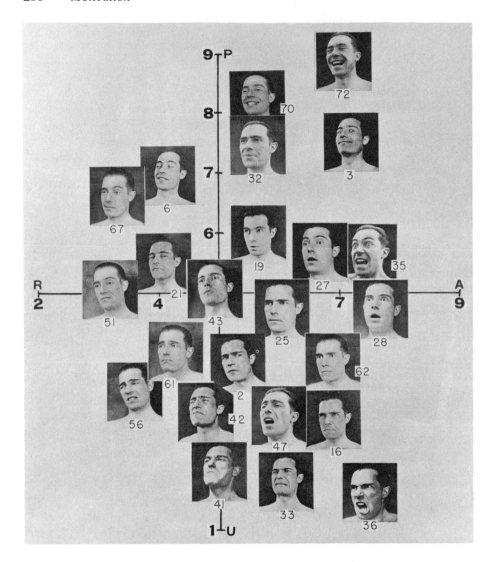

FIG. 7–12. Schlosberg created this graph by plotting the errors in judgment made by subjects guessing the emotions being expressed. The photos are positioned on pleasantness-unpleasantness and acceptance-rejection dimensions. The greater the errors in judgment, the closer to the center of the graph the photos are placed. (Schlosberg, 1952)

When people judge the characteristics of feelings portrayed by photographs, they must use their own feelings of similar experiences as a guide. Thus the facial expression data provide a clue to private feelings. We can suggest, then, that two important dimensions of our personal feelings are intensity and affect.

What Are the Physiological Bases
of Motives and Feelings?

We have discussed two parallel kinds of events: First, on a behavioral level, we are able to infer motives from the kinds of goals, positive and negative, the organism seeks and avoids. The strength of the motive is inferred from the degree of arousal of the organism and the persistence of his behavior. Second, from people's judgment of facial expressions we find that people distinguish a variety of the feelings that they themselves have experienced on the basis of the intensity of the feeling and of whether it is pleasant or unpleasant. Finally, we can take the two dimensions that we have looked at both behaviorally and introspectively and study their physiological basis. What are the physiological accompaniments of the feelings of pleasantness one obtains upon reaching a goal? What are the physiological aspects of arousal which can accompany the activation of strong motives and intense feelings?

A POSSIBLE PHYSIOLOGICAL BASIS FOR AFFECT

In Chapter 3, we mentioned that the hypothalamus is associated with motivation, and that electrical stimulation can produce eating, drinking, sexual behavior, or behavior that seems to reflect fear and rage. Two psychologists wondered whether the effects of electrical stimulation could be studied just like any other incentive.

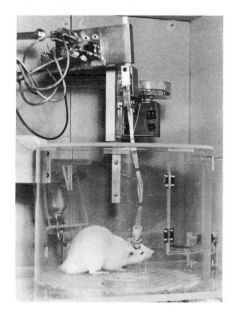

■ Olds and Milner (1954) implanted electrodes into many of the subcortical areas of rats' brains. Then they placed the rats in a Skinner box and arranged the circuit so that each time a rat pressed the bar, he administered to himself a minute electrical impulse for about half a second (see Fig. 7–13). The results with some electrode placements were quite startling. The animals pressed the bar for electrical stimulation at higher rates than for any other known incentive, sometimes as high as 5000 times an hour. They ignored food, water, mates—they just pressed the bar until they collapsed from exhaustion. When they recovered, they resumed bar pressing. ■

FIG. 7–13. This rat can press a bar to either deliver, or prevent delivery of, a minute electrical impulse to certain areas in his brain. The apparatus shown here is similar to that used by Olds and Milner (1954) to study effects of electrical stimulation. (Photo courtesy of Dr. J. Olds)

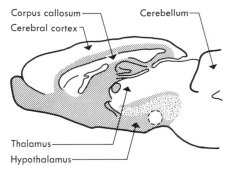

FIG. 7–14. The areas of the brain for which rats seek either to receive or to avoid electrical stimulation. Rats will press a bar at a very high rate in order to receive stimulation in the area shown by striped shading. They will also press a bar to avoid stimulation in the area shown by dotted shading. (After Olds, 1958)

Figure 7–14 shows the areas (shaded) in which high self-stimulation was discovered. As you can see, the septal area is one of the areas in which the animals stimulated themselves at high rates. It is located immediately in front of the hypothalamus.

Olds (1960) wondered whether self-stimulation rates would vary with motivation. He tested some animals who were hungry, others who had been castrated.

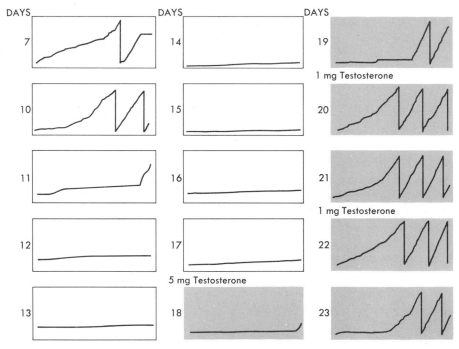

FIG. 7–15. The effect of testosterone levels on self-stimulation in an area near the hypothalamus. The animal was castrated seven days prior to the day of the first record. The records are cumulative response curves of the type discussed in Chapter 5. As you can see, bar pressing falls to almost zero two weeks after castration, but climbs again to a high rate following injections of the male hormone, testosterone. (After Olds, 1960)

He found that self-stimulation rates in certain areas of the hypothalamus did vary with these manipulations (see Fig. 7–15).

Olds infers that when the brain centers indicated in Fig. 7–14 are stimulated, the rats feel pleasure and that self-stimulation areas are those that are active when we feel pleasure as a result of normal events. The hunger and castration data suggest that different motives may be associated with different "pleasure centers."

Have similar centers been located for negative affect? In a series of studies, Miller and his colleagues have shown that animals will avoid mild electric stimulation to certain brain areas just as they would avoid a painful stimulus (Miller, 1958; Delgado, Roberts, and Miller, 1954). The negative areas are illustrated in Fig. 7–14.

Although it is impossible to know what an animal feels during stimulation of his brain, these data do suggest that the feelings, pleasure and pain, are associated with subcortical areas in the brain.

THE PHYSIOLOGICAL BASIS OF AROUSAL

When we look at someone and say he is excited, we infer his aroused state from many characteristics: a flushed face, sweaty palms, rapid breathing, tensed muscles. These signs are behavioral manifestations of an active sympathetic nervous system.* Sympathetic nervous system activity speeds up the heartbeat. It causes the liver to release sugar into the blood stream, and this permits greater energy to be used. It causes the blood to clot more quickly so that wounds will be less damaging. It stimulates the thyroid gland so that metabolism is increased; breathing rate and muscular tenseness increase.

An additional result of sympathetic nervous system activity is an increase in the secretion of epinephrine from the adrenal glands. As we pointed out in Chapter 3, epinephrine circulating through the blood has the same effect as the sympathetic nervous system, thus augmenting the nervous system messages.

In the aroused organism, there are also changes in brain activity. The activity of the reticular formation of the brain increases, thus bombarding the cortex with nonspecific activity. It is interesting that an injection of epinephrine into the blood supply near the reticular formation will have the same effect.

All these physiological changes produce an organism which is aroused for sudden and violent action, both physically and mentally.

IS THE AROUSAL PATTERN ACCOMPANYING MOTIVES AND FEELINGS ALWAYS THE SAME?

We have seen that there is a common physiological pattern associated with emotions and activated motives. But is this pattern always the same for everyone under all conditions?

---

* The sympathetic branch of the autonomic nervous system was introduced in Chapter 3, pp. 63–64.

A number of investigators have suggested that individuals differ in the degree to which autonomic functions are activated in motivating situations. Regardless of the source of arousal, some people respond with more activation of some sympathetic functions than others. Thus one person may tend to show a much accelerated heart rate, but little change in breathing during a variety of arousing situations. Others may show greatest change in blood pressure or muscle tenseness. Still others show no consistent pattern (Lacey, Bateman, and Van Lehn, 1952, 1953).

Other investigators have tested the hypothesis that different *sources* of arousal will produce differences in the physiological arousal pattern. We mentioned in Chapter 3 that anger and fear reactions seem to be related to similar but different hormones secreted by the adrenal gland; fear is associated with epinephrine and anger with norepinephrine (see pp. 62–63). Mandler and his colleagues (1961) have recorded different physiological patterns from subjects with anxiety about sex and from those with anxiety about aggression.

Despite this evidence for a degree of physiological differentiation between sources of arousal there are enough common elements that we can still properly speak of a basic physiological arousal pattern. In fact, there is some evidence that when we feel aroused, we will label the arousal with the emotion which is appropriate to the situation. Here is an experiment which demonstrates this phenomenon:

■ Seven groups of subjects agreed to participate in a drug experiment. The subjects in each of the groups were then given an injection of epinephrine. Groups I and II (the informed groups) were told that the drug would have the side effects of increased heartbeat, tremor, and flushing. Groups III and IV (the ignorant groups) were told nothing about side effects. Group V (the misinformed group) was told that the side effects of the drug were numbness and placidity. Groups VI and VII were given placebos.

After these instructions and the injection, each subject was asked to wait in a room for the remainder of the experiment. Each subject was met in the waiting room by someone who was presumably another subject, but who was actually working for the experimenter. For groups I, III,

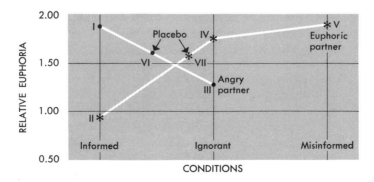

FIG. 7–16.   The amount of euphoria reported by the seven groups (see text above) in the experiment of Schachter and Singer. (After Schachter and Singer, 1960)

and VI, the confederate expressed anger and hostility, criticizing the experimenter and the experiment. For groups II, IV, V, and VII the confederate acted joyfully euphoric, flying paper airplanes, playing with equipment, etc. Each subject was observed and scored for the degree to which he joined the confederate in angry or euphoric behavior. Then the students filled out a questionnaire in which they reported their feelings of happiness and irritation. They were then told the purpose of the experiment. The results from the questionnaire are plotted in Fig. 7–16. As you can see, the feelings of the misinformed groups and the ignorant groups tended to be much more influenced by the behavior of the confederate than those of the informed groups. Also plotted in this figure are the reports of two groups who were given a placebo of salt water rather than epinephrine. You can see that they were less influenced by the confederate than the ignorant groups, who received epinephrine. (Schachter and Singer, 1962). ∎

Schachter and Singer interpret their results in this way. When we feel the concomitants of arousal, we search for a possible cause. Those subjects who had been told of the true effects of the drug could thus attribute their aroused state to the drug. Those who did not know the effects of the drug interpreted their aroused state in terms of the situations in which they found themselves. Those with a euphoric partner interpreted their own arousal as euphoria; those with an angry partner interpreted their own arousal as anger.

The Phenomena of Motivation: an Integration

The phenomena we have just presented reveal what a complex construct *motive* must be. In the brain are stored many expectancies of affect, ranging from expectancies of pleasantness from food to expectancies of unpleasantness from an inconsistent view of the world. These expectancies are activated by the

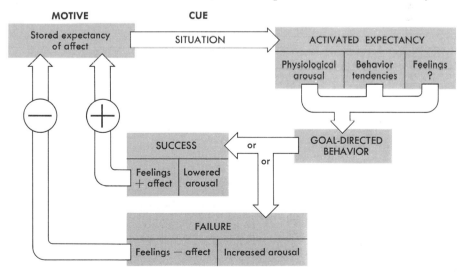

FIG. 7–17.   The hypothesized events in the arousal of a stored motive and the subsequent satisfaction of this motive or its nonsatisfaction.

situation, either inside the organism, as in thirst, or outside the organism, as in sensory deprivation. The activated expectancy consists of several components: often, but not always, it is accompanied by a feeling reflecting the motive; at the same time the physiological arousal pattern appears, probably in proportion to motive strength; finally, learned, and perhaps some unlearned, actions are performed in relation to the aroused feelings and to the appropriate goal. The effects of success or failure in achieving the goal are also complex. First, success is usually accompanied by pleasant feelings; failure, by unpleasant ones. These feelings provide feedback to the stored expectancy. Pleasant results will increase the expectancy of pleasantness; unpleasant results bring about the expectancy of unpleasantness from the situation. The physiological arousal pattern will also change; especially with failure, which may produce a new increase in arousal, along with feelings of perhaps anger or fear. We can summarize these relationships as shown in Fig. 7–17.

The Dynamics of Motivation

If we observe the behavior of the people around us and think of the motivation for their behavior, we are almost sure to be struck by the fact that a person has a number of motives, and that his behavior varies from time to time depending upon what motive is activated. Thus the college man may devote himself wholeheartedly to his date on Friday and Saturday, and on Monday be almost as intent on a chemistry experiment. His behavior suggests that different motives are influencing his behavior in different situations. Another man in the same chemistry class spends most of his time moving around the class visiting other students. Apparently, his motives differ from those of the more serious students. What causes a particular motive to become active? What accounts for the strength of activated motive? How does motive strength affect performance? These are basic questions in the dynamics of motivation.

Which Motives Will Be Activated?

Our first problem is that of selection of motives. Each of us has many stored motives. Why is it that some are called into action in a particular situation while other important motives may have little influence on our behavior in this situation? Two major factors determine which motives are called into play: stored motive strength and cues in the situation.

STORED MOTIVE STRENGTH. A situation may include cues to several motives. Some motives are so strong that they tend to be elicited even though there are cues for other motives in the situation. Thus a person may be motivated to study a book even in a crowded snack bar where there are cues to many other important motives. One important determiner of the strength of a motive is the proportion of previous times that a change in affect has occurred in this situation. A child who has been rewarded many times for getting A's is more likely to be motivated for school work than the child who has seldom been rewarded for high grades. Similarly, the child who is generally rewarded for learning new things is likely to develop a stronger motive for knowledge than the child who is frequently scolded for asking foolish questions.

A second determiner of the strength of a motive is the degree of change of affect which has previously occurred. Suppose, for example, that we are dealing with the learning of the achievement motive. When the child gets good grades his parents reward him with approval. The greater their joy at his achievement, the stronger his achievement motive is likely to become.

THE ROLE OF CUES. Cues play a threefold function in the activation of motives. First of all, they activate the stored expectancies of affects. The activating cues may be either in the external situation or in the organism. For example, the announcement that a test is to be given in the next hour may act as a cue for the individual's achievement motive, while a phone call from a pretty girl may act as the cue for affectional or social motives. Both of these are external cues. On the other hand, the hunger motive may be elicited either by stomach contractions or by the sight of some favorite food—the first is an internal cue; the second, external.

The cues which elicit a motive are those which in previous experiences have preceded or accompanied pleasure or unpleasantness. Thus stomach contractions or the sight and smell of food arouse the motive for eating because time after time the pleasure of eating has followed stomach contractions and the sight and smell of food.

Second, the cues from the situation provide information about the *probability* of reaching the goal of the motive in this situation. Generally, the more cues in the situation related to motive satisfaction, the greater the perceived probability of reaching it. Thus the probability of eating dinner is high when there is food in sight, when one hears the call "Dinner!" and when one is also

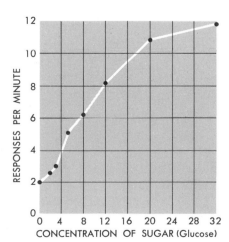

FIG. 7–18. The effect of sugar concentration on bar pressing in rats. The greater the concentration of the sugar, the higher the bar-pressing rate. The differences in performance in situations that reward with low and high concentrations may be attributed to differences in the aroused motives produced by the attractiveness of the reward. (After Guttman, 1954)

stimulated by hunger pangs. An illustration of this factor is the phenomenon that under certain conditions the closer one comes to a goal the stronger his motivation. A rat will run faster as he approaches the end of a maze. Similarly, the study behavior of students is an example of their increasing motivation for grades as the grading period approaches. This increase in motivation as one approaches a goal is called a positive *goal gradient*. In terms of the factors we have discussed, we can see that the closer one comes to a goal, the more cues to the goal are present, and the more closely these cues have been associated with change in feeling. Thus the activated motive becomes stronger.

Finally, cues provide information about the amount and quality of the incentive. The greater the incentive, the stronger the aroused motive. A dollar reward will produce a more motivated person than a penny reward. See Fig. 7–18 for a similar phenomenon in rats.

The Activation of Motives: a Summary

We have theorized that three factors affect the strength of activated motives in a situation: First, stored motives of different strengths are brought by the individual to the situation. One or more of these stored motives will be activated by cues. Second, the perceived probability of reaching the goal of the motive is cued by stimuli in the situation, and third, the expected amount of satisfaction from reaching the goal is aroused in the individual by cues. Thus the strength

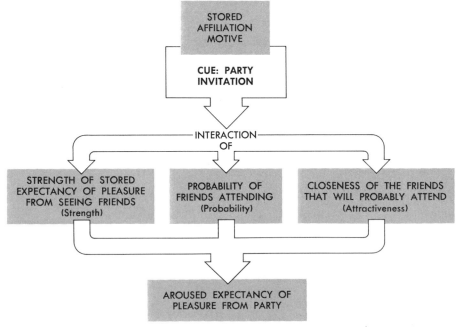

FIG. 7–19. The interaction between the stored motive and the situation, which results in an aroused motive.

of an aroused motive depends on an interaction between stored motives in the organism and the cues in the situation.

A specific example using the affiliation motive is diagrammed in Fig. 7–19.

How Do Motives Affect Performance?

MOTIVE STRENGTH AND THE EFFICIENCY OF PERFORMANCE

We noted earlier in this chapter that the use of learned skills to reach a goal is one indication of an activated motive. Now we may ask: What is the relation of the strength of the activated motive to the efficiency of performance? Will the hungriest rat run fastest in a maze? Will the man with the highest achievement motivation be the most efficient in solving problems?

The answers to these questions depend upon two factors: the degree of arousal associated with the activated motive and the complexity of the task to be performed. Mild arousal tends to improve performance. It increases muscle tension via the sympathetic nervous system and cortical activity via the reticular formation. However, high arousal is disruptive to purposeful activity. The symptoms of arousal draw attention to themselves and distract the person from his task.

The more difficult the task, the greater the disruptive effects of high arousal. Complex tasks require close attention, which is impossible when the effects of arousal are dominant.

■ These relationships between strength of motivation, task complexity, and performance are illustrated by an experiment done by Broadhurst (1957). He trained rats to swim underwater

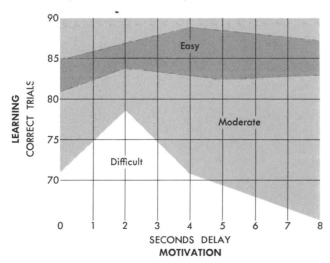

FIG. 7–20. The effects of different levels of motivation on efficiency in learning to solve easy, moderate, and difficult problems, as determined by Broadhurst's experiment. (After Broadhurst, 1957)

through a maze for the reward of getting out of the water. The maze was Y-shaped, and after the choice point, the rat was confronted by two doors. The door which led out of the water was indicated by a light. The difficulty of the task was varied for different groups of rats by varying the intensity of the light from dim, to moderate, to bright. The dimmer the light, the more difficult it was for the rat to discriminate the illuminated door from the dark door. The rats' motivation was varied by their being submerged for a period of 0, 2, 4, or 8 seconds prior to swimming the maze. Broadhurst's results appear in Fig. 7–20. As you can see, when the problems required easy and moderate discrimination, higher motivation led to faster learning. However, when difficult discrimination was required, both low and high motive strengths led to less efficient learning than medium levels. ■

These results in the rat study are reminiscent of the results found in the studies relating anxiety to performance in human beings, which we described in Chapter 1. There we saw that high anxiety led to the best performance in a simple task, but that moderate levels of anxiety led to the best performance in complex tasks.*

MOTIVES AND THE SELECTION OF BEHAVIOR

We have already spoken of the dangers of invoking a special motive, or an instinct, for each act we want to explain. This leads to two generalizations:

1. A motive can determine many acts. For example, the achievement motive can influence studying hard, seeking opportunities to compete, etc.

2. An act can be determined by many motives. Studying hard can be influenced by achievement motivation, motivation for approval, motivation for prestige, etc.

Not only is the relationship between type of motive and type of act complex, but also the relationship between strength of motivation and behavior is not as simple as it may at first seem. In general, it is true that the stronger his motivation, the more active the person becomes and the harder he works to achieve his goal. But because the manner in which we satisfy motives is learned, in some cases increased motivation may not result in increased activity. The strongly motivated fisherman, for example, may learn to be very still when a fish approaches his bait, even though the sight of the fish increases his motivation. In addition, increased motivation may not produce increased effort when the situation has elicited both motives for approach and motives for avoidance. Generally, we speak of motives associated with tendencies to approach a goal as positive motives, while motives to avoid an object or situation are called negative motives. Let us look at these two types of motives in more detail.

One of the important reasons for distinguishing positive and negative motives is that they affect behavior differently. A person who has a strong desire for affiliation and a person with a strong fear of rejection will both be more highly

---

* See pp. 14–15.

motivated in a group than the person with little affiliation motivation. But the individual with the positive motive is much more likely to attempt to attract attention than the one who fears rejection, while the individual who fears rejection will be more likely to conform to group norms and to avoid being different. We have already discussed similar differences in the positive achievement motive and its negative counterpart, fear of failure.

Another important way in which the two classes of motives differ is in their change of relative strength the closer one gets to the goal. Positive and negative motives ordinarily differ in the *rapidity* with which they become stronger. If, for example, a student needs to prepare for an examination but finds the subject matter boring, the positive motive is stronger as he plans his evening work; however, as he gets closer to actual studying the negative motives become relatively stronger and stronger, so that he thinks of other things to do instead of studying. The strength of negative motivation shows a sharper increase close to the goal than does the strength of positive motivation or, in other words, the gradient is steeper.

FIG. 7–21. A harness apparatus such as this was used by Brown to test strength of approach and avoidance. (Photo courtesy of Dr. Neal E. Miller)

■ This phenomenon has been demonstrated with rats. Brown (1948) trained one group of rats to run down an alley to receive food in a goal box. He trained another group of rats to escape from a goal box, in which they were shocked, by running down an alley. Then he tested the strength of approach in the first group and the strength of avoidance in the second group. He did this by attaching a harness to the rats (see Fig. 7–21) and measuring the strength of their pull either toward or away from the goal box. He took measurements at several points in the alley. As might be expected, the closer the rats in the first group were to the goal box in which they had been fed, the harder they pulled toward it. Similarly, the closer the rats in the second group were to the goal box in which they had been shocked, the harder they pulled to get away from it. However, as can be seen in Fig. 7–22, the slope of the avoidance gradient is steeper than the approach gradient. That is, close to the goal, the avoidance tendency increases more sharply than the approach tendency. ■

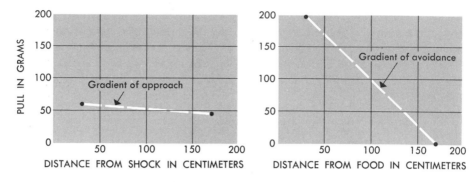

FIG. 7–22. The relationship between the strength of pull and the distance from the goal box in the approach and avoidance situations. (After Brown, 1948)

Another characteristic of negative motives is that their extinction is slower than that of positive motives. To try to overcome a child's fear is a more difficult task than to get him to dislike something he has previously liked. The reason for this is also fairly clear. When a positive motive is involved, the individual continues to get to the goal and has many chances to find that it is no longer satisfying. Since negative motives, however, are associated with avoidance of the goal, the negatively motivated individual is unlikely to find out that the goal is no longer unpleasant. We described experimental demonstrations of this phenomenon in our discussion on extinguishing avoidance behavior. We see a practical application of this principle with farmers using electric fences. Many farmers have found that after a period of use it is no longer necessary to keep current in the fence because once animals have learned to avoid it, they are unlikely to learn that it no longer shocks.

SUMMATION AND CONFLICT. When two or more motives may be satisfied by the same goal, their strength is summated. For example, a student may work harder to get a good grade if the grade will not only satisfy his achievement motivation but also bring his grades up to the level needed to get into a fraternity, thus helping satisfy his affiliation motivation.

Since more than one motive may be elicited in the same situation, it is apparent that motives will sometimes conflict. Psychologists have distinguished three types of conflict; these are illustrated in Fig. 7–23. When a child has to decide whether to spend his money for a whistle or a candy bar, he is experiencing an approach-approach conflict. Another type of conflict the child may experience is that between two negative avoidance motives, such as washing his face or getting punished. In the approach-approach conflict, the child usually makes a choice and the conflict is ended, for he no longer has any money with which he might buy something else; in psychological terms, the cues to the conflict are removed by the choice.

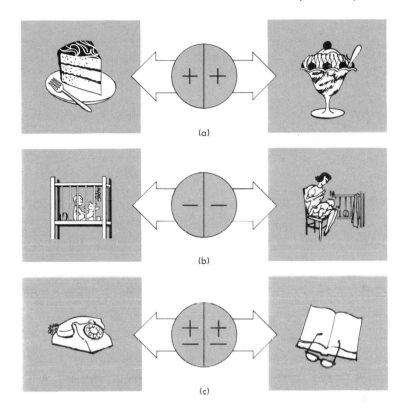

FIG. 7–23. Examples of three types of conflict: (a) Approach-approach: choosing between desserts in a restaurant. (b) Avoidance-avoidance: choosing between remaining confined or being spanked. (c) Approach-avoidance: choosing between a social evening and failing an examination or a dull evening of study. (This might be called a double approach-avoidance conflict since each choice has both attractive and repulsive elements.)

The avoidance-avoidance conflict may be resolved in the same manner. However, in these conflicts there is also a strong tendency for the individual to try to avoid both unpleasant activities by doing something else. When the person makes a choice in avoidance-avoidance situations, then the closer he gets to the unpleasant consequences he has chosen, the more unpleasant it seems. At the same time as he gets farther from the other alternative it seems less unpleasant. Thus, if he cannot escape from the situation he is likely to vacillate between the two choices.

One of the most difficult conflicts to resolve is that involving one or more objects which arouse both negative and positive motives. As we have seen, such a combination of positive and negative feeling is called *ambivalence*. To an adolescent, anticipated sexual activity, for example, may involve both anticipation of pleasure and guilt, or fear. The resultant state of conflict may be very difficult to resolve because the positive motivation keeps him from leaving the situation, while the negative motivation becomes stronger as he approaches the goal. As a result, he is likely to alternately approach and avoid the goal.

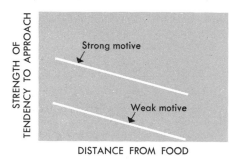

FIG. 7–24. Motive strength changes the height but not the slope of the approach gradient.

■ This vacillation has been demonstrated in the study of approach-avoidance conflicts in rats. Earlier we described Brown's procedure for establishing the fact that the avoidance gradient is steeper than the approach gradient. Later studies have shown that the *height* of both the approach and avoidance gradients depend on the intensity of the motive. Thus the maximum speed of a rat who has not been fed for one hour is slower than the maximum speed of the rat who has not been fed for five hours (see Fig. 7–24). Miller and his associates studied rats who were first trained to eat in a goal box and then were shocked while in the same box. This set up an approach-avoidance conflict about the goal box. As you might expect, when either the motive for food or the expectancy of shock is very mild, the organism responds on the basis of its strong motive. This situation is diagrammed in Fig. 7–25.

However, if the two motives are more equal in strength, the result is vacillation. In terms of approach-avoidance diagrams, we see vacillation when the gradients of approach and of avoidance cross at some point. This means that far from the goal, where the approach tendency is higher than the avoidance tendency, the rat will continue to approach; close to the goal, where

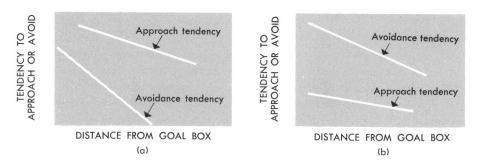

FIG. 7–25. Outcomes when both an approach and an avoidance motive of different strengths are aroused. (a) With a strong approach tendency and a weak avoidance tendency, the organism will approach the goal. (b) With a strong avoidance tendency, the organism will avoid the goal.

the tendency to avoid is stronger than the tendency to approach, the rat will move away from the goal. Thus Miller predicted that the rat would vacillate at the points at which the gradients crossed (see Fig. 7–26). Studies of the points around which rats stopped approaching and began to avoid confirmed Miller's prediction. (Miller, 1959) ■

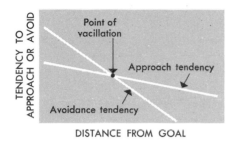

DISTANCE FROM GOAL

FIG. 7–26. Outcome of an approach-avoidance conflict when the two motives are about equal. The organism will vacillate about the point where the two gradients intersect.

The vacillation and the consequent inability to resolve such a conflict are frustrating. When possible, a compromise solution is reached. One of the ways in which human beings handle such conflict is to *repress*, or become unaware of, motives which cannot be tolerated. While the person is unconscious of such a repressed motive, it may still influence his behavior. Because ambivalence, conflict, and unconscious motives are so important in behavior, they will be discussed in more detail in Chapter 11, "Frustration."

The Development of Motives

WHAT IS UNLEARNED? Each baby is born with drives, such as hunger, thirst, and avoidance of pain, which arouse him to activity. The drive state is often unpleasant, and reduction of the drive is pleasant. In addition, there are other unlearned sources of pleasure: the feel of a soft warm body, moderate changes in stimulation, the taste of sweet substances. Unlearned sources of unpleasantness include pain, cognitive inconsistency, and certain stimuli, such as bitter substances and repeated vertical movement (as the pitching of a ship).

The facial expressions associated with emotions also have unlearned components. This has been determined by studying people who do not have the opportunity to observe the facial expressions of others; that is, the deaf and blind. Observation of a child both deaf and blind revealed that she frowned when she was displeased and laughed clearly and musically when pleased.

Another way of studying the problems of what is unlearned would be to see how much variation we find in different cultures. If people in all cultures express emotions in the same way, we might suppose that patterns of emotional expression are inherited. If, however, they differ, learning must be a factor.

Cross-cultural studies find instances supporting both hypotheses. Tears, for example, seem to be a universal expression of grief. However, in contrast to our culture, in some Chinese cultures, anger is expressed by staring with fixed eyes, by laughing, or by fainting. In these cultures, the Chinese servant smiles when he is being scolded or when he is reporting some calamity to his superiors. These studies imply that there are both learned and unlearned aspects to emotional expression.

Not all the unlearned emotional expressions appear at birth. The infant's emotional development is characterized by increased *differentiation*. At birth his only emotional reaction is a rather diffuse excitement and crying. By the age of three months, distress and delight have become differentiated. By the age of six months, fear, disgust, and anger can also be distinguished, while the one-year-old has added to this list signs of affection (Bridges, 1932).

Finally, a baby is born with two tendencies that form the bases of motivational development. First, he has a tendency to seek pleasure and avoid pain. Second, he has the capacity to *learn* the conditions which surround his positive and negative goals.

The Role of Punishment and Reward

As the infant matures, he is exposed to a complex pattern of punishments and rewards. He learns to select his behavior in accordance with the contingencies. Generally, an act which has been rewarded once in a situation is less likely to be rewarded if it is repeated immediately. For example, a mother may welcome her child to her lap, but if he wants to sit in her lap all the time, he is likely to be forcibly detached. Similarly, the child who continually seeks approval finds that the more he seeks approval, the less likely he is to attain it. Much of the child's learning must thus be similar in many ways to that of the pigeons trained under schedules of partial reinforcement, where reinforcement is not dependent upon the number of responses given (an interval schedule). The whining, nagging child, on the other hand, may have learned responses similar to those of pigeons reinforced after a number of responses (a ratio schedule).*
More often, however, the child's learning involves discriminating between situations in which one type of striving is rewarded and situations in which it is punished or at least not rewarded. Thus for each motive the individual learns a countermotive or balance that comes into action whenever there is danger of overemphasizing behavior leading toward one goal.

To the prospective parent, the complexity of the task of developing motives and countermotives is almost frightening. Recalling our earlier discussion of positive and negative motives, we see that there is an additional complexity involved. Since the generalization gradient is ordinarily steeper for negative

---

* See p. 123 for partial reinforcement curves.

motives than for positive motives, negative motives are likely to be used in controlling immediate behavior problems. Most of us are likely to be most concerned about changing a child's motivation when his behavior is annoying, and consequently we are likely to use punishments or threats as providing the most information and most effective control to stop the annoying behavior. However, there may be unforeseen results of an overemphasis of threat of punishment. Baldwin (1948) observed 67 four-year-olds at play and at home. Children whose parents used strict, severe, discipline were better behaved than those from more democratic homes, but they were also less curious, sociable, and spontaneous. The pattern of rewards and punishments used by a parent to control specific behaviors may thus have unintended general effects.

The Principle of Secondary Reinforcement

One of the most important principles in the development of motives is that pleasantness and unpleasantness become associated with new, formerly neutral, stimuli. Any stimuli which are consistently present when pleasure occurs come to be pleasurable in themselves. A dog barks with joy when he sees his master, even when the master does not bring food. On the other hand, something which has consistently been a barrier to satisfaction or has been associated with distress tends to arouse unpleasant feelings by itself. As we stated earlier, the formerly neutral cue that now serves as a goal is called a *secondary reinforcer.*

It is usually the baby's parents who remove distress and bring about pleasant feelings—feeding him, changing his diapers, cuddling him. Life seems much more pleasurable to him if his parents are nearby and approve of his activities. Before long, parental approval becomes a secondary reinforcer, a goal in itself. As the child generalizes from his parents to other people, the close relationship between himself and his mother and father may become the basis of his general orientation toward others. If this analysis is correct (and it is only theoretical), the principle of secondary reinforcement is one foundation of social motivation.

We see the importance of the same principle in another situation: A child works hard at learning how to read in order to gain the approval of his mother and his teacher. Thus reading behavior is one of the events that regularly precedes an experience of pleasure. By the association of the reading with the pleasure of approval, reading itself begins to produce a feeling of pleasure. What was once an instrumental act to achieve a goal now becomes a goal in its own right. We see the same phenomenon in adults. The accumulation of money may begin as a means to an end—security, status, comfort—but may become an end in itself. Because patterns of behavior learned as instrumental habits can develop motivational value, it is often difficult to draw the line between motives and habits. For our purposes, we will call a learned pattern of behavior a *habit* when it is used to reach a goal and we will call it a *goal* when it has become pleasurable in itself.

Finally, the principle of secondary reinforcement helps to explain why people often risk pain as they strive for goals. Why, for example, does the gambler continue gambling despite continued losses? Why will a person accept a new job with more problems and more responsibility? Granted that there are certain possibilities for pleasure in such situations, they still look like exceptions to our rules.

However, if we look at the principles by which a stimulus becomes rewarding, we can understand why a small amount of pain or anxiety could become pleasurable. You can undoubtedly remember times when it really felt good to be hungry, because you could see the turkey and mashed potatoes all ready to be served. Similarly, remember that many of our pleasures come about from resolving problems. Thus in the life of the relatively successful person, anxiety has usually been associated with the pleasure that is the result of a problem solution. Anxiety (in a mild form) then becomes a cue to pleasure rather than a determent. Consequently, even mild anxiety conforms to our general principle that any cue regularly preceding positive affect comes to elicit positive affect itself. There are good psychological reasons why people are willing to take up activities about which they feel anxious and in which they may fail.

CONTIGUITY AND DISTANT GOALS

As we implied in discussing motive strength, contiguity of the cue to pleasure or pain is also important in determining its ability to arouse motivation. A cue which has been perceived a long time before a change in feeling takes place will be less strongly associated with the change of feeling than one which immediately precedes the feeling change. However, such distant cues can eventually be associated with the feeling change, and the individual may learn to expect that the reward will occur later. The human being's ability to use language to represent distant goals and to conceptualize the relation of subgoals to final goals helps bridge the time gap.

The child must learn to forego present pleasure for distant goals early. One of the first of such demands arises in toilet training. While toilet training seems a simple matter of learning motor control, it is more than that, for it is one of the earliest instances of the child's motives coming into conflict with a social norm, and of his being punished for nonconformity or rewarded for conformity.* Elimination is one of the basic human needs. Society, speaking through the child's mother, decrees that certain controls must be placed on the expression of this need. Our culture begins toilet training much earlier than most. Almost as soon as the infant can sit up, his mother begins his training. While mothers

---

* We suspect that problems associated with the child's feeding himself are even more important for many families, but toilet training was emphasized by Freud and consequently has been studied more.

in primitive cultures typically start such training at 18 to 30 months of age, American mothers sometimes begin when the child is 8 or 9 months old. Because maturation is incomplete, training is more difficult and takes much longer than in other societies.

Toilet training often begins by rewarding performance with such concrete rewards as candy or cookies and punishing transgressions by a spanking or severe expressions of displeasure. As training progresses, however, more and more emphasis is placed on verbal rewards such as "That's a *good* boy!" and "You're a *big* boy!" Increasing use is made of guilt and shame as punishment: "Aren't you ashamed of yourself, a big boy like you acting like a baby?" As the rewards and punishments become less concrete and more and more emphasis is placed on the child's own responsibility and his own feelings of goodness or shame, he gradually is motivated to control elimination himself and feels ashamed when he transgresses.

This early social learning is typical of the tremendous amount of learning of social motives and social norms which the child must accomplish before he is accepted into society. Variations in training result in distortions of norms or rebellion against them. Some of the long-lasting conflicts and frustrations may have their roots in the social learning which takes place in the first few years of life.

As a child experiences a variety of punishments and rewards, he begins to categorize goals and the situations in which goal attainment is likely. Sometimes the basis of categorization is the similarity of pleasant situations, and we call this category of motives an *interest*. For example, a child who enjoys an erector set, model airplanes, and a wood-burning kit would be described as having an *interest in mechanical things*. He will probably seek other situations which similarly provide an opportunity for him to make something with his hands.

Sometimes a child learns that he can get similar rewards from many diverse situations. The goal is abstracted from the many ways of attaining it and becomes the object of a *general motive*. For example, the pleasure of success and parental or peer approval may be associated with such situations as winning a spelling bee, getting an "A" on a test, or winning a race. Even though a school boy may have used a variety of behaviors to attain success in such situations, they have in common the element of achievement in competition. In new achievement situations the boy will be motivated by the expectation of the same sort of pleasure he received from success in the earlier achievement situations. One reason the child develops a general competitive achievement motive is because his parents or other parents see certain situations as achievement situations, and not only reward him similarly for behavior in all of them but label them with the same words. The development of a general achievement motive is thus much like the development of a concept such as "dog" or "food" in that common elements come to be abstracted and generalized.

"Good" and "Bad" as General Motives

Two of the broadest and most important motivational categories a child learns are those labeled "good" and "bad." These, like other general motives, are learned from a variety of experiences with adults and peers in which punishment and reward follow a consistent pattern and in which the same words "good" and "bad" are used consistently. Let us look for a moment at some of the simplest examples of such learning.

Some of the child's experiences carry natural immediate punishments for being bad. A child, for example, is likely to be attacked if he attempts to take another child's toy. Other concepts of good or bad are less likely to be learned from the realistic results of behavior but must be learned from parental admonitions. For example, the child does not learn that stealing is naughty from his experiences with a stolen toy, but rather from warnings or from the punishment when he is caught. The parent must not only administer rewards and punishments for "good" or "bad" behavior performed in the parents' presence, but must also reward the child for "good" behavior performed when parents are not present. Thus the parent who is attempting to teach a child to control his aggression punishes the child for hitting little brother even though the parent was out of the room when the act occurred. From the principle of contiguity, we would expect such delays in punishment or reward to be relatively ineffective. However, the parent overcomes this disadvantage to some extent through the use of words reconstructing the situation and telling the child what he is being punished for.

Thus punishment is associated with "bad behavior" and the general category "bad." Soon the behavior itself becomes a cue for unpleasantness and the child feels distressed when he has done something that he himself places in the "bad" category. This is the genesis of guilt which threatens self-punishment in the face of temptation. Similarly, a child learns to feel pleasure when he behaves in ways that belong to the category "good."

Individual Differences

THE MEASUREMENT OF INDIVIDUAL DIFFERENCES. One of the most universal findings in the study of motivation is the existence of widespread individual differences. Even in rats an experimenter has observed that preference for food varies within a group that has been uniformly deprived. In this case, preference was measured by observing the amount of time spent with food as opposed to a toy or a playmate (Allison, 1964). Allison's apparatus is diagrammed in Fig. 7–27.

However, not all motives are so easily assessed. We have already described the more complex projective tests that have been used to measure motives. We shall now look at some of the questionnaire methods that have been developed.

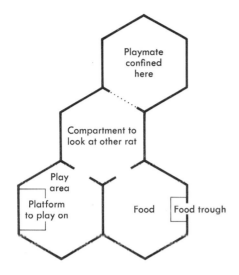

Playmate
confined
here

Compartment to
look at other rat

Play
area

Platform
to play on

Food   Food trough

FIG. 7–27. The floor plan of the apparatus used by Allison to measure individual differences in the motives of rats. The
proportion of time a rat spent in each
chamber gave a measure of his motive
strength. Allison found differences in rats
even though they had been deprived of
food the same number of hours. (After
Allison, 1964)

The Allport-Vernon Scale

The problem of identifying these general classes of goals has attracted many
philosophers and psychologists. The word most often used to refer to such
a general category of goals sought by many members of a society is "value."

■ One of the best-known classifications is that of the philosopher Spranger, who felt that there
were six basic human values: theoretical, economic, aesthetic, social, political, and religious.

"1. *The theoretical.* The dominant interest of the theoretical man is the discovery of truth. In
the pursuit of this goal he characteristically takes a 'cognitive' attitude, one that looks for iden-
tities and differences; one that divests itself of judgments regarding the beauty or utility of objects
and seeks only to observe and to reason. Since the interests of the theoretical man are empirical,
critical, and rational, he is necessarily an intellectualist, frequently a scientist or philosopher. . .

"2. *The economic.* The economic man is characteristically interested in what is useful. Based
originally on the satisfaction of bodily needs (self-preservation), the interest in utilities develops
to embrace the practical affairs of the business world—the production, marketing, and consump-
tion of goods, the elaboration of credit, and the accumulation of tangible wealth. . .

"3. *The aesthetic.* The aesthetic man sees his highest value in *form* and *harmony.* Each single
experience is judged from the standpoint of grace, symmetry, or fitness. He regards life as a
manifold of events; each single impression is enjoyed for its own sake. He need not be a creative
artist; nor need he be effete; he is aesthetic if he but finds his chief interest in the artistic episodes
of life. . .

"4. *The social.* The highest value for this type is love of people, whether of one or many,
whether conjugal, filial, friendly, or philanthropic. The social man prizes other persons as ends,
and is therefore himself kind, sympathetic, and unselfish. He is likely to find the theoretical,
economic, and aesthetic attitudes cold and inhuman. . . In its purest form the social interest is
selfless and tends to approach very closely to the religious attitude.

"5. *The political.* The political man is interested primarily in *power.* His activities are not
necessarily within the narrow field of politics; but whatever his vocation, he betrays himself

as a *Machtmensch*. . . There are, however, certain personalities in whom the desire for a direct expression of this motive is uppermost, who wish above all else for personal power, influence, and renown.

''6. *The religious*. The highest value for the religious man may be called unity. He is mystical, and seeks to comprehend the cosmos as a whole, to relate himself to its embracing totality. Spranger defines the religious man as one 'whose mental structure is permanently directed to the creation of the highest and absolutely satisfying value experience.' Some men of this type are 'immanent mystics,' that is, they find their religious experience in the affirmation of life and in active participation there. The 'transcendental mystic,' on the other hand, seeks to unite himself with a higher reality by withdrawing from life; he is the ascetic, and like the holy men of India, finds the experience of unity through self-denial and meditation.'' ■ *

Allport, Vernon, and Lindzey (1960) took Spranger's classification as the basis of their *Study of Values*, a test of people's values. They realized that Spranger's descriptions represented ideal types, rather than a classification into which all people could be fitted. Thus their purpose in the test was to assess the relative importance of the six values to the people taking the test.

Some research results suggest that the test did tap values in the way intended. For example, artists, who would be expected to be high in aesthetic values, do obtain high scores on the Allport-Vernon-Lindzey test. Similarly, clergymen score highly on religious and social values; and business administration students produce high scores on economic values.

Interest Tests

Because motivation is so important in determining behavior, differences in motives may account for differences in success in a vocation. Thus both employers and vocational guidance counselors use tests which help reveal some of the individual's motives. Some of these tests are called *interest* tests because they measure motivation by asking what classes of activities a person prefers.

One of the most widely used interest tests is the "Strong Vocational Interest Inventory" (Strong, 1941, 1943). This test includes such things as checking one's liking for or interest in a large number of occupations, school subjects, and amusements. It also asks the individual being tested to choose which of ten famous men he would like to have been. By comparing the testee's interests with those of men successful in a given vocation and also by assessing his abilities, the individual's success in a given job can be predicted fairly well. For example, research with the Strong inventory revealed that men who stayed with a particular occupation had, while in college, achieved interest test scores that were more similar to the scores of men successful in that occupation than to the scores of men in different occupations. Their scores were also more similar to the scores of those currently successful in that field than were the scores of men who began in that field but switched over to another job. More-

---

* Allport, G. W., *Personality*. New York: Holt, 1937. Reprinted by permission.

over, scores in early adulthood correlate highly (0.80) with scores 18 years later (Strong, 1955). This indicates that vocational interests are quite stable for most people.

Not only are interests stable; there are also consistent differences in interests among groups. For example, as we might expect, men and women in our culture differ in a number of significant ways. As compared with women, men are more interested in mechanical, scientific, and adventurous activities, as well as political, legal, and selling occupations. Women are more interested in musical, artistic, literary, social service, and clerical activities.

When changes in interests or motives do take place, they usually do so slowly and in response to consistent, persisting pressure. Studies of changes in values held during college life indicate that the typical student changes little over four years unless he attends a college whose students take pride in their uniqueness and who consistently represent certain goals. For example, students at Ivy League schools are likely to shift from an initial interest in science to a later interest in humanities during their collegiate careers.

Sources of Individual Differences

Though each person's motive structure is unique and depends in part on his unique experiences, we can trace some individual differences between people to the family, the subculture, and the culture of which they are a part. We have already noted the differences in the affiliation motive in first-born and later-born children in the same family.

Although the achievement motive is common throughout our culture (perhaps because of common emphasis on achievement in baby care, education, business, and even religion), we can still find differences in the motives of people of different social classes. Middle-class children score higher in the achievement motive than lower-class children do. This result can be related to the fact that middle-class parents have higher aspirations for their children than lower-class parents do. They try to implant in their children the desire to get ahead. While lower-class parents may also want their children to get ahead, they place much less stress upon it. Success seems so difficult to attain that there is little use in trying.

Even the extent to which one is motivated by hunger, sex, or some other motives based on an unlearned need is determined to a high degree by his culture. Some needs are fulfilled almost automatically and consequently do not have a great deal of importance in determining people's behavior. Need for oxygen is satisfied so easily that advertisers do not try to appeal to it. Poems are not written about it, and most people do not daydream about it. Hunger is also not as important a motive in a society such as ours as it is in a society where most people do not get enough to eat. On the other hand, in our society much emphasis is placed on sex, and a good deal of our training is devoted to teaching children acceptable sexual attitudes and behavior.

Practical Applications

All complex behavior can be understood in terms of attempts to satisfy motives. Often our attempts to deal with people are thwarted by the apparent lack of purpose in their behavior. So long as we feel that their behavior is meaningless, we will have difficulty in understanding it and changing it. As soon as we recognize that the behavior is directed toward satisfaction of some motives, we can look for the motives being satisfied and may get some insights which will help us cope with the behavior.

In any culture certain sets of motives are common, strong, and significant. To know what such motives are enables us to deal more effectively with the people of that culture. By your knowledge of motives which are common in our culture, you may adjust your own behavior so that these motives are not frustrated in the people with whom you associate. For example, in industry, employees bring their entire repertory of motives to their jobs, and their productivity and job satisfactions depend upon satisfaction of motives like affiliation, recognition, autonomy, and achievement, and not just upon economic benefits. The employer who understands this will be more effective than one who does not.

Throughout this chapter we have referred to the implications of motivational principles for the rearing of children. In Chapter 5 we discussed the relative uses of rewards and punishments. The general conclusion was that rewards are most effective when there is some particular thing you want the child to do; punishments are most effective when there is some particular thing you do *not* want the child to do. From our study of motivation it is also clear that for a "reward" to be effective it must satisfy a motive. This may seem obvious, yet parents often forget that very young children have not yet learned to be motivated for verbal rewards or punishments, while an older child may be highly motivated for social rewards.

Finally, motivational principles may provide a basis for understanding our own behavior.

Summary

Concepts

Motive. An expectancy of pleasantness (positive affect) or unpleasantness (negative affect) ; a person may or may not be conscious of his motives

Incentive or *goal.* An object that gives rise to affective feelings in an individual

Contact comfort. The satisfaction in a baby monkey derived from clinging to a warm, soft object

Emotion. A feeling which is accompanied by characteristic behavioral and physiological events

Goal gradient. The tendency for motivation to increase as the organism approaches the goal

Conflict. The simultaneous arousal of two or more motives involving mutually exclusive goals

Interest. A category of positive motives involving similar activities and objects

General motive. A category of motives that have in common an abstract goal; the activities and situations involved may be very diverse

Value. A general motive usually common to many members of a society

Principles

1 Psychologists use the concept of *motive* to account for the energy, the direction, and the persistence of behavior.

2. Motives are inferred from observing an organism's use of learned behavior in a situation, from the direction of behavior in a choice situation, from an organism's persistence in pursuing a goal, and, in human beings, from projective tests.

3. The major human motives include motives related to physiological needs, social motives, motives for self-esteem, and motives for competence in dealing with the environment.

4. Conscious feelings frequently accompany the arousal and the satisfaction of motives.

5. Motives and feelings may be described in terms of at least two dimensions: pleasantness-unpleasantness and intensity. Each of these dimensions may have a physiological correlate.

6. The arousal of a stored motive depends on stored motive strength and the cues in the situation which provide information about the attractiveness of the goal and the probability of reaching it.

7. The effect of arousal on the efficiency of performance depends on the complexity of the task. With complex tasks, medium arousal is optimum.

8. Positive and negative motives differ in several ways: the gradient of avoidance is steeper than the gradient of approach; negative motives are more difficult to extinguish; and the behavior induced by each differs.

9. Conflicts are usually resolved on the basis of the stronger motive. When the two motives have about equal strength, the outcome is either a compromise or vacillation.

10. A child is born with (a) the tendency to experience certain events as pleasant, others as unpleasant, (b) the capacity to display the unlearned components

of emotional expression as he matures, (c) the tendency to seek pleasure and avoid pain, and (d) the ability to learn the conditions which lead to positive goals and those that lead to negative ones.

11. The principle of secondary reinforcement helps to account for the development of some of the social motives, the transformation of an instrumental act to a goal in itself, the apparent contradiction of a person risking pain and failure, and the existence of distant goals, despite the importance of temporal contiguity in learning.

12. There are tests for measuring individual differences in values and interests.

Suggested Readings

ATKINSON, J., *An Introduction to Motivation*. Princeton, N.J.: Van Nostrand, 1964.

McCLELLAND, D. C. (ed.), *Studies in Motivation*. New York: Appleton-Century-Crofts, 1955. This book and the preceding one stress human motives, such as affiliation, achievement, and power.

BINDRA, D., *Motivation*. New York: Ronald, 1959. Describes how psychologists approach motivation from the study of animals and a behavioristic point of view.

YOUNG, P. T., *Motivation and Emotion*. New York: Wiley, 1961. Emotions are given more emphasis.

McCLELLAND, D. C., *The Achieving Society*. Princeton, N.J.: Van Nostrand, 1961. Shows how the concept of achievement motivation has been studied cross-culturally and how this motive can be related to economic development in a society.

HARLOW, H. F., "The nature of love," *Amer. Psychologist*, 1958, **13**, 673–685. An entertaining article about Harlow's experiments with artificial monkey mothers.

chapter 8

action: learning and performance

chapter 8

THE PHENOMENA OF ACTION

THE DYNAMICS OF ACTION

THE DEVELOPMENT OF ACTION

INDIVIDUAL DIFFERENCES

PRACTICAL APPLICATIONS

In the last two chapters we have seen that a person's behavior depends on his perception of the situation and on his motivation. Perception and motivation give us a good start toward explaining behavior, but it is also apparent that each person has a repertoire of habits which can be used to satisfy his motives. A single motive might be satisfied by any one of many different acts; conversely, the same act may be used at different times to satisfy different motives.

The Phenomena of Action

Acts are patterns of behavior. Some acts, such as reflexes or instinctive behavior, are primarily determined by the situation and the inherited structure of the organism. Most acts are learned ways of satisfying motives. Swatting a mosquito, going to a movie, putting on a shoe, and writing a letter are all acts. As we saw in Chapter 5, the size of the unit of behavior we define as an act depends upon our purposes. In one study we may wish to predict whether a person will press button A or button B, and the act is pressing a button. In another study we may wish to predict whether a person will study or play cards, and our "acts" are studying or card playing. An act is simply a convenient unit of behavior, usually defined with reference to the environment. Uttering a word, saying a phrase, speaking a sentence, or delivering a speech may all be acts depending upon the sorts of antecedents and effects we wish to study. These act units are patterns of movements arbitrarily selected from the continual flow of activity.

What Is the Physiological Basis of Action?

Just as an understanding of receptors was useful as a background for our study of perception, so an understanding of effectors is a useful background for the study of action.

The effectors are muscles and glands. Nerve impulses travel from the motor cortex, down through the brainstem and spinal cord, to motor neurons terminating in muscles. Similarly, lower centers, such as the hypothalamus, send messages which result in glandular secretion. In the glands, as we saw in Chapter 3, the nerve impulse results in a change in the secretion of a fluid which plays a part in physiological functioning. In the muscles, the neural signal results in contraction or relaxation of muscle fibers in movement.

Muscles

The use of muscles is important not only for the resulting effect on the environment but also for the effect on the muscle itself. When a muscle is exercised, nourishment from the bloodstream strengthens it; lack of exercise results in weakness and wasting away (atrophy from disuse). This is of interest not only in its own right but also because early psychologists and educators sought an analogy between neural and muscular functioning, thinking of certain learning experiences as providing mental exercise and of forgetting as being due to disuse, just as muscular atrophy results from disuse.*

There are three types of muscles: heart (cardiac), smooth (visceral), and striped (striated) (see Fig. 8–1). The heart muscles contract rhythmically at a moderate speed. The smooth muscles are found in the stomach, intestines, blood vessels, and other visceral organs. Their response is also slow and rhythmic.

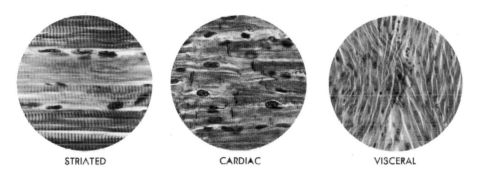

STRIATED   CARDIAC   VISCERAL

FIG. 8–1. The three types of muscle as they appear under a microscope. (Photomicrograph of striated muscle, courtesy of Ward's Natural Science Establishment, Inc.; others, courtesy of General Biological Supply House)

Smooth and heart muscles have been called "involuntary" because their contraction is usually automatic in accordance with the metabolic processes. However, this does not mean that smooth and heart muscle action cannot be modified by learning. The method by which this has most often been demonstrated is classical conditioning.† Heart rate has been conditioned to a neutral stimulus, such as a clock, by using shock as an unconditioned stimulus. The constriction of blood vessels has been elicited by a buzzer, after a period of training in which the buzzer was always followed by placing the subject's hand in ice water (Menzies, 1937). Smooth muscle and heart muscle action can also be brought under instrumental control. The learning of bladder and bowel control provides two common examples of voluntary control of smooth muscle. Hnatiow and Lang (1965) have shown that heart muscle action can also be changed voluntarily. Their subjects were able to increase the steadiness of their heart rate (reduce the variability) by watching recordings being made of their heartbeats. Interestingly, none of the subjects could explain how they were able to do so. Thus, although it can be done, it seems to be much more unusual and difficult

---

* We shall take up the problem of forgetting from disuse in Chapter 9.
† Classical conditioning was described in Chapter 5.

to bring smooth and heart muscles under instrumental control—that is, to use them to achieve goals for which one is motivated—than striped muscles.

Striped muscles are the muscles that move our arms, legs, neck, and other parts of our body, and hence are the ones involved in most acts. They are made up of bundles of muscle fiber. Each individual fiber operates on the principle of the all-or-none law: it either completely contracts or completely relaxes. Usually some of the muscle fibers in a striped muscle are contracted, although the majority of the fibers are relaxed. This phenomenon is called *muscle tone*. Alert, energetic people tend to maintain a high level of muscle tone which permits quick, decisive action. However, an excessively high muscle tone, as in the case of an overly anxious person, makes smooth, coordinated, and meaningful movement difficult. On the other hand, people who fail to use their muscles regularly usually have low muscle tone, which also makes sudden, rapid, and coordinated movements difficult.

A muscle can pull but not push; hence movements require two sets of opposing muscles. To bend your arm at the elbow, you use the biceps muscle; to extend your arm, you use your triceps muscle, which pulls in the direction opposite to the biceps. Since muscles are in opposition, when both sets of muscles are tense, individuals are actually pulling against themselves. Usually when we speak of conflict, we are referring to conflict of motives and habits, which we conceptualize as being stored in the central nervous system. But when opposing sets of muscles are tensed simultaneously, the conflict is manifested at the effector level, too.

What Are the Dimensions of an Act?

We can describe an act in terms of the strength with which it is performed, in terms of its precision, and in terms of time.

STRENGTH. One dimension by which an act can be described is the strength or force with which it is performed. Typically, this is measured by a gauge or other device calibrated in terms of the amount of weight necessary to produce the same effect. For example, if we say that the grip strength of industrial workers varies from 75 to 170 pounds, we mean that a load of 75 to 170 pounds placed on the handle would have an effect equal to that of the subjects' squeezing (Morgan *et al.*, 1963).

When we compare the relative strength of different types of actions, we find that a shoulder action is generally about one and one-half times stronger than an elbow action. In using the arms to exert force with a bended elbow, strength is greatest when the elbow is bent at right angles.

Since feet are used to make important responses in driving automobiles or airplanes, it is interesting to find that the average person can exert a force with his legs that is greater than his own body weight. One study showed that for most subjects the maximum momentary force exerted by either leg ranged from 465 to 655 pounds. Maximum force was exerted when the leg was only slightly bent (160 degrees).

PRECISION. A second characteristic of responses is *precision*. Most muscular movements are not perfectly steady. If you stick out your finger and try to hold it steady, it will tremble back and forth about 10 to 12 times per second. Heavier parts of the body have a slower rate of tremor. But tremor increases during emotions or fatigue, so that performance on tasks requiring great precision is likely to be more affected by these factors than is performance not requiring precision.

One type of act requiring precision is reaching out to adjust a particular control mechanism. This is the sort of movement involved in flying an airplane or controlling a bulldozer or crane. It involves the steady contracting of one or more sets of muscles while the opposing muscles simultaneously relax. Sometimes one must make such movements without looking. Studies of such movements indicate that we tend to overshoot short movements and undershoot longer movements. Generally we do better on movements that lead away from the body than on those that move toward the body. The direction of movement is most accurate when the movement is directly in front of the person and below shoulder height.

The precision of movements is aided by kinesthetic and visual feedback on the progress of the movement. There will be dramatic examples of the effects of disturbance of this feedback later in this chapter. However, precision is not entirely dependent upon such feedback. Some very quick movements can be made very precisely in less than the reaction time for kinesthetic stimuli (about $\frac{1}{8}$ second). A skilled violinist can make 16 finger movements per second. Thus each of his movements cannot depend on feedback from the previous movement; the neuromuscular pattern must be preset to be reeled off in sequence.

TIME MEASURES. One of the simple, yet very revealing, dimensions of an act is the time it takes to complete it. We notice that we have increased our skill often by just seeing how much less time it takes to carry out the act.

You may think that once you have learned a skill well, you no longer can improve on your performance. However, studies of the time taken to complete a skilled act have shown that people continue to improve over millions of repetitions (Fitts, 1964). For example, Crossman (1959) studied workers in an industrial plant whose job was to roll cigars. Even after a full year of practice, the workers continued to improve in terms of time and therefore in terms of numbers of cigars produced. After about five years, their time had almost reached an absolute minimum because of the time needed by the machine with which they were working.

REACTION TIME. Another useful measure of performance is reaction time. Reaction time is defined as the time from the onset of the stimulus to the onset of the response. In a typical reaction-time study a person sits before a lever and a screen. As soon as he sees a light flash on a screen, he is supposed to depress the lever. A precision timer is electronically started simultaneously with the flash of light and stopped by the depression of the lever, yielding the reaction time.

Reaction time varies with the kind of signaling stimulus used. In general, reaction time to sound is faster than that to light. Furthermore, it varies with the kind of response required. Lifting a finger is accomplished slightly more quickly than raising a foot.

By recording electrical potentials in receptors, in the brain and in the muscles, it is possible to tell what accounts for this time. For example, when a light strikes the eye, electrical activity in the visual cortex begins about 0.02 to 0.04 second later, while direct stimulation of the optic nerve results in activity only 0.002 to 0.005 second later. In the ear, on the other hand, activity in the auditory nerve starts only 0.001 to 0.002 second after the sound strikes the ear. The ear thus sends off its messages to the brain faster than the eye does. On the response side, nerve conduction from the brain to the fingers takes 0.010 to 0.015 second. The difference in reaction time for lifting a finger and lifting a foot is about the same as the difference in the time for a nerve impulse to travel to the finger and to the foot. The amount of time taken to get the response started depends upon the motion required, but it is clear that over half of the simple reaction time for most movements is taken up by activity in the brain, rather than by activity in sensory and motor nerves. This suggests that we can learn something about the complexity of the cognitive processes in a task by studying reaction time.

For example, the reaction-time task can be made more complex by having the subject sit before a panel on which one of several lights can flash, and asking him to press a different key in response to each light.

■ Hick (1952) used this type of apparatus and varied the number of stimuli which might be flashed during different periods in the experiment. During one period, the subject knew that either one of two lights would flash, and he was to respond by depressing one of two keys. During various other periods of the experiment, the number of possible stimuli (and responses) was 3, 4, 5, 6, 7, 8, 9, and 10. (During each period the subject knew the number of stimuli to which he might have to respond.) Hick's results are plotted in Fig. 8–2. They show that reaction time increases as the number of possible stimulus-response combinations in the experiment increases. In fact, the reaction time varies directly with the logarithm of the number of stimulus alternatives in the situation. ■

However, task complexity cannot be measured in number of stimuli and potential responses alone. Some stimulus-response combinations are easier to per-

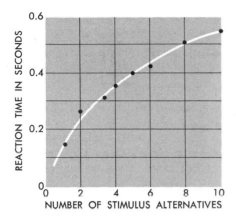

FIG. 8–2. The increase in reaction time as the number of stimulus alternatives increases. (After Hick, 1952)

form than others, and this too is reflected in reaction time. For example, you can repeat the one of ten numbers you have just heard faster than you can depress the one of ten levers corresponding to the spoken number. But you can depress the one of ten levers that vibrates, faster than you can say the number of the lever that vibrated. The psychological closeness of stimulus and response is called s-r *compatibility*. The greater the compatibility of the task the shorter the reaction time (Fitts and Seeger, 1953). See Fig. 8–3.

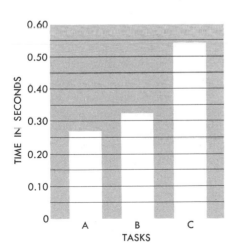

FIG. 8–3. Reaction time for three tasks, each involving the same number of stimulus alternatives (nine) but differing in compatibility. Task A is pointing at a light. Task B is pointing at a light without seeing one's hand. Task C is pushing a finger key in response to the onset of a light. (Task A after Hick, 1952; Tasks B and C after Fitts and Peterson, 1964)

Reaction time varies with age; it is slowest for young children and for older persons. Slowing in reaction time with age is relatively slight until a person reaches age fifty or sixty, but certain types of reaction, such as that involved in tracking a moving target, drop off more rapidly than the simple lifting of a finger.

Dimensions of Action: Implications

Our brief survey of the dimensions of an act has revealed several principles important for an understanding of action. First, the same performance can be measured in a number of ways. We usually choose a convenient measure; thus, for example, the best performance in the 100-yard dash is measured in seconds. In other situations we measure performance in terms of precision or accuracy. In marksmanship one's performance is measured in terms of accuracy in hitting a target. Sometimes a third measure of performance, *endurance*, is used. For example, the performance of a soldier on a forced march may be evaluated primarily in terms of his endurance. Sometimes, although rarely, a measure of force may be used. In many tasks, performance is measured by some combination of these measures; for instance, typing performance is often measured in words per minute, with a deduction for errors.

Second, whenever we look at an individual's performance, we need to take into account the nature of the task itself. Some movements are easier to make than others, some are more easily controlled, some can be exerted with greater strength, and some are made more easily in response to certain stimuli. It is apparent that knowledge of these response characteristics can be of great value to the designer of machines requiring human operators.

However, given the same task, different people will respond differently. To understand why, we have to look at events occurring inside the organism. We shall do this in the following section.

The Dynamics of Action

What Determines the Selection of an Act?

Some acts depend chiefly on the inherited structure of the organism and his perception. Reflexes and instinctive behavior are almost automatically called forth by stimuli in the environment. However, most actions are selected by an individual from many possible alternatives on the basis of his perceptual, motivational, and habitual expectancies. This is our major theoretical assumption for act selection. To put it another way, acts are selected on the expectancy—conscious or unconscious—that the future can be controlled to some extent by present action.

THE ROLE OF PERCEPTION. The first step in striving toward a future goal is information about the present situation. Much of this information comes from perception. For example, one driver approaching a dark spot on the pavement may swerve his car because he perceives the spot as a hole. Another driver approaching the spot does not swerve because he perceives it to be a spot of tar. Presumably the skill and motives of the drivers are similar. Their acts have differed because of differences in perception.

A second function of perception in act selection is to constantly inform an individual about the effects of his acts as he moves toward his goal. This permits him to change behavior as the situation changes. Let us observe, for example, the behavior of a quarterback.

■ He receives a direct pass from center and cuts to his right. The play calls for a pass, but looking downfield he sees no receiver open. He then swings around and runs full speed toward the goal line. His blockers take out the opposing end and linebackers, but two defensive backs charge toward him. He cuts sharply toward the center of the field, and as the backs head in, cuts back to the right and outruns the backs. ■

In Chapter 5 we introduced the concept of feedback to describe the process by which a system may adjust its operation to changing conditions and its own changing state. The touchdown run illustrates such use of continuous feedback, as the quarterback continually adjusts his behavior in terms of his own position relative to that of the other players. Thus just as homeostasis involves a feedback system for physiological maintenance, so unlearned and learned acts help to maintain the individual's relationship to his environment, by adjusting constantly to informational feedback from the effectors and from the environment.

Acts which are linked together so that each act gives rise to cues for the next are called *serial acts*. We do not usually think of such acts as a series of movements integrated by stimuli, because we are often unaware of the stimuli. In learning skilled acts, many of the important cues are kinesthetic, and we are usually unaware of these. For example, in riding a bicycle we turn to the right by first turning to the left. The equilibratory sensations serve as cues to the act of turning to the right. We learn to respond to these cues even though we normally do not pay very much attention to them.

Even a well-practiced serial act like speech is highly dependent on sensory feedback, in this case, auditory feedback. As we speak, we constantly hear the sound of our own voice. What happens when this sound is delayed so that there is a short lag between our saying a word and our hearing what we say?

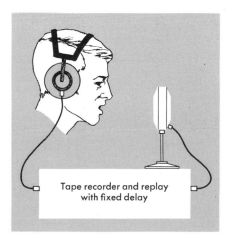

Tape recorder and replay with fixed delay

FIG. 8–4. The apparatus for studying delayed auditory feedback. Through the earphones, the subject hears his own voice slightly delayed.

■ This was studied by having college students read written material into a microphone which was connected to a tape recorder. Through earphones the subjects heard the words they had spoken played back fractions of a second later (see Fig. 8–4). Delays of as little as $\frac{1}{5}$ second resulted in severe disturbances of speech. Speech became slower and louder. There were frequent errors—omissions, additions, and substitutions. A very common finding was that subjects tended to repeat syllables in such a way that it appeared they were stuttering. (Lee, 1950, Smith, 1962) ■

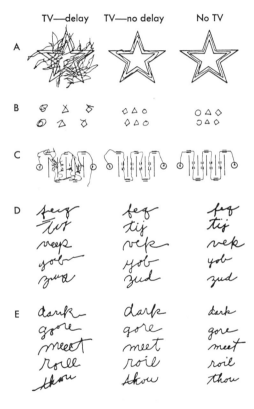

FIG. 8–5. A sample of the type of performance under different types of visual feedback: delayed visual feedback on a television monitor, visual feedback from the television monitor without delay, and ordinary feedback (the subject watches his hand directly). The tasks are: (A) tracing a star between two outlines, (B) copying shapes, (C) tracing through the double lines of a maze pattern, (D) writing nonsense syllables, and (E) writing words. (From K. U. Smith, *Delayed Sensory Feedback and Behavior*. Philadelphia: Saunders, 1962. Reproduced by permission.)

Similarly, Smith (1962) found that if a person did not see the results of his own writing immediately, but watched his writing appear on a television monitor $\frac{1}{2}$ second after he wrote it, his writing became quite distorted. The effects of delayed visual feedback of $\frac{1}{2}$ second on tracing a star, copying shapes, tracing between dotted lines, and writing words are shown in Fig. 8–5. These results provide further examples of how perception of one's acts serves as a continuous guide to movement.

In observing a serial habit in action we are likely to overlook the fact that serial habits are usually very flexible; thus the movements in the series may vary widely, depending upon the continuous information from the receptors which is used in directing the act toward its goal. It is therefore a mistake to think of each movement in a sequence as being rigidly associated with a particular cue from the preceding movement, or to think of the entire sequence as being determined by the cue which initiates it. Rather a movement is guided by a fairly flexible and complex series of cues and time relationships that extend not only backward to the immediately preceding stimuli but also forward to the anticipated movements to follow.

This forward-looking aspect of action is illustrated by Woodworth's concept of *two-phase movement* (Woodworth, 1958). By "two-phase movement," he means that for many acts the initial movements are preparatory and may be in a direction opposite to the ultimately desired movement. For example, if we want to hit someone, we first move our fist and arm back before sending it forward into his jaw. Thus at any moment in time the movements of the skilled performer are guided not only by the last preceding movement but also by the movement expected to follow.

Moreover, the performer may be attending to cues at one point in time which will determine responses to be performed later. For example, the skilled musician ordinarily is reading the music several notes or measures ahead of the music he is performing. The degree to which he reads ahead probably depends upon the degree to which the music is conventional; studies of other skilled performances suggest that the units of information that can be retained are relatively long for familiar sequences. Hence we would expect a musician to be able to read very little ahead of his performance in unfamiliar modern music, where the sequences are less predictable. Examples such as these indicate that execution of an act involves integration of a very complex matrix of stimuli and movements which reach both forward and backward in time.

A third function of perception in act selection is to provide information about stimuli which are associated with appropriate goals. Sometimes these cues are outside the organism, as in the case of a restaurant sign. Sometimes the cues come from conditions inside the organism, as in the case of the rat who learned to turn left when hungry and right when thirsty in a maze. In both cases the cues have become associated with goals via learning, and so they are no longer meaningless stimuli but activators of motivational expectancies.

MOTIVATION. We have already described in detail the role of motivation in act selection in Chapter 7. Let us review some of the major points here.

Motives have three major functions in the selection of an act. First of all, the presence of an activated motive arouses a person, preparing him for action both physiologically and psychologically.

Second, a motive provides the goals toward which actions will be directed. For example, the acts a student utilizes in the classroom depend on the motives he has. If he is interested in a course, he uses acts of listening, note taking, and participation in discussion. On the other hand, if he is not interested, he may use attention-getting acts such as asking irrelevant questions, making audible comments to his neighbors, or moving in his seat. Though he may not be aware of it, the acts were selected in accordance with the relative strengths of his motives for achievement, curiosity, affiliation, attention, and others.

Third, the strength of the aroused motive will determine the persistence and flexibility with which a goal will be pursued. The higher the motive strength, the greater the persistence. This persistence does not always lead to improved performance, however. Extremely high levels of motivation prevent the variation in action necessary to solve complex problems.

HABIT STRENGTH. In Chapter 5, we hypothesized that for each act there is stored in the brain an act tendency, which we call an s-r-s relationship. This means that we store in our brains memory traces of the acts we perform in particular situations and the effects of the acts. A more common term for the same kind of construct is *habit*.

However, any situation provides cues that may have been associated with many different habits. In the case of a simple maze, both a left-turning habit and a right-turning habit have been associated with the choice point for a rat. Which habit will be utilized in the action depends in part on *habit strength*. Presumably, if all other conditions are equal, a person will perform the acts with the greatest habit strength.

Habit and its associated habit strength are constructs and any statement made about their values must, of necessity, be theoretical. Thus a heated controversy grew out of the question, "Under what conditions will habit strength be increased?" One view stated that mere repetition of an act increased both the habit strength and the performance of an act, regardless of the consequences (Thorndike, 1913). Another theorist, Hull (1943), stated that habit strength would be increased only when the acts were followed by reinforcement.* Tolman (1951), one of Hull's leading theoretical adversaries, agreed that reinforcement affected performance, but felt that repetition alone was enough to increase habit strength.

From our own evaluation of the evidence, we find that our position is closer to Tolman's than to Hull's. We interpret the many experiments on this problem, such as the latent learning experiment described in Chapter 5,† as indicating that reinforcement, in Hull's sense of drive reduction, is not necessary for learning. We interpret a habit as an s-r-s relationship. Thus the consequences of a response are part of the habit. This implies that the consequences of an act must be the same on each trial, if repetition is to increase habit strength. In other words, confirmation of the expectancy that the act in question will have a particular consequence is necessary. In the latent learning study the rats not only repeatedly moved through the maze, but they learned which movements led to

---

* Hull's definition of reinforcement was any stimulus which reduced a drive.
† For a description of the latent learning study, see pp. 117–118.

particular parts of the maze. If the same turn at the same spot had led to different parts of the maze on different trials, the rats could not have learned where different parts of the maze were in relation to one another. You will recall that in Chapter 5 we distinguished between informational and affective feedback. What we are saying here is that it is the informational feedback that is crucial for habit strength. The affective feedback, we noted in the last chapter, strengthens the motive to reach the goal.

ACTION DECREMENT. An apparent exception to the principle of repetition is this: If a rat in a maze turned left at the choice point on trial 1, he will most likely turn right on trial 2. This tendency not to repeat the identical action just completed is called *action decrement.** Action decrement dissipates with time. The longer the time between the two maze trials, the more likely it is that the identical action will be repeated (see Fig. 8–6).

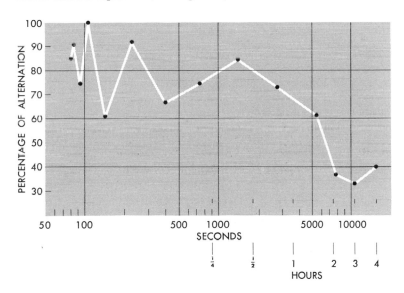

FIG. 8–6. The tendency of rats to alternate between right and left turns on two successive trials as a function of the time between the two trials. The greater the time interval between the two trials, the smaller is the tendency to alternate. (After Walker, 1956)

An interesting example of the tendency to avoid repetition comes from observing people calling the toss of a coin "heads or tails." On each trial there is an equal chance that the coin will fall so that either the head or the tail side shows. Successive tosses are unrelated. However, people who have seen the coin

* Another term for the same phenomenon is *reactive inhibition.*

falling heads up are more likely to call "tails" on the following toss. The fact that gamblers make their bets as though the coin had a tendency to alternate is called the *gambler's fallacy*.

LEAST EFFORT. Another of the general principles of act selection is that, other things being equal, whenever either of two acts can be used to reach a goal, that act is chosen which requires the least effort. This is sometimes called the *law of least effort*. Thus, in going to class on the ground floor, most people would not take a route which would involve climbing to the second floor and then descending to the ground floor again. In many situations, however, acts may involve more than one form of satisfaction. Thus rats will often choose to take a longer novel route to a goal just as a Sunday driver may take the scenic instead of the direct route. This is not an exception to the law of least effort, since the longer route satisfies the additional goal of stimulus change.

The Efficiency of Performance of a Selected Act

Many of the same factors that determine which act will be selected also affect the efficiency with which the selected act is performed. Let us look at these and other factors and their influence on performance.

PERCEPTION: THE EFFECT OF IRRELEVANT STIMULI. In Chapter 6, "Perception," we studied factors influencing attention. It is evident that anything attracting one's attention will distract one from the task. Hence, changing stimuli and intense stimuli are more distracting than constant and weak stimuli. Furthermore, sounds tend to be more distracting than light or touch stimuli, as we saw earlier. In addition, a stimulus of the same type as that to which one is responding is more distracting to a perceiver than a stimulus from a different modality. For example, sounds are more distracting when someone is listening to something, but irrelevant lights are more distracting when someone is looking at something.

As the situation becomes increasingly more complicated, with many distractions, we might expect to find performance further impaired. In general, our expectation is supported by research findings. However, distraction sometimes seems to improve performance. This result seems to occur because people may make a special effort to overcome distraction, and because people may become so adapted to distracting stimuli in their working environment that it is "distracting" to work without them.

SET. The efficiency of performance also depends on the degree to which the total organism is prepared for it. The function of warning signals is to establish the appropriate set; i.e., to prepare a person for the events that are about to occur and the response he will be required to make. The effects of set are revealed in reaction time studies. If the subject is warned two to four seconds before the signal to which he is to respond, his speed of reaction will be much improved. For example, studies of football charging show that the players charge more quickly if a key signal is given two numbers before the starting number.

MOTIVATION. As we have noted several times earlier, the effect of motivation on performance depends on the complexity of the task. In very simple tasks the higher the motivation, the better the performance. For example, people who are more anxious are faster in a response to avoid a painful stimulus than the less anxious are. While high motivation improves the performance of simple, well-learned tasks, it impairs performance of more difficult, complex tasks. Some football coaches have applied this principle in preparing their teams for important games. If the team is very tense, the coach plans that the first sequence of plays will be familiar ones, rather than newer, more difficult ones. With familiar plays, the tension may be helpful. Once the initial tension has been reduced, newer plays can be run.

MUSCULAR FACTORS. Some of the factors influencing performance originate in the condition of the muscles themselves. If muscles are weakened by illness or if neural connections are not made, performance of the act will be disturbed. Diseases which attack the nervous system, such as infantile paralysis or locomotor ataxia, obviously affect performance. Damage to the brain by disease or injury also may affect performance. For example, the paralysis of the person who has suffered a "stroke" is caused by the destruction of the motor area of the cerebral cortex just in front of the central fissure.

Fatigue is another physiological factor which we should expect to influence performance. However, it is important only in activities involving the use of large muscles for an extended period of time or in those requiring great precision. Most of what we call fatigue is simply lack of motivation or boredom. Since variability seems to be a basic goal of human behavior, sameness of perception, motivation, or action is likely to lead to feelings of fatigue. Therefore, if we remove all of the distractions from a work situation, the effect may be opposite to that we intended. One of the problems in highway planning is to remove distractions, and yet avoid "highway hypnosis"—a condition of half sleep resulting from lack of new stimuli. (Note the relationship between this and our discussion of sensory deprivation in the preceding chapter.)

Separating the Factors in Act Selection and Performance

We have seen that perception, set, motivation, habit strength, action decrement, and least effort are all factors that influence the selection and performance level of an act. By listing the factors separately, we do not mean to imply that they do not interact in complex ways. Perception and set depend, in part, on which motives are active. The performance of an act may in itself become a goal.

The multiplicity of the factors and their interaction leaves the psychological scientist with a problem. He can only *observe* the *performance* of an organism. How can he know, for example, whether it is low habit strength or low motivation that is causing poor performance?

The principal solution has been to try to hold all the other factors constant while systematically varying one of them. For example, if we wanted to study the effects of motivation on performance, we would use a skill that all the subjects had learned equally well, establish similar sets in the subjects with instructions, and allow only motivation to vary. One reason that so many studies have been done with animals is that it is easier to control these factors with them. For example, we can ensure that all our rats have had the same amount of experience and practice in a maze, and vary motivation by using different eating schedules.

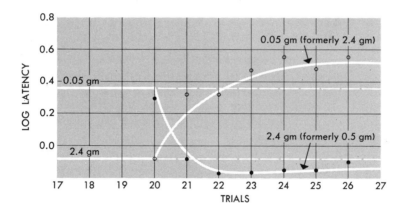

FIG. 8–7. Changes in performance with changes in the incentive in Zeaman's experiment. On trial 20 the group of rats that had been receiving the smaller reward now received the larger one and their latency decreased; that is, their speed increased, from this trial on. Similarly, when the rats receiving the larger reward on early trials found a smaller reward after trial 20, their latency increased. (After Zeaman, 1949)

■ An excellent demonstration of separating out the various factors in performance comes from a study by Zeaman (1949). Zeaman trained some rats to run down a runway for a reward of 0.05 gram of food; another group of rats to run down the same runway for a reward of 2.4 grams of food. Both groups of rats increased their speed (decreased their latency) during the early period of training, but after about 15 trials, the speed hardly changed at all. However, the speed maintained by the 2.4-gram group was considerably greater than the speed maintained by the 0.05-gram group. This might suggest that the greater the reward, the better the learning. However, Zeaman showed that this interpretation was incorrect. He did this by changing the amount of reward from the twentieth trial on. The group that had received the smaller reward now received the larger one, and conversely. Zeaman's results appear in Fig. 8–7. As you can see, changing the amount of reward changed the performance considerably. ■

We saw earlier that reward was not necessary for learning, though it was necessary for performance. Zeaman's study shows that the performance, not learning, varies with the *amount* of reward. It also shows another technique by which the motivational and the habit-strength factors can be separated experimentally.

Failure to take into account all the possible factors can lead to unexpected and seemingly unexplainable results.

■ In 1939, a series of studies was undertaken to determine the effect of light illumination on production at the Hawthorne plant of Western Electric Company. Employees assembling electrical fixtures first worked in an illumination measured as 24 foot-candles of light, then 46 foot-candles, and then 70 foot-candles. Each increase in illumination resulted in an increase in production. Illumination was then decreased. However, production continued to increase until the illumination had dropped to three foot-candles. Then the workers said they could no longer see what they were doing. (Roethlisberger and Dickson, 1939) ■

How can we explain the fact that decreases in illumination (up to a point) did not reduce the efficiency of production, but actually increased it? The answer came from an examination of the total situation. The workers who participated in the study were given more attention and more variety than they ever had gotten in their daily routine. This increased their motivation to such a level that it overrode the variations in performance due to perceptual factors alone.

The "Hawthorne effect" is now so well known that every experimenter considers and attempts to control the motivational effects of his experiment. Without such controls the effect of the purported independent variables would be impossible to estimate. This is important to remember when reading studies of the learning of acts, which we take up in the next section.

How Actions Can Be Modified: the Aquisition of Skills

THE SEQUENCE OF ACTION: TRIAL AND ERROR

As a result of an act, the situation and the organism are changed and new acts are called forth. For example, an act may result in attainment of the goal; then the following acts that are selected involve dealing with the goal. If the goal were food, once the food had been obtained, acts of eating might be selected.

In other cases, the act selected is ineffective in attaining the goal; hence a new act is selected. If the new act is not effective, still another act is selected. Thus a child trying to get out of a playpen will first pull at the sides, then try to lift his foot over the side, then try to squeeze his leg out between the bars, and finally cry for "Mommy." This process, called *trial and error*, involves selecting successive acts according to the principles of act selection we described earlier. As each act fails to bring the goal, it is abandoned, and another act is performed, until finally the goal is reached.

Trial-and-error learning can be studied by observing animal learning. Some of the earliest studies, by the psychologist E. L. Thorndike, involved cats that were, at separate times, enclosed in a puzzle box (see Fig. 8–8). In order to open the door of the box and obtain the food outside, the cats had to pull a loop of cord. Thorndike described the behavior of his cats as follows:

■ "When put into the box the cat would show evident signs of discomfort and of an impulse to escape from confinement. It tries to squeeze through any opening; it claws and bites at the bars or wire; it thrusts its paws out through any opening and claws everything it reaches; it continues its efforts when it strikes anything loose or shaky; it may claw things within the box. It does not pay very much attention to the food outside, but seems simply to strive instinctively to escape from confinement. The vigor with which it struggles is extraordinary. For eight or ten minutes it will claw and bite and squeeze incessantly." (Thorndike, 1898) ■

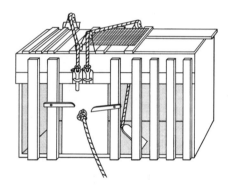

FIG. 8–8. The puzzle box. Thorndike studied trial-and-error learning by watching the movements of cats learning to escape from the box. (Thorndike, 1911)

Sooner or later the cat claws the loop; the door opens, and the cat comes out and gets the food. When put into the box again, the cat goes through much the same kind of act sequence, but is likely to hit the loop sooner. After many such trials, the cat, when placed in the problem box, pulls the cord quickly and walks out the door.

While the sequence of acts used by the cat in the problem box may appear to be random, it is not. Our principles of act selection apply here as well as elsewhere. The act which occurs is the one with the greatest habit strength associated with the goal and the situation. When it fails, the act with the next-greatest habit strength is selected, and so on to the third act, the fourth act, and succeeding acts. When the "correct" act finally occurs, the next act of walking out is selected in terms of the new situation of having the door open.

The occurrence of an act in such a sequence affects its habit strength in future similar situations. When the cat is placed in the problem box again, those responses which previously were unsuccessful tend to have less habit strength than on the first trial, and the correct act tends to have greater habit strength. Thus, other things being equal, the correct act will occur sooner on later trials, as can be seen in Fig. 8–9.

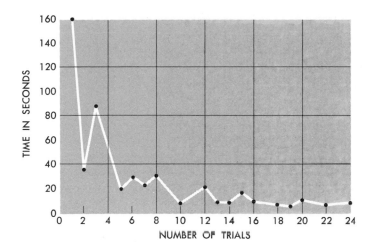

FIG. 8 9. The course of trial-and-error learning in a single
cat learning to escape from a puzzle box. (After Thorndike,
1911)

LEARNING SKILLS

The general principles of learning discussed in Chapter 5 can be applied to such
simple act-selection situations as that of the cat in the problem box or the rat
in a simple maze. However, there are additional special problems involved in
learning acts that must be simultaneously or sequentially coordinated. When
such complex series of acts are valued by society and judged against a standard
of excellence, we call them *skills*. Those involving muscular coordination are
called *motor skills*. Talking, typewriting, baseball playing are examples of the
variety of skills most of us learn. Learning a new skill is much like learning to
escape from a problem box, in that a great deal of trial and error is involved.
The child learning to catch a baseball makes many movements in the early trials.
Some combinations of movements are successful and others are not. Those
movements which result in dropping the ball tend to be abandoned; those which
result in catching the ball are repeated.

THE METHOD OF SUCCESSIVE APPROXIMATION. In learning very complex skills,
simple trial and error may be inefficient because the correct responses occur so
rarely. For example, it would probably be inefficient to begin a jet fighter pilot's
training by giving him a plane and telling him to learn to fly it by trial and
error. In some training situations in which the correct combination of responses
is extremely low in habit strength, another method of learning must be used.
One of the most effective is the *method of successive approximation*.

    The key to the method of successive approximation is to increase the habit
strength of the components of the desired skill through training simpler ap-

proximations of desired acts. As training proceeds, the response to be reinforced is changed, approaching the complex situation by gradual steps. For example, if we were to try to teach pigeons to play table tennis, simple trial-and-error methods would probably never work. However, B. F. Skinner has used successive approximations with much success in teaching such unusual skills.

What steps could one follow in teaching a pigeon to play table tennis? Try as you read this description of procedures to anticipate each next step.

■ Since pigeons tend to peck at strange objects, we might first shape food into round pellets resembling a table-tennis ball and place a pellet on the table to be used for the game. When the pigeon has developed a consistent habit of pecking at these balls, we might then roll the food ball toward the pigeon, letting her eat the food if she pecks the ball before it rolls off the table. Next, we could substitute a real table-tennis ball, feeding the pigeon whenever she pecks the moving ball. When this habit is established, we might then cease rewarding the pigeon except when the ball she has pecked rolls off the opposite end of the table. When she has learned to peck the ball toward the other end of the table, she is ready for the game, and all we need do is put another pigeon who has been similarly trained on the other side of the table. When one pecks the ball so that it rolls off the other side of the table, she is fed, and the result is a game like that depicted in Fig. 8-10. ■

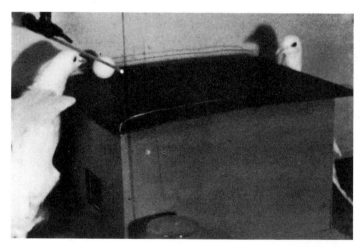

FIG. 8–10. Two pigeons playing table tennis. They were trained by the method of successive approximations. (Photo courtesy of Dr. B. F. Skinner)

The techniques of successive approximation have been successfully used to train animals for exhibition and have also been useful in teaching difficult motor skills to humans. In some respects, the training for jet fighter pilots resembles the method of successive approximation, for the pilots begin their training in ground school and progress from simpler training planes to the more difficult combat planes.

FEATURES OF THE TRAINING PROCESS

WHOLE VERSUS PART LEARNING. Another question which has perplexed psychologists and educators for a long time is this: Should a person trying to learn a new skill learn it one part at a time, or try to learn the whole skill at once?

The method of successive approximation often makes effective use of a part approach to learning. On the other hand, studies of the teaching of typing indicate that it is much more efficient for the beginning typist to begin typing words than to begin with separate practice on each letter. Thus, there are examples of effective learning with either method.

The solution to the problem of whole versus part learning seems to be this: When a skill can be performed with some success from the beginning, it is more efficient to train on the whole skill, even though it may seem difficult. When, however, the skill is so difficult that initial trials produce no success, it is more efficient to train on parts. Learning to swim, for example, seems to proceed most rapidly when the components of breathing, back and arm stroke are learned separately. For some skills a combination of whole and part learning may sometimes be helpful; that is, one may practice the whole first, then select difficult parts for separate practice.

TRANSFER OF TRAINING. As you read the description of the method of successive approximation, you may have related the principles to the concept of *generalization*, for the success of each step of training depends upon the pigeons' ability to generalize from the simple situation to the more complex ones.

While generalization often contributes positively to learning, it may also have negative effects. For example, if you have learned to type with a standard typewriter and now begin typing with an electric machine, you will find that your old habit of lifting your hand to pull a lever to return the carriage at the end of each line *interferes* with the new response of pressing the carriage-return key. Since many habits have been learned and practiced throughout our lifetimes, the designer of new equipment must take account of these lifetime habits. The effects of previous training on performance of a new skill is called *transfer of training*. When previous training aids the learning or performance of the skill, we speak of *positive transfer;* when interference results, we call it *negative transfer*.

What factors determine the amount of transfer? In terms of our study of generalization, you know that similarity is a major factor. In general, the more similar two skills are, the more transfer occurs. However, this does not tell us whether the transfer will be positive or negative.

Let us consider some examples of positive and negative transfer to see if we can determine what the differences are. An example of positive transfer is the ease with which the boy who has learned to play baseball can learn to play softball. Negative transfer is illustrated by the difficulty one has in putting his key in the ignition of a new car when the switch of his old car was in a different position.

In softball, the batting and fielding responses required are similar or identical to those required in baseball, and the chief difference is in the situation. On the other hand, in inserting the ignition key in a new car, the old and new situations are similar but the responses are different. This leads us to the following generalizations. *When the response is the same in the new situation, the more similar the new situation to the old one, the greater the positive transfer.* As you can see, this is simply the phenomenon of generalization. Thus we expect positive transfer from baseball to softball.

When, however, *the stimuli are similar and the responses differ, the more the situations are similar, the more interference* (or negative transfer) *occurs.* Thus we expect a high degree of negative transfer when the location of the ignition switch is changed. Unfortunately, for those making practical use of these two principles, most situations involve similarities and differences in both stimuli and responses, so that the only way of determining the resultant transfer is to test it. Some examples of positive and negative transfer in language learning are listed in Fig. 8–11.

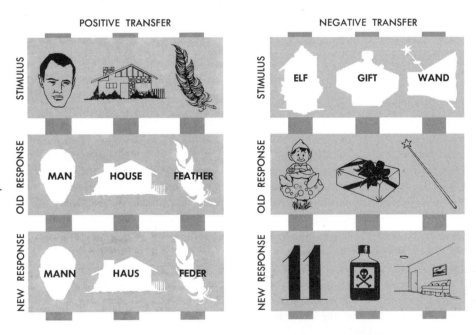

FIG. 8–11.   Positive and negative transfer in learning a new language such as German. Some words are alike in both appearance and meaning in the two languages; here there is positive transfer. Other words have the same or similar spelling but have entirely different meanings: in German, *elf* is the number eleven; *gift* means poison, and *wand* means wall. Such words would produce a negative transfer.

THE EFFECT OF REPETITION. In order to learn a skill, a large amount of repetition is usually necessary, since, as we have seen, habit strength depends upon successful repetitions. Yet the phenomenon of action decrement, the tendency to not repeat an act just performed, suggests that performance will be less successful with increasing repetition. If this is the case, are we not defeating our purposes by practicing a desired response? Fortunately, the answer is not a simple "yes"; action decrement is more temporary than habit strength and thus tends to die out over time. This has an interesting implication for arranging learning conditions.

SPACED VERSUS MASSED PRACTICE. The decrease of action decrement over time helps us answer a question which has intrigued psychologists for many years. *If an individual can spend only a limited time in practicing a skill, how should he distribute his time?* For example, if one can spend eight hours in practice, should he spend one hour a day for eight days or spend eight hours practicing on one day?

When the question is put in such an extreme form, two factors affecting the effectiveness of the practice are immediately apparent. One of these is fatigue. Long practice may build up so much fatigue that less progress is made. A second factor is motivation. In long practice sessions, motivation may not remain so high as for shorter ones. In addition, however, we need to consider action decrement. Research demonstrates that even with high motivation and low fatigue, massed practice is likely to be less efficient for learning than spaced practice. The reason is now clear. Action decrement tends to disappear between trials when practice is spaced and tends to build up when practice is massed. Thus spaced practice is generally more efficient for learning than massed practice (although at certain stages of learning, massed practice may be effective). A fourth factor influencing the effectiveness of distributed practice is interference from other response learning. When there is such interference, it seems to produce less adverse affects with distributed (spaced) practice (Underwood and Schulz, 1961). Perhaps all these factors contributed to the following discovery:

■ In World War II, psychologists were asked to work out improvements in training procedures for radiomen. The basic training consisted of learning the dots and dashes corresponding to the letters of the alphabet. Using the usual methods of training, 28 percent of the students could learn these well enough to receive five words a minute by the end of the seventh day. By changing training procedures to utilize psychological knowledge about learning, a psychologist was able to improve learning so that 50 percent of the students could receive five words a minute after seven days of training.

The method did not require the students to put in more time. In fact, at the time when the study of radio schools began, the students were required to practice sending and receiving code seven hours a day, five days a week, plus four hours on Saturday, during the first five weeks of the eight-week course. During the last three weeks of the course the students learned about procedures, equipment, and other topics. On the basis of psychological theory, the experimenter suspected that equally good results could be obtained with a shorter work day. Hence he set

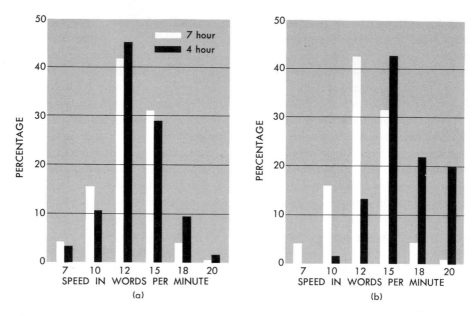

FIG. 8–12. The speed of receiving radio code achieved by men in a group who practiced four hours a day and men in a group who practiced seven hours a day at two points during training: (a) after five weeks and (b) after eight weeks. (After Keller and Estes, 1945)

up an experimental class in which the code training was on a schedule of four hours a day, six days a week, spread over the whole eight weeks. At the end of five weeks this group was compared with a comparable group which had been studying seven hours a day. The results showed that the four-hour group did just as well as the seven-hour group (see Fig. 8–12a).

At the end of the eight weeks, comparisons were again made. Now the four-hour group was clearly superior to the seven-hour group (see Fig. 8–12b).

It appeared evident that three hours a day of the normal training had been wasted and that increased mastery of the code could be attained by spreading the practice time over the whole eight weeks. (Bray, 1948) ∎

REMINISCENCE. The superiority of distributed practice is probably related to another characteristic of motor-skill learning. Ordinarily, we expect forgetting to begin as soon as practice stops, but sometimes instead of the individual doing more poorly when he begins again, he actually does better than he was doing when he stopped practicing. This phenomenon is called *reminiscence*. Reminiscence occurs after rather short rests (up to five minutes in one experiment) and is more likely to occur after massed practice than after spaced practice. It looks as though fatigue, action decrement, or interference from competing responses may die out more rapidly than the learning of the correct responses, and thus account for reminiscence. But even though we have known about reminiscence for years, we still are not sure of the explanation, and so it remains an interesting research area.

LEARNING SKILLS: A SUMMARY. We have seen that new skills may be acquired through trial and error. The method of successful approximations is more effective than trial and error because many errors can be avoided through controlling the sequence of learning. Whether a skill should be practiced as a whole or practiced in parts depends on the success with which the whole can be performed. If the skill is so difficult that practice produces little success, it is likely to be more efficient to practice parts; on the other hand, even though the task may be difficult, whole practice is likely to be more effective if some initial success is likely.

Transfer of training to a new task depends upon similarity. If the responses required are the same, then the more similar the situations, the greater the positive transfer; if the responses are different, then the more similar the situations, the greater the negative transfer.

Because repeating an act increases fatigue, reduces motivation, increases action decrement, and may build up incorrect responses, spaced practice is ordinarily more effective than massed practice.

How Can Act Learning Lead to Flexibility in Behavior?

When a person learns to make a response in a situation, he has actually learned more than to make an isolated response in a unique stimulus situation. First of all, he tends to make the same response in similar as well as identical situations. Someone who has learned to play a piano will probably also be able to play a harpsichord. You will recall that we called this phenomenon stimulus generalization.

Second, as we act in a situation, we learn the *effects* of our actions. Sometimes different actions will produce the same effects. For example, moving a piece on a chessboard will have the same effect whether the actual movement is done with your left hand or your right hand. As we grow up we learn many actions that will produce the same results, and if, for some reason, we are prevented from performing one action, we can produce the desired effect with another one. When a person has learned that several actions will have the same result in a situation, we say he has learned a *habit family*. Usually the habits in a habit family have different habit strengths, so that the one with the greatest habit strength will be performed first. If that one fails, the one with second-greatest habit strength will be performed, and so on.

Finally, in learning to make a response to a stimulus, a person may learn a more general relationship between his environment and his actions (Miller, Pribram, and Galanter, 1964). He learns to pattern his behavior in such a way that it shows some general relationship to the stimulus situation. One common example of this sort of behavior is imitation.

■ The situation in which the children were to respond consisted of a room with two chairs in two of the corners, a box being placed on each chair. The children were told that there was candy in one of the boxes. One child was told ahead of time which box to open. He was given the first turn to find the candy while the other child watched. Then the second child was given an opportunity to find the candy. If the second child went to the same box as the first he found a piece of candy. Although on the first trial most of the children did not imitate the "leader," by the third trial most of them did copy his performance. Then the situation was changed so that the children had to select the correct box from four boxes arranged in a square. In this new situation 75 percent of the children imitated the leader.

Another group of children was trained *not to imitate*, i.e., they found candy only when they chose the box that had not been selected by the leader. In a new situation, 100 percent of the children continued not to imitate. (Miller and Dollard, 1941) ■

Both the children who were rewarded for imitating and the children who were rewarded for not imitating learned something more than just to make a response to a stimulus. They learned to vary their responses in relation to the behavior of the leader. When an organism learns to vary his behavior so that his response in a new situation bears the same relationship to it as a previous response did to an old situation, we say he has learned *a general habit.**

The use of general habits that are based on the relationship between symbols and the "real" world lies at the base of many human activities—from the child who responds to verbal directions to the contractor who creates a house according to an architect's blueprint. Though the specific directions or the specific blueprint was never presented before, still the child and the contractor can act appropriately in relation to the situation.

General habits are probably learned through learning specific habits that have similar stimulus-response relationships. After several specific experiences of success via imitation, a child learns to imitate in a new situation. After many specific experiences in which a child learns the relationship between words and acts, he learns to follow new directions.

Note that, in each case we have mentioned, the action performed in accordance with the general habit was already in the response repertoire of the organism. In the example of classroom imitation, the children already know how to walk, pick up a box, etc. Similarly, the contractor already knows how to use a variety of materials in a variety of ways. A child who has never learned how to play a violin could not imitate Isaac Stern no matter how strongly his general habit of imitation is activated by the situation.

A person can respond in accordance with general habits without being able to articulate the relationship on whose basis he is responding. For example, a child learns to say "I run," but "he runs," long before he can state the rules of grammar which underlie his general habits of speech. Given a verb he has never heard before, a child will conjugate it according to the rules of regular verbs (Brown, 1958). Verbalization of the principle involved is a higher level of abstraction which he learns later on.

---

* The term "general habit" was introduced in Chapter 5, p. 132.

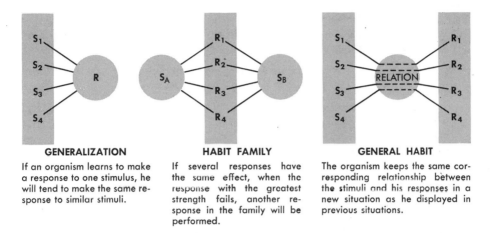

GENERALIZATION

If an organism learns to make a response to one stimulus, he will tend to make the same response to similar stimuli.

HABIT FAMILY

If several responses have the same effect, when the response with the greatest strength fails, another response in the family will be performed.

GENERAL HABIT

The organism keeps the same corresponding relationship between the stimuli and his responses in a new situation as he displayed in previous situations.

FIG. 8–13.   Three processes involved in the selection of acts.

Act Learning and the Flexibility of Behavior: a Summary

Through most of this chapter, we have discussed actions in terms of simple act expectancies (s-r-s relationships). In this last section, we looked at the more complex structures which underlie the tremendous flexibility of behavior, especially human behavior. Through the mechanism of stimulus generalization, a habit learned in one situation can be applied to another. Because of the habit family, if one approach to a goal fails, we are capable of using another. And through the learning of general habits, we can use the effects of previous learning, yet vary our own actions in accordance with changing situations. These mechanisms are summarized in Fig. 8–13.

The Development of Action

Infancy

The newborn baby comes into the world with a repertoire of "wired-in" innately coordinated acts. Within a few hours after birth he sneezes, yawns, cries, turns his head, puts his thumb in his mouth, and jumps when a loud noise is made nearby. When his lips are touched, he begins sucking. If he is dropped into a pool of water, he moves his arms and legs in a dog paddle and swallows very little water. Another reflex is illustrated in Fig. 8–14.

Despite his repertoire of reflexes the human being comes into the world relatively ill-equipped for looking after himself. Much of his activity is uncoordinated. He kicks, twists, turns, cries, and moves all of the muscles in his body. He makes the movements which will eventually go into his repertoire of acts, but the movements are random, diffuse, and unrelated to the situation. His repertoire of coordinated responses to stimuli is extremely limited. Out of his mass of incoherent movements must develop all of the acts which are essential if a person is to live successfully in our complex society. Except for the small number of inborn coordinated responses, all other acts must be learned.

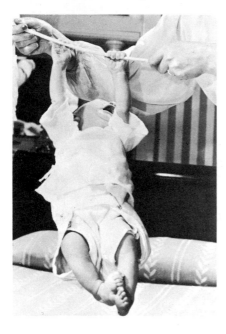

FIG. 8–14. A baby will reflexively grasp at an object and support his own weight. (United Press International photo)

The process of development involves both increasingly complex integrations and increasingly precise differentiation of responses. When the infant is disturbed, he moves all over. His legs kick; his hands paw at the air; he cries. Out of these mass movements, specific acts are differentiated. Clumsy pawing at a toy gives way to clearly differentiated reaching and grasping of the toy. The process of integration of movements into acts occurs almost simultaneously with the differentiation we have just described. Thus the child who has learned to differentiate movements of fingers and arm soon integrates these movements into the act of feeding himself, coordinating movements of the eye with movements of the hand and arm. Although babies differ in the rate at which maturation proceeds, the sequence is the same for all babies.

The amount of change necessary is most noticeable when one compares the helplessness of the human infant with the independence of other young animals. While the human infant does not walk until he is about a year old, the guinea pig will walk at birth, and other mammals walk soon after birth. Despite his ability to suck and swallow, the newborn human is utterly incapable of getting his own food, while the newborn chick is able to peck grain and seeds with fair accuracy during the first day of his life.

Because of the human's helplessness, he has relatively little fixed behavior at birth, and the baby's behavior can be influenced by his parents as well as by other environmental stimuli. In short, he can learn. Therefore as the baby develops, the inconsistent, uncoordinated movements of hand and feet change to coordinated acts of grasping and crawling. By the age of two months the baby will wink when an object approaches his eye (Preyer, 1882). This is one of the first signs of behavior based on an expectancy about the environment, and it is expectancies which will increasingly guide the child's behavior.

When he comes into the world the baby has the potential for all the *movements* which will be required of him, but acts develop through the organization of these movements into integrated muscle patterns related to particular stimuli and expectancies. Learning rather than instinct determines the situations in which these acts are used. Of course, maturation frequently determines when the learning experiences are most profitable.

Learning Specific Acts

While maturational processes of differentiation and integration are taking place, the baby is also learning specific acts. Such learning begins at a very early stage. In an experiment by Dorothy Marquis (1941), very young infants less than 10 days old were placed on different feeding schedules. One group was fed every three hours, one group was fed every four hours, and one group was fed whenever it was hungry. When the babies who had been on the three-hour schedule were switched to a four-hour schedule, they began crying and became very active three hours after their last feeding. The four-hour group did not increase rapidly in activity until almost four hours after feeding. The group which was fed whenever it was hungry tended to become active between three and four hours after the last meal. These results indicate that these very young babies had *learned* to adapt to their respective feeding schedules.

In another experiment Marquis sounded a buzzer five seconds prior to each feeding of ten infants who were from two to nine days old. Within five days eight of the infants began to make sucking and mouth-opening responses as soon as they heard a buzzer, while a control group who had heard the buzzer, but not in connection with feeding, did not respond. Both of these experiments indicate that infants are capable of learning even in the first few days of life. This early learning, taking place in the repeated situations of feeding, elimination, and bathing is the basis of later more complex learning.

MATURATIONAL LIMITS. The development of many skills and general habits depends upon maturation. For example, as we saw in Chapter 4, one of the first complex skills which the child develops is walking. Before the child can walk, simpler skills must mature. One of the baby's first accomplishments is his ability to hold up his head without support. Next he becomes able to support his trunk with his arms. Then he develops the ability to sit alone and to maintain his balance in a sitting position. These, plus many other skills, are necessary if the child is to walk. The parent who tries to hurry the child's walking prior to the development of this sequence is doomed to failure.

CULTURAL DETERMINANTS. However, it is probable that many complex skills could be learned at an earlier age than they usually are. In these cases, even though the child's neuromuscular maturation may be adequate, learning does not take place until society, in the form of parents or playmates, gives the opportunities and reinforcements for developing the skill. For example, in a study of maturation and learning by McGraw (1935), a boy was taught to roller-skate before he reached the age of two. Assuming that McGraw's subject was typical, the capacity for learning roller-skating exists long before most children learn it in our culture.

Maturation and Learning: a Reprise

It might be useful here to review and illustrate once again the complex interrelationships between maturation and learning that we discussed in Chapter 4. Some classic studies in the area deal with the development of the chick's pecking ability.

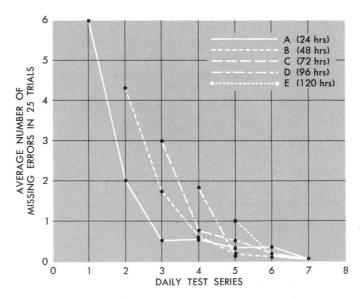

FIG. 8–15. The effect on their pecking abilities of keeping chicks in the dark. Group A was kept in a dark room for 24 hours after hatching; Group B was kept in the dark room for 48 hours; Group C, 72 hours; Group D, 96 hours; and Group E, 120 hours. (Cruz, 1935)

■ Cruz (1935) and Padilla (1930) raised several groups of chicks in the dark. One group of chicks was brought out into the light to obtain food by pecking the first day after birth and thereafter obtained all their food by pecking. A second group was brought out the second day; a third group the third day, and so forth. During the time before the chickens were brought into the light, they were fed in the dark. If maturation were the sole determinant of pecking ability, four-day old chicks brought into the light for the first time should peck as accurately as chicks that had already been pecking for four days. On the other hand, if practice alone is the determinant, chicks brought into the light on the fourth day should be no better when brought out than chicks which are newly hatched. If practice is necessary during a critical period, soon after birth, chicks that do not get the opportunity to practice should be worse than other chicks that began practicing at the critical time.

As indicated in Fig. 8–15, both maturation and practice were operating. Chicks that began pecking the third day were not as accurate as three-day-old chicks that had been pecking three days, but were more accurate than newborn chicks. As the graph indicates, maturation was effective for five or six days. Chicks kept in the dark for eight days showed malcoordination. Chicks delayed for 14 days were completely unable to peck. Some of this group died of starvation even though the ground was covered with grain. Others had to be taught to peck by training on soft mash. *When practice was delayed beyond the critical period, capacity waned.* ■

Does this remind you of our earlier discussion of imprinting? You will recall that in the imprinting studies, lack of stimulation at the appropriate time resulted in a permanent failure of attachment to the imprinted cue.

FIG. 8–16. These three children were hidden by their mother in a house for 11 years. Their unusual gestures and expressions are one effect of their isolation. They also seemed retarded in physical development. The girl on the left is 16 years old, the boy, whose height is only 3 ft 11 in., is 14, and the girl on the right is 13. (Wide World Photos)

This example deals primarily with a simple motor response; however, the effects of practice and learning in childhood are also important for more complex behavior. Early learning aids later learning. Not only are connections established which permit easier and more accurate transfer, but early perceptual learning aids later learning by giving experience in discriminating the cues to which responses must be learned. Thus the person who gets a late start, whose environment failed to provide learning opportunities in early childhood, is handicapped in later learning (see Fig. 8–16).

■ One of the most dramatic illustrations of such a handicap is furnished by the "wolf children" of India (Singh and Zingg, 1942). Two girls were found in 1920 living in a cave where they were being cared for by a wolf along with her own cubs. The children were raised by Rev. A. L. Singh, who observed their development. They appeared to be one and a half and eight years old at the time of their discovery. Whether the two children were abandoned together or the older one had been abandoned earlier is not known. The younger died within a year because of her difficulty in adjusting to the new diet. However, the older girl, Kamala, survived for over nine years and was cared for by Mrs. Singh. The effect of her experience is indicated by the fact that even though she eventually learned to walk she could never run on two feet. In time, however, Kamala learned to show affection and to speak a few words. While we have no way of assessing this child's inherited capacities, it seems possible that some of her difficulty in learning, as compared to two- and three-year-old normal children, was related to the lack of practice in her early environment. ■

There are many difficulties in evaluating reports such as this. One of them is that the cases are so dramatic that it is difficult to disentangle objective observations from the natural awe and wonder of those interacting with the children. Another difficulty is that the individuals caring for the children are under great pressure to capitalize on their notoriety. Most important is the lack of knowledge of the children's background and of the age at which they were abandoned. Consequently, studies of "wolf children" cannot by themselves give much support for or against a psychological theory. This much seems to be reasonably sure from the cases reported above and other such cases. Children have survived in the wild for a significant period. These children typically show considerable retardation and have great difficulty in learning many of the skills necessary for socialization. Because these observations fit in with controlled studies of the effects of early experience in lower animals, many authorities now believe that the retardation may be partly accounted for by a lack of appropriate early experience.

The Development of Speech

The principles of learning and development which we have been discussing can be clearly seen in the development of speech. Here maturation and the learning of specific habits are necessary before the complex general habits can emerge.

As we have seen, the newborn infant's responses are uncoordinated and un-differentiated. Among his responses to various stimuli are vocal sounds. Matu-rational factors limit the sort of sounds the baby makes. The area in the brain that controls speech develops later than other motor areas of the brain, and the muscles and structures involved in speech also change as the infant matures. In the beginning most of his sounds are single vowel sounds, but as maturation proceeds he begins using his lips and tongue to produce a consonant like "mah." At about the age of six or seven months he begins stringing these simple syllables together. When he says "ma-ma-ma," he hears the sound "ma-ma-ma," so that the sound "ma-ma-ma" becomes associated with the act of producing the sound.

Vocalizations probably have special significance for the child. Usually his mother has talked to him as she cared for him. The sound of the human voice has frequently been associated with reduction of pain or some form of pleasure. Furthermore, the infant's own crying or other vocalization has brought his parents to satisfy his needs. Thus we should expect him to be motivated to repeat the sequence of acts which result in vocalized sounds. This hypothesis, suggested by Mowrer (1950), is supported by the observation that deaf children babble much less than normal children. They have not associated sounds with satisfaction. They have few sources of feedback. Consequently, spontaneous vocalizations would be unlikely to be repeated.

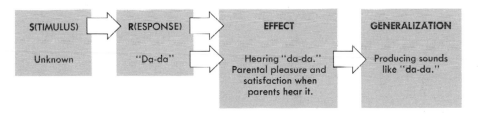

FIG. 18–17   Instrumental conditioning as one process involved in language learning.

In addition to the probability that vocalizations "sound good" in themselves because of their associations with pleasure, these vocalizations also sometimes produce marked effects upon the behavior of parents. When the baby says "da-da," his parents come running, happy because he has said "Daddy!" and the baby hears them make sounds similar to those which he has said himself with such good effect. Thus his behavior has stimulated responses from important people. The learning situation is illustrated in Fig. 8–17, which follows the s-r-s-a paradyme suggested for instrumental conditioning in Chapter 5.

As a result of such rewards, the strength of the habit of saying "da-da" is stronger the next time Daddy appears. As similar situations occur day after day, the baby eventually responds consistently with "da-da" when Daddy ap-pears. Thus by a pattern of attention and reward the baby learns to repeat some sounds and to omit others.

■ A similar phenomenon has been demonstrated in the laboratory with college students as subjects. The students were asked to say individual words as they thought of them in succession. Whenever a student in the experimental group said a plural noun, the experimenter responded by saying, "mmm-hmm." If the student said any word other than a plural noun, the experimenter said nothing. The experimenter was uniformly silent to all the words spoken by a control group. As you can see in Fig. 8–18, the frequency of saying plural nouns gradually increased for the experimental group but not for the control group (Greenspoon, 1955). Just as the students changed their word patterns in accordance with the effects produced by words, so the baby tends to repeat sounds that bring about the desired behavior from his parents. ■

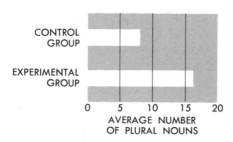

CONTROL GROUP

EXPERIMENTAL GROUP

0   5   10   15   20

AVERAGE NUMBER
OF PLURAL NOUNS

FIG. 8–18. The effect of reinforcement on saying plural nouns. The chart shows the average number of plural nouns spoken by subjects in a five-minute period after 25 minutes of training. The experimenter reinforced subjects in the experimental group—but not subjects in the control group—when they uttered plural nouns during training. (After Greenspoon, 1955)

The physical process of speech development itself seems simple, but it is actually a remarkable feat of coordination. Muscles of the chest must be coordinated in expelling air through the vocal cords, which in turn are controlled by some 19 muscles. These must be coordinated with muscles controlling the lips, teeth, tongue, and mouth if sounds are to be formed into words. Certain maturing patterns seem to go together naturally, and language utilizes these to make learning easier. For example, in almost all languages there are words for mother and father with sounds like "ma-ma" and "da-da" or "pa-pa" since these are among the baby's first syllables. When these syllables are used with others, the complexity of patterns of movement involved becomes greater.

The discriminations involved are also extremely complex. For example, the child must learn not only to discriminate between the sound of "d" and "t" but also to differentiate the responses involved in producing the sounds. In addition he must learn to associate the word with the thing it symbolizes. It is generally reported that he begins to use words as symbols between the ages of nine and fifteen months. After the baby has learned his first word, his new words are at first added very slowly. Typically, there are still only five or six words in his vocabulary six months after the first word has been spoken. The baby gets a great deal of practice in using these words. In addition to the probability that both maturation and his previous learning enable him to vocalize a good deal, his parents, proud of his new accomplishment, continually test and exhibit his vocabulary. The rewards for these particular sounds serve as incentives for repeating them. Since each time they are repeated the child hears the sound he has made, their habit strength increases above that of his other vocalizations, and potentially meaningful sounds are thus made more and more frequently.

At the same time that the baby is learning to say "da-da" when his mother says "da-da," he is also learning in several ways a general habit of imitation of speech which is highly rewarded. When the baby makes a sound, he hears the sound, and frequently his mother and father repeat the sound. Thus hearing sounds is associated with producing sounds. By the age of six to twelve months, he frequently imitates sounds. Other events provide occasions for another sort of imitation; when the child performs an act, he usually sees the movement that he is making. Consequently, the sight of motion becomes the cue to the motion. It is then not difficult for cues involved in seeing others do something to become the cues to doing the same thing. This general habit of imitation, both of speech and action, is frequently rewarded.

Other general habits learned during the early years of life also contribute to the development of speech. At about the age of a year and a half to two years, the child's vocabulary suddenly spurts upward. As a result of learning to identify a few objects by words, the child seems to develop a general habit of identifying objects by words. He now begins to ask for the names of objects and to take great pleasure in identifying the pictures in his picture book. In the years following, he not only learns to use many new words, but he also builds up general habits of grammar, which he uses in forming sentences.

To summarize: In our study of the development of language we have seen how maturational factors determine the kinds of sounds the infant can make, while the association of the sounds with satisfaction motivates the infant to repeat these sounds and increase their habit strength. In addition, the feedback obtained by hearing the sounds he makes provides a situation in which learning is facilitated. The learning of specific words leads to a general habit of using words to identify objects, and then to general habits of grammar and sentence structure.

Individual Differences

The English language contains many words which describe characteristics of action in which individuals differ. When psychologists investigated some of these characteristics, they discovered that the characteristics were not as general as everyday language implied. Let us look at some of the terms that are commonly used to describe differences in the actions of people.

ACTIVITY. One characteristic of a person's action that does show some consistency is *activity*. Among infants this is one of the most noticeable characteristics differentiating one baby from another. Since differences appear at such an early age, it is probable that there are basic inherited differences in this characteristic. However, as the individual grows older, these inherited biological characteristics, other physiological factors, and learning interact to determine the individual's activity. The functioning of the thyroid gland, for example, affects the rate of metabolism and the resulting degree of activity. Undersecretion of the thyroid generally results in lessened activity, while oversecretion causes a person to become jumpy and restless. But even when individuals do not differ in amount of thyroid secretion, they may still differ in activity as a result of differences in learning. For example, lower-class children differ from middle-class children in that they use their bodies much more actively in expressing their feelings. Such differences must arise from the differences in training between lower-class and middle-class children.

ATHLETIC ABILITY. In our culture, the skills required for superior performance in sports like football, baseball, or basketball are highly valued. The boy who is a good football player is encouraged to try out for the baseball team. We might thus expect him to develop general athletic ability. Statistical analyses of various tests of athletic and motor ability, however, reveal that there is no general athletic ability. Skill on tasks requiring large-muscle coordination is found to be independent of skill on tasks requiring fine sensory-motor coordination. Different sports and even different positions on the team may require different combinations of these abilities as well as strength and speed. Athletic ability is thus not a single characteristc but a combination of several, and the degree of relationship between ability in two sports depends on motivational factors and the degree to which they require the same component abilities.

While tests of strength, speed, dexterity, and coordination enable us to make better-than-chance predictions of athletic skill, they are unable to predict who will be a record breaker. This will not be surprising to those readers who have followed a sport over a period of time. In football, as in every other sport, fine prospects who possess all of the abilities necessary for success never make the varsity. This points to the importance of motivation in the development of ability. In most situations, the limits of capacity are not reached because there is not enough motivation to push an individual to the practice necessary for maximum achievement. The persons outstanding in certain athletic abilities, as in other abilities, tend to come from regions or social classes which particularly reward practicing and developing these abilities. Thus Australia produces an unusually high proportion of outstanding tennis players, and Japan and Australia produce great swimmers.

MANUAL DEXTERITY. As our discussion of athletic ability implies, motor abilities are not as general as we might expect. The abilities underlying skill in various tasks tend to be fairly specific. One of these is manual dexterity. In everyday language we often talk about a boy as being "good with his hands," and this may refer to manual dexterity. But tests show that people who can use their arms and hands well to manipulate large objects are not necessarily high in finger dexterity, the ability to manipulate small things skillfully with one's fingers. For example, people who are good at bolting two boards together are not necessarily good at putting something together with a screw driver.

Practical Applications

Individual Applications

CHILD REARING. Since act selection depends upon perception, motivation, and habit strength, a person's selection of acts can be influenced by influencing these factors. For example, if a parent is trying to teach a child to be neat, he can change the child's motivation by using rewards or punishments; he can also change the child's habit strength by training. Parental training of children is sometimes inefficient because of failure to provide motivation. In other cases, the training fails because the child does not know what to do or does not have the act in his repertoire.

Typically, however, parents set up the learning situation so that the desired response is probable. For example, in training a baby to come when the mother holds out her arms, the mother usually begins by holding out her arms when the child is already crawling toward her. Thus the sight of open arms becomes a cue for going to mother, and the reward of being cuddled creates a motive for the act. Here, the parent uses the principles of learning which we have been studying.

Developing Skills

Almost everyone would like to improve his skill in some area. In some cases we should like to add new skills to our repertoire or to teach a new habit to a child or pet. Our study of habit formation gives many clues to development of a skill.

Practice (repetition) *with immediate feedback of results is the most important principle of improvement.* We saw in Chapter 5 the importance of immediate feedback in training riflemen. When marksmanship training was changed so that the marksmen could see where each of his bullets hit, accurate shooting was achieved much more rapidly. Similarly, in learning to play golf, practice is the first essential for improvement. In golf, feedback of results is almost always immediate. However, the performance is so complex that it is often difficult for the beginning golfer to make the necessary corrections in his actions. An important function of a teacher in golf or in other skills is to help the learner discriminate the movements which are causing his errors. One of the difficulties in learning by observing an expert is that the beginner fails to observe the important components of the act. Thus a second important principle of skill training is that *coaching should help the learner discriminate critical components of the skill.*

Earlier in this chapter we read of two pigeons which had learned to play table tennis. As we saw, Skinner, who trained them, used the technique of successive approximations. This technique consists of teaching first a simple act. Then a simple change or additional act is added to the original act. More variations are added until the final complex act has been learned.

The same technique can also be used by an individual who wishes to develop a complex skill, such as playing the piano. The principle involved here is one based on our earlier discussion of whole versus part learning. *Learning should begin with units which can be practiced with some success.*

The old adage "practice makes perfect" is not an adequate guide to learning a skill. To be effective, the practice must be on the right act. Practicing something over and over without instruction and with little feedback may simply "stamp in" bad habits that will interfere with learning more efficient habits.

A corollary of this principle is that guidance in the correct performance is most effective if given early in learning. Thus it is usually more efficient to get professional instruction when you are beginning to learn golf or any new skill, instead of after you have learned it by yourself.

A closely related corollary is less well substantiated but offers exciting possibilities. Intellectualization of skills can reduce training time on the job. When pilots in training were told what to expect, what cues to look for, and what responses they were to make, the air time to solo an airplane was reduced to three or four hours (A. C. Williams, unpublished). This, of course, is closely related to our earlier statement that verbalization of principles and concepts speeds learning.

Even though we have advised beginning training with units simple enough so that correct responses are likely to occur, from our study of transfer you will recognize that training which brings in steps not included in the final act is likely to be inefficient. Looking at the keys when learning typing will hinder rather than aid later performance, because it brings into the serial habit steps that are not included in the ultimate serial habit. There is one exception to this generalization. This is in training on a new task where a good deal of negative transfer is expected from previous learning. One way of reducing this negative transfer is to increase the subject's ability to discriminate between the critical stimuli. This technique, called *stimulus predifferentiation,* involves training the individual to make two differing simple responses to the two critical, but similar, stimuli before training on the new task begins.

A fourth principle of skill learning is: *In learning a skill, it is better to train with natural units than to break the task into artificial parts which later must be combined.* To learn golf by practicing first the back swing, then hitting the ball, then the follow through, would be inefficient. The learning of typing is greatly improved when the training system uses practice on ordinary words and sentences rather than individual letters and nonsense syllables.

A fifth principle which is important for learning skills is illustrated by the experiment in the training of radiomen which we cited earlier. The success of this training was based on application of the principle that *under most conditions spaced practice is more efficient than massed practice.*

Breaking an Undesired Habit

Frequently we are more interested in breaking old habits than in forming new ones. Guthrie and Edwards (1949) described three methods of breaking habits.

The *first* is to give the stimulus for the undesired response at a time when some incompatible response is taking place. This provides a good opportunity for learning the incompatible response in place of the undesired one. Thus a child afraid of the water may lose his fear response if in active play at the beach he chases a ball into shallow water.

The *second* is to repeat the cue for the habit until fatigue or action decrement prevents its occurrence. Thus if one is in the habit of typing "hte" for "the," one method of correcting it is to type "hte" over and over again. This is probably effective not only because it induces action decrement but also because it brings the cues into consciousness again. "Breaking" a horse by forcing a saddle on him and riding him until quiet acts occur is a good example of this method.

The *third* method is to give the stimulus for the habit with such slight intensity that the act does not occur. Gradually, the stimulus intensity may be increased until finally it no longer elicits the habit, even at normal intensities. This was the technique used to extinguish a young boy's fear of a rabbit. (The study was described in Chapter 7.)

A *fourth* technique, not discussed by Guthrie and Edwards, is probably more commonly used than the other three. It is to change the individual's motivation. Parents utilize this principle when they offer children rewards for breaking habits of tardiness or untidiness.

Social Applications

The principles of action can also be applied to the field of equipment design. For example, certain movements are easier to perform or to coordinate than others because of the structure of the human body. The standard typewriter keyboard is poorly designed for human abilities. The fingers which are used most are not those which are the most agile. A keyboard which permits a maximum number of successive movements by fingers on the opposite hand or by nonadjacent fingers and a maximum use of the "home-row" keys has been devised. Using this keyboard, high school students were able to type 40 words per minute after 26 class periods of instruction, while students using the standard keyboard averaged only 35 words per minute after 180 class periods of instruction (Dvorak *et al.*, 1936). However, it has been found that there is a large amount of negative transfer when typists trained on standard keyboards are asked to switch to the new keyboard.

As jobs become more complex, more and more attention is being given not only to designing equipment men can use, but also to training. The principles of skill learning, which we have discussed, are utilized in such training programs. Thus attention is given to providing prompt feedback of results to the trainee, to setting up the training program so that the sequence of learning is effective, and to the use of knowledge about spaced and massed practice.

Probably the most well-developed area of application of our knowledge about action is in the identification and measurement of important motor abilities. Aptitude tests are used to predict later performance. Tests of motor abilities and mechanical aptitude are widely used in industry and the Armed Forces for selection and assignment of personnel. The training psychologist attempts to devise training programs that will produce efficient operators, despite the difficulty of the task or the type of person to be trained; the personnel psychologist attempts to select people whose abilities will enable them to perform the task with a minimum of training; and the engineering psychologist attempts to design equipment which can be operated by as many people as possible with as little training as possible. The better each psychologist performs his task, the easier is the task of each of the others.

Summary

Concepts

Reaction time. The time interval between onset of the stimulus and the beginning of the response

Stimulus-response compatibility. The psychological "closeness" between a stimulus and the response to it

Serial act. A group of acts which occur in sequence in such a way that the stimuli produced by each act serve as cues for the successive act

Two-phase movement. Acts in which the initial movements are preparatory and perhaps opposite to the ultimately desired movement

Action decrement. The tendency of an organism not to repeat the identical action just completed; the tendency decreases as the interval between the two acts increases

Law of least effort. The tendency to choose an act which accomplishes the goals of the organism and which requires the least effort

Trial and error. A process of problem solving in which a sequence of acts is performed until one act produces the goal. On succeeding attempts to solve the same problem, the goal-producing act occurs earlier and earlier in the sequence

Successive approximations. A method of training an organism to perform a complex serial act by selective reinforcement—early in training, the organism is rewarded for any act which remotely resembles the final act; as training proceeds, the response which is reinforced changes, becoming more and more like the desired final act

Transfer of training. The effect of earlier learning on present learning; transfer is *positive* if the earlier learning makes present learning easier; *negative* if the earlier learning makes present learning more difficult

Habit family. A group of habits which produce the same result

General habit. The learned act tendency which results in a person's maintaining the same relationship between corresponding stimuli and responses in a class of situations

Principles

1. There are three types of muscle: heart, smooth and striped; modification of responses involving smooth and heart muscles is most easily accomplished via classical conditioning; of responses involving striped muscles, via instrumental conditioning.

2. Acts can be described in terms of the strength and precision required, in terms of the time taken to complete them, and in terms of the time interval between the stimulus and the act (reaction time).

3. Reaction time often reflects the psychological complexity of the task.

4. Some factors influencing act selection are perception, motivation, habit strength, action decrement, and least effort.

5. The role of perception in the selection of acts is to provide information (i) about the situation, (ii) about the effects of each act in relation to the goal, and (iii) about the nature and location of the goal.

6. Motivation affects act selection in that it determines the degree of arousal of the organism, the goals to be sought, and the persistence and flexibility with which they are sought.

7. We hypothesize that the strength of a habit depends on the number of times its performance has been followed by informational feedback. Whether or not the act based on the habit is performed depends on affective feedback.

8. The efficiency with which a selected act is performed depends on distraction from irrelevant stimuli, motive strength, and muscular factors.

9. Positive transfer tends to occur when the old and new learning situations require the same responses; negative transfer tends to occur when the two situations require different responses to similar stimuli.

10. If the whole act can be practiced with some success, practicing the entire act seems to be more effective than practicing the components separately.

11. Spaced practice seems to be superior to massed practice; this phenomenon may be partially due to action decrement.

12. The development of acts in infancy is marked by increased differentiation and integration.

13. The development of certain acts requires practice at particular maturational periods.

14. There are consistent individual differences in activity and manual dexterity; athletic ability does not appear to be a single characteristic.

15. Undesired habits may be eliminated by (i) presenting the stimulus for the habit when an incompatible response is occurring, (ii) presenting the stimulus when the undesired response is fatigued, (iii) presenting the stimulus at such low levels that the response does not occur, then gradually increasing it, and (iv) changing motivation.

16. The principles of action have been applied to the selection and training of personnel and to the design of equipment.

Suggested Readings

GAGNÉ, R. M. and E. A. FLEISHMAN, *Psychology and Human Performance*. New York: Holt, Rinehart, and Winston, 1959. An introductory textbook stressing the topics of this chapter.

WOODWORTH, R. S., *Dynamics of Behavior*. New York: Holt, Rinehart, and Winston, 1957. This final statement of one of the great names of psychology includes a good deal on action.

chapter 9

cognition: memory, language, and meaning

chapter 9

Part 1. Memory

THE PHENOMENA OF MEMORY

THE DYNAMICS OF MEMORY

THE DEVELOPMENT OF MEMORY

INDIVIDUAL DIFFERENCES

PRACTICAL APPLICATIONS

Part 2. Language and Meaning

THE PHENOMENA OF LANGUAGE

THE DYNAMICS OF LANGUAGE:
THE ANALYSIS OF MEANING

THE DEVELOPMENT OF LANGUAGE

INDIVIDUAL DIFFERENCES IN LANGUAGE

IMPLICATIONS

In the last chapter, we dealt with mental processes that are directly reflected in behavior—the determinants of skilled performance. However, many activities, especially human activities, result from complex mental processes that are not so easily made directly observable. In terms of the computer analogy we described in Chapter 3, behavior resulting from the "higher mental processes" involves more activity inside the machine. In terms of your own experience it involves more conscious thought. We shall look at these processes in the next two chapters. Problem solving and decision making will be discussed in Chapter 10. Here we shall look at the processes of memory and symbolic representation with language.

PART 1. MEMORY

Without our ability to remember past experience, we would be wanderers in a world perpetually new to us. Each situation would require reflexive or random behavior. In fact, it is typical of human beings to regret that their memories are not better. We forget names; we mislay keys; wedding anniversaries slip by; and such slips of memory not only cause embarrassment, but may be inconvenient or damaging. The student who is faced with final exams is coming to grips with the basic problem of remembering. How can he learn so that he will remember when he is confronted with the exam questions? Why has he forgotten what was said in the lectures early in the term? At the same time, memory for some things is remarkably good. Even after years in which one has never ridden a bicycle, he can usually ride again with little relearning. How can such persistence of learning be explained? These very practical questions are the basis for much of the research and theory which will be presented in this chapter.

We have, of course, discussed memory in virtually every preceding chapter, since all learning—all the effects of experience—involves memory. A young girl may be bitten by a dog and carry a fear of dogs throughout her life. Similarly, memory may be revealed by the ease with which a former tennis player learns table tennis, by the recognition of a familiar face, by the tendency to think we've met someone before if he has familiar features, or by our ability to rememorize a poem learned in childhood, as well as by our ability to recall the date when

Columbus discovered America. Memory may be revealed by stimulus generalization or by transfer to a new learning task, as well as by the performance of a conditioned response. Our usage of the term "memory" is thus broader than that of everyday usage, for we are including not only recall of past experience but also *any evidence of learning*.

The Phenomena of Memory

Types of Memory

There are a variety of ways of differentiating between types of memory. One way in which memories can be classified is in terms of time: some memories are very temporary; others are more enduring. For example, one may look up a telephone number, remember it long enough to dial the number, but then be completely unable to recall it. Such immediate memory is called *short-term memory*. On the other hand, an adult may recall a poem or song learned in childhood, even though he has not heard or practiced it for many years. Such *long-term memories* may differ from short-term memories in method of storage, and individuals with high ability in one type may not exhibit this same high level in the other.

Memories also may vary in the degree to which they resemble the original perceptions. Some of our memories are vivid. We can recall clearly the sights, sounds, and even the smells of some exciting event. But other memories may influence our behavior even without our awareness. All of us have had experiences of entering a strange place and feeling that we have been there before, without having a clear memory of it, or have met a stranger and had an immediate reaction of like or dislike without knowing why. This sense of familiarity sometimes experienced in a new situation has been noted for many years. The French call it *déjà vu* ("previously seen"), and Plato used it as part of the basis for his belief that he had previously lived in other bodies. *Déjà vu* illustrates the phenomenon (called *redintegration*) that a part tends to reinstate the whole. If some aspects of a new situation are familiar, the whole situation seems familiar. Similarly, if some mannerism or characteristic of a person is like that of one's father or of someone else to whom he had an emotional response, he tends to make a similar response to the new person. Memories may thus vary from those of which we are largely unaware, to those which are very vivid.

One of the most unusual phenomena of memory is the ability of some children to look at a picture for a brief period of time and then describe all the details in the picture from memory. Whereas most people remember only the features that attracted their attention, the child with *eidetic imagery* seems to be able to see the whole picture in his mind. Such "photographic," or eidetic, memory is not uncommon in children of ages six to twelve, but rather rare in adults, which suggests that its loss may be related to the development of abstract thinking.

Rote memory, such as is involved in a person's memorizing something without understanding it, is different from memory in which the task is to remember the sense, or meaning, of what was learned. People who are good at rote memorization do not necessarily do well on tests of meaningful memory, and vice versa. The relationship between rote memory and meaningful memory depends to some extent on the learning task as well as on the test of memory. Thus a student who memorizes the details of a course may do well in some types of courses with some types of examinations but poorly in a different course, or even in the same course, if the examination requires thought instead of mere rote learning. The score of the student who tries to get only the "sense" of the text and lectures also depends on the content and examinations. If what the teacher expects is unclear, we may find no correlation between these abilities. If the teacher indicates that he expects both types of learning, we would probably find a positive correlation. McClusky (1934) showed that students who prepared for an objective test performed better on such a test than on an essay test covering the same material. Students who prepared for an essay test did well on both essay and objective tests.

THE MEASUREMENT OF MEMORY. From these examples of different types of memory it is clear that we use the construct *memory* to describe a wide variety of phenomena. Although we ordinarily think of memory as a conscious process, we measure human memory not only by what a person can *recall* when he is asked to remember something, but also by his *recognition* of the correct response, as in a multiple-choice test question. A still more sensitive measure of memory is the amount of *saving* there is in relearning something, when the time or trials required in relearning are compared with the time or trials required to learn it originally.

The Experiments of Ebbinghaus

The first psychologist to study memory systematically was Herman Ebbinghaus (1885). He did a remarkable series of studies, using himself as both experimenter and subject. The task he set for himself was learning and relearning lists of nonsense syllables. As a measure of memory (and forgetting), he observed how long it took him to relearn the list. If he forgot nothing, it would take him no extra time to reproduce the list perfectly. (The savings measure of memory was first used by Ebbinghaus.)

Why did Ebbinghaus use nonsense syllables? He wanted to use verbal materials which would have three characteristics: (1) The material should provide a large pool of items that are approximately equally difficult to learn and remember. (2) The items should have little or no meaningful association. (3) They should be items with which an adult subject has had little or no experience.

Therefore, instead of analyzing his memory for words or sentences, Ebbinghaus constructed syllables by using all combinations of two consonants separated by a vowel that did not spell a word. He memorized lists of these nonsense syllables, such as *pif* and *qax*, and tested his recall after various periods of time by seeing how long it took him to relearn the list. His results are plotted in Fig. 9–1. As you can see, after one hour, about half of the material had been forgotten (that is, he had to practice the list for half as much time as he had practiced it in the original learning in order to reproduce it perfectly), after nine hours, 65 percent of the material had been forgotten. Ebbinghaus also compared his memory for nonsense syllables with his memory for meaningful material (verses of *Don Juan*) and found that he remembered a larger percentage of the meaningful materials, but the general shape of the curve of forgetting was the same in all of his experiments.

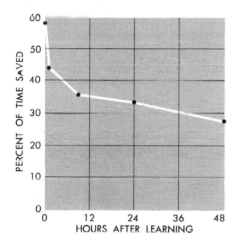

FIG. 9–1. The results from Ebbinghaus' study on the forgetting of nonsense syllables. Ebbinghaus compared the amount of time needed to relearn a list to the amount of time needed for the original learning. The percent of time saved on the relearning of different lists after different time intervals is plotted. (After Ebbinghaus, 1913)

However, Ebbinghaus ran into one puzzle which he was unable to solve. Although 65 percent of the learning had been forgotten after nine hours, only 66 percent had been forgotten after twenty-four hours. This would not have bothered Ebbinghaus if the forgetting during the next day had also turned out to be very small. But after another day he found that 72 percent had been forgotten. Ebbinghaus was puzzled. In terms of all his other results more should have been forgotten between nine and twenty-four hours. As you can see from Fig. 9–1, the curve is just not what one would expect in that period. Eventually, Ebbinghaus concluded that he must have made an error, and went to his grave without solving the puzzle. Much of the research following Ebbinghaus' work was devoted to extending and understanding his pioneer studies. In the next section we shall see how some of the problems raised by Ebbinghaus were solved by later psychologists.

The Dynamics of Memory

Memories consist of stored perceptions, concepts, motives, and habits. Over time these elements of memory interact with one another and with the continuous flow of on-going experience. In this next section we shall document the effects of this interaction.

How Does Time Change Stored Memories?

About thirty-five years after the Ebbinghaus experiments, Jenkins and Dallenbach (1924) investigated the mysterious lack of memory loss in the period between nine and twenty-four hours after learning. They hypothesized that the memory loss between learning and testing were due, not to the passage of time alone, but to what the subjects *did* in the intervening period. In particular, they studied the effects of two different kinds of intervening activity: normal daytime activity and sleep. The results clearly showed that less was forgotten when sleep was the intervening activity between learning and memory testing. On the basis of their work, Jenkins and Dallenbach concluded that *interference* is the major cause of forgetting. The lack of memory difference between nine and twenty-four hours in the Ebbinghaus data could be accounted for by the fact that much of that time had been spent sleeping.

When an activity following learning interferes with the subsequent memory for that learning, we call the effect of the intervening activity *retroactive inhibition*. The Jenkins and Dallenbach study shows that sleep produces less retroactive inhibition than do normal activities.

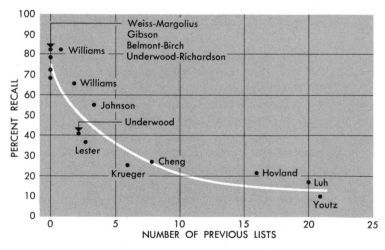

FIG. 9–2. The percentage of items recalled after one hour by subjects on different studies depended on the number of previous lists of similar items the subject in the study had memorized. (After Underwood, 1957)

There is also another source of interference. Early learning sometimes inter-feres with later learning. This kind of interference is called *proactive inhibition*. The importance of proactive inhibition as a factor in forgetting was pointed out in a penetrating analysis of a number of forgetting studies by Underwood (1957). Underwood noticed that in different studies of forgetting, researchers reported different amounts of forgetting after one hour. The losses ranged from 80 percent to 25 percent. One explanation for this result was that different re-searchers used different kinds of materials. But Underwood had another idea. He checked to see how much experience the subjects in each study had had with the kinds of material they were memorizing. If they were memorizing a list of nonsense syllables, how many previous lists had they memorized? If they were memorizing number pairs, how many previous sets of pairs had they memorized? Underwood found that the more experience subjects had had with the kinds of materials they were memorizing, the *poorer* the memory for the newly learned list after an hour had elapsed (see Fig. 9–2). Further study showed that one kind of error frequently made was to recall an item from an earlier learned list instead of the newly learned one. These results strongly suggest that pro-active inhibition is a major factor in forgetting. The experimental designs of proactive- and retroactive-inhibition studies are summarized in Fig. 9–3.

	RETROACTIVE INHIBITION				PROACTIVE INHIBITION		
	PERIOD 1	PERIOD 2	TEST PERIOD		PERIOD 1	PERIOD 2	TEST PERIOD
EXPERIMENTAL GROUP	Learn A	Learn B	Test for recall of A	EXPERIMENTAL GROUP	Learn B	Learn A	Test for recall of A
CONTROL GROUP	Learn A	Irrelevant activity	Test for recall of A	CONTROL GROUP	Irrelevant activity	Learn A	Test for recall of A

FIG. 9–3. The experimental designs for demonstrating interference processes in memory.

One determinant of the degree of interference produced by proactive and retroactive inhibition is how well the tasks involved are learned. For example, in retroactive studies, if the early task is well learned and the study of the later task is only beginning, there is very little interference. With partly learned tasks interference increases with increased practice of the less well-learned task until both tasks are equally well learned. Practice on the task beyond this point now has the effect of reducing the degree of interference. For example, a student who has taken a year of French and then selects a year of German will probably find that studying German will interfere with his memory of French. However, if he first learned French very well or if he learns German very well this inter-ference will be reduced.

These phenomena are essentially of the same sort as those discussed in the last chapter under the topic of transfer. Retroactive and proactive inhibition are processes causing negative transfer. As we saw in our study of transfer, similarity is one of the important factors determining the degree of interference or facilitation. If the stimuli are different and the responses the same, as in learning to translate other languages into English, the degree of facilitation is related positively to the *similarity* of the *stimuli* in the two tasks. Thus knowing French facilitates translation of similar Spanish words with the same meaning into English. If the *stimuli* are the same and the responses different, interference occurs. The more similar the responses that the two tasks require, given identical stimuli, the greater the interference. Thus some knowledge of French or German may interfere when one is trying to translate English into Spanish. We would expect that a knowledge of Arabic would cause less interference.

The Effects of Time Alone

Proactive and retroactive inhibition are processes that occur *over time*. But the astute student may ask, "What about time alone? Don't we forget some things just because time has passed and our memories have gradually faded?"

This is a good question, and one which psychologists have been concerned about ever since they began studying memory. The evidence is not clear-cut. Old people sometimes feel that they can recall childhood events clearly. Similarly, hypnotized subjects apparently recall clearly details of childhood experiences, but studies suggest that many of the vivid details are reconstructed or fabricated by the subject (Stalnaker, 1932). While we are not usually able to check the validity of such anecdotal accounts, a few experiments have shown that memories may persist over a relatively long period. One of the most dramatic was an experiment carried out by Burtt using his own son as a subject.

■ Burtt read Greek passages of *Oedipus Tyrannus* to his son when the boy was between the ages of 15 and 36 months. When the boy was $8\frac{1}{2}$ years old, he memorized one-third of these passages and other passages which had not been previously learned. At age 14, the lad memorized another one-third of the passages and some more new ones. At age $8\frac{1}{2}$ he required 317 repetitions to learn the "familiar" passages and 435 repetitions to learn the new ones—a saving of 27 percent. By age 14, however, the saving was only 8 percent. (Burtt, 1941) ■

It appears that there may be some sort of deterioration in memory over time. On the other hand, since a living organism inevitably encounters new experiences, it is almost impossible to prove whether interference alone or simple disuse and the passage of time account for forgetting. One pair of experimenters, however, devised an ingenious experimental test of the "time-decay" hypothesis.*

---

* The time-decay hypothesis states that some forgetting occurs as the result of passage of time alone, if the material is not practiced. However, the memory is stored in the brain and, if it is not used, the trace of it will decay as time passes.

■ Minami and Dallenbach (1946) found that cockroaches remained inactive if placed in a dark, damp place. They then trained cockroaches to avoid a corner of their cage where they would be shocked. After training, half of the cockroaches were placed on a treadmill in a dry lighted cage, where the cockroaches remained fairly active. The remaining cockroaches were placed in a damp dark passageway, where they remained inactive. If disuse is important, both groups should forget. The results were like those of the sleep experiments: The inactive cockroaches showed some signs of forgetting for the first hour or so, but during the remainder of the inactive period there was little forgetting. The active cockroaches, on the other hand, showed increasing forgetting with increasing time. ■

We can conclude that the passage of time alone does not seem to produce much, if any, forgetting. Interference from other learning seems to be a much more important factor.

Time Decay and Short-Term Memory

Some psychologists have suggested that experience is being stored in the brain in a two-stage process. According to this theory, when the original experience occurs, certain neurons in the brain are active. This temporary activity is responsible for short-term memory. If the same neurons are active many times, a structural change takes place in the neurons which accounts for long term memory long after the temporary activity has ceased. Thus, short-term and long term memory are seen to involve different processes and principles.

One suggestion was that short-term memory does decay simply as a result of the passage of time, whereas long-term memory does not. A study by Peterson and Peterson (1959) seemed to support the time-decay hypothesis. They exposed a single three-letter nonsense syllable to college students for ½ second and asked students to recall them 3, 6, 9, 12, 15, and 18 seconds after presentation. To prevent rehearsal in the few seconds intervening between presentation and recall, the students were asked to count backward by 3's from a three-digit number. As you can see in Fig. 9–4, over half of the students were unable to recall the nonsense word after only 6 seconds had elapsed!

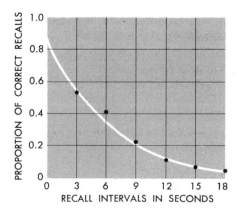

FIG. 9–4. The recall of a single three-letter nonsense syllable for different time intervals, according to Peterson and Peterson (1959).

The Petersons' study lends support to the idea that the memory of one brief presentation decays with time. However, in doing this study, the Petersons did not control the number of previous nonsense syllables their subjects had been asked to remember. Keppel and Underwood (1962) hypothesized that proactive inhibition might account for the result. They reasoned as follows: All of the subjects in the earlier Peterson experiment participated in several presentations made at different time intervals. One subject would be shown and asked to recall one nonsense syllable 3 seconds after presentation, shown another nonsense syllable and asked to recall it after 6 seconds, etc. Now, most theorists agree that for long-term memory, the amount of proactive inhibition increases as the retention interval increases. Thus proactive inhibition causes more interference if recall takes place a week after learning than if it takes place a day after learning. If we make the same assumption for short-term memory, we would expect that nonsense syllables which had to be recalled after 18 seconds would show the effects of interference from earlier trials more than those which had to be recalled after 3 seconds. Thus the Petersons' results could be accounted for by proactive inhibition. To test their explanation of these results, Keppel and Underwood did an experiment of their own. They used the same procedure as the Petersons, with the exception that only three time intervals were used: 3, 9, and 18 seconds. There were three different nonsense syllables. The crucial part of their experimental design was that they systematically varied the number of syllables previously learned as well as the time interval; that is, some subjects recalled the first syllable after 3 seconds, the second after 9 seconds, and the third after 18 seconds. Another group of subjects recalled their first nonsense syllable after 18 seconds, their second nonsense syllable after 9 seconds, and their third after 3 seconds. In fact, every combination of the three time intervals was tested. This enabled the experimenters to separate the effects of proactive inhibition from the effects of time decay alone. Their results appear in Figure 9–5. Only the top curve shows the effects of time without the effects of proactive inhibition. As you see, the effects of time are much smaller than the Peterson study suggested. The two lower curves show the effects of having learned either one or two syllables earlier. This really affects recall. As predicted, the longer after presentation the material is recalled, the greater the effects of proactive inhibition.

A further study by Murdock (1961) showed that if simpler material is used with the Peterson procedure—a common word rather than a nonsense syllable—there is almost no decrement in short-term memory after 18 seconds. This suggests that the letters in the nonsense syllable do not form a unit in the manner that a word does and thus each letter interferes with recall of the other.

A more direct test of whether single presentations lead to temporary brain activity which dissipates with time or to some permanent storage is contained in a study by Hebb (1961). He asked subjects to recall once several series of digits immediately after they heard each series. Each digit series was long enough that no subject could remember all the items perfectly after only one presentation. Hebb then interspersed the same digit series several times among many different series. If the single presentation did not lead to any permanent storage, the subjects should do no better the second time they came to a given series of digits than they did the first time. However, Hebb discovered that each time the subjects were asked to repeat the same series their retention improved, even though they did not recognize the digits as familiar. This implies that the passage of time did not erase the memory of the series, even though the digits were presented only once. Thus though you cannot recall the phone number you heard and repeated two weeks ago, some permanent storage of it has taken place in your brain.

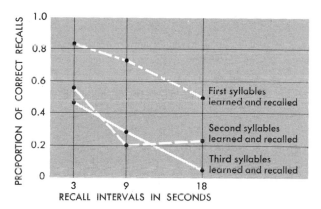

FIG. 9–5. Proactive inhibition in short-term memory. Subjects recalled the first nonsense syllable they learned (top line) better than the second and third syllables they learned. The effect was produced at all three recall intervals tested. (After Keppel and Underwood, 1962)

All these studies suggest that the same factors that influence short-term memory also influence long-term memory, and there is no need to assume that the two are different processes. Time decay is unimportant compared to interference effects. On the other hand, it is easy to see why the two types of memory appear to be different. Normally, when we have seen material we want to remember, we rehearse it many times. This rehearsal increases the strength of the memory and makes it less susceptible to the interference effects of proactive and retroactive inhibition. As you will remember, we said that the better learned the material, the less other learning can interfere with it. We can summarize the studies on both long-term and short-term memory by saying that time alone does nothing to memory; processes occur in time which interfere with memory.

How Do Motives Affect Memory?

The degree to which a person remembers an event depends in part on his motivation at the time of the event. Events which were pleasant, which were related to a person's positive goals, will be remembered better than unpleasant anxiety-provoking events. Sigmund Freud first suggested this relationship from his observation of neurotic patients. He noted that his patients tended to be unable to remember events which were anxiety-laden. Freud used the term *repression* for this tendency to "forget" something which aroused anxiety.

Note that Freud is not saying that anxiety erases the memory. The memory of the event is still stored in the brain and still affects behavior. In fact, Freud suggests that repressed events are usually the basis of neurotic behavior. Severe anxiety prevents the *recall* of the event. In Freud's own words, "The essence of repression lies simply in the function of rejecting and keeping something out of consciousness." You may remember that we described a similar mechanism in perception. Just as perceptual defense prevents a person from seeing anxiety-arousing material, so repression serves to prevent a person from remembering such material.

Repression and motivated forgetting in general are theoretical mechanisms. In addition to Freud's case histories, what evidence do we have for assuming their existence? Part of the evidence comes from the psychological clinic. Some amnesia cases have been interpreted as the result of experiences which caused so much anxiety that all memories of the event were repressed. Other evidence for these mechanisms comes from the laboratory. Postman and Schneider (1951) showed that individuals remember words related to their strongest values better than words related to other values. In Chapter 1, we described a study which revealed that children tend to remember pleasant experiences longer than unpleasant ones. Experimental evidence for motivated forgetting is accumulating.

How Do Perception and Categorization Affect Memory?

In Chapter 6, we noted that what we perceive depends in part on how we relate sensory input to categories we have learned in the past. The more familiar a stimulus, the more well-defined the category to which the stimulus belongs, the more easily it is perceived. We find a similar phenomenon in memory. As children, we learn both the categories labeled by language and the general habits of grammar. If we compare memory for different kinds of material in adults, we find that words are more easily remembered than nonsense syllables, sentences are more easily remembered than an equal number of single words, and related sentences are more easily remembered than unrelated sentences (Lloyd, 1960). The more familiar the categories into which memory materials are placed and the smaller the number of categories, the better the memory.

The Lloyd study suggests that categorizing facilitates memory. Another demonstration of how memory functions via categorization comes from a study by Bousfield (1953).

■ An experimenter read a list of 60 words to a group of subjects. The list was a random inter-mingling of words from four categories: professions, names, animals, and vegetables. The subjects then wrote down as many of the 60 words as they could remember. An examination of the lists of words the subjects wrote showed that the students did *not* tend to write down words in the order in which they heard them. Rather, they tended to list groups of words from the same *categories* together, although these words appeared in different parts of the list; e.g., lion, tiger, and leopard would be recalled one after another. ■

We can interpret this experiment as an indication that we remember in terms of the categories into which we organize events.

Just as categorization permits economy in perception, so it permits economy in memory. If we were to read short lists of numbers to you and then ask you to repeat them, you would probably have little difficulty in remembering lists of 4 and 5 numbers, but as the length of the lists increased you would have more and more difficulty until on some of the lists with 8 or 9 numbers, you might not even remember 4 or 5 of them. Clearly our immediate memory has a limited capacity (known as the *memory span*) and when that capacity is exceeded, memory functions inefficiently. Yet if we were to read a list of numbers, 2-4-6-8-10-12-14-16-18-20-22-24 . . . , you would be able to repeat back as long a list as we wished to read. Has your memory span suddenly increased? No, you do not remember each number individually; you remember that you heard even numbers beginning with 2 and ending with 24. Because you were able to ab-stract a relationship between the stimuli, you actually had to remember only three things; the category of even numbers and two boundaries.

However, our tendency to remember in terms of categories may lead not only to more efficient memory but also to distortion. Sir Fredrick Bartlett, a British psychologist, demonstrated this effect by studying memory for a rather compli-cated story. Here is an example of Bartlett's results:

■ The original story was as follows:

THE WAR OF THE GHOSTS

One night two young men from Egulac went down to the river to hunt seals, and while they were there it became foggy and calm. Then they heard war cries, and they thought: "Maybe this is a war party." They escaped to the shore and hid behind a log. Now canoes came up, and they heard the noise of paddles, and saw one canoe coming up to them. There were five men in the canoe, and they said:

"What do you think? We wish to take you along. We are going up the river to make war on the people."

One of the young men said: "I have no arrows."

"Arrows are in the canoe," they said.

"I will not go along. I might be killed. My relatives do not know where I have gone. But you," he said, turning to the other, "may go with them."

So one of the young men went, but the other returned home.

And the warriors went on up the river to a town on the other side of Kalama. The people came down to the water, and they began to fight, and many were killed. But presently the young man heard one of the warriors say: "Quick, let us go home; that Indian has been hit." Now he thought: "Oh, they are ghosts." He did not feel sick, but they said he had been shot.

So the canoes went back to Egulac, and the young man went ashore to his house, and made a fire. And he told everybody and said: "Behold I accompanied the ghosts, and we went to fight. Many of our fellows were killed, and many of those who attacked us were killed. They said I was hit, and I did not feel sick."

He told it all, and then he became quiet. When the sun rose he fell down. Something black came out of his mouth. His face became contorted. The people jumped up and cried.

He was dead.

After an interval of 20 hours one subject produced the following first reproduction:

THE WAR OF THE GHOSTS

Two men from Edulac went fishing. While thus occupied by the river they heard a noise in the distance.

"It sounds like a cry," said one, and presently there appeared some men in canoes who invited them to join the party on their adventure. One of the young men refused to go, on the ground of family ties, but the other offered to go.

"But there are no arrows," he said.

"The arrows are in the boat," was the reply.

He thereupon took his place, while his friend returned home. The party paddled up the river to Kaloma, and began to land on the banks of the river. The enemy came rushing upon them, and some sharp fighting ensued. Presently, someone was injured, and the cry was raised that the enemy were ghosts.

The party returned down the stream, and the young man arrived home feeling none the worse for his experience. The next morning at dawn he endeavored to recount his adventures. While he was talking something black issued from his mouth. Suddenly he uttered a cry and fell down. His friends gathered around him.

But he was dead.

Eight days later this subject remembered the story as follows:

THE WAR OF THE GHOSTS

Two young men from Edulac went fishing. While thus engaged they heard a noise in the distance. "That sounds like a war cry," said one, "there is going to be some fighting." Presently, there appeared some warriors who invited them to join an expedition up the river.

One of the young men excused himself on the ground of family ties. "I cannot come," he said, "as I might get killed." So he returned home. The other man, however, joined the party, and they proceeded on canoes up the river. While landing on the banks, the enemy appeared and were running down to meet them. Soon someone was wounded, and the party discovered that they were fighting against ghosts. The young man and his companion returned to the boats, and went back to their homes.

The next morning at dawn he was describing his adventures to his friends, who had gathered round him. Suddenly, something black issued from his mouth, and he fell down uttering a cry. His friends closed around him, but found that he was dead." ■*

* Bartlett, F. C. (1932), "The War of the Ghosts," *Remembering: A Study in Experimental and Social Psychology*. London: Cambridge University Press, 65–67. Reprinted by permission.

If we compare the two reproductions to the original story, we can see how categorization leads to changes in memory over time. The story becomes progressively more logical and more concise. Irrelevant details and inconsistent elements drop out. Familiar activities like fishing are substituted for the more unfamiliar, hunting seals. And the story conforms more to the kinds of cause-effect relationships with which we are familiar.

A similar phenomenon has been demonstrated in memory for visual forms. If people are asked to reproduce pictures they have seen earlier, we get results as shown in Fig. 9–6 (Gibson, 1929). As you can see, inconspicuous irregularities tend to disappear over time. This tendency is called *leveling*. On the other hand, noticeable irregularities are accentuated or *sharpened*. Again these results can be explained in terms of categorization. A figure is seen as a "circle with a hump" and is produced in terms of "circle" and "hump" categories from memory.

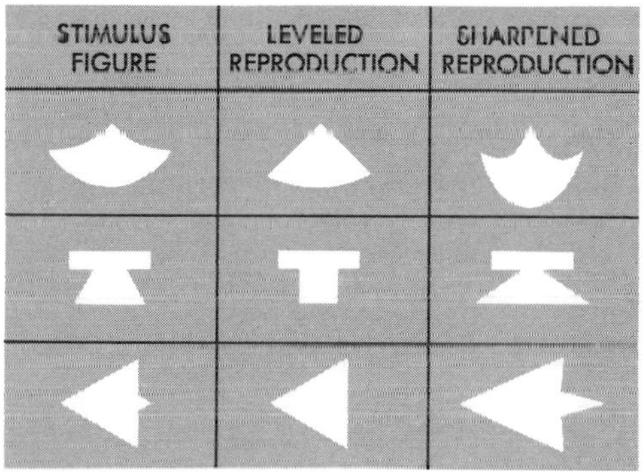

STIMULUS FIGURE	LEVELED REPRODUCTION	SHARPENED REPRODUCTION

FIG. 9–6. Some leveled and sharpened reproductions. The stimuli shown are similar to the ones used by Gibson (1929).

However, this does not mean that the only aspects of a figure that are remembered are those that fit into categories. Prentice (1954) showed that while visual forms tend to be reproduced in terms of categories, subjects can still *recognize* which of a number of similar figures they originally saw. This seems to suggest that an object is remembered (as it is perceived) in terms of categories *plus* salient differences *plus* minor irregularities. The first two aspects mentioned are remembered better and longer, and it takes a more sensitive measure of memory to reveal that the minor details are also stored in the brain.

Set and Memory

In our discussion of latent learning in rats, in Chapter 5, we noted that the rats learned although there was no immediate motivation for performance. Psychologists have studied an analogous situation in human beings: *incidental* versus *intentional* learning. This problem is studied by presenting the same material to two groups of subjects: one group is asked to learn it; the other group is asked to look at it (perhaps to encircle certain items or perform some other task which ensures that the subjects have perceived the material). Then both groups are tested for recall. As you might expect, a number of experiments have shown that both groups show some memory for the material. However, the intentional-learning group is usually superior to the incidental-learning group (Postman, 1964). There are several possible reasons for the superiority of intentional learning. First, we saw earlier how quickly material consisting of several items, which is presented only once, is forgotten when rehearsal is prevented. We would expect that subjects instructed to remember would be induced to rehearse, whereas those who had no instructions would not rehearse. Second, the intentional-learning subjects would have a greater tendency to categorize material, to try to find relationships among items, and to find devices that would facilitate remembering (Deese, 1964). Finally, we would expect the intentional-learning subjects to pay closer attention to the stimulus material, thereby increasing the effectiveness of presentation. Thus our knowledge of the factors influencing memory would have predicted the obtained result: that the *set* produced by instructions to learn facilitates memory.

How Are Memories Aroused?

Earlier we said memory was any evidence of prior learning. Defined in this way, the term refers to some observable behavior. In ordinary language, memory also refers to a private experience in which a person recalls an event without saying anything. But whether or not the private experience is included in a definition of memory, recall can be considered an act, and the factors that are responsible for arousing a particular sequence of recall are identical to those responsible for the selection of any other act: present perceptions, motives, and sets interact with stored percepts, motives, and habits. A hungry man is likely to remember a fine meal he once ate; the sight of an airplane may recall an exciting plane trip; thinking of one former classmate elicits memories of others. Although we can demonstrate the effects of the various conditions on observable acts only, we can reasonably infer that the memories in our private thoughts are aroused in a similar way.

The Development of Memory

In Chapter 8, we saw that even in the first days of life, babies learn to adjust to feeding schedules. This change of behavior as a result of experience indicates that memory must exist in at least a primitive fashion. The first signs of recognition are likely to be cessation of crying when the mother or the bottle appears. Such a reaction is reported as occurring between the ages of 12 and 18 weeks. By the age of six months the baby seems able to recognize familiar people, and by the age of one year he can remember for 30 seconds in which of three boxes a toy was placed. A child of two or three can remember from one to three days under which of three plants a cookie has been hidden. As the child matures we see an increase in both the length of time he can retain prior experiences and the complexity of the exprience he can store and recall.

One reason for the child's increase in memory is that he is forming more and more concepts which enable him to remember more economically. The appearance of language accelerates this trend. As we saw in the last chapter, the average child speaks his first word at the age of 9 to 15 months. The first words are learned very slowly. Within six months following the first word, only five or six more words are added to the spoken vocabulary of most children. Since language development depends on experience, it is not surprising that the most common concepts in the speech of young children deal with mother, home, father, and sisters or brothers.

Between the ages of 18 and 42 months one of the most exciting periods in all of child development occurs. Gradually, the child becomes aware that sounds have meanings and objects have names. He has learned to label concepts with words. This is a far greater achievement than it might first appear to be. In fact, the phenomenon of meaning is so complex that psychologists are just beginning to understand the processes involved. We shall take a closer look at the ways in which psychologists have studied meaning in Part 2 of this chapter.

Individual Differences

As we saw earlier, psychologists studying individual differences have found it useful to distinguish between different kinds of memory.

Rote memory is measured by tests of learning to repeat verbatim a group of meaningless words. *Meaningful memory* is measured by measures of recall of a passage the subject reads, hears, or memorizes.

Because memory is so important for adjustment to one's environment, tests of memory are commonly included in intelligence tests and a memory (M) factor emerges in analyses of intelligence.

PHYSIOLOGICAL DIFFERENCES RELATED TO MEMORY. Almost everyone has read of a case of amnesia caused by a blow on the head. Similarly, we have heard of older people whose memory is failing. In both cases we assume that individual differences are related to brain functioning. But how is memory dependent on the brain? What part or parts of the brain are involved?

Since it is difficult to conduct well-controlled studies with human beings who have suffered brain damage, much of the work on the CNS and memory has been done with the animals which most closely resemble man. One of the first experiments involved letting monkeys see under which of two cups food was hidden. The monkey, however, was not allowed to go to the food for several seconds. As we saw earlier, normal monkeys can be delayed for several minutes or even hours and still find the food. Monkeys with injuries in the frontal lobe, however, cannot remember the correct cup even after a delay of only one minute. These results indicate that recent memory is affected by the functioning of the prefrontal area of the brain (see Fig. 9–7), but this and other experiments also indicate that it is not affected by injuries to other areas of the brain.

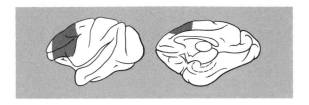

FIG. 9–7. Injury to the (shaded) cortical areas in monkeys impair their ability to remember even for a few seconds under which one of two cups food is hidden. (Pribram, 1955)

Amnesia is a relatively complete loss of memory in people. Sometimes amnesia involves forgetting the events which immediately preceded some physical or psychological shock, sometimes events immediately following such a shock, and sometimes some events in childhood or earlier life. Experiments with electric shock and rats indicate that memory of experiences is lost if the experiences are immediately followed by a shock administered to the brain. Since the shock does not affect experiences which precede it by an hour or more, these experiments suggest that some time is needed after learning in which to fix or consolidate memories. The rat study provides a rationale for assuming that amnesia for immediately preceding events may be caused by a psychological shock similar to the disruption produced in this experiment.

One of the curious aspects of amnesia is that the amnesic loses specific memories but not general concepts. He may forget his name but still knows that he is a man. He may forget the date but still know the order of months of the year. Our understanding of amnesia in human beings is complicated by the fact that amnesia often occurs without injury or physical shock to the brain. In such cases it appears that the motivational factors in memory act to prevent recall of experiences which arouse anxiety. As we saw earlier, this process of forgetting due to motivation is called repression, and it will be described in more detail in Chapter 11, "Frustration."

ALCOHOL. Another way of studying the relationship of CNS functioning to memory and thinking is to study the effect of drugs. For example, it is generally believed that alcohol impairs ability to think clearly. One of the best experimental studies of this problem indicates that alcohol administered at a rate of approximately 4 ounces of whiskey for a 165-pound man produces 11- to 25-percent loss in efficiency on such tasks as coding words and substituting digits for symbols—tasks which require immediate memory (McFarland and

Barach, 1936). The researchers believe that alcohol has these effects because it impairs oxidation in the brain. When alcohol was administered while the subject was breathing air whose oxygen content was increased, the bad effects were reduced.

Practical Applications

Personal Applications

Probably everyone would like to improve his memory. Can this be done? Experimental evidence indicates that there are limitations upon the degree to which memory can be improved by practice.

■ Experiments by Gates and Taylor (1925) showed that groups of children who were given practice in memorizing series of digits were able to do better on a test of immediate recall of a group of digits than a group of children who had no practice. However, on another test four and a half months later there was no difference between the groups. ■

This study suggests that memory capacity *per se* is not improved by practice. One can, however, improve one's retention of material by applying some of the learning techniques discussed in Chapter 8—spaced learning, learning natural wholes rather than parts, active learning, etc.

There is probably a limit to the number of separate things we can remember. As the individual learns more concepts, we would expect interference between them. However, memory is facilitated if one can organize the concepts into groups by developing relationships between them. Thus remembering the concepts red, orange, yellow, green, blue, and purple would be difficult if we regarded each of them as an isolated experience. But when we group them as colors and think of the relationships between them, it is easy for us to remember them. The concept "color" has not simply added another isolated notion in the mass of concepts we possess, but is a new thing which relates and organizes a group of concepts.

Even materials which are not naturally related themselves are remembered more easily if some artificial relationship can be applied. The familiar mnemonic devices are examples of this principle. It is easier to remember the notes of the lines and spaces of the musical staff by remembering <u>E</u>very <u>G</u>ood <u>B</u>oy <u>D</u>oes <u>F</u>ine and <u>FACE</u> than to remember the individual letters, E, G, B, D, F, and F, A, C, E. Laubach (1960) is using this principle to teach people how to read. Figure 9–8 shows examples of his system.

STUDY HABITS. These suggestions for improving memory obviously have direct implications for the college student who is trying to improve his study habits. For example, the value of organizing concepts suggests that the efficient student attempts to *organize* and relate the materials he must learn. Because of interference when many unorganized bits of information are learned at the same time,

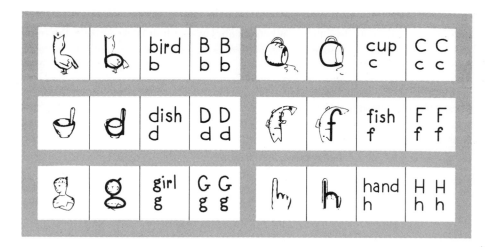

FIG. 9–8. The use of mnemonic devices in the teaching of reading. By relating both the sounds and the shapes of letters to words whose meanings people already know, the letters are learned more easily. (From *Symbology*, © 1960 by the Art Directors Club of N.Y., edited by Elwood Whitney, reprinted by permission of Hastings House, Publishers, Inc.)

the student should attempt to *select* the main points of the lesson. Just as in memory span the addition of a digit beyond the memory span causes the number of digits remembered to drop sharply, so when the student attempts to remember too many details, he becomes "mentally dazzled" and is likely to forget all of them. This, in turn, is related to the principle of *meaningfulness*. Since meaningful material is so much more easily remembered than meaningless material, it is obviously wiser to spend time trying to get a clear understanding of difficult material than to attempt simply to memorize it without understanding.

Social Applications

In addition to personal applications, our study of memory and concept formation also has broad social applications.

MEMORY AND TESTIMONY. Our courts place a good deal of weight on the testimony of eyewitness observers of a crime or accident. How accurate is such testimony? In 1923, psychologist Hugo Münsterburg described the following demonstration:

■ There was, for instance, two years ago in Göttingen a meeting of a scientific association, made up of jurists, psychologists, and physicians—all, therefore, men well trained in careful observation. Somewhere in the same street there was that evening a public festivity of the carnival. Suddenly, in the midst of the scholarly meeting, the doors open, a clown in highly colored costume rushes in in mad excitement, and a Negro with a revolver in hand follows him. In the middle of the hall first the one, then the other, shouts wild phrases; then the one falls to the ground, the other jumps on him; then a shot, and suddenly both are out of the room. The whole affair took less than twenty seconds. All were completely taken by surprise, and no one, with the exception of the President, had the slightest idea that every word and reaction had been rehearsed beforehand, or that photographs had been taken of the scene. It seemed most natural that the President should beg the members to write down individually an exact report, inasmuch as he felt sure that the matter would come before the courts. Of the forty reports handed in, there was only one whose omissions were calculated as amounting to less than 20 percent of the characteristic acts; fourteen had 20 to 40 percent of the facts omitted; twelve omitted 40 to 50 percent, and thirteen more than 50 percent. But besides the omissions there were only six among the forty which did not contain positively wrong statements; in twenty-four papers up to 10 percent of the statements were free inventions, and in ten answers—that is, in one-fourth of the papers more than 10 percent of the statements were absolutely false, in spite of the fact that they all came from scientifically trained observers. ∎*

Psychologists have carried out a number of such studies of the ability of people to testify about a movie or rehearsed intrusion which they have witnessed. The results of such studies show that a good part of such testimony is inaccurate and becomes increasingly so with the lapse of time. Some of these inaccuracies are due to faulty observation, but many inaccuracies are due to the sort of distortions which occur in all memory. Usually the witness has had no set to observe carefully and to remember accurately. In experiments in which students knew they were supposed to remember as much as possible, they recalled only half of the facts on the average and of those recalled only 90 percent were accurate. With questioning, the average student recalled 75 percent of the facts but made more errors. The degree of inaccuracy is related to the way in which the questions were asked. For example, here are four ways of asking a question (Morgan, 1941):

∎ 1. *Determinative type of question.* Example: Did the man wear a hat?
   2. *Disjunctive type of question.* Example: Did or did not the man wear a hat?
   3. *Expectative type of question.* Example: The man wore a hat, didn't he?
   4. *Implicative type of question.* Example: What color was the man's hat? ∎

As you can guess, these are in order from most to least accurate answers. Experiments show that leading questions, such as, "Didn't another car pass by just before the accident?" are likely to be answered "Yes" if the accident occurred on a busy street. Once this false recollection is reported, it tends to become fixed and appear later without questioning, and other details are "remembered" to make it consistent. The degree of inaccuracy is also affected by the type of situation observed. If the scene arouses emotion, recall is likely to be more inaccurate. As we should expect, errors in recall increase over time. Thus a long delay between a crime and the trial is likely to increase the probability of errors in testimony. Fortunately, the witness is able to some extent to

---

* From Münsterberg, H. (1923), *On the Witness Stand.* New York: Doubleday. Reprinted by permission.

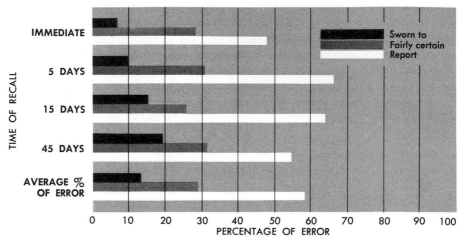

FIG. 9–9. The certainty with which subjects mistakenly recall events. Although they are "fairly certain" with a great percentage of error, the subjects are willing to swear to only a small percentage of their erroneous memories. (After Dallenbach, 1913)

judge which of his memories are most accurate (see Fig. 9–9). However, he makes errors even about facts which he is willing to swear to.

One of the ways in which the courts surmount such barriers to accuracy is through comparison of the stories of several witnesses. Since the factors producing error may operate differently for different people, facts upon which witnesses agree are more likely to be accurate than those which only one witness remembers. However, even in this case it is a fallacy to equate human memory with a perfect automatic recording device of experience.

PART 2. LANGUAGE AND MEANING

The Phenomena of Language

Experiences are stored in the brain according to previously formed categories. These categories may be perceptual, motivational, actional, or conceptual. We saw in Chapter 5 that animals demonstrate the ability to respond in terms of a learned conceptual category: A monkey was able to solve a problem on the basis of the concept "oddity." However, human beings are unique in that they are able to express these categories with words. This greatly expands the kinds of concepts that can be learned, remembered, and manipulated. It would be possible, for example, to form the concept "chair" without the word "chair," but without words we could not communicate this concept to another person easily. If the concept were an abstraction like "good" or "evil," it would be almost impossible to develop and test the concept without words. Words and language are the tools with which much of our thinking is done.

In calling language a uniquely human phenomenon, we are not implying that animal communication does not occur. It does. Bees communicate the location of a feeding place to one another with a tail-wiggling dance. At the sight of a predator, a small bird will cry out in a way that serves to warn other members of his species of danger. Both types of communications are examples of instinctive responses to a situation which serve as automatic cues to other members of the species.

If you have a pet dog, you may have noticed that at certain crucial times, the dog will signal you in a way that makes you understand he needs to go outside. He may stand at the door and whine, for example. This is also communciation, and, in this case, the dog's behavior is learned, not reflexive. Vicki, the chimp who was raised in the Hayes' home like a baby,* actually learned to say three words: "Mama," "Papa," and "cup." She used the three sounds indiscriminately whenever she was in distress.

Human language is unique not because it permits communication or because it is learned. The special features of language are (1) the many elements which can be combined and recombined in many different ways; (2) the existence of grammars which specify the rules of combination; and (3) the complex relationship between the words which make up the language and the "real" world, a relationship we call *meaning*.

The Dynamics of Language: the Analysis of Meaning

If we were unwilling to make any inferences about mental events, we could look at words as elements of behavior. Words are stimulus input for the listener or reader; they are responses for the speaker or writer. However, noting the physical characteristics of a spoken word gives us little information about the nature of meaning. The words *Bahnhof* and *railroad station* have few physical characteristics in common, yet most people familiar with both English and German would agree that they have the same meaning.

We get a closer approximation to the meaning of *meaning* by thinking of a word as a stimulus or response or an element of thinking which "stands for" a category. In this sense, a word is a shorthand substitute for all the properties that are associated with the category the word labels. When you say a word, you are trying to activate a similar category in the mind of your listener. When

---

* Vicki was introduced in Chapter 4, p. 82.

we say that *railroad station* and *Bahnhof* have the same meaning, we are actually saying that the use of two words in English and in German activate similar categories in the minds of the New Yorker and the man from Berlin.

Linguists distinguish two kinds of meaning for a word. The *denotation* of a word is usually defined as "what the word indicates" or "what the word points to." The *connotations* of a word are its associations and emotional implications. For example, the words *bathroom* and *powder room* have similar denotations, but their connotations are quite different.

Our category theory of meaning includes both denotation and connotation. Let us look, for example, at a word like *textbook*. The category *textbook* includes certain perceptual properties like the general shape, size, texture, the appearance of words and pictures, etc. These are the kinds of properties that can be communicated to another person by pointing at them. The linguist would call them the *denotative aspects*. However, each of us also associates other properties with this category: boring, grades, studying, test, anxiety, etc. Such properties would be considered *connotative*. Note that the connotation of the word will be quite different for different people. Note also that not every word category necessarily has significant perceptual properties. What could we point at in our environment which would serve as even a partial definition of *justice, may be, the,* or *infinite?* These are categories whose defining properties are almost purely conceptual.

The Measurement of Meaning

Recently psychologists have become interested in the possibility of measuring various aspects of meaning. In particular, Osgood (1952) has developed an instrument, the *semantic differential,* which measures the connotative meaning of

ROSEBUD

Angular	_____	Rounded
Weak	_____	Strong
Rough	_____	Smooth
Active	_____	Passive
Small	_____	Large
Cold	_____	Hot
Good	_____	Bad
Tense	_____	Relaxed
Wet	_____	Dry
Fresh	_____	Stale

FIG. 9–10. A sample page from Osgood's *Semantic Differential.* The respondent is asked to place a check in the space on each line which represents the word's position on the continuum defined by the opposite adjectives. (From Osgood, C. E., "The nature and measurement of meaning," *Psychol. Bull.,* **49,** 197–237, 1952. Reprinted by permission.)

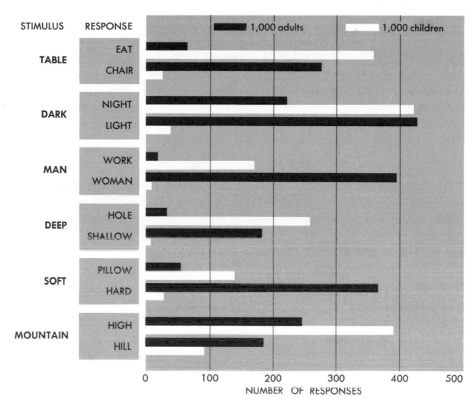

FIG. 9 11. Some frequent associations to common words for children and adults. Note that adults have a greater tendency to respond with opposites and that children have a greater tendency to respond with a word that completes a phrase (e.g., dark night). (After Woodworth, 1938)

words. In taking the semantic differential, the subject rates words in terms of properties like rough-smooth, bad-good, clean-dirty, etc. Figure 9–10 shows a sample page of the test. Surprisingly, most people have little difficulty in rating words on such characteristics. A factor analysis* shows that the ratings given a word by a subject can be summarized by a score for each of three factors: *Evaluative* (the good-bad, pleasant-unpleasant dimension), *potency* (strong-weak dimension), and *activity* (fast-slow, active-passive dimension). For example, one subject's semantic ratings showed the word *rosebud* connoted good, impotent, passive; *hero* was good, potent, and active; *fate* was somewhat bad, indifferently potent, and quite passive; and *quicksand* was bad, strong, and passive. The semantic differential provides a measure of meaning which makes it possible to study both the differences between people rating the same word and the relation between the meanings that different words have for a single person.

---

* The statistical technique of factor analysis is discussed in Chapter 12. For further details, see also Appendix I.

We can interpret the semantic differential as an instrument which makes observable some of the properties of a word category. If we assume that categories with similar properties tend to be aroused by one another, we would expect that hearing a word would make a person think of other words that would be rated similarly on the semantic differential. This hypothesis was tested by using one of the oldest methods in psychology: the word-association method. In a word-association experiment, a subject hears or sees a stimulus word and responds by saying the first words he thinks of. For example, people hearing the stimulus word *table* usually respond with the word *chair*. See Fig. 9–11 for some stimulus words and their most common associates. Pollio (1963) studied the semantic-differential ratings of 52 common words and the first words given in association to them. He found significant correlations between the ratings of the stimulus word in terms of the evaluative, potency, and activity dimensions, and the ratings of the response word in terms of these dimensions. Even though the semantic differential captures only a few of the properties of a word category, we can use it to uncover some interesting relationships among the words and among the categories these words have come to represent.

The Development of Language

How does an arbitrary sound come to have meaning? One method psychologists have used to study the development of meaning was the observation of subjects learning the "meaning of nonsense syllables." In one of these experiments the subject would see a card with drawings of faces, swastikas, triangles, or odd-shaped figures and be told that this was a "LORB." Another card would then be exposed, labeled as "DWIN," and each subsequent card would contain an example of a concept to be learned. This situation is similar to that a child finds himself in as he hears many different words which he has to learn to relate to the variety of experiences he is exposed to.

Heidbreder (1946, 1947) found that the ease of word-concept formation was greater for concrete objects and for familiar things than for more abstract concepts. Furthermore, she found that those subjects who actively tried out hypotheses about the concept learned more rapidly than subjects who passively waited for the concepts to become clear. Some of the figures Heidbreder used are shown in Fig. 9–12.

An experiment by Cahill and Hovland (1960) showed that the rate of learning a concept meaning is heavily dependent on memory. In most concept-formation experiments a card is presented to the subject and he is told, "This is (or is not) a WIB" (or whatever the label of the concept is), and the card is removed. In Hovland's experiment, the cards were presented and then left in view for half of the subjects. These subjects learned the concepts much more rapidly than subjects for whom the conventional procedures were used. This indicates

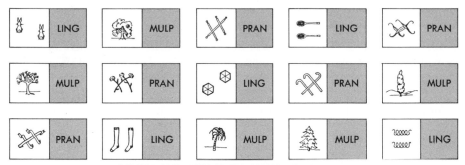

STIMULI AND ASSOCIATED NONSENSE SYLLABLES

FIG. 9–12. What is a LING, a MULP, and a PRAN? These are some of the stimuli and nonsense syllables Heidbreder used to study concept formation. The concept MULP was learned faster than PRAN, which was learned faster than LING. (After Heidbreder, 1946)

that concept formation depends on memory just as memory is dependent on concepts.

Another series of experiments of Hovland and Wiess (1953) showed the relative effectiveness of different kinds of experience in learning the meaning of a word. Suppose for example, that you are trying to learn the concept "WEX." You do not know that "WEX's" are red squares, but you do know that you are to learn a concept involving two characteristics. When you are shown a black circle and told that this is not a "WEX," you do not know whether "WEX's" are not black or are not circles—all you know is that this black circle is not a "WEX." However, when you are shown a red square and told that it is a "WEX," you can now identify other "WEX's." The negative example eliminated only one of several possibilities. If the cards involved not only form and color but also size, a medium-sized red square would not give us complete information because we would not know whether the correct concept was red squares, medium-sized squares, or medium-sized red figures. But a second positive instance containing a large red square would be enough to enable us to identify "WEX's" as red squares. With most everyday concepts the possible wrong examples are much more numerous than the number of right examples, and it is thereby more informative to get an example of what something is than what it is not. However, a negative example can be constructed so that it eliminates as many alternatives as a positive example does. For example, in a coin toss we learn just as much by hearing that the coin did *not* fall tails up as we do by hearing that it fell heads up.

Hovland and Wiess designed experiments to test the effect of positive and negative instances. They found that the greater the information given by a positive or negative example, the more value in learning. When positive instances contained less information than negative instances (i.e., when there were many kinds of right examples and only a few things that the concept was not), negative instances now helped learning more than positive ones. After finding that positive instances were more effective in experiments in which positive instances provided more information than negative instances, Hovland and Wiess now asked, "Will the advantage of positive instances disappear if we construct concepts for which positive and negative instances convey the same amount of information?" Their results showed that even when information was controlled, people learned the meaning of a word more easily from positive instances than from negative ones. The order, as well as the number, of positive and negative instances is important. Huttenlocher (1962) reports that a negative instance followed by a positive instance is extremely effective for concept formation; in fact, it may lead to better concept formation than two successive positive instances.

All these studies help to show how meaning can be learned by experience with labeled examples of concepts. But we do not learn the meanings of words solely from actual experiences. Often we learn the meaning of a word from its association with other words. Experiments by Pollio (1963) and Staats and Staats (1959) demonstrate how nonsense syllables can acquire meaning by association.

■ In Pollio's experiment, three nonsense syllables were flashed on a screen for five seconds each. While each nonsense syllable was on the screen, the experimenter read nine words. The subjects were explicitly told *not* to attempt to memorize either the words or the syllables, just to look and listen. For one nonsense syllable, the nine words read had "bad" connotations, like the words *sickness* and *trouble*. For one syllable, the nine words read had "good" connotations, e.g., *sweet* or *beautiful*. For a third syllable, the words read were neutral. After this procedure the subjects were asked to give word-associations to the nonsense syllables for about 20 seconds. Pollio found that about half the words given in association to a syllable were some of the original nine words paired with that syllable. The rest of the words (other than the original nine stimulus words) given in association to the syllable tended to have the same evaluative connotation ("good" or "bad") as the original words paired with the nonsense syllable. In an earlier study using a similar procedure, Staats and Staats showed that a nonsense syllable which had been paired with "good" words was judged as being pleasant while a nonsense syllable which had been paired with "bad" words was judged as being unpleasant. ■

Both these studies suggest that a person can acquire meaning for a formerly meaningless sound from other words he hears or sees at about the same time.

Earlier we mentioned that the relationship between a word and its meaning is arbitrary. A person learns to respond to a word, not in terms of its physical characteristics, but in terms of its symbolic meaning. The dominance of the symbolic properties over the physical characteristics of a word develops gradually. This was demonstrated in an experiment on *semantic generalization*.

The subjects for this study were 8, 11, 14, and 19 years old. Written words such as *won* were paired with a mild electric shock for each subject. The

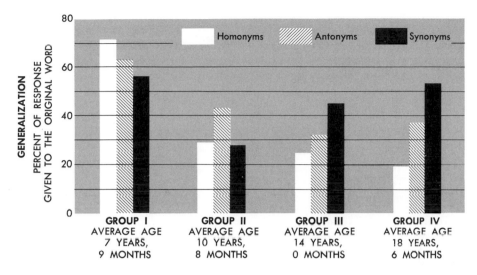

FIG. 9–13. The amount of generalization in different age groups to words that sounded like the word to which the response was trained (homonyms), to words opposite in meaning to the training word (antonyms), and to words similar in meaning to the training word (synonyms). (After Riess, 1946)

response that was measured was the change in skin resistance (a drop in skin resistance is an unconditioned response to shock). The experimenters then measured skin resistance in response to other written words which had never been paired with shock, for example, *one, lost,* and *beat.* As you can see, the first word sounds just like *won,* but its meaning is unrelated to the original stimulus. The second and third words are related to the original stimulus in meaning: *lost* is an opposite and *beat* is a synonym. Figure 9–13 shows the stimulus to which the skin response was greatest in each age group. The youngest children showed the greatest generalization to the word that *sounded* the same. Older children generalized more to words that were meaningfully related to the original stimulus but which had little physical resemblance to it.

Stages in the Development of a Child's Vocabulary

Over a period of two years the average child's vocabulary increases on the average of almost two words a day—from 22 words at 18 months to 1220 at 42 months (Smith, 1926). Note that this curve of development fits with the implications of the theory that early learning is important for later learning. Presumably, early words must be learned by sheer repetition, each word having to build up its own neural pattern. But as the child's vocabulary grows, new words can be associated with words the child already knows, and learning is therefore speedier. As the child learns these words, the learning of more new words becomes even easier and we thus get the positively accelerated curve seen in the first three years of language development.

As his vocabulary grows, the child's use of vocabulary is also changing. At the age of two, the average length of sentences is two words. At five, the average length is five words, and compound sentences are used. The tasks shown in Fig. 9–14 illustrate the typical child's development in comprehension.

AGE $2\frac{1}{2}$	He can identify objects by their use, and will point to a cup when his mother says, "Show me what we drink out of."
AGE $3\frac{1}{2}$	He begins to develop abstractions, and can point to the correct stick when asked, "Which is the longer?"
AGE 4	He can answer the question, "Why do we have houses?"

THE FOLLOWING ITEMS ARE FROM INTELLIGENCE TESTS

AGE 6	"I want to find out how many words you know. When I say a word, you tell me what it means. What is an orange? What is an envelope?"
AGE 9	"Bill Jones' feet are so big that he has to pull his trousers on over his head. What is foolish about that?"
AGE 12	"What do we mean by courage? . . . charity? . . . defend?"
AGE 15 (Average adult)	"What is the difference between (a) laziness and idleness? (b) poverty and misery?"

FIG. 9–14. Tasks which reflect conceptual development, and the average ages at which children can perform them.

As the child learns words and learns to name the objects around him, he gradually develops concepts of the relationships between these objects and of the nature of the world in which he lives. He also gradually learns the relationship between a word and the concept to which it refers. According to Piaget (1928, 1950, 1952) the younger child (up to age seven) thinks that by learning the name of a thing he has discovered its essence. The name is an explanation. "If there weren't any names, how could things be made?" At this stage the child believes that names belong to things. The name comes from the thing and cannot be changed. However, by the age of seven or eight the child develops the idea that names were invented by the makers of things. Thus God or the first men invented names for the things they made. It is not until age nine or ten that the average child regards names as man-made and not necessarily connected with the creation of the thing named. These stages are not absolute, and there are differences in the age at which children develop particular ways of thinking about different things. Nevertheless, Piaget's stages suggest common trends in the development of conceptual thinking.

The Development of Grammar

Learning a language involves more than simply learning the meanings of words. One feature of human language is that it has a structured grammar which provides rules for combining words into sentences. Some time between the ages of two and five, children accomplish the tremendous feat of learning the rules by which words are combined into sentences. There are several hypotheses about how this could occur: (1) The child strings together words randomly, but is only reinforced for grammatical structures. Therefore ungrammatical structures disappear. (2) The child imitates the phrases of his parents. As imitation increases, more and more grammatical phrases appear. (3) The child constructs his phrases on the basis of a primitive grammar which gradually evolves into a more complex grammar. The latter theory suggests that a child is born with the capacity to make primitive discriminations between the uses of words. As soon as he utters two words together, they are related by some rule.

One of the chief ways of studying children's language is by recording their spontaneous utterances. Such recordings show that children begin to say two-word phrases at about the age of two years. *From the very beginning*, the two words are not simply random words from the child's vocabulary. Here are some examples* of early multiword utterances taken from recordings of children's speech:

> two boot
> a gas here
> here tractor
> bye-bye celery
> this dolly
> all gone shoe

One characteristic of these phrases is that they do express a thought. They are not random chains of words. This suggests that the first hypothesis is inadequate to account for the development of grammar. In fact, these early phrases have some of the qualities of adult language in a telegram; that is, articles, prepositions, and auxiliary verbs are frequently omitted. Of course, ungrammatical constructions that an adult would not use (two boot, a gas here) also appear. These are phrases that the child did not hear from adults, and therefore he could not simply be imitating what he hears. Rather, the phrases suggest that the child is constructing original phrases on the basis of a primitive grammar.

What are the rules of this grammar? If we analyze the patterns of words that children use in their first phrases, we can see that some words are used much more frequently than others—*this, that, a, my, pretty, big, all gone, see*—

---

* These examples are from Miller and McNeil (in press).

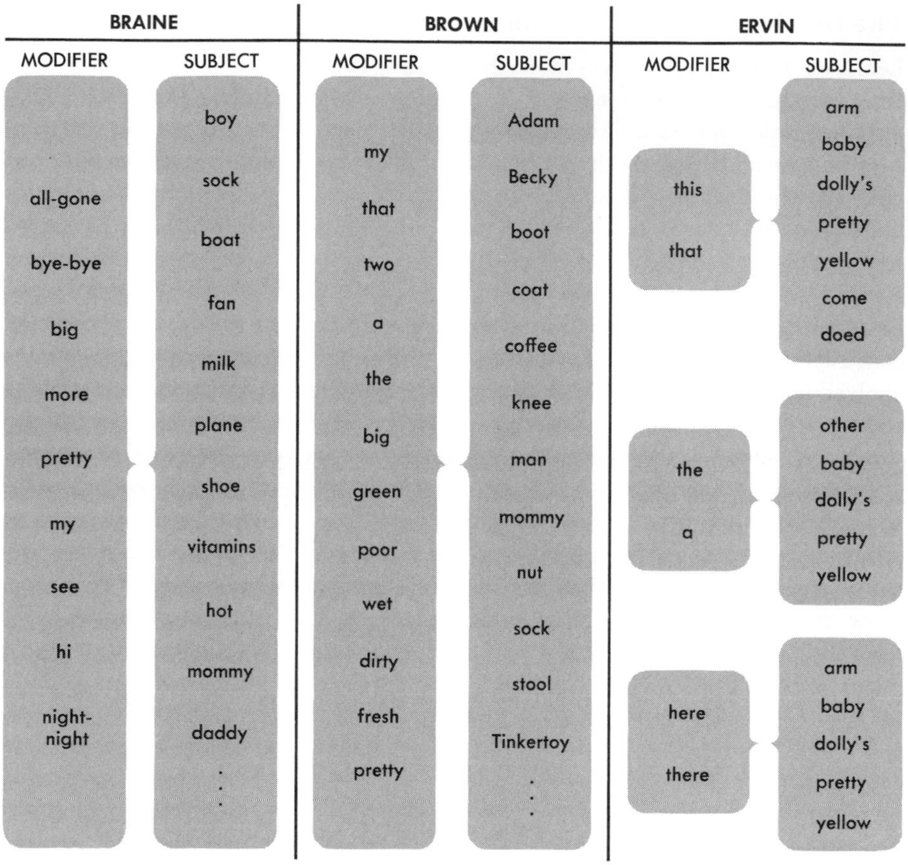

BRAINE		BROWN		ERVIN	
MODIFIER	SUBJECT	MODIFIER	SUBJECT	MODIFIER	SUBJECT

FIG. 9–15. The subject and modifier words used by children in early two-word utterances, as observed by three investigators. In their phrases, the children used any one of the modifier words in conjunction with any one of the subject words in the adjoining column. (After McNeil, 1966)

these words are used more frequently and in a greater variety of situations than words like *shoe, dolly,* and *truck.* The words which are less frequent and more situation-specific are most usually what in adult grammar we would call nouns or subjects. The other words might be called modifier or operator words; they tell something about the subject word. Subject and modifier words recorded in three observation studies of children's speech are summarized in Fig. 9–15.

The two-word utterances of children frequently consist of a modifier word and a subject word. Phrases consisting of one or two subject words also occur ("Truck, mommy!" would be an example). However, a child almost never utters a phrase consisting of two modifier words. Thus we can infer a rule by which children construct two-word phrases: a phrase consists of either modifier and subject or subject and subject.

As the child grows older, both the length of his phrases and the complexity of his grammar increase. One phenomenon is the appearance of inflections of verbs and nouns. At first a child uses a single word such as *cry* to stand for *cry, cried, will cry, is crying*, and so on. Similarly, he uses the same word for singular and plural nouns. By the age of four or five, he has learned to inflect his verbs and nouns. This is not simply a matter of having memorized the correct forms for each individual word, as the following study shows.

This is a wug.

Now there is another one.
There are two of them.
There are two _____.

■ Berko (1958) showed little children pictures like the one presented in Fig. 9–16 and said things like: "This is a wug. Now there are two of them. There are two_____." The child would normally fill in the word *wugs*. This indicated that they spoke as if they knew the rule for forming plurals. With similar types of material Berko showed that four-year-old children can construct plural and possessive endings on nouns, the past tenses of verbs, and comparatives and superlatives of adjectives according to the regular rules of English. ■

FIG. 9–16. The kind of material Berko used to study the grammar of children. (From Berko, Jean, "The child's learning of English morphology," *Word*, 14, 150–177, 1958. Reproduced by permission.)

Note that the children are putting correct endings on words they are hearing for the very first time. Thus in a child's learning of a language, we see not only the acquisition of elements—learning the meaning of words—but also the immediate imposition of categorization and structure. This structure takes the form of unverbalized grammatical rules which become more differentiated as maturation and learning proceed.

Individual Differences in Language

MEANING. Within a given culture, many people have similar experiences involving the use of words. To the extent that this occurs, the same words have common meanings to all. In addition, however, each individual's experiences differ somewhat from those of other people, and to the extent that the experiences he includes under the label of a particular word are different from those of other people, the meanings of that word will be unique. Thus to a person who has heard compositions by Schönberg, the word (and concept) "music" will have a different meaning from that of people who have heard only folk music.

Measures of Language Differences

Because language and concept formation are so important in many intellectual tasks, it is not surprising to find that most intelligence tests* include tasks designed to measure these abilities. Let us look briefly at some of them.

VERBAL ABILITY. The man in the street tends to judge the intelligence of someone he meets by the man's language. While such judgments are likely to be influenced by many irrelevant factors, there is some justification for using vocabulary as a measure of intelligence, because thinking requires the use of concepts, and ordinarily our concepts are verbal. Since concepts are so important in intellectual functioning, the more concepts an individual has at his disposal, the better able he should be to solve intellectual problems. Because most concepts are verbal, vocabulary items are indirect tests of conceptual development.

Items like the following are used in testing the verbal factor in intelligence.

VERBAL ANALOGIES†

In the following exercise, find the word at the right which is related to the third word in the same way that the second word is related to the first.

1	2	3	4	5	6	7	8
fish	water	bird	blue	robin	ocean	sky	high
mayor	city	captain	ship	private	general	store	lieutenant

DISARRANGED SENTENCES

In the sentence below the words are mixed up. When the words are put in the right order, they read, ''Chicago is a large city.'' This statement is true. Therefore, a plus sign (+) is written in the parentheses.

(+) Chicago large a city is

Mark the following sentences yourself. Put a plus sign (+) in the parentheses if the sentence is true. Put a minus (—) sign if it is false. Do *not* take time to write out the sentence in the correct order.

(   ) white blackboard the is
(   ) is falling rain water
(   ) fly some can birds

As the examples indicate, this verbal factor involves verbal and grammatical relations, not just knowledge of words in isolation. Thus it is even more clearly a test of conceptual ability.

---

* We shall discuss the concept of intelligence and ways of measuring it more fully in Chapter 10.
† Thurstone, L. L. (1938), "Primary Mental Abilities," *Psychometric Monog.* 1–4, **44, 48**. Reprinted by permission.

As our folklore would lead us to suspect, girls are slightly superior to boys in verbal ability. There is, of course, a great deal of overlap between the distributions for boys and girls, so that many boys are more verbal than most girls. But generally girls talk earlier and continue to do superior work in spelling and in English courses in school. Even as adults they tend to be superior on the verbal sections of intelligence tests, although this may be largely because of the superiority of girls over boys on words having to do with people (Coffman, 1960).

Frequently, differences are found between social classes and between urban and rural residents on tests of verbal ability. This does not mean that people in the working class or those who live in rural areas are inferior in their ability to form concepts. Rather, it indicates that rural and working-class environments may not provide opportunities for children to learn the type of concepts contained in the test. This may make the tests invalid for certain purposes, but insofar as knowledge of the type of concepts sampled by the test is important for success in a particular situation, such as college, the person who lacks these concepts will be handicapped, and the test may thus be a good predictor of performance.

NUMERICAL ABILITY. A second conceptual ability in which people differ is *numerical ability*. It is measured by intelligence test items such as those shown in Fig. 9–17 (Thurstone, 1938).

Is this addition right or wrong?

42
61
83
176

Mark every number that is exactly three more than the number just before it

4 11 14 10 9 12 16 10 3

FIG. 9–17. These two items are similar to ones used to test numerical ability.

■ Most of us have known people who were excellent in English, but "just couldn't do math." Statistical studies bear out our common-sense notion that although numerical and verbal ability are correlated, they are not closely related. At first glance it seems strange that we should have one ability for dealing with verbal concepts and a different ability for handling numerical concepts. Coombs (1941) hypothesized that numerical ability was not just ability to deal with numbers but was actually the ability to manipulate concepts according to well-learned systems, i.e., addition, subtraction, and multiplication. To test his hypothesis he devised a system for combining letters, and trained subjects to use this system in solving problems. His hypothesis was confirmed, for he found that the better his subjects learned the system, the more highly their performance correlated with tests of numerical ability. Thus "number ability" seems to consist of a sort of mental agility in dealing with concepts related by well-learned rules. We might expect it, then, to be related to the ability to learn grammar. ■

Hence, although correlated with verbal ability, number ability seems to be fairly distinct from verbal ability, which involves knowing individual words and their relationships.

Differences in Word Association

Earlier we mentioned word association as a way of measuring meaning. In this test, as you may remember, the subject is asked to respond to each of a list of words with the first word that comes into his mind. Within a given culture certain responses can be predicted. For example, to the word *dark* the most frequent response is *light*. Men differ from women in their associations. To the word *garden*, boys are more likely than girls to respond *woods*, and girls are more likely than boys to respond *flower*. Psychotic patients give a higher percentage of unusual responses to such a list than normal subjects do. Blocking on a word, apparent misunderstanding, or an unusual psychogalvanic response may point to a topic arousing emotion (Jung, 1918).

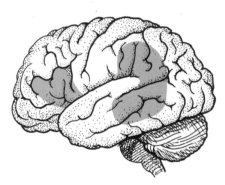

FIG. 9–18. The shaded areas indicate regions of the cortex where electric stimulation and injury produce a deficit in language functions. (After Penfield and Roberts, 1959)

Physiological Differences

We mentioned in Chapter 3 that certain areas of the cortex are related to language functions. These areas are diagramed in Fig. 9–18. For most people, the language function is not localized in both cerebral hemispheres, but rather only in the left hemisphere. Injury to these areas leads to a condition called *aphasia*. Aphasia may take the form of an inability to understand words or talk or write. Sometimes the aphasic individual may be able to speak words but unable to group them into sentences. In the aphasiac, words seem to be disassociated from their function and meaning.

Implications

We have pointed out that words permit the symbolic manipulation and the communication of concepts. We have also pointed out that some concepts are formed *because* of the existence of a word in the language. This suggests that the way we think actually depends in part on the structure of the language we speak. For example, the words which parents use in training their children reveal cultural differences in expected behavior.

In English we tell children to "Be good!" The French mother admonishes her child, "Be wise!" or, "Be well-behaved!" Scandinavian mothers say, "Be kind, be friendly!" "Be in line!" says the German parent.* Such differences in reprimands must affect the child's conception of ideal behavior.

Whorf (1956) has suggested that the English-language emphasis on subject-predicate leads us to read into nature entities which perform miracles, while the Hopi Indian, whose language is not so concerned with space or time, simply describes the phenomenon. In the Hopi language verbs are used to describe what we represent by nouns like *lightning, wave,* and *flame.* Putting these into a noun, or "thing," class—as we do—simply doesn't make sense to the Hopi, and we, on the other hand, find it difficult to see why it is unnecessary to say *lightning flashes,* which seems a redundancy to the Hopi. As we saw in Chapter 2, space and time are always found together in Hopi, and the idea of relativity, which is difficult for us to grasp, is built into Hopi language and thus into Hopi thinking.

In our own society, our system of free public education is based upon the assumption that an effective democratic society is dependent upon the ability of our citizens to communicate in terms of symbols with common meanings. Schools broaden the range of concepts which each child possesses. Through courses such as those in science and social science, schools develop concepts which enable the child to make discriminations and categorizations, and to see relations—accomplishments he would probably never be able to attain if he stayed in his home environment. Through the humanities, the child learns concepts and symbols which enable him to communicate more effectively with others and to enrich his view of the world.

Summary

Concepts

Memory.   Any evidence of prior learning

Redintegration.   The tendency of a part to reinstate the memory of a whole

Short-term memory.   Memory for items immediately after presentation

Long-term memory.   Memory which persists over days, months, or years

* From the recording, "The Ways of Mankind." Chicago: Center for the Study of the Liberal Education of Adults.

Retroactive inhibition. The deleterious effect produced by interspersing an activity between learning and recall

Proactive inhibition. The deleterious effect of earlier learning on the recall of later learning

Repression. The inability to recall material which is associated with high anxiety

Incidental learning. Learning which takes place without the set or instruction to learn (as opposed to intentional learning)

Denotation. That aspect of the meaning of a word which refers to what the word indicates

Connotation. That aspect of the meaning of a word which refers to the associations and emotional implications of the word

Aphasia. The inability to speak, write, or understand the meanings of words—resulting from brain injury

Principles

1. Memory can be measured by assessing a person's recall of material, his recognition of it, or by the amount of savings in relearning.

2. Time decay has little effect on either long-term or short-term memory; interference from proactive and retroactive inhibition is a much more important factor in forgetting.

3. There is both some clinical and some experimental evidence for motivated forgetting.

4. Memories tend to be organized in terms of previously-learned categories. This results in increasing the amount of material that can be memorized, but it may also result in distortion.

5. The increase in a child's capacity to remember parallels the development of concepts that may be used in categorizing experiences.

6. Witnesses to an event are usually unable to recall all the details of the event accurately.

7. Human language differs from animal communication in that language involves many elements, which are combined in many different ways according to fixed rules, and which convey meaning.

8. Language development in children involves learning both the meanings of words and the rules of grammar.

9. Two processes in the development of meaning which have been studied in the laboratory are: (i) learning concept names from their presentation with specific examples and (ii) learning the meanings of nonsense syllables from their presentation in contiguity with other words.

10. From the time a child produces two-word utterances, he appears to be constructing his phrases on the basis of a primitive grammar. As maturation and learning proceed, the grammar becomes more complex and differentiated.

11. Some tests of individual differences in language, such as those of verbal and numerical abilities, are used as parts of intelligence tests.

Suggested Readings

EBBINGHAUS, H., *Memory: A Contribution to Experimental Psychology*, 1885, trans. by H. A. Ruger, and C. E. Busseneus. New York: Teachers College, Columbia University, 1913.

The topic of human learning is another of the active research areas in present-day psychology. One way of reviewing the latest findings would be to look at the recent issues of the *Journal of Experimental Psychology*, *American Journal of Psychology*, or the *Journal of Verbal Learning and Verbal Behavior*.

BROWN, R., *Words and Things*. Glencoe, Ill.: Free Press, 1958. Contains one of the most readable discussions of language.

CHASE, S., *Power of Words*. New York: Harcourt, Brace and World, 1954. Another very readable book.

cognition: reasoning, problem solving, decision making, and intelligence

THE PHENOMENA OF PROBLEM SOLVING

THE DYNAMICS OF PROBLEM SOLVING

INDIVIDUAL DIFFERENCES IN PROBLEM SOLVING

chapter 10   THE DEVELOPMENT OF THINKING

PRACTICAL APPLICATIONS

As you progress further and further through this book, you may have been noticing that the behavior we discuss becomes more and more complex. At the bottom of this "hierarchy of behavior" is behavior based on conditioning. Here an organism acts on the basis of having learned that one stimulus is a signal for another or that a certain response in a given situation will have a certain effect. Slightly more complex is the serial act we discussed in Chapter 8, in which a whole series of responses follow one after the other to produce a smooth coordinated act. In Chapter 9, we looked at concept formation in language. This requires that a person abstract certain properties from diverse situations and respond to them with a common label, a word.

The Phenomena of Problem Solving

In this chapter we shall look at behavior that is based on even more complex thinking processes (see Fig. 10–1). Once a person has learned some concepts, he begins to discern relations between these concepts. A child, for example, may learn the relationship between the concepts "Mother," "Father," "Husband," and "Wife." We then say he has learned a *rule*. When he learns several rules, he can use them to deduce new rules. Or he may see how he can apply the rules he has learned to attain goals for which he is motivated. Such behavior is called problem solving and decision making.

Let us look at several specific examples of these more complex forms of behavior.

■ Frank Smith, the president of a small company, was faced with a difficult decision. An expensive new machine would undoubtedly reduce labor costs for his company, but the capital outlay required was so great that the other company officers were divided on the desirability of its purchase.

To further complicate his decision, the operators of the present machines would need to be retrained and some of them would have to be shifted to other jobs. This might create bad morale among the employees.

To make his decision he needed additional information. What were the facts about the cost of the machine and the costs that would be reduced by use of the machine? At what levels of production would it be efficient? For this information he turned to other officers of the firm, and it became clearer that the machine would be financially worth while only if production increased. Thus Mr. Smith was left with the problem of estimating the probability that additional production would be needed for a long enough period to justify purchase of the machine. His associates were of less help in answering questions about the effect of the change upon morale, but were inclined to think that the men would not like it. His personnel manager was able to give him more information about the amount of training necessary to learn to operate the new machine.

As Mr. Smith tried to weigh the values of efficient operation versus happy workers, an idea came to him. Last year when a change in the administrative structure seemed to be necessary, he had found that a free discussion of the problem with all of the officials involved had resulted in a solution which was accepted much more readily than he had anticipated. Could the same technique be tried with his workers? ■

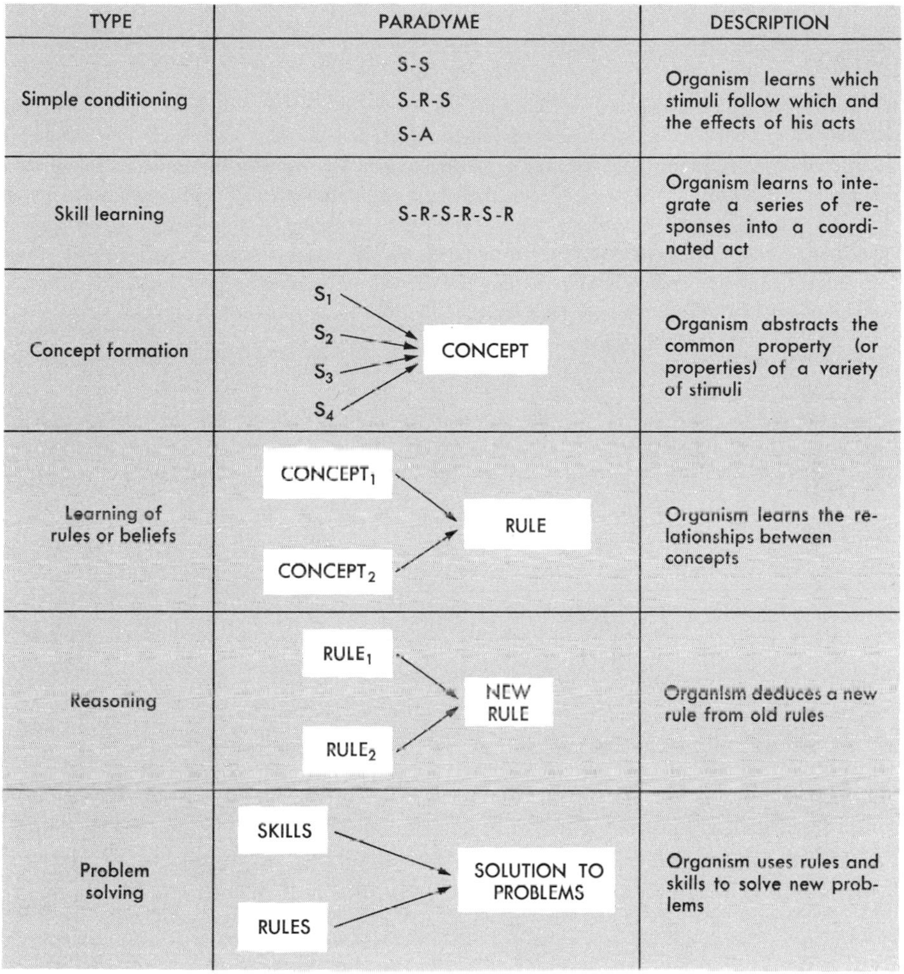

TYPE	PARADYME	DESCRIPTION
Simple conditioning	S-S S-R-S S-A	Organism learns which stimuli follow which and the effects of his acts
Skill learning	S-R-S-R-S-R	Organism learns to integrate a series of responses into a coordinated act
Concept formation	S_1 S_2 S_3 S_4 → CONCEPT	Organism abstracts the common property (or properties) of a variety of stimuli
Learning of rules or beliefs	$CONCEPT_1$ $CONCEPT_2$ → RULE	Organism learns the relationships between concepts
Reasoning	$RULE_1$ $RULE_2$ → NEW RULE	Organism deduces a new rule from old rules
Problem solving	SKILLS RULES → SOLUTION TO PROBLEMS	Organism uses rules and skills to solve new problems

FIG. 10–1. The hierarchy of learning. (After Gagné, 1964)

■ Bob, a psychology student, is trying to design an experiment to determine whether or not people can learn from records played while they are asleep. He is confused, however, by the problem of how to keep his subjects from waking up when he begins to play the record. Unfortunately, many of his subjects wake up and spoil the experiment. What can he do? Various possibilities present themselves—playing the records softly, giving his subjects sleeping pills, playing music at the same time as the lesson. Each of these ideas is rejected. Suddenly he gets an idea. He will play the radio all night long for several nights before the experiment so that his subjects will get adapted to sleeping while hearing music and voices. On the night of the experiment, the lesson will simply be played in place of a program. ■

■ Linda is faced with an important decision. Her parents would like her to study something practical like nursing or teaching. She is interested in history and would like to take a liberal arts curriculum. What should she do? The decision occupies much of her thoughts for weeks. Finally, she decides to enter an education school with a major in history. ∎

∎ Bill is a subject in an experiment. He is seated in front of an experimental slot machine. He has a number of poker chips which he feeds into the slot machine. After he has fed in a number of chips, a red light goes on which informs him that enough chips have been fed in. He must then press one of two buttons. Sometimes after pushing a button the machine will produce a number of chips; sometimes nothing happens. At the end of the experiment Bill will be able to cash in his chips for money. On one day of the experiment the left button will pay off 60 percent of the time and the right 40 percent; on another day the left will pay off 30 percent of the time and the right 70 percent. The experimenter finds that Bill chooses the left button slightly over 60 percent of the time when it pays off 60 percent, and only 20 percent of the time on the 30 percent payoff day. ∎

What are the elements involved in such problem solving?

First, we have the *weighing of goals*. Frank Smith had to weigh the goal of efficient operation versus the happiness of his workers. People differ in their solutions to problems partly because they have different goals or different methods of weighing them. You may remember that we conceptualized situations in which there are conflicting goals in Chapter 7; a person may be faced with an approach-approach conflict, in which he must choose between two strongly attractive goals; an avoidance-avoidance conflict, in which he must choose between two unpleasant alternatives; or an approach-avoidance conflict, in which he has ambivalent feelings toward a single goal. The most difficult situation is the double approach-avoidance conflict, in which a person must choose between two goals, each of which arouses ambivalent feelings. Thus the goal of becoming a doctor may involve not only positive anticipations of financial rewards and opportunity to serve, but also fears that one will be unable to handle the responsibilities of a doctor. On the other hand, the goal of becoming a businessman also arouses both positive and negative expectations. The resulting choice between becoming a doctor or a businessman is one which is not easily resolved.

A second element necessary for problem solving is *the discovery of appropriate means* to the goals. In some cases, discovery of the appropriate alternative is the key to the decision. For example, Bob, the psychological experimenter, made his decision easily once he thought of how to keep his subjects asleep. In other kinds of problems, the alternative means to different goals are evident from the beginning of the problem and the difficult part of the problem is in reconciling various goals. In Linda's case, the decision was between known alternatives that involved goals so nearly equal that a decision was difficult.

Once alternative routes to different goals are discovered, the decision maker considers another factor. This is the *assessment of the probability* that a given course of action will reach the goals most valued. Frank Smith has to estimate the probability that buying the machine will result in greater efficiency. Bob has to estimate the probability that his possible solution will prevent his subjects from awakening. Linda has to estimate the probability of completing college. Bill estimates the probability of a payoff. These estimates are not always conscious. We might ask each of them why he acted as he did and get an answer like "It just seemed like a better bet," but we will find that probability helps explain decisions whether the estimate is conscious or not.

With this introduction, you may well be wondering how this is different from our previous discussion of action in Chapter 8; there too we talked about weighing values and the probable effectiveness of instrumental acts. Noting the common theory underlying these topics is an important basis for your understanding of this chapter, for the distinction between them is certainly not an absolute one. In this chapter we are principally dealing with situations in which the action depends on very complex mental processes; the chief focus of interest is not on the action *per se,* but on the manipulation and reorganization of stored concepts, motives, habits, and rules which precede the action. We call such mental manipulation and reorganization *thinking.*

We shall draw on two different lines of research in this chapter. The process of utilizing information for the discovery of alternative solutions to reach a goal has been studied under the title *reasoning. Decision making* is a term usually applied to the weighing of goals and assessing the probable success of known alternatives. *Problem solving* is the application of both types of thinking. Although research on reasoning and decision making has sometimes been carried on quite separately, real-life problem situations involve both, and in this chapter we hope to present a description of thinking which integrates these two areas of research.

The Dynamics of Problem Solving

What Determines the Discovery and Choice of an Alternative?

In situations requiring reasoning, one can make a mistake either because (1) his perception of the situation is faulty in that he misses some information necessary for solution of the problem, or because (2) he is motivated to choose an incorrect alternative, or because (3) he fails to perceive the relationship between his past experience and the present problem, or because (4) he fails to utilize the available information logically. Thus our previous discussions of perception, motivation, learning, and memory are relevant to an understanding of problem solving. Let us now briefly consider how these four factors—perception, motivation, past experience, and logic—affect our choice of alternatives.

Perception

As in habit selection, one of the most important factors determining the discovery and choice of an alternative is perception.

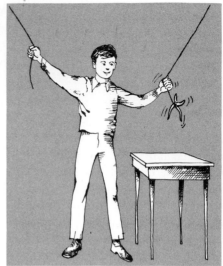

FIG. 10–2. The two-string reasoning problem. The subject's task is to tie the two strings together.

■ A good example of such an effect is illustrated by a subject's performance on Maier's two-string reasoning problem. For this problem, the subject was taken into a room where two strings were hanging from the ceiling. In the room was a chair, a pair of pliers, and several other objects. The subject was told that his task was to tie the strings together. He took one cord in his hand and tried to reach the other. He found that he could not quite reach the string (see Fig. 10–2). Spying the chair, he attempted to stand on the chair and reach the strings, but this too was impossible. (Note that the first direction of thought was cued off by the perception of the strings, the second direction by the perception of the chair.) After the subject had been thinking for some time, the experimenter walked to the window of the room and brushed against one cord so that it began swinging back and forth. Within a few seconds, the subject picked up the pliers, tied them to the cord, set the cord swinging, grasped the other cord, reached out with his other hand to catch the swinging cord, and solved the problem.

Perception of the swinging cord served as the cue to the correct direction of swinging. Surprisingly enough, most of the subjects, when questioned about how they arrived at their solution, did not remember having seen the string swinging. Apparently the cues which influence the direction of thinking may not be consciously perceived. (Maier, 1931) ■

In problem solving, as in our study of generalization and transfer, we again encounter the problem of perception of similarity. In problem-solving situations, similarity to previous situations is not great enough to lead immediately to a well-learned response. Rather, the problem solver must perceive both how the situation resembles and how it differs from previous situations. *Gestalt* psychologists have emphasized the importance of a new perceptual organization, or insight, in successful problem solving.

Motives

Since motives influence perception, they affect the discovery of alternatives. They also affect the choice of alternatives, since many alternatives have motivational value in addition to their value as means of reaching the goal. In some problem situations certain alternatives are not selected because they are immoral; in other cases certain alternatives may be appealing simply because they are more interesting or challenging than others. The crossword-puzzle addict may know that he could find a missing word in the dictionary, but rejects this alternative as unsporting.

Objective values may not correspond to the values a person considers in making a decision. From the standpoint of a mathematician it would be silly for anyone to bet a penny against a nickel if the odds were 10 to 1 against him. Yet some people do bet at such odds. What seems to happen is that the bettor figures, "If I lose, it's only a penny, but if I win, I can get something worth while for my nickel." Similarly, even though in the long run a 50–50 chance of winning $20 has the same value as 1 chance in 10 of winning $100, some individuals will consistently prefer the long odds, while others will prefer the more conservative bet. Studies of parimutuel betting on horse races show that, in general, bettors tend to underbet horses with short odds and overbet horses with long odds.

Studies have shown that individuals differ in their motivation for different kinds of risks.

■ Experiments (Coombs and Pruitt, 1960) indicate that some individuals prefer bets where neither the possible gains nor losses are very great, while others prefer bets where the possible outcomes range from substantial losses to substantial gains. They also found that some individuals prefer long shots with big potential payoffs, while others prefer bets with a high probability of winning even though the amount to be gained is relatively little. The latter results are common in decision-making research.

The tendency to choose alternatives with very high or very low probabilities of success is related to motivation. Individuals who are motivated by fear tend to choose either a "sure thing" or a very difficult task, while people motivated positively tend to choose tasks with 50–50 probabilities of success. Thus in the experiment we described earlier (McClelland, 1958) children were given the opportunity to practice a ring toss game with a choice of standing one to seven feet from the target. Children who had scored high in fear of failure tended to stand either very close or very far from the target, while those who had made a high score on a test of achievement motivation chose to toss from the middle distance. ■

Past Experience

One may perceive a problem, be motivated to solve it, but fail for one or more of three reasons relating to past experience.

1. He may not have learned the principle involved.

2. He may know the principle involved but not see how to apply it.

3. His past experience may point so strongly to one wrong alternative that he fails to consider the right one; i.e., he may have a strong incorrect-act tendency.

We shall examine each cause of failure in turn.

Our first source of failure is lack of knowledge. We have already discussed the development of concepts and principles in the last chapter, so we will not repeat that discussion here except to remind you that past experience enables the individual to form concepts or principles which he can use in new problem situations.

The second source of failure, difficulty in applying a known principle in new situations, is dependent upon two factors: the individual's ability to think logically (to be discussed later) and the manner in which the relevant principle was learned. A concept learned from varied instances is more likely to be applied in new situations than one learned from a restricted range of examples (Wolfle, 1935).

The third cause of failure is one in which previous experience may actually inhibit the solution of a problem.

■ Birch and Rabinowitz (1951) gave subjects the two-string problem described earlier, in which the task is to tie together the two hanging strings. In their test only two weights were available; one was an electrical switch, the other an electrical relay.

Before the test, some of the subjects solved a problem involving the completion of an electrical circuit by installing a switch. Others completed a circuit by the use of a relay.

When both groups were tested on the two-string problem, the results showed that those who had used a switch in the wiring diagram tended to use the relay for the weight for the pendulum, while those who had previously used a relay in wiring now used a switch for a weight. ■

Having used an object one way tended to prevent its use in a different way in solving the problem. In this case, previous experience limited the subject's performance in problem solving.

Logic

In problem solving a person uses information that he has learned previously. He combines facts acquired from a variety of sources in order to reach a conclusion. Thus a very important phase of problem solving is the manner in which a person puts together available information and reaches a conclusion.

Logicians and mathematicians have studied the structure of deduction—of reaching conclusions given certain assumptions. Using the work of the logician, psychologists have studied the kinds of logical errors people tend to make in reaching a conclusion. Let us look, for example, at a common form of argument called the *syllogism*. The syllogism consists of two premises (assumptions) and a conclusion. Here are three syllogisms in symbolic form:

	All A's are B's.
Syllogism 1	All B's are C's.
	Therefore, all A's are C's.

	All A's are B's.
Syllogism 2	All C's are B's.
	Therefore, all A's are C's.

	Some A's are B's.
Syllogism 3	Some B's are C's.
	Therefore, some A's are C's.

Logically, the conclusion of Syllogism 1 follows from its premises, but the conclusions of Syllogisms 2 and 3 do not necessarily follow from their premises. In Syllogisms 2 and 3 if we substitute the word freshman for *A*, student for *B*, and human being for *C*, the arguments appear valid. However, we can also substitute dog for *A*, animal for *B*, and cat for *C* and we then can see how the conclusion does *not* necessarily follow from the premise. We can diagram syllogisms in terms of overlapping circles, as in Fig. 10-3.

How well can people judge the validity of an argument? This depends partly on how the argument is presented. People usually can judge the validity of a

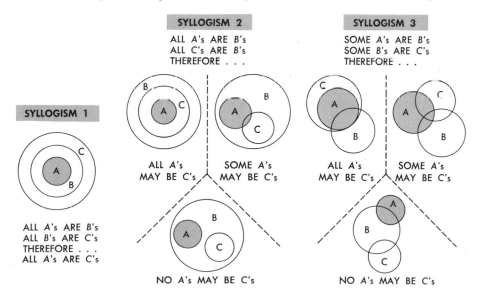

FIG. 10–3. Various ways of diagramming the same syllogisms.

conclusion better if it is presented in terms of words rather than letters. Arguments taking the form of Syllogisms 2 and 3 are often judged to be valid (Wilkins, 1928). One reason given has been called "the atmosphere effect." Affirmative premises seem to set up an expectancy of an affirmative conclusion. Negative premises seem to set up an expectancy of a negative conclusion (Morgan and Morton, 1944). It is interesting that the most common form of logical error is overgeneralizing (attributing properties to a group when the facts do not warrant it, as in Syllogisms 2 and 3) and that people are often 100 percent confident that such illogical conclusions are valid (Dawes, 1964).

Some logical errors come not from the form of the argument, but from emotional bias associated with the content. Look at these two syllogisms:

> All members of the John Birch Society are conservative.
> Barry Goldwater is conservative.
>
> Therefore, Barry Goldwater is a member of the John Birch Society.
>
> All members of the Communist Party favor increased welfare laws.
> Norman Thomas favors increased welfare laws.
>
> Therefore, Norman Thomas is a member of the Communist Party.

Both of these arguments are invalid; yet psychological studies suggest that a person's political beliefs will influence his judgment of the validity of the conclusion. If he is strongly motivated to accept a conclusion, he will tend to do so despite the fact that the information given does not justify it, more so than he would if the argument were stated with neutral terms (Morgan and Morton, 1944; Lefford, 1946; Thistlewaite, 1950). One can readily see the effects of such emotional bias in evaluating information prior to making a decision such as whom to vote for.

Logic and Probability

Another series of studies has shown how people make decisions based on knowledge of probabilities. For example, earlier we described the behavior of the psychological subject, Bill, who learned that pressing one button (the left button) on a machine would pay off 60 percent of the time, and pressing the other would pay off 40 percent of the time. Bill decided to press the left button about 60 percent of the time. Is this the way to get the largest number of payoffs?

Let us say Bill is allowed to press a button 100 times. If he presses the left button 60 percent of the time, with 100 choices he will press it 60 times. Now the left button pays off 60 percent of the time so Bill will receive chips from the left button 60 percent of 60 times or 36 times. He presses the right button 40 percent of the time, or 40 times in this case. The right button produces chips 40 percent of the times it is pressed, so Bill will receive chips 16 times from the right button (40 percent of 40). All together Bill will receive 36 + 16 or 52 payoffs by dividing his choices into 60 for one button, 40 for the other. Actually, he would have received 60 payoffs if he had pressed the left button 100 percent of the time.

Psychological studies have shown that Bill's behavior is not unusual. Given two choices with various probabilities of success, people tend to choose each alternative the same proportion of the time as the probability of payoff. Such behavior is called *probability matching* and is typical of human beings, although it does not logically lead to maximum success.

We see a similar phenomenon when people are given a choice of playing different probability games.

■ In an experiment by Cohen and Hansel (1958), people were given their choice between a single drawing of lots in which they had one chance in ten of winning, or ten drawings in different boxes in each of which they had one chance in 100. Most people chose the ten drawings, even though the chances of winning are mathematically equal in the two alternatives. In a second operation, subjects were given their choice between drawing one slip from a box containing ten slips or drawing ten from a box containing 100, returning each slip before drawing the next. In this case, most people's decisions were influenced by such factors as the number of tickets. ("I'm more likely to get one out of ten than one out of 100, no matter how many draws I have in each case.") ■

Individual Differences in Problem Solving

Reasoning and decision making are highly valued in our culture. Consequently, the sources of individual differences are of real social concern. From our analysis of decision making we can see that differences in decisions may result from (1) differences in motivation, (2) differences in the amount of information (perception-memory) one has upon which to base estimates of the probability of success, (3) differences in the ability to use past experience in constructing or deducing a rule or principle which applies to this situation, (4) differences in the ability to apply the rule in this situation, and (5) differences in the ability to shift from one possible solution to another when necessary. We have discussed some of these differences among people in earlier chapters. However, individual differences in problem solving have been studied not only as a composite of these five elements, but also as an overall characteristic of a person. This overall ability to solve problems is sometimes called *intelligence*.

What Is Intelligence?

There has been a great deal of confusion about the definition and measurement of intelligence. You probably have a concept of what you think intelligence is, but your concept of an intelligent person may be different from that of someone else. Nor have psychologists agreed on a single meaning for the term. Here are some of the definitions of intelligence given by psychologists:

■ "... the capacity to learn."

"... the ability to carry on abstract thinking."

"... the global capacity of the individual to act purposefully, to think rationally, and to deal effectively with the environment."

"... the ability to undertake activities that are characterized by (1) difficulty, (2) complexity, (3) abstractness, (4) economy, (5) adaptiveness to a goal, (6) social value, and (7) emergence of originals, and to maintain such activities under conditions that demand a concentration of energy and a resistance to emotional forces."

"... the ability to understand and deal with persons, things, and symbols." ■

As you can see, different psychologists emphasize different aspects of the problem-solving process in their definitions of intelligence. But there is one thing all these definitions have in common: They all refer to something unobservable, not to what a person *does*, but to his capacity or ability. A frequent assumption implicit in these definitions is that intelligence is an inherited capacity which determines a person's potentialities and his limits.

The Measurement of Intelligence

If we look at the history of intelligence testing, we see that the measurement of intelligence has had little to do with the theoretical definitions of intelligence.

Intelligence testing began in 1904 when the Paris school authorities asked psychologist Albert Binet to devise a way of separating normal from feebleminded children. Feebleminded children were to be put in special schools, but normal children who did not learn, because of inattention or naughtiness, were to remain in school with the other children.

Binet's problem was a very practical one and his solution was also a very practical one. He and his protégé, Simon, invented a test which was made up

BINET SCALES

AGE 7	AGE 9
1. Shows right hand and left ear 2. Gives description of pictures 3. Executes three commissions given simultaneously 4. Gives value of three single and three double sous 5. Names four colors: red, green, yellow, blue	1. Makes change from twenty sous 2. Defines names of familiar objects in terms superior to use 3. Recognizes all nine [French] coins 4. Gives months of the year in correct order 5. Comprehends and answers easy problem questions

FIG. 10–4. Some items from two of the age scales of Binet's original test. (From Freeman, F. S., *Theory and Practice of Psychological Testing*, third edition. New York: Holt, Rinehart, and Winston, 1962. Reprinted by permission.)

of a variety of problems, ranging from very easy to very difficult ones. The items included tasks in such areas as vocabulary, information, rote memory, and verbal comprehension of sentences (see Fig. 10–4). Binet and Simon tried out their problems on many children of different ages, and found out what could be performed by the average child of each age. The tests then could be used to tell whether a child could perform the tasks appropriate to his own age. If a child failed to perform the majority of tasks that most children of his age could, he was said to be subnormal. If a child solved problems that were beyond children of his own age, he was said to be brighter than normal.

Until Binet's time, many people thought that there was a distinct qualitative difference between the feebleminded and the normal child. If a child were feebleminded, he could not learn in school. If he were normal, he should do all right in school. Binet, however, discovered that the children he tested didn't fall into distinct classes. Rather, there were continuous degrees of difference leading from low to average and from average to high intelligence. Performance of an unselected group of children of a given age on an intelligence test showed many children scoring around the average, slightly fewer on each side, and fewer and fewer further from the average or mean score (see Fig. 10–5). Thus we see that scores on intelligence tests are, like ability test scores, distributed in an approximately normal distribution.

Binet could now tell the school authorities that many children, although not feebleminded, still were not able to do the problems solved by average children of the same age. This information alone was helpful, but a problem remained, "What could these children do?" Here Binet had a brilliant inspiration. He knew what tests the average children of each age group could pass. Some eight-year-old children could pass only the tests which the average five-year-old passed, others could pass these tests and also the tests of the six-year-olds, and still other eight-year-olds could pass the tests for seven-year-olds but not those

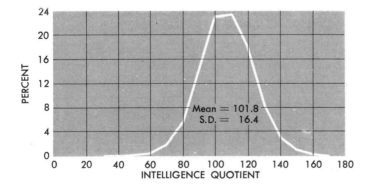

FIG. 10–5. A typical distribution of intelligence test scores from an unselected group. (After Terman and Merrill, 1960)

for eight-year-olds. Why not call the level of tests a child could pass his *mental age?* A nine-year-old child with a mental age (M.A.) of six would be capable of doing first grade work in school, but not of doing fourth grade work. The mental age was thus very useful in helping place children with others of equal ability, and tests were constructed to fit each year up to about age fifteen. In constructing the tests, psychologists found that scores increased more slowly after age thirteen and that relatively little increase occurred after age fifteen.

But merely knowing a child's mental age is not all that we need. Obviously, we can expect more in the future from a boy of six with a mental age of nine than we can from a boy of fifteen who also has a mental age of nine. A measure of intelligence must involve both mental age and chronological age. These two ages have been combined into a single index of brightness—the intelligence quotient, or I.Q., which is the mental age divided by the chronological age, then multiplied by a hundred (to eliminate fractions):

$$\text{I.Q.} = \frac{\text{M.A.}}{\text{C.A.}} \times 100.$$

Thus a boy with a mental age of nine and a chronological age of six has an I.Q. of 150;

$$\text{I.Q.} = \frac{9}{6} \times 100 = 150.$$

A boy with M.A. = 9 and C.A. = 15, has an I.Q. of 60;

$$\text{I.Q.} = \frac{9}{15} \times 100 = 60.$$

Since intellectual development slows down in the teens, the normal adult would appear to have a lower I.Q. as he grew older if we used the same formula for adults as for children. If a person's mental age at 20 were 15 and at 32, 16, it would appear that he has become much less bright even though he has really not lost but gained. In order that the normal I.Q. for adults will also be 100, a C.A. of 15 is used for adults. Thus a person 25 years old with normal intelligence still has an I.Q. of 100, since he has a mental age of 15 and is assigned a C.A. of 15;

$$\text{I.Q.} = \frac{15}{15} \times 100 = 100.$$

Since Binet's work, both kinds of tests and the use of tests to measure intelligence have increased tremendously. Binet's tests and their subsequent translations and revisions were developed and tested on school children. Other tests were developed mainly for testing adults; some of these put less emphasis on verbal ability and symbolic problems and more on performance of mechanical tasks. Some were designed for group testing (the Binet test had to be administered individually). Some even appeared in Sunday supplements of newspapers! The scores of each of these tests are usually called intelligence quotients. Tests which are carefully developed usually correlate with each other, but a person will not necessarily show the identical I.Q. on every test. For example, the correlation between a person's score on the Stanford-Binet Intelligence Test and the Wechsler Adult Intelligence Scale (two of the most widely used intelligence tests) is about 0.6, a figure indicating some variation in scores from test to test. Other correlations are given in Fig. 10–6.

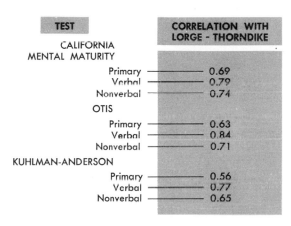

TEST	CORRELATION WITH LORGE - THORNDIKE
CALIFORNIA MENTAL MATURITY	
Primary	0.69
Verbal	0.79
Nonverbal	0.74
OTIS	
Primary	0.63
Verbal	0.84
Nonverbal	0.71
KUHLMAN-ANDERSON	
Primary	0.56
Verbal	0.77
Nonverbal	0.65

FIG. 10–6. The average correlations between the Lorge-Thorndike Test and other tests commonly given in schools. Three areas were considered: correlations with tests given in primary grades, correlations with the verbal sections of other tests, and correlations with the nonverbal sections of other tests. The verbal and nonverbal correlations were determined for grades 4 through 12 only. (After Lorge and Thorndike, 1957)

The Binet test and its revisions have been widely used in schools. They have been quite successful in predicting a child's level of performance in school at a later age. The correlation between the Stanford-Binet test and school grades is about 0.5. The Army intelligence test, the Army General Classification Test, has been useful in predicting which recruits will be successful in officer candidate school. There is no question that the intelligence test movement has provided useful tools in many areas.

However, a major question remains. Do the instruments that carry the label "intelligence test" measure the capacities that are usually defined as intelligence? The answer is clearly "no." These tests do not measure a capacity; they measure performance on particular tasks. An underlying assumption is that everyone born with a capacity has had an opportunity to develop his potential. In devising intelligence tests to measure these factors, psychologists have attempted to use only items upon which everyone has had an equal opportunity for practice. For example, some tests include problems in arithmetic, others involve giving synonyms or antonyms of several words. Such problems are included on the assumption that everyone taking the test has had an equal opportunity to learn the words of our language and to learn how to add and subtract. It is also assumed that those individuals who have achieved the most, given this opportunity to practice, are those with the most intelligence. In interpreting results of these tests, however, people often forget that they are not valid in comparing groups which have not had equal experience with the sort of problems involved in the test. This is important to keep in mind as we turn to group differences in intelligence.

Group Differences in Intelligence

Once intelligence tests became available it became possible to study individual and group differences in intelligence. Many studies dealt with this problem. In Chapter 4 we saw how intelligence tests were used in attempts to determine whether or not there were racial differences in intelligence. Some of the same problems arise in evaluating other group differences.

Sex

In constructing intelligence tests, items which favor either girls or boys are eliminated; thus one finds few differences between the sexes in intelligence as measured by intelligence tests. There are, however, a number of indicators of real sex differences in problem solving.

Coeds, for example, have more difficulty in shifting set than do male students (Guetzkow, 1948; Sweeney, 1953). Other studies have also revealed inferior problem-solving performance by women. It has been suggested that this may be the result of anxiety. In our society men are supposed to be superior, and it may be that women feel that being able to solve problems too well is un-feminine. Those women who scored highest in a test of femininity tended to perform most poorly in problem solving (Milton, 1957). When women's anxiety about problem solving was reduced by a group discussion, their performance improved (Carey, 1958).

Socioeconomic Status and Urban-Rural Differences

In considering racial differences in intelligence, we saw that results are not clear because of educational and cultural differences between the races. Within American society we have differences in culture between nationality groups, between urban and rural residents, between inhabitants of different geographical areas, and perhaps more important, between different socioeconomic classes. Thus even though the relationship of socioeconomic status to intelligence has been the subject of much research, the conclusions drawn are limited by the difficulty of finding problems based on common cultural background. For example, rural children attain lower average I.Q.'s than city children on most tests. This may be due to the fact that most intelligence tests have been made up by city dwellers and validated on city children. Because country children have different experiences, they may be handicapped on the usual intelligence tests.

Similarly, the results of studies agree that intelligence test scores vary from one class to another, with a greater percentage of bright children in families of high socioeconomic status and a greater percentage of feebleminded children in families of lower socioeconomic status. But all studies find a wide range of intelligence in all social classes.

Some people have used social-class differences in intelligence as an argument for limiting the birthrate in the lower classes. Figures on the birthrates in various educational levels would lead one to expect that the intelligence of the total population would decrease as a result of high birthrates in the lower social classes. However, the Scottish Council for Research in Education conducted a very careful study of the intelligence quotients of all Scottish children in certain age groups in 1932 and again in 1947. The results showed that not only had no drop occurred in the intelligence quotients of Scottish children, but there was even a slight increase in mean test score. The increase in mean test score may be due to improvements in education.

The relationship between socioeconomic status and intelligence test scores is thus not one of simple cause and effect. Even though the proportions may differ, every level of intelligence can be found at each social level. Since both heredity

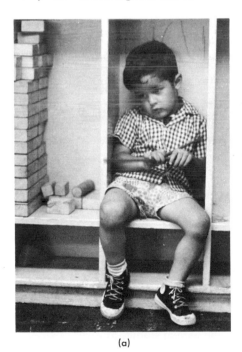 

(a) (b)

FIG. 10–7. A boy who is enrolled in Project Head Start. He is shy and withdrawn his first day (a), but he soon participates in activities that increase his range of experiences (b). (*Life* Magazine © 1965 Time, Inc. All rights reserved.)

and environment differ from one social class to another, the effects of heredity and environment are intermingled. To the handicap of poor heredity may be added the handicaps of poor home life and poor schooling, and since present intelligence tests are not culture-free, the child whose home training and schooling have not been normal may be handicapped in solving many intelligence test problems.

Does this mean that we can dismiss low intelligence test scores among culturally deprived groups? Not at all. We have seen that intelligence tests are fairly accurate predictors of intellectual functioning in some situations—particularly in school. The individual whose background has handicapped him in solving the problems on intelligence tests may find himself equally handicapped in dealing with many problems in the culture within which the test was standardized. Thus, lower-class children who make low scores on intelligence tests will probably also do poorly in school and in business.

Recently, our government has undertaken programs whose purpose is to counteract the snowballing effects of cultural deprivation in a child's preschool years. In Project Head Start, preschool children are given experience with toys, books, and games with which most middle-class children have contact in their own homes. The hope is that these experiences will give the formerly deprived child both the motivation and the skills that will enable him to benefit more from his formal education when he attends public school later on. Figure 10–7 shows one child on his first day in a Head Start center and on a later day when he has become accustomed to his new world.

The Stability of Intelligence

Does the I.Q. change? We have already said that intelligence tests predict achievement in school and other situations, which implies that I.Q.'s are relatively constant. Nevertheless, one occassionally reads of some treatment which has produced a marked change in I.Q. With the widespread use of intelligence tests in the schools, it is important for parents to know how much change to expect in their children's I.Q.'s.

First, it should be pointed out again that tests of intelligence are constructed on the assumption that those tested have had the same degree of experience with the problems used. Thus some studies demonstrating changes in I.Q. may be accounted for by differences in practice on the sort of problems used in tests, or by an actual effect of environment upon intelligence. This last interpretation suggests that what one does may increase or decrease his general intellectual ability. This interpretation is supported by the animal studies of early experience which we cited earlier, and by a few studies of children.

A second factor affecting changes in intelligence test scores is that intelligence tests measure performance on several kinds of tasks: verbal, spatial, memory, and reasoning. In choosing the items, the test maker is faced with the problem of *sampling*. How many problems should he use from each factor? If he uses a great many spatial problems, the person with high spatial ability will have an advantage over the person with great verbal ability, who would do better on a verbal test. In the early days of test construction, the primary purpose of the tests was to predict school achievement. Hence the factors important in school were given the most emphasis, even before these factors were clearly known. As a result, verbal factors are emphasized highly in most present-day tests. But because the test items vary somewhat from test to test, some changes in I.Q. may simply be due to changes in factors measured in the tests at different ages. Even on the best tests one can expect on the average a change of about five points between two administrations of the test.

From your study of motivation, you can probably guess that differences in motivation may also account for apparent changes in intelligence. A child's motivation for taking intelligence tests may vary from time to time, so his score may be lower than it should be when his motivation is low. On the other hand, when parents have stressed the importance of achievement to such an extent that the child is anxious about the tests, his anxiety may produce poor intelligence-test scores.

INTELLIGENCE: A SUMMARY. We have seen that the term *intelligence* can refer to three different characteristics of a person: His inherited capacity to learn, think, and solve problems; his normal level of performance on certain kinds of tasks; and his intelligence-test score. If a person never has the opportunity to develop his capacities, there is no test in the world which will be able to determine what his inherited abilities were. However, given a "normal" cultural environment, people of different capacities will profit differentially. By sampling from the kinds of problems associated with school and vocational success, the psychologist constructs an intelligence test. To the extent that a person is optimally attentive and motivated, the intelligence-test score will reveal a person's performance level on the kinds of tasks sampled in the test.

Intelligence Tests and Creativity

We have noted that the tasks that make up the items in intelligence tests were selected partly on the basis of their success in predicting school achievement. A factor analysis of intelligence test items reveals that they sample performance requiring several basic abilities: verbal ability, word fluency, numerical ability, spatial ability, reasoning, and rote memory. (We noted individual differences in some of these abilities in the last chapter.) As you may remember, the items which tap these abilities are rather simple and straightforward. Each has a clearly prescribed correct answer.

Recently, some psychologists have become concerned that standard intelligence tests fail to capture one important aspect of problem-solving ability: creativity, the ability to construct new and original solutions to problems. Creativity involves at least two aspects. One of these is flexibility—the ability to change from one approach to another. The other is originality—the ability to discover new alternatives.

Rokeach (1960) has executed a series of studies exploring characteristics of individuals differing in flexibility. Individuals whom Rokeach calls "rigid" have difficulty changing their approach or set. Their difficulty lies in the ability to analyze a problem rather than in synthesizing its elements.

One of the tests commonly used to determine the degree to which an individual is affected by set is the following (Luchins, 1942):

■ You are to suppose that you have three empty water jars of known capacities in quarts and an unlimited supply of water. Your problem is to use these jars to obtain a specified number of quarts of water. In Fig. 10–8 the letters A, B, C represent the three jars and the numbers below them their capacities. The fourth number is the number of quarts you are to obtain. For example: you are to get 100 quarts of water. You have three empty jars which hold 21, 127, and 3 quarts, respectively. To solve this problem, fill the 127-quart jar (B); from it fill the 21-quart jar (A). This leaves 106 quarts in B. From B, fill the 3-quart jar (C) twice. The required 100 quarts are left in B. ■

PROBLEM	CAPACITY OF JARS (quarts)			SOLUTION REQUIRED
	A	B	C	
1	21	127	3	100
2	18	43	10	5
3	9	40	6	19
4	20	59	4	31
5	23	49	3	20
6	15	39	3	18
7	28	76	3	25

FIG. 10–8. Luchins water-jar problem. The first four problems are most easily solved by one approach; the others, by a different approach. (Luchins, 1942)

It is quite normal to continue using the habits of $B - A - 2C$, even when it would be quicker to simply take $A - C$. In the first four problems one develops a *set* to solve the problems by the former method, and this set increases the tendency to think in a particular direction.

Persons high in reasoning ability are just as susceptible to set as those low in reasoning ability; i.e., both groups are equally likely to solve Problem 5 by the formula $B - A - 2C$. However, individuals high in reasoning ability are better able than poor reasoners to change direction when it is required, as on Problem 7 (McNemar, 1955).

A strong motive, such as anxiety, is likely to interfere with an individual's ability to shift to new alternatives. For example, a number of studies suggest that individuals high in anxiety over achievement do not change their approach on the water-jar problems.

Originality involves the ability to create new and unusual alternatives. Guilford (1959) and his colleagues (1957) have assembled a number of tasks designed to measure originality. One such task, for example, asks subjects to devise titles for plots; another requires them to answer "What would happen if all national and local laws were suddenly abolished?" Trained judges can agree on ratings for answers.

Both originality and flexibility emerged as characteristics of creative people in a series of studies by Barron (1958) and his associates. Barron assembled two groups of people from many professions: mathematics, literature, architecture, and science. One group included people who were recognized by their fellow professionals as being creative; the other group consisted of people of similar training and experience, but who were not recognized as creative contributors to their fields. Both groups of people were highly intelligent; there was no significant difference in their I.Q. scores. However, the studies revealed that the creative people were likely (1) to be able to integrate diverse stimuli, (2) to be high in energy, (3) to be high in the ability to think of many different words quickly, (4) to be dominant and assertive, (5) to be impulsive, (6) to be interested in music, art, literature, and social service activities, (7) to prefer complex to simple stimuli, (8) to be generally effective in performance in different kinds of situations, and (9) to be less susceptible to social influence in making decisions.

The study of creativity is currently a very active area in psychology and the results that are emerging are, as you can see, of much interest. As yet we know only a little about how creativity may be nurtured in schools and homes.

Functioning of the CNS

Individual differences in problem solving must in some way be related to brain function. But what is this relationship? Is reasoning ability localized in one part of the brain? To answer these questions we must turn to studies of patients who have suffered brain damage as the result of tumors, wounds, or brain operations. Since reasoning seems to be more characteristic of the species that have evolved a highly developed frontal lobe of the cerebral cortex, it is natural to hypothesize that reasoning is related to frontal-lobe functioning.

According to Goldstein (1939), who studied many patients with frontal-lobe defects, such patients can deal very well with simple, concrete problems. What they lose is an ability to take an abstract attitude toward a problem. Thus they are ineffective in reasoning because they cannot think of what they *might* do; they have to perform the action itself. For example, a frontal-lobe patient can drink a glass of water, but if you ask him to demonstrate with an empty glass how he would drink, he becomes confused. He can take a key from the doctor's hand and unlock a door, but without the key he is unable to demonstrate the movements involved when doors are unlocked. He simply can't think about things which are not real and concrete.

In many ways this behavior is similar to that of lower animals who have difficulty abstracting. Generally speaking, we find more ability to abstract as we go up the phylogenic scale. Other animals can learn simple rules and apply them in simple situations, but they are much inferior to man in these abilities. They must act out hypotheses in overt behavior, while man is better able to test hypotheses in his mind.

Goldstein's work indicates that injuries to the brain result in particular kinds of difficulties in thinking, but does not indicate that reasoning is localized in one region. Further research by Halstead (1947) and his associates suggests that there is no specific localization of a specific intellectual process, but that particular areas of the cerebral cortex are of greater importance for particular functions. For example, in support of Goldstein, Halstead found that injuries to the frontal lobe are particularly detrimental to abstraction. Injuries to the left hemisphere are more damaging to logical verbal ability than are injuries to the right hemisphere.

The Development of Thinking

When the newborn human infant comes into the world, his capacity for thinking is obviously limited. The cortex of the brain is not yet fully developed. As we saw in Chapter 4, the long period of human development permits the flexibility of behavior that is an outstanding characteristic of human beings. While hereditary factors are undoubtedly extremely important in determining the mental ability of a person, the early years of life are also important in mental growth.

An examination of the intelligence-test scores of adopted children sheds some light on this issue. Studies by Skeels, Skodak, and others have indicated that while children's I.Q. ten or more years after adoption correlated significantly with their true mother's I.Q.'s, the I.Q. was approximately ten points higher than would have been predicted on the basis of their heredity alone. Children of feebleminded mothers placed in adoptive homes before the age of six months made normal scores on intelligence tests two to four years after placement. This, of course, cannot be attributed solely to environmental influences, since as we saw in our discussion of heredity, the ordinary chance recombinations of genes might be expected to result in more nearly normal intelligence tests scores. However, environmental factors seem highly probable in accounting for the fact that, of these children, those placed in homes of higher socioeconomic status tended to have higher intelligence test scores than those placed in homes of lower status. From these studies the investigators concluded that a favorable adoptive environment contributed to the development of intelligence (Skodak, 1938, 1950; Skeels, 1938). Further evidence on this point is found in a study by Wittenborn (1956) who found that the I.Q.'s of adopted children depended on the age at which the child was placed in an adoptive home. The younger the child at adoption, the higher his later intelligence test score.

What do superior homes do to influence intellectual functioning? This is still an unanswered question. It may be that more emphasis is placed on language. It may be that they simply give enough attention and love so that there is less anxiety and the child feels freer to try new possibilities. Without further research we are unable to determine whether any or all of these conditions are important. We do, however, have some interesting research findings which are relevant.

■ Researchers at the Fels Research Institute (Kagan, Sontag, Baker, and Nelson, 1958; Sontag, Baker, and Nelson, 1958) studied the intellectual development of a group of children tested periodically for several years. They found that many children changed significantly over the years. Children who were assured, who enjoyed competition and problem solving, and who were liked by others, tended also to improve in I.Q. On the other hand, after entering school, children whose mothers overprotected them tended to decrease in I.Q. ■

Work on the effects of experience on intelligence should not be interpreted as meaning that one's intellectual performance is determined solely by his experience as an infant or child. Research to date indicates that effective intelligence is the result of heredity-environment interaction. Even when identical twins who had been separated in infancy were reared in different homes, they tended to resemble each other closely in I.Q., which suggests that heredity is very important. But the way in which hereditary potential develops is, as we have seen, dependent upon the individual's environment.

Periods in the Development of Intelligence

Piaget has suggested that intellectual development in children can be divided into four major periods (Flavell, 1963). The *sensory-motor* period takes place in the first two years when the infant develops simple perceptual and sensory-motor skills. He also learns about the permanence and constancy of objects in this period. The chief accomplishment of the *preoperational period* (from age two to about age seven) is the acquisition of language, particularly naming objects and manipulating them symbolically.

In the *concrete operations* period (from about seven to eleven), the child learns to use more abstract concepts in interpreting his experiences. The difference between a preoperational child and a child in the period of concrete operations is illustrated in the following two demonstrations:

■ Children are shown two identical beakers, each filled with water to the same level. The children agree that the two beakers contain the same amount of water. The children then watch as water from one of the beakers is poured into a container that is much taller and narrower

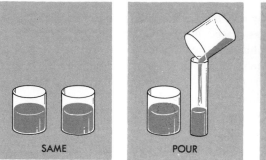

FIG. 10–9.   One of the problems Piaget and Inhelder used to study the development of thinking in children. (After Piaget and Inhelder, 1962)

than the original beakers. Naturally, the water level is higher in the narrower container. Now the children are again asked which container holds more water. Younger children (below the age of seven) tend to say that the taller container now has more water because the water is higher. Older children say there are equal amounts of water in each container because the amount was not changed by putting it in a new container (see Fig. 10–9). Similarly, if children are shown equal lumps of plasticine and one lump is then molded into a long, thin string, younger children will say there is more clay in the long thin lump than in the other. (Piaget and Inhelder, 1962) ∎

The difference between the younger and older children, according to Piaget, is that the younger children are unable to overcome their perceptual impressions of amount. The older children have learned the concept of conservation: that amounts do not change when they are transformed in various ways. This concept enables them to interpret their perceptual experiences in a new way. Piaget believes that such concepts are learned through actions. Children learn the principle of conservation, for example, by doing things like molding plasticine into different shapes. By making the same lump assume many different shapes, the child obtains the concept of conservation despite the transformation.

The *period* of *formal operations*, which takes place between the ages of about twelve to fifteen years, is marked by an even greater ability to use abstract concepts. Now the child is not only able to apply concepts in a given situation, but he is also able to conceptualize a variety of possibilities, given a problem. Furthermore, he is able to eliminate them in a systematic logical fashion.

∎ Huttenlocher (in press) gave children between the ages of six and 12 this problem: She showed them a light bulb and two switches, and she told them that one of the two switches operated the bulb. It was the children's job to determine which switch operated the light bulb by moving only one given switch. She used four conditions of presentation: (1) The light was off when the child received the problem, and moving the one switch turned it on. (2) The light was on at the beginning, and moving the switch turned it off. (3) The light was on at the beginning, and moving the switch had no effect. (4) The light was off at the beginning, and moving the switch had no effect. The conditions are listed in the order of the complexity of the inferences required by the child to solve the problem in each case. It takes fewer conceptual steps to infer that a switch turns on a light if one sees the turning of the switch resulting in light than if one sees the movement of the switch turning off the light. Similarly, it takes fewer conceptual steps to make inferences about a switch whose movement has an effect than to see it have no effect and to have to infer that the other switch is the one which works. Huttenlocher found that six-year-olds had no trouble solving the problem under condition (1). But the greater the number of conceptual steps involved, the more difficulty they had. On the other hand, twelve-year-olds had no trouble solving the problem under any of the conditions. ■

The twelve-year-old children were able to conceptualize all the possible combinations of switches and bulb; the six-year-olds were more bound to the concrete events before them.

Although we have given specific ages for each period, neither Piaget nor any other investigator considers these ages as absolute. The reason for dividing intellectual development into periods is to point out that this, like motor development, follows an ordered sequence, in which some periods necessarily precede others.

If such an ordered sequence does exist, we should be able to discern it in cultures whose handling of intellectual development is quite different from that of Western culture, e.g., in cultures in which there is less formal schooling. There is only a small amount of such data available. One study by Goodnow (1963), reported by Brown (1965), involved the testing of children in Hong Kong on problems requiring concrete operational thinking. Four groups were tested: Chinese and European children, some of each with formal schooling and some without. Although there were some deviations, the author concluded that there was remarkable similarity in the performance of children of different nationality and education.

A number of investigators have wondered what the effects would be of training children who are in one period in the skills normally appearing in a later period. The results, in general, have depended on how close the children were to the next period. Children who were far away from the transition benefited little from training; children who were close to transition to the next period showed some signs of accelerated development (Brown, 1965).

Training prior to "intellectual readiness" may cause children to state correct answers, but as Smedslund (1961) showed in the following study, it does not change their modes of thinking.

■ Smedslund used the plasticine problem with preoperational and operational children. He showed the children two identical balls and then altered the shape of one of them. The children would have to guess whether the two lumps still had the same weight. Then he actually weighed the two lumps on the scale, so that the children could see the result. This training resulted in correct answers, even in preoperational children. Smedslund now put in an "extinction" trial. Unbeknownst to the children, he removed a piece of plasticine when he molded it into a new shape. On these trials the scale showed that the two lumps were not of equal weight. The preoperational children showed no surprise and immediately went back to their old ways of judgment. The operational children were surprised and made comments like "a little piece must have fallen on the floor." But they continued to judge weight on the basis of conservation. ∎

These results suggest that training prior to a period of readiness is uneffective. The phenomenon is reminiscent of the critical periods in sensory-motor development and in imprinting, which we described earlier. As in these earlier examples, we suspect that the intellectual critical periods depend on both biological maturation and on experience. In the case of operational thinking, this experience might be wide, and involve many different materials and contexts, all illustrating a particular relationship.

Thinking in Adolescence and Adulthood

Descriptions of intellectual development usually end with adolescence. During adolescence the curve of mental development, as measured by intelligence tests, begins to level off. There have been relatively few studies of mental changes in adulthood. Studies of the peak creative productivity of scholars in different fields have suggested that the peak varies from field to field. For example, according to one study, in poetry the age of greatest productivity is 25–29; in chemistry, 30–34; in medicine, 34–39; in mathematics and astronomy, 40–44 (Lehman, 1953). One is tempted to hypothesize from such figures that the age of peak creativity is later in fields that require the greatest use of previous knowledge and past experience. However, we really know little about the reasons for such differences between fields.

Thinking in Old Age

Until recently, psychologists believed that all aspects of thinking, except information, decreased with age, leveling off in the teens and beginning to decline in the mid-twenties. Recent research, however, suggests that intellectual ability actually continues to improve with age, unless brain damage occurs as a result of circulatory difficulties. Bayley (1955) retested a group of adults who were identified in childhood as being unusually intelligent; she found that rather than experiencing a falling off in intelligence as they got older, these individuals showed gains in intelligence up to age 50 and beyond. Other studies indicate that the same result holds for individuals of average intelligence.

Once again, however, we would point to the importance of environment in determining the direction of this trend. We would expect individuals in intellectual pursuits to be more likely to add to their store of concepts than the individual in a repetitive job. From our analysis of decision making, it makes sense that increased experience and an increased storing of concepts should result in more effective thinking. Thus even though the older person may lose flexibility, his increased experience may compensate for this. However, the older person may become so accustomed to relying on experience that he fails to take a problem-solving attitude.

The chief cloud upon this generally sunny picture of thinking in old age is that many older persons suffer from circulatory ailments. Since brain functioning is the basis of thinking, it would appear that any impairment of circulation in the brain would result in impaired thinking. However, Aring (1957) reports that he finds no relationship between brain damage and intelligence in old age, so that this supposed cause of decrement may not have the effects we would expect.

Another possible handicap to intellectual functioning in old age is impairment of sensory functions. Not only do sensory malfunctions limit the older person's ability to obtain information from his environment, but any great reduction in sensory input may affect intellectual functioning in a manner similar to that observed in sensory deprivation experiments.

To sum up, the individual's increasing experience results in generally improving problem solving through the life span on problems requiring utilization of previous experience. Increased experience, however, also may result in decreasing flexibility, thus handicapping the individual on new problems in which his previous experience is irrelevant or tends to interfere.

Practical Applications

Our analysis of the factors involved in decision making indicates the kinds of difficulties which interfere with effective decision making.

One of the most common difficulties is our tendency to confuse means and ends. Often after the decision is made, the decision maker is not really sure why he did what he did and is unhappy with the results. Improving one's decision making in such cases involves analyzing the problem in terms of probable outcomes in order to eliminate attractive alternatives whose consequences are unsatisfactory.

A second barrier to effective decision making is inadequate information. A careful study of the problem may indicate possibilities which were not immediately apparent. Education and experience are clearly of practical importance in the development of principles which can be applied to new problems. Thus we should not be surprised that scholars in one field are not necessarily capable decision makers in other fields. To improve, however, they need only to acquire more information.

A third barrier is that in applying rules to new situations, we frequently fail to note the likenesses and differences between the problem situation and the situations in which the principles were learned. Situations arousing emotions are particularly likely to cause faulty discrimination and differentiation.

A fourth failure is failure to change direction. In discussing reasoning, we pointed out that success in reasoning depends upon one's ability to change his approach to the problem—to change "direction." As we saw earlier, one factor influencing ability to change direction is anxiety.

A fifth barrier to effective reasoning is emotional bias. As we have seen, one's motivation affects the way he perceives situations, his choice of response, and his thinking. Closely related to this is the tendency to be influenced by immediate rewards present in the situation. Abstractions and symbols are helpful because they help the individual take the problem out of the present situation and look at it with less constraint from emotion.

Child-Rearing Practices

If early experiences affect later intelligence, the implication for child rearing is immediately apparent. A stimulating environment increases the opportunity for the child's intelligence to develop. This does not mean, however, that parents should pursue a completely *laissez-faire* policy—permitting children unlimited freedom to get into mischief. As we saw in our discussion of curiosity in Chapter 7, anxiety is likely to occur when the situation is so novel that the organism cannot cope with it. We saw earlier in this chapter that one of the most important barriers to effective thinking is anxiety. To be free from anxiety, the child needs a sense of security in his parents' love, and their support in his explorations, as well as their protection from overwhelmingly difficult problems.

Sontag's research cited above indicates that the child also needs motivation for achievement if he is to develop his intellectual resources; hence the conditions for learning the necessary achievement motivation are also indirectly relevant to the development of problem-solving ability.

Social Applications

One use of information about problem solving and decision making is in the application of formal rules of decision strategies to complex problems of military or industrial operations. While such operations research owes much of its procedures to mathematics, psychologists have contributed knowledge of the characteristics of humans as decision makers to studies of how decisions should be made in large operations.

Understanding thinking has important values in predicting success in situations involving the use of problem-solving or decision-making ability. Intelligence tests, for example, are useful aids in predicting success in college. Typically, the correlation between an intelligence test and college grades is about 0.5, so that intelligence tests are helpful in identifying the ablest students. Although there are few well-established principles to guide us, American citizens realize that human talent is our most valuable resource and that one of our most critical social problems is that of identifying, developing, and utilizing this talent most effectively.

What are the implications of the research on problem solving for education? Our study suggests that education should provide opportunities to practice problem solving, should not encourage blind obedience, should help students clarify their values, should attempt to destroy stereotypes, should provide information, and should attempt to reduce anxiety.

In a study of outstanding scientists, Roe (1953) noted that these men had had early opportunities to learn that they could find things out for themselves. While it is important that we help develop students' abilities to analyze critically an experiment or literary production, too much emphasis upon a critical approach may interfere with the student's own creativity. Perhaps we should give students more exercises in writing proposals for new work or more experience in solving problems through the use of different approaches.

In reporting a long-term study of Vassar students, Sanford and his colleagues (1956) report that the college environment shielded students from experience with complex, difficult, and frustrating situations. They suggest that colleges need to challenge students by presenting problems which cannot be solved by simply doing what the students have done in the past.

Summary

Concepts

Thinking. The manipulation and reorganization of concepts, motives, habits, and rules

Decision making. The weighing of goals and the assessment of the probable success of known alternatives

Reasoning or *logic.* The utilization of information to reach conclusions

Probability matching. The tendency of an individual to choose an alternative the same percentage of time as that alternative leads to success

Intelligence quotient (I.Q.). An index of intelligence derived from a test; in children's tests it is usually calculated by dividing mental age by chronological age and multiplying by 100

Principles

1. Some components of problem solving are the weighing of goals, the discovery of appropriate means to goals, and the assessment of the probability that a given course of action will lead to the chosen goals.

2. The manner in which a person solves problems depends on his perception of the problem, his motives (including his motives for taking risks), past experience, and his use of logic.

3. Intelligence has been theoretically defined as an overall ability to solve problems: measures of intelligence assess the performance of individuals on tasks involving intellectual functions. The degree to which the measure reflects inherited ability depends on the test used, and on the past experience and the motivation of the person taking the test.

4. Creativity involves two aspects of problem-solving ability not usually measured in intelligence tests: flexibility—the ability to change from one approach to another—and originality—the ability to discover new alternatives.

5. Some observations of brain-injured patients suggest that deficits in abstract thinking may be related to frontal lobe injury.

6. Intellectual development in children may be divided into four periods which involve progressively increasing ability to use abstract concepts, relationships, and strategies.

7. The individual's increasing experience from childhood to old age results in generally improving problem solving on problems requiring the use of past knowledge, but this increasing experience may also reduce flexibility.

8. The knowledge of problem-solving principles can be applied to personal problems, to corporate and military decisions, and to the improvement of education.

Suggested Readings

JOHNSON, D., *Psychology: A Problem Solving Approach.* New York: Harper, 1961. Another elementary textbook that uses a problem solving approach.

HUMPHREY, G., *Directed Thinking.* New York: Dodd & Mead, 1948. A very readable book of practical information on thinking.

Many of Piaget's books have been translated into English and give interesting examples of his studies of children's thinking. An excellent summary of Piaget's work is found in FLAVELL, J. H., *The Developmental Psychology of Jean Piaget.* Princeton, N.J.: Van Nostrand, 1963.

chapter 11

frustration and the mechanisms of defense

chapter 11

WHAT ARE THE SOURCES OF FRUSTRATION?

WHAT ARE THE REACTIONS TO FRUSTRATING
SITUATIONS?

THE DEVELOPMENT OF REACTIONS TO
FRUSTRATING SITUATIONS

INDIVIDUAL DIFFERENCES

PRACTICAL IMPLICATIONS

In Chapter 10, we dealt with one kind of behavior when an individual's attainment of a goal is blocked—problem solving. Unfortunately, problem solving does not always achieve the desired goal. Sometimes a solution seems impossible, and the problem persists unsolved over a long period. The state of the individual in the face of strong, persisting, unsatisfied motives is called *frustration*. The sources of frustration and reactions to it are the subject matter of this chapter.

What Are the Sources of Frustration?

The usual source of frustration is a barrier, an impediment to the satisfaction of a motive. We can distinguish three major types of barriers: (1) situational, (2) interpersonal, and (3) intrapersonal. Let us look at some examples of each of these.

There are two kinds of *situational barriers*. One is a simple *physical block* to reaching a goal. A man who has lost his keys and stands in front of the locked door to his home faces such a barrier. So does a child who cannot reach a toy which has fallen a few feet from his playpen. Masserman (1961), who induced frustration in cats in different ways, used a physical barrier in one case: he locked the container in which cats had been trained to find food.

Another situational barrier is *situational ambiguity*. If the situation does not provide clear cues, it may be impossible to reach one's goals. For example, the motorist, on his way to keep an important appointment in a strange city, may experience frustration when road signs do not provide the information he needs. Pavlov (1927) demonstrated the effects of ambiguous cues in the behavior of dogs. They were trained to salivate when they saw circles and to refrain from salivation when they saw ellipses. When the ellipses presented became so circular that the dogs could not distinguish them from circles, the dogs' behavior showed signs of frustration.*

The situational ambiguity may be in the cues in the environment, or it may be in the feedback that the situation provides to a person's behavior. Thus, if a child is sometimes punished and sometimes rewarded for the same act under the same conditions, he is likely to experience frustration. Maier and his students have made a series of studies on the behavior of rats who were both punished and rewarded for the same behavior on different trials. We shall describe this work later in the chapter.

The second major category of barriers to motive satisfaction consists of *interpersonal barriers*. An interpersonal barrier is one in which motive satisfaction is prevented either by a person or by a group of people. Many of our motives are social and require other people for satisfaction. For example, a girl's longing for her parents' approval may be thwarted by their excessively high standards. Other people may also stand in the way of satisfaction of

---

* Pavlov's experiment was described in greater detail in Chapter 7, p. 219.

nonsocial motives. A person belonging to a minority group may be prevented from joining a swimming club by the members. He faces an interpersonal barrier to the satisfaction of a chiefly nonsocial motive.

The third major category of barriers is the *intrapersonal* barriers. These are barriers to motive satisfaction within ourselves. We can distinguish two kinds of intrapersonal barriers. Sometimes we cannot reach our goals because of some deficiency, a physical handicap, or a lack of skill. The former athlete, wounded in battle, who can no longer be a star, provides an example. The immigrant who is unable to communicate with the people around him provides another.

A second kind of intrapersonal barrier to satisfying a motive is the presence of another conflicting motive. A student wants both to attend a party and to study for an important examination. A child with only a nickel to spend desires both some candy and a cardboard toy. The classic example of an intrapersonal

SITUATIONAL BARRIER

INTERPERSONAL BARRIER

INTRAPERSONAL BARRIER

FIG. 11–1. The types of barriers that produce frustration.

barrier leading to frustration is the adolescent who desires to satisfy his sexual urges but who also desires even more to avoid behavior which he believes to be sinful.

The foregoing classification of barriers into three types is certainly not an absolute one. Often it is difficult to pinpoint the barrier as being one or the other. Frequently, the barrier is a combination of the physical situation, the social environment, and factors in the person himself. For example, the teenage girl who lives on a farm may be prevented from reaching her goal of popularity by a combination of her physical distance, the apathy of her peers, and her own fear of being rejected. Nevertheless, the distinction among the three types of barriers is a useful one in that it enables us to clarify the potential sources of frustration. These sources are summarized in Fig. 11–1.

The Freudian Theory of Conflict

It is the third type of barrier, conflicting elements within the person himself, that Freud stressed in his theory of personality. Sigmund Freud was a medical doctor who specialized in the treatment of patients with psychological disorders. His method of treatment, *psychoanalysis*, involved listening to his patient's accounts of their dreams, their memories of early childhood, and other free associations. During these treatment sessions, as he listened to his patients, he also began to formulate a general theory on the nature and dynamics of human personality.

Freud (1923) conceptualized personality as being divided into three major systems: the *id*, the *ego*, and the *superego*. At birth, the *id* makes up the entire personality. It is principally a reservoir of unconscious instinctive urges which demand immediate gratification. Thus, whenever the tension level of the organism is raised by an urge, the id seeks immediate tension reduction. This demand for immediate gratification is called the *pleasure principle*.

However, the id is ill equipped to reduce tension as the pleasure principle demands. It has no skills for adapting the organism to conditions in his environment. For this reason, a new subsystem of personality, the *ego*, develops. The ego is the part of personality that has commerce with the real world. Its function is to perceive conditions accurately and to plan action in such a way as to achieve as much gratification as is realistically possible. The ego rejects the pleasure principle and instead heeds the *reality principle*: gratification of basic urges must be postponed until the proper conditions in the environment make this gratification possible. This means that the ego must control the id's impulsive, but unrealistic, demands.

One of the aspects of the world that the ego perceives is the moral code of the parents. At first, the child obeys this code in order to gain the approval and avoid the wrath of his parents. But by the mechanism of identification, to be considered later in this chapter, the child internalizes these rules in the third major system of personality, the *superego*. The superego has two subsystems:

the *conscience* and the *ego ideal*. The conscience encompasses all the moral prohibitions which derive from the actions and statements for which the child has been punished. In particular, the child was probably punished for giving expression to his sexual and aggressive impulses, and hence the conscience contains prohibitions against such expressions. If the prohibitions of the superego are violated, then the person feels guilt, a kind of punishment meted out by the superego. The superego may even have prohibitions against feeling sexual and aggressive impulses at all, so that the mere awareness of such impulses produces guilt. Thus, it is inevitable that the demands of the superego clash with those of the id.

The other subsystem of the superego, the ego ideal, corresponds to the individual's conception of what is morally good. As the ideals and expectations of one's parents are internalized in the ego ideal, the motivation for good behavior becomes self-rewarding. On the other hand, if a person fails to behave in accordance with his own ego ideal, he will feel evil and unworthy. Earlier, we suggested that among the most important threats to an individual is a threat to his self-esteem. In Freudian terms, we would say that self-esteem is lowered when the person does not conform to his own ego ideal. However, it may not be realistically possible to behave in accordance with the ego ideal; this would lead to ego-superego conflict. The ego ideal may also demand suppression of id impulses, leading to superego-id conflicts.

The arbiter of the clash between the various parts of the personality is the ego. It must weigh the various demands and prohibitions of the different systems and resolve them in some way. One of the greatest threats to personality occurs when the ego can no longer control the other subsystems. Feelings of anxiety serve as a warning signal that the ego is about to lose control. The defense mechanisms, which we shall discuss later in the chapter, were conceived of by Freud as ways adopted by the ego to defend itself against anxiety.

■ You may have noticed that the terms Freud uses are quite different from the kinds of terms we have been using. Id, ego, and superego almost appear to be characters with "personalities of their own." Freud did not intend this to be so. He saw the three parts of personality as three systems whose processes followed different principles. However, he described the systems in terms of images, and analogies rather than with precise terms and careful definitions. Thus his theory does not conform to the model that modern philosophers of science present for scientific theory. Nevertheless, Freud was a keen observer and a tremendously creative thinker. His ideas have provided a challenge for all people interested in the nature of human personality. His work contains kernels of numerous hypotheses which suggest experiments to modern behavioral scientists. Much of our discussion of the reactions to frustration can be traced directly or indirectly to the influential writing of Sigmund Freud. ■

We began this section by saying that Freud saw intrapersonal conflict as the basis of all frustration. Now that we have described the systems of personality, we can see that Freud included all three types of barriers under the intrapersonal rubric. Id-superego conflicts correspond to the intrapersonal barrier produced by conflicting motives. The intrapersonal barrier produced by some sort of deficiency may be either an id-ego or an ego-superego conflict. In both cases, the executor of personality is incapable of fulfilling the demands of another system of his personality. Freud might also call the social and situational barriers ego-id or ego-superego conflicts because the ego perceives that the environment cannot satisfy the demands of the impulsive id or the high-minded superego.

Problem Solving versus Frustration

Barriers normally lead to problem solving. An unexpected barrier will often lead to more persistent attempts to reach the goal (Lambert and Solomon, 1952). Under what conditions, then, will the attempt to solve the original problem be abandoned? The underlying condition that produces frustration is a combination of strongly aroused motives that are persistently driving toward certain goals and the lack of perceivable means of reaching those goals. Note that this analysis specifies the person's own assessment of whether his motives can be satisfied, rather than the objective probability of satisfaction as the key factor.

What Are the Reactions to Frustrating Situations?

When a person is exposed to a physical or psychological stressor, his body mobilizes for defense. Hans Selye (1950), a physician, developed the concept of the general adaptation syndrome to describe the body's common reaction to all types of stressors. According to the theory of the general adaptation syndrome, our physiological adjustment to stressors occurs in three stages: (1) an initial alarm reaction during which certain organs of the body are alerted (such as the arousal of the sympathetic nervous system), (2) a stage of resistance, during which these organs function at abnormal levels for a prolonged period of time to maintain defense against the stress (such as increased production of white blood cells), and (3) a stage of exhaustion, when the body's resources against stress are exhausted (see Fig. 11–2).

Our psychological reactions to frustrating situations follow an analogous sequence.* The initial reaction is a heightened state of arousal which may be manifested as aggression, flight from the situation, or diffuse anxiety. None of these reactions normally change the frustrating situation. However, the organism now has an additional problem to cope with—the anxiety which results from his inability to reach his goals. People often diminish this anxiety by distorting some aspect of their thinking. Such a distortion is called a *defense mechanism*. The use of defense mechanisms corresponds to the stage of resistance in the general adaptation syndrome. However, if the psychological stress situation is

---

* Masserman (1961) has also drawn an analogy between the general adaptation syndrome and frustration.

extremely serious, then the defense mechanisms are insufficient, a person's psychological resources are exhausted, and he becomes maladjusted. We shall be concerned with the first two stages in this chapter.

As we saw in Chapter 7, an immediate reaction to frustrating situations is anger and aggression. This aggression may be directed against any available object. However, unchecked individual aggression cannot be tolerated if a society is to survive. Therefore, in every society the expression of aggression is controlled by cultural norms. We are taught from early childhood that the expression of aggression, such as pounding on little brother's head with a hammer, is "bad." We do not feel free to express our aggression in frustrating situations.

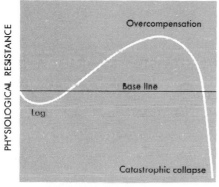

FIG. 11–2. Selye's theory on the resistance of the body to increasing stress. We can summarize psychological reactions to frustrating situations by postulating an analogous sequence. (From Miller, 1955)

This adds another conflict to the frustration causing the original anger; the new conflict is between one's motive for aggression and fear of punishment. The punishment feared is not necessarily physical punishment, but may be fear of guilt feelings arising from one's own concept of "good" behavior.

Another immediate reaction to frustrating situations is an attempt to withdraw from the situation. However, this reaction, like aggression, usually cannot solve the problem. The motives that produced the frustration persist unsatisfied. The student who copes with a conflict between studying boring material or failing an important examination by going to the movies has not really solved his problem; he is faced with the same frustration as soon as he returns from his temporary escape.

A third reaction to frustrating situations is fear, perhaps anxiety.* The feeling is familiar to all of us: a pounding heart, trembling, a knot in the bottom of our stomachs, perhaps thoughts of dread and helplessness in our minds. In addition to the difficult problem which we were unable to solve, we are faced with the fact that we were incapable of solving it, and consciously or unconsciously we fear for our psychological integrity—our self-esteem and feelings of com-

---

* You may remember that we are using the term *fear* when a person understands the object and reason for his fear; *anxiety* is the same feeling without this understanding.

petence. Such anxiety for a prolonged period is intolerable. Now the major problem for the anxious individual changes from his original goal to protecting himself from his overwhelming anxiety. One common solution is some form of reality distortion by means of a defense mechanism.

How Do Defense Mechanisms Function?

The primary function of defense mechanisms is to protect the individual from his anxiety by a distortion of normal perception, motivation, memory, thinking, or action. For example, the person with a conflict about aggression may not recognize intentional insults (perception); he may distort his interpretation of his own feelings so that they are less threatening (motivation); he may not remember the insults later (memory); he may interpret his own hostile retorts as appropriate wit (perception and thought); or he may seize on a minor comment his child makes the next day and spank him for it (action).

As we shall see, behavior which in one situation may be classified as a defense mechanism may in another situation be used as an ordinary act. The distinction must be made largely on the basis of the individual's awareness of the purposes of his behavior, i.e., whether or not the individual has deceived himself about external reality or about his own feelings, motives, or behavior. A related criterion is the normality of the individual's emotional reactions, since the absence of a normal emotional response may be a symptom of some unconscious distortion. Because the classification of a person's particular behavior as a defense mechanism requires some knowledge about an individual's motivation and awareness, the uninformed observer is likely to be inaccurate in his analysis of defense mechanisms. Nevertheless, it is possible to make some inferences from behavior. For example, when an individual is in a situation which would cause crying or extreme sorrow in others, and he remains unmoved, one would suspect that a defense mechanism is being used. Similarly, the individual who appears to be unafraid in a situation which normally elicits fear from others may be using a defense.

How can we justifiably say that the individual's awareness of his own behavior is distorted or that an individual has an unconscious motive, when the person himself denies it? This question is basic to our study of frustration, and the answer to it is consistent with our previous discussions of psychological assumptions. Motives and defense mechanisms are constructs; we infer them from behavior, and our analysis of them is theoretical. Sometimes the individual accepts the psychologist's inferences, but this is not so important to the psychologist as the result of these inferences, i.e., whether or not they enable him to make better predictions of behavior.

Types of Defense Mechanisms

Psychologists frequently divide defense mechanisms into two major categories (White, 1963; Blum, in press): those which involve complete *blocking out* of some psychological process and those which involve *substitution or distortion.* The first category, blocking out, is often considered the primary defensive process, because all defense mechanisms involve some blocking. The substitution defenses give, in addition, disguised expressions to the process being blocked. Some theorists suggest that the second category of defenses is even more anxiety-reducing than the first. Not only is the unacceptable material blocked from consciousness but the barriers causing the conflict are partially surmounted. For example, a man with a conflict about expressing aggression toward his father may reduce his anxiety not only by expelling the idea of hostility toward his father from consciousness, but also by expressing aggression toward a substitute object, such as his elderly next-door neighbor.

The Primary Defenses: Denial, Repression, Isolation

One of the most common and most fundamental of these defense mechanisms is *denial.* Denial consists of a person's not admitting to himself consciously that painful facts exist. Thus the anxious student may say to himself, "I'm doing great. I haven't got any problems." Yet he may be late in turning in assignments, too sick to go to an exam, and jittery when called upon in class—all behavioral evidences of anxiety. Freud notes that the statement, "How lovely that I've not had one of my headaches for a long time," is actually the first announcement of a new attack.

We find an example of denial in a description of behavior in German concentration camps during World War II. In the camps, the prisoners were subjected to prolonged, persistent, and horrible forms of inhuman treatment by their captors. Direct retaliation meant certain death. Here is how Bettelheim (1947), a psychologist who was a prisoner, describes his thoughts and feelings:

■ "The author's thoughts and emotions during the transportation were extremely detached. It was as if he watched things happening in which he only vaguely participated. Later he learned that many prisoners developed this same feeling of detachment, as if what happened really did not matter to oneself. It was strangely mixed with a conviction that 'this cannot be true; such things do not happen.' Not only during the transportation, but all through the time spent in camp, the prisoners had to convince themselves that this was real and not just a nightmare. They were never wholly successful. The feeling of detachment which rejected the reality of the situation might be considered a mechanism safeguarding the integrity of the prisoners' personalities." ■*

When a person fails to remember an anxiety-arousing experience, he is using the defense of *repression.* The man who forgets an appointment with a dentist, the student who forgets that he has received a warning letter about his academic

---

* From Bettelheim, B., "Individual and mass behavior in extreme situations," in E. E. Maccoby, T. M. Newcomb, and E. L. Hartley, *Readings in Social Psychology.* Holt, 1947. Reprinted by permission. This footnote applies also to those passages quoted on pp. 387–388 and 393.

standing, the woman who forgets that her old beau is now married—all these people may be repressing memories that cause anxiety. Evidence for the existence of such a mechanism comes from both the laboratory and the psychiatric clinic. We described the experimental evidence in our discussion of motivated forgetting in Chapter 9.

A clinical example of repression comes from the study of soldiers who acquire amnesia of events during combat. These men struggle to remember what has just happened to them, but they cannot, although their comrades can tell the psychologist or psychiatrist in charge exactly what happened. Usually, a combination of psychotherapy and drug therapy can gradually restore the repressed material to consciousness. Grinker and Spiegel (1945) report that as more and more material is remembered by the patient, he becomes increasingly more anxious. This finding supports our notion that repression has the function of reducing anxiety.

Isolation is a defense in which the affect associated with an idea is blocked out. The person using isolation may admit unacceptable feelings intellectually, but he does not experience them emotionally. Because the idea and the feeling are walled off from each other, the isolator avoids the anxiety appropriate to his thoughts. For example, a student who has studied psychology may come to a psychotherapist and say in a matter-of-fact way, "I hate my father." Although the student can talk about his problem in intellectual terms, he has blocked out the strong emotional feelings that must accompany such a shocking statement.

Defenses Involving Distortion and Substitution

As we said earlier, these defenses not only involve ejecting a thought, memory, or emotion from consciousness, they also involve a disguised or substitute expression of the blocked thought, memory, or emotion.

Displacement is a distortion of the normal goal of a motive. A substitute object replaces the true, but inaccessible or threatening, goal. A childless woman may displace her desire for a baby by lavishing attention on a pet dog. The child who has been chastised by his mother displaces his anger to a toy by riding his bicycle over a stuffed teddy bear. Analogous behavior was found in a white rat who had been trained to strike another rat.

■ Miller (1948) placed two rats in a cage. The wire-grid floor of the cage was electrically charged. The rats were shocked until the rat being studied struck the other. The rat soon learned to display this aggressive behavior whenever he was put into the cage with another rat. In addition to the second rat, a plastic doll was then placed in the cage. The rat ignored the doll and continued his aggression against the other rat. However, when the second rat was removed, the remaining rat then directed his aggressive behavior against the "innocent" doll. The rat's response had been displaced to the only accessible object (see Fig. 11–3). ■

The rat in the above example was prevented from expressing direct aggression because of a situational barrier: the other rat was not present. In human beings, the barrier preventing the person from reaching the goal object is usually not a physical one, but an intrapersonal one: a conflicting avoidance motive. For example, a child will not express direct aggression toward his mother because the conflicting motive, fear of punishment, is stronger.

FIG. 11–3. Displacement of a rat's aggression from another rat to a rubber doll. After being trained to strike the other rat to avoid shock, Miller's rat strikes at the doll when the other rat is removed. (Photos courtesy of Dr. N. E. Miller)

If displacement can sometimes be interpreted as the resolution of an approach-avoidance conflict, then from our previous analysis of approach-avoidance conflicts, we should be able to learn something about the object the frustrated organism will choose as its target. Miller (1948) has presented just such an analysis.

You may remember that experiments suggest that the gradient of approach is steeper than the gradient of avoidance. This was demonstrated in a study in which the strength of pull toward a food reward or away from a box with an electrified floor was measured at varying distances from the food or shock. Thus approach and avoidance gradients were measured at *different distances* from the goal.* If we make the assumption that the shapes of the gradient are approximately the same when we measure approach and avoidance to objects that are increasingly *similar, rather than increasingly close* (in distance), to the

* This experiment was described in greater detail in Chapter 7, p. 241.

object of the conflict, then we could conceptualize the conflict as shown in Fig. 11-4. In this diagram, we are using the example of the man who feels hostility toward his father, but who also feels that such hostility is an unacceptable feeling toward a parent. He is generalizing these feelings toward people similar to his father, such as his uncle and his boss. However, Miller hypothesizes that approach tendencies are generalized over a wider range than avoidance feelings. Therefore, if the response involved is hostility, it is likely that it will be displaced toward an object that is similar enough to elicit approach and dissimilar enough not to give rise to avoidance. Thus Miller might predict that the man will show hostility toward his neighbor.

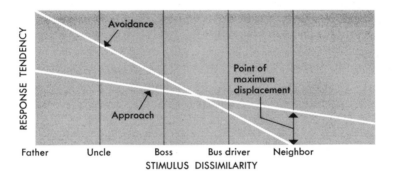

FIG. 11-4. Displacement conceptualized as an approach-avoidance conflict. A man feels hostility toward his father (approach tendency to displaying aggression) but feels guilty about it (avoidance tendency). Both tendencies generalize, but the approach tendency generalizes over a wider range, as the longer line indicates. The point of maximum displacement is the point at which the approach tendency minus the avoidance tendency is greatest. (Suggested by Miller, 1948)

This analysis is a good example of the combination of experimental and clinical approaches. The mechanism of displacement was first described in a clinical context as a defense against anxiety in which the object is disguised. The experimental analysis suggests what the characteristics of this displaced object are likely to be.

We have just seen that displacement involves the substitution of another object for the true object of a motive. In *projection*, the person distorts the *agent* of the unacceptable thought or motive. He fails to see himself as a person who has an anxiety-producing thought or feeling; he attributes the unacceptable thought or feeling to someone else. In a sense, he is ejecting the unacceptable thought by giving it to another person. The anxiety is reduced when the projector sees someone else as experiencing the threatening feeling. For example, a man whose ego ideal is to be a tolerant, easygoing father reacts to his son's irritating, annoying behavior by thinking, "I'll bet my wife could just about kill that kid now." In this case he has projected his own feelings onto his wife.

■ Sears (1936) demonstrated projection in a study involving college students. The students were asked to rate themselves and one another on four undesirable traits: stinginess, obstinacy, disorderliness, and bashfulness. Some students who were given high ratings in these traits by their peers, showed that they were aware of these qualities in themselves by giving themselves high self-ratings in these traits, too. The interesting results, however, come from students who were given high ratings in one of these traits by their peers, but who did not rate themselves highly in this trait. These students, who did not show awareness of their undesired trait, tended to rate *other* students more highly in the undesired trait than the rest of the group did; that is, they projected the undesired trait onto their fellow students. ■

Identification is almost the opposite of projection. Whereas in projection a person ejects an unacceptable impulse by attributing it to another person, in identification a person acquires some characteristics he desires by dissolving the barriers between himself and another person. He mentally equates his own self, his ego, with that of another person, the model. The values, triumphs, and failures of the model become the identifier's own values, triumphs, and failures. The identifier usually imitates the model, his dress, gestures, and actions.

In discussing identification as a defense mechanism, we have to distinguish between it and normal imitation. Identification is more than simply modeling yourself after someone you admire. In identification there is such a distortion of thought that someone else's goal achievements serve to substitute for personal motive satisfaction. In the mind of the identifier, the model is actually part of the identifier's view of himself.

Adolescents provide common examples of identification. In these intervening years between childhood and maturity, the adolescent's goals are often adult goals, but he has no realistic way of satisfying them. By identifying with a teacher, an athlete, a singer, or a playboy, the adolescent can achieve the independence, the success, and the popularity in fantasy that are realistically impossible to him.

Temporary identification accounts for some of our enjoyment and absorption in fictional media. The goals and emotions of the hero and heroine on the screen become our own as we sit in a movie theatre, and thus we laugh and cry as we watch their adventures.

A special type of identification is *identification with the aggressor*. In this case, an individual is in a situation in which he has strong motives to retaliate against someone who has shown aggression toward him, but he cannot do so because of the power of the aggressor over him. One way of resolving this conflict is to "acquire" the power of the aggressor by identifying with him. Again we turn to Bettelheim's description of life in a concentration camp for a dramatic example:

■ "The prisoners suffered from the steady interference with their privacy on the part of the guards and other prisoners. So a great amount of aggression accumulated. In new prisoners it vented itself in the way it might have done in the world outside the camp. But slowly prisoners accepted, as expression of their verbal aggressions, terms which definitely were taken over from the vocabulary of the Gestapo. From copying the verbal aggressions of the Gestapo to copying their form of bodily aggressions was one more step, but it took several years to make it. Old prisoners, when in charge of others, often behaved worse than the Gestapo because they considered this the best way to behave toward prisoners in the camp . . .

"Old prisoners tended to identify with the Gestapo not only in respect to aggressive behavior. They tried to arrogate to themselves old pieces of Gestapo uniforms. If that was not possible, they tried to sew and mend their uniforms so that they would resemble those of the guards. When asked why they did it they admitted that they loved to look like one of the guards . . .

"Often the Gestapo would enforce nonsensical rules, originating in the whims of one of the guards. They were usually forgotten as soon as formulated, but there were always some old prisoners who would continue to follow these rules and try to enforce them on others long after the Gestapo had forgotten about them. These prisoners firmly believed that the rules set down by the Gestapo were desirable standards of human behavior, at least in the camp situation. Other areas in which prisoners made their peace with the values of the Gestapo included the race problem, although race discrimination had been alien to their previous scheme of values." (Bettelheim, 1947) ■

In *rationalization,* a person does not distort the agent or the object of a thought or action; he replaces the true anxiety-arousing reason for this action with a more acceptable one. The college student who receives an unexpected low grade in a course may think to himself, "Grades are not a good measure of a person's knowledge, anyway." The famous fable of the fox and the unreachable bunch of grapes has the old fox rationalizing that "the grapes are probably sour anyway."

This defense mechanism illustrates again that we seek consistency between our thoughts and our actions. If the true reason produces too much conflict, we will substitute another one. A similar phenomenon can be produced experimentally with hypnosis.

■ One of the authors' friends related this experience. He was in an experiment on hypnosis. While he was under hypnosis, the experimenter told him that as soon as the word "table" was spoken, he would walk across the room and take off the sweater he was wearing. The experimenter also told our friend that he would not remember why he was doing it. In the post-hypnotic session, the experimenter used the word "table" in the context of ordinary conversation. As soon as he heard the word, our friend rose and said, "Boy, it's getting warm in here." Then he walked across the room and took off his sweater. According to our friend, he really did feel warm and his behavior was motivated by his feelings of warmth. ■

Another defense which involves denial of a forbidden motive is *reaction formation.* This defense, however, goes beyond the simple denial of one's motives to the development of behavior displaying the opposite motives. Thus the person with aggressive urges which he does not dare to express may not only deny them, but actually become very mild and kindly. Similarly, people who resent a democratic form of government may become superpatriots. In the concentration camp, reaction formation may have been involved in some of the old prisoners' submissiveness to the guards.

Substitution is a defense in which a new act is substituted for one which aroused anxiety or guilt. Substitution is likely to occur when a frustrating situation lasts over a long period of time, so that the substitute behavior can be rewarded and identified. In a frustrating situation, satisfaction of any motive by any act reduces discomfort, whether or not the motive satisfied is related to the motive of the act which was frustrated. Hence substitutions can be set up almost by chance. However, the behavior used is frequently related to the frustrated response.

Sublimation, which is one type of substitution, involves adopting constructive activities or goals in place of threatening or punished actions. Thus an individual with basic aggressive urges might channel these into constructive activities as a literary critic or as a surgeon. Although sublimation is generally regarded as one of Freud's more speculative notions, it, like displacement, can be interpreted in terms of approach-avoidance conflicts. In these terms, if the generalization gradient for pain were sharper than that for pleasure, the *net* pleasure would be greater for some activity related to, but not close to, the forbidden goal itself. Sublimation provides added satisfaction because the new goal is socially approved. Thus the new motive is likely to bring social rewards, rather than the punishment associated with the original motive.

Another way of obtaining substitute satisfaction when success in the real world is impossible is through *fantasy.* Here, thought provides a substitute for action. All the joys of goal attainment without the feared punishments can be fancied by the daydreamer. One of the best fictional examples of the use of fantasy can be found in *The Secret Life of Walter Mitty,* written by James Thurber.

Figure 11–5 shows the frequency of certain types of daydreams experienced by college students. As you can see, sexual daydreams and fantasies about vocational success are among the most frequently reported. Probably these are two areas in which motives are often frustrated. This interpretation gains support from the "semistarvation" studies, in which fantasy was a reaction to a situation known to be frustrating.

■ During World War II, a group of conscientious objectors agreed to participate in an experiment designed to study the effects of prolonged food deprivation. The men's diet was just adequate for keeping them alive, but was never sufficient, and the men were constantly hungry. Among the men's responses to this frustration were hoarding silverware, developing an interest in reading recipes and cookbooks, pinning pictures of lavish meals from magazines on the walls, and daydreaming about sumptuous feasts. (Guetzkow and Bowman, 1946) ■

In substitution, sublimation, and daydreaming, a thought or action similar to the anxiety-arousing action substitutes for it. In another mechanism, *regression,* the behavior used to avoid anxiety has a totally different form. In some cases, when the more recently learned skills for problem solving fail, the individual displays more immature forms of behavior. His behavior increasingly resembles

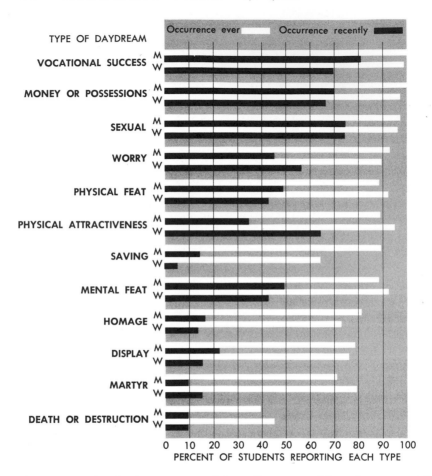

FIG. 11–5. The daydreams reported by college men (M) and women (W). The figure shows both the daydreams that have occurred recently and those that have occurred at any time. (After Shaffer and Shoben, 1956)

that of a young child or infant. This return to a more immature form of behavior is called regression. A classic example of regression is provided by an experiment by Barker, Dembo, and Lewin (1941).

■ Preschool children were observed as they played with moderately attractive toys. Their behavior was rated by observers for constructiveness. Then the children were admitted to another part of the room previously hidden by a screen where they found more interesting and more attractive toys than their former playthings. They were permitted to play with the more enticing toys for fifteen minutes, after which time they were returned to their original play area with the less attractive toys. They were now separated from the attractive toys by a wire screen, which left the desirable toys in full view but out of reach. The experiment was designed to produce frustration by placing a physical barrier between the children and favorite toys. In this situa-

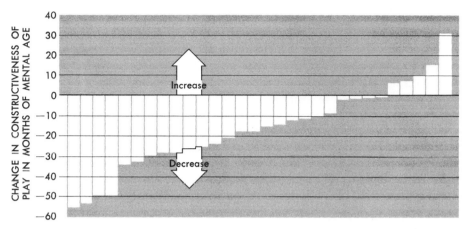

FIG. 11–6. The change in the constructiveness of the play of each child (represented by a bar) as a result of a frustrating situation. (After Barker, Dembo, and Lewin, 1941)

tion, most of the children displayed behavior more infantile and less constructive than their behavior with the same toys earlier. If we compare constructiveness scores before and after playing with the more attractive toys, we find that after frustration was induced, the constructiveness scores were significantly lower than in the earlier play period (see Fig. 11–6). ∎

Why regressive behavior occurs is still a moot point in theory. One can speculate that regression is a form of withdrawal; by "becoming an infant again," the individual returns to a period when someone else was responsible for his needs and maintenance. Although the behavior is no longer appropriate to the situation, when other means fail, habits which led to motive satisfaction at an earlier period of life once more become aroused. Another possible theory is that regression is simply a disruption of learned habits by a strong motive. According to this hypothesis, frustration itself cues primitive responses.

The Appropriateness of Defenses

Beginning students of psychology are generally made anxious by the discovery that they have been using certain defenses themselves. Psychologists are partly to blame for this in their tendency to contrast defenses and problem solving. The fact that the mechanisms were discovered in clinical studies of abnormal people adds to the anxiety. Thus psychology students sometimes hurl the defense labels at adversaries in arguments (e.g., "That's just projection!") so that the titles of the defenses take the place of the simpler words more commonly used to express aggression.

It is true that if a defense mechanism helps an individual remain unconscious of some aspect of reality, he is less able to use all his resources to deal with his problem. But everyone uses defenses. They are *normal* ways of coping with frustrating situations. It is not the presence or absence of the use of defense mechanisms which distinguishes the healthy from the unhealthy person, but rather the appropriateness of the defense in the situation in which it is used. Anxiety is not only an unpleasant feeling but is also detrimental to the organism's adequate functioning, so that, in some cases, it may be healthier to defend against anxiety than to continue to be anxious. For example, a student who represses his anxiety about sex might be better able to cope with examinations than one who is aware of his anxiety. A football player who displaces his hostility against his parents to his opponents may be acting more adaptively than the man who expresses this hostility directly.

Defense mechanisms play an important role in the normal development of personality. Children, to whom parents are seemingly omnipotent, become civilized human beings partly through identification with them. Anna Freud (1937) points out that many of the anxiety-arousing conflicts of adolescence can be worked out intellectually only if isolation temporarily blocks the disrupting emotions involved.

Defenses become pathological when they create problems that are more serious than the problems they solve. For example, the person who displaces his aggressions from his employer to his wife may make his home life so unpleasant that this becomes a serious problem. One sign of the unadaptive use of defenses is the failure to use different defenses in different situations. The normal person is more likely to employ a variety of defenses whereas the maladjusted person is more likely to be rigid, employing the same defense in appropriate and inappropriate situations alike (Shire, 1954). Finally, if in order to solve one problem, the distortion of reality is so great as to impair effective behavior in other areas, the defense mechanism is obviously a sign of maladjustment.

Before you decide, however, that all you have to do is select your defense wisely, let us recall that defenses are not consciously chosen. Unless the person fully believes the distortions his anxiety has produced, they fail to protect him. Why one defense rather than another appears is a question that has not been completely answered. We present the evidence that exists and our own speculations and questions in the following section.

Why Is a Particular Defense Mechanism Selected?

While there are many different defense mechanisms, those listed are typical ways in which a person protects himself from anxiety. When one considers the number of defense mechanisms which the individual might use in dealing with his anxiety, an immediate question comes to mind: What determines which defense mechanism a particular person uses in any situation? For example, why did the old prisoners in the concentration camp react with identification instead of fantasy?

The Situation

As in the case of other general modes of behavior, defense mechanisms are elicited by cues in the situation. The primary cues are those associated with anxiety. Cues which have previously been associated with the reduction of anxiety by a defense mechanism will probably tend to elicit the same defense mechanism in later situations.

The situation itself may provide cues, making a particular defense more probable. For example, a projective test provides the opportunity for an individual to satisfy frustrated motives in fantasy. Bettelheim's description of concentration-camp life provides another example. In the following excerpt, note how the behavior of the Gestapo produced a situation which facilitated the development of regressive behavior in the prisoners who were under their control.

■ "The prisoners developed types of behavior characteristic of infancy or early youth. Some of them have been discussed, such as ambivalence to one's family, despondency, finding satisfaction in daydreaming rather than in action. During the transportation, the prisoners were tortured in a way in which a cruel and domineering father might torture a helpless child; at the camp they were also debased by techniques which went much further into childhood situations. They were forced to soil themselves. Their defecation was strictly regulated. Prisoners who needed to eliminate had to obtain permission of the guard. It seemed as if the education to cleanliness would be once more repeated. It gave pleasure to the guards to hold the power of granting or withholding the permission to visit the latrines. This pleasure found its counterpart in the pleasure the prisoners derived from visiting them, because there they could rest for a moment, secure from the whips of the overseers.

"The prisoners were forced to say 'thou' to one another, which in Germany is indiscriminately used only among small children. They were not permitted to address one another with the many titles to which middle- and upper-class Germans are accustomed. On the other hand, they had to address the guards in the most deferential manner, giving them all their titles.

"The prisoners lived, like children, only in the immediate present; they lost the feeling for the sequence of time; they became unable to plan for the future or to give up immediate satisfactions to gain greater ones in the near future. They were unable to establish durable object relations. Friendships developed as quickly as they broke up. Prisoners would, like adolescents, fight one another tooth-and-nail only to become close friends within a few minutes. They were boastful, telling tales about what they had accomplished in their former lives, or how they succeeded in cheating guards. Like children, they felt not at all set back or ashamed when it became known that they had lied about their prowess.

"Another factor contributing to the regression into childhood behavior was the work the prisoners were forced to perform. Prisoners were forced to perform nonsensical tasks, such as carrying heavy rocks from one place to another, and back to the place where they had picked them up. They were forced to dig holes in the ground with their bare hands, although tools were available. They felt debased when forced to perform 'childish' and stupid labor, and preferred even harder work when it produced something that might be considered useful. There seems to be no doubt that the tasks they performed, as well as the mistreatment by the Gestapo which they had to endure, contributed to their disintegration as adult persons." (Bettelheim, 1947) ■

Motivation

We do not know whether particular kinds of motives tend to elicit particular kinds of defenses. For example, does the threat of pain tend to elicit defenses different from the defenses elicited by simply preventing a person from attaining a desired goal? Does frustration of a very strong motive result in a defense different from that elicited by a mild frustration?

There is some evidence that the nature of the distortion is related to the motive frustrated. However, there seems to be no built-in relationship such that threat to a particular motive inevitably results in a particular defense. On the basis of present knowledge, we would guess that the individual tends to use particular defenses against particular kinds of anxieties as a result of learning.

What is the relation between strength of aroused motivation and defense? Clark and Sensibar (1955) studied this relationship by using this procedure. They showed an experimental group of men pictures of nude women, and a control group some neutral pictures. This was done to vary the strength of aroused motivation in the two groups. Now both groups were shown a standard set of pictures (the Thematic Apperception Test) and each subject was asked to write a story about each TAT picture. The stories the subjects wrote were scored in two ways. First, the amount of overt sexual context in each story was determined. The subjects in the group who had seen the nudes before writing their stories used *less* overtly sexual content than the control group. Second, the amount of disguised sexual symbolism in each story was determined. The group which had seen the nude pictures tended to use more disguised, sexually symbolic material in their stories than the group which had seen the neutral pictures. This study fits the Freudian theory. The stronger the sexual motivation (in a situation where its expression is not approved of), the more anxiety and guilt is aroused; the greater the anxiety, the greater the tendency to repress the sexual impulses and to permit their expression only in disguised form.

■ The research also raises an important methodological question. If the sexual symbols are disguised, how can we know that one group uses more of them than another? Would it not be easy for scorers to perceive sexual symbols in the stories in which they expect them? In this study, the experimenters handled this dilemma by listing the objects which Freud and his students have suggested as sexual symbols. They then eliminated those symbols which actually appeared in the pictures themselves. Symbolism was scored only if the symbol was used in some action which could be interpreted as symbolic. Scorers were then trained to score the stories for these symbols. This procedure would be useless if different scorers obtained different results; however, the experimenters found that their scorers' scores correlated 0.82. The scorers now scored all the stories, without knowing which stories came from which group. ■

In this study, increasing strength of motivation resulted in a greater tendency to express the motive symbolically rather than in more direct words.

Types of Conflict Induced

Studies of children's play suggest that choice of reaction to frustration may depend upon the type of frustration or conflict.

■ Children were observed in a large playroom that was equipped with a number of attractive toys. Five conditions were used:

1. Two adults ordered a child to play with a particular toy.
2. Two adults ordered a child not to play with a particular toy.
3. One adult ordered a child to play with one toy; the other adult ordered the same child to play with a different toy.
4. One adult ordered a child not to play with a toy; the other adult then countermanded the order.
5. (Control) The adults talked to each other, without giving any orders.

Under the "control" (5) and "agree-positively" (1) conditions, play continued at the child's normal level of maturity. The other conditions produced a reduction in constructive play. Condition 2 tended to produce inactivity and nervousness, while conditions 3 and 4 (disagreement) produced unconstructive, vacillating behavior. (Meyers, reported in Lewin et al., 1944) ■

These children had similar motives, but their reaction to frustration depended upon the type of frustration imposed. We would suspect that the type of defense mechanism elicited in a frustrating situation may similarly depend upon the type of frustration. Likewise, conflict between two positive motives might lead to defenses different from those resulting from conflict between two negative motives. Conflict between act tendencies or plans might produce defenses different from those produced by conflict between motives. Perceptual discrepancies may produce yet other defenses. Unfortunately, this is an area which is still largely unexplored by researchers, and there is little evidence to either support or reject these speculations.

The Developmental Stage of Strongest Frustration

Sigmund Freud theorized that different defenses are learned at different periods of an individual's development. During each developmental stage—early infancy, later infancy, early childhood, and later childhood—a child is likely to face certain typical frustrating situations and, at various stages, he is equipped with different skills for coping with these frustrations. If we hypothesize that a person learns best the defenses which in the past have been most effective in reducing anxiety, we would expect that people who experienced a great deal of frustration at any particular stage of development would be likely to exhibit the defenses learned in that period more frequently than others. It is for this reason that we shall now consider the development of reactions to frustrating situations.

The Development of Reactions to Frustrating Situations

Early Infancy

Freud (1905) pointed to certain common frustrations which every child in our culture experiences. For example, all infants must learn to eat solid foods rather than milk. If weaning is harsh and abrupt, this may be a period of frustration for the infant. Freud called the early period, during which the child's chief pleasures come through the mouth, the *oral stage*. At this time the child is just beginning to distinguish reality from unreality. When he closes his eyes some things go away, but other images (imaginary) stay. If frustration at this stage is severe, does the child learn to prefer fantasy? The answer to this question is still unknown. In any case, closing the eyes, fainting, dependency and daydreaming are forms of defenses which the infant can use in frustrating situations, since it is during this period of his life that he is beginning to learn basic discriminations; that is, to distinguish between himself and his environment, between reality and fantasy, between sleeping and waking, between his mother and other people, and between the present and other times. These reactions are the prototypes of the defenses of denial and fantasy. Studies of the story endings told by children who were asked to complete a story about a frustrating situation show that denial is used less as children grow older. This, too, suggests that denial is a primitive defense mechanism learned early in life. (Douglas, 1958)

Later Infancy

Another early frustration involves toilet training. According to Freud, defecation is a major source of pleasure for the young child. In our culture, as we have already seen, parents attempt toilet training at a relatively early age, and the child is thus faced with a problem which he often lacks the ability to handle. At this stage (called the *anal stage* by Freud) the child has learned to discriminate between himself and the outside world and is learning that people in the outside world make demands of him. They ask him to release his bowels at specified times and places. Freudian theorists have suggested that just as he learns to control ejection of bodily contents, he learns to eject bad thoughts, attributing them to other people, and this is the manner in which *projection* develops.

As the infant grows and begins to do things for himself and to differentiate himself from his environment, he becomes more aware of barriers and of the things or people that are frustrating him. The most frequent situations causing anger during the first two years are those involving routine care such as dressing, bathing, and toilet training. In the second year, conflicts with parental authority are among the leading causes of outbursts (Goodenough, 1931). Temper tantrums appear at about the age of 14 months and reach a peak at the age of two years.

Because aggressive impulses are so common in this period, methods of handling relations with authority and aggressive urges begin to be learned.

The two-year-old can talk, and the development of certain defense mechanisms probably depends on his ability to talk and to understand his parents. Before he rationalizes, for example, he has probably learned that his parents will accept a good reason in place of a socially unacceptable, but true, reason. This perhaps is followed by his own acceptance of reasons that do not damage his developing self-esteem.

One of the most puzzling defense mechanisms is *reaction formation*. How can one possibly learn to do the opposite of what he really wants to?

Actually, the learning of reaction formation is not as complex as one would expect. In much of our learning, we learn an act and its opposite at almost the same time. Among the first language relationships learned are opposites. We learn to classify things into two opposing classes—black-white, good-bad, etc. Learning experiments have shown that children learn reversed relationships more easily than other relationships, as soon as they have learned the words appropriate to the problem (Kendler and Kendler, 1959). We can speculate on the manner in which this may apply to defenses. A child may have discovered that, even before he does something, his mother warns him to avoid it. It seems almost as though she can read his mind. One way of escaping punishment is to do the opposite of what he feels—in fact, to have the opposite feeling. If, instead of hitting little brother, he shows affection toward him, he is rewarded. In other situations, he also finds that he is rewarded for doing the opposite of what he feels, and thus a tendency to generalize this behavior to new situations may develop. Such a generalized response to frustration is what we have called reaction formation.

Fantasy is another defense that involves thinking, and as we would expect from our study of the development of thinking, it seems to increase in frequency from the preschool to the school years. One form of fantasy which is particularly prevalent in the preschool years is the imaginary companion. For most children the companion is an imaginary playmate who is always available to play with. In some cases, however, the imaginary companion is a more powerful person who will protect the child or punish those who frustrate him. Presumably, such fantasies diminish during the school years as the child becomes better able to cope with the world around him and gains more satisfactions from playing with real companions.

The Oedipus Complex

The third major problem which Freud identified is that of the child's relation to his parents, particularly with respect to his sexual impulses. According to Freud, the child's love for the parent of the opposite sex is closely tied to his developing sexual impulses. About the age of three or later, his attachment to his mother (in the case of boys) begins to encounter barriers due to his mother's attachment to his father, and according to Freudian theory, the result is hate and jealousy of the father. Freud used the term *Oedipus complex* to describe this combination of love for the mother and jealousy of the father. Because of the father's greater power, the child is likely to imagine that the father will inflict dire punishment for successful competition. In fact, according to Freudian theory, the boy may even fear loss of his sexual organs. In the face of such threats, the child's only way out is to give up competition with the father and try to become like him. Ideally, the child resolves the conflict by identification with the father and repression of his sexual impulses.

The research evidence supporting Freud's theory of the Oedipus complex is meager. Cross-cultural studies suggest that hostility to the father is certainly not a universal phenomenon, but that it may be limited to cultures in which the father is the chief disciplinarian (Malinowski, 1927). There is some evidence that in the later preschool and early school years there are marked increases in nightmares, in fear of the dark, and in fears of imaginary creatures; Freudian theory would interpret these as indications of the repressed fear of the father.

The Persistence of Defenses

One of the puzzling aspects of defense mechanisms, as compared with other general habits, is their strength and persistence. Particularly in the case of unadaptive rigid defenders, the use of the mechanisms brings continual trouble and unhappiness. The individual who continually rationalizes soon finds that no one believes his excuses. Yet he continues to believe them himself. This persistence in the use of a defense mechanism is an example of *fixation.*

Freud used *fixation* in a rather special sense to refer to the tendency of an individual to maintain unaltered an idea that is attached to a basic impulse or to continue to use a form of behavior learned in connection with an early conflict which was never resolved. Freud thought of fixation as a sort of halting of development at a particular stage. According to this view, defense mechanisms persist because the individual has not solved the underlying problem. While in Freudian theory, fixation refers to persistent attempts to achieve immature aims, most other theorists have used the term to refer to any rigid irrational persistence of behavior, such as defenses. Both Freudian and non-Freudian uses of the term *fixation* have the common meaning of rigid persistence, but the Freudian usage refers much more to infantile attachments, while the non-Freudian usage refers to behavior.

Looking at defense mechanisms as forms of behavior, we are using *fixation* in the latter sense when we ask, "Why does fixation occur? Why do not defense mechanisms extinguish?" This is a fascinating research problem that is still not completely solved, even though we are able to study it under laboratory conditions.

■ Among the most dramatic laboratory examples of fixation is the behavior of rats in a problem situation that is unsolvable. Maier and his students (Maier *et al.,* 1940) trained rats to jump to either of two windows. One window was covered by a card with a black circle, the other by a card with a white circle (see Fig. 11–7). When the rat made the correct choice, the card fell down, and the rat could eat the food behind it. When the rat made an incorrect choice, the window was locked and the rat bumped his nose and fell. After they had learned this, the rats were frustrated by the locking of both cards in place so that no matter where the rat jumped, he bumped his nose against a card and fell into a net below.

(a)

(b)

FIG. 11–7. The behavior of a fixated rat. Even when the rat can see the food in the left window, he persists in jumping to the right. (Photos courtesy of Dr. N. R. F. Maier)

In this situation the rats tried to withdraw from the problem; they were unwilling to jump. When they were forced to jump, they developed fixations. Instead of jumping first to one window and then to the other, the rats now developed consistent behavior patterns. For example, one rat might always jump to the right, another always to the left.

Maier now made the problem solvable, so that when the rat jumped to the black circle card, the card fell down and the rat could again get to the food. The window with the white circle remained locked. After several trials in which the black circle was on the right and the rat was rewarded, the black circle appeared on the left. The rat would look longingly at the black circle, would edge over to it—and then jump to the right and bang his nose against the other card. Even when the left window was completely open so that the food was visible, the rat continued to jump to the right. Only with long special training was Maier able to break these fixations. ■

Maier suggests that such frustration-instigated behavior is qualitatively different from motivated behavior. One of the major differences is its persistence and rigidity despite changes in the situation. Maier places heavy emphasis upon individual differences in susceptibility to frustration. When their responses fail to solve the problem, some individuals become frustrated and become fixated in a given mode of behavior.

The fixation illustrated by Maier's rats is an example of the rigidity of behavior which seems characteristic of the frustrated person. Perhaps the persistence of the defense mechanisms, which also provide only partial satisfaction, is an analogous phenomenon.

Individual Differences

Frustration Tolerance

Whether or not they accept all aspects of Maier's theory, most psychologists agree that individuals differ in their ability to withstand frustrating situations. During World War II, this was particularly evident in individual differences exhibited by the men in their ability to endure the stress of battle. Some soldiers developed symptoms of severe maladjustment during their training in the United States. Others became ill at embarkation points. Still others developed symptoms as they waited to enter battle. Some became ill during the first battle. Others became incapacitated after several days of fighting. The longer the troops were kept on the battle line, the greater was the incidence of "battle fatigue." (Stouffer, 1944)

Similarly, an analysis of the life histories of 90 German Jews subjected to Nazism indicated that some reacted to stress by planning and by arranging to leave Germany; others became apathetic; some displayed aggression; some displaced their aggression; some regressed.

Psychologists have accounted for such differences in the ability of individuals to tolerate frustrating situations by postulating individual differences in *frustration tolerance.* This concept implies a general resistance to anxiety aroused by the appearance of barriers. Before we go on with the discussion of frustration tolerance, we should point out that this general concept may not apply to every situation, and that, in some cases, it may be more appropriate to take into account the significance of a particular barrier to the individual. For example, many soldiers were well able to tolerate the danger and other stresses of war, but were not able to tolerate situations involving killing enemy soldiers. Similarly, one may have a good deal of frustration tolerance in most situations but be particularly vulnerable to frustration arising from confrontation with an authority figure (this was fairly common among returned veterans). Nevertheless, the concept of frustration tolerance seems to describe a relatively general and enduring characteristic of an individual. Many theorists have accepted the concept and have gone on to try to account for the individual differences in frustration tolerance.

Different theorists have emphasized different factors in the development of frustration tolerance. Three factors that are frequently mentioned are (1) hereditary and other prenatal differences, (2) the trauma of birth, and (3) experiences involving frustrating situations in childhood.

Children seem to differ in the amount of anxiety they display, even in the first hours following birth. Although many theorists point to heredity and prenatal conditions as causes of these differences, Otto Rank, one of Freud's students, suggested that the process of birth itself may be responsible. Before birth, according to this theory, the baby lives in an environment in which all his needs are completely satisfied. However, the process of birth involves great pressure, a lack of sufficient oxygen, and other stresses. These events cause the baby to experience his first anxiety. The shock experienced at birth provides the baby with a reservoir of anxiety which is released throughout life. Rank's theory implies that the more stressful the birth process, the more likely the child will feel anxiety in frustrating situations later on.

This hypothesis finds little experimental support. There do not seem to be significant differences in anxiety between babies born naturally and those born by Caesarean section. It seems probable that most of the differences that appear at birth are inherited or perhaps determined by prenatal conditions, such as biochemical conditions in the uterus produced by the mother's emotions.

Even though heredity and prenatal events may affect the frustration tolerance of an individual, the influence of environment begins to make itself felt from the very moment of birth onward. While the baby's needs were continually satisfied before birth, after birth he must often wait to be fed, may experience pain, and feel either too warm or too cold. Even during the first week of life babies show evidence of frustration. If the bottle is taken out of a baby's mouth, he cries. A source of satisfaction has been withdrawn, he is frustrated, and he has a built-in response to frustration.

Families differ greatly in the attention given to their babies. If his needs are taken care of promptly and consistently, he soon develops enough sense of security to be able to wait a few minutes to be fed. (This usually occurs about the age of three months.) Parental consistency in rewards (and also in punishments) lays the foundation which determines the security with which the individual faces the inevitable conflict between his biological needs and the demands society (through his parents) makes on him. The infant faces weaning, toilet training, learning to feed himself, training to control his sexual curiosity, and training to restrain his aggressive impulses. All of these are experiences which bring problems of adjustment, which test the child's ability to deal with frustration, and which develop his frustration tolerance.

Apparently, frustration tolerance is learned by success in dealing with such problems. The danger of pushing the infant to develop new skills is that he will lack the ability to handle the frustration, and thus will learn to use defense mechanisms regularly rather than problem solving when he faces a problem situation. The infant who must cope with frustrating situations that he cannot handle learns to abandon problem solving in such situations.

On the other hand, the child faced with problems which are too easy becomes bored. The child learns frustration tolerance by being challenged by difficult problems which he can solve. It is probably in these early frustrating situations that the individual learns the particular habits of problem solving or of defense which he will later use in frustrating situations.

Sociological Differences in Defenses

Because defenses are learned, it is not surprising that individuals reared under different conditions use different defenses. Recent research has revealed that lower-class individuals tend to use defenses different from those used by middle-class individuals. Earlier we spoke of frustrations involving external barriers versus those involving internal barriers. The lower-class individual is much more likely to have to face external, environmental frustrations, while the conflicts of the middle-class person are likely to be internal ones. The lower-class person thus would be expected to learn to use defenses which distort reality, such as denial or fantasy. The middle-class person, however, needs self-control and hence is more likely to use repression, reaction formation, or other mechanisms which involve distortion of motives. Some support for these hypotheses may be found in responses of school children to projective tests (Miller and Swanson, 1960).

We also find sociological differences in the tendency to express or disguise aggression. Lower-class people are more likely to express aggression freely and overtly than are middle-class persons. The middle-class person, on the other hand, learns to inhibit direct aggression and instead to express hostility verbally and symbolically (Miller and Swanson, 1960). In his circles, a social slight may be just as damaging as a punch on the jaw.

The middle-class individual is also more likely to feel guilty about aggressive impulses and to repress and disguise his aggression.

Practical Applications

Personal Uses

Probably the most important consequence of learning about frustration is that one begins to understand that behavior which may appear to be stupid, irrational, or mean is often a response to a frustration. The importance of understanding these causes of behavior is that with such understanding one may change the resulting behavior by (1) changing the situation so that either the source of the frustration is removed or another defense is chosen, or (2) by changing the individual so that he can deal with the source of the frustration constructively, e.g., by teaching him a new skill. Let us suppose, for example, that we observe aggressiveness and unfriendly behavior in a certain group of children. Looking at the situation to determine the cause of the frustration, we may note that their teacher is very authoritarian. If we now train the teacher to handle the children in a less authoritarian fashion, we may find that the children will become much more cooperative.

Child Rearing

If our theory is correct, parents can increase their children's frustration tolerance by providing solvable problems for their children. Individuals who are unable to tolerate frustration may be grouped into two classes: those who faced too many unsolvable problems in childhood and those who faced too few problems. Thus both neglected and overprotected children have more difficulty in handling frustrating situations than do children who have developed realistic confidence in their ability to solve problems.

Social Implications

Social conditions often cause frustration for members of society. For example, the "cold war" poses a threat to everyone. The result is widespread use and social acceptance of certain defense mechanisms. Thus displacement of aggression against some common object may be widely prevalent in a culture faced by a serious threat. This common social phenomenon, called scapegoating, was recognized in Biblical times and is illustrated by the witch hunts of Salem and the Communist scares of post-World War I and post-World War II periods. The analogy between displacement on the personal level and prejudice on the social level has frequently been pointed out. The validity of such analogies is difficult to test. One heroic attempt was a study sponsored by UNESCO which was designed to compare reactions to the Russian threat in different European countries. The results were not uniformly in support of the hypothesis. Nevertheless, some attempts to reduce prejudice have indicated that it is useful to take account of the possible relation between frustration and prejudice. We shall return to this relationship in Chapter 16.

Summary

Concepts

Frustration. The state of the individual in a situation in which strong motives are blocked and problem-solving behavior is abandoned

Defense mechanisms. General habits which block or distort a psychological process in order to protect the individual against anxiety

Fixation.   Rigid, irrational persistence of an act

Frustration tolerance.   The general resistance of an individual to anxiety in frustrating situations

Principles

1. The source of frustration may be a situational barrier, an interpersonal barrier, an intrapersonal barrier or a combination of these. Motive conflict, an intrapersonal barrier, is an especially frequent source.

2. The individual's reactions to frustrating situations may be divided into three stages: (i) an alarm reaction during which a heightened state of arousal is manifested in increased persistence, aggression, withdrawal, or anxiety; (ii) a stage of resistance in which the individual defends himself against anxiety by the use of defense mechanisms; and (iii) a stage of exhaustion in which the individual succumbs to psychological maladjustment.

3. There are two categories of defense mechanisms: *primary* defense mechanisms, which involve the complete blocking out of a psychological process (denial, repression, and isolation), and *secondary* defense mechanisms, which involve distortion of a psychological process (displacement, projection, identification, rationalization, substitution, fantasy, regression).

4. Defense mechanisms are normal ways of coping with frustration.

5. The factors which may influence the selection of one defense mechanism rather than another include: the cues in the situation, the individual's motivation, the type of conflict involved, and the learning experiences of the individual in childhood.

6. Individuals differ in frustration tolerance and in the kinds of defenses they display.

Suggested Readings

Freudian theory has such an important influence on many aspects of contemporary culture that every educated person should have some understanding of Freud's basic ideas. There are paperback editions of summaries of Freud's theories, as well as of Freud's own writings. Among these are:

BRENNER, C., *An Elementary Textbook of Psychoanalysis.* New York: Doubleday-Anchor A102.

HALL, C. S., *A Primer of Freudian Psychology.* New York: New American Library, Mentor MD271.

RICKMAN, J. (ed.), *A General Selection from the Works of Sigmund Freud.* New York: Doubleday-Anchor A115.

FREUD, S., *Psychopathology of Everyday Life.* New York: New American Library, Mentor MD67.

FREUD, S., *General Introduction to Psychoanalysis.* New York: Washington Square Press W599.

FREUD, S., *Origin and Development of Psychoanalysis.* Chicago, Ill.: Regnery, Gateway 6009.

FREUD, A., *The Ego and Mechanisms of Defense.* New York: International Universities Press, 1946. A classic monograph on defense mechanisms by Sigmund Freud's daughter.

The concentration-camp experiences cited in this chapter are discussed in more detail in BETTELHEIM, B., *The Informed Heart.* Glencoe, Ill.: Free Press, 1960.

THE PERSON   PART 3

**the person: personality characteristics
and their assessment**

chapter 12

HOW CAN PERSONALITY TRAITS BE IDENTIFIED?

HOW CAN PERSONALITY TRAITS BE ASSESSED?

HOW ARE PERSONALITY TRAITS USED
TO PREDICT BEHAVIOR?

CAN PERSONALITY TRAITS HELP TO PROVIDE
A DESCRIPTION OF A TOTAL PERSONALITY?

Up to this point we have been concerned chiefly with general laws that are common to the psychological functioning of everyone. Although we have referred to differences between people in connection with each psychological process we have discussed, the focus of attention has been the process itself— perception, motivation, learning, thinking, frustration. In the following chapters we shall focus our attention on the *individual*. This chapter will deal with ways of describing and assessing general individual differences; Chapter 13 will trace the psychological development of the individual.

We shall use the term *personality* to refer to the unique organization of relatively enduring psychological characteristics possessed by an individual, as revealed by his interaction with the environment. This definition takes into account several factors: (1) No two people are exactly alike; each person has a unique pattern of psychological characteristics. (2) Each person maintains a certain consistency, an identifiability that endures through time, by which he can be recognized. (3) To understand personality we must not only identify an individual's psychological characteristics, we must also discover how they relate and interact with one another; personality is *organized*. (4) Personality and the characteristics and organizations to which it refers are *constructs*; we infer them and their properties from observable behavior.

Much of what we have already discussed belongs in the personality category. All of an individual's percepts, motives, habits, concepts, and defenses are part of his personality. Why, then, do we discuss personality separately?

We have seen how a person's acts depend on his previously learned percepts, motives, habits, and concepts as these are aroused by a given situation. If we knew all these tendencies were in an individual, we could probably predict his behavior with some accuracy. However, for an individual about whose background we do not have exact knowledge, can we make any general predictions about his behavior tendencies in a variety of situations? Will Howard enjoy being a teacher? Is Carl likely to become a leader in the boys' club? Will Barbara and Eddie be happy in their marriage? Which of the recruits will be able to withstand the most severe combat stress without neurotic breakdown? In order to begin to answer such questions, most personality psychologists infer units that are more general and more complex than the constructs with which we dealt earlier.

We can approach the question of personality description from another point of view. The English language contains almost 18,000 words which differentiate people from one another (Allport and Odbert, 1936). Many of these words imply characteristics which are much more general than the ones we have been discussing. In fact, frequently a single word is used to characterize an entire person. We speak of "heroes," "rogues," and "villains," of a woman who is a "motherly type," of a "true scholar." These words are labels for categories or *types* of people. Presumably, either a person belongs in such a category or he

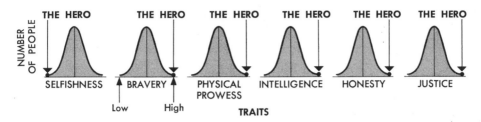

FIG. 12–1. Why type descriptions have declined in psychology. Types usually include in their descriptions only the fraction of the population who are extreme on a number of dimensions, while most people are moderate on most dimensions.

does not. He either is or is not a rogue; he is or is not a true scholar. Other words in the language refer to more specific characteristics or *traits* of individuals; we speak of a person as honest, sociable, artistic, etc. None of these adjectives are discrete categories to which a person does or does not belong. Rather, each refers to a *dimension* which a person possesses to a high, moderate, or low degree. A person may be very sociable, moderately honest, and not very artistic. (Incidentally, although these traits are more specific characterizations of people than types, they are classifications which are usually more general than percepts, habits, and motives. When we refer to a person as being very artistic, we are at once saying something about the way he sees, what his motives are, how he thinks, and how he typically acts.)

Psychologists have naturally been interested in the extent to which these common language designations actually refer to general consistencies that can be discerned in the behavior of people. In general, *traits* have proved to be more useful in scientific descriptions than *types*. This should not be surprising. A type, such as the "hero," is a person who ranks high on a number of trait dimensions: he is very brave, very strong, highly intelligent, extremely honest and just, and very unselfish. However, most people are not extreme, but moderate, on most traits. Therefore type designations which refer to people who are high on a number of dimensions really refer to only a very, very small number of people; most people cannot be categorized as a type. Figure 12–1 illustrates this point graphically.

In this chapter, then, we shall look at how psychologists have used the concept of trait to describe personality and to predict behavior. We define a personality trait as a combination of perceptual, conceptual, motivational, and act tendencies that give rise to a general behavioral disposition. We have already discussed one trait, intelligence, during our review of the individual differences in problem solving.*

---

* In including intelligence as a personality trait we are following Guilford (1959). Some psychologists prefer to limit personality traits to the *noncognitive* traits.

How Can Personality Traits Be Identified?

With almost 18,000 words in the English language for describing personality, the psychologist is faced with the problem of identifying and measuring a small number of traits which will be useful in describing individuals and predicting their behavior. There are at least three different methods by which psychologists have identified traits: the *empirical method,* the *statistical method,* and the *theoretical method.*

The *empirical method* identifies traits by looking at groups that are known to differ. This is the method Binet used to identify and assess intelligence. He knew that ten-year-olds, on the average, should have a higher mental age than six-year-olds, and he looked for tests on which ten-year-olds would perform consistently better than six-year-olds. Other personality traits have been identified in the same way. For example, it is appropriate to assume that people who are confined to mental hospitals differ in important personality characteristics from the general population. Thus tests which differentiate between the two groups point to significant personality characteristics.

A second method, the *statistical method,* involves finding statistical consistencies underlying behavior in a variety of test situations. A good example of this method is *factor analysis.* In factor analysis, the first step is to administer items from many different tests to a large group of people. The answers given on the various items are then correlated with one another. This produces clusters of items that are correlated with each other but which do not correlate with some of the items in other clusters. A person can then examine in what way the items in a cluster are similar to each other but different from the items in other clusters. The dimension that describes item similarity within a cluster suggests a dimension of personality. For example, suppose that we administer seven tests and find that they correlate with one another as shown in Fig. 12–2. We can deduce

	A	B	C	D	E	F	G
A		+0.7	+0.8	+0.8	−0.1	0.0	0.0
B			+0.9	+0.7	0.1	0.2	0.0
C				+0.8	−0.2	−0.1	−0.1
D					0.0	−0.1	0.2
E						0.6	0.7
F							0.7
G							

FIG. 12–2. A group of correlations among six tests. A factor analysis of these correlations would reveal two underlying factors: One factor emerges from the high correlations among A, B, C, and D; another factor emerges from the high correlations among E, F, and G. (From Cattell, 1965)

that tests A, B, C, and D are tapping one dimension and that tests E, F, and G are tapping another dimension. We can diagram the intercorrelations as shown in Fig. 12–3. The area in which the tests overlap shows the degree to which the tests are measuring a common dimension or, in the terminology of factor analysis, a common factor.

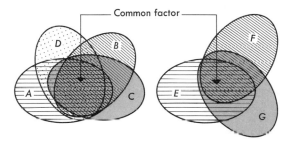

FIG. 12–3. The correlations among the tests A, B, C, and D and among tests E, F, and G of Fig. 12–2 can also be represented as overlapping circles. The area of overlap represents the degree to which the tests reflect a common factor.

It was the factor-analytic technique that enabled Thurstone (1938) to divide intelligence into seven primary abilities. It was also by this technique that several dimensions of maladjustment were identified as independent of one another, as we shall see below.

The third way to identify personality traits is by the *theoretical method*. A psychologist's theoretical conceptions of personality may suggest the importance of certain traits. For example, Freud's theory suggests that dependence (which Freud saw as originating in the oral stage) is an important dimension. Jung theorized that introversion and extroversion provided significant personality descriptions.

Many traits have been identified by these methods and tests have been developed to measure them. Some of these tests have shown many interesting relationships between the traits and behavior; others have not and have been discarded. One reviewer (Mann, 1959) noted that over 500 different measures of personality were referred to in research material published between 1900 and 1957, but only a quarter of these were used in more than one study. Some may have been poor measures; others may have measured traits which had few relationships to other elements of personality or to behavior. Since we are dealing with fairly general characteristics of individuals, we should be able to approach personality characteristics from a number of different angles and converge upon certain common basic elements, but as yet there is no well-established list of dimensions useful enough in understanding behavior to be usable by all theorists and researchers. However, there are some dimensions which have emerged in a number of studies. We shall discuss several of these in the following pages.

Some Dimensions of Personality

An empirical problem recognized by society is the problem of maladjustment. Some people require treatment in a hospital because of difficulties in adjustment; others are able to carry on their daily work despite many frustrations. Psychiatrists and psychologists diagnose two classes of maladjustment:* *neurosis,* a disorder in which people show disturbed behavior but in which they can still remain in society, and *psychosis,* a maladjustment so severe that institutionalization is necessary. In the past, some psychologists believed that people with the same personality traits became neurotic and psychotic, that psychosis was simply a more severe manifestation of the same type of personality disorder as neurosis. Statistical analysis of a variety of tests showed that this was not so.

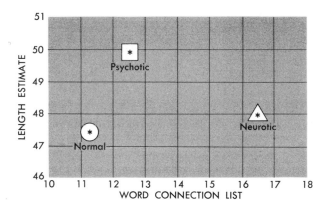

FIG. 12–4. The average score of normals, psychotics, and neurotics on two tests. On the word-connection list test, which is a multiple choice form of a word association test, neurotics achieved a significantly higher score than either normals or psychotics; on the length estimate test, which is plotted on the graph in terms of amount of overestimation, psychotics were significantly higher than either neurotics or normals. (From Eysenck, H. J., *The Scientific Study of Personality.* Macmillan, 1952. Reprinted by permission.)

■ Eysenck (1952) administered a great many tests to normal people, to those who had been diagnosed as psychotic, and to those who had been diagnosed as neurotic. When Eysenck correlated and factor-analyzed his results, he found that certain tests differentiated psychotic patients from normal people and neurotics, and other tests differentiated neurotics from normal people and psychotics. Figure 12–4 shows the average scores of the three groups on two different tests—one on which psychotics differ significantly from normals and neurotics; the other on which neurotics differ significantly from normals and psychotics. Eysenck's conclusion, based on evidence such as this, was that two different personality dimensions were needed to account for the data: neuroticism and psychoticism. ■

---

* Types of maladjustment are discussed more fully in Chapter 14.

EMOTIONAL STABILITY–NEUROTICISM. Eysenck's first factor, emotional stability–neuroticism, has emerged in several studies.* Cattell (1957) interprets the dimension as a sort of psychological exhaustion—the degree to which the person has been beaten down by stress. Cattell's own work with factor analysis indicates that there is an "anxiety" factor separate from Eysenck's factor, although the two factors are positively related.

Psychoanalytic theory also differentiates neurosis from psychosis. The theory interprets neuroses as resulting from failure of the normal defense mechanisms (such as sublimation) to control inner impulses and reactions to external stimuli (Fenichel, 1945). This failure may result either from an overload of external stress or from such a residue of unresolved conflict that even normal external stresses cannot be handled. This description does not differ greatly from that proposed by Cattell, or from Eysenck's description of neuroticism as being analogous to brittleness in metal. In this sense, an individual's place on the neuroticism dimension is an index to the amount of additional stress he can stand without breaking.

What characteristics tend to accompany a low position on the emotional stability–neuroticism dimension? The person who is low in emotional stability tends to show dependence, low energy, and narrow interests, and usually does not belong to groups. His perception is likely to be handicapped by poor sensory acuity, and particularly by poor night vision. He tends to be anxious and to have little frustration tolerance. At the other end of the scale is the emotionally stable person. He is likely to have a cheerful, even disposition which is not disturbed by distractions or stress. Persons who are high in emotional stability are likely to state that they can study with a radio on and that they do not mind interruptions; and objective tests indicate that the effect of noise on them is indeed less detrimental than the effect of noise on individuals who rank toward the neuroticism end of the scale. This trait is thus particularly relevant to behavior in stressful situations.†

The words *tends* and *likely* are used intentionally in the preceding discussion. It is important to realize that personality traits do not usually come in black-and-white categories. A person who is high in intelligence tends to solve problems better than a person of less intelligence, but he does not solve every problem better than his compatriot. Similarly, when we say that the person low in emotional stability tends not to belong to groups, we do not mean that all persons low in emotional stability belong to no groups at all; some undoubtedly belong to many. What we mean is that, *on the average,* people low in emotional stability belong to fewer groups than do people in general. We need to remember that real people are complex and that when we identify characteristics

---

* The studies used different methods of trait identification.
† As we discuss each trait, we shall try to point out the kinds of situations in which behavior mediated by the trait is most relevant.

associated with a particular trait, we are speaking of behavior probabilities of better-than-chance, but still far from perfect, predictability. In fact, correlations between neuroticism and the characteristics mentioned above are quite low; typically on the order of 0.2 to 0.3. The nature of the factor-analytic approach to personality is that the most general factors are identified by the common relationships of large numbers of relatively low correlations.

REALISM–PSYCHOTICISM. Eysenck's second dimension of personality, realism–psychoticism, is related not only to an important social criterion, severe maladjustment, but also appears to be related to one of the key concepts in psychoanalytic theory—the ego. According to this theory, the ego is that part of the personality which maintains contact with external reality. Psychosis, according to psychoanalytic theory, is a state in which the ego fails to function in a mature fashion. In some senses the psychotic individual is one whose ego has regressed to a primitive, infant-like state.

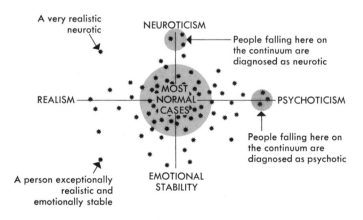

FIG. 12–5. A possible distribution of individuals on the emotional stability-neuroticism and the realism-psychoticism dimensions.

Both Eysenck's and Cattell's work show the realism–psychosis dimension as a continuum in which normal people score at many different points. Individuals scoring at one extreme of the dimension tend to come to public attention and to be diagnosed as psychotic (see Fig. 12–5). Eysenck and Cattell have also demonstrated that individuals who are at the psychotic end of the dimension tend to show poor concentration, poor memory, lack of fluency, and low dexterity. At the high, realistic, end of the dimension are individuals likely to have good judgment of reality, good concentration, and good memory. Scores on this dimension correlate positively with success in flying training (Cattell, 1957). Unfortunately, we still do not have any very clear ideas about what sorts of situations particularly reveal behavior mediated by this personality dimension. Theory suggests that the trait is relevant to any situations requiring realistic, well-timed responses to the external world.

EXTROVERSION–INTROVERSION. A third dimension appearing in the work of Cattell and Eysenck is a trait that was first identified by a personality theorist. The trait, extroversion–introversion, was first proposed by the Swiss psychologist Carl Jung (1923). Jung described introversion as a trait characterized by being interested primarily in one's own thoughts and feelings, and extroversion as a trait characterized by directing one's interest toward other people and the external world. Jung's writings inspired many psychologists to attempt to develop measures of extroversion–introversion. A serious blow was dealt the theory when Guthrie (1927) and Guilford (1934) demonstrated that these tests did not show a high degree of correlation with one another. However, recent studies, both by factor analysts and by other personality researchers, have brought extroversion–introversion back onto the psychological stage.

One reason why the extroversion–introversion concepts declined was that these concepts were used to categorize people into types. The layman was likely to say, "Is he an extrovert or an introvert?" and to believe that he understood an individual as soon as he had found out what type that individual was. One was either an extrovert or an introvert. But this dichotomy turned out to be of little value. When it comes to extroversion and introversion, as in the case of almost all personality traits, most people fall between the extremes. Nevertheless, we can differentiate characteristics of people at the extremes. The person toward the introversion end of the dimension is more likely than the extrovert to prefer music which is quiet. The introvert is likely to prefer different kinds of humor (see Fig. 12–6). He is also likely to have feelings of inferiority. His level of aspiration tends to be unduly high, yet he underrates his own work. He is likely to be more persistent and intelligent than the extrovert.

The extrovert, on the other hand, is likely to possess a high degree of spontaneity. People toward the extroverted side of this dimension tend to be practical, little concerned with abstract theory, less self-sufficient and more likely to have mood changes than introverts. They seem to be more susceptible to changes in stimulation than introverts. The situations in which this trait is particularly relevant are probably those involving choices between responding to internal or social cues, with the extrovert being more responsive to social or other external stimuli.

Although the dimension of extroversion–introversion has persistently reappeared in analyses of personality tests, it would be a mistake to think of it as a highly unified, very specific dimension. As we would expect, it can be separated into more specific dimensions (such as thinking introversion and social introversion). Performance on the various tests of extroversion–introversion are usually positively, but not highly, correlated (Carrigan, 1960).

WHICH JOKE SEEMS FUNNIER TO YOU?

A. 'Aren't you getting tired of this bachelor life, Bill?' asked his friend, Jack.
'Certainly not,' replied Bill. 'What was good enough for my father is good enough for me!'

B. Kind neighbour (to little boy eating an apple): 'Look out for the worms, Sonny.'
Little boy: 'When I eat an apple, the worms have to look out for themselves.'

JOKE *A* IS APPRECIATED MORE BY EXTROVERTS; JOKE *B* BY INTROVERTS—AS A RULE.

A. 'I'm looking forward,' she said, 'to my twenty-fifth birthday.'
'Aren't you,' suggested her escort, 'facing the wrong direction?'

B. 'For goodness' sake, use both hands!' exclaimed the girl in the car.
'I can't,' said her escort, 'I've got to steer with one.'

JOKE *B* IS THE EXTROVERT CHOICE; JOKE *A* THE INTROVERT.

FIG. 12–6. People on the introversion side and those on the extroversion side of the continuum tend to prefer different types of humor. (From Cattell, R. B., *The Scientific Analysis of Personality*. Baltimore: Penguin Books, 1965. Reprinted by permission.

Again a reminder: We speak here of characteristics differentiating people at the extremes of the dimension; one should remember that most people fall between these extremes.

INDEPENDENCE–DEPENDENCE. Many psychologists have suggested that another important dimension of personality is independence. Independence is presumed to account for individual differences in the ability to work without close supervision and to resist pressures to conform. Psychoanalytic theorists have emphasized the importance of conflicts about dependence in problems of adjustment. According to psychoanalytic theorists, the infant has such a compelling need for his parents' love that he learns patterns of passive receptive dependence upon them, which are difficult for the individual to give up when he is expected to learn new, more mature, patterns of independent behavior. Factor-analytic studies have not identified this dimension as clearly as others we have discussed. Nevertheless, several studies report a factor which seems to involve independence-dependence (Cattell, 1957; Guilford, 1959; French, 1953). The situations particularly relevant to this dimension would presumably be those involving work with or without direction, and involving social pressures.

OTHER DIMENSIONS. We have listed only four of the thousands of names of personality traits in our language. There are undoubtedly others which we might well have included. Aggressiveness and anxiety are two that are frequently cited, but we have already treated them in the chapter on motives. Dependability (or conscientiousness) is another which is of much interest. Rigidity has been used in many studies. Honesty is an example of a number of traits which have importance for ethical standards. We shall discuss some work related to this trait later on. While we cannot include a detailed discussion of every trait, we hope that our discussion of emotional stability, realism, extroversion, and independence will communicate, in addition to the specific information about these traits, the following general themes:

1. what we mean by a personality trait, particularly the notion of dimensions, rather than dichotomous categories;
2. the manner in which personality traits are identified;
3. that traits are not generally highly correlated with one another, which makes it impossible to categorize people into simple types;
4. that different traits become relevant in different situations.

How Can Personality Traits Be Assessed?

Perhaps our introduction to the identification and assessment of personality traits has made it sound like a very difficult and complex process. It is. Nevertheless each of us is continually engaged in the business of assessment. When we meet someone new, we try to "size him up"—to judge whether or not he would be a good friend, or a good person with whom to work or to do business. Typically, we are not aware of the factors that influence our judgments. We simply "feel" that the person is likable, or crafty, or trustworthy.

In this section we examine various procedures, ranging from the simple methods of assessment commonly used in sizing up a new acquaintance, such as judging from appearance, to more formal methods of assessing personality characteristics, such as personality tests. As we look at each source of information, we shall ask, "What, if anything, is this method good for? What dimensions does it tap?" At the same time we should also remember that in many cases specific measures of perceptual differences, motives, or skills may be much more reliable and useful than assessment of general personality characteristics. A personality test offers no magical way of unraveling the complexities of the person. However, personality tests are methods of eliciting behavior in more or less controlled situations. Their usefulness in prediction depends to a large extent on the validity of the theory which links behavior on the test with the behavior to be predicted.

Characteristics of Effective Assessment Methods

The psychologist, in developing methods of assessing personality, strives for *reliable* and *valid* measures. The consistency of a measure is called its *reliability*.

For example, if we measure a person's height several times, we get about the same results time after time; i.e., the measure gives stable results. We can thus say that our measure is reliable. However, if a professor graded his papers by throwing them down the stairs and giving the highest grades to those reaching the bottom, his grades would be unreliable because it is unlikely that he would get the same results if he threw them a second time. If a measure will not give consistent results, its usefulness is obviously limited.

How truly a method measures what it is supposed to measure is called its *validity*. Grading history papers by counting the spelling errors would give reliable results, but they would not be valid; i.e., they would not truly measure what the students had learned about history. The lines on one's hands are not good measures of personality; they have low validity as personality measures. A good set of bathroom scales has high validity in measuring weight; it correlates highly with other measures of weight.

In order to determine a test's validity we need some criterion against which we can check it. There are several types of criteria and therefore several types of validity (Cronbach, 1960). We shall discuss three types which are important in the construction of personality tests: (1) *predictive validity*, (2) *concurrent validity*, and (3) *construct validity*.

We can consider predictive and concurrent validity together. Here there is a clear criterion, external to the test, against which the test can be measured. A test's *predictive* validity is established when it does, in fact, successfully predict some future behavior from the person's test score. For example, intelligence tests have predictive validity if they can predict later school performance. A valid test of psychoticism would predict which people in the general population would be most likely to require care in a mental hospital. A test shows *concurrent* validity if it successfully discriminates between people who are known to be different at the time they take the test. For example, if a test of neuroticism were given to a group known to include both normals and neurotics, it would show concurrent validity if neurotics scored significantly higher in neuroticism than normals.

Frequently, when one attempts to assess personality traits by means of a test, there is no simple external criterion by which the test can be validated. For example, there is no clear-cut external criterion for dependence versus independence. If the personality trait in question is derived from a theory, the test of the trait may show *construct* validity; that is, the scores on the test conform to the hypotheses of the theory. For example, Freud hypothesized that dependency was related to frustration during the oral period. Thus a test of dependency would show construct validity if people who had high scores on the test had histories of frustrating experiences during the first year of life.

A special kind of construct validity which has been important in personality testing is *factorial* validity. The personality-trait theorist assumes that if clusters of items have high intercorrelations, they tap some underlying dimension of personality. Thus, if items which suggest dominance have high intercorrelations, the trait theorist would claim factorial validity for dominance. The problem with this type of validity, unless the trait is also validated by means of some criterion in addition to intercorrelation, is that we have no way of knowing what is responsible for the underlying consistency among the tests. In the case of dominance, is the common dimension of the tests actually dominance rather than some other trait? There is no way of determining this by factorial validation alone. For this reason, Cattell has suggested that we may not want to *name* factorially discovered traits at all. We could simply give each trait a number and find a relationship between it and a certain kind of behavior without naming the trait!

You may have noticed that the types of criteria for validating tests of personality traits are similar to the methods we described earlier for identifying personality traits. Empirical criteria, psychological theory, and statistical techniques, such as factor analysis, are involved in both processes. In fact, a test which has been useful for identifying a trait may contain items which are equally useful in assessing that trait later on.

Another characteristic of a test is its *sensitivity*. A test on which everyone made the same score would not be very useful. The good test should discriminate between people (validly, of course), but how wide a range of personalities should it cover? A fever thermometer is sensitive over a wide range of temperatures but relatively insensitive to hour by hour temperature changes of healthy people. Similarly, a test designed to discriminate between normals and psychotics might be relatively insensitive to personality differences within the normal range. A valid test need not be uniformly sensitive. In selecting students for academic scholarships to college, we would try to design a test which would discriminate very well between students with high ability, but we would not care about discriminating between those of average and low ability. Such a test, when given to high school seniors, might well produce an asymmetric distribution of scores with a big hump at the low end and a long tail at the high end of the distribution.

The concept of sensitivity is closely related to validity, since a test cannot predict very well if it lacks sensitivity to the differences necessary for predicting the criterion. Sensitivity also bears a relationship to reliability, because a test, in addition to being sensitive to differences between individuals, may be sensitive to differences in an individual from one time to another. Since personality traits are elicited by situational cues, we may be interested in how much some characteristic varies because of situational differences. If we loosely define reliability to mean "consistency over time," this means that a sensitive instrument will appear to be unreliable. For this reason we need to extend our definition of reliability to mean "stability of test scores over time in the same situation when no true change has occurred in the trait being measured."

In interpreting psychological tests, one needs to consider *test norms*. For example, suppose that Johnny solved six of ten problems correctly. Did he do well or poorly? Actually, we have no way of knowing from the number of correct answers alone. The problems may have been very easy; they may have been very hard. We need to know how other children of Johnny's age or grade did; their performance gives us the test norms.

The easiest way to compare children would be to rank each of the children 1, 2, 3, 4, etc., in the order of their test scores. In tests which large numbers of people are taking, however, ranking is no longer practical; hence percentile ranks are used. A person's *percentile rank* (or *centile*) is a number indicating the percentage of people taking the test whom he equals or excels. Thus a person whose score was the middle score would have a percentile rank of 50. If his score was above the scores of 75% of those taking the test, his percentile rank would be 75, and so forth.

However, a percentile rank does not mean much unless one knows something about the group on which the norms are based. For example, a college student who scored at the 99th percentile on a mathematics test would not be proud if he learned that he was being compared with first-grade arithmetic students. Similarly, the person who scores at the 50th percentile for the general population on an intelligence test will rank below the 50th percentile for high-school seniors, and his percentile rank as compared with college students will be even lower. On one widely used group test of intelligence, for example, the person at the 50th percentile for college students excels 82 percent of the general population on the test; and at some colleges, the student who ranks at the 95th percentile for the population as a whole will have a percentile rank of 50 in comparison with other students in his college. Thus we see that when one interprets a percentile rank, it is important to know the standardization group; i.e., the group with whom one's score is being compared.

Informal Methods of Judging Personality

As we noted earlier, everyone is a personality assesser. Many of us take real pride in our ability to judge other people. Most of us assess well enough so that we are seldom surprised by the behavior of our friends or relatives. Some of us use physique as a guide; others use facial characteristics, speech habits, age, race, sex, social class, or occupation. Few could specify precisely what cues they are using in judging personality. We succeed as well as we do largely because we have a good deal of feedback from continued observations of the behavior of friends and acquaintances and, as our assessment changes, we soon forget the early errors. Nevertheless, it may be helpful to look at the validity of some of the methods commonly used in judging personality.

ARE PHYSICAL CHARACTERISTICS GOOD INDICATORS OF PERSONALITY? Physique is an appealing method of categorizing people because body build is so much more obvious than scores on a complex personality scale. One of the recent attempts to relate personality dimensions to bodily dimensions is that of Sheldon. He differentiated three dimensions of physique. The *endomorph* has a round body with small bones, smooth skin, and little hair. The *mesomorph* has large bones and well-developed muscles. The *ectomorph* is straight and slender (Sheldon *et al.*, 1940).

Sheldon's theory and his research suggested that the endomorph is likely to love comfort, good food, and good company, and to express his feelings easily. The mesomorph tends to be active, athletic, and dominant. The ectomorph tends to avoid company and to be inhibited and restrained (Sheldon and Stevens, 1942). Further research by Sanford (1943) showed some positive correlations between the tall, thin body type and ratings of guilt and self-suf-ficiency, characteristics which seem to be related to our dimension of introversion. Other investigators, however, have found only chance relationships between body types and personality. Thus Sheldon's techniques for measuring body type have not come into wide use, and people who base their everyday judgments of personality on physique alone are not likely to make very valid assessments.

Although body type is not a very valid indicator of personality, it is easy to see why some relationship might be found. Not only is it possible that genetic factors determining personality are associated with those determining physique, but also constitutional factors are important in determining the roles we play. The correlations between physique and ratings of personality may be a function of social expectations of a person's behavior. A study by Wells and Siegel (1961) showed that subjects rated the psychological characteristics of silhouettes somewhat as Sheldon would have rated them; i.e., the ratings were based on body type. Endomorphs were rated as more good-natured, more warm-hearted, and lazier than others; ectomorphs were rated as more tense, more ambitious, and quieter than others; mesomorphs were rated as more masculine, more adventurous, and more self-reliant than others. Given these expectations, we might predict that people would learn to behave some-what like the cultural stereotypes. For example, a strong active boy is likely to be permitted by his parents to be self-reliant and dominant. This analysis would account for some of the relationships that have been found. But in terms of our present knowledge, physical characteristics alone do not seem to satisfy our historic desire for a quick, simple method of assessing personality.

USING SOCIOLOGICAL (DEMOGRAPHIC) VARIABLES IN ASSESSING PERSONALITY. Some people judge personality in terms of such easily recognized characteristics as age, sex, social class, occupation, or race. Because the norms of behavior differ for members of different groups, knowing a person's occupation or social class may be helpful in assessing some of his personality characteristics and predicting his behavior.

Age. The different roles our society assigns to people of different ages make for important differences in behavior. The adolescent, for instance, typically has strong needs to express independence of authority, while the older person is more likely to have accepted his role in society and to conform to society's expectations. The older person is likely to be more conservative than a young person. He is likely to be more deliberate, and to deal with one stimulus at a time.

Sex is another important index of personality factors. As we saw in Chapter 2, the Cultural Background of Behavior, some personality characteristics that we associate with sex are the result of cultural learning; others may be influenced by basic biological factors. In any case we can predict some behavior simply on the basis of sex differences. Thus women are, in general, more verbal, more emotional, more introverted, and less flexible than men. Women tend to score higher on scales of anxiety than do men. They also tend to have more difficulty in shifting set in problem solving.

A third characteristic which is easily assessed is *socioeconomic status*. People in the middle class are more likely than people in the lower and upper classes to be characterized by a strong motive for achievement (Rosen, 1956). In addition, as we saw earlier, the mode of expressing aggressive urges varies with socioeconomic status. The person in the lower class learns to express his aggressions fairly directly, often by actual physical violence; the middle-class person is taught to control his expression of aggression, and when he does release it, he uses words rather than blows. People in different social classes differ even in the types of mental illness they tend to develop. Because the group norms of the lower class differ from those of the middle class in so many ways, knowledge of social class is useful background information in assessing personality and predicting behavior. But there are such big differences between people within a particular social class that generalizations to individuals are not very dependable.

Another variable which may be used in assessing personality characteristics is *occupation*. In general, white-collar workers tend to be more conservative than blue-collar workers, even when both receive the same pay. People in different occupations also tend to have different interests and values, as we saw in Chapter 7.

Race is also frequently used as an index of personality. As we have already seen, race is not a good predictor of intelligence, and no major inherited racial differences in personality characteristics have been established. When differences between races apparently do exist, they frequently are related to differences in social class more directly than to differences in race. In fact, the difficulty of equating environmental variables makes studies of racial psychological differences almost impossible.

AN EVALUATION OF SOCIOLOGICAL VARIABLES. In the preceding paragraphs we suggested that there is some predictive value in knowing the groups into which a person may be categorized. However, these variables alone are inadequate predictors of the personality of an individual because (1) they ignore the wide range of individual differences within each group, (2) they tend to obscure the tremendous overlap of characteristics of people between groups. The assumption that, because a variable has some usefulness in predicting certain average characteristics for a large group of people, it can also provide accurate information about an individual, is an erroneous and dangerous one.

Formal Personality-Assessment Techniques

In discussing physiological and sociological categories as cues to personality characteristics, we have been approaching the task from the standpoint of informal, face-to-face evaluations of other people. But now we turn to the more formal types of assessment devices: methods developed and used by psychologists.

INTERVIEWS. One of the most obvious ways to obtain information about someone is to ask him questions. Such informal interviews are a common procedure in selecting people for admission to college, for jobs, or as recipients of research grants.

The interview has a number of advantages. It is a very flexible means of getting information, of following up interesting points, and of exploring meanings. A friendly and understanding interviewer can elicit franker statements than an impersonal instrument can (Kahn and Cannell, 1956). Furthermore, an interviewer observes not only an individual's verbal answers to his questions, but other reactions as well. For example, the act of hesitation by an individual in answering a question may provide as much information as the content of the answer itself.

Despite these advantages, researchers find that informal interviews are not good predictors of specific outcomes.

■ One of the most intensive studies of the value of various methods of assessing personality was carried out by Kelly and Fiske (1951). In a carefully controlled study, they used various methods of assessing personality to predict the success of students intending to become clinical psychologists. As criteria, Kelly and Fiske used not only measures of knowledge but also ratings of professional competence by supervisors and colleagues. The staff members "were generally of the opinion that the interviews were the most valuable part of the assessment program." Yet the results of the research showed that the interview was actually of little value in making accurate predictions. Thus the interview lacks validity as a device for predicting success in clinical psychology. The Strong Vocational Interest Inventory, on the other hand, proved to have a number of significant relationships to the criteria of success. The investigators concluded that the interview is not so much a device for assessment of personality as a technique of gaining confidence in one's judgment. Perhaps it is too difficult for one person to simultaneously determine: (1) the important dimensions of a situation, (2) how best to assess these dimensions with face-to-face questions, and (3) how to weigh the answers to predict one particular outcome. Informal interviewing is still an art rather than a precise scientific instrument for assessing personality. ■

Name of student . . . .

A—How are you and others affected by his appearance and manner?	☐ Sought by others ☐ Well liked by others ☐ Liked by others ☐ Tolerated by others ☐ Avoided by others ☐ No opportunity to observe	Please record here instances on which you base your judgment.
B—Does he need frequent prodding or does he go ahead without being told?	☐ Seeks and sets for himself additional tasks ☐ Completes suggested supplementary work ☐ Does ordinary assignments of his own accord ☐ Needs occasional prodding ☐ Needs much prodding in doing ordinary assignments ☐ No opportunity to observe	Please record here instances on which you base your judgment.
C—Does he get others to do what he wishes?	☐ Displays marked ability to lead his fellows; makes things go ☐ Sometimes leads in important affairs ☐ Sometimes leads in minor affairs ☐ Lets others take lead ☐ Probably unable to lead his fellows ☐ No opportunity to observe	Please record here instances on which you base your judgment.
D—How does he control his emotions?	☐ Unusual balance of responsiveness and control ☐ Well balanced ☐ Usually well balanced ☐ Tends to be unresponsive ☐ Tends to be over emotional ☐ Unresponsive, apathetic ☐ Too easily depressed, irritated or elated ☐ No opportunity to observe	Please record here instances on which you base your judgment.

FIG. 12–7. A portion of a commonly used rating scale, the ACE Personality Report, Form B. (Reproduced by permission of American Council on Education)

One of the problems with informal interviews is that there is no standard situation by which to compare the interviewees. Each conversation between interviewer and interviewee is qualitatively different. One method for improving the effectiveness of the interview as a predictor is to use standard questions. This permits a comparison of the responses of various people to the same general stimulus situation. When standard questions are used, the interview loses some of its spontaneity and flexibility. This loss is compensated for by the increase in comparable quantitative data, which permits more precise prediction.

RATING SCALES. One of the tasks of the interviewer is to assess the interviewee's personality by observing his behavior in the interview situation. From our discussion of personality dimensions, it is clear that the usefulness of observation will depend on the extent to which the situations observed provide cues for the dimensions which the observer wishes to assess. For example, after a single interview an observer can hardly make judgments about extroversion as accurate as his judgments might be if he saw the person in a variety of social situations. This is particularly true when the interviewee knows what characteristics the interviewer considers desirable.

In order to avoid these pitfalls, personality assessers have developed rating scales. A rating scale is so constructed that it enables someone who knows the person being evaluated very well, and who has observed his behavior in many situations, to rate him on various personality characteristics. Figure 12–7 shows a sample rating scale.

One of the major problems in using such scales is *halo effect*. Halo effect is the tendency of an observer to allow judgments of a number of specific characteristics to be affected by his general like or dislike for the person, or by his impression of some dominant trait like social poise or verbal ability. Thus, if we like a person, we may rate him high on all characteristics, even though he may not excel in everything.

One can partially surmount this difficulty by asking several observers to rate the same person. The degree of rater agreement gives us an estimate of the reliability of the rating scale. If ratings lack interobserver reliability, they are not very useful, since there is no way of determining whose ratings are the most valid.

One possible cause of rater disagreement is that the trait names used on the rating scale have different meanings for different raters. One of the most prevalent difficulties encountered by someone who is trying to construct a rating scale (or any type of questionnaire) is that a word or question will have different meaning for the test constructor than for the person answering the question. A person learns the meaning of words which describe personality by observing behavior and hearing it described by those words. Thus the more nearly the question asked of the rater refers to observable behavior rather than to an abstract trait, the more likely that it will be answered reliably and validly.

THE USE OF STANDARD SITUATIONS. Another possible source of rater disagreement is simply that the raters have observed behavior in different situations. The obvious solution to this problem is to set up standard situations. When the Office of Strategic Services (OSS) assessed the personality of candidates for important secret World War II jobs, it attempted to overcome some of the difficulties of observation by setting up standard situations in which each candidate was observed. These situations were carefully chosen to elicit the dimensions which were believed to be important for success in the OSS. The following is an example of the tests.

■ Ostensibly this was a test of the candidate's ability to direct two helpers in building with him a frame structure out of simple wooden materials. Actually the situation was not so benign as it first appeared. To be sure, it was a test of leadership, but more truly it was intended to be a test of emotional stability and frustration tolerance. Energy and initiative in carrying out the work and the social relations of the candidate with his helpers were also rated.

The building materials for this test were wooden poles of two lengths (five and seven feet), wooden blocks with sockets into which the poles could be fitted, and small pegs to hold the poles and blocks together. This equipment was a great magnification of the "tinker-toy" sets of childhood. With this, each candidate was directed to build a five-foot cube with seven-foot diagonals on the four sides.

In his instructions the candidate was told "This is a construction problem, but even more important than that, it is a test of leadership. I say that because it is impossible for one man working alone to complete this task in the ten minutes allotted to do it. Therefore we are going to give you two helpers who work here on the estate. You are to be supervisor, their boss. You are to guide them in their work, but as foreman, you will follow more or less of a hands-off policy. Let them do the manual labor. You can assume that they have never done such work before and know nothing about it. Any questions? (Final pause to amplify any details not understood by the candidate.)

"All right. It is now ten o'clock. You have just ten minutes in which to do the job. I'll call your two helpers."

At this, the two assistants, who had been working in the barn, were asked to come out and help the candidate. They complied, but waited for him to take the initiative. These two members of the junior staff traditionally assumed the pseudonyms of Kippy and Buster. Whoever played the part of Kippy acted in a passive, sluggish manner. He did nothing at all unless specifically ordered to, but stood around, often getting in the way, either idling with his hands in his pockets or concerned with some insignificant project of his own, such as a minute examination of the small-scale model. Buster, on the other hand, played a different role. He was aggressive, forward in offering impractical suggestions, ready to express dissatisfaction, and quick to criticize what he suspected were the candidate's weakest points.

The two assistants, by their secret instructions, were not permitted to disobey orders, and they were supposed to carry out whatever directions were given to them explicitly. Within the bounds of this ruling, though, it was their function to present the candidate with as many obstructions and annoyances as possible in ten minutes. As it turned out, they succeeded in frustrating the candidates so thoroughly that the construction was never, in the history of S (the camp), completed in the allotted time.   (From the OSS Assessment Staff *Assessment of Men: Selection of Personnel for the Office of Strategic Services.* New York: Rinehart, 1948. Reprinted by permission.) ■

The OSS used, as observers, psychologists who had been trained in what to look for as well as in the use of the rating scales which were employed. Unfortunately there was little systematic appraisal of the success of the assessment in predicting future behavior, so that the validity of this particular study is uncertain. However, the program did suggest an interesting way to combine observation of behavior and rating techniques.

In addition to ratings by experts and by colleagues, there is a third method: rating of oneself. Such self-ratings were used in the OSS project, and also in the research project concerned with the prediction of success in clinical psychology. Despite the likelihood of bias in one's own estimate of himself, in the clinical psychology study, self-ratings turned out to possess as much validity as ratings by experts.

PERSONALITY QUESTIONNAIRES. One instrument of personality assessment which is often used is the personality questionnaire. Here the respondent answers questions about himself by marking the appropriate alternative. A personality questionnaire can be considered a technique for obtaining samples of verbal behavior in response to standard verbal stimuli.

The questionnaire has a number of advantages. It is easy to administer, and it can be scored objectively. The objective scoring categories yield results which permit the establishment of test norms and the comparison of individuals and groups. Once the criterion of validation has been determined, it is easy to determine whether the scores meet the criterion.

Different personality tests have been constructed and validated on the basis of different criteria. Some have used empirical criteria leading to predictive and concurrent validity. Some have used statistical criteria leading to factorial validity. Some have used theoretical criteria leading to construct validity. We shall describe a questionnaire in each of these categories.

The *Minnesota Multiphasic Personality Inventory*, which is frequently referred to by its initials MMPI, consists of 550 statements. Some examples of the items are:

(a) I daydream very little.
(b) I sometimes put off till tomorrow what I should do today.
(c) I enjoy detective or mystery stories.
(d) I feel uneasy indoors.

The person taking the test sorts cards containing such statements into three piles: one for true statements, one for false statements and one for statements he feels he cannot answer.

The 550 items were selected because they differentiated between normal people and nine different groups of psychiatric patients; that is, each group has a different pattern of answering the questions. Certain items are good in differentiating one group from normals, others are good differentiators of other groups. Therefore the patterns of answers are divided into nine different scales, one for each psychiatric classification. For example, the paranoia scale, which is made up of selected items, separates people who are suspicious to a pathological degree from normals. The psychopathic deviation scale separates people who are completely unconcerned about the morality of their behavior from normals. Figure 12–8 shows the average scores of normal adolescents and juvenile delinquents on the nine scales.

The two profiles show *average* scores. On every scale, there are some normal people whose scores almost reach the pathological scores. This finding emphasizes again that these combinations of items measure dimensions of a personality characteristic, not discrete types.

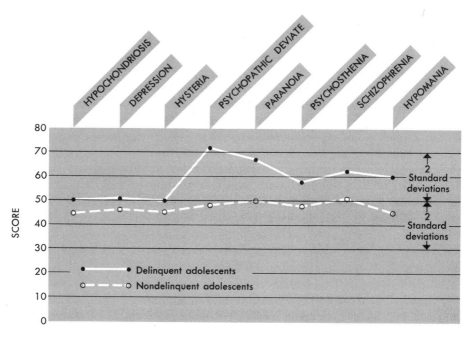

FIG. 12–8. The MMPI profiles of normal and delinquent adolescents. Note that the two groups differ from each other the most on psychopathy. (After Hathaway and Monachesi, 1953)

Note that the items were not selected because it seemed that they might show paranoia or psychopathy or any other psychiatric symptom. Nor was any theory employed to determine which items should indicate a form of maladjustment. The criterion was entirely empirical; those items which do successfully differentiate paranoids from normals were put into the paranoia scale regardless of the content.

The Cattell 16 Personality-Factor Test was developed by factor analysis. Cattell (1957) began with the list of trait names from Allport and Odbert (1936) and added words frequently used in psychological and psychiatric literature. Cattell and his students grouped all the words that were synonyms, discarded some words entirely, and wound up with a list of 171 characteristics. Then he obtained ratings for 100 adults on these characteristics and factor-analyzed the results. Finally, he sought questionnaire items that correlated highly with the factors which emerged from the factor-analysis of the ratings. The result was the Cattell 16 Personality-Factor Test. The factors measured by the scale include emotionality, excitability, dominance, cheerfulness, and hypersensitivity. Figure 12-9 shows certain words used in the ratings as well as some of the questionnaire items related to the factor of dominance versus submission.

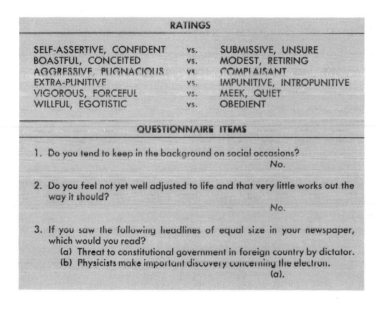

RATINGS		
SELF-ASSERTIVE, CONFIDENT	vs.	SUBMISSIVE, UNSURE
BOASTFUL, CONCEITED	vs.	MODEST, RETIRING
AGGRESSIVE, PUGNACIOUS	vs.	COMPLAISANT
EXTRA-PUNITIVE	vs.	IMPUNITIVE, INTROPUNITIVE
VIGOROUS, FORCEFUL	vs.	MEEK, QUIET
WILLFUL, EGOTISTIC	vs.	OBEDIENT

QUESTIONNAIRE ITEMS

1. Do you tend to keep in the background on social occasions?
   No.

2. Do you feel not yet well adjusted to life and that very little works out the way it should?
   No.

3. If you saw the following headlines of equal size in your newspaper, which would you read?
   (a) Threat to constitutional government in foreign country by dictator.
   (b) Physicists make important discovery concerning the electron.
   (a).

FIG. 12-9. Some ratings and some questionnaire items related to the dominance-submission dimension. These are similar to items used in the Cattell 16 Personality-Factor Test. (From Cattell, R. B., *The Scientific Analysis of Personality.* Baltimore: Penguin Books, 1965. Reprinted by permission.)

The Edwards Personal Preference Schedule is an example of the theoretical method of test construction in which the person who makes up the test includes items designed to expose particular personality characteristics. In this case the test is based on the system of motives originally proposed by Murray (1938). Table 12-1 lists the needs, proposed by Murray, which Edwards incorporated into his questionnaire. The test consists of pairs of statements, and the re-

TABLE 12-1   List of Murray's Needs*

Abasement.   To submit passively to external force. To accept injury, blame, criticism, punishment. To surrender. To blame, belittle, or mutilate the self.

Achievement.   To accomplish something difficult. To master or organize physical objects, human beings, or ideas. To overcome obstacles and attain a high standard.

Affiliation.   To draw near and enjoyably cooperate or reciprocate with an allied other (an other who resembles the subject or who likes the subject). To please and win affection. To adhere and remain loyal to a friend.

Aggression.   To overcome opposition forcefully. To fight. To oppose or punish another.

Autonomy.   To get free, shake off restraint, break out of confinement. To avoid or quit activities prescribed by domineering authorities. To be independent and free to act according to impulse. To defy convention.

Counteraction.   To master or make up for a failure by restriving. To obliterate a humiliation by resumed action.

Defendance.   To defend the self against assault, criticism, and blame. To conceal or justify a misdeed, failure, or humiliation.

Deference.   To admire and support a superior. To praise, honor, or eulogize. To yield eagerly to the influence of an allied other. To emulate an exemplar.

Dominance.   To control one's human environment. To influence or direct the behavior of others by suggestion, seduction, persuasion, or command. To dissuade or restrain.

Exhibition.   To make an impression. To be seen and heard. To excite, amaze, fascinate, entertain, shock, intrigue, amuse, or entice others.

Harmavoidance.   To avoid pain, physical injury, illness, and death. To escape from a dangerous situation. To take precautionary measures.

Infavoidance.   To avoid humiliation. To quit embarrassing situations or to avoid conditions which may lead to belittlement: the scorn, derision, or indifference of others. To refrain from action because of the fear of failure.

Nurturance.   To give sympathy and gratify the needs of a helpless object: an infant or any object that is weak, disabled, tired, inexperienced, infirm, defeated, humiliated, lonely, dejected, sick, mentally confused. To assist an object in danger. To feed, help, support, console, protect, comfort, nurse, heal.

Order.   To put things in order. To achieve cleanliness, arrangement, organization, balance, neatness, tidiness, and precision.

Play.   To act for "fun" without further purpose. To like to laugh and make jokes. To seek enjoyable relaxation of stress. To participate in games, sports, dancing, or cards.

Rejection.   To exclude, abandon, expel, or remain indifferent to an inferior object. To snub or jilt an object.

Sentience.   To seek and enjoy sensuous impressions.

Sex.   To form and further an erotic relationship. To have sexual intercourse.

Succorance.   To have one's needs gratified by the sympathetic aid of an allied object. To be nursed, supported, sustained, surrounded, protected, loved, advised, guided, indulged, forgiven, consoled.

Understanding.   To ask or answer general questions. To be interested in theory. To speculate, formulate, analyze, and generalize.

---

* Murray used the word *need* in the same way we have been using *motive*. (After Murray, 1938)

spondent must choose which of the pair he prefers. Examples of items from the Edwards test appear in Fig. 12–10.

LIMITATIONS OF PERSONALITY QUESTIONNAIRES. Because a questionnaire is such a straightforward, easily constructed method of assessing personality, hundreds of them have been constructed and many have been widely used. But they still have some liabilities. One problem in interpreting a person's questionnaire responses is the tendency of some subjects to agree with *any* opinion or statement, regardless of its content, and the tendency of some other subjects to disagree regardless of content (Messick and Jackson, 1961). This tendency to acquiesce (and the opposite tendency) can distort the test scores if the interpreter of the test is not aware of it.

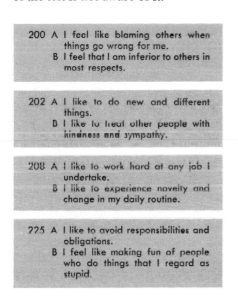

200 A I feel like blaming others when things go wrong for me.
    B I feel that I am inferior to others in most respects.

202 A I like to do new and different things.
    B I like to treat other people with kindness and sympathy.

208 A I like to work hard at any job I undertake.
    B I like to experience novelty and change in my daily routine.

225 A I like to avoid responsibilities and obligations.
    B I feel like making fun of people who do things that I regard as stupid.

FIG. 12–10. Some items from the Edwards Personal Preference Schedule. (Reprinted by permission of Psychological Corporation)

Another problem is that a person's score on a test depends in part on his willingness to tell the truth about himself. Frequently when a person takes a personality test he is motivated by the desire to present a distorted picture of himself. For example, a person applying for a job wants to present a socially desirable picture of himself. A person seeking help at a psychiatric clinic may intentionally try to present a highly unfavorable picture of himself.

Some designers of personality tests have tried to take these problems into account. For example, the Edwards Personal Preference Schedule gives respondents choices in pairs of statements that have been equated for social desirability. The MMPI has fifteen items which constitute a "lie" scale. These items describe minor faults characteristic of almost everyone. [Item (b) in the sample items on page 429 is an example of a lie-scale item.] If a person puts many of these items into a false category, the interpreter of the test concludes that the respondent's answers reflect an attempt to make a favorable impression. Such solutions are not always possible, and even some of the best of the current personality tests are susceptible to some faking. Thus personality questionnaires are most useful in situations in which the test taker is motivated by a wish to give a true picture of himself.

PROJECTIVE MEASURES. Because answers to questionnaires can be faked, and because such tests tend to provide information primarily about those aspects of personality which are conscious or are easily observed, psychologists have sought more indirect measures: projective tests. These tests attempt to alleviate both of the above drawbacks. Because they are so different from other devices used to measure personality, they seem mysterious and almost magical to the layman. They are, however, based on psychological principles with which you are already familiar.

As we have seen, perception is influenced by motivation. We have also seen that when we ask a person a direct question about his personality he may utilize his defense mechanisms to avoid damage to his self-esteem. Hence his answers are not always objectively true. Projective tests are based on the principle that the individual will reveal his deepest characteristics and feelings when his behavior is most unrestricted. From our study of perception you will recall that perception is largely determined by characteristics of the stimulus object, but that when the stimulus is ambiguous, motivation and previous learning or other individual factors are likely to influence interpretation. If we point to a picture of a chair and ask a patient what it is, he will probably answer "chair," and we learn very little about his personality. If we ask him "How are you?" he is likely to answer "Fine, thank you." On the other hand, if he is asked to do something for which there are no well-learned conventional responses, his feelings, motives, and personality characteristics are likely to guide his response. For example, we might ask a subject to describe another person. Insofar as our subject's description differs from that of other people's descriptions, we can obtain a measure of his personality.

In most projective tests the stimuli used are ambiguous; i.e., they have little apparent meaning. In *Van Lennep's Room Test*, subjects are asked to tell about a room, as pictured in Fig. 12–11. The descriptions subjects have given include such varied responses as the following.

■ "A friend's room, where the man is a guest."

"A room which is a historical museum visited by the man."

"A room which is a stage, watched by a large number of people."

By a shy girl: "The curtains had to be drawn so that she might be separated and undisturbed behind them."

By a paranoid (an abnormally suspicious person): "The curtains had to be removed because somebody might hide behind them." ■

FIG. 12–11. Van Lennep's room test. What story would you tell about this room? (Photo courtesy of Dr. D. J. Van Lennep)

So the same picture had different meanings for different people, depending on their motives and past experience.

Similarly, if we ask a person to tell what he sees in an ink blot, most of what he says must come from himself; not much is determined by the objective characteristics. Of course, some ink blots *do* look like bats or bears or birds, and the tendency to perceive, or not to perceive, such resemblances is one of the characteristics noted by the tester. By using the same ink blots for all people tested, psychologists can estimate how much of the perception of the ink blot is related simply to the stimulus characteristics of the blot and how much to the personality of the individual. The projective tests, then, give the subject more freedom of response than personality questionnaires do. His responses may vary on many dimensions, even though he is scored only on particular dimensions.

One of the most widely used projective personality measures, the *Rorschach Test*, actually uses ink blots as stimuli. If one drops a blot of ink on a paper and then folds the papers over upon the blot, he will find when he opens the paper something similar to Fig. 12–12.

What does the figure look like to you? To one person it might seem to be a raccoon skin; to another it might appear to be a teddy bear, with two paws, looking over a fence; to another it might look like two little boys back to back, with balloons in the shape of cows. There is no right or wrong answer. Different people see such blots differently. Some people see mostly small details;

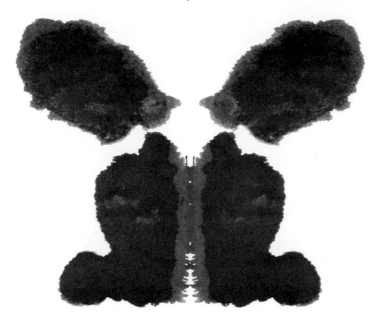

FIG. 12–12.   An ink-blot similar to the ones found in the Rorschach ink-blot test.

others see moving animals; still others see human figures. A Swiss psychiatrist, Hermann Rorschach, developed a series of such blots, and theorized that many of the underlying aspects of personality would be revealed in the way one responded to the ink blots.

Some standardized scoring methods have been developed for the Rorschach test. For example, when the person being tested reports that the ink blot resembles a person doing something, his response is scored as M; then the number of M responses for all the blots is totaled. Other responses are similarly categorized. Such dimensions of personality as conscious and unconscious anxiety, hostility, and creativity are believed to be revealed by the Rorschach test.

In the Rorschach test, as in the interview, the information gathered is synthesized by the person giving the test. This means that scoring involves subjective interpretation and provides an opportunity for the tester to project his own characteristics into his interpretation. No statistical norms exist for the Rorschach test, and all attempts at validation have been relatively unsuccessful. Recently, Holtzman (1959) has developed a new ink-blot test whose scoring system incorporates many of the hypotheses suggested by the theory and results of the Rorschach test. However, the administration and the scoring are more standardized in the new test. This has enabled Holtzman to begin to collect data on norms and to provide a firmer basis for future validation.

The Thematic Apperception Test, called the TAT, was the first test designed to tap the needs hypothesized by Murray. (The Edwards Personal Preference Schedule, which we described earlier, is an objective test developed later to measure the same needs.) The TAT consists of a series of pictures such as the sample shown in Fig. 12–13. The subject is asked to tell a story explaining the picture. The stories are interpreted on the assumption that themes prominent in these stories are reflections of motives important in the story-teller's life. (We described the scoring system for achievement motivation in Chapter 7.) Though there is some evidence that TAT scoring is reliable, there is little evidence of validity.

FIG. 12–13. A sample picture from the Thematic Apperception Test series. (Reprinted by permission of the publishers from Henry A. Murray, *Thematic Apperception Test.* Cambridge, Mass.: Harvard University Press, copyright, 1943, by the President and Fellows of Harvard College.)

Although projective measures have not been very successful in predicting behavior related to personality traits, many clinical psychologists feel that they are useful. In addition, some of them have proved effective for specific purposes in research. For example, the TAT is often used in research on achievement motivation.

OBJECTIVE MEASURES OF BEHAVIOR. Although all methods of measuring personality are essentially methods of measuring behavior, tests which involve nonverbal behavior in a standardized situation have been classified as *objective tests of behavior*.

Classic examples of such tests are the tests of honesty and self-control devised by Hartshorne and May (1928). Hartshorne and May attempted to measure honesty and self-control by setting up carefully controlled experimental situations in which presence or absence of these traits could be measured objectively. For example, children were given a classroom test. The papers were collected and the answers copied. The papers were then returned to the students, and the children were asked to score their own papers according to the correct answers given by the teachers. The child's score was then simply the number of answers which were changed or copied from the teacher's key. Other kinds of deceits which the experiment made possible at different times were: adding to one's work after time was called, faking the solution to a puzzle, cheating in games, and stealing money.

The results were disappointing to Hartshorne and May. Children who cheated in one situation did not necessarily cheat in another. The average correlation between tests of dishonesty was 0.23. The investigators concluded that honesty is not a generalized personality trait, but that honesty in any given situation depends on which behavior has been learned for that situation.

Modern statistical techniques have altered this interpretation. We mentioned earlier that factor analysis is often used to find underlying consistency among rather low correlations. When Burton (1963) reanalyzed Hartshorne's and May's data using factor analysis, he concluded that there *was* an underlying honesty factor to which each of the tests was related. According to Burton, behavior in tasks which permit cheating is determined by two categories of factors: a general honesty factor and factors specific to the situation.

The objective tests used to measure honesty have an obvious logical relationship to the trait being measured. Cattell (1965) and Eysenck (1952) have found that scores on certain objective tasks correlate with other indicators of personality traits even though there is no obvious relationship between the trait and the task. Emotional stability, realism, extroversion–introversion, and independence are among the dimensions for which batteries of objective tests have been devised. For example, when tests of dexterity are scored for speed and accuracy, extroverts do better on speed measures, introverts do better on accuracy. Similarly, people who are high on the dimension of neuroticism tend to have poorer scores on tests of two-hand coordination than emotionally stable people.

The advantage of such tests is that they are objective. Scores can be obtained which are not likely to be biased by the scorer's knowledge of the subject. Further, since the relationship of test scores to personality is not evident, there is less likelihood that the subject will fake his response. In fact, in most cases, he cannot simply decide to get a high score and do so, because the test requires maximum performance. Any one behavior test typically has only a low relationship to a particular personality trait. Thus when we measure a particular trait we need to obtain several types of measurements of objective behavior, establishing the validity of each in combination with the others to be included in the test battery. This is costly and time-consuming, but it is one of the fronts along which progress is being made (Cattell 1955).

Personality Assessment: a Summary

Varied methods of assessing personality are available, but each has certain advantages and disadvantages. Sociological variables, for example, are easily ascertained, but stereotypes are likely to distort judgments based on them. Interviewing a subject seems to strengthen confidence in judgment and understanding of a subject, but not to improve specific prediction of the subject's behavior. Ratings of observed behavior are subject to "halo effect" and to difficulty in sampling relevant situations, but normally involve behavior similar to that to be predicted. Personality questionnaires sample a wide variety of situations and behaviors but can sometimes be faked to give a good impression. Projective tests, although they have not been well validated, permit deeper characteristics to appear. Behavioral tests are difficult to fake; however, they are often difficult to administer.

Since one ultimate use of personality assessment is the prediction of behavior, the choice of an assessment technique often depends on the use to which the information is to be put. We thus turn now to a more extended consideration of problems of prediction.

How Are Personality Traits Used to Predict Behavior?

As we saw earlier, even when we have accurate measurements of personality characteristics, the task of making a prediction is difficult. The person who is assessing personality for purposes of prediction normally has three major tasks:

1. He must know which personality dimensions or traits are important to the determination of behavior in the situation for which he is trying to predict. (Note that this implies an assessment of the situation!)
2. He must assess these personality dimensions.
3. He must decide how to weigh the relative importance of each dimension in order to predict a particular kind of future behavior in the situation.

THE IMPORTANCE OF THE SITUATION. Trying to predict behavior simply by learning the important traits or dimensions of an individual's personality is usually unsuccessful unless one also considers the situation in which the individual is to act. The most common misuse of assessment has occurred when the examiner has assumed that a person with a high degree of a particular trait will manifest it in every situation. As we have already seen, this is not necessarily the case, and some trait assessments which have apparently turned out to be incorrect have been due to a lack of consideration of the situation for which predictions were made; the history of honesty tests is a good example of this. In predicting behavior one must evaluate the potentiality of the situation to elicit the values or traits constituting the personality, what Cattell (1965) calls the *psychological meaning* of a situation.

It would be helpful if we could classify situations in terms of dimensions just as we classify personalities. For example, situations may be characterized by greater or lesser degrees of freedom of choice of behavior or by warmer or colder interpersonal relations. A number of experiments have shown that our ability to predict behavior is improved when we consider variability both in individuals and in situations. There are situations in which practically everyone displays a particular kind of behavior; there are people who are so rigid that they display a particular kind of behavior in many situations. But there remain many situations where people act differently. For example, suppose that we wish to predict student ratings of the value of three courses: French, mathematics, and psychology. One such study (McKeachie, 1961) found that in general women students give more favorable ratings than men. But we can improve our predictions significantly if we also know each student's motive for affiliation, for in psychology the men who were high in the affiliation motive rated the course highest, while those who were low in the affiliation motive were less favorable. Knowing more about differences in situations, we can further improve predictions. Men who are high in the affiliation motive do best (in terms of grades) in classes taught by friendly, "warm" instructors.

PURE VERSUS MIXED MEASURES. Even when the situation for which we wish to predict behavior is quite clearly defined and limited, the problem of combining all we know about a person and deciding how much weight to give each dimension is difficult. Since predictions of behavior almost invariably involve consideration of a number of dimensions, it is frequently most efficient to use tests which are not pure tests of single dimensions, but rather involve the combination of a number of dimensions which are needed for important situations. For practical purposes the primary criterion for choosing a measure is that it makes valid predictions. Hence many of the selection tests used in industry represent combinations of abilities and personality traits rather than "pure" measures of a particular personality dimension.

STATISTICAL VERSUS CLINICAL PREDICTION. Because most predictions involve integrating a great deal of information, many psychologists have argued that only the human brain can successfully perform this task. Meehl (1954) has been particularly interested in determining which parts of assessing and predicting the psychologist can do effectively, given the results of objective tests and what computers can do more efficiently, given the same results. Meehl has collected a number of studies which compare predictions based on a statistical combination of several personality indices with the predictions of clinicians who have the same and perhaps additional data available. In almost every study, the statistical prediction was as good as, or superior to, the intuitive judgments of clinicians.

■ For example, Meehl describes a study by Wittman in which both psychiatrists and statisticians, using a statistical formula, predicted the degree of improvement of hospitalized schizophrenic patients. The statistical formula combined 30 variables which could be gleaned from the case history. Some of these variables were objective, such as marital status and duration of psychosis, while other variables depended on interpretations by the person writing the history, such as whether the patient was more anal- than oral-erotic. Of course, the same data were available to psychiatrists who made their prognosis without a formula. The results appear in Fig. 12–14. The figure shows that, in every category, the prediction by formula was superior to the intuitive combination of variables by the psychiatrists. ■

FIVE-STEP CRITERION CATEGORIES	NUMBER OF PATIENTS RATED	PERCENTAGE OF HITS BY SCALE	PERCENTAGE OF HITS BY PSYCHIATRISTS
REMISSION	56	90	52
MUCH IMPROVED	66	86	41
IMPROVED	51	75	36
SLIGHTLY IMPROVED	31	46	34
UNIMPROVED	139	85	49

FIG. 12–14. Clinical versus statistical prediction. The number of "hits" correct prognoses—by the objective scale exceeded the number of "hits" by the psychiatrists. (After Wittman, 1941)

Does this then mean that we should attempt to do away with people as judges of other people? No. As we have shown, we can successfully relieve the interviewer or judge of some of the task. But thus far our objective formulas are useful only in limited areas. Moreover, we not only lack adequate personality measures but also lack prediction equations for most of the situations for which we wish to predict. Furthermore, it is not usually economical to devise statistical formulas which take into account every possible special circumstance. It is these rare special circumstances which create situations which only human beings can detect. If we were trying to develop a test to pick mailmen to deliver mail during the Christmas rush, we could probably devise instruments which would predict very well for most cases, but an applicant with a broken leg, even though he passed the tests, would be eliminated by an interviewer. The chief danger in human assessment, however, is that the interviewer or assessor will overweigh unusual characteristics. When Meehl says that statistical prediction is superior to clinical prediction, he is talking about the *combining* of variables, not about measuring individual personality traits. There are many traits for which no valid tests are available. As we saw earlier, clinical ratings on such traits can be combined with objective test scores, resulting in more accurate predictions.

Examples of Successful Prediction

The importance of establishing and accurately measuring the basic dimensions of personality is illustrated by the many practical applications of such knowledge. Let us look at two examples.

PREDICTING ACADEMIC SUCCESS

It is of great value to a college to be able to predict which students will not attain passing grades. The expense of teaching a failing student is great not only in terms of extra time required of instructors and counselors but also because, when the teacher has several poor students in a class, his explanations to them are likely to be boring to the good students. Thus the interest and learning of the good students is impaired. More important, the frustration of failure may be damaging to the students. Therefore, both from the standpoint of the college and the student, intelligence tests are valuable.

We have pointed out that the interest in individual differences in intelligence stemmed largely from a desire to predict success in school. How well have Binet and his successors succeeded in this task?

Many of the readers of this book will have encountered one of the intelligence tests for college freshman, such as the Scholastic Aptitude Test of the College Entrance Examination Board. Figure 12–15 is a chart showing the scores of students on such a test and their grades in the first year of college.

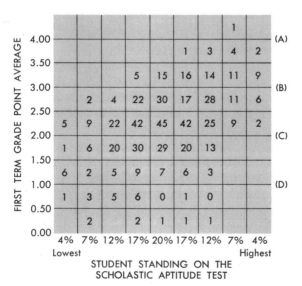

FIG. 12–15. The relationship between a student's standing on the Scholastic Aptitude Test and his average grades in his first term in college. (After Tyler, 1965)

We see that all but one of the students in the upper four percent, according to college student norms, made an average of 2.00* or better, whereas only 5 of the 13 students in the lowest four percent made averages of 2.00. Thus it appears that the intelligence test does not predict college grades perfectly, but that there is some relationship between the score on the intelligence test and college grades (about 0.4 to 0.5).

---

* Grade point averages are calculated at many schools based on the following scale: A = 4.00, B = 3.00, C = 2.00, and D = 1.00.

During World War II, the Army General Classification Test was given to ten million men. This test was made up of verbal, numerical, and spatial problems. One of the purposes of the test was to predict success of men in army training schools. The AGCT possessed high validity for predicting success in Officer Candidate School. Of those scoring over 140 on the tests, 91 percent received commissions. Of those scoring under 110, only 48 percent graduated and were commissioned.

PREDICTION OF MARITAL ADJUSTMENT

Can we predict whether or not two persons will be happy if they marry? Not as much work has been done on this problem as might be expected in light of its importance. Nevertheless, tests have been developed which predict marital adjustment with a moderate degree of success. Kelly (1939, 1955) studied 300 engaged couples and made follow-up studies two years and 20 years after marriage. He found that the personality tests predicted marital happiness as well as high school grades predict college grades (correlation about 0.5). Among the best predictors in such tests are questions about the happiness of the young couple's own families. Items assessing emotional stability have also proved to have some validity.

Can Personality Traits Help to Provide a Description of a Total Personality?

We have seen that combinations of scores on personality measures can be used to predict the behavior of groups of people in a particular situation. But there are many cases in which the psychologist is not so much interested in predicting which army recruits will be most successful officers or which couples will have happy marriages as he is in describing and understanding one person. In the following section we shall examine how studying the kinds of traits we have been discussing contributes to the understanding of an individual.

The Problem of Unique Traits

Some psychologists have pointed out that the description of an individual in terms of common dimensions must necessarily be incomplete. Each person, according to this view, has some traits he does not share with any other person. These unique traits would not emerge in studies which identify traits by comparing the responses of large groups of people. Such traits are formalized in our language by naming them for the people who uniquely possess them. For example, we speak of the Kennedy style, Xanthippian nagging, etc. According to this position, these special traits, although they may be related to common traits, have unique nuances (Allport, 1961).

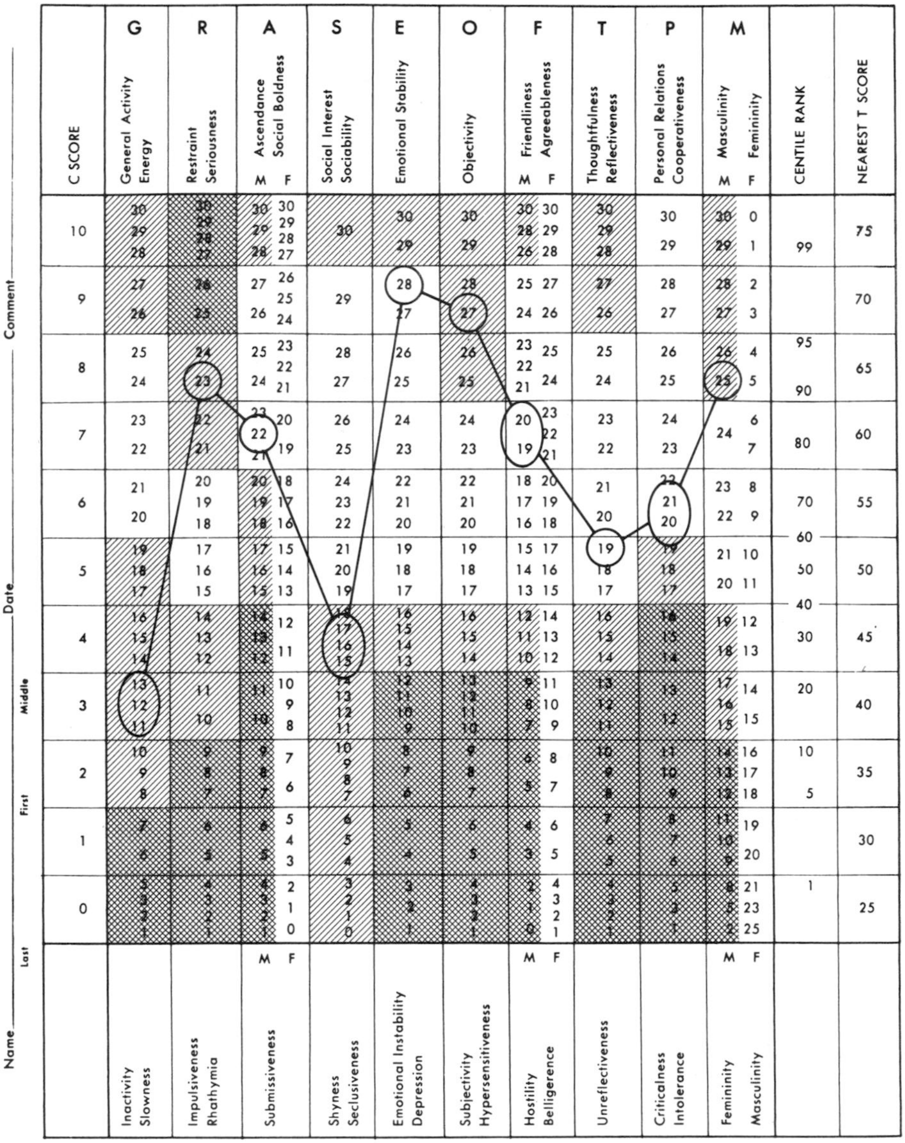

	G	R	A	S	E	O	F	T	P	M		
C SCORE	General Activity Energy	Restraint Seriousness	Ascendance Social Boldness (M F)	Social Interest Sociability	Emotional Stability	Objectivity	Friendliness Agreeableness (M F)	Thoughtfulness Reflectiveness	Personal Relations Cooperativeness	Masculinity Femininity (M F)	CENTILE RANK	NEAREST T SCORE

(data grid of scale values)

| | Inactivity Slowness | Impulsiveness Rhathymia | Submissiveness (M F) | Shyness Seclusiveness | Emotional Instability Depression | Subjectivity Hypersensitiveness | Hostility Belligerence (M F) | Unreflectiveness | Criticalness Intolerance | Femininity Masculinity (M F) | | |

FIG. 12–16. One individual's personality profile based on his answers to items in the ten scales of the Guilford-Zimmerman Temperament Survey, a personality questionnaire. (Copyright 1955, Sheridan Supply Co., Beverly Hills, Calif. Reproduced by permission.)

The approach that emphasizes the uniqueness of each individual personality is called the *idiographic* approach. Instead of studying individuals by looking at their scores on common personality measures, the idiographic psychologist looks at personal documents such as autobiographies and diaries, and to case histories for unique themes consistently appearing in the life of a single individual. However, despite the special attention given to each individual, such study has not led to improved prediction about individuals.

Few psychologists would argue with the statement that every individual is unique. However, many psychologists would argue that it is more fruitful, both for understanding and prediction, to capture the individual's uniqueness by means of descriptions in terms of common traits. For example, Cattell (1965) points out that everyone's nose has a different shape and everyone's fingerprints have a unique pattern of lines. Yet both can be described in terms of common physical dimensions. Similarly, the personality psychologist hopes to be able to describe the unique personalities of individuals in terms of common personality traits. Although people are described on the basis of common dimensions, each person's *pattern* of traits may be unique.

The Organization of Personality Traits

The pattern of a person's personality traits as revealed by tests is usually summarized in a personality profile. Given only a dozen or two dozen basic traits, the variety of patterns is enormous. There are enough possible patterns so that each individual could exhibit a profile unique to himself. Figure 12–16 shows an example of the profile of a person's personality.

Although a personality profile provides information about a person's position in regard to each trait, it tells us little about how the traits are organized or how they interact. One contribution of the idiographic approach has been to point up the fact that not every trait has the same significance to those who are trying to understand the personalities of many individuals. Conrad (1932) demonstrated this point with the following study.

■ Three teachers rated preschool children on 231 common traits. The correlations between the teachers' ratings were low, the median correlation being about 0.5. But the teachers were also asked to put stars beside their ratings on the traits which they considered "of central or dominating importance in the child's personality." On the starred traits, the inter-rater agreement was 0.95. ■

More recently psychologists have become interested in seeing whether they can find consistent differences in the organization of personality traits in different people. For example, psychologists have had some success in showing that the organization of traits in women seems to be different from that in men (Beloff, 1958; Kagan and Wallach, 1964; Livson and Bronson, 1961). Livson's and Bronson's study suggested that social adjustment and control of impulses were related in boys but that social adjustment was related to impulsiveness, not control of impulses, in girls. Research on differences in the organization of personality characteristics is still in its infancy, and we can expect exciting developments in this area in the next few years.

Summary

Concepts

Personality. The unique organization of relatively enduring characteristics possessed by an individual as revealed by his interaction with this environment

Personality trait. A combination of perceptual, conceptual, motivational, and act tendencies which gives rise to relatively stable, consistent behavioral dispositions in a class of situations

Reliability. The degree to which a test produces the same results in the same situation over time (assuming that no true change has occurred in the trait being measured)

Validity. The degree to which a test measures what it is supposed to measure as determined by a criterion; an empirical criterion in the case of predictive and concurrent validity—a theoretical criterion in the case of construct validity, and a statistical criterion in the case of factorial validity

Sensitivity. The range over which a test measures differences

Halo effect. The tendency of a rater to allow an overall judgment of a person to influence the ratings on particular traits

Idiographic approach. The approach to psychology which emphasizes the uniqueness of each personality and which uses methods such as the analysis of personal documents to understand a person's uniqueness.

Principles

1. Descriptions of personality in terms of types have declined because types include only a few people who are at the extremes of a number of personality-trait dimensions.

2. Personality traits have been identified and validated on empirical, statistical, and theoretical criteria.

3. Each personality trait represents a dimension on which an individual can score at any point.

4. Physical and sociological characteristics are inadequate bases for determining a person's personality characteristics.

5. Among the formal assessment techniques—interviews, ratings, personality questionnaires, projective tests, and objective tests of behavior—each has advantages and disadvantages. Interviews and projective tests have uncertain validity, though they are flexible and unstructured, thus permitting deep characteristics to emerge; ratings and questionnaires are objective and most easily validated, but are subject to halo effect and faking, respectively; objective measures of behavior are frequently difficult to administer.

6. Different personality traits become relevant in different situations; hence predictions based on traits are improved if the psychological meaning of the situation is known.

7. In many studies a statistical combination of personality variables produced more accurate predictions than clinical judgment based on the same variables.

8. There are individual differences in the *organization* of personality traits.

Suggested Readings

For material on the factor-analytic approaches to personality, read the following:

CATTELL, R. B., *The Scientific Analysis of Personality* Baltimore: Penguin Books, 1965.

EYSENCK, H. J., *The Structure of Human Personality*. London: Methuen, 1953.

Another more general approach is McCLELLAND, D., *Personality*. New York: Holt, 1951.

An idiographic orientation is found in ALLPORT, G. W., *Pattern and Growth in Personality*. New York: Holt, 1961.

the development of the person

chapter 13

EARLY INFANCY

THE SECOND YEAR

EARLY CHILDHOOD

LATER CHILDHOOD

ADOLESCENCE

ADULTHOOD

OLD AGE

The psychological differences between an infant and an adult are tremendous. The infant is helpless; the adult is independent, able to provide for himself. The infant is unaware of other people; the adult adjusts his behavior to the demands of society. The infant is unaware of himself as a person; the adult values his own identity. The infant has no conception of the future; the adult works for goals which are years ahead of him. The infant is not aware of differences between people; the adult develops friendship, loyalties, and love for others. The infant lives in a world of sensations and feelings; the adult lives in a world of ideas and values. This "miraculous" transformation takes place gradually as the individual learns to use his genetic endowment to cope with his physical and cultural environment.

In each of the chapters dealing with our basic constructs, i.e., percepts, motives, habits, etc., we have briefly discussed their developmental aspects separately. Now we want to draw together all these aspects and look at the developing person as he matures through infancy, childhood, and adolescence.

Early Infancy

The newborn infant is ill-equipped to face the world alone. His sensory apparatus is still not completely functioning. Both vision and hearing are less discriminating than those of an older child. His nervous system is immature, and he is unable to exert voluntary control over many of his muscles. Even if he could control them, his muscles are weak and he is unable to move any distance under his own power. The dimensions of space and time are without meaning to him. Periodically his stomach walls contract, or a pain or some other stimulus disturbs his womb-like existence and he cries and squirms until the disturbing feeling is gone. He may sleep 19 or 20 hours a day, waking only for brief periods for feeding. The development of a child's sleep cycle is depicted in Fig. 13–1.

His repertoire of responses is limited, but these few responses perform crucial functions. When he is hungry, if his cheek is touched, his head turns and his mouth opens to grasp the touching finger. When his lips or mouth are touched, he begins sucking. If you place your finger in his palm, he grasps it.

If he is to survive, his physical needs, such as hunger, thirst, and breathing must be satisfied. And despite the infant's lack of resources, his needs are satisfied. Five or six times a day he is fed. Someone miraculously appears when he cries, no matter what the hour of day or night. Whatever he needs appears as if by magic. But despite his apparent power he is, of course, helpless. One of the major trends of development is from the helplessness of the infant to the competence and adequacy of the mature adult.

The young baby is impatient. When he is hungry, he wants to be fed *now*. Within a few weeks his visual acuity develops to the point that he can see details of a face above him, but it is not until he is about three months old that he begins

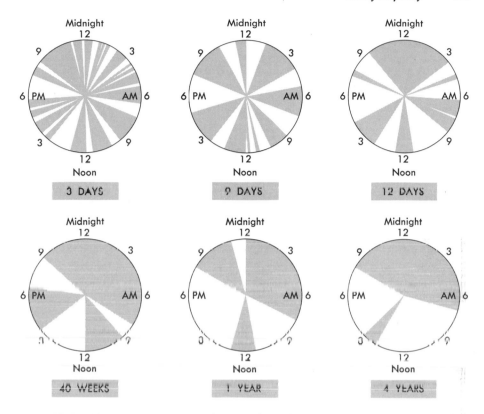

FIG. 13-1. Changes in a child's sleep cycle with age. Sleep periods are shaded.

to quiet when he sees his mother coming to feed him. This marks the beginning of one of the most important attributes of the civilized human being, the ability to anticipate and to wait.

Individuality in Infancy

Despite these common, primitive modes of interacting with his surroundings, each baby copes with his environment differently. One infant eats well, another does not. One is active; another placid. One is happy; another cries a great deal. While differences between newborn babies are smaller than those between older children, babies do display individual characteristics which distinguish them one from another. These early characteristics show some stability. Thomas (1963) collected ratings of a number of infants on such traits as social responsiveness, mood quality, distractibility, and persistence. The babies were rated on six different occasions during their first two years. Throughout this period, successive ratings for each infant were consistently similar to that infant's earlier ratings.

Thus the developing person is not a passive recipient of environmental influences. Development is an active process. Sometimes we attribute adult individuality to environment alone, forgetting that the environment which contributed to development was itself influenced by the characteristics of the baby. For example, if a baby laughs and gurgles whenever he hears music, he is actually rewarding his parents for providing music and is encouraging them to provide it more frequently. Similarly, if the baby does not eat well, the mother becomes anxious. She is likely to blame herself. Her concern and anxiety may be communicated to the baby and in turn increase his difficulty in adapting to his environment. On the other hand the happy, healthy baby eases the normal anxiety of the mother and she begins to relax, to develop more confidence in her ability to be an adequate mother, and to enjoy caring for the baby.

The Impact of the Environment

To what extent can the nature of the environment affect an infant who can hardly perceive, or control his muscles, or conceive of the future? Both clinical observation and precise experimentation demonstrate the importance of the environment even in these earliest months of life.

Spitz (1945) studied babies in two institutions as well as control groups of infants reared in their own homes. In one of the institutions, which we will call the Nursery, infant mortality was low.

■ "The problem here (in the Nursery) is not whether the children walk or talk by the end of the first year; the problem with these 10-month-olds is how to tame the healthy toddlers' curiosity and enterprise. They climb up the bars of the cots after the manner of South Sea Islanders climbing palms. Special measures to guard them from harm have had to be taken after one 10-month-old actually succeeded in diving right over the more than two-foot railing of the cot. They vocalize freely and some of them actually speak a word or two. And all of them understand the significance of simple social gestures. When released from their cots, all walk with support and a number walk without it."*

In the other institution, called the Foundling Home, children showed susceptibility to infection and illness. Many of the babies died. Those that survived developed slowly; of the 26 children between one-and-a-half and two-and-a-half years of age, only two could walk or speak any words. ■

What had caused these differences? Could hereditary factors account for these findings? The parents of the babies in the Nursery were delinquent girls, many of whom were feeble-minded. In the Foundling Home the parents were of varied backgrounds, some similar to the parents of the Nursery children. Others, however, were normal mothers who were simply unable to support their children.

* From Spitz, R. A., "Hospitalism," in O. Fenichel *et al.* (eds.), *The Psychoanalytic Study of the Child*, Vol. 1. New York: International Universities Press, 1945. Reprinted by permission.

Although it seems unlikely that hereditary factors could account for the superior health and development of the Nursery children, we do not know enough about the parents to eliminate this as a possibility.

Could the differences be due to sanitary conditions? Both institutions sterilized bottles and prepared adequate foods to meet the needs of the individual child. Hygienic conditions were carefully maintained. Both institutions provided adequate medical care. Hence it seems unlikely that hygienic features could account for the differences in the babies' development.

What differences did exist which might account for Spitz' observations? Two factors seem to be of particular importance. One of these was the degree of stimulation. In the Nursery every child had toys to play with and could see out of his crib into a corridor with mothers and their babies bustling around; he could see and hear other babies in their cribs; he could see trees and sky outside. However, in the Foundling Home few children had toys to play with, and sheets were hung over the foot and sides of the beds so that the babies could see only the ceiling.

The second factor was the care of the child. In the Foundling Home the 45 babies were cared for by six nurses. In the Nursery each baby was cared for by its own mother or by another of the girls in the institution. Because the mothers had few other interesting activities they spent much time with their babies and gave them a great deal of attention, cuddling, and care.

The Spitz observations were neither well-controlled nor clearly reported, but they do suggest interesting hypotheses. Not only do they suggest hypotheses about the importance of perceptual stimulation and maternal care but also the more general hypothesis that there may be critical periods in the development of the child. How can we test these hypotheses? We obviously cannot set up a controlled experiment with human infants. However, two lines of study help to clarify the issues. One is a series of animal studies in which the experimenter can manipulate the relevant conditions. The other is a series of observations of children in institutions in which certain conditions varied naturally. Here is some of the evidence:

White rats, reared in an environment which provides varied visual and tactual stimulation, are, when mature, more intelligent and less emotional than other white rats who have been restricted in infancy (see Fig. 13–2). (Levine, 1960; Beach and Jaynes, 1954) Similar experiments with dogs indicate that, as compared with dogs raised in a varied environment, dogs reared in a restricted environment are not only less intelligent but are also socially deficient. For example, the restricted dogs are more likely to ignore strange dogs (Clarke *et al.*, 1951). Studies of cats reared in darkness showed that early visual pattern stimulation is important for subsequent eye coordination and discrimination of movement. Animals reared in darkness do not show normal fear responses to strange objects (Riesen, 1961). That such results may be generalized to human infants is indicated by the studies reviewed in Chapter 10, which showed that early adoption of children was related to the development of intelligence. Early stimulation and freedom thus appear to be important factors in development.

We also have evidence from animal research about the second factor that might account for Spitz' results. In Chapter 7, "Motivation," we described how monkeys seemed to have a need for cudding, and the presence of their terry-cloth "mothers" seemed to give them security enough to explore the environment rather than to cower in a corner. Thus "mothering" is probably also important in the development of emotional security.

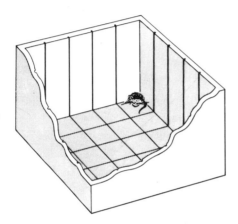

FIG. 13–2. The Open Field Test, which is a test for emotionality in rats, is based on the finding that nonanxious rats tend to explore a new environment, while anxious rats tend to huddle in a corner. Thus the number of squares a rat traverses in a set period of time is an index of emotionality. Rats who received daily tactual stimulation in infancy tended, as adults, to explore many more squares than non-stimulated rats. Here, an adult rat who received little tactual stimulation in infancy is shown in the open field test. (After Levine, 1960)

But "mothering" involves more than tactual contact such as that the baby monkeys obtained from their terry-cloth mothers. The monkeys raised with terry-cloth mothers got along fine in infancy, but as compared with monkey-mothered monkeys they later showed some interesting deficiencies. They tended to be retarded in play activities; they more frequently exhibited rocking, self-hugging, biting themselves, inward-directed activity; and, most important, they failed to develop normal friendly relationships with other monkeys. As they matured to adulthood the cloth-mothered monkeys were ineffective sexually and were inadequate mothers (Harlow, 1961).

These results are similar to those obtained when monkeys are reared in isolalation (Mason, 1961), and no doubt have already reminded you of the imprinting studies reported in Chapter 4. You will recall that in such species as ducks, chicks, and fish, an animal may be attached to a "parent" object if it is exposed to that object during a brief period in infancy and will follow that object some time later, even after being separated from it for a long time. Like Harlow's monkeys, animals imprinted in this manner fail to develop normal gregarious and sex responses to members of their own species. Among monkeys the critical period for such experience does not seem to be as fixed as it is in the species used in imprinting research, but once an infant monkey has been exposed to a real monkey mother, it is difficult to satisfy him with a terry-cloth substitute.

■ A study of institutionalized children by Pringle and Bossio (1960) also suggests that the same institutional situation will have different effects, depending on the ages at which the children entered it. The investigation involved testing children between the ages of eight and 14 on both intellectual and personality development. Some of the children had been in the institution since before their fifth birthday; others had come to live there after their fifth birthday. There were both intellectual and emotional differences between the two groups. Whereas the two groups were comparable on nonverbal sections of the intelligence test, the earlier-entering children performed more poorly on the verbal section of the intelligence test and on other tests of language development. Furthermore, a larger number of the earlier-entering children showed anxiety about adult affection, restlessness, depression, and hostility to adults and children. ■

Bronfenbrenner (in press), after reviewing a number of studies on institutionalized children, concluded that the most serious and long-lasting consequences followed institutionalization before the age of six months.

If one of the causes of the poorer intellectual and emotional development of institutionalized infants is lack of stimulation, their development should be facilitated by additional stimulation. Casler (1965) demonstrated that this could be done. He gave one group of institutional babies extra tactile stimulation for a period of 10 weeks. Then he administered the Gesell developmental schedule to these infants and to other infants who had not received the special treatment. Casler found that the babies who experienced the extra stimulation reached a higher level of development than the other babies.

These studies show the general effect of an infant's environment on his development. They imply that despite his apparent oblivion to many events around him, the infant is extremely sensitive to the people and the things with which he has contact. The degree of this sensitivity is suggested by some observations by Escalona (1945).

■ In a prison nursery a baby's preferences for orange juice versus tomato juice corresponded to the preference of the nurse who regularly fed him. When three of the babies were switched to the care of a woman with the opposite preference, these babies' preferences changed to match those of their new nurses. ■

It is difficult to see how the baby knew which juice his nurse preferred. We can only guess that the nurse or mother communicates her feelings to an infant through the way she holds him, through her facial expressions, tone of voice, degree of impatience, or other physical ways. This also seems to account for the following observation.

■ The babies in the prison nursery seemed much more likely to have upset stomachs on Thursday than on other days of the week. Since there seemed to be no difference in food or routine on Thursdays, Escalona looked elsewhere for the cause. She found that Thursday was the day on which the parole board met. Many of the mothers were concerned about their chances for parole and as a result tension was high. Apparently this tension was communicated to the babies and then was revealed in their digestive disorders. ■

While such observations are not conclusive, it seems probable that the mother's feelings are communicated to her baby. The studies suggest that some influences on an infant's personality development may be unverbalized and unintentional. Basic parental attitudes may be communicated even though the mother, herself, may not be aware of them.

What sort of conclusion can we draw from all these observations? We have two sources of evidence; studies of naturally occurring variations in infants' environments, such as those reported by Spitz and Escalona, and experimental studies of animals, such as those of Levine and Harlow. Both sources of data suggest that visual, tactual, and social stimulation are important factors in intellectual development, in the emotional security of the infant, and in determining later social responses.

The Development of Physical Self-Awareness

During early infancy the baby chews on his big toe and cries because something hurts, but keeps on chewing because he does not realize that he is biting his own toe. Differentiation of one's own body from the environment is obviously not well developed at this age. He feels one hand with the other, each hand feeling and being felt. Only his own body (not an external object) possesses this characteristic of feeling when it is touched and it is from such exploration that he learns the boundaries of himself. By the age of six months he has begun to solve the problem of discriminating himself from others and he not only knows that his toes are part of himself, but distinguishes people from other external objects, recognizes his parents, and may be shy with strangers.

Feeding Practices

Freudian theory suggests that a major part of a baby's pleasure in this early period comes from eating and other oral stimulation. It further suggests that frustration surrounding eating could have profound effects on later behavior. As a result of such theorizing a number of students have examined a variety of practices to see if any generalization could be made about their effects on later development. For example, some psychologists hypothesized that breast feeding would lead to greater emotional security than bottle feeding. Efforts to verify this hypothesis have been generally negative (Orlansky, 1949). Other psychologists have examined weaning as an event with later repercussions. When a baby nurses, he gets not only nourishment but also physical contact with his mother. At weaning the latter source of gratification is removed. Therefore, it has been suggested that the earlier weaning takes place, the more likely it is that the event will leave an emotional scar. Again, however, careful research has not demonstrated such simple relationships (Caldwell, 1964).

In analyzing these negative results, most psychologists agree that the important variable is probably the general attitude of the parents rather than any specific practice. With either breast or bottle feeding the mother may be either confident, relaxed and loving, or rigid, cold, and rejecting. Heinstein (1963) found that the most important single variable associated with feeding which related to later maladjustment was the warmth or coldness of the mother—as evaluated by an interviewer—rather than type of feeding and age of weaning. Another study suggests that the age at which weaning is begun is not nearly so important as the amount of frustration connected with it. Children who have experienced severe frustration in nursing and weaning are more likely to be dependent than other children (Sears *et al.*, 1953).

The Development of Trust

Erikson (1963) has suggested that in each stage of development, the individual must cope with a critical problem whose resolution results in the development of an important personality characteristic. In this earliest period of living, Erikson believes, the child develops a basic sense of trust or mistrust. Periodically the infant feels the discomfort of hunger or cold or pain from illness. Frequently he is exposed to unfamiliar people and places, and mother occasionally disappears. If the child discovers that these temporary frustrations will be overcome, and that he can rely on his providers, his environment, and himself to restore consistency and continuity to his life, he develops a basic sense of trust in the world and himself.

Erikson's ideas are supported by clinical observations by Spitz. Spitz (1946) described the reactions of six- to eight-month-old children who were suddenly separated from their parents for about a month. Here is a typical description:

■ "White female. Intelligent, friendly child who smiles easily and ecstatically at the approaching observer. No notable event in the course of the first seven months. At this time (seven months) a change occurred in the child. The observers got the feeling that the child was apprehensive. A week or two later the change was accentuated. The temper of the child had become unequal. She still was most friendly to the observer, but as often as not broke out crying when the observer approached closer. After another two weeks she could no longer be approached. No amount of persuasion helped. Whenever approached she sat up and wailed. Two weeks later, she would lie on her face, indifferent to the outside world, not interested in the other children living in the same room. Only strong stimulation could get her out of her apathy. She would then sit up and stare at the observer wide-eyed, a tragic expression on her face, silent. She would not accept toys, in fact, she withdrew from them into the farthest corner of her bed. If the approach was pressed she would break into tears. This went on until the child was nine months old."* ■

In such cases, the infants had learned to expect the continuing presence of a loving mother. Her disappearance and the consequent disappearance of her love

---

* From Spitz, R. A., "Anaclitic depression," in O. Fenichel *et al.* (eds.), *The Psychoanalytic Study of the Child*, Vol. 2. New York: International Universities Press, 1946. Reprinted by permission.

destroyed the developing sense of trust which could be regained only by the restoration of someone's consistent presence and love. Interestingly, these emotional reactions to separation do not occur if separation occurs before six months. However, in terms of later development, the earlier separation has more serious consequences (Bronfenbrenner, in press). Thus the development of trust during the first six months is advantageous even if it is followed by temporary emotional upheaval due to temporary separation.

Unless a child can develop some inner expectancies which are closely related to outer reality, his first experiences will teach him that he is a helpless creature in a confusing, unstable world. There is even some evidence that consistent *rejection* by parents produces less anxiety and confusion than vacillation between love and rejection (Hutt and Miller, 1949). This discussion does not imply that parents can be or should be completely consistent. The baby must learn, too, that his environment will not provide perfect sameness. But if a baby grows up experiencing a world in which frustrations will be overcome, in which he can depend on continuing care and love from his parents, he develops a sense of trust which may provide emotional support throughout his life.

The Second Year

In the second year, a child acquires many new skills, faces physical and parental restrictions more frequently, and becomes increasingly more aware of himself as an independent individual.

Walking

We have already discussed the maturational and learning process involved in the development of locomotion (see Fig. 13–3). Here walking is important to us as a skill which greatly changes the infant's relation to the world around him. Now that he can stand on his own feet, he is able to exert much more control over his environment. He is no longer quite so dependent on his mother. The first step not only marks progress in locomotion, but is also a step toward independence, and his parents' joy reinforces the child's feeling of mastery and self-esteem in his still developing skill. By the age of 16 months, when most children are walking, the child continually practices his newfound skill and his mother often has difficulty keeping track of him.

The development of walking increases the child's freedom to explore and manipulate his environment. But with the increased freedom comes increased awareness of restriction. The child is prevented from walking into the street, from touching an electrical outlet, from pulling down a lamp. Typically, a middle-class child will face more restrictions than a lower-class child, since in a middle-class household, furniture, lamps, knickknacks and books are highly valued. Of course some restrictions are necessary, both for the maintenance of order in the home and for communicating the fact that behavior must be governed by

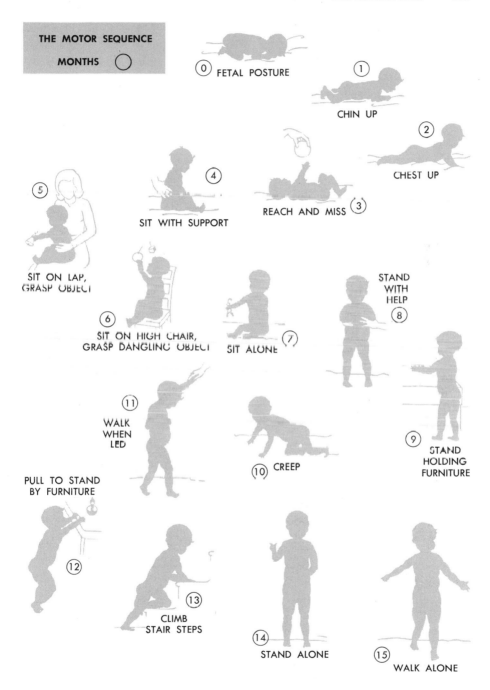

THE MOTOR SEQUENCE

MONTHS ◯

0 FETAL POSTURE

1 CHIN UP

2 CHEST UP

3 REACH AND MISS

4 SIT WITH SUPPORT

5 SIT ON LAP, GRASP OBJECT

6 SIT ON HIGH CHAIR, GRASP DANGLING OBJECT

7 SIT ALONE

8 STAND WITH HELP

9 STAND HOLDING FURNITURE

10 CREEP

11 WALK WHEN LED

12 PULL TO STAND BY FURNITURE

13 CLIMB STAIR STEPS

14 STAND ALONE

15 WALK ALONE

FIG. 13–3. The locomotor sequence which culminates in walking. (Adapted from Shirley, Mary, *The First Two Years: A Study of Twenty-Five Babies*, 1931. Courtesy of University of Minnesota Press.)

certain rules. These restrictions need not be harmful so long as the child finds some *consistency* in the limits that are placed on him, and so long as these limits are not so restricting that they prevent opportunity for normal exploration and mastery of the environment.

As the child learns to walk, the mother's satisfactions and frustrations change. She is no longer the protector of a completely helpless baby. Some mothers long for the past satisfaction of caring for the young infant and resent his growing independence. Others try to spare him the normal frustrations of living. When such attitudes are expressed with constant assistance and restriction, the child is likely to become dependent, feeling incapable of coping with any problem alone. This is particularly likely to occur when the child is suffering from some injury or disease. Parents of a handicapped child may do so much for him that he fails to develop his potential and learns to accept a completely dependent role.

Cleanliness Training

The second year of life also brings another social demand upon the developing baby. Toilet training may begin late in the baby's first year, and it is usually completed in American society by the third year. The difficulty of this problem for the child depends upon his degree of maturation when training is begun. Sears *et al.* (1957) found that children whose toilet training is initiated at an unusually early or an unusually late age showed the most emotional upset during training.

One of the most important aspects of toilet training is that to some degree the child is able to control the situation and to test his growing sense of independence. He can express his feelings toward his mother or father by his cooperation or lack of cooperation in toilet training. Nothing angers a parent more than to have a good dress or carpet soiled by a child who is supposed to be toilet trained. Thus the toilet training situation may be one which provides a learning experience in reactions to authority. Investigations of child rearing practices indicate that this is particularly true by the age of one-and-a-half to two. Most mothers do not hold the very young child responsible for such accidents, but they interpret accidents in older children as disobedience and punish children accordingly. A typical answer to the question, "What do you do about it when she has accidents after she is mostly trained?" is "I would reprimand and scold her, and if that didn't work, then I'd give her a few slaps on the behind."

In toilet training, as in feeding, the details of the training procedure seem to be less important than the interpersonal context in which training occurs. When the mother is relatively cold and unaffectionate, the more severe the toilet training, the more likely the child is to become emotionally upset. However, severity seems to make little difference for children of warm, affectionate mothers. (Sears *et al.*, 1957)

Learning to Feed Himself

Another important skill for the child is feeding himself. This is not a completely happy experience for either parents or child. After all, the child has developed considerable skill first in sucking and then in drinking and eating food from cups and spoons held by his mother; now he is asked to give up this pleasurable, easy method of satisfying hunger for one which is much less efficient and which also gets him into trouble more often.

However, he is also motivated to master the feeding situation himself. Spoons and glasses are complex tools for the one- to one-and-a-half-year-old, but to make them work may be a stronger motive than hunger at times. His clumsy messiness is likely to be irritating to his parents. They are pleased that he wants to feed himself, but displeased when he spills his milk. In fact his messiness may cause his mother to feel that it is more trouble to clean up after him than to feed him, and consequently she may discourage him from feeding himself. Other mothers may force the child to feed himself, but punish him when he spills things. Here again is a situation, repeated a thousand times a year, in which the child's attitudes and behavior are shaped by his parents in the development of independence.

Language Learning

A language opens up tremendous new possibilities for the child. During the first year of his life, words have been used to control him as well as to encourage him. Now he can use words to attract attention. He can ask for things and sometimes receive them. He can think and communicate his thoughts. He can refer to himself. We should not assume that his self-concept has been nonexistent prior to this time, for his parents' love and care have already laid the basic foundation for his self-acceptance and self-esteem. But as he acquires language his parents are able to use words to describe him and his actions, and he begins to build into his self-concept more differentiated aspects of his "goodness," "badness," "cuteness," and "boyness." All of these are important in developing his concept of himself in relation to the world he lives in.

Sibling Rivalry

Often at this age another problem faces the first child. A second baby is born. The first child has been an only child. All of his parents' love and attention have been his. This may be one factor which is responsible for the result we described earlier: the older children tend to develop a motive for affiliation which leads them to seek companionship in times of stress to a much greater extent than their younger siblings (Schachter, 1959). Now the older child must share his parents' love with someone else. What will he do? In some cases he competes for attention. Sometimes the competition takes the form of extra-good behavior, over-helpfulness, and perfect obedience. In other cases the demand for attention may take the form of "bad" behavior which not only expresses aggression but which is so annoying that the parents are forced to pay attention.

The more closely people are associated the more likely they are to come into conflict, but also the more necessity there is for control of aggression. In our society, direct aggression against younger brothers or sisters is likely to be severely punished, and the child is taught that he is supposed to "love brother." Other societies handle sibling rivalry differently. For example, the Kwoma tribe in New Guinea praises older children for bullying younger children so long as no serious injury is done. As a result the Kwoma youth does not learn to feel guilty and remorseful about rivalry with his siblings. Even within our culture, parents handle sibling rivalry differently. When the mother is over-solicitous or discipline is inconsistent, rivalry seems to be accentuated (Sewall, 1952). Thus, although the rivalry situation is similar in all families with more than one child, the manner in which the situation is handled may differ from culture to culture and family to family.

General Trends

Two general themes throughout all these specific problem areas are the growth of the child's awareness of himself and his abilities, and an increase in the amount of discipline which thwarts the growing autonomy.

THE EFFECT OF PUNISHMENT. Freudian theory suggests that severe discipline at this stage is conducive to long-lasting personality distortions. That a child experiences some punishment is inevitable. For example, yanking a child away from a car may be punishing but it is also effective in saving his life. But the child who is punished a great deal begins to see himself as "bad" on the one hand, and defends himself with hostility and aggression toward others on the other hand. At least clinical observations would suggest this.

Some survey evidence indicates that attempts to control behavior with punishment alone are not even effective for producing the desired change.

■ A group of researchers interviewed 379 mothers in two suburban New England towns to find out what their child-rearing practices were and what effects these practices had on their children. One of the variables studied was the amount of punishment used. They concluded that punishment is "ineffectual over the long term as a technique for eliminating the kind of behavior toward which it is directed." Mothers who reported using a high level of punishment in toilet training ended up with bedwetting children; mothers who reported punishing dependency reported their children were more dependent than other children; mothers who reported punishing aggressive behavior severely in early childhood reported more aggression at the time of the interview than did other mothers. (Sears, Maccoby, and Levin, 1957) ■

The interview study, which is necessarily limited by the degree of accuracy of perception and the willingness of the mothers to be truthful, is supported by other studies. One of the outstanding findings is that children who are disciplined by physical punishment tend to be more aggressive than others *even if they are being punished for aggression** (Sears *et al.*, 1962, Eron *et al.*, 1961). There are three hypotheses to account for this finding (Becker, 1964): (1) the frustration-aggression hypothesis, (2) the imitation hypothesis, and (3) the reinforcement hypothesis.

(1) The frustration-aggression hypothesis assumes that aggression is a natural outcome of frustration (Dollard *et al.*, 1939). Since physical punishment is frustrating, the effects of punishment would be to increase aggression, no matter what the punishment is given for.

(2) The imitation hypothesis states that children who experience aggression through physical punishment become aggressive because they are imitating the behavior of their parents. A study by Bandura, Ross, and Ross (1963a) shows that children do, in fact, imitate aggression that they observe:

■ Nursery school children were divided into three groups. One group saw a film showing an adult being aggressive toward a large plastic inflated doll, the other group saw a film showing a nonaggressive adult. A third group did not see either one. All the children were then mildly frustrated. The children who had seen the aggressive adult tended to show the most aggression; the children who had seen the nonaggressive adult were least aggressive. In addition, the children who saw the aggressive adult on the film tended to imitate the exact forms of aggression they had seen. Figure 13–4 shows some frames of the films that the children saw and some frames of films taken of the children's behavior. ■

(3) The reinforcement hypothesis states that parents who use physical punishment on their children also tend to encourage their children to be aggressive toward their peers. There is mixed evidence for this hypothesis. Bandura (1960) found that mothers who were highly punitive were more permissive when their sons expressed aggression toward peers and siblings. This was not true of highly punitive fathers. Becker *et al.* (1960) found that a mother who uses a great deal of physical punishment also believes that her children should "fight for their rights" among their peers.

Whatever hypothesis turns out to be correct (and it is likely that all three will play a role in the explanation), it is clear that wide use of physical punishment may do more to teach aggressive behavior than to teach the child to avoid the specific acts for which he is being punished.

---

* This relationship is found in the early years of infancy and childhood. There is some evidence that continued punishment for direct aggression during the school years does lead to displaced aggression. (Sears, 1961)

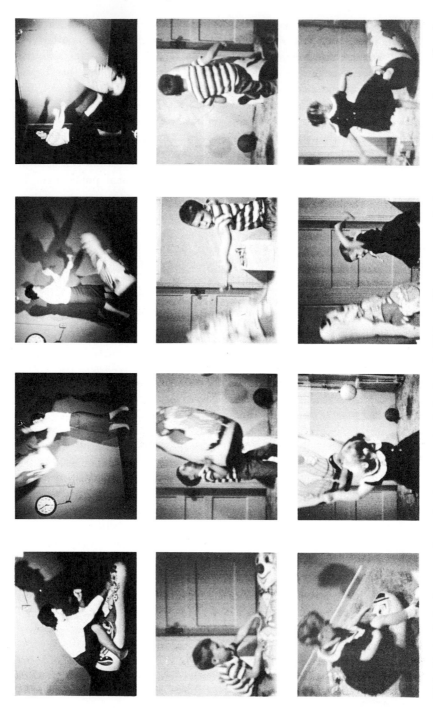

FIG. 13–4. Imitation as a factor in the aggressive behavior of children. The top rows of pictures are frames from a film the children saw. The other two rows show the behavior of children after seeing the film. Note the similarities. (Photos courtesy of Dr. A. Bandura)

AUTONOMY AND NEGATIVISM. As we pointed out earlier, in this period of life the child is likely to receive more punishment than he did earlier, because he is capable of doing much more than he did earlier. He can move across the room when he wishes and feed himself. He can control his bowels, and he can control his parents' attention. He can break toys and he can make his little brother cry. Each day he explores both his freedom and his limits.

Frequently this exploration manifests itself by a period of negativism. Every parental suggestion is greeted by "No." While this is frustrating to the parents, it probably is an important step in the development of self-awareness and independence. Such negativism typically reaches its peak between the ages of two-and-a-half and three-and-a-half and then normally declines. Although negativism is annoying, parents who know that such a stage is common can tolerate it with some amusement. For other parents, however, negativism represents a severe threat to parental authority and the parent may act vigorously and forcefully.

Erikson (1963) summarizes these trends by pinpointing this age as one of growing autonomy pitted against growing shame and doubt. He says: "This stage becomes decisive for the ratio of love and hate, cooperation and willfulness, freedom of self-expression and its suppression. From a sense of self-control without loss of self-esteem comes a lasting sense of good will and pride; from a sense of loss of self-control and of foreign overcontrol comes a lasting propensity for doubt and shame."

Early Childhood

The years between infancy and school age are marked by continued improvement in muscular control, language facility, and thinking skills, by increase in self-assurance and/or guilt, and by a growing identification with adults.

Modesty Training

As part of his explorations of his body the young child is likely to become interested in his genital organs and in those of his parents and of other children. The child's first display of sexual interest may be an unhappy experience. His parents are likely to be surprised and afraid. They may respond with excitement and severe punishment. As a result the child may inhibit expression of sexual interest or even repress his sexual urges. As he grows older, the continued silence of parents about sex and their attempts to reduce sexual stimulation may increase the child's uncertainty and consequent anxiety about sex. In place of building up positive understanding, his parents communicate their attitude of disapproval. Because of the child's lack of knowledge it is not surprising that the functions of excretions and sex are often confused and both are seen as being "nasty." In the study of New England mothers (Sears *et al.*, 1957), to which we referred earlier, it became clear that the mothers, too, closely associate toilet training and sex training. Mothers commented frequently on problems of maintaining privacy in the bathroom and training children not to urinate outdoors. Their answers indicated a dual concern about toilet training and modesty in exposing the genitals during elimination. If the parent communicates a great deal of concern and anxiety to the child, there may be effects upon the child's self-esteem, and some theorists have suggested that the parents' attempt to restrict the child's knowledge and curiosity in this area may be generalized to inhibit his curiosity and realistic perception of other aspects of life.

INCREASED USE OF VERBAL DISCIPLINE. When a child has reached the age of three, he is usually able to understand both verbal commands and verbal rewards and punishments. It may be a much more severe blow to hear mother say, "We don't like little boys who . . ." than to feel a slap. Where withdrawal of love is frequently used as a punishment, the child may develop a strong fear of rejection.

Identification and the Development of Internal Standards

At first, the "do's" and "don't's" of behavior are restrictions external to the child which prevent certain actions. If a two-year-old child wants a cookie, he tries to climb up to the cupboard, even if his mother is present. A few months later, he remembers past punishments, and he will try to take cookies only when mother is gone. Still later, he goes into the kitchen, looks at the cookie jar, and says "No, no, no!" He has now not only learned to distinguish punished from unpunished acts, but he has accepted his parents' concept of right and wrong as his own.

This acceptance is part of the general process of identification. You may remember that we have already discussed identification as a defense mechanism in which a person satisfies his unresolved motives by considering someone else's accomplishments as his own. However, in the development of a child, identification is a normal process, in which the child takes over the habits, values, and attitudes of one of his parents. Parents often see the products of identification as their child displays their less desirable habits and gestures with disturbing accuracy.

There are two general theories of identification. The learning-theory explanation looks upon identification as an extension of the general habit of imitation. If a mother shows affection for her daughter and becomes a frequent source of motive satisfaction, her presence and her actions themselves become rewarding. When the child adopts her behavior and her thinking, she is reinstating her mother's pleasurable presence and rewarding herself. Note that the little girl will imitate aspects of her mother's behavior for which she may never have been externally rewarded, according to this theory. However, some imitated behavior will be explicitly rewarded, strengthening the tendency to imitate. In particular, a boy will probably be rewarded more for imitating his father and a girl for imitating her mother. Freudian theory derives identification from the child's envy of his parents' powers and privileges. This envy may not be expressed through direct aggression, for such aggression would be punished either physically or by withdrawal of love. This conflict is resolved by attempting to become like the powerful parent. In boys, identification with the father is the resolution of the "Oedipal situation," in which the boy envies his father's position with his mother and fears his power. In girls, a somewhat more complicated process is believed to result in identification with the mother.

Some studies seem to favor the learning-theory explanation. In a projective doll-playing test, boys whose fathers were warm and permissive tended to play the role of the father more frequently than boys with cold, punishing fathers (Sears *et al.*, 1953). In another study, nursery school children tended to imitate a young woman who paid attention to them and frequently rewarded them in play more than they imitated the behavior of someone who watched but did not interact with them (Bandura, 1962).

One experiment was designed to test whether an adult rival or an adult who dispensed rewards would be chosen for imitation.

■ The experimental situation provided the child with a model "family." One adult distributed rewarding objects such as cookies and toys. The other adult competed with the child for these rewards. Now the child watched the two adults guessing which box contained the prize. Both adults chose the correct box, but prior to making a choice each one selected an individual "thinking cup" and went through a distinctive ritual of phrases and gestures. Then the child was asked to participate in the guessing. He was scored for the number of words and gestures of each model he imitated. The children imitated the rewarding adult significantly more frequently than they imitated the rival adult. (Bandura, Ross, and Ross, 1963b) ■

Freudian theory suggests that the mechanism of identification produces the genesis of morality and guilt as the child takes over his parents' values. Recently there has been much research on the factors that lead to internal standards and guilt in children. Often these studies involve either asking children to complete a story in which the central character obviously has committed a transgression (see Fig. 13–5), or asking them what they would do if they found

Timmy's mother asked him to watch his baby brother while she went to the attic to find something. He said that he would, and his mother went upstairs. Then some of Timmy's friends rang the bell and asked Timmy to come out and play. Timmy put on his coat and went outside with his friends. What happened next?

FIG. 13–5. A story that might be used to study the development of guilt in children. (Suggested by the work of Kohlberg, 1963)

themselves in a situation in which they had obviously "done wrong." Then the answers are rated for degree of guilt versus fear of detection and external punishment. The consistent finding in these studies is that the children who show internalized standards tend to come from different kinds of homes than children who show fear of external retribution. The children who show internalized standards tend to have warm affectionate parents, who frequently use praise, who generally do not use physical punishment, and who explain the reasons for their actions. The children who show little guilt generally have parents who are unaffectionate, arbitrary, and physically punitive. (Sears, 1957; Burton, *et al.*, 1961; Aronfreed, 1961) If identification is the chief mechanism for the formation of conscience, these results also suggest that warmth and praise are more likely to result in identification than punitiveness.

At the same time that the child becomes more self-restricting to avoid guilt, he becomes capable of wider achievement as a result of his growing skills. Erikson (1963) believes that this is the stage during which the child must resolve the conflicting tendencies of increasing initiative and increasing guilt. If he can learn to balance the two tendencies so that neither overwhelms the other, he is on his way to becoming an adult who can both find opportunities for achievements and maintain moral integrity.

Later Childhood

If all goes well, the child who completes the pre-school years has (1) differentiated himself from the environment, (2) developed a capacity for affection, (3) learned some of his parents' most important attitudes, (4) developed some degree of independence in feeding, toilet training, etc., (5) developed some ability to perceive the world realistically, and (6) mastered some skills with which to cope with the environment. Now the child is ready for some systematic instruction which will prepare him to become a functioning member of society. This is true in all cultures, although the instruction is not always formally institutionalized in preliterate culture (Erikson, 1963). In our society, the child enters school. He must learn how to work and how to get along with other children and a teacher.

Now the child is judged according to his mastery of skills, and his own achievements are compared with those of his peers. These experiences are important in influencing his developing motivation for achievement balanced against a fear of failure (or in Erikson's terms, the balance between a sense of industry and inferiority). The child's awareness of his own abilities relative to the problems he must solve and relative to his peers is reinforced by the many competitive testing situations both in and out of school. Most children learn to adjust their goals to their own abilities. If a child experiences failure, he tends to lower his aspiration; if he succeeds, he will try to do even better the next time (e.g., Sears, 1940, 1941). Out of such experiences of success and failure the child learns to incorporate his skills and abilities within his self-concept. Thus not only is he learning to adjust his goals to his abilities, but also his picture of himself is becoming more complex and highly differentiated. Now parental stimulation, encouragement, support, and love are more important than ever. If, for example, the child is slow in developing, or below average in ability, he is much more likely to experience failure in striving for achievement, and thus is less likely to develop a strong positive need for achievement. If, on the other hand, he is confident of his parents' love and can maintain his self-esteem despite occasional failures, he may still develop habits of persistence and hard work to achieve his goals.

However, during the school years the home is no longer the only major source of information, activities, attitudes, and values for the child. His peers now play an increasingly important part in his life. Ordinarily, while he is in elementary school and junior high, his closest associates are children of his own age and sex (Lenton, 1962). Throughout this period, his attachments to his friends will become more pronounced, the activities of his social group will become more organized, he will spend more time with his friends away from home, and his friends will have an increasingly greater influence on him (Anderson, 1939; Wright, 1956).

Other important sources of information and values for the school-age child are the mass media. He finds role-models in the heroes of folklore, books, movies, and television. Through his vicarious experiences in fiction, he learns the sort of behavior which is valued in his culture. Increasingly television is becoming the major mass-medium influence on children. More than 90 percent of the homes in the United States have a television set. The average American child spends approximately one sixth of his waking hours watching television. His television watching reaches a maximum while he is in the sixth to the eighth grades at school (Schramm, Lyle, and Parker, 1961). Such a pervasive influence must affect the values, beliefs, and actions of those exposed to it. However, as Maccoby (1964) points out, the same programs will have different effects on different children. For example she cites the work of Riley and Riley (1954), which showed that children who have few friends tend to daydream about a program after seeing it, while more social children will not. The child's sex also influences the effect of a program on him. After watching the same show, boys tend to remember best the aggressive actions of a male hero and girls tend to remember best the romantic content associated with a heroine (Maccoby and Wilson, 1957). Thus the mass media do not necessarily have a unified mass effect, though they certainly play some role in the life of every child in a modern American community.

The school-aged child must not only cope with these relatively new influences, he must also cope with old problems and situations which may become more difficult as a result of his increasing age. Because he is stronger, his parents find it more difficult to deal with his aggression. Because he is more conscious

of the relationship between himself and others and of the value of competing,
sibling rivalry is intensified. Because he is better able to consider other people's
feelings and to accept group goals, he can participate more fully in groups,
and the conflicts between peer group norms and parental desires develop. The
very fact of developing maturity inevitably brings new conflicts and problems.

Adolescence

Adolescence is a period of transition. Erikson calls it a period of role confusion
out of which should emerge identity. The individual who has previously accepted his role as a child now attempts to adopt aspects of the role of an adult.
But the new world of adulthood is an unfamiliar one to the adolescent. It is
not clear to him how far he can go. He can no longer get into the movies for
the child's price, but he cannot get married, buy liquor, or hold a full time job.
His parents tell him that he is old enough to accept responsibility, but refuse to
let him take the family car.

While he ventures into the unknown world, his own body, which has hitherto
been a relatively stable base, is changing rapidly. The adolescent is not sure
of what his body can do. He feels clumsy and ill at ease. He recognizes his
sexual maturing and is likely to worry about it.

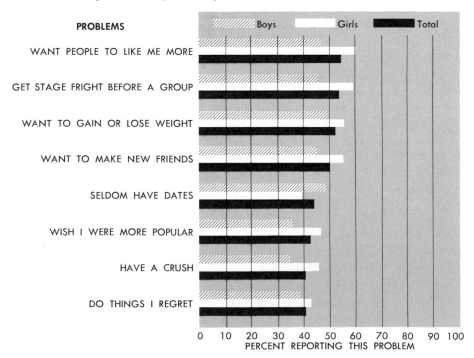

FIG. 13–6. The eight problems most frequently reported by a group of adolescent
boys and girls. (After Remmers and Radler, 1957)

At the same time that the adolescent has increased need for help, there is increased pressure upon him to become more independent. As he approaches adult size, he and society expect that he will make more of his own decisions. As he tests out his independence, he frequently comes into conflict with parental demands. Oftentimes his parents have not accepted his maturity. They still see him as a big *boy*, while he would like to be seen as a young *man*. Even when parents are wise and reasonable, there are conflicts, for the demands of the adolescent are often attempts to prove to himself that his parents still care for him and want to look after him.

As the adolescent breaks away from the support of the home, he seeks support elsewhere, usually in his peer group. The things he most frequently mentions as problems are related to social relationships (see Fig. 13–6). So strong may be his fear of rejection by the group that he may attempt to conform in every way possible to the norms of the group. Thus he *must* have the haircut or style of clothing which is the current fad. His concern about superficial matters helps him to avoid anxiety about underlying problems. He must become an individual and he expresses this drive for independence in the extremes of fashion to which he conforms. But he must be different only in ways acceptable to his peers. On the other hand, his parents remain the most important influence in political and economic matters and the most important advisers on personal problems (see Fig. 13–7).

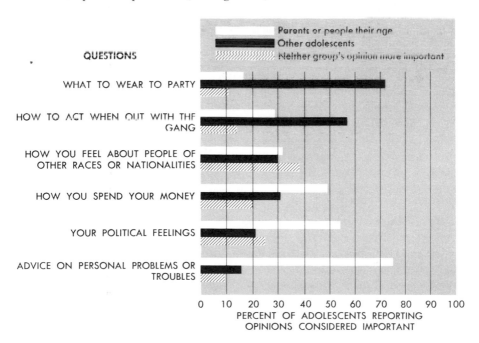

FIG. 13–7. The groups whose opinion are most important to adolescents with regard to specific problems. (After Remmers and Radler, 1957)

As compared with himself at a younger age, the adolescent is quicker to learn and better able to generalize. His intelligence is nearing that of maturity. Many adolescents gain satisfaction from testing out their minds in long, abstract, intellectual discussions. Inhelder and Piaget (1958) call it the metaphysical age, since it is a time of theorizing about the nature of man, good and evil, love, and social systems. New ideas are grasped and the need for independence plus the interest in thinking may cause a family to enter a series of debates between stodgy conservative parents and the young reformer.

The adolescent's physiological sexual maturing is only one aspect of the process of establishing his own identity as a man or woman. One of the difficult problems for adolescents is that girls normally mature earlier than boys. Since the adolescent male wishes to conform to our cultural norms of masculine strength and dominance, it is disturbing both to the girl and the boy when the girl looms a foot higher than her male classmate. Early maturing tends to be socially advantageous for boys but less so for girls (Jones, 1949).

Within a sex, individual differences in rate of maturing are social as well as physiological. For example, one study compared the interests of girls who had had their first menstrual period with those who had not yet begun to menstruate. The girls who had menstruated were more interested in their appearance and in the opposite sex, less interested in physical activities, and more interested in imaginative activities (Stone and Barker, 1939).

Because attitudes toward masculinity and femininity are closely related to other sexual attitudes, the adolescent may show a good deal of ambivalence about assuming the role of man or woman. Behavioral reactions may range from clinging to childhood, through over-identification with the parent of the same sex, to rejection of one's own sex role. But as problems are solved, individuals become able to establish their own identity within their own sex role. Here, as at other stages of development, the normal person is not one who never has problems but one who resolves his problems as he develops.

Two problems that may be faced by the late adolescent are those of college adjustment and vocational choice. We shall now look at them in greater detail.

College Adjustment

The late adolescent who goes to college has an excellent opportunity to meet people from different cultural backgrounds, to discuss new experiences and insights, and to learn more about his cultural heritage. Such opportunities should help the student achieve a higher level of adjustment. But college itself presents adjustment problems. College has been described as a social device for prolonging adolescence. Whether or not this description is true, it does point to one of the sources of conflict for the college youth. By postponing the time when he can support himself, going to college keeps the student economically dependent on his parents. College takes the youth out of the home, and hence reduces his parents' opportunities to exert control over his behavior, but most parents feel that if their money is being used, they should continue to have some voice in its disposition.

College students are, on the average, more intelligent and wealthy than persons who fail to continue their education. We have statistics on such objective characteristics but we know much less about the goals of students in going to college. Undoubtedly, many go to college in order to prepare themselves for greater vocational achievement. Others see college as a means of gaining greater status. Still others go because their friends are going or because they want to develop social skills. Some go because they enjoy studying and learning.

Since students differ in their motivation for attending college, they tend to select different colleges. Colleges develop reputations which attract a particular type of student. Thus one college is known as a place for having a good time while another has the reputation for emphasis on intellectual effort, with little attention to personal appearance or having "fun." Though entering freshmen still differ in motivation and ability, existing group norms may exert pressure toward social activities while norms at another college may emphasize scholastic work (Pace and Stern, 1958).

Every college, however, still includes students differing greatly in motivation, and as a result they tend to focus their efforts in different areas of campus life. For example, while students with strong power motivation are motivated to succeed in extra-curricular activities, other students are motivated for success in sports, social success, or academic achievement. Although students' needs change during their four years of college as a result of pressures from other students and from the faculty, they are by no means homogeneous as they receive their diplomas.

College grades do not predict later success perfectly. Since grades measure attainment of only one class of goals, albeit an important one, they are not highly useful in predicting in situations which require other motives and skills. For example, the student with a strong power motive may satisfy this motive through leadership in extra-curricular activities, spending only enough time in course work to maintain his eligibility. Despite his average grades, he may, in later life, do well in a position providing opportunities to satisfy his motive for power.

PROBLEMS OF ADJUSTMENT. Because he feels a little lost and lonesome, the college freshman is particularly sensitive to the possibility of being disliked and rejected. Thus he is especially susceptible to pressures from the group. He tries to adopt college norms as he sees them. Because those things stand out in his perception which differ from the norms of his home groups, he is likely to feel that he must make some quite conspicuous changes in his behavior. For example, courtship behavior is frequently more public in college than in high school. The freshman couple who must approach the girl's dormitory through a line-up of couples kissing good-night are likely to feel both anxious and confused about how to end their date. Drinking may also be a problem for some students. While colleges differ greatly in norms about drinking, the freshman is likely to misperceive the norms of his own institution. A survey of students of representative colleges by a research team showed that about 25% of these students were total abstainers. Over 50% of the men and 70% of the coeds drank less than once a month. Nevertheless, the freshman who sees that drinking is not disapproved, is likely to overestimate the social presure toward drinking and to feel anxious about whether or not his own drinking behavior conforms to his peers' expectations (Strauss and Bacon, 1953).

In the classroom, too, the college student's behavior is affected by anxiety. In order to stay in college, the student must make acceptable grades. This may produce a state of conflict. On the one hand his long-term goals demand good grades; on the other hand his great need for emotional support from his fellow students demands that he not spend too much time in study.

For example, girls often feel faced with a conflict between high achievement and popularity with the opposite sex. While the evidence does not support their belief, some girls feel that successful academic competition with boys is inversely related to number of dates.

As we saw in Chapter 6, some students are dominantly motivated by expectations of success while others, equally concerned about achievement, are dominantly motivated by fear of failure. While both kinds of students will study, the student with positive expectations is much more likely to work effectively. On the other hand, the student who fears failure becomes distraught when he is under pressure. This emotional disturbance interferes with his thinking, and makes him uncomfortable. He escapes from this painful situation as quickly as possible. In a study in which the time of leaving the final examination was recorded, it was found that those who were high in fear of failure were significantly more likely to turn in their papers early than those who had a positive motive for achievement (Atkinson and Litwin, 1960).

In dealing with conflicts arising in college, students use the same types of mechanisms that individuals use in other conflict situations. Every campus has its quota of withdrawn students who have retreated from their problem to isolation or to the companionship of a group of students from similar backgrounds. Similarly the campus rebel handles his conflicts by attacking authority and tradition, while the "Big Man on Campus" may escape the same conflicts by frantic involvement in extra-curricular activities.

WHAT FACTORS DETERMINE THE STUDENT'S SUCCESS IN COLLEGE? One of the most important factors in determining the student's academic success is his intelligence. As we have seen, the correlation between intelligence test scores and grades in college is about 0.5. Another factor determining success in college is the student's motivation. But this is not as simple a relationship as that between intelligence and grades. For example, the achievement motive is an important motive, but unless academic achievement is instrumental to satisfaction of this motive, the student with high achievement motivation may direct his energies to other kinds of achievement. For some students, conscious or unconscious motivation to resist parental pressure may conflict with motives for achievement. Because getting good grades may be instrumental to satisfaction of a number of different motives, measures of single motives have not been very useful in predicting grades in college.

Still another factor of success in college is the student's repertoire of general habits for study. As we have seen, psychologists have had a good deal of success in determining what methods of study are most effective, and the less intelligent student using efficient learning methods may do as well scholastically as the brighter student who uses poor methods.

Despite the problems which college poses, the average student masters them and emerges from four or more years of college a somewhat more mature individual. The graduating senior knows more than he did when he entered college, and he has typically developed new and more diverse interests. In some students, at least, these interests seem less a reflection of current fads in the peer group than a representation of greater personal independence and educability. Although the basic values of students seem typically to be little changed by college, there is evidence of some development. Seniors, for example, tend to be more tolerant than freshmen. They tend to be less authoritarian, more curious, and more independent. Studies of Vassar students (Sanford *et al.,* 1956) suggest that as compared to the freshman, the senior has a much clearer perception of herself and feels freer to express herself in relations with others. She is more aware of, and more willing to admit, difficulties in adjustment.

Vocational Choice

In some societies the problem of vocational choice scarcely exists. Son follows father with little thought of the possibility of entering another vocation. In our society, however, where families often encourage children to "better" themselves, and a variety of occupations are available to each young person, the problem of vocational choice is a very serious one for many adolescents of both sexes. One-third to one-half of all college students are in the process of choosing vocations while they are in college (Webb, 1949). In fact, college counseling services find this to be one of the major problems college students bring to them. Here we see once again a way in which a given society may be predisposed toward certain adjustment problems.

The adolescent is frequently worried by the fact that he is not sure which vocation he wishes to enter. His parents are likely to have certain vocational goals for him, or at least they want him to decide early so that he can begin his vocational training early. Yet he feels that his choice of vocation is important in determining the course of all his future life, and he is expected to make this decision at a time when he lacks information about the demands of possible vocations, and when he is also most unsure of his own abilities. With his self-concept thus unstable and ambiguous, and his concept of vocational demands also unclear, he cannot easily make rational, confident decisions about his future.

In our society the desire for achieving higher status is one of the most important factors in vocational choice. While the youth has learned the patterns of behavior necessary to conform to the norms of the social class in which he was reared, he is urged to aim higher in the social strata—to choose a vocation with greater prestige than that of his father, one which will demand that he learn new norms. A national survey of 14- to 16-year-old boys revealed that 40% of the boys of this age aspire to enter professions. While some of these boys realize that they may change their minds, the fact that only about 7% of adult males now hold professional positions indicates that many will be disappointed (Survey Research Center, undated).

In choosing a vocation, the youth is likely to be conscious of stronger interest in some areas than in others, but to be uncertain about his abilities in the fields which are of interest. Fortunately, vocational interests are positively, though not highly, correlated with abilities. As we saw in Chapter 7, individuals who score high for a particular vocation on the Strong Vocational Interest test not only are more likely to stay in that vocation but also are more successful in the vocation. Because a person is likely to be rewarded for doing good work, he is likely to enjoy activities at which he is talented.

Just as positive and negative motives affect academic performance differently, so too are they important in affecting vocational decisions. Students who fear failure are less realistic in assessing their own interests and abilities in relation to the vocation they choose than are students with positive achievement motivation (Mahone, 1960). Frequently we hear of lower-middle-class upward-striving parents who push their son into medicine or one of the other professions, but young people from the upper socioeconomic classes also find that parental and peer-group pressures limit their range of choice. Studies of upper-class college students showed that they were less likely than other students to choose vocations fitting their measured interests. Moreover, on a follow-up 14 years later, members of the upper-class group were significantly more discontented with their jobs than were the other students (McArthur, 1954, and Stevens, 1955).

■ Roe (1953) looked at the backgrounds of many successful scientists to seek out developmental trends. Her studies indicate that successful scientists typically showed early talent, which was encouraged and rewarded. The typical scientist was the oldest child in his family, often the only child. His childhood was not a happy one. Frequently he was a "sickly child" and felt lonely and "different" from other children, partly, perhaps, because of his unusually high intelligence. (This suggests the hypothesis that relative isolation in childhood is conducive to scientific interests and productivity.) He read a great deal. In high school and college he was shy and had few dates.

Usually he discovered his scientific interest in his junior or senior year of college and from that time on worked at it seven days a week. Time that most people devote to social activities, the young scientist devoted to his work, and usually he was rewarded for his work by a teacher who encouraged and stimulated him. Thus the scientist avoided situations which would have aroused his anxiety and instead developed an even greater interest in activities which brought him satisfaction. ■

Roe's study of scientists supports other studies showing that differing vocations make differing demands, offer different satisfactions, and thus appeal to individuals of differing personalities. Vocational choice, therefore, represents an expression of personality factors formed throughout childhood. A study of lawyers, dentists, and social workers (Nachmann, 1957) revealed that in the families of lawyers, as compared with the other groups, fairness and reason were emphasized, aggressive impulses were accepted, verbal skills were stimulated, and the father was likely to have been a strong, dominant figure. In choosing law as a profession the young man thus chooses a profession which permits and rewards verbal aggression and which satisfies needs for justice which may have been developing since his childhood.

This is not meant to imply that the motives satisfied by work are all unique and unconscious. Interviews with large numbers of workers suggest that fulfillment of motives for recognition, independence, and achievement are important in general employee satisfaction and that employees are aware of it. When these motives are frustrated, employees quit.

In a study of why people leave jobs, interviewers who questioned workers a year after they had quit found that common reasons were that they had not liked the company, were dissatisfied with working conditions, or had disliked the person working on the next machine.

This same study showed that quitting was also related to ability. On routine jobs the persons who quit tended to be the more intelligent workers, while the less intelligent workers were more likely to quit complex jobs. Lack of adjustment to work is thus likely to result from a poor match between the worker's abilities and motives and the satisfaction the job provides (Brayfield and Crockett, 1955; Wickert, 1951).

Adulthood

There is no definite age at which adolescence ends and maturity begins. Ideally the end of adolescence finds the person to be aware of himself and to value himself; he has the capacity to love another; his personality is integrated and relatively free from damaging conflict; he is independent, able to make decisions for himself; his decisions are based on realistic perception of the environment and the possession of the knowledge and skills necessary for environmental mastery (Jahoda, 1959). Of course, individuals differ in the degree to which they achieve these goals, but in general, adolescence, despite its storm and strain, results in progress toward them.

Marriage

MATE SELECTION. The young adult usually marries and has a family. In our society, each person chooses his own mate, though there are, of course, indirect pressures from family and friends which affect the choice. There are two general theories of mate selection: one can be summarized by the saying, "like marries like"; the other by the saying, "opposites attract." There is some evidence that each theory is correct in some respects. Men and women who marry tend to be similar in age, religious and socioeconomic background, education, and place of residence prior to marriage. Furthermore, they tend to be of the same general intelligence level, to have similar interests, and to have similar attitudes on political and social issues. (See, for example, Burgess and Wallen, 1944)

However, Winch (1958) points out that these similarities are in sociological and cognitive characteristics, but not in personality or motivational characteristics. He proposes a theory of complementary motives: that a person falls in love and marries someone whose motives are complementary in such a way that when one partner satisfies the other's motives, he simultaneously satisfies his own motives, too.

■ Winch tested his theory by assessing the motives of 25 married couples. He used Murray's list of needs (see Table 12–1), and the Thematic Apperception Test was one of the assessment instruments. Winch hypothesized that he would find complementary motives in the couples; for example, that someone with strong dominance would tend to be married to a person with strong deference motives; that a nurturant wife would tend to have a husband who had strong succorance motives; that a man with high achievement motivation would be married to a woman who aspired to status. The results showed that complementary motives did occur more frequently in marriage partners than would be expected by chance, though, of course, the complementarity of motives in marriage partners was far from perfect. ■

On the basis of his results, Winch concluded that complementarity was one of many factors influencing mate selection.

EXPECTATIONS OF MARRIAGE. Both the bride and the groom come to marriage with expectations of what marriage will be like. Some of these expectations are influenced by personality characteristics, such as dependence. Others are the result of differences in home background. In many families of two generations ago, both partners expected the husband to be dominant in decision making and the wife to be responsible for the home and family. Today some men and women in our culture retain these expectations while others expect the man to help in household duties and child rearing. More and more women expect to work after marriage except when the children are very young. Since our patterns of husband-wife relationships are changing, the expectations of husband and wife may differ, resulting in unhappiness and conflict. Probably one of the reasons that short acquaintanceship and dating decreases the likelihood of successful marriage (Burgess and Wallen, 1953) is that long acquaintanceship may reduce the likelihood of wide errors in expectations of the way one's mate will behave after marriage.

AREAS OF CONFLICT. In a relationship as pervasive and intimate as marriage, it seems inevitable that some disagreements arise, even when the couple is compatible. Blood and Wolfe (1960) studied the problems which led to disagreements by interviewing a number of wives in the Detroit area. They found that money was the most frequently mentioned source of conflict (one quarter of the wives reported this). Other frequent sources of disagreement were the discipline of children, the type and amount of recreation, and "personality clashes." In-law problems, the roles of husbands and wives, politics, and religion were much more minor. Interestingly, sex, which some authors consider a major factor in marital adjustment, was infrequently mentioned as a cause of disagreement. It is interesting, too, that 15 percent of the women interviewed reported *no* major source of disagreement at all.

Happy marriage, like success in other areas of adjustment, is the continuation of a series of experiences in relating satisfactorily to others. During the years of marriage, personality changes may continue which had their genesis in earlier developmental processes, and as we might expect, happily married couples tend to converge. While there is no conclusive evidence, what data are available suggest that happiness in marriage is positively related to good adjustment in other areas (Kelly, 1941). Erikson (1963) points out that marriage provides an opportunity for mutual satisfaction in deepest intimacy. But marriage vows do not guarantee this situation. A person must be sure of his own identity in order to be able to share his life and to commit himself to another. Otherwise fear of loss of self-identity will cause him to retreat into himself and to isolate himself from his partner.

Generativity

Much of the psychological study of development ends with the resolution of adolescent conflicts. Problems in adulthood are usually traced to failures earlier in life. However, maturity too brings new problems and new adjustments, which themselves require careful analysis.

For example, in both his work and his family, the adult has the opportunity to contribute to the generations that will follow him. The guidance and care he gives to his children, the fulfillment he finds in creating and producing in his occupation help to give his life continuity and meaning. It has been suggested that without some way of relating oneself to the next generation, of contributing to the future, the passing years may bring with them a sense of stagnation and uselessness (Erikson, 1963).

Old Age

Old age brings new problems, some of which are physical. Many people suffer from failing vision or increasing deafness. Muscular responses are weaker. To some extent the problems of adjustment are not quite so great because we expect that older people will be slower and weaker. But these physical changes are gradual and the older person may not recognize or accept his aging because it is not a clearcut change.

In addition to his physical difficulties the older person faces other major changes in his life. Children grow up and leave home. Sexual functioning declines. The man may retire from his job. A man who has worked 8 hours a day for 40 years often feels useless and bored when he retires, just as the woman who has been caring for her children feels lost when the last child leaves home. Retirement is significant not only because the individual must now find some way to fill an additional 8 hours a day, but also because one's sense of worth depends upon being engaged in productive work.

The roles of husband and wife are likely to change during this period. Whereas the man is likely to be dominant during the earlier years of marriage, both husband and wife see the wife as becoming dominant in old age (Neugarten and Gutman, 1958). Whether this is because of changes in the secretion of sex hormones, the generally better health of women, the man's loss of self-esteem and purpose when he retires, or some other factor, such a change involves learning new adjustment skills in family relationships.

The older individual is likely to become dependent upon his family for financial or physical help. With our cultural value of independence, the dependency status is one which arouses many conflicting feelings, and the resulting irritability may cause even greater problems in the older person's relationship with his family. Moreover, our values of productivity, service, and outgoing social activity are those modeled after the well-adjusted middle-aged person. They may be inappropriate for the elderly, but they are so widely held that the older person's self-esteem suffers from his diminishing capabilities to attain these goals. The older person faces these problems of adjustment with reduced abilities to adjust to new situations. As we saw earlier, the older person's sensory and motor abilities are likely to decrease in his later years. His habits are so well learned that it is difficult to change them.

Despite all these problems, later years may be pleasant and productive. Social stimulation and emotional support from family and friends are particularly important. Interviews with some 70-year-old men and women on how they spend their time suggest the significance of family relationships to older people.

■ "My son-in-law is all thumbs when it comes to fixing things around the house, so I help him out whenever I can."

"My grandchildren like to raid the cookie jar, and it really keeps me hopping to keep ahead of them with my baking."

"My daughter and I do the marketing together."

"Yes, since I retired I have a lot of free time. What I do with myself? Well, you know—just putter around, watch TV and sometimes go for a walk. And I like to spend as much time with my kids and grandkids as I can. That's what *means* the most to me." ■*

Integrity Versus Despair

A problem present throughout adulthood, which may come to a crisis in the middle and final years of adulthood, is the growing awareness of death. In youth, an individual can look forward to almost infinite opportunities, in adulthood only a few of these are realized, and in old age comes the awareness that many possibilities have been passed by. However, if a man can look back upon his life as the meaningful fulfillment of his potentialities as a human being, he will not envy youth nor need he fear death. Here is how Erikson discusses this final crisis of development, despair versus integrity:

■ "Despair expresses the feeling that time is now short, too short for the attempt to start another life and to try out alternate roads to integrity.

"Although aware of the relativity of all the various life styles which have given meaning to human striving, the possessor of integrity is ready to defend the dignity of his own life style. . . . For he knows that an individual life is the accidental coincidence of but one life cycle with but one segment of history and that for him all human integrity stands or falls with the one style of integrity of which he partakes. . . . In such final consolidation, death loses its sting." ■†

What Is Emotional Maturity?

There is no single scientific answer to this question. The answer to this question depends partly on a person's values and his philosophic view of human nature. However, if we examine the ideas of many thoughtful psychologists, we do find some convergence of ideas (cf. Allport, Rogers, White, Erikson). Here, then, is a reasoned consensus of how emotional maturity may be described.

First, let us mention a few factors that to us are *not* criteria of maturity. Maturity does not imply complete conformity, nor does it necessarily imply the

---

* From Thompson, W. E., and G. F. Streib, "Meaningful activity in a family context," in R. W. Kleemeier, *Aging and Leisure*. New York: Oxford University Press, 1961. Reprinted by permission.

† From Erikson, E., *Childhood and Society*. New York: Norton, 1963. Reprinted by permission.

attainment of material success. Furthermore, a person does not reach maturity because he has had no difficult problems nor because he has never been torn by serious conflict. Rather, maturity is attained by grappling with each developmental conflict so that its resolution may contribute to the evolving personality (see Fig. 13–8). We believe that as people approach emotional maturity, they will tend to have these characteristics:

1. *Independence.* The mature person emerges from the dependency of childhood to independence, making his own decisions according to his own standards.

2. *Environmental mastery.* This implies the ability to see the world realistically, to think rationally, and to use the resources of environment and self to be productive and creative.

	1	2	3	4	5	6	7	8
MATURITY								INTEGRITY vs. DISGUST, DESPAIR
ADULTHOOD							GENERATIVITY vs. STAGNATION	
YOUNG ADULTHOOD						INTIMACY vs. ISOLATION		
ADOLESCENCE					IDENTITY vs. ROLE DIFFUSION			
LATER CHILDHOOD				INDUSTRY vs. INFERIORITY				
EARLY CHILDHOOD			INITIATIVE vs. GUILT					
THE SECOND YEAR		AUTONOMY vs. SHAME, DOUBT						
EARLY INFANCY	TRUST vs. MISTRUST							

FIG. 13–8. The primary conflicts in the various periods of life as conceptualized by Erikson (1963). Although Erikson associates each conflict with a particular period of development, he also suggests that each conflict may have precursors in an earlier period and a derivative in a later period. The empty squares above and below each primary conflict are meant to represent these precursors and derivatives.

3. *The capacity for love.* The mature person has the capacity and the desire to share with others, to give of himself to his family, his friends, and to his society.

4. *Identity: self-awareness and self-esteem.* Under this label we include a complex of attitudes toward self: the ability to perceive one's own characteristics accurately, accepting all the aspects of oneself without repression, valuing one's own worth as a unique human being.

5. *Integration.* As a mature human being experiences his environment and himself, he searches for a unifying view of the world which gives meaning to his individual acts and to a total life.

Summary

Principles

1. Some individuality is evident in early infancy, which suggests that the developing person is not simply a passive recipient of environmental influences.

2. The infant's physical, intellectual, emotional, and social development requires varied sensory stimulation and a close social relationship during the early months of life.

3. The specific practices involved in weaning and toilet training are less important in terms of later development than the emotional context in which they are carried out.

4. Continued use of physical punishment as discipline for a child increases his tendency to be physically aggressive.

5. Experiments suggest that warmth and praise are more likely to lead to identification and the development of internalized standards than are cold, inconsistent discipline and physical punishment.

6. During later childhood, the sources of information, activities, opportunities for achievement, and values expand from the home to include school, peer group, and mass media.

7. Adolescence is a period of physiological, social, and intellectual transition.

8. New problems and conflicts develop in adulthood when the individual must cope with college and/or employment, marriage, a family, and old age. Maturity is not indicated by the absence of conflict in these areas, but by its satisfactory resolution.

Suggested Readings

ERIKSON, E. H., *Childhood and Society*. New York: Norton, 1963. A more complete statement of Erikson's theory of development.

HOFFMAN, M. L., and HOFFMAN, L. W., *Review of Child Development Research*. New York: Russell Sage Foundation, 1964. An excellent review of recent experimental results.

AUSUBEL, D. P., *Theories and Problems of Child Development*. New York: Grune and Stratton, 1957. An excellent reference source.

maladjustment

chapter 14

NEUROSES

PSYCHOSOMATIC DISORDERS

PSYCHOSES

CONDUCT DISORDERS

At the end of the last chapter we listed five characteristics which we believe to be signs of mature adjustment. These characteristics are ideal traits and no one acquires all of them in full measure. We can think of adjustment as a continuum with ideal maturity at one end, maladjustment at the other, and with most people's adjustment falling somewhere between the two extremes. In general, we call a person maladjusted if he is incapable of coping with the world or with his own impulses realistically and flexibly without doing damage to himself or to others. The borderline between normal and maladjusted behavior is not a well-defined one, but we can identify some cases that clearly belong in the maladjustment category. Let us look at some illustrative case histories:

■ M. E. had just been released from the Navy, but he felt no elation. He looked at his civilian clothes and felt as though he were a stranger. He knew that he should go to his home to see his folks and his girl friend, but he just did not want to bother. He rented a room and went to bed. In the morning he sat up and thought of getting something to eat, but did not really care about eating. He began to dress, but when he came to the necktie he realized that he had to choose which one to wear. He thought about it. His thoughts moved slowly. Finally, after sitting and thinking for an hour, it no longer seemed worth while, and he rolled back to bed.

For several days this continued. Some days he ate, others he did not. His beard had grown, his clothes were wrinkled; his spirit seemed to have vanished.

Gradually he improved. One day he shaved, and was shocked at the thin pale cheeks that he uncovered. He began to leave his room and to eat regularly. He thought about going home, and the thought was pleasant. He packed his bags, went to the railroad station, bought a ticket, and boarded a train for home. As he traveled across the country, he was impressed as never before by the beauty of the countryside. He noted with appreciation the beauty of the young women who occasionally walked through his car. His spirits mounted as he thought of the joy of returning home. He began to wish that he had taken a plane instead of a train.

Upon arrival home, he greeted his family joyously and began a speedy round of meeting his old acquaintances. When he discovered that one of his old friends was in another city, he flew there to see him. He went out on dates every night and often routed his friends from their sleep for some new adventure. He put through long-distance calls to his former Navy buddies and asked their cooperation in his rather vague but enthusiastically described plan for a new business. If they refused he became very angry, and when his parents suggested that he take it easy, he became very angry with them. His pace became more and more feverish. His ideas and speech were sometimes so rapid as to be incomprehensible. Finally, his parents took him to a physician who recommended his commitment to a mental hospital. ■

▨ Anne is a housewife, the mother of six children. She is now in the hospital complaining of backaches, vomiting, severe headaches, and general weakness and tiredness. Medical examinations can discover no physiological basis for her complaints. Her case history shows that in addition to her hospitalization at the time of the birth of each of her children, she has been operated on six times for various complaints with no improvement. A social worker discovers that each of the latter hospitalizations has been preceded by her husband's dismissal from a job. ■

■ Mike is 12 years old. He has always been quiet and obedient. He seldom plays with the other children, and when his mother suggests that he go outside to play, he often sneaks back to his room. His teachers say that he is one of the best-behaved children in his class, but that he does not always pay attention. His parents are disturbed by the fact that he insists on their setting a place at the dinner table for Jimmy, an imaginary friend. Sometimes Mike seems to be talking to himself, but he reports that he is talking to Jimmy or to an angel who sits on his doorknob. When asked what the angel says, he replies, "Meatballs." ■

■ Ace is a 16-year-old boy who has always been in trouble. His record includes truancy, running away from home, and petty theft. His father, a widower, says he tries to discipline the boy whenever he misbehaves but "the whippings don't do nothing." Ace's latest clash with the authorities came after he and three of his friends were ejected from a taproom for being underage. Five hours later, Ace was arrested for car theft. ■

Each of these cases involves a different form of maladjustment. In each case we can identify some bizarre or inappropriate actions which are symptoms of maladjustment. However, let us look at another example:

■ "C" is a young man who is very proud. He is relatively well-to-do and insists on giving other young men generous gifts. When they give him something, he insists on giving them something of even greater value. One day he invited several of his associates to dinner and during the dinner burned all of his possessions with no apparent concern. ■

The behavior of C seems to us as maladjusted of any of the four cases cited previously. Yet C was a member of the Kwakuitl Indian tribe, and was displaying a prescribed social behavior. In Kwakuitl society one gained prestige through the "potlatch," a feast at which one gave his friends valuable presents and displayed his contempt for wealth by destroying it. If one's competitor could not return an even more valuable gift or give a bigger potlatch, he lost prestige. Thus, in Kwakuitl society the behavior of C would have been accepted as normal and commendable. This example serves as a reminder that in order to evaluate behavior in terms of adjustment, we need to know the context of the behavior, including the customs and norms of the society in which the behavior occurs.

What Are the Forms of Maladjustment?

Behavior which we label maladjusted can have a number of causes. It may be the result of normal learning in an unusual environment. It may be a manifestation of nervous-system disorder. Or it may represent the breakdown of normal problem-solving ability and normal defense mechanisms which have failed to protect the individual from his anxiety.

Whatever the origin of the conditions, students are often surprised to discover some similarity between the maladjustments described in a psychology text and their own behavior. Partly this is like the medical-student syndrome, in which the student feels as though he is stricken with each disease he reads about. And partly this is because of the continuity of normal and abnormal behavior. The symptoms of maladjustment are normal mental processes which, for some reason, have become exaggerated and distorted. Thus recognizing some of the symptoms described below should not disturb you. The fact of self-awareness is itself a sign of mature adjustment.

We can classify maladjustment into four categories: (1) neurosis, in which a person develops a crippling symptom of psychological origin; (2) psychosomatic disorders, in which a physical ailment can partially be traced to psychological stress; (3) psychosis, in which a person withdraws from reality into a private fantasy world; and (4) conduct disorders, such as antisocial behavior. As we take up each form of maladjustment, we shall describe and illustrate the condition involved, discuss its possible causes, and describe the methods that are used in order to remove the condition.

Neuroses

A neurosis is a form of maladjustment in which the individual is handicapped by psychological or physical symptoms although he is usually capable of functioning without hospitalization. About 3 to 4 percent of the population is estimated to be neurotic to the extent that the individual's condition seriously interferes with his work and social adjustment.

A neurosis may be manifested by a variety of symptom complexes. The American Psychiatric Association has classified the symptom types of neurosis as follows:

> Anxiety reaction
> Phobic reaction
> Depressive reaction
> Dissociative reaction
> Obsessive-compulsive reaction
> Conversion reaction
> Psychoneurotic reactions

To a psychologist, a simple listing of types of neurosis is disturbing. Classification systems such as that above are convenient methods of grouping and communicating about maladjusted people, but symptoms are dependent variables with respect to the factors of greatest psychological interest. They are the outward signs of the neurosis—the covering which can be understood only with respect to the underlying factors which have determined them. Thus, although we will give examples of these symptoms, you must remember that they are the outcomes of stress, frustration, and conflict. In Chapter 11 we compared psychological adjustment to the Selye adaptation syndrome. In this analysis, neurosis represents the third stage, that in which the adjustment mechanisms have broken down. Although we cannot discuss each of the above reactions in detail, we will identify each and give examples of some.

An *anxiety reaction* is illustrated in the following case:

■ A married woman, whose life was complicated by her mother's living in the home, complained that she felt tense and irritable most of the time. She was apprehensive lest something happen to her mother, her husband, her children, or herself. She had no definite idea what it was that she feared might happen. She suffered from occasional attacks in which her heart pounded, and she could not seem to get her breath. Often she broke out in a profuse perspiration. Her mouth seemed always dry, even though she drank a great deal of water. ■

The woman in this case illustrates the free-floating anxiety which is typical of the anxiety reaction: feelings of fear and helplessness for no apparent reason. Many of the physical symptoms of this reaction are the normal concomitants of high arousal: accelerated breathing and heartbeat, excessive perspiration, heightened sensitivity to stimuli, and inability to sleep regularly. Although anxiety is a central element in neurosis, anxiety itself is not necessarily a neurotic symptom. What identifies the neurotic reaction is persistent anxiety in situations that are not really dangerous. In anxiety reactions the defense mechanisms have failed at least partially so that the anxiety emerges, but since the neurotic does not remember the specific cause of the anxiety, he feels trapped by unknown forces.

Phobic reactions are persistent, strong, unreasonable fears. Claustrophobia, for example, may involve fear of small enclosed places. Other phobias may involve fear of water, crowds, noise, etc. Although the fears are quite specific, the person suffering from a neurotic phobia is unable to account for his fear. Phobias, especially those of severely disturbed neurotics, sometimes expand, so that as time passes, the fear generalizes to more and more objects. Ross (1937) gives this example:

■ A man developed a phobic reaction toward the number 13. At first he controlled his fear by staying in bed on the thirteenth of each month, thus avoiding contact with calendar and newspaper dates.

One day he realized that the word twenty-seven had thirteen letters, and he began spending two days a month in bed. Later he avoided passing a sign which had thirteen letters in it that hung on his normal route to work; he began to hop over the thirteenth step in each flight of stairs, to count his footsteps, to count streets. Finally all his actions revolved around his phobia. ■

The phobia is like the anxiety reaction in that the individual becomes very anxious in situations where the feared stimulus is present. But the phobia has the advantage that the individual can often avoid the feared situation, so that some peace can be achieved. In a sense he has displaced his feelings from the real source to a less threatening one. Moreover, the style of life required in avoiding the feared situation may offer satisfactions of its own.

Depressive reactions are characterized by feelings of sadness, worthlessness, and lack of energy. While everyone develops symptoms of depression in certain situations, persisting depressive reactions are more severely incapacitating and the reactions are disproportionate to objective events.

Neurotic depressions typically involve partially repressed guilt. By expressing his feeling of inferiority and worthlessness, the neurotic depressive obtains from his family and friends assurances that he really needn't feel guilty or inferior and thus gains temporary relief. But as he continues to express his self-depreciation, his friends are likely to lose patience, and his belief that he is beyond hope is confirmed.

Dissociative reactions are neuroses characterized by a loss of personal identity. Amnesia is one of the more common forms. Here a person selectively forgets; he is unable to remember his identity, although he does remember how to speak, how to dress himself, how to function. Often amnesia results from a conflict that is resolved by behavior which expresses the repressed motive without exposing the amnesiac to the anxiety or guilt that would be felt if he acted in the same way in his own identity. Thus one can, in a state of amnesia, escape from a situation without having to face the conflict and its associated anxiety. In using the defense mechanisms of denial and repression, the dissociated neurotic not only shuts out the conflict but also his own involvement in it. Sometimes amnesia is coupled with a fugue state in which a person takes on a new identity as well as forgetting his old one. In extreme cases, two or more personalities may exist relatively independently of one another. Such Dr. Jekyll and Mr. Hyde cases are quite rare, however.

Obsessive-compulsive symptoms frequently occur together in neuroses. An *obsession* is a persistent, irresistible idea. A *compulsion* is an irresistible act tendency or behavior pattern, which is repeated over and over again.

■ This pattern is illustrated by the case of a 13-year-old boy who was constantly preoccupied with the thought that he wanted to hurt other people. Whenever he saw someone asleep, he was struck by the thought that he had killed him. He was a very conscientious, religious boy, and he went to confession frequently. In his religious observances he felt compelled to make the sign of the cross three times instead of once as other people did. He refused to watch deaths portrayed in movies and television because he thought they were real. He also was afraid of bumping people and hurting them and for this reason he avoided crowds and all the usual boyhood sports. ■

Behavior such as this is indicative of a conflict and we can see elements of displacement of aggression and of reaction formation. By continual attention to religion and avoiding other people, the boy avoids anxiety about his more basic problems.

In a *conversion reaction* or *hysteria* a person develops physical symptoms in the absence of any true physical pathology. The reaction may take the form of a paralysis, an anesthesia (loss of some sensation), or another set of physical symptoms. The case of Anne, the housewife with recurrent physical symptoms, is an example of this neurosis.

Conversion reaction can be recognized by the fact that the disorder often is physiologically incorrect. For example, a person with a "glove anesthesia" feels no sensation in the area which would be covered by a glove. However, the dis-

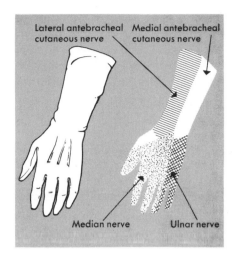

Lateral antebracheal cutaneous nerve

Medial antebracheal cutaneous nerve

Median nerve

Ulnar nerve

FIG. 14–1. Glove anesthesia can be easily diagnosed as a hysteria, since the area over which a person has no sensation does not correspond with the distribution of nerves, which is diagrammed on the right, but with the area a glove would cover, as shown on the left. (From Sanford, 1965)

tribution of sensory nerves makes an organic anesthesia over this specific area very improbable (see Fig. 14–1).

One of the features of conversion reaction is the person's apparent indifference to his symptoms and his resistance to cure. The layman is likely to conclude that the patient is deliberately pretending to have imaginary symptoms. This is not the case. Rather, the symptoms are the result of unconscious psychological processes over which the patient has no control. His physical symptom shows that he is disabled and reduces anxiety by enabling the individual to avoid situations or behavior which would activate his conflict.

Psychoneurotic reaction, the last category, is a catch-all classification including other emotional disturbances which present mixed symptoms from the foregoing classes.

The Causes of Neurosis: the Anxiety Theory

The symptoms of neurosis show wide variation. However, most psychologists agree that neurotic symptoms are a result of underlying, unresolvable anxiety that arouses conflict. Like defense mechanisms, the symptoms often represent denials and distortions of reality, but they are more persistent, more rigid, and more incapacitating.

White (1963) points out that the neurotic symptom may reflect three phases of the unresolved conflict. It may be a part of the normal response to anxiety; it may be a means for avoiding the anxiety by denial and distortion; and it may be an expression of the original conflict that produced the neurotic reaction. Most often the symptoms combine all three phases. In the anxiety reaction, the patient represses the conflict, but expresses his anxiety both physiologically and psychologically. The housewife whose mother came to live with her was torn by her ambivalent feelings toward her mother. Her feelings of rejection of her mother were unacceptable and had to be repressed. The anxiety connected with her feelings toward her mother, however, emerged in the anxiety reaction.

In a phobic reaction, a person displaces the true source of his anxiety to another object. Usually the feared object has some associative relationship to the true source of the anxiety. For example, the man who feared the number 13 was disturbed about childhood sexual escapades he had had with a superstitious housekeeper. His guilt was so strong that he repressed all memory of it, but the anxiety connected with it was channeled into a phobia with superstitious content.

Neurotic depressions have been interpreted as self-punishment because of guilt, often about hostile impulses. Instead of expressing his feelings of aggression, the depressed patient turns his hostility onto himself. Dissociative reactions may represent an escape from unsolvable problems by denial of one's identity. Obsessive-compulsive reactions may be seen as recurring attempts to undo unacceptable thoughts and acts. The boy with obsessions about hurting people and with compulsions to perform rituals was torn between hate for his parents and his training that a person should love his parents. Here the idea of hurting his parents was transformed into the recurring thought that he was actually hurting others. He tried to undo his evil thoughts and acts by over-conscientious religious acts. And in conversion reaction the anxiety is displaced into a physical symptom. Anne, the mother of six who became ill each time her husband was fired, was plagued by insecurity which was intensified by her husband's failures. Her father, too, had been an unreliable breadwinner and he periodically had deserted his family.

The Problem of Symptom Selection

In each case, we can see a relationship between the anxiety and the symptom. However, it has been difficult to establish why a given patient developed one neurotic symptom rather than another. Why did Anne have a conversion reaction, whereas the 13-year-old boy developed obsessive-compulsive symptoms? Why does anxiety lead one patient to a phobia and another patient to chronic anxiety reactions? There are several hypotheses to account for symptom selection. The *genetic hypothesis* states that people are genetically predisposed toward certain neurotic symptoms. Just as some people are born with a hereditary predisposition toward tuberculosis, so some people are born with a predisposition toward a conversion reaction, according to this interpretation. Whether or not the predisposed neurosis appears would depend on environmental factors. The *learning hypothesis* states that the specific symptom depends on the habits and general habits learned by the patient. If a person has been highly rewarded for being sick, his neurosis would probably be manifested in a conversion reaction; if he has been rewarded for self-criticism, perhaps he would become neurotically depressed, according to the learning hypothesis. The *developmental-stage hypothesis* first put forth by Freud states that the kind of symptoms developed depends on when in the patient's life history the neurotic conflict developed and on the nature of the conflict. For example, Freud believed that obsessive-compulsive symptoms were the result of unresolved conflicts from the anal stage. In this period children must learn how to obey rules, how to be orderly, and how to control their aggressions. Failure to solve conflicts associated with such learning would be manifested by the patient's compulsively following irrational rules of his own making.

Unfortunately, the available data do not permit clear support for any of these hypotheses. We know that neurotic parents tend to have neurotic children with somewhat similar symptoms, but this could be accounted for by any one of the three hypotheses. Some neurotic disorders are unknown in certain cultures; for example, obsessive-compulsive neuroses are uncommon among Kenyans (Coleman, 1950). Conversion reactions tend to be more common among patients from the lower economic and educational levels, and anxiety reactions and compulsive symptoms are more typical of middle-class people. However, these differences could be the result of hereditary differences, or differential reward patterns, or different kinds of experiences connected with the early developmental stages, or some combination of the three.

The Neurotic Paradox

One of the puzzling aspects of neurosis is that the symptoms are usually not completely successful in protecting the individual from his anxiety; neurotics usually report feeling generally unhappy. Furthermore, the symptoms themselves add new problems for the patient. Why, then, do the symptoms persist? The most plausible explanation is that they provide immediate partial relief from the anxiety, and the motive for avoidance of anxiety is so strong that even partial alleviation is sufficient to maintain the neurotic behavior. Like the dogs in the avoidance box who fail to extinguish learned fears, the neurotic's avoidance of his conflict is so strong that he cannot face it and resolve it. The fact that the symptom provides immediate partial reduction of anxiety adds to the symptom's persistence. The neurotic may then find that his symptoms lead to new problems, but such unpleasant side effects are usually delayed. From the work of experimental psychologists we would expect that the *immediate* consequences would have the more powerful effect.

The Onset of Symptoms

The anxiety theory of neurosis traces the disorder to unresolved conflicts. However, no one is capable of solving every problem successfully. Why do some people develop symptoms while others can tolerate conflict? One factor appears to be amount of psychological stress to which a person is exposed. Evidence for this factor comes from studies of the incidence of neurosis in World War II soldiers. Some soldiers developed neurotic symptoms while in the United States; more developed them in Europe before combat; still more developed them in combat, and the longer the combat service, the fewer escaped neurotic symptoms. In short, the incidence of neurosis varied directly with the amount of stress.

But why did some soldiers develop neurosis before going overseas while others did not develop a neurosis despite months of combat? It is apparent that factors within the individual must account for this. We do not yet know the degree to which hereditary factors enter in. Identical twins are somewhat more alike than fraternal twins in tests differentiating neurotics from normals, which would indicate that heredity may be a predisposing factor in neurosis (Eysenck and Prell, 1951; Cattell, Blewett, and Beloff, 1955). Factors in the life history of the individual, however, seem to be more strongly related to ability to withstand stress. Neurotics report having had many more childhood fears than normal individuals. It may be that they simply are more likely to remember childhood fears than are other people. On the other hand, it may be that this indicates a lack of security in the family which gave the individual less strength to handle current anxiety. This second interpretation is supported by the work of clinical psychologists and psychiatrists who often trace neurotic symptoms in an adult patient to problems left unresolved in adolescence, childhood, and even infancy.

These two factors—amount of current psychological stress and frustration tolerance—combine to determine whether the resultant anxiety will produce symptoms. In some cases, a person with a moderate amount of frustration tolerance who is exposed to extreme psychological stress may develop neurotic symptoms. Such a neurosis is called a *traumatic* neurosis and is illustrated by the following case:

■ A 23-year-old flier was a fighter bomber pilot in World War II. He was eager to go overseas and was enthusiastic about his missions. In combat he attacked his targets with tenacity and while he had momentary periods of anxiety, even when he returned with flak holes in his plane, he was generally relaxed.

The first time he was really shaken was on his 39th mission. He was attacking an important airdrome and was so intent on destroying it that he pulled out of his dive too low and was caught in the explosion of his own bomb.

Although he was temporarily stunned, he brought his disabled plane back to his base. However, his confidence in his own ability was shaken and he determined to keep a tighter grip on himself. All went well until his 42nd mission when he became so intent on strafing a troop concentration that he failed to notice a mountain ahead and only at the last terrified moment was able to slip by it.

Now, with two narrow escapes from death, he began to dread going on missions. He lay awake at night thinking of flying, and seeing the mountain before him. When he fell asleep, he dreamed that his plane had been hit and was falling but that he could not get out of it. He frequently awoke in a cold sweat. During the day he stopped playing cards because he could not relax. Surprisingly, he felt more relaxed in his plane than on the ground and continued carrying out his missions, successfully. After his 54th mission he decided to talk his problem over with the Flight Surgeon.

The Flight Surgeon permitted him to continue flying but his efficiency began to deteriorate. On one occasion, he forgot to pull his bomb release switch, on another he forgot to strafe. His flying in formation and landings became poorer and poorer. When he was not flying he suffered from periodic attacks of anxiety. Finally, after his 65th mission, he was grounded and sent home. ∎*

On the other hand, neurotic symptoms may also be triggered by a rather mild stress in a person of low frustration tolerance already burdened with a great deal of repressed anxiety. The woman who developed conversion symptoms each time her husband lost his job illustrates such a combination of factors. Such neuroses have actually developed over a long period of time, although the onset of symptoms may be sudden.

The foregoing analysis of neurosis is based on observations made by clinical psychologists and psychiatrists in the course of treating neurotic patients. Although there is some disagreement about the kinds of conflict that produce neurotic symptoms, most psychologists accept the interpretation that symptoms are a manifestation of the patient's attempts to cope with overwhelming anxiety.

The Treatment of Neurosis: Psychotherapy

The most common treatment for neurosis is psychotherapy. There are a number of types of psychotherapy, but they are similar in that they rely upon talks between the patient and the psychotherapist. Psychotherapy is sometimes used with psychotic patients in conjunction with medical therapies. It is commonly used in the treatment of neuroses. Even more common is short-term counseling or psychotherapy, which is used with fairly normal individuals facing common problems, such as vocational choice, marital dissatisfaction, or child-rearing difficulties.

The classic form of psychotherapy is *psychoanalysis,* based on the theories and techniques developed by Freud. Freud taught that adult neuroses could always be traced to infancy and childhood experiences. In one of the developmental stages—the oral, anal, or Oedipal stages—according to Freud, the motive for expression of sensual urges conflicts so much with parental admonitions that the sensual motives are repressed, and thereafter much "psychic energy" must be devoted to defending against these threatening motives. The psychoanalyst attempts to reduce the patient's defenses and to bring the repressed material into consciousness so that the patient can recognize it and deal with it. In order to discover the nature of repressed material the psychoanalytic patient learns to free-associate: to say everything he is thinking, withholding nothing, no matter how irrelevant, bizarre, or embarrassing it may seem. The psychoanalyst accepts

* Excerpted from Grinker, R. R., and J. P. Spiegel, *Men Under Stress.* Philadelphia: Blakiston, 1945. Reprinted by permission.

all the patient reveals without shock or censorship. He has been trained to recognize the distortions and symbols that emerge in free associations to memories and dreams. Gradually, he teaches his patient to recognize the emotional significance of his behavior and the patient begins to find more appropriate ways of dealing with his problems. Timing is extremely important, for premature interpretation would lead only to denial, hostility, and confusion.

As therapy proceeds, a complex emotional relationship develops between the patient and his analyst. Freud called this relationship *transference* because he believed that it represented the patient's transference of childhood feelings toward his parents onto the therapist. When transference occurs, the patient is able to partially relive his childhood conflicts and to work them through.

Once the patient has been able to face and resolve the sources of his anxiety, he no longer needs to express his problem through neurotic symptoms, and they should disappear.

A complete psychoanalysis usually consists of four or more interviews a week for several years, and costs thousands of dollars. Freudian psychoanalysts do not usually treat psychotic or feeble-minded patients because of the difficulty these patients have in verbalizing their feelings. Because psychoanalysis is not applicable to all types of maladjustments and is so long and expensive, the number of patients treated by psychoanalysts is only a small proportion of the mental patients under treatment.

The first psychoanalysts were students who had been psychoanalyzed by Freud; these in turn trained other students as they psychoanalyzed them. As psychoanalysis spread, some of the analysts modified classical Freudian theory. For example, Adler believed that neurosis was not so much the result of conflict about sensual urges as it was an outgrowth of feelings of inferiority all young children feel. Some later analysts focused on social relationships in childhood as the basis of later disturbances (Horney and Sullivan). The various "schools" of psychoanalytic thought have in common the idea of the origin of neurosis in very early childhood experiences and the basic techniques of psychoanalytic therapy such as free association. Although the number of psychoanalysts is still very small (less than 1000 in the American Psychoanalytic Association) many psychiatrists, clinical psychologists, and social case workers base their procedures upon psychoanalytic theories.

A different theory and practice of psychotherapy was developed by Carl Rogers, who calls his method *client-centered* or *nondirective* therapy. Rogers assumes that within each person, there is a potential for a mature, healthy personality. If a person is permitted to explore his own thoughts freely in the presence of a sympathetic, accepting helper, the person himself will be able to work out his emotional problems. The therapist trained in client-centered therapy learns to control his natural tendency to advise, or to direct or reinterpret his client's statements. Rather, his only statements summarize and clarify the feelings that patient expresses. As the therapist shows that he accepts the patient's feelings, ideas, and actions, without reservation, the patient finds that he too can accept these aspects of himself. Now he can use his growing self-knowledge to cope with and solve his original problem.

Client-centered therapy was developed by an academic psychologist and its techniques are sometimes used in psychological clinics connected with universities. The average number of contacts between therapist and patient (or client, as Rogers prefers to call him) is about 10. Some psychologists criticize the theory behind this type of therapy on the basis that the therapist probably unconsciously directs the statements of his patients by his facial expressions and even by his "mmm-hmm." These critics point out that verbal behavior can be controlled by subtle words and gestures, so that the therapy is not as non-directive as it seems. (For an experiment demonstrating the subtle control of verbal behavior, see page 292.)

There are several striking differences between psychoanalytic and client-centered therapy. The psychoanalyst traces his patient's problems to an earlier period of his life; the nondirective therapist is most interested in his client's present ideas and feelings. The psychoanalyst consciously directs his patient to particular subjects, prompting him to use free association, and to interpret memories, dreams, and slips of the tongue in terms of Freudian theory; the client-centered therapist tries to avoid structuring the patient's utterances in any way. His only interpretations are his attempts to restate the feelings this patient has expressed.

Despite these differences both in theoretical background and in technique, there are many common features. Both forms of psychotherapy rely on a voluntary relationship between a person who seeks help and a professional trained to give such help. In both, the means to this help is verbal communication between therapist and patient. In both, the therapist provides an atmosphere in which the patient feels free to put into words the ideas and emotions which he has previously felt unable to express to others. And both provide an opportunity for gradual emotional change as a result of this unique relationship between patient and therapist.

Varieties of Therapy

Many therapists would not classify themselves in either the classic psychoanalytic category or the client-centered category. Rather, they use elements of both, depending on their own inclinations, the specific patient, and the problem. Because the personality of the therapist is such an important element in the treatment, there is some justification to the statement that there are as many different kinds of therapy as there are therapists.

Therapy with children presents particular problems since, first, the child has not chosen to initiate therapy and second, he does not have the verbal skills to express his feelings. For this reason a new technique, *play therapy*, was de-

(a) The therapist presents his young patient with a doll family: father, mother, daughter, and son.

(b) The young patient expresses her hostility toward her mother by making the girl doll stamp on the head of the mother doll.

FIG. 14–2. The use of play therapy to permit a child to express her problems. (Photos courtesy of Dr. J. C. Solomon)

veloped. Here the child is given an opportunity to express, work through, and resolve his problems using dolls and other play materials as well as words (see Fig. 14–2).

Another variant of psychotherapy originally developed as a response to the length and costliness of psychotherapy. In *group therapy*, several patients meet in a group with a single therapist. This type of therapy is particularly effective

(c) The therapist presents a scene in which the family is about to board a streetcar. The young patient makes the car "run over" the mother and the little brother.

(d) A close-up of the results of (c). Father and daughter stand by as the car runs over mother and brother.

for patients with less severe problems who require social support and an opportunity to test social reality.

There are many other variations and techniques, too numerous to describe. However, we do want to mention a recent development in the treatment of neurosis and other maladjustments which is becoming increasingly more influential. In our discussion of symptom selection, we noted that the learning hypothesis states that a neurotic symptom can be considered a habit, and that the patient's particular symptoms depend on the acts for which he has been rewarded or punished. This would imply that the neurotic symptom could be eliminated by using the principles of learning: reinforcement, extinction, successive approximations. The application of these principles to clinical patients is called *behavior therapy*.

One of the symptoms for which behavior therapy seems to be particularly effective is the phobia. In accordance with the theory that neurosis is the product of learning, the behavior therapist considers a phobia a learned fear and he seeks to eliminate it by extinction and relearning. In Chapter 7, we saw how a little boy's fear of a rabbit was alleviated by extinction and successive approximation. While the little boy was eating (an act considered incompatible with fear) a white rabbit was placed in a corner of the room. The boy continued to eat and showed no sign of fear. On succeeding days the rabbit was placed closer and closer to the little boy; this was done so gradually that his fear of the rabbit eventually dissolved.

The principles applied here are (1) finding a response incompatible with fear, and (2) eliciting that response as the stimulus situation becomes increasingly close to including the object of the phobia. Wolpe (1958) has used the same techniques in a more typical psychotherapeutic situation with phobic patients. His first step is to identify the situations in which the patient feels intense, moderate, and low anxiety. Then he teaches the patient muscular relaxation— another act incompatible with anxiety. The crucial step is to have the patient practice muscular relaxation while imagining situations that gradually approach those that formerly produced anxiety. Wolpe reports a high percentage of success using this treatment.

Other applications of learning theory involve rewarding a patient when his behavior is free of symptoms, and occasional use of aversive conditioning. (The latter has been used in treatment of alcoholism and homosexuality.) Notice that the behavior therapist does not make any assumptions about the underlying causes of the neurosis as many psychoanalysts and psychologists do. For him the symptom *is* the neurosis; and eliminating the symptom constitutes curing the neurosis. Psychoanalytically oriented psychologists contend that eliminating symptoms without considering the underlying conflict would merely result in the formation of a different symptom. Thus far such an outcome has not been reported, and a lively controversy between behavior therapists and more traditional therapists continues.

Some psychologists consider the techniques of behavior therapy not as a substitute for traditional therapy but as an additional tool for use in appropriate cases. When a symptom is very incapacitating, when the patient is unable to talk about his symptoms without being overcome by anxiety, traditional therapy may be more successful if the symptoms are first eliminated.

The Effectiveness of Psychotherapy

It is extremely difficult to give a precise evaluation of psychotherapy for neurotics, or to compare the relative success of particular techniques or theories. Different therapists do not have comparable groups of patients. They do not regularly compare their records. Control groups that would permit us to estimate the number of spontaneous recoveries are difficult to obtain. A few surveys seem to suggest that 60 to 70 percent of the patients who seek and complete treatment of some sort are cured or greatly improved. Traumatic neuroses which develop in adults seem to have an even greater chance of being reduced or eliminated (Eysenck, 1961).

Explanations of neurotic behavior are still theory, and the techniques developed to alleviate symptoms grew up in the absence of complete knowledge, without the benefit of scientific verification. Nevertheless, if a person is disturbed about his symptoms and his anxieties and decides to seek professional help, his chances for improvement are good.

Psychosomatic Disorders

We saw earlier that high arousal is accompanied by bodily changes such as increased heartbeat, secretions of adrenalin, and high blood pressure. Prolonged maintenance of high arousal keeps the body's stress mechanisms working at a continually high level, and may lead eventually to over-reaction and organ damage or malfunction. Such disorders include high blood pressure, skin disease, migraine headaches, asthma, and ulcers (Selye, 1956). Because psychological stress is one source of high arousal, in some cases these conditions may be the result of emotional problems, although there are many other possible causes for these conditions. When psychological problems are a major factor in organic pathology, the patient's condition is referred to as a *psychosomatic disorder*. As an example of the interaction of physiological and psychological factors in psychosomatic disorders we shall examine these factors in conjunction with peptic ulcers.

The immediate physiological cause of peptic ulcers is clear. A peptic ulcer is a crater-like wound in the lining of the gastrointestinal tract, usually caused by excessive secretion of digestive juices. A series of animal experiments performed by different investigators have attempted to track down just why this oversecretion of digestive juices takes place. Studies of rats have shown that some strains of rats are born with a greater tendency toward ulcers than others (Sines, 1961). In his experiments on the general effects of stress, Selye (1956) demonstrated that animals who are exposed to extreme physical stress such as prolonged cold temperatures tend to develop ulcers. And experimental psychologists have shown a relationship between psychological stress and ulcers (Brady, 1958).

■ Brady's studies followed the development of ulcers in monkeys. These monkeys had been trained to avoid an electric shock by pressing a lever. If the monkey failed to press the lever, he received a brief shock every 20 seconds or at some other regular interval. The monkeys quickly learned to press the lever regularly in order to avoid the shock. But many of these monkeys also developed ulcers.

Were these ulcers simply the result of being shocked? To find out, Brady and his associates experimented with pairs of monkeys, one of whom could prevent the shocks both to himself and his partner by pressing the lever (see Fig. 14–3). Thus both monkeys received the same number of shocks. The monkey who pressed the lever to avoid shock, however, was the one who tended to get ulcers.

FIG. 14–3. A pair of monkeys used in Brady's experiment on ulcers. The monkey on the left, "the executive," can prevent the regular electric shocks for both monkeys by pressing the lever in front of him. The monkey on the right can do nothing to prevent the shock; his lever is not connected with anything. (From Brady, 1958. Photo courtesy of the Medical Audio Visual Dept., Walter Reed Army Institute of Research)

Brady's group carried out further experiments to find out what additional factors were important in producing ulcers. One of these was the rhythm of work and rest. The original experimental monkeys had worked 6 hours and rested 6 hours. Changing this period reduced ulcers. Monkeys with 18 hours on and 6 hours off did not develop ulcers, nor did monkeys with 30 minutes on and 30 minutes off. Further investigation showed that the increased secretion of acid gastric juices built up during the rest period (see Fig. 14–4). ■

It may be that during the stress period, gastric secretion is inhibited. When the stress period is over, the body may overcompensate by secreting excess amounts of acid. This would suggest that ulcers are most likely to develop in a person who experiences frequent, intermittent stress situations.

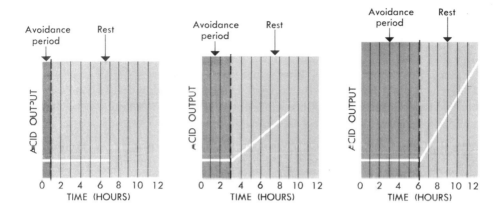

FIG. 14–4. Acid output in the stomach of "executive" monkeys as a function of the schedule of avoidance sessions and rest periods. Note that the increase in stomach acidity occurred during the rest period, after a sustained period during which the monkey had to press the bar continually to avoid shock. (From Brady, J. V., "Ulcers in executive monkeys," *Sci. Amer.*, October, 1958. Reprinted by permission.)

Some human case histories also suggest a relationship between psychological stress and ulcers. Here is an illustration:

■ Sammy G. came from a wealthy family. His father, a self-made man, had built up an internationally famous marine salvage company. He was away from home a great deal, visiting his branch offices throughout the world, and Sammy and his mother did not see too much of him. The family had servants and Sammy's mother, with little to do, devoted much of her time to Sammy. Until he was nine, his mother had Sammy tutored at home and it was only upon his father's insistence that Sammy was finally sent to a local school. Sammy's mother herself drove him to and from school and also stopped by every day to have lunch with him, so that he had little contact with his fellow pupils outside class. When Sammy went away to college, his mother wrote to him daily and drove up and spent every weekend with him. When Sammy was a senior, his father died of a heart attack and Sammy suddenly found himself owner of a huge commercial enterprise. Sammy's uncle (his mother's brother), who had been executive assistant to Sammy's father in charge of the home office, helped Sammy take over the business. Sammy devoted himself to the job with tremendous energy and soon became regarded as "a chip off the old block." Sammy's uncle, satisfied that Sammy was capable of taking over the reins of the company, retired and went to live in Switzerland. Six months after his uncle retired, Sammy developed stomach ulcers and had to be hospitalized. ■

In this case, it is quite likely that Sammy G.'s anxiety about assuming full responsibility and his unconscious desire for dependency were contributing factors to the development of ulcers.

However, this again raises the question of symptom selection. Why did Sammy G. react by developing ulcers rather than some other psychosomatic disorder? There are several hypotheses. The *weak-link* hypothesis states that Sammy G. developed ulcers because he already had a physiological tendency toward ulcers which was manifested during a period of stress. The *learning hypothesis* suggests that the ulcer patient may previously have been rewarded for stomach trouble. The *emotional-link* hypothesis states that certain emotions automatically lead to increased gastric secretions. The ulcer would be a natural concomitant of certain strong feelings while other psychosomatic disorders would be the result of other strong emotions. Finally, the *psychoanalytic hypothesis* would examine an ulcer symptom just as it would a neurotic symptom, looking at gastric malfunction as a manifestation of the failure to resolve oral conflicts, particularly those revolving around dependency.

The genetic study in rats we mentioned earlier supports the weak-link hypothesis. The emotional-link hypothesis finds some support in the observations of Wolf and Wolff (1942). One of their patients was a man whose esophagus had been so severely burned that scar tissue completely closed the passage. Surgeons created a stomach fistula in order to feed him. This also gave investigators an opportunity to study his stomach secretions. They found increased acidity when the man was angry and resentful but a marked drop in acidity during periods of fear or sadness. The proponents of the psychoanalytic hypothesis point to cases of ulcers which have been successfully treated by psychoanalysis when other medical therapies produced only temporary alleviation (Alexander, 1932). Again the data suggest that no single hypothesis is sufficient to account for all the facts.

The Treatment of Psychosomatic Disorders

Psychosomatic disorders involve both true organic damage and psychological problems. Their treatment therefore necessitates both the medical and the psychological attacks. Medical therapy can alleviate and control the condition, e.g., prevent increased stomach acidity with drugs for ulcers, clear the bronchial passageways in asthma. However, if the causes of the condition are not removed, the disorder will recur. Thus the psychological stress precipitating the condition must also be considered. Sometimes it can be removed by changes in the patient's situation, for example, by lessening the burdens of responsibility on an ulcer-ridden executive. Or psychotherapy may be useful in that it permits the patient to resolve the problem which is producing the emotional tension.

The analysis and treatment of psychosomatic disorders serve as a reminder that the organism cannot neatly be separated into mind and body. Mind depends on nervous-system activity, and the nervous system has complex interrelationships with all the organ systems of the body.

Psychoses

The psychoses are the most serious forms of maladjustment. It is the person with a psychosis who in everyday language is called "crazy" and who is likely to be pronounced legally insane. Psychosis is marked by such deterioration of cognitive and emotional faculties that the psychotic becomes incapable of normal functioning.

Most of the patients in mental hospitals are psychotics. Currently there are about 500,000 patients in mental hospitals in this country, and Cameron (1963) estimates that if sufficient facilities were available 1,500,000 more would be committed. About one person in twelve becomes so maladjusted at some point during his life that he requires hospitalization.

Psychoses are divided into two major categories: organic and functional. *Organic psychoses* are those in which some physiological injury or disease is clearly an important factor. *Functional psychoses* are those in which there is no evidence of brain damage.

Organic Psychoses

Damage to the nervous system which results in bizarre behavior typical of psychosis may be caused by the circulatory disturbances of old age, syphilitic infection, brain tumor, accidental injury, or nervous system disease. The symptoms often include impairments of orientation and comprehension, disturbed judgment and thinking, and inappropriateness of affect (Coleman, 1956). The severity of the disturbance depends not only on the nature and extent of physical injury but also on the prepsychotic personality of the patient and the current environmental circumstances. A person whose brain is not functioning efficiently might not have difficulty in solving the problems of everyday life. But if there are additional problems of adjustment, as in old age, and this is coupled with reduced problem-solving ability, maladjustment is not surprising. We see an interaction of factors in the following case of senile deterioriation:

■ "The patient was 65 years old when her only son died from influenza at the age of 39. Shortly thereafter her relatives noticed that she was less alert, less attentive, and less active than she had been prior to her son's death. Her memory began to grow weaker. Four years later her husband died at the age of 70 from cancer of the colon. The shock of his death led to a severe depression. During this depressive period she lapsed into a semiconfused state. Her mind would wander, and her memory became less and less dependable. Because of inability to care for her own needs, she went to live with her daughter-in-law, who cared for her as well as she could under the circumstances. Her mental condition grew worse as time went on. Habits of eating, sleeping, cleanliness, and elimination gradually deteriorated. Lapses of attention and memory became more frequent, more severe, and more disconcerting. For about two years prior to hospitalization she had to be closely watched and supervised, for her extreme forgetfulness endangered her life and that of the other members of the household. She would turn on the gas stove and leave it on without remembering that she had done so. She would eat a hearty meal and a few minutes later ask for food, complaining that she had not eaten all day. She had a voracious appetite, consuming about four times as much food as she was used to eating before her illness. She talked to herself more and more frequently in a loud tone of voice, especially at night after everyone retired. She was not particularly intractable, but at times she behaved like a naughty child. She imagined that she saw strange people in the house and heard their voices.

"About six months before her admission to the hospital her memory failed almost completely. She was confused and irrational. The day after her return from a three months' rest in Florida she could not recall having been to Florida and insisted that she had never been there. The mere presence of her grandchildren annoyed her. She constantly complained of being mistreated by them, although there was no evidence to support her complaints. She often expressed the wish that she were dead, but made no attempts at suicide. She grew restless and irritable and was very much dissatisfied without apparent reason. She acquired the odd habit of tearing up newspapers and toilet tissue. She spoke of her dead husband as if he were alive; she steadfastly refused to believe that he had died because she "saw him, talked to him as he was leaving for work and returning from his office." Since she required more care than could be provided at home, the family physician recommended that she be committed to the state hospital. Her age at the time of commitment was 72." ■*

TREATMENT OF ORGANIC PSYCHOSES. The treatment and prognosis for organic psychosis depend upon its cause. Some organic psychoses have practically been eliminated. For example, the psychosis pellagra was found to be a disease caused by a nutritional deficiency: lack of vitamin B-2. When the diet of the patients suffering from pellagra was supplemented with this vitamin the symptoms disappeared. The incidence of general paresis, the psychosis associated with the final stages of syphilitic infection, has been greatly reduced by prevention and by early detection and treatment with drugs. Other organic psychoses stem from circulatory or other causes of deterioration. Prognosis for improvement is poor under usual conditions of care. Many patients with organic damage can, however, function happily and productively with special attention.

Functional Psychoses

The two most common types of functional psychosis are *schizophrenia* and *manic-depressive psychosis*. Out of any hundred people, one or two develop manic-depressive psychosis and two or three, schizophrenia. About one-fourth of the first admissions to mental hospitals are for schizophrenia and about one-sixth are diagnosed as manic-depressive. In this country there are about 250,000 people presently hospitalized for schizophrenia.

* From Jastak, J., "Senile Psychosis," in A. Burton and R. E. Harris (eds.), *Case Studies in Clinical and Abnormal Psychology*. New York: Harper and Bros., 1947. Reprinted by permission.

Schizoprenic patients may exhibit a wide variety of symptoms, all of them characterized by an apparent lack of coherence between the individual's thoughts and feelings and his reactions to his environment. Psychologists usually distinguish four symptom types: (1) The *simple* schizophrenic shows disturbances of thinking and attention, apathy, and blunted affect. Onset is gradual; the patient gradually withdraws more and more from the outside world. The case of Mike, the quiet, obedient 12-year-old boy illustrates this type. (2) The distinguishing characteristics of the *catatonic* schizophrenic are peculiar gestures and postures, and stereotyped actions. Occasionally, the patient goes through phases of catatonic excitement and stupor. The excitement phase is marked by uncontrollable bursts of energy during which the patient may endanger his own life and those of others. The stupors, which are much more common and more prolonged, are periods during which the patient remains in one position for days and does not move or speak. He may be limp, allowing someone to place him in any position, or he may actively resist any change in position. (3) The *paranoid* schizophrenic has a well-developed delusional* system often accompanied by hallucinations. His delusions usually involve the idea that he is being persecuted; many paranoids invent elaborate systems of plot and counterplot. The following conversation between doctor and patient includes many of the elements of the paranoid form of schizophrenia.

■ *Doctor:* What's your name?
Patient: Who are you?
Doctor: I'm a doctor. Who are you?
Patient: I can't tell you who I am.
Doctor: Why can't you tell me?
Patient: You wouldn't believe me.
Doctor: What are you doing here?
Patient: Well, I've been sent here to thwart the Russians. I'm the only one in the world who knows how to deal with them. They got their spies all around here, though, to get me, but I'm smarter than any of them.
Doctor: What are you going to do to thwart the Russians?
Patient: I'm organizing.
Doctor: Whom are you going to organize?
Patient: Everybody. I'm the only man in the world who can do that, but they're trying to get me. But I'm going to use my atomic bomb media to blow them up.
Doctor: You must be a terribly important person, then.
Patient: Well, of course.
Doctor: What do you call yourself?
Patient: You used to know me as Franklin D. Roosevelt.
Doctor: Isn't he dead?
Patient: Sure he's dead, but I'm alive.

---

* A delusion is a false belief maintained despite contrary evidence or logical absurdity.

Doctor: But you're Franklin D. Roosevelt?

Patient: His spirit. He, God, and I figured this out. And now I'm going to make a race of healthy people. My agents are lining them up. Say, who are you?

Doctor: I'm a doctor here.

Patient: You don't look like a doctor. You look like a Russian to me.

Doctor: How can you tell a Russian from one of your agents?

Patient: I read eyes. I get all my signs from eyes. I look into your eyes and get all my signs from them.

Doctor: Do you sometimes hear voices telling you someone is a Russian?

Patient: No, I just look into eyes. I got a mirror here to look into my own eyes. I know everything that's going on. I can tell by the color, by the way it's shaped.

Doctor: Did you have any trouble with people before you came here?

Patient: Well, only the Russians. They were trying to surround me in my neighborhood. One day they tried to drop a bomb on me from the fire escape.

Doctor: How could you tell it was a bomb?

Patient: I just knew. ■*

(4) The *hebephrenic* displays inappropriate smiling and laughter, bizarre ideas, and incoherent, disorganized speech in which he may make up new words (called neologisms). The following is a reproduction of a conversation between a doctor and a Negro patient with hebephrenic symptoms:

■ *Doctor:* How old are you?

Patient: Why, I am centuries old, sir.

Doctor: How long have you been here?

Patient: I have been now on this property on and off for a long time. I cannot say the exact time because we are absorbed by the air at night, and they bring back people. They kill up everything; they can make you lie; they can talk through your throat.

Doctor: Who is this?

Patient: Why, the air.

Doctor: What is the name of this place?

Patient: This place is called a star.

Doctor: Who is the doctor in charge of your ward?

Patient: A body just like yours, sir. They can make you black and white. I say good morning, but he just comes through there. At first it was a colony. They said it was heaven. These buildings were not solid at the time, and I am positive this is the same place. They have others just like it. People die, and all the microbes talk over there, and prestigitis you know is sending you from here to another world . . . I was sent by the government to the United States to Washington to some star, and they had a pretty nice country there. Now you have a body like a young man who says he is of the prestigitis.

Doctor: Who was this prestigitis?

Patient: Why you are yourself. You can be a prestigitis. They make you say bad things; they can read you; they bring back Negroes from the dead. ■†

---

* From Coleman, J. C., *Abnormal Psychology and Modern Life*, second edition. Chicago: Scott, Foresman, 1956. Reprinted by permission.

† From White, R. W., *The Abnormal Personality*, second edition. New York: Ronald, 1956. Reprinted by permission.

Although these four symptom types are useful for classification and description, many patients do not clearly fit one category or another. In fact, it is sometime difficult to determine whether a patient should be classified as a schizophrenic or as a manic-depressive.

The *manic-depressive* psychoses are characterized by extreme distortions of feeling—extreme depression, extreme elation, or periodic mood swings from one to the other. The manic patient is highly energetic, optimistic, and self-confident, and may become violent if blocked. His flights of fantasy may include elaborate plans and delusions of great wealth, status, or competence. On the other hand, the depressed patient is very, very dejected; his movements and speech are very slow; he is slow to initiate activity; he feels that his life has been worthless, that he has done much harm and little good. Depressed patients sometimes attempt to commit suicide. Although some patients are depressed and others are manic, sometimes a patient will have cycles of manic phases alternating with depressed phases. M. E., the returning Navy man described in the chapter introduction, was probably suffering from a manic-depressive psychosis.

The Causes of Functional Psychoses

Unfortunately it is not possible to give a definite answer to the question: What causes psychosis? We have three lines of evidence which give us some idea of the factors which may be involved.

1. STUDIES OF FAMILY HISTORY. The family histories of psychotic patients often show other cases of psychosis. For example, Kallman (1953) collected data which show that 0.85 percent of the general population becomes schizophrenic; but in families where one parent is schizophrenic, 16.4 percent of the children also develop schizophrenia. He also found that 14.7 percent of the fraternal twins born to schizophrenics will become schizophrenic, as contrasted with 85 percent of the identical twins born to schizophrenics. This latter finding has been used to support the hypothesis that functional psychoses are primarily inherited disorders. Other studies of family history do not show concordance rates as high as Kallman's but they show the same trends. Similar evidence has been presented for the inheritance of a predisposition to manic-depressive psychosis. While such studies are significant, they are not conclusive, for environmental factors in families of schizophrenic parents or siblings are less than ideal. Even the comparisons of fraternal and identical twins, which offer stronger evidence, cannot get around the possibility that the environments of identical twins may be more similar than those of fraternal twins.

2. CASE HISTORIES. The case histories of psychotics suggest the importance of environmental factors in the development of psychosis. Consider, for example, the following case.

■ Clara and Doris were identical twins. Their father, a logger, was an alcoholic; their mother had been a dancer before marriage. According to Clara's reports, the mother was so upset when the father left that she burned down the house and put the children in an orphanage. At this time Clara and Doris were not yet two years old. Within a year both girls were adopted and did not see each other again until they were about 30.

Clara was adopted by a family with no other children. Her foster father owned a small store, and the family lived over the store. He liked building things, and Clara spent much time with him. Clara's childhood was fairly happy, even though her mother kept her close to home and permitted only one special chum to come into the house very much. She was never punished, and her parents were generous with her. At the age of 15 or 16 Clara began to work in a factory and held various unskilled jobs until she married at the age of 17. She joined the Lutheran church, belonged to the Ladies' Aid and two lodges, and handled her children easily, giving them a good deal of freedom. She was very talkative, lighthearted, and spontaneous but had good self-control.

Doris was adopted by a carpenter's family. They had two daughters and a son and seemed to have always regarded Doris as a burden. Doris' foster parents were very strict, and Doris was punished frequently and severely. Doris started her schooling at the age of six, but hated it, and was often kept after school for mistakes. When this occurred, she was whipped as soon as she got home and put to bed with nothing to eat until the following noon. Doris held various jobs until she married at the age of 23. Her husband was a shell-shocked veteran of World War I, who worked only intermittently, so that they were in constant financial distress.

While Clara's health was generally good, Doris suffered from many illnesses and injuries. She was subject to nervous spells and was finally admitted to a state hospital for treatment of manic-depressive psychosis. ■*

Since Clara and Doris were identical in heredity, the fact that Clara did not become psychotic while Doris did is evidence that environmental factors enter into the development of psychosis. A number of reviewers suggest that certain kinds of infantile experiences are associated with the later development of psychosis. The mothers of schizophrenic children are typically rejecting, perfectionistic, moralistic, and dominating (Coleman, 1956). Psychoanalysts usually interpret psychosis as arising out of problems in the oral stage of development and view the symptoms as a return to infantile modes of perceiving, thinking, and behaving.

There is little evidence that environmental stress precipitates the onset of psychotic episodes. For example, we saw earlier that during World War II, the incidence of neurosis increased the longer the troops were in combat. There was no comparable increase in psychosis (Stouffer, 1949).

3. DRUG STUDIES. Recently several drugs have been discovered which, in very small amounts, produce psychotic-like episodes in the recipient. Here, for example, is how a clinical psychologist describes his thoughts and feelings under the influence of lysergic acid.

---

* Adapted from Burkes, B. S. and A. Roe, "Studies of twins reared apart," *Psychol. Monogr.*, **63**, 5 (No. 300), 1949.

■ "Beginning with the physiological sensations, I was shortly flooded by a montage of ideas, images, and feelings that seemed to thrust themselves upon me unbidden. I had glimpses of very bright thoughts, like a fleeting insight into the psychotic process, which I wanted to write down or report to Dr. Krus. But they pushed each other aside. Once gone, they could not be recaptured because the parade of new images could not be stopped. At this point I should have settled back to enjoy a dreamlike or perhaps hallucinatory fantasy. As an introspective clinical psychologist, however, I tried to think. I tried to think about the meaning of the experience, about the integrity of the self, and about the difference between sanity and insanity. These can be troublesome thoughts when one is lucid. When they become the content of an uncontrolled, free-wheeling flight of ideas, they become frightening. The issue of mastery over apperception became an issue of selfhood. I had lost the observer role. I could tell myself that people recover from the LSD reaction. At the same time, I was informed enough to realize that I was taking it harder than most people do. Perhaps I would be the historic exception who did not recover. As a dynamically oriented psychologist, I now became disturbed that I could entertain such a possibility. By this time, I had superimposed a real psychogenic anxiety on the effects of the drug itself—and Dr. Freeman took me in hand. It was not until I slept, and awoke the next morning, that I felt myself again." ■*

The discovery of these drugs has heightened speculation that some metabolic imbalance is responsible for functional psychosis. A great deal of research has been devoted recently to finding biochemical differences between psychotics and normals, particularly in adrenal functioning. No such differences have been definitely established as yet (Kety, 1959) but the research continues in the hope of finding a chemical abnormality which can then be treated with chemotherapy.

The Treatment of Functional Psychoses

Because he is incapable of caring for himself and because he may be a danger to himself or to society, the psychotic is usually hospitalized. Some hospitals provide little more than custodial care, but others provide a variety of medical and psychological techniques. Psychotherapy is difficult because the psychotic's condition sometimes precludes the establishment of a therapeutic relationship. Many of the medical therapies are designed to give the patient sufficient hold on reality so that psychotherapy can proceed. Medical therapies are carried out by psychiatirsts, medical doctors who are specialists in the treatment of mental illness.

One such medical technique is electroshock therapy. Here, a convulsion-producing electric shock is applied to the patient's head. Shock therapy has been found useful mainly for shortening the duration of psychotic depressions. No one knows, however, what the physiological effects of shock therapy are or why it produces the results it does.

---

* From Bennett, C. H., "Drugs and I," in *Drugs and Behavior*. New York: Wiley, 1960. Reprinted by permission.

Electro- and insulin-shock therapy developed in the absence of any other means for coping with psychotic patients. Today, these techniques are being replaced more and more with drug therapy—tranquilizers for the overexcited patients and stimulants for depressed patients. Specialized techniques of psychotherapy for psychotics are also developing.

Of course, the crucial test of all of these means of therapy is their success in helping or curing psychosis. Unfortunately, there is little evidence of their effectiveness as compared with spontaneous recovery levels. However, recovery rates are much better than the layman usually believes, and discharges from the hospital are increasing. Today about 90 percent of the schizophrenics who receive early treatment and almost 100 percent of the manic-depressive patients are sufficiently improved to be discharged from the mental hospitals (Coleman, 1963).

Conduct Disorders

This category encompasses many heterogeneous disorders such as sexual deviations, alcoholism, drug addiction, and criminal behavior. These maladjustments are defined in terms of a set of symptoms, which may arise from a variety of causes. As an example of a conduct disorder, we shall examine the causes and treatment of juvenile delinquency.

A juvenile delinquent is identified in legal rather than psychological or medical terms: he is a youth or adolescent who has been convicted of committing a crime. There may be a variety of psychological factors which culminate in the same type of behavior.

In a search for the causes of delinquency, one outstanding fact is that delinquency is not distributed equally among the total population. The delinquent tends to come from a congested, poverty-stricken area in a city. (Figure 14–5 shows the concentration of delinquency in certain areas of Chicago.) In such areas, young people often congregate in gangs whose norms are to flout the norms and laws of the larger society. The *dissocial* delinquent is a youngster with strong loyalties and deep emotional attachment to his peers. He has learned to distrust established institutions and expect little from them. He clashes with society because the values of his subculture are in conflict with the laws of the land. Once he has gotten involved in lawlessness, problems snowball, making it more and more difficult for him to stay out of trouble. How a normal young man can become involved in delinquent behavior is illustrated by the case of Smokey.

■ "Smokey, a Negro boy of 17, had been born in Florida but brought to New York City by his parents when he was a small child. Father, mother, and five children, of whom Smokey was the eldest, lived in a housing project in a gang-ridden area of Brooklyn. Smokey's life had a number of stabilizing elements: his parents were both present in the home; they were interested in and

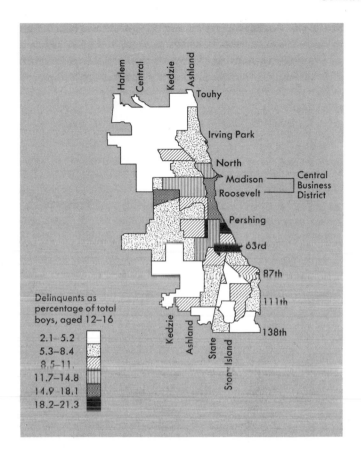

FIG. 14–5. The distribution of juvenile delinquency in Chicago. The greatest percentage of delinquency is found in the areas that are not far from the central business
district. (From Cavan, R. S., *Juvenile Delinquency*. Philadelphia: Lippincott, 1962.
Reproduced by permission.)

concerned for their children, holding them under strict discipline. The father, a machinist, supported
the family, and the children were adequately clothed. Smokey loved his mother and was respectful
and affectionate toward his father. He did not want to do things to hurt them. In addition to
attending school, Smokey held a part-time job as a messenger boy. He looked forward to the
day when he might become a policeman. He had a girl with whom he went steadily, and he looked
forward to marriage in the future. All these things point toward a well-organized adolescence
and a stable and conventional future.

"However, Smokey also had experiences and relationships that pulled him in the opposite direction. At the age of 13 he found that he could not remain outside a street gang without repeatedly
being beaten up. He therefore joined one of the stronger gangs and became a leader. He felt
responsible for his gang and its reputation and he came to depend on it for affection, approval,
and status. He had not been able to avoid all delinquency and was on probation. His parents

knew he belonged to a gang but did not know it was a "bopping" gang, that is, one that included gang fights in its regular activities.

"Soon after he had related these facts to a reporter who had befriended him, a critical event happened which broke the slender threads that held him to a conventional life and future. He had beaten up a boy and taken money from him, both serious offenses. He was arrested, and his parents learned of his life with the gang. His father had to borrow $300 for bail. Since the housing project had a policy of ordering out any family who had a child in trouble, the family was given an eviction notice to move within two months. His parents therefore were angry with him. The move would entail more debt, since some private apartment owners require a preliminary payment of several hundred dollars as "key money." He was in jail a week and therefore lost his job. With his world tumbling around him, Smokey saw no reason to continue school. And in addition to these disturbing events, Smokey's girl, aged fifteen, told him she was pregnant. He therefore stopped going with her.

"The sudden change precipitated by his assault on the other boy was more than Smokey could handle. He gave up and turned in the direction of personal disorganization and seemingly toward more crime. He increased his drinking, which had been moderate before, and lost status with his gang, which became involved in more fighting. He became belligerent and ready to fight anyone. The reporter noted that in all probability when his case comes to trial he will be sentenced to prison unless he is again placed on probation; he is now past the age for the juvenile court. If Smokey had grown up in a different neighborhood he might have passed through adolescence without any difficulty." ■*

Smokey's case is not unique. Two different studies (Riess, 1952; Hewitt and Jenkins, 1946) indicate that over 60 percent of the delinquents studied did not show personality maladjustments.

The *antisocial delinquent,* on the other hand, is one who suffers from emotional conflict and anxiety. He expresses his problems by striking out against society. Ace, the 16-year-old boy described at the beginning of the chapter, probably belongs in this category. Ace's criminal acts not only conformed to gang norms but also provided a way of expressing his hostility to his father and to authority in general. Several investigations suggest that family relationships in which the father is harshly critical toward his child and severe in his discipline, while he himself fails to embody the rules of society, provide particularly fertile ground for the development of a delinquent (Aichorn, 1935; Bandura and Walters, 1959). In such a case, a boy has little hope of gaining his father's approval and love; he has no adequate model after whom to pattern his behavior, and no one to selectively praise, reprove, and correct his behavior fairly. Other typically delinquent-producing homes are ones in which there is no father at all to provide a model. These family patterns are not restricted to any social class; however, they are more prevalent in the lowest socioeconomic group.

---

* From Cavan, R. S., *Juvenile Delinquency.* Philadelphia: Lippincott, 1962. Reprinted by permission.

Although we separated delinquents into either dissocial or antisocial types, it is quite likely that some interaction between social conditions and family relationships most frequently produces delinquency. Most children, even in high-delinquency neighborhoods, do not become delinquent. It has been suggested that cohesive affectionate families, fair and consistent discipline, and parental interest in children's activities are factors which serve to deter young men and women from lawless activities even when social pressures for them are strong (McCord, McCord and Zola, 1959). On the other hand, the child who feels deprived of love and who learns to hate authority as a result of his experiences at home will be most likely to use the outlets against society that are available in the subculture of the slum.

A third kind of delinquent fits into the psychiatric classification of *psychopath*. A psychopath is a person who has failed to interiorize norms or values. He seeks immediate gratification of his own desires regardless of the consequences for others. The classic description of the psychopath states that he appears emotionally warm and charming but that he is incapable of close interpersonal relationships. If he becomes involved in crime, it is probably as an individual, not as part of the gang.

The cause of psychopathic development is not known. Some researchers believe that the psychopath's brain does not function normally. They point out that the behavior may develop following brain tumors, head injuries, or diseases like encephalitis and that the incidence of abnormal EEG waves is greater among psychopaths than among normals (White, 1963). Other investigators emphasize childhood rejection as the reason the psychopath failed to interiorize any set of moral standards (Karpman, 1951). Neither explanation has received general acceptance. One reason it has been difficult to gather evidence is that many psychopaths never come to the attention of legal authorities and the proportion of psychopaths among juvenile delinquents is small (White, 1963).

Because the psychopath is unmotivated for psychotherapy and because the etiology of the disorder is not clear, it is extremely difficult to correct the condition. One recent approach has been to try to create a therapeutic community in which the psychopaths work, participate in group therapy, and become increasingly more responsible for their own activities (Jones, 1953, 1962).

The Treatment of Delinquency

The juvenile delinquent who has come to the attention of the courts several times is likely to be taken from his community and placed in a reformatory or training school. Today, emphasis in these correctional institutions is placed on rehabilitation both by vocational training and by counseling. However, there are many inherent difficulties in the rehabilitation process. Being placed in the institution confirms the delinquent in his self-perception of rejection by society. He is placed among other, perhaps more experienced, delinquents who give support to his lawless values. The adults who are trying to change him have a completely different set of standards and represent another agent of authority. Thus it is not surprising that over half the children who appear in juvenile court are repeaters.

Nevertheless, a number of experimenters have tried to use the period during which the delinquent is in a training school to establish the kind of environment which would turn the youths away from a criminal career. In doing so they try to compensate for inadequate childhood experiences by providing an environment which is marked by affection and permissiveness, firm insistence on a few essential rules, presence of identification figures, and opportunities for interesting constructive activities (Aichorn, 1935; Redl and Wineman, 1952). Group therapy is often used to try to change the prevailing delinquent attitudes into more constructive ones. Unfortunately, these programs require a large and well-trained staff and a willingness to experiment and to fail. The society at large is often unwilling to finance them. For example, the Redl and Wineman experiment ended after two years for lack of funds.

But the greatest challenge so far as delinquency is concerned is prevention. Recently several experiments have been conducted to try to reduce the amount of delinquency in a slum neighborhood through social service and recreation programs. Many of these have produced disappointing results (Powers and Witmer, 1951). For example, a well-controlled experiment in providing a friendly counselor for predelinquents failed to produce a significant difference in delinquency over a ten-year period, although the program may have helped the younger boys and those who received intensive counseling (McCord and McCord, 1959). Other experiments report some degree of success. Bandura and Walters (1963) describe a program which uses behavior principles to help to "socialize" potential delinquents.

■ Slack and Schwitzgebel rented an old store in a "hard-core" delinquent neighborhood. They paid neighborhood boys to serve as subjects. In addition to money, the boys were also given candy and cigarettes. After a period some boys began to come to the store regularly and would cooperate for social approval alone. The therapists had the boys participate in a variety of activities, some of which taught them skills they could use for later employment. The psychologists reported that the boys no longer considered avoiding work as a goal and that they participated less in delinquent activities. ■

No long-term study has been done on this type of experimental program, but the early reports are encouraging. If the public continues to support programs of many types aimed at preventing delinquency—despite the possibility and even the probability of failure—we can be optimistic about diminishing the proportions of what today remains a major social problem.

Summary

Concepts

Neurosis. A maladjustment which does not require hospitalization but in which a person is handicapped by one or more of the following symptoms: diffuse anxiety in situations that are not dangerous (anxiety reaction), a persistent irrational fear (phobia), irrational depression (neurotic depression), loss of personal identity (amnesia), recurrent irresistible ideas (obsession) and acts (compulsion), physical symptoms in the absence of pathology (conversion reaction)

Psychotherapy. A category of treatment methods for psychological disorders for which the primary technique is conversation between the patient and the therapist; the category includes *psychoanalysis,* developed by Sigmund Freud, and client-centered therapy, developed by Carl Rogers

Psychosomatic disorder. An organic disorder of which psychological problems are a major cause; examples of possible psychosomatic disorders are ulcers, asthma, and high blood pressure

Psychosis. A maladjustment in which the individual loses contact with reality and usually requires hospitalization. The two major types are the *organic* psychoses, which can be traced to physiological causes, and the *functional* psychoses, such as schizophrenia and manic-depressive psychoses, which have no evident physiological causes

Conduct disorders. A heterogeneous category of disorders, including juvenile delinquency and criminal behavior, alcoholism, drug addiction, and sexual deviation

Principles

1. Adjustment can be considered a continuum with ideal maturity at one pole and maladjustment at the other.

2. The evaluation of a person's adjustment depends not only on a person's behavior, but also on the context in which it occurs.

3. Most psychologists consider neurotic symptoms to be a result of underlying anxiety caused by unresolved frustration, though there is no generally accepted theory to account for the development of one symptom rather than another.

4. The onset of symptoms in neurosis seems to result from an interaction between frustration tolerance and current psychological stress.

5. Psychosomatic disorders involve organic pathology, which results from over-reaction of the body's physiological defense against stress.

6. Functional psychoses appear to develop as a result of hereditary predisposition, a poor environmental history, and unknown psychological and, perhaps, physiological factors.

7. Psychoses are treated by a combination of medical therapy, which may include the widespread use of drugs, and psychotherapy.

8. The definition of juvenile delinquency is a legal one—a youngster who has been apprehended for breaking a law. The possible causes of delinquent behavior include social conditions, such as a slum culture, and disturbed family relationships, such as the absence of an effective adult male role model.

Suggested Readings

Two very elementary and readable books by Dr. G. H. PRESTON are *Psychiatry for the Curious*. New York: Rinehart, 1943; and *The Substance of Mental Health*. New York: Rinehart, 1943.

Among the most widely used textbooks of abnormal psychology are CAMERON, N., *Personality Development and Psychopathology: a Dynamic Approach*. Boston: Houghton Mifflin, 1963; WHITE, R. W., *The Abnormal Personality*. New York: Ronald, 1963, third edition; and COLEMAN, J. C., *Abnormal Psychology and Modern Life*. Chicago: Scott, Foresman, third edition, 1964.

The most convenient source of Freudian theory is probably FREUD, S., *A General Introduction to Psychoanalysis*. New York: Garden City, 1938. Freud's observations of his patients and the theories he devised to account for them form the background for much of the current work in this area. One of the classic expositions of psychoanalytic theory is by one of Freud's students, FENICHEL, O., *The Psychoanalytic Theory of the Neuroses*. New York: Norton, 1946.

chapter 15

interpersonal relations

SOCIAL PERCEPTION AND JUDGMENT

MOTIVATION AND GROUP MEMBERSHIP

chapter 15 GROUP ACTION

THE INDIVIDUAL IN THE GROUP: THE PROBLEM
OF LEADERSHIP

In our study of psychology we first analyzed psychological processes within an individual. Then we looked at the individual as a total personality and examined his overall development and adjustment. Throughout, we have emphasized the effect of other people on an individual's behavior and the effect of the cultures and subcultures in which he lives. But now we shall change the focus of our attention from the individual human being to the relationships between an individual personality and his social environment. The social environment includes both the other people he encounters, singly or in groups, and social institutions such as government and the mass media.

The study of groups and other social systems is in the province of sociology; the study of the individual personality is in the province of psychology. Thus the study of the relationships between individuals and social systems—social psychology—is on the borderline between the two fields and the concepts developed in such a study serve as a bridge between them.

The areas of social psychology that we have chosen for discussion in this text are those that complement our study of human behavior and experience with a social dimension; that is, they are those areas which are closer to psychology than sociology. We shall try to demonstrate that certain psychological principles are easily applied to social phenomena as well as to point out some of the unique consequences of social interaction. In this chapter we shall examine the processes of perception, motivation, and action in a social context, concluding with the personality differences and the group. In the following chapter we shall look at attitudes and attitude change.

Social Perception and Judgment

Other people constitute a significant part of every human being's environment. Our reaction to others depends to a large extent on how we perceive and judge them. Sometimes the basis for our perception of another person is actual experience with him. Frequently, in this era of mass media, we form our impressions of public figures by reading about them, hearing them speak, and seeing pictures of them. However, the principles of social perception from actual contact and other cues overlap, and we shall present data about both.

What Is the Relation Between Person Perception and Object Perception?

You may recall that we described the phenomena of perception in Chapter 6. Most of the experiments we cited to illustrate perceptual principles employed inanimate objects as stimulus materials. However, the same principles apply to perception when a person is the stimulus object. Social perception, like all perception, is organized, involves the activation of previously established categories, and is affected by the set and the motivation of the perceiver.

SOCIAL IMPRESSIONS AND ORGANIZATION. We can get some insight into how people integrate discrete observations into the perception of a personality from the following experiment by Asch (1946).

■ An experimenter read lists of personality characteristics to a group of college students. Each list was supposed to enumerate the characteristics of an unknown person. For example one list was: energetic, assured, talkative, cold, ironical, inquisitive. The students were then asked to write a description of this person. Here are two sample impressions given in response to the above list:

1. He seems to be the kind of person who would make a great impression upon others at a first meeting. However, as time went by, his acquaintances would easily come to see through the mask. Underneath would be revealed his arrogance and selfishness.

2. He impresses people as being more capable than he really is. He is popular and never ill at ease. Easily becomes the center of attraction at any gathering. He is likely to be a jack-of-all-trades. Although his interests are varied, he is not necessarily well versed in any of them. He possesses a sense of humor. His presence stimulates enthusiasm and very often he does arrive at a position of importance. ■

You can see that the bits and pieces provided by the adjective list have been woven into a meaningful, organized pattern, and that new characteristics, such as humor, which fit into the pattern have been attributed to the person, although they did not appear in the original list.

Social Perception and Set

As in all perception the set induced immediately prior to the presentation of a stimulus object influences perception of it. This phenomenon was demonstrated for social perception by Kelley (1950) in the following study:

■ Students were introduced to a guest instructor by one of two kinds of notes, the two being identical except that in one the stimulus person was described among other things as being "rather cold" whereas in the other form the phrase "very warm" was substituted. The content of the "rather cold" version is as follows:

"Mr. ——— is a graduate student in the Department of Economics and Social Science here at MIT. He has had three semesters of teaching experience in psychology at another college. This is his first semester teaching Ec. 70. He is 26 years old, a veteran, and married. People who know him consider him to be a rather cold person, industrious, critical, practical, and determined." (Kelley, 1950) ■

Students who had information that the instructor was "warm" rated him after the class period as more considerate, less formal, more sociable, more popular, better natured, more humorous, and more humane than did students who had received the "cold" introduction. Furthermore, students who had received the "cold" introduction tended to participate less in the class discussion than people who had received the "warm" introduction.

The Use of Previously Formed Categories

Earlier, we emphasized the importance of categorization for experiencing a stimulus complex as a meaningful percept. Similarly our judgments of people depend in part on the social categories we have formed. For example, in Chapter 2 we defined a social role as a prescribed pattern of behavior for a given position in society. For each social role with which we are familiar, we develop a pattern of expectancies which colors our impression of a person executing that role. When someone is introduced as a professor, the perceiver has a ready-made set of judgments into which his new acquaintance is fitted; the same man dressed in shorts, mowing a lawn, and introduced as "Bill" may evoke quite different perceptions.

A study by Haire and Grunes (1950) shows the resistance of subjects to modifying their impressions of a person even if objective information contradicts the expectancies associated with a role.

■ Two groups of college students were presented with a description of a factory worker. The only difference between the descriptions given to the two groups was that the description for group I included the adjective *intelligent* while the description for group II did not. The subjects then wrote a short paragraph giving their impressions of the person just described. The authors describe the typical group II impression as follows:

"Virtually every description would fit into the pattern of a typical American Joe: likable and well liked, mildly sociable, healthy, happy, uncomplicated in a sort of earthy way, not very intelligent, but trying to keep abreast of current trends, interested in sports, and finding his pleasures in simple undistinguished activities."*

These responses confirmed the investigators' hypothesis that intelligence was not a trait expected of someone in the role of factory worker. The subjects in group I tended to modify the trait of intelligence so as to make it conform to those they associate with the role. (He is intelligent, but not too much so) or to alter the role (such as by making the man a foreman). ■

We see another example of categorization influencing social perception in the use of racial, religious, and national stereotypes. A stereotype is a pattern of characteristics uniformly attributed to all people belonging to a particular group. Katz and Braly (1933) and, more recently, Gilbert (1951) have shown that college students do tend to characterize members of racial and national groups in a consistent fashion when they are asked to check the traits that are typical of each. For example, in the earlier study, Italians tended to be described as impulsive, musical, and imaginative, and Negroes tended to be characterized as happy-go-lucky, musical, and superstitious (Katz, 1933). Such stereotyped expectancies affect the perception of an individual belonging to a minority group in much the same way as an expectancy of warmth or coldness affected

---

* From Haire, M., and W. F. Grunes, "Perceptual defenses: processes protecting an original perception of another personality," *Hum. Relat.*, **3**, 403–412 (1950).

perception of an instructor in the study described above. (For example, see Weissberg and Proshansky, 1963.)

Social Perception and Motivation

Our own motives and emotions also influence our impressions of other people, as the following study suggests.

■ Feshbach and Singer (1957) showed two groups of students a film of a young man performing a number of mechanical tasks. On the pretext that the experiment dealt with the effect of distraction on personality judgment, the subjects in one group were given eight electric shocks during the film. Following the film showing, the students were asked to judge the man in the film on how fearful he was in the situations portrayed in the film and how fearful he was in general. The subjects who had been shocked tended to judge the film character as more fearful than the unshocked group in both general fearfulness and in the situations seen in the film. ■

Unique Features of Social Perception

Although all the principles of object perception also apply to person perception, some features are unique to the interpersonal situation in which one human being perceives another. First, the perceiver (Mr. P) attributes psychological processes to the human stimulus object (Mr. O). Another person is perceived as having motives, emotions, expectancies, intentions, etc. Although a perceiver may occasionally attribute such processes to an inanimate object (this car just does not *want* to start), they are ordinarily attributed only to human beings.

One psychological process that perceiver, Mr. P, perceives in the human stimulus object, Mr. O, is perception. Mr. P is not only aware of Mr. O as part of the perceptual environment; he is at the same time aware that Mr. O also perceives his surroundings and that he, Mr. P, is one object in Mr. O's perceptual environment. In other words, as we watch others, we observe them watching us. Second, Mr. P perceives Mr. O as an initiator of action. Human beings, like inanimate objects, may help a perceiver to satisfy his goals, or may prevent him from doing so, but only another human being is seen as an *initiator* of activity which may help or thwart. Finally, in interpersonal perception, Mr. O is continually changing in response to Mr. P's actions. A faint smile or a slight frown on Mr. P's face may completely alter Mr. O's behavior, hence Mr. P's perception of Mr. O.*

These three characteristics point to the complexity of the processes involved in social perception. Yet most of us are sufficiently accurate in our perceptions

---

* Although we have been analyzing the interpersonal situation from the point of view of one person as perceiver (Mr. P) and the other person as object (Mr. O), it is important to realize that each person in the situation is simultaneously both perceiver and object. Mr. P is an object of perception and Mr. O is a perceiver.

of others that smooth interpersonal relationships are possible. Some psychologists have been especially interested in factors influencing the accuracy of social perception and we shall take up their work in the following section.

What Determines the Accuracy of Social Perception?

As you can see from our comparison of person and object perception, the research on social perception has utilized a number of kinds of situations in order to study the process. People have been asked their impression of other people after hearing an adjective list, seeing a picture, hearing voices, interacting for the first time with a new person, or after a lengthy acquaintance. One factor determining the accuracy of social perception is the *nature of the information* on which the perception is based.

When the only information on which to base judgments is a photograph, certain facial characteristics are associated with certain personality characteristics. For example, bright, widened eyes are seen as being associated with conscientiousness and sincerity. Similarly, individuals with smooth skin, smiling mouth, and good grooming are judged to be intelligent, gay, and refined. Women with relaxed mouth, much lipstick, and thick lips are perceived as being feminine and "sexy."

From studies of the relationship of facial and physical characteristics to personality we would suspect that there is in fact no true relationship between relaxed mouths or thick lips and femininity. Thus the individual who uses such a theory is likely to have distorted perceptions of women. However, it would not be surprising if there were some low positive correlation between physical characteristics and the personality traits they are presumed to indicate, for the individual's self-concept is determined to some extent by others' expectations of him. Thus the cultural norms about the relation of physical characteristics and personality may determine whether or not such a relationship exists. In other words, since people build their self-concepts from the percepts of others, social perceptions may make themselves come true to a small extent.

The more information the perceiver has about the situation to which the person is responding, the more accurate are the judgments about the person. For example, you may have had some difficulty judging the feelings expressed by the three girls pictured in Fig. 7–10 on page 228. A look at the complete photograph, which is shown in Fig. 15–1, and the knowledge that this photograph was taken during an appearance by a popular singing group called The Beatles, will enable you to realize that all three girls are probably experiencing similar emotions—commonly called "Beatlemania." Your perception has become more accurate as a result of understanding the situation in which the person is responding. Similarly, early studies of judging the emotions expressed by infants showed that interjudge agreement was much higher when the perceivers saw the situation in which the emotion was aroused.

Two experimenters (Allport and Cantril, 1934) were interested in the accuracy of social perception when the only cues to the people being judged were their voices. The speakers read prepared material, so that vocabulary and grammar could not serve as sources of information. The subjects were asked either to match the voices with a personality sketch or to judge the speaker on a number of dimensions. On the basis of the data, the experimenters concluded that the subjects were able to make a few correct judgments about the speaker. The judges were able to match such characteristics as age and dominance more correctly than would be expected by random matching. As you might expect, matching was more accurate to a brief personality sketch than to individual personality dimensions.

FIG. 15-1. The emotional reactions of some adolescent girls attending a performance of the singing group, The Beatles. The emotional reactions of the three girls in the foreground—without the contextual background provided here—were shown in Fig. 7-10, p. 228. (Wide World Photos)

Of course, we do not always make judgments of other people solely from photographs or from voices, although our perceptions of public figures are often based on this sort of information. More normally, we perceive people with whom we interact over a period of time. Thus *length of acquaintance* is another variable which has been studied. Common sense would suggest that the longer two people know each other, the more accurate are their perceptions of each other. However, there seems to come a point in the course of the relationship after which continued interaction does not increase accuracy. For example, Hollander (1956) reported that the accuracy of judgments made by students in an Officer Candidate School after three weeks of acquaintance and after six weeks were about the same.

How can we explain this result? If the people judging one another have known each other for a long time and like one another, two other sources of error reduce accuracy. First, a person tends to see his close friends as more similar to himself in attitudes than they really are (Mellenger, 1955). Second, a person tends to judge the people he knows and likes more favorably than warranted on all evaluative traits. This is an example of the *halo effect* we mentioned earlier.

We can see the halo effect distorting social perception in the following study by Zillig (1928).

■ Two groups of children were selected from a class. One group consisted of children who were widely liked by their classmates; the children in the second group were generally disliked. Both groups performed exercises before the remainder of the class. The liked group had been trained to perform deliberately poorly, the disliked group to perform perfectly. Nevertheless, the observers tended to report that they had ''seen'' the children they disliked performing poorly and the children they liked performing well. ■

This study demonstrates again that present perceptions depend, in part, on previously formed judgments. We can see, then, that the accuracy of the perception of a person is strongly influenced by *the accuracy of early impressions*.

For example, Kelley (1950) obtained student ratings of instructors' personalities after the first class period and again after 15 class periods. In general, the students' first impressions tended to persist. Of three instructors who were rated on 22 traits, there were no significant changes in rating for one, eight changes for another, and six for the third.

The manner in which later information about a person is fitted into one's first impression is illustrated by a study in which subjects wrote their impressions of a person after listening to a series of adjectives about him. The adjective list read to one group was: "intelligent, industrious, impulsive, critical, stubborn, envious." To another group the series, "envious, stubborn, critical, impulsive, industrious, intelligent" was read. The words were identical except for order, but the impression of the group to whom the first series was read was of an able person who possesses shortcomings "which are not serious enough to overshadow his merits." The second group's impression was of a person who is a problem and has abilities "hampered by serious difficulties." The newer information about the person's characteristics was fitted into the impressions formed from the earlier information.

First impressions have the greatest effect on later perception when the perceiver is forced to make a judgment based on minimal information. In one experiment (Dailey, 1951), judges were asked to predict the responses of subjects once after receiving a small amount of information and once again after receiving additional information. Another group of judges made only a single judgment after receiving all the information. The results showed that the initial judgments seriously limited the accuracy of the judgments made after receiving additional information. On the other hand, the overriding influence of first impressions can be minimized by warning observers that information which is presented first tends to have disproportionate influence on personality judgments (Luchins, 1957).

Who and what are being judged also influence the accuracy of perception. Surface traits that are directly related to behavior are easier to judge than inner feelings (Hollingsworth, 1922). Likewise, some people provide cues that lead to more accurate perception than others. For example, one investigation revealed that personal likes and dislikes were much easier to predict for some people than for others. (Taguire, Kogan, and Bruner, 1955).

Finally, psychologists have investigated *individual differences* in social perception. In particular, they have raised the question of whether there is any general ability for accuracy in social perception.

The investigation of this problem has an interesting methodological history. Early investigators were troubled by the criterion problem. In order to check the accuracy of social perception, we have to ask perceivers to judge some characteristic that can also be measured objectively. In the first experiments on individual differences, the problem was solved by asking the perceiver to judge how another person would respond to a personality questionnaire. Such a study did reveal that some people could judge better than others.

The people superior in making such judgments showed two personality characteristics. First, they tended to be better adjusted than the less accurate perceivers. This result confirmed the experimenter's expectations that realistic perception should correlate with adjustment. Second, the superior judges tended to answer questions about themselves in a manner more similar to the group average than poorer judges. (Dymond, 1950)

At this point, however, let us stop and think about our interpretation of these results. Is there any other way such results could have been attained? Most people rate themselves as well adjusted on a set of items concerning personality. Now suppose that they are asked to judge how other persons rated themselves. If a person tends to fill out the questionnaire for other people pretty much as he filled out his own, he will obtain a high score on social sensitivity, for since other people also see themselves as relatively well adjusted, his predictions will be close to the actual ratings others gave themselves. Such a person may not really be sensitive to others, but may simply be going around assuming that everyone else is like himself. Similarly, one can appear to be a good judge of group opinion if most people in the group are like him. Analyses by Meehl (1954) and by Cronbach and Gage (1955) indicated that this indeed occurs. The inaccurate person is likely to be one who overemphasizes differences between people or who overestimates the importance of certain variables he can detect. In one experimental program for training medical students in physician-patient relationships, the group receiving training actually became worse in predicting patient responses to personality scales than a group which had no training. The reason for this painful result apparently was that the trained group perceived more differences between people as a result of training and as a result made bigger errors than the control group (Crow, 1958). A person *appears* to be the most sensitive perceiver and best judge of other people if he sees them as being similar to himself. Moreover, the average man is likely to be better able than the deviant person to predict a group of scores, simply because he is close to the average.

These measures, then, did not seem to tap the accuracy of person perception, as was originally hoped, and experimenters saw the need for developing tasks in social perception in which the perceiver's similarity to the people being judged would not be a factor. One such task was for the perceiver to rank several interviewers in terms of how he thought they would rank him on some trait. In this case, the correlation between perceived ranking and true ranking would provide a measure of accuracy of social perception.

Just as in the early research, some people proved to be consistently accurate in such discriminations. However, the persons who were accurate in terms of predicting people's responses on the average were not necessarily high in sensitivity to differences between people in the group as revealed by ability to rank others accurately. In fact, in an experiment carried out by Bronfenbrenner, Harding, and Gallwey (1958) the two abilities were found to have a correlation of -0.26, i.e., there was a slight tendency for the person who was more accurate in judging the average response of the group to be less accurate than the average in perceiving differences between members of the group. Another finding was that the people who were sensitive to interpersonal differences were likely to be described by other group members as "shy" and to be rated unfavorably by other group members.

In reviewing the data on the question of whether accuracy in social perception was a consistent trait, Guilford (1959a) came to the following conclusion:

■ "The most appropriate conclusion to draw at present is that if there is a generalized ability to judge people, it is a poorly organized trait in most individuals. It appears for the most part that abilities of this kind are specific, depending upon many circumstances, such as the combination of rater and ratee, the kind of judgment required, and the information available." ■*

Motivation and Group Membership

Our perception of the physical environment depends, in part, on which aspects of the environment we attend to and where our goal seeking has taken us. Similarly, our social environment depends, in part, on which people we choose

---

* From Guilford, J. P., *Personality*. New York: McGraw-Hill, 1959. Reprinted by permission.

for associates. Each person grows up in some social group which he has not chosen—usually he grows up in a family. In the course of his development, he learns that some of his motives are more easily satisfied in conjunction with other people, sometimes in formal, sometimes in informal groups. As an adult, he usually lives in a new family group; to provide for the basic needs of his family he often associates himself with a production group; and he may spend some of his leisure time as a participant in a voluntary group.

The group membership patterns of the average American city dweller were studied in two surveys taken in Detroit (Axelrod, 1956, Freedman, 1952). The investigators reported that eight out of ten residents interviewed belonged to some formal organization. Over one-half of the people interviewed belonged to churches, and about two-thirds belonged to some other organization. Men are more likely to belong to organizations than women, although more women than men belong to churches. Among men living in the Detroit area the most common form of membership other than church is the labor union.

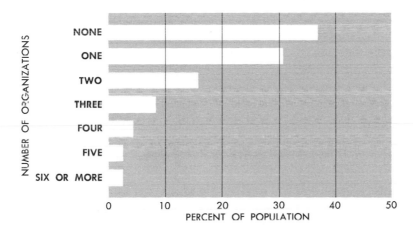

FIG. 15–2. The number of organizations to which various percentages of the city population belong. The data for this figure come from a survey carried out in Detroit. (After Axelrod, 1956)

Figure 15–2 shows the number of organizations to which various proportions of the population belong. The notion that Americans are great joiners is not supported by the Detroit survey. The average Detroiter belongs to only one organization, as we see in the figure. Furthermore, only about 30 or 40 percent of the people attend meetings of groups frequently and only about one-fifth of the members of a group are active outside meetings. In the Detroit survey about one-fourth of the members of a group reported that they had attended no meetings in the previous three months, and another third that they had attended only one or two meetings.

SELECTED CHARACTERISTICS	PERCENT WHO ARE MEMBERS	PERCENT WHO ARE VERY ACTIVE
FAMILY INCOME		
Under $3000	42	8
$3000–3999	66	9
$4000–4999	67	14
$5000–5999	62	12
$6000–6999	65	12
$7000 and over	81	21
EDUCATION		
0–6 years	52	2
7–8 years	60	9
9–12 years	63	14
Some college	78	19
OCCUPATION OF FAMILY HEAD		
Service worker or laborer	50	19
Operative	40	8
Craftsmen, foremen, etc.	40	11
Clerical, sales, etc.	62	21
Professional, managers, and proprietors	61	11

FIG. 15–3. Some characteristics of group members. These data are from the same survey cited in Fig. 15–2. (After Axelrod, 1956)

As Fig. 15–3 indicates, people with higher incomes and education are more active in groups than those low in these respects. Interestingly, the participation patterns of Negroes and whites are similar despite differences in income. The relation of age to participation is also interesting. Activity in groups increases with age up to the forties, but in the 50-year-olds it begins to drop, and drops even more sharply in the sixties. Only one-sixth of the people above 60 attend group meetings.

In addition to his formal memberships, the average person meets with other people on a regular but informal basis. The Detroit studies showed that most people get together with relatives at least once a week and get together with friends at least once a month.

Why Do People Join and Remain in Groups?

The behavior of joining a group can be analyzed just like any other act. Group membership becomes a goal for an individual because he perceives that group membership will directly or indirectly provide positive affect. The incentive value of a group may lie in the fact that the individual's goals are identical with the *goals of the group.* For example, a person who values citizen participation in a democracy may join a group formed to encourage voting on election day. A group may be attractive to a person because he enjoys the *activities* which group membership permits him to take part in. If a man likes to play chess, he will probably be motivated to join a chess club. A group may attract a member because he enjoys being with the other members of the group; he perceives the group as a means for satisfying his *affiliation* motives.

On the other hand, the factors which make a group attractive to an individual may have little to do with the actual goals and activities of the group. A person may seek group membership because of its prestige in the eyes of others. Thus a coed choosing whether or not to join a sorority may be influenced not only by her desire to enjoy sorority parties but also by the prestige she feels she would enjoy by being able to say, "I'm a Xi Xi Xi." Or a person may find a group attractive because it provides an opportunity for achieving goals different from those of the group as a whole. A salesman may use a club membership to get business contacts, for example.

The central role of motivation in choosing among alternative group memberships is illustrated in the following study:

■ French (1956) brought together a group of people, some of whom had high achievement motivation, others of whom were distinguished by high affiliation motivation. They were then asked to choose which people they would prefer to associate with at future meetings. The high-affiliation subjects tended to choose people they liked, whereas the high-achievement people tended to choose the best performers. ■

As with all incentives, the greater the perceived probability that group membership will satisfy a member's motives, the greater the probability that membership will remain a goal for him. Direct support for this principle comes from the following study.

Ross and Zander (1957) measured several motives, such as those for autonomy, recognition, and fair evaluation, given by employees for joining a business organization. They also obtained the employees' estimates as to whether these motives would be satisfied by working for the organization. Over a period of time, a number of employees left the company. A comparison of the men who stayed and those who left showed that the strength of the various motives was approximately the same for the two groups. However, they differed in estimated probability of motive satisfaction. Those who remained had estimated higher probabilities that the motives would be satisfied by employment in the company.

What Is Group Cohesiveness?

We have just discussed the attraction of a group for an individual in terms of his motivation. However, it is also possible to distinguish one group from another in terms of its attractiveness for all its members. This characteristic is called *group cohesiveness*. Of course, the cohesiveness of a group depends upon the motives of each individual in the group, but as we shall see, some interesting results emerge when group cohesiveness itself is used as a dependent variable.

Operationalizing Cohesiveness

In different situations experimenters have used a number of different measures to assess cohesiveness. In formal organizations cohesiveness can be measured by looking at turnover, absenteeism, and payment of dues. Mann and Baumgartel (1952) showed the relation of one such overall measure, absenteeism, to individual motivation for a job. They found a significant relationship between rate of absence in various parts of the company and expressed satisfaction with regard to supervision, fellow workers, and the type of work.

White and Lippitt (1960) devised measures of cohesiveness based on the principle that the more cohesive a group, the more its members would tend to associate themselves with the group in speech. Thus the number of times the word *we* rather than *I* was used provided one measure of cohesiveness. Group-oriented remarks and friendly remarks provided two other measures. Dimock (1937) reasoned that in a cohesive group a member's ten best friends would tend to come from among the other members of the group. Thus the proportion of "in-group" friendship choices would provide a cohesiveness measure.

■ Such data can be diagrammed in a chart called a *sociogram*, such as the two illustrated in Fig. 15–4. Each group member is designated by a circle. Whenever a member chooses another member as one of his best friends, an arrow is drawn toward the circle representing the person chosen. The sociogram of a highly cohesive group will have many arrows; one which is not cohesive will have few. ■

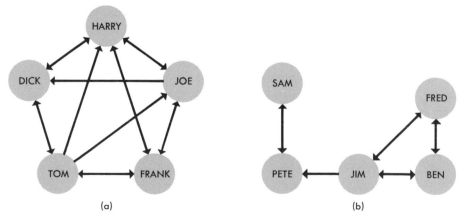

FIG. 15–4. Sociograms of two groups. Each member is represented by a circle, and each arrow indicates a friendship choice. Two-way arrows indicate mutual choices. According to one measure of cohesiveness, group (a) is more cohesive than group (b).

In order to study cohesiveness in newly formed groups, some experimenters use questionnaires. In one study subjects were asked to indicate whether they wanted to remain members of the group, how often they wanted the group to meet, and whether they wished to ask others to stay in the group. The pooled responses for all the people in one group were then analyzed to yield an overall cohesiveness score.

As you can see, experimenters have developed different measures of cohesiveness for different kinds of groups. Although they each tap different observable aspects of the group, they all, in one way or another, give some indication of the attractiveness of the group for its members.

Some Factors Influencing Cohesiveness

COMMON FATE. One major factor in determining the cohesiveness of a group is the degree to which individual members feel they *share a common fate* with the other members. For example, friendly interaction among a crew of garment workers increased when they were all given a raise by the management. This indication that their fortunes would rise together was the factor that increased cohesiveness (Thibault and Willerman, reported by Cartwright and Zander, 1960). Similarly, a common threat to a group increases cohesiveness. When Japanese-Americans were threatened during World War II, they organized themselves in cohesive groups.

Sherif and Sherif (1953) manipulated cohesiveness in a boy's camp by using this principle. They divided the boys into two rival teams. As the teams competed on a number of tasks, each team became more cohesive, and rivalry between the teams became more intense. For example, when a tournament was arranged between the "Eagles" and the "Rattlers," there were few signs of sportsmanship. The Eagles were soon calling the Rattlers "stinkers" and "cheaters," and after one game they burned a banner left by the Rattlers. The next morning the Rattlers seized the Eagles' flag. Hoards of green apples were collected for ammunition, and scuffles and raids became commonplace. However, a series of incidents arranged by Sherif and Sherif changed the camp from two highly cohesive groups, each shutting out the other, into a more harmonious single group. The camp water supply system "broke down," and the two groups volunteered to search for the trouble; working together, they located and fixed it. When a truck which was to go to town for food would not start, both groups used their tug-of-war rope to tow and start it.

At first, peace was maintained only while the two groups were actually working together, but gradually the members of the two groups became more friendly. Eventually the groups asked to "treat" or entertain each other, and even asked to go home on the same bus rather than on separate buses.

So long as the boys on the two teams felt they shared a common fate with only their own teammates, camp membership as a whole induced little cohesiveness. But when events convinced the boys on both teams that they shared a common fate, that they would succeed or fail together, the cohesiveness of the camp as a whole increased.

CLARITY OF GOALS AND MEANS. Given the principle that perception of common goals increases cohesiveness, the following relationships are not surprising: The better the individuals in a group understand the group goals, the means by which the goals can be achieved, and how their personal actions contribute to the goal, the greater the cohesiveness of the group. Raven and Rietsma (1957) tested these principles in the following experiment:

■ Each subject was told he was working in conjunction with three other people. He was asked to cut different geometrical shapes out of cardboard and told that other people would use the shapes he cut out. Some of the subjects were clearly informed that the shapes were being used to build houses, and specific requests for particular shapes were explained. The others were given no indication of the product, and requests for specific shapes were arbitrary. Those subjects who had a clear idea of the group goal and their individual contribution differed from the un-informed group in their answers to a questionnaire that followed the task. They tended to express stronger feelings that they were members of a group and to express greater concern for the achievement of the group goal. ■

This result is consistent with findings in an industrial setting that morale is higher when the reasons for changing procedures are explained.

Cohesiveness and Amount of Interaction

It has been suggested that the more the members of a group interact with one another, the greater the cohesiveness of the group. A classroom study by Bovard (1956) supports this hypothesis. He compared the expressions of liking for fellow classmates in a group discussion class with those in a teacher-centered class. The students who had interacted with one another in discussions had had higher liking scores.

However, there is an important exception to this principle. In the Sherif and Sherif study the boys from opposing teams interacted frequently to hurl insults at one another. Obviously, these contacts did not increase camp cohesiveness. In fact *unpleasant interaction* decreases cohesiveness, rather than increasing it.

Group Action

As we noted earlier, people come together into groups for several different reasons. In general we can distinguish between *task-oriented* groups, whose primary purpose is to perform a specific task, and *interaction-oriented* groups, whose primary purpose is to provide an opportunity for people to interact with one another. A production unit in a company is an example of a task-oriented group; a social club is an example of an interaction-oriented group. Many groups have goals which include both functions. For example, a benevolent organization may be set up both to do good works in the community and to provide an opportunity for congenial interaction. But whether or not social interaction is one of the primary functions of the group, an important aspect of the behavior of almost every group is the manner in which its members communicate and interact with one another.

What Is Social Interaction?

The term "communication" implies a sender, a message, and a receiver. In a sense, all perceptions are examples of communication—the stimulus object is the sender, the physical energies to which we are sensitive are the message, and the perceiver is the receiver. When both sender and receiver are organisms, the communication may be designated as social communication. Note that social communication can take place whether or not sender and receiver are present simultaneously. For example, a writer can communicate with readers separated from him in time and space. When each organism in the group is simultaneously sender to the others and receiver from the others, we speak of *social interaction* (see Fig. 15–5).

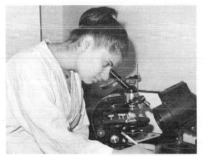

COMMUNICATION

SOCIAL COMMUNICATION

SOCIAL INTERACTION

FIG. 15–5. Three kinds of communication. (Top and left photos by United Press International)

The Nature of the Message

Two people looking at one another without speaking may be interacting. For example, in a pediatrician's office, two mothers each holding an infant may be looking at one another. Mrs. L. looks first at Mrs. D's baby, then at Mrs. D's face and smiles. Mrs. D nods her head, looks at Mrs. L's baby and smiles. Here messages have been sent and received by both women and interaction has taken place. The messages sent and received in this case were nonverbal.

In human social interaction, the messages exchanged usually depend to a large extent on the medium of language. You may recall from our previous discussion that one unique feature of social perception is the human perceiver's awareness that he shares with his object a similar way of perceiving and conceiving of the world, simply because both are human. Furthermore, both have probably learned a common set of symbols to describe their percepts and concepts, i.e., a language. When the sender is aware of the effect his message will have on the receiver, the communication is *intentional*. To the extent that common symbols have different meanings to sender and receiver, the communication fails. For example, the message "The man who stole the package was really an honest man" may have no meaning for some people, but may convey information to others. For some people the concept of an honest man automatically excludes anyone who would steal.

The skill of producing the desired effect in others through communication is a learned skill. Gradually, we learn to understand how our words (and gestures) convey information. Examples of failures of communication among children are instructive. For example, Piaget (1959) told children the following story:

■ "Once upon a time, there was a lady who was called Niobe, and who had 12 sons and 12 daughters. She met a fairy who had only one son and no daughter. Then the lady laughed at the fairy because the fairy only had one boy. Then the fairy was very angry and fastened the lady to a rock. The lady cried for ten years. In the end she turned into a rock, and her tears made a stream which still runs today."

The child then told the story to another child as in the following account by an eight-year-old:

"Once upon a time there was a lady who had 12 boys and 12 girls, and then a fairy boy and a girl. And then Niobe wanted to have some more sons. Then she was angry. She fastened her to a stone. He turned into a rock and then his tears made a stream which is still running today." ■*

The problem in the explanation was not that the child has not understood the original story. But the child sender assumed that the pronouns he used and the omitted referents would be clear to the other child because they were clear to him (the sender). Piaget concluded that children often fail to communicate with one another because each is shut up in his own point of view and is not able to take into account the other's perspective. Adults are more likely to have learned

---

* Piaget, J. P., *The Language and Thought of the Child*, third edition. London: Routledge and Kegan Paul, 1959. Reprinted by permission.

how to use language so that the explanation communicates the desired message despite the difference in perspective between sender and receiver. Of course, some adults are much more skilled in communicating than others. Effective communication thus depends upon ability to take the role of the other, to have reasonable ideas of the way in which he categorizes incoming information.

How Has Communication in Groups Been Analyzed?

Psychologists have developed methods to study both the direction and the content of group communication.

THE CHANNELS OF COMMUNICATION IN SMALL GROUPS. In some groups, every member communicates with every other member. In other groups, interaction between members is more restricted. In a given group, if one member ever communicates with another, we say that a *channel of communication* exists between them. Obstacles to communication channels may be physical. For example, it is physically impossible for a listener to communicate with a radio announcer. The obstacles may also be psychological, as when a student is afraid to speak to a famous professor.

The overall pattern of communication channels in a small group is called a *communication net.* The diagrams in Fig. 15–6 show the communication nets for three kinds of college classes (lecture, teacher-centered question-and-answer, and group discussion).

The effects of various communication nets on group action can be studied experimentally by opening and closing channels of communication. For example,

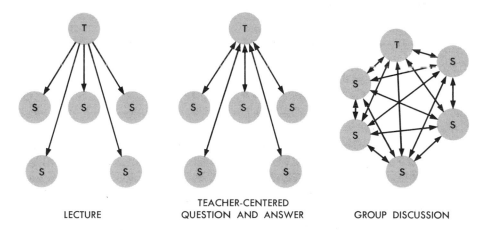

LECTURE

TEACHER-CENTERED
QUESTION AND ANSWER

GROUP DISCUSSION

FIG. 15–6. Channels of communication in three types of classroom procedures. An arrow from one person to another indicates that the former communicates with the latter. For convenience, only five students appear in each diagram.

Leavitt (1951) controlled the channels of communication in the following way:

■ Five people are seated around a table, but they are separated from one another by vertical partitions. There are slots in the partitions through which notes can be passed from one person to another. By varying the pattern of open and closed slots, various communication nets can be established. Five experimentally produced nets are diagrammed in Fig. 15–7. ■

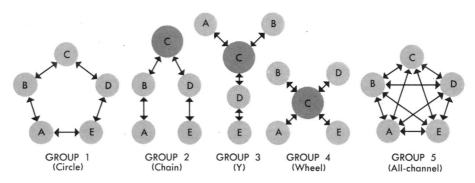

FIG. 15–7. Some communication nets that have been studied experimentally. In this experiment, described above, five people sat around a table and passed notes to one another through openings in vertical partitions. (After Leavitt, 1951)

The *conductivity* of a communication net refers to the freeness of interaction. It is measured by the proportion of actual communication channels to the potential number of communication channels. In each of the five-person groups diagrammed in Fig. 15–7, the potential number of channels is the same, 20. However, there are many more actual channels in Group 5 (20) than in Groups 1 (10), 2 (8), 3 (8), or 4 (8).

In one study Leavitt (1949) examined the relationship between conductivity and satisfaction in the group. He found that the greater the conductivity of the communication net, the more the members of the group liked the task and the more satisfied they were with it. Leavitt also found that the position a person had in the communication net was related to his satisfaction. The more central an individual's position—that is, the more people he could communicate with directly or through an intermediary—the better he liked the task and the more satisfied he was with the job done. The central positions in groups 2, 3, and 4 are emphasized in Fig. 15–7. We shall return to the effect of communication nets on group action in our discussion of productivity.

CATEGORY ANALYSIS IN SMALL-GROUP COMMUNICATION. We can describe interaction in a group even more precisely, if we can find a way to specify the *type* of messages exchanged. One such system was developed by Bales (1950). He divided communications made in face-to-face groups into 12 mutually exclusive and exhaustive categories. Every sentence uttered by any member of the group could be placed in one of these categories (see Fig. 15–8).

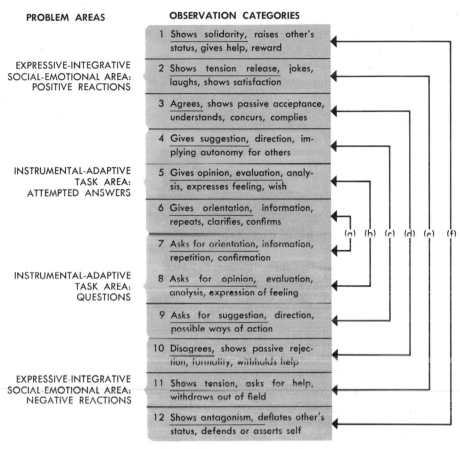

PROBLEM AREAS   OBSERVATION CATEGORIES

EXPRESSIVE-INTEGRATIVE
SOCIAL-EMOTIONAL AREA:
POSITIVE REACTIONS

1 Shows solidarity, raises other's status, gives help, reward

2 Shows tension release, jokes, laughs, shows satisfaction

3 Agrees, shows passive acceptance, understands, concurs, complies

INSTRUMENTAL-ADAPTIVE
TASK AREA:
ATTEMPTED ANSWERS

4 Gives suggestion, direction, implying autonomy for others

5 Gives opinion, evaluation, analysis, expresses feeling, wish

6 Gives orientation, information, repeats, clarifies, confirms

INSTRUMENTAL-ADAPTIVE
TASK AREA:
QUESTIONS

7 Asks for orientation, information, repetition, confirmation

8 Asks for opinion, evaluation, analysis, expression of feeling

9 Asks for suggestion, direction, possible ways of action

EXPRESSIVE-INTEGRATIVE
SOCIAL-EMOTIONAL AREA:
NEGATIVE REACTIONS

10 Disagrees, shows passive rejection, formality, withholds help

11 Shows tension, asks for help, withdraws out of field

12 Shows antagonism, deflates other's status, defends or asserts self

(a) (b) (c) (d) (e) (f)

FIG. 15–8. The categories Bales used to study small-group interaction. Pairs of categories are relevant to different aspects of group functioning: (a) orientation, (b) evaluation, (c) control, (d) decision, (e) tension-management, and (f) integration. (From Bales, 1950)

With such a category analysis it is possible to map the sequence of communication in a small group. Bales has found, for example, that when a member of a group attempts a solution to a problem, the common reaction is one of approval. On the other hand, a communication which shows antagonism is most likely to be followed by another communication expressing antagonism. Generally, when a person makes a suggestion which produces a negative reaction, he changes his suggestion, which produces another reaction. Schachter (1951) has found that if someone's opinion disagrees with the average group opinion, a great deal of communication is directed toward him. If he persists in his disagreement, after a period he is ignored.

It is also possible to summarize the type of interaction that has taken place in a group by looking at the total number of acts in each category. This in-

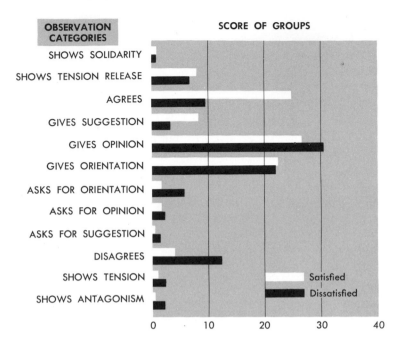

FIG. 15–9. Differences between a satisfied and a dissatisfied group in the content of their interaction, as revealed by Bales' system of categories. (After Bales, 1952)

formation can be summarized in a graph. Figure 15–9 shows the interaction of two five-person groups. One group was satisfied with the group functioning; the other was dissatisfied. Note that the outstanding difference between the two groups is in amount of agreement and disagreement.

What Are the Characteristics of a Productive Group?

In a task-oriented group, the evaluation of the success of the group depends not only on the satisfaction of the members, but also on the objective product of group action. The product is not necessarily an object, although it may be, as in the case of a sewing circle or a manufacturing company. The product of the group may be a solution to a problem, such as how to reduce the cost of a loaf of bread. The product may be a creative one, such as new ideas for an advertising campaign. Or the task of the group may be to reach unanimous agreement (consensus) on a problem that has no absolutely right or wrong answer. The verdict of a jury is an example of this sort of group product. In the text below we shall refer to these types of groups as object-producing, problem-solving, creative, and consensus groups, respectively.

INDIVIDUAL VERSUS GROUP PRODUCTIVITY. Six men can perform a task either individually or by coordinating their efforts in a group. Under which condition will the product be superior? The answer to this question depends on both the nature of the task and the nature of the individuals making up the group.

Let us assume, for example, that a group has the task of constructing complex machines. The quantity and quality of production may be improved by a division of labor. Then each member can concentrate on his component of the machine and perfect his contribution. Presumably this would lead to increased production. However, if one member of the group were considerably less skilled than the rest and produced his component more slowly, it is conceivable that a composite product from each man working alone could be superior to the group product. To the extent that the progress toward the product depends upon the work of the least-skilled members, and to the extent that a wide disparity exists between the least- and most skilled members, the superiority of group productivity over individual productivity diminishes.

Shaw (1932) investigated group versus individual productivity in problem solving.

■ Individuals and groups of four students of the same sex and intelligence were given problems such as the following to solve:

"On the A side of a river are three wives and their husbands. All the men but none of the women can row. Get them across to the B side of the river by means of a boat carrying only three at one time. No man will allow his wife to be in the presence of another man unless he is also there."

Shaw found that the groups were more likely to arrive at a correct solution than were individuals, and that the average time of solution was less for groups. On many problems, but not all, the best individual was as good as the groups. ■

However, groups do not have an advantage on all types of problems. With a very simple task such as finding the sums of pairs of one-digit numbers, individual performance is as good as group performance. An analysis of the proceedings in the four-person group set up in Shaw's experiment suggests one reason why the type of problem she presented was solved more efficiently by the group.

■ The problems presented all required a series of steps, each one of which had to be correct before the next step could be taken. Thus the speed with which incorrect steps were recognized was crucial. In the groups, a false start suggested by one member of the group was readily recognized as incorrect by another member. Individuals working alone tended to persist in the wrong direction for a longer period. ■

Thus one advantage of group problem solving is the possibility of criticism which prevents persistent activity in the wrong direction.

Another type of problem in which group superiority has been demonstrated is the solution of a crossword puzzle (Thorndike, 1938). Here the advantage lay in the heterogeneity of the group, for different members could contribute solutions to different parts of the puzzle. A word with which one member was unfamiliar was familiar to another. If the task is one in which the skills and knowledge of a variety of members can be pooled to contribute to the product, group performance in problem solving is likely to be superior.

In tasks requiring sustained creative effort, however, individuals may be superior to groups. In the Thorndike experiment mentioned above, groups and individuals were also asked to construct a crossword puzzle. Here the individuals proved to be superior. The multiplicity of suggestions from the heterogeneous group could not be coordinated, and one person's suggestions interfered with those of another. One person working alone could perceive an overall pattern while designing parts. This finding corroborates the observation that our finest works of art are most often produced by individuals, not teams.

The sum of the work of individuals proved superior to the group product in another creative task. Taylor (1958) observed that individuals working alone could produce more ideas on a subject than the same number of individuals working in a group. Apparently the group discussion had the effect of inducing the same lines of thinking, thus limiting the range of ideas. Each individual working alone also tended to follow a given line of thinking, but each individual's set was different.

Thus the question, Are groups more productive than individuals? has no simple answer. Factors such as the characteristics of the task and the combinations of individual differences in the group interact. When specialization is advantageous, groups are superior, if one poor performer does not hold up production. In step-by-step problems, groups may be superior because of mutual criticism leading to early abandonment of false starts. A task which permits a group to take advantage of the heterogeneity of its members will be performed better by a group. On the other hand, individuals are likely to be superior in very simple problems and in tasks requiring sustained coordinated creative effort.

Some Factors Influencing Productivity

COHESIVENESS AND PRODUCTIVITY. Since cohesiveness is the attraction of the group for its members, it might be expected that the greater the cohesiveness of the group, the greater the group productivity. This hypothesis failed to be confirmed in two studies, one in which the product was performance in a military drill (French, 1951) and one in which the product was group-written essays. (Darley, Gross, and Martin, 1952)

Schachter and his associates (1958) hypothesized that the reason for these unexpected results was the failure to take into account the fact that the actual group goal might be different from the task assigned to the group. If this is the case, cohesiveness may have the effect of decreasing productivity. Their hypothesis was tested by artificially constructing two high-cohesiveness groups and two low-cohesiveness groups. In one group of each type, the goal of the group was maximum productivity. (The goals were induced by sending notes, presumably from other group members but actually from the experimenters.) In the other pair of groups, the induced group goal was minimum productivity. A comparison of the productivity before and after induction of the group goal shows the following results: Both groups whose induced goal was high productivity did, in fact, increase production, with the high-cohesiveness group showing a slightly greater increase. And both groups that had minimum productivity as the induced goal decreased production, but the high-cohesiveness group slowed down considerably more than the low-cohesiveness group (see Fig. 15–10). In general, the results support the hypothesis that the effect of cohesiveness on productivity depends on the degree to which the actual group goal is superior performance on the assigned task.

		GROUP GOAL FOR PRODUCTIVITY	
		Maximum	Minimum
COHESIVENESS	High	+5.92	−2.16
	Low	+5.09	−0.42

FIG. 15–10. The change in productivity as an interaction between cohesiveness and the induction of a group goal. The data came from the experiment by Schachter *et al.* (1958).

We see this phenomenon in action in a work group studied by Roethslisberger and Dickson (1939). All the workers in the group received the same pay based on group productivity. However, the workers believed that if an excessive amount of work was turned out, the piecework rate would go down. Thus the group goal was to keep production within a certain range. Both slow workers, dubbed "chiselers," and unusually fast workers, dubbed "slaves" or "speed kings," were subjected to group pressure. Thus cohesiveness does affect production in object-producing groups, sometimes in unexpected directions.

When the group task is to reach consensus on an issue, we also find differences that depend on cohesiveness. Gerard (1954) found that members of a highly cohesive group will disagree as readily as members of less cohesive groups. However, members of the more cohesive group will make more persistent attempts to reconcile their differences, and disagreements are abolished more easily. Thus if reaching consensus is the goal of the group, the more cohesive the group, the more easily consensus is reached.

COMMUNICATION AND PRODUCTIVITY. Psychologists have been interested in whether or not there is an optimum communication net for a small group as far as problem solving is concerned. In particular, the circle, the wheel, and the all-channel net have been compared in terms of their efficiency for problem solving.

■ Shaw (1954) gave five marbles to each member of a small group. The participants were told that all members had one and only one marble of the same color. The task was to determine the common color. The participants could communicate with one another with written messages. In every problem the all-channel net proved to be the most efficient. However, whether or not the circle or the wheel was more efficient depended on the complexity of the problem. When the colors of the marbles were easily labeled as red, blue, yellow, etc., the wheel was the more efficient net; when the colors were more difficult to name, such as blue-green and red-orange, the circle communication net was superior. ■

Why was the circle superior for complex problems? In the wheel, the person in the "hub" position serves as the collector and integrator of information. When the received information is ambiguous and the integration job is extremely complex, the central coordinator becomes overloaded and the wheel becomes inefficient.

Why is the all-channel net consistently most efficient? Several psychologists have suggested that the all-channel net permits the group to organize itself into the communication net most efficient for the particular problem (Guetzkow and Simon, 1955). If the potential for free communication does not result in the establishment of a more restricted communication network, the efficiency of the all-channel net is reduced (Guetzkow and Dill, 1955).

GROUP PROCEDURE AND PRODUCTIVITY. Groups vary in the procedures they use to carry out their functions. Sometimes one person is in charge of the task and closely directs the work of subordinates. Sometimes no one person is in charge, but the group proceeds on the basis of previously formalized rules. Sometimes neither leader nor rule book is present to determine group action. Which kinds of procedures lead to greatest productivity?

■ One of the classic studies in this area was carried out by Lewin, Lippitt, and White (White and Lippitt, 1960). They studied four boys' clubs. Each of these clubs had an "authoritarian" leader, a "democratic" leader, and a "*laissez faire*" leader for periods of six weeks each. The authoritarian leader took responsibility for assigning tasks, giving praise and criticism, and demonstrating methods of work. The democratic leader encouraged the group to decide on its own activities. He participated with the group and left members free to work with whomever they pleased. The *laissez faire* leader played a completely passive role, leaving complete freedom for individuals or groups to decide activities and procedures. He supplied information, helped when asked, and was friendly, but otherwise played no active part in the group. See Fig. 15–11. The same persons served as an authoritarian leader for one group during the first six weeks, as a *laissez faire* leader for the second six weeks, and a democratic leader for a third period of six weeks. Since each individual leader took on each of the possible leadership roles, the results could not be attributed to the personality characteristics of the leader.

The differences between the groups in the different conditions were remarkable. Under an authoritarian leader groups showed either of two responses, a submissive reaction or an aggressive reaction. In the submissive groups, members showed little interest in their work until the leader arrived. As soon as he arrived, he began directing their work, giving each boy detailed instructions about what to do. The boys obeyed with little evidence of resentment. In the aggressive-

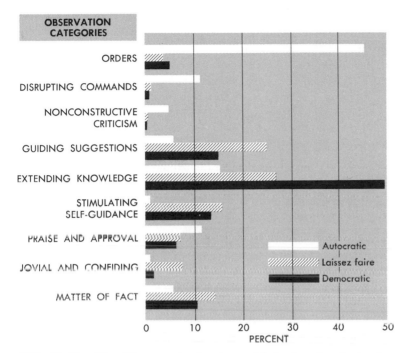

FIG. 15–11. The differences in the observed behavior of authoritarian, democratic, and *laissez faire* leaders, in terms of the time spent on each category. (From White and Lippitt, 1960)

authoritarian groups, the boys voiced resentment toward the other groups and only by firmly outlining the day's work could the leader head off an attack. The boys argued with one another even though they eventually settled down to work. Under *laissez faire* leadership the group lost interest. The boys typically paid little attention to the leader and were unable to agree on a plan for their activities. Under democratic leadership the same groups showed enthusiasm for the work as well as increased good will toward each other.

The purpose of each group was both social and productive. In the latter role the group members performed such crafts as glass-painting and soap-carving. From the point of view of time spent on productive activity, there were noticeable differences between the groups. When the leader was present, for example, the authoritarian groups spent the largest percentage of their time on production (74 percent in the submissively reacting groups and 52 percent in the aggressively reacting groups); the democratically led groups spent 50 percent of their time on productive work and the *laissez faire* groups were productive only 33 percent of the time. When the group leader was out of the room, however, productive time in the two authoritarian groups dropped sharply (from 74 percent to 29 percent and from 52 percent to 16 percent), while the productive time of the democratically led groups dropped only slightly (from 50 percent to 46 percent). The leaders further reported that both production and play were more creative in the democratic groups than in the authoritarian groups, and that the creativity in the democratic group was more sustained and more practical than in the *laissez faire* group. ∎

What were the factors which made for high productivity in the authoritarian and democratic groups? As distinguished from members of the *laissez faire* groups, the authoritarian and democratic group members knew what to do. In the authoritarian group, this was possible because the leader told them what to do. In the democratic group the members themselves decided on both the group goals and means, so they were likely to understand them. Other research also suggests that an important factor in group productivity is clarity of procedures. For example, studies of business and government conferences showed that the successful conferences were those with orderly problem-solving procedures.

Two of the features that made the democratic groups superior in some ways were the participation of the group in decision making, and the interest and friendliness of the leader. Other results also support these two characteristics as factors tending to increase productivity.

■ In an industrial experiment, management tried two ways of introducing a change in production method. Some groups were told by their foremen that a change in operations was needed. Other groups were asked to participate in discussions on how the change should be made. Production in most of the "told" groups fell below standard production rates after the change was instituted, whereas the production of the participating group climbed sharply. (Coch and French, 1958) ■

Similarly, the influence of friendly and interested leaders in increasing group effectiveness has been demonstrated in both industrial and military settings (Likert, 1958). For example, in a study of railroad section gangs, workers in high-production groups more frequently described their foreman as taking a personal interest in them (Kahn and Katz, 1960).

One other factor that may make a democratically led group superior to either a *laissez faire* group (in which there is no leader) or an authoritarian group (in which there is no member participation in decision making) is that the leader provides an opportunity for presentation of a minority opinion.

■ Maier and Solem (1952) made a comparison between groups in which elected representatives served as observers in a problem-solving task and groups in which the elected representatives were asked to serve as discussion leaders. The groups that had a discussion leader produced more correct answers than the *laissez faire* group. An analysis of interaction in the two kinds of groups showed that in the led groups, a minority of one who had the correct answers had more opportunity to state his opinion and discuss his reasoning. In the *laissez faire* group the majority opinion dominated most of the discussion. ■

These results suggest that democratic procedures may be most effective in a number of situations. However, we should note that all these studies were carried out in this country, where the culture is democratic and democracy is a value. Nevertheless, our analysis suggests that such procedures should be effective wherever the group wishes to take advantage of the skills and knowledge of *each* member in every phase of the task. In an authoritarian group, all the idea-generating and decision-making functions rest in one individual. In a *laissez faire* group, valuable minority opinion may be lost and the group lacks sufficient direction.

Democratic procedures are not necessarily desirable for every group and every kind of task. In a large organization a number of central decisions have to be made and passed down; classroom activities are determined in part by the curriculum, etc. But even here the interest of the leader and some participation by the members produce a better-motivated and perhaps more productive group.

The Individual in the Group: the Problem of Leadership

In our discussion of group procedure, we used the term *leader* to refer to people in several different kinds of relationship to the group. In the boys'-club experiment, the leader was an adult who was responsible for the conduct of the children. In the railroad work crew, the person called leader was the foreman— a peer of the workers who had been elevated to a position of higher authority by forces outside the group. In the small-group problem-solving study, the leader was a member of the group selected by the group to represent it. What do all these positions have in common? A person is usually designated as the leader of a group if he has *more influence over the behavior of the members* than anyone else in the group. Sometimes the leader acquires this influence as a result of his assigned role in an already structured group—for example, a policeman directing traffic, a teacher in a classroom, a chef in the kitchen. Sometimes the group has no predetermined structure and the leader emerges from the group.

THIRTEEN FUNCTIONS OF LEADERS

1. EXECUTIVE
2. PLANNER
3. POLICY MAKER
4. EXPERT
5. EXTERNAL GROUP REPRESENTATIVE
6. CONTROLLER OF INTERNAL RELATIONS
7. PURVEYOR OF PUNISHMENTS AND REWARDS
8. ARBITRATOR AND MEDIATOR
9. EXEMPLAR OR MODEL
10. SUBSTITUTE FOR INDIVIDUAL RESPONSIBILITY
11. IDEOLOGIST
12. FATHER FIGURE
13. SCAPEGOAT

What Are the Functions of a Leader?

The leader, whether designated or emergent, exerts influence over the other group members in the course of fulfilling one of a number of functions. Krech, Crutchfield, and Ballachey (1962) distinguish 13 possible leader functions (see Fig. 15–12). Of course, not all leaders perform all these functions in every group, and the relative importance of each function varies according to the nature of the group.

FIG. 15–12. A "leader" can serve many different functions in a group. (From Krech, Crutchfield, and Ballachey, 1962)

■ Halpin and Winer (1957) sought to derive the underlying dimensions of leadership functions. They collected questionnaire responses on the leaders in a number of different structured groups: in industry, in the Air Force and Navy, in school systems, and in colleges. By factor-analyzing the results they found they could describe most of the activity of leaders in terms of two basic dimensions: (1) Consideration, which includes such activities as rewarding a task performed well by a group member, tolerating or not tolerating disagreement, supporting or failing to support the actions of the members when they are challenged from outside, and showing or not showing friendly interest in group members. (2) Initiating structure, a dimension which captures the degree to which the leader plans and directs activity in the group. Figure 15–13 shows how democratic, authoritarian, and *laissez faire* leaders might be described in terms of the two basic dimensions of leadership activity. ■

All leadership functions are not necessarily carried out by a single person even in well-structured groups with a designated leader. When the designated leader in a well-structured group fails to perform his functions, a second leader may emerge. For example, the men in railroad section gangs were asked whether one man in the section spoke up for the men when they wanted something. They said that the foreman (the designated leader) usually performed this function, but that when he did not, a new leader emerged from the group who did take on this responsibility. (Katz, Maccoby, Guren, and Floor, 1951)

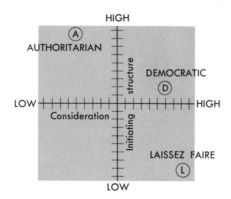

FIG. 15–13. The possible positions of an authoritarian (A), a democratic (D), and a *laissez faire* (L) leader on the two underlying dimensions of leadership: consideration and initiating structure. (After Gagné and Fleishman, 1959)

In his analysis of unstructured small groups, Bales found that two leaders often emerged. One person was characterized by the group as doing the most to guide the discussion and as having the best ideas. This person was not, however, usually best liked. The function of resolving tensions and preserving group unity fell to another group member who was usually chosen as the one best liked by his fellow members. It is interesting to note that in an unstructured group two different people often emerge as the executors of the two kinds of activity that were derived by Halpin and Winer to be the underlying dimensions of leadership.

Who Will Emerge as the Recognized Leader
of an Unstructured Group?

After the members of an unstructured group have interacted for a period, a structure emerges, with a leader, some "key men" and some followers. Sherif and Sherif (1953) observed how the boys in their experimental camp organized themselves with a group structure. They noticed that the highest status position—leadership—and the lowest status positions were established first, with intermediate positions remaining ambiguous for a longer period. Their theoretical picture of the "crystallization" of two group structures appears in Fig. 15–14.

Some psychologists have wondered whether they could predict, on the basis of specific personality characteristics, which person would become leader of a given group. Is there a single "leader" personality?

A number of investigations, each studying different groups, have been carried out. Mann (1959) reviewed the literature in this area and found some traits that are mentioned consistently as characteristics of leaders. Leaders tend to be somewhat more intelligent, better adjusted, more dominant, more masculine, less conservative, and more socially perceptive than the other members of the

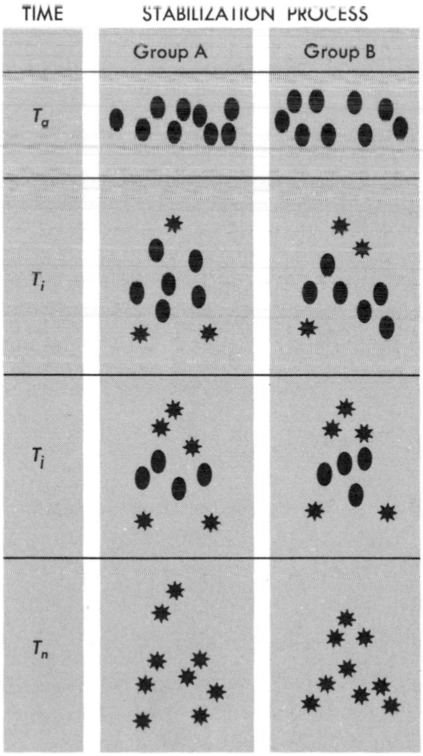

FIG. 15–14. The emergence of structure in two originally unstructured groups. The people whose status has been established are indicated by stars. The high- and low-status people are the first to establish their status. (After Sherif and Sherif, 1953)

group. Note that this is not simply a list of personality characteristics of an individual, but a list of relationships between the individual and the group. The leader tends to be *somewhat* (but not very much) more intelligent than the other members, for example.

This suggests that there is no single leader personality for all groups. The kind of person who becomes leader depends on both the characteristics of the group members and the nature of the group task. This principle is supported by studies which show that leadership ratings for the same person vary when groups are confronted with different tasks. The average correlation in one such study was 0.67, for example (Gibb, 1949).

■ Carter (1953) studied leadership ratings in the same group following six different tasks: reasoning, intellectual construction, clerical work, discussion, motor cooperation, and mechanical assembly. When he factor-analyzed the results, he found that leadership ratings were highly intercorrelated within two kinds of tasks: one person tended to be leader in intellectual tasks, another tended to be leader in tasks involving object manipulation. He concluded that given a particular group, who will be leader depends to some extent on the *general* nature of the task. ■

THE IMPORTANCE OF SPECIAL KNOWLEDGE. If the nature of the task influences who becomes leader, it is quite likely that the person who does become leader combines certain personality characteristics with some special skills for the task. The importance of expertise in leadership is illustrated in the following study:

■ Children who seldom assumed leadership were taken aside and given special training. The training consisted of teaching these children how to play certain games. When the children were returned to their normal group, and the group members began playing these games, the children with special training assumed leadership (Jack, 1934). ■

Sometimes the special knowledge that "creates" a leader is access to information. For example, in Leavitt's study of problem-solving groups using various communication nets, the person most frequently perceived as leader was the person who had access to communication from more people than anyone else, i.e., the person in the most central position.

The interaction of special knowledge and personality in determining leadership is illustrated in this study by Berkowitz (1956).

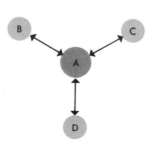

College students were assessed for the trait of dominance. Then the experimenter constructed a number of four-person groups, each with one person high, one person low, and two people moderate in dominance. The experimental group

FIG. 15–15. The channels of communication in Berkowitz's experiment. (After Berkowitz, 1956)

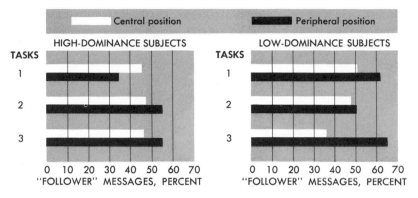

FIG. 15–16. The interaction of dominance and a person's position in the communication net on the proportion of "leader" and "follower" messages sent. (After Berkowitz, 1956)

was given problems to solve, with each person having some information necessary to solve the problem. Communication was permitted to flow in a wheel pattern, as shown in Fig. 15–15. In half the groups the high-dominance person held the central (A) position; in half the groups the low-dominance person held the central position.

The messages sent from one group member to the others were divided into two categories: those relaying information and those initiating communication. Berkowitz interpreted messages in the first category as evidence of followership and messages in the second category as evidence of leadership. The results for three successive tasks appear in Fig. 15–16. Note that low-dominance people show more followership behavior in the followership position than high-dominance people in the same position. Both types show more leadership when they are in the leadership position. On the first task, the high-dominance people showed more leadership than the low-dominance people, but this effect disappeared by the second task.

If such a group had been entirely unstructured, the dominant person would probably have assumed leadership in every case. But assigning the preferred central position to a low-dominance person seems to have made a leader out of a follower.

Leadership and Followership

Our discussion of personality and role in the group has been limited thus far to leadership. But a leader must have followers and the question arises: What are the characteristics of an effective follower?

■ One of the few studies on this question was done by Hollander and Webb (1955). The subjects for the study were graduating naval cadets who had just completed a 15-week course in an Officer

Candidate School. Each cadet was asked to nominate three of his fellow cadets whom he considered best qualified to lead a special military mission. Then the respondent was asked to place himself in the position of leadership and to select the three cadets whom he would most want as part of his unit and the three whom he would least want. Finally the respondent was asked to name his three best friends. The resultant correlations appear in Fig. 15–17.

LEADERSHIP	VS.	FOLLOWERSHIP	0.92
LEADERSHIP	VS.	FRIENDSHIP	0.47
FRIENDSHIP	VS.	FOLLOWERSHIP	0.55

FIG. 15–17. The relationships (indicated by correlations) among cadets' choices for leaders, followers, and friends. The figures indicate that each cadet tends to choose the same people to be his leaders and his followers, but he may choose different people for his friends. (After Hollander and Webb, 1955)

Note that the relationship between leadership and followership choice was extremely high, showing that cadets generally chose the same people as most effective leaders and followers. Note also that again, friendship was not the chief determinant of leadership. The selection of both leaders and followers was more than a mere popularity contest.

Our survey of the problem of leadership has shown what a complicated problem is the question, Who will be the leader? First, there are a number of different leadership functions, all of which are not necessarily performed by a single person. Second, the person who exhibits the most leadership behavior in one group may not do so in another group. Both the nature of the group and the nature of the task help to determine who will be the leader in a specific group.

Summary

Concepts

Social psychology. The study of relationships between individuals and social systems

Cohesiveness. The overall attractiveness of a group for its members

Social interaction. Communication among individuals who both send and receive messages

Communication channel. The existence of communication between two people in a group

Communication net. The channels of communication in a group; the number of channels compared to the number of potential channels is the conductivity of the communication net

Task-oriented group. A group whose primary goal is to perform a specific task, such as producing something, solving a problem, providing ideas, or reaching a consensus

Interaction-oriented group. A group whose primary goal is to provide opportunity for social interaction

Leader. A person who has more influence over the members of a group than any other member; this may involve a number of different functions

Principles

1. Social perception is similar to object perception in that it is organized, involves activation of previously established categories, and is affected by the set and motivation of the perceiver. It differs in that the object of social perception is also a perceiver, and an initiator of action, and is continually changing in response to the perceiver's actions.

2. The accuracy of social perception depends on: (1) the nature of the information; (2) the length of acquaintance (to a degree); (3) first impressions; and (4) who and what are being judged.

3. There are individual differences in the accuracy of social perception, but different people are the most accurate in different kinds of judgments.

4. People join groups because their goals match those of the given group, because they enjoy its activities, because of affiliation motives, and for idiosyncratic reasons.

5. Cohesiveness is influenced by the degree to which members feel they share a common fate, the clarity of goals and means, and the amount and type of interaction.

6. Interaction in a small group can be described in terms of the freedom of communication within it, and the types of communication.

7. The amount of productivity of a group depends on an interaction among the group goal, its cohesiveness, the type of interaction, the procedures, and types of leadership.

8. The two major dimensions of leadership are consideration and initiating structure.

9. Who emerges as a leader of a group depends on both the personality characteristics of its members and the nature of the group.

Suggested Readings

MACCOBY, ELEANOR, T. M. NEWCOMB, and E. HARTLEY, *Readings in Social Psychology*, third edition. New York, Holt, 1958.

For some of the most advanced thinking about social perception, read TAGURI, R., and L. PETRULLO (eds.), *Person Perception and Interpersonal Behavior*. Stanford, Calif.: Stanford University Press, 1958.

CARTWRIGHT, D., and A. ZANDER, *Group Dynamics*. Evanston: Row Peterson, 1960. A good collection of studies on small groups.

chapter 16

the person and society

WHAT IS AN ATTITUDE?

HOW ARE ATTITUDES MEASURED?

ARE THE VARIOUS COMPONENTS OF ATTITUDES
CONSISTENT WITH ONE ANOTHER?

HOW ARE ATTITUDES FORMED?

chapter 16   HOW ARE ATTITUDES ORGANIZED?

HOW DO ATTITUDES CHANGE?

WHAT FACTORS CONTRIBUTE TO COMPLIANCE?

We have come full circle in our study of psychology. In Chapter 2, we took a brief look at the impact of culture on the individual, but there were many unanswered questions about the processes involved. We hope that the subsequent material helped you to fill in those gaps. Now once again we shall take an explicit look at the relationships between an individual and his society.

We have noted frequently that a person learns concepts, motives, habits, and beliefs in a social context. Many of the important objects and events that are the content of this learning have social significance. Social psychologists have studied the ways people comprehend their social environment through the study of attitudes. The first part of the chapter is devoted to this work.

The social environment may have a powerful impact on a person's behavior. In fact, social pressures sometimes induce behavior quite untypical of the individual. In the latter part of the chapter, we shall look at two demonstrations of this phenomenon and some factors influencing it.

What Is an Attitude?

Through our experiences in our environment, we acquire many different expectancies about a particular object. The configuration of all of a person's expectancies about an object makes up his *attitude* toward the object. Thus we define an attitude as an organization of concepts, beliefs, habits and motives* associated with a particular object. For example, when we refer to a person's attitude toward a piece of cake, the attitude might have the following components: the concept of cake being any dessert containing sweet dough, the belief that a piece of cake has many calories, the tendency to buy a piece of cake every morning during a coffee break, and the affective expectancy that cake tastes very good. The concepts and beliefs associated with an attitude are often referred to as the *cognitive component* of the attitude; the habits, as the *action component*; and the motives, as the *affective component* (Katz, 1960). Most frequently social psychologists study attitudes toward socially significant objects; for example, groups, such as racial and religious minorities, or social systems, such as democracy and communism, or social issues, such as birth control and disarmament.

The Dimensions of an Attitude

THE AFFECTIVE COMPONENT. Attitudes vary from one another in a number of different ways other than their specific content. Two of the dimensions of attitudes—intensity and position—refer to the affective component. *Position* refers to the degree of expectancy of pleasantness or unpleasantness associated with the object. The strength of the affective expectancy is the *intensity* of the attitude. For example, a child's attitude toward a physician about to give him an injection

---

* We previously defined concepts, motives, habits and beliefs in expectancy terms.

may include a very strong expectancy of a moderate amount of pain. Thus the position of the object on the affective dimension is moderately negative but the attitude is very intense.

■ A study by Suchman (1950) suggests that position and intensity are often related. In particular, Suchman determined the attitudes of men in the Army toward the Women's Army Corps and toward their Army jobs. He also asked the men how strongly they felt about their positions. For the most part, the men who expressed extreme positions—either very favorable or very unfavorable—stated that they felt strongly about the issue. The men who expressed more moderate attitudes toward the WAC and toward their jobs also tended to express less intensity about the attitude (see Fig. 16-1). ■

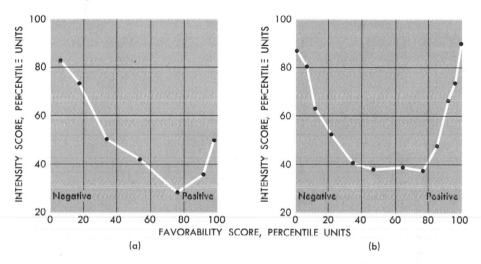

FIG. 16–1. The relationship between intensity and position of the attitudes of soldiers toward two objects: (a) the Women's Army Corps and (b) their Army jobs. In general, extreme positions are accompanied by more intense attitudes. (After Suchman, 1950)

THE COGNITIVE COMPONENT. Several attitudinal dimensions are related to the cognitive component of the attitude. The *specificity* of the concept of the object is one dimension. For example, a person may have an attitude toward Frank Sinatra, toward singers in general, toward performers, or toward celebrities. The *degree of differentiation* of an attitude refers to how many beliefs and concepts are associated with the object. For example, a violinist's attitude toward Beethoven is much more differentiated than that of a person who has had little experience with music.

THE ACTION COMPONENT. Attitudes differ in their relation to overt behavior. Some attitudes have many habits associated with them, others have few. Sometimes the only action associated with an attitude is its verbal expression. This verbal expression of an attitude is called an *opinion*. However, the action component of an attitude may be much more differentiated, and may include a variety of act tendencies. For example, most people have favorable attitudes toward one political party. These may be expressed simply by a vote on election day, or by heated discussions with associates, or by active party work during the political campaign.

How Are Attitudes Measured?

The measurement of attitudes presents the same problems as the assessment of any psychological construct. Is the measure reliable? Does the measure produce the variation in scores implied by the theoretical analysis? Does it provide a valid basis for prediction? Some instruments and procedures have been quite effective in solving these very difficult problems.

Attitude Scales

Frequently a person's position on an attitude is measured by asking the respondent to indicate his agreement or disagreement with a number of statements dealing with the same subject. The major problem for the developer of an attitude scale is to select a series of statements that will have the following characteristics.

(1) An attitude scale should discriminate between people holding different attitudes. Some general statements will be accepted by people who might hold a variety of positions. For example, in an attitude scale toward war the statement, "War should be avoided if possible" would probably be accepted by people of varying attitudes. Different people would attach different interpretations to the phrase "if possible," and the statement would therefore not help us to infer a person's attitude toward war with precision.

(2) The scale should cover the entire range of positions on the attitude. A scale on political attitudes should not only be able to discriminate Democrats from Republicans, but also the radical from the moderate conservative, the liberal from the left-wing radical.

(3) It should avoid statements that imply positions on several attitudes simultaneously. If a statement implies positions on several attitudes, it is difficult to know which of the attitudes determined the response to it. For example, this item was eliminated from an attitude scale on the church because of such ambiguity:

■ "I believe that the church has a good influence on the lower and uneducated classes but has no value for the upper, educated classes." (Thurstone and Chave, 1929) ■

This statement confounds attitudes toward the church with attitudes toward people of different socio-economic classes.

One of the early investigators who undertook to solve these problems was Thurstone (1929) who used the following procedure. A series of statements

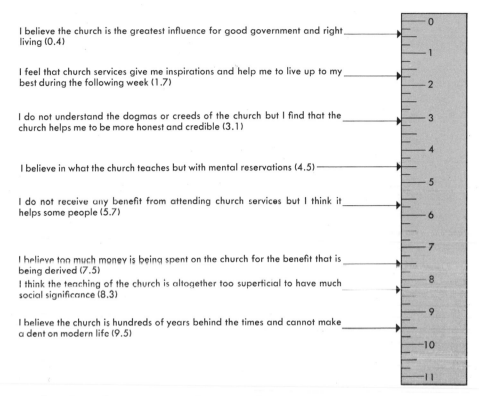

I believe the church is the greatest influence for good government and right living (0.4)

I feel that church services give me inspirations and help me to live up to my best during the following week (1.7)

I do not understand the dogmas or creeds of the church but I find that the church helps me to be more honest and credible (3.1)

I believe in what the church teaches but with mental reservations (4.5)

I do not receive any benefit from attending church services but I think it helps some people (5.7)

I believe too much money is being spent on the church for the benefit that is being derived (7.5)

I think the teaching of the church is altogether too superficial to have much social significance (8.3)

I believe the church is hundreds of years behind the times and cannot make a dent on modern life (9.5)

FIC. 16–2. Some statements from the equal-appearing interval scale by Thurstone and Chave on attitudes toward the church. The scale value of each statement appears in parentheses and is indicated on the "attitude yardstick." (After Thurstone and Chave, 1929)

representing a variety of opinions on a subject were gathered together. Then a group of people were asked to sort the statements into eleven categories, the first category for statements representing the most favorable attitude toward the subject, the sixth category representing a neutral attitude, and the eleventh category representing the most unfavorable attitude. The judges were not asked to express their own attitudes but to decide the extent to which each item expressed a favorable or unfavorable position. Moreover, the judges were not instructed to place an equal number of statements in every category. However, judges who put more than 30% of the statements in a single category were eliminated as careless judges.* After a number of judges had sorted out the

* Later studies have shown that one effect of eliminating judgments from subjects who put many statements into a single category is to discard the judgments of subjects with extreme positions on the attitude, e.g., anti-Negro white subjects in judging statements about Negroes. Thus these studies showed that a person's own attitude does affect his rating of an item. (Hovland and Sherif, 1953)

statements, Thurstone was able to calculate a scale value for each statement—namely, the average category number to which the statement had been assigned. There was a great deal of variability in the categories to which judges assigned some statements and there was substantial agreement on others. By eliminating the high-variability statements, Thurstone was able to collect a group of statements that unambiguously represented points along a wide range of positions toward an attitudinal object. Figure 16–2 gives examples of statements and their assigned scale value derived from this procedure. Thurstone's procedure has been called *the method of equal-appearing intervals,* since the result is an attitude yard-stick with equal attitude differences represented by equal distances on a scale. An attitude scale constructed in this way can now be used to assess a person's attitudes by asking him which of the items he agrees with.

The method of equal-appearing intervals places statements on a position continuum from favorable to unfavorable. A person's position can be ascertained by discovering which of the statements he will accept. Another method of determining a person's position on an attitude was developed by Likert (1932). Here the scale is constructed from a number of statements, each of which clearly represents either a favorable or unfavorable attitude. People helping in the construction of the scale state individually the degree to which they agree or disagree with the statements. For example, the following items come from a Likert scale on internationalism.*

In the interest of permanent peace, we should be willing to arbitrate absolutely all differences with other nations which we cannot readily settle by diplomacy.

Strongly approve (1)	Approve (2)	Undecided (3)	Disapprove (4)	Strongly disapprove (5)

The United States should have the largest military and naval air fleets in the world.

Strongly approve (5)	Approve (4)	Undecided (3)	Disapprove (2)	Strongly disapprove (1)

We should be willing to fight for our country whether it is in the right or in the wrong.

Strongly approve (5)	Approve (4)	Undecided (3)	Disapprove (2)	Strongly disapprove (1)

Our country should never declare war again under any circumstances.

Strongly approve (1)	Approve (2)	Undecided (3)	Disapprove (4)	Strongly disapprove (5)

* From Murphy, G., and R. Likert, *Public Opinion and the Individual: A Psychological Study of Student Attitudes with a Retest Five Years Later.* New York: Harper, 1939. Reprinted by permission.

A person who loves his fellow men should refuse to engage in any war, no matter how serious the consequences to his country.

Strongly approve	Approve	Undecided	Disapprove	Strongly disapprove
(1)	(2)	(3)	(4)	(5)

A score of 1 is given for the most favorable attitude on each statement toward internationalism, whether it is indicated by strong agreement with a favorable statement or strong disagreement with an unfavorable statement.

The responses of the subjects on the items are then correlated. If all the statements are measuring the same attitude, there should be a high correlation among the responses to the statements: people with a strongly favorable attitude toward internationalism should reveal this in their answers to all the relevant statements. Thus item scores that do not correlate highly with total scores on the other items are eliminated. The items that remain now make up an attitude scale that can be used to determine a person's attitude on an issue.

Guttman (1950) developed still another way of selecting statements to reflect a single attitude. He reasoned this way: Someone with a strongly favorable attitude toward an object, for example, dogs as pets, will accept statements that are both mildly favorable toward dogs and strongly favorable toward them. For example, he would agree both that a seeing-eye dog may be very helpful to blind people and that the loyalty and affection of a dog undoubtedly make him a man's best friend. Someone with a mildly favorable attitude might agree with the first statement about dogs but not the second. If a series of progressively more favorable statements could be collected, such that a person with a strongly favorable attitude would accept all of them and someone with a strongly unfavor-

	PERSON	1 (MOST FAVORABLE ITEM)	2	3	4	5	6 (LEAST FAVORABLE ITEM)
PERSON WITH MOST FAVORABLE ATTITUDE	A	+	+	+	+	+	+
	B	—	+	+	+	+	+
	C	—	—	+	+	+	+
	D	—	—	—	+	+	+
	E	—	—	—	—	+	+
	F	—	—	—	—	—	+
PERSON WITH LEAST FAVORABLE ATTITUDE	G	—	—	—	—	—	—

FIG. 16–3. The theoretical response patterns of people of different attitudes to the items on a Guttman scale.

able attitude would accept few or none, then the number of accepted statements could be a measure of attitude. Ideally, the responses of people having a range of opinions will fall in the pattern illustrated in Fig. 16–3. In selecting a set of statements for measuring a single attitude by the Guttman method, the investigator discards statements which, in pretesting, produce response patterns widely deviant from the ideal pattern.

The Bogardus Social Distance Scale, which measures attitudes toward national, racial, and religious groups, provides an example of a series of statements that fits Guttman's criterion. In this scale, respondents are asked to indicate the degree of relationship to which they would admit members of a given group. If the scale were used to assess attitudes toward foreigners, it might appear in the following form:

I would willingly admit foreigners:

> 1. to close kinship by marriage
> 2. to my club as personal chums
> 3. to my street as neighbors
> 4. to employment in my occupation
> 5. to citizenship in my country
> 6. as visitors in my country.

Notice that a person who accepted statement 1 would accept all the others. A person who accepted number 3, but not number 1 and 2, would also accept statements 4–6.

Are the Various Components of Attitudes Consistent With One Another?

Attitude scales determine a person's position on an attitude via his acceptance or rejection of statements. Sometimes these statements directly reflect the affective component: "Foreigners frighten me." Sometimes they reflect the cognitive component: "I believe the church has done a great deal to eliminate poverty and misery." Sometimes they reflect the action component: "I would welcome a conscientious objector to my house as a friend." All these measures are used, however, to determine a person's position—from favorable to unfavorable—toward an attitude object. Thus a basic assumption is that there is consistency aomng the motives, beliefs, and habits that are associated with a single attitude object.

■ Supporting evidence for this assumption comes from a study by Campbell (1947). He asked high school and college students to respond to statements about five different racial and national groups. Included among the statements were items tapping the affective component (statements of like and dislike), items tapping the cognitive component (beliefs concerning the morality and intelligence of the groups), and items tapping the action component (social distance scales similar to the Bogardus scale described above). The responses tapping the various components were then correlated with one another. High correlations would indicate that a person who expressed a liking for a minority would also believe that this minority showed intelligence and high moral standards. Furthermore, he would permit close social relationships with that minority. Conversely, high correlations would imply that a person who expressed dislike of a group would also have unfavorable beliefs about the group and would maintain great social distance. Campbell found that the average correlations among the components (with one exception) were between 0.50 and 0.65, indicating a trend toward consistency. ■

Attitudes and Action

In Campbell's study, all the components of the attitude were assessed by the verbal report of the respondent. However, a more direct way to measure the action component is to observe the behavior of a person toward the object of the attitude. The first studies that compared verbal measures of the action component with observations of actual behavior were very discouraging to those who had developed attitude scales.

■ La Piere (1935) spent two years travelling around the United States with a young Chinese student and his wife. During the course of the trip, the companions visited many hotels and restaurants. Although La Piere had been concerned about the reception Orientals would receive at these establishments, he found that they were almost always received politely and that, with but one exception, they were given service and accommodations at each place visited. Six months after the trip La Piere sent questionnaires to many of the establishments he and his friends had visited. Among the questions was: "Will you accept members of the Chinese race as guests in your establishment?" Over 90 percent of the replies to this question were "No." One establishment replied "yes," and the remainder were undecided. Thus out of the 128 restaurants and hotels polled, 118 stated that they would not serve Orientals. Yet 117 of these establishments gave service to Orientals who requested it. ■

A similar study, which dealt with serving Negroes in restaurants, yielded similar results. Restaurant proprietors who failed to answer a request for reservations for a group including some Negroes did, in fact, serve a party of three, consisting of two white women and one Negro woman, when they appeared at the restaurant in person (Kutner, Wilkins, and Yarrow, 1952).

Does this inconsistency between verbal statement and action imply that verbal measurements of attitude are invalid? Does it mean that attitude measurements are useless in the prediction of behavior? Let us take a second look at these apparently inconsistent results. La Piere found that most of the places that said the Chinese couple would not be served did, in fact, serve them. In the Kutner study, all the restaurants that refused the reservations for a racially mixed party did, in fact, give service to such a party. *However, in neither study did the restaurant agent who agreed verbally to serve the mixed group fail to do so in the face-to-face situation.* So if there is an inconsistency, it is only in one direction: people who express verbal prejudice do not necessarily act on it.

The apparent inconsistency disintegrates even further when we consider the relationship between behavior and a construct such as attitude. Theoretically, a number of factors inside and outside the organism combine to produce behavior. In our discussion of performance, for example, we saw that a habit will not be performed in the appropriate situation without appropriate motivation. Failure to perform does not necessarily imply that the organism does not have the habit in his repertoire.* Similarly, failure to act consistently in accordance with an expressed attitude does not mean that the person does not really hold the attitude.

Campbell (1963) suggests a very ingenious explanation for the results of these and other attitude studies which takes into account both the unidirectional nature of the inconsistency between attitude and action, and the characteristics of a construct. He points out that in the case of a children's arithmetic test, a child who succeeds in answering only two items correctly out of four is not necessarily inconsistent in arithmetic. If he gets the two easier problems correct, but misses the two more difficult problems, we would interpret his score as an indication of the level of his ability. In the same way, reasons Campbell, we can think of various degrees of attitude toward minority groups. Then we can examine specific situations to see how difficult it would be to express the attitude through action. The more difficult the situation, the more extreme the attitude would have to be in order for it to be expressed in action. And only if an attitude were acted on in a difficult situation and not acted on in an easy situation could we say that action and attitude were truly inconsistent.

Thus we can look back at La Piere's data and ask, which was more difficult in 1935: to state in reply to a mailed questionnaire that the restaurant would prefer to avoid serving Chinese people—or to confront three well-dressed people in a restaurant with other customers present and say "I am sorry; we don't serve Orientals"? As Campbell points out, the restaurant manager would be inconsistent only if he agreed to accommodate the people in the mail questionnaire and refused to serve them when they appeared in person. The face-to-face situation represented a higher hurdle—required a more extreme attitude—than either the mailed questionnaire or the phone call situation.†

Evidence for this "situation-hurdle" interpretation comes from the following observations:

■ Minard (1952) studied race relations in a small coal-mining community in West Virginia both by observation and by interview. He found that the patterns of segregation and integration were different in the mines, where most of the men worked, from the patterns in the town, where they lived. The mine was integrated, with equal status and equal pay for equal work. The town maintained segregation. Each day, the white workers went from an environment in which equality

---

* See, for example, the latent learning studies described in Chapter 5 on pp. 117–118.
† With the passage of the Civil Rights Act of 1964, including a public accommodations provision, the height of various hurdles has probably changed.

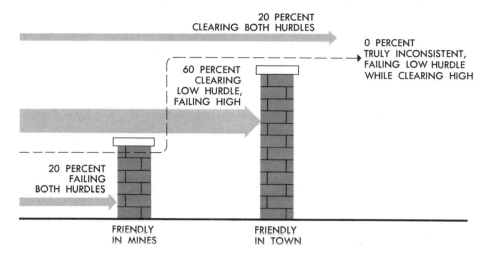

FIG. 16–4. Campbell's interpretation of Minard's data. The actions of the miners are not inconsistent, since the higher the hurdle, the fewer the people whose actions clear the hurdle. But no one whose actions clear the high hurdle displays actions which fail to clear the lower one. (After Campbell, 1963)

was the norm to one in which Negroes were considered inferior. This situation produced an interesting interaction between attitude and behavior. Twenty percent of the white miners had very favorable attitudes toward Negroes and acted in accordance with their attitudes both in the mine and in the town. Twenty percent had extremely unfavorable attitudes toward Negroes and acted accordingly all the time. The remaining sixty percent simply shifted their behavior toward Negroes when they left the mine, treating Negroes as equals while at work and treating them as inferiors in the town. ■

Campbell (1963) interprets Minard's observations in the following way: Treating Negroes as equals in town represents a difficult hurdle, since it means breaking the traditions of the community. Only 20% of the miners had attitudes favorable enough to get beyond such a barrier. The mines, on the other hand, represent a very low hurdle, so much so that 80% of the workers—both those favorable toward Negroes and those whose attitudes are intermediate—show behavior that normally would indicate lack of prejudice. Note that no white worker treated the Negro as an equal in town and as an underling in the mine; such behavior would show true inconsistency between attitudes and behavior. See Fig. 16–4.

How Are Attitudes Formed?

In a sense, you already know the answer to this question. We defined an attitude as an organization of concepts, beliefs, habits, and motives associated with an object. Thus the formation of an attitude consists of acquiring various concepts, beliefs, habits, and motives—learning processes which we discussed in detail in earlier chapters. Here, then, we shall review and summarize some of the processes that result in attitude formation. The organizing principle for our summary will be the motivational basis of attitudes.

The Motivational Basis of Attitude Formation

The affective component of an attitude—the component considered by many psychologists to be at the core of the attitude—may be associated with any one or several of the many human motives. Katz (1960) suggests that the dynamics of attitude formation and change are probably different for attitudes with different motivational bases. In his analysis, Katz distinguishes between four different motivational bases for attitudes: (1) utilitarian (2) value-expressive (3) ego-defensive (4) knowledge.

An attitude with a *utilitarian* basis is one that is associated with the survival, safety, and some of the social motives of the individual. The object of the attitude is perceived as a goal or as a means to a goal related to such motives. A worker's favorable attitude toward a law that will benefit him economically is an example. A child's favorable attitude toward candy is another. Katz suggests that a person acquires utilitarian attitudes through experience with the object. The nearer the object, and the less ambiguous the relation between it and motive satisfaction, the stronger the probability of acquiring a very favorable attitude. Similarly, the more closely an object is associated with negative affect, the more likely the development of an unfavorable attitude. A child's negative attitude toward animals may have been acquired from some unpleasant experiences with a snarling dog, for example.

A *value-expressive* attitude is based on a person's motive for self-esteem and self-actualization. We suggested earlier that each person comes to identify certain general goals as values and to develop the concept of an ego-ideal. In our discussion of development, we pointed out that each person seeks to develop an identity, a concept of self in which he has pride. Both a person's sense of identity and his feelings of self-esteem depend, in part, on the relations of his actions to his values and of his self-image to his ideal. Thus those attitudes that exemplify his values and his ego-ideal will enhance his feelings of self-esteem. A person who values world law will find satisfaction in expressing favorable attitudes toward the United Nations, for example. We suspect that the formation of value-expressive attitudes depends on an individual's perception of the relation between the object, the attitude, and his ideal of himself.

Much of the development of a child's ego-ideal depends on his parents. As part of the process of identification, the child comes to view the values and attitudes of his parents as representing the ideal. Thus he enhances his self-image when he adopts the attitudes of his parents as his own. This process can help to account for the finding by Remmers and Radler (1957), cited earlier, that there are very strong correlations between the attitudes of high school children and their parents on a number of public issues. Of course parents are not the sole models for identification. For example, adolescents often identify with their peers or with older adults other than parents. In this case, the attitudes of these people would serve as the basis for the development of some value-expressive attitudes.

Ego-defensive attitudes are also related to the motive for self-esteem, but they defend the ego in a negative way. They are formed in conjunction with processes defending the person from his own anxieties; i.e., defense mechanisms. For example, a number of psychologists have suggested that prejudice toward minority groups in some people may represent a projection or a displacement of feelings of hostility and inferiority onto a minority. In one study of anti-Semitism, Campbell (1947) found that people who were dissatisfied with their own economic condition tended to express more hostile attitudes toward Jews than those who were satisfied. In another study, Frenkel-Brunswick and Sanford (1945) found that anti-Semitic girls tended to express more repressed aggression, suspicion, and jealousy in projective tests than did tolerant girls. Stricker (1963) found that the subjects who had watched an aggression film made higher scores on a prejudice questionnaire. These studies do not prove that the prejudiced attitudes were based on defense mechanisms, but the observed relationships are consistent with such an interpretation, at least in some cases—if not in all instances.

Attitudes with a *knowledge* basis are acquired in conjunction with competence motives, specifically the motives to acquire a clear, stable, and consistent picture of the world. For every person there are some attitudinal objects with which he has had little experience and about which his information is sparse or ambiguous. This situation coupled with the motive for knowledge sets the stage for attitude formation. It is quite likely that the person will fill out this gap in his picture of the world (1) by actively seeking more information, which will permit attitude formation by one of the other principles discussed (such as seeking actual contact leading to a utilitarian attitude), or (2) by adopting toward the object the attitudes of the people around him, or (3) by adopting an attitude toward the object that is consistent with the rest of his thinking.

It has been suggested that attitudes formed on the basis of national stereotypes exemplify (2)—adopting the attitudes of others (Katz, 1960, Lippmann, 1922). There are many nationalities with whom we, as individuals, have little contact and about whom information is either almost nonexistent or contradictory. The stereotypes that are part of our culture and that are communicated to us by the social environment help to stabilize and clarify our images of the people of the world. Think about the sources of your own attitudes toward Indians, for example.

A study by Morrissette (1958) illustrates (3)—consistency—as a basis for attitude formation.

■ College women were given a hypothetical situation: Three girls who had been roommates for several months had solved the problems of living together successfully, and had grown to like each other very much. One of the roommates had to withdraw from the household, leaving a vacancy.

Now the subjects were asked to picture themselves becoming the third roommate. They were to imagine that they met one of the remaining girls, Carol, and that they were very favorably impressed with her. The task of the subjects was to predict their attitudes toward the other remaining roommate, Helen. The results were clear: 91 percent of the subjects predicted that they would like Helen. Since the subjects had no objective information about Helen, they formed an attitude toward her that was consistent with their attitude toward Carol and Carol's attitude toward Helen. ■

How Are Attitudes Organized?

THE CENTRALITY OF ATTITUDES. Some attitudes have little effect on a person's thinking and behavior; others have a major effect on both processes in a variety of situations. The greater the effect of an attitude on a person's psychological processes, the more central it is. Newcomb (1965) suggests that the centrality of an attitude depends in part on the strength of the motives associated with the object, and in part on how persistently present the object is in the individual's environment.

One technique for determining which attitudes are central is the funnel technique. Here, an interviewer begins his interview with a very general question and proceeds to more specific ones. The rationale for using this method to get an index of centrality is that the more central an attitude is for an individual, the more likely it is that the attitude will be expressed in answer to a general question that permits a wide variety of attitudes to be expressed. An attitude which has very little effect on a person's thinking and behavior will probably not be expressed unless aroused by a specific question.

■ Stouffer (1955) collected data from open-ended interviews which showed the relative centrality of attitudes toward American Communists. Early in the interview the respondent was asked: "What kinds of things do you worry about most?" Most people mentioned personal and economic problems. Less than 9 percent of the people mentioned world problems in answer to this question. Less than 1 percent specifically mentioned communism. Then the people were asked, "Are there other problems you worry or are concerned about, especially political or world problems?" Now 30 percent mentioned world affairs and 6 percent specifically mentioned communism. In answer to the question "How great a danger do you feel American Communists are to this country at the present time?" 43 percent replied a great or a very great danger. Thus close to half the people expressed a negative attitude toward American Communists, but the attitude was not as central to their thinking as were attitudes toward their family and work.

To ask a very specific question like the last one independently of the others may paint a very false picture of the centrality of attitudes in the respondent. ■

Attitude Systems

Some attitudes are closely related to one another. That is, they share common or similar concepts, beliefs, motives, and habits. We can think of such a cluster of attitudes as an *attitude system*. In other cases, a single attitude may be relatively isolated. For example, a voter's attitude toward a party's candidate for national office usually is closely related to the voter's attitudes toward the economic philosophy of the party, the party's legislative record, and its traditional stand on foreign policy. However, in the 1952 and 1956 elections, as we saw in Chapter 1, the attitudes of some voters toward President Eisenhower were isolated from their attitudes toward the Republican Party.

Note that the closeness of relationship among attitudes does not necessarily reflect the true relationship between the objects of the attitudes. The same person may, on one hand, express anti-Semitic attitudes and, at the same time, express favorable attitudes toward a particular Jewish person. The objective fact that a friend is a member of the Jewish community does not necessarily prevent the individual from isolating the two attitudes.

The Study of Ethnocentrism

One attitude system that has been studied intensively by psychologists is ethnocentrism. The overall study began with an investigation into anti-Semitism as an attitude. Adorno *et al.* (1950) designed attitude scales in which subjects were asked to express their feelings, beliefs, and prescriptions for action about Jews. They found quite a bit of consistency in the various attitudinal components. Now the investigators questioned whether anti-Semitism was part of a larger attitude system that included hostility toward all outside groups. Thus they constructed an ethnocentrism scale that measured attitudes toward Negroes, foreign nationalities and other minority groups. They found high correlations among the three attitudes as well as high correlations between the ethnocentrism scale (*E*-scale) and the original anti-Semitism scale. This supports the hypothesis that ethnocentrism (or lack of ethnocentrism) constitutes a consistent attitude system.

The authors now further hypothesized that ethnocentrism was itself a component in a still more encompassing attitude system, which might be summarized as receptivity to fascistic ideas. This larger system includes many anti-democratic and pro-authoritarian attitudes. For example, favorable attitudes toward strict obedience and tendencies to evaluate people as either "good" or "bad" are components in this system. The scale measuring these attitudes was called the *F*-scale, and was considered a measure of authoritarianism. Again, the authors found high correlations between the *E*-scale and the *F*-scale. Now the authors interviewed subjects who were the highest 25 percent and the lowest 25 percent on the ethnocentrism scale to see the relationship of personality characteristics to this attitude system. They found that the people high in ethnocentrism tended to be rigid, to reject their socially unacceptable impulses, and to externalize them through projection. Furthermore they found differences in the subjects' childhood situations which would result in such personality differences. Thus the authors concluded that the ethnocentrism attitude system was ego-defensive in nature.

You should not conclude from this study that all racial prejudice is a part of an authoritarian attitude system. Critics of the authoritarian study point out that the subjects in that study were a special group. That is, they were non-Jewish, white, middle-class Americans from California and the Pacific Northwest (Hyman and Sheatsly, 1954). For different individuals, the same attitude may be a part of a different attitude system and may have been formed in conjunction with different motives.

■ Pettigrew (1958) compared anti-Negro attitudes and authoritarianism in four groups: South African students, American students, small town adults in the southern United States, and small town adults in the northern United States. Within each cultural group, authoritarianism and prejudice against Negroes were positively correlated. However, Pettigrew also compared the groups with one another and found that (1) there were no differences among the groups on authoritarianism, and (2) there were significant differences among the groups in prejudice. The South African and southern U.S. groups were significantly less tolerant toward Negroes. Thus, given a South African and an American student equal on the authoritarianism scale, the South African is likely to show more prejudice. His attitude toward Negroes is an expression of his society's norms as well as of his unique personality structure. ■

How Do Attitudes Change?

Advertisers spend millions of dollars trying to change the attitudes of consumers toward their products. Politicians try to establish favorable attitudes in voters toward themselves and their positions. Various organizations have as their aim the changing of people's attitudes toward mental health, minority groups, seat belts in automobiles, church attendance, alcohol, and the possibility of curing cancer. The area of attitude change is one of considerable social importance, and psychologists have spent considerable research time in isolating the variables involved.

Changing the Cognitive Component

Frequently, attempts at attitude change take the form of providing new information. People interested in advancing automobile safety quote figures which demonstrate fewer fatalities when seat belts are worn. A governor running for re-election will give evidence to support his contention that his state's economy is better than ever. The assumption is that a change in a person's belief will change his position toward the attitude object.

The Nature of the Message

One of the first problems encountered when a person attempts to change attitudes by communicating new information is this: should he simply present his arguments and evidence, or should he present both sides of the issue, specifically refuting the arguments of the opposition. The effects of presenting one side of an argument versus two sides were studied in research carried out with soldiers during World War II.

Soldiers were presented with arguments for the position that the war with Japan would continue for a long time after the surrender of Germany. One group listened to a fifteen minute talk supporting this position. A second group heard the same talk, but was also given some arguments supporting the idea that there would be an early end to the war. The participating soldiers estimated the length of the war with Japan both before and after hearing the talks. Both techniques were effective overall. However, a close analysis of the data showed a difference in reaction depending on the *original* position of the men (see Fig. 16–5). Of those men who originally thought the war with Japan would be more than two years long, more increased their estimates after the one-sided communication. Of the men who originally estimated the war would continue for less than two years, more increased their estimates after the two-sided communication. (Hovland, Lumsdaine, and Sheffield, 1949).

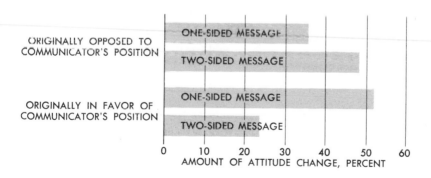

FIG. 16–5. The interaction between the nature of the message (one-sided versus two-sided) and the initial attitudes of the men listening to the message. Those who were originally opposed to the message exhibited a greater change in their attitudes after hearing the two-sided message. (From Hovland, Lumsdaine, and Sheffield, 1949)

This study suggests that a one-sided communication is most effective in strengthening a person's attitude which is already in the desired direction, whereas a two-sided presentation is more effective in reversing a person's position.

A later study showed an additional bonus for two-sided communication: greater resistance to counterpropaganda.

■ Lumsdaine and Janis (1953) conducted this study before the announcement that the Soviet Union had exploded an atomic bomb. Two messages were prepared. One argued that it would be impossible for the Soviet Union to build large numbers of A-bombs. The other argued first that large-quantity Soviet A-bomb production would be possible; then it argued that such production would *not* be possible and refuted the earlier affirmative arguments. The subjects were four groups of high school students; two groups heard the one-sided message, and two groups heard the two-sided message. A week after the message was presented, the students filled out a questionnaire indicating their opinions. Just before the questionnaire was given out, two of the four groups were given a second message which took the position that the Soviet Union had in fact developed an A-bomb and would be producing the bombs in large quantity. This message was intended as counterpropaganda. The results are presented in Fig. 16–6. For the groups who heard one of the two original messages, but not the counterpropaganda message, the one-sided and two-sided presentations were about equally effective. However, there was a dramatic difference between the two kinds of messages in establishing resistance to counterpropaganda. The two-sided message proved far more effective in "inoculating" the subjects in resistance to counterpropaganda, since it alerted them to the possibility that there were opposing arguments and provided answers to them. ■

Frequently a person strengthens his arguments for a position by citing the agreement of a source of great prestige. Hovland and Weiss (1951) experimentally investigated the effects of the attributed source on the amount of attitude change produced by the message. College students read messages of which half were quotes attributed to a prestigious and trustworthy source and the other half were attributed to untrustworthy sources. As you might expect, questionnaires taken immediately after the messages revealed that the quotes attributed to high-prestige sources led to significantly greater amounts of attitude change than the low-prestige sources. Four weeks later, a second questionnaire was administered to test for longer range attitude change, and now the investigators were surprised by the results. Although there had been no intervening messages,

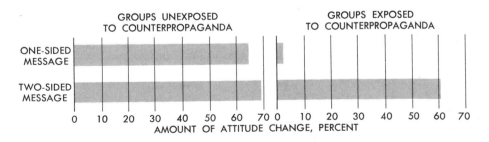

FIG. 16–6.   Resistance to counterpropaganda in relation to the nature of the message (one-sided versus two-sided). The two-sided message produced much greater resistance to counterpropaganda. (From Lumsdaine and Janis, 1953)

the subjects' attitudes showed definite changes. The attitudes originally influenced by the high-prestige source showed a *decrease* in amount of agreement, while the attitudes originally influenced (to a small extent) by the low-prestige source showed an *increase* in amount of agreement (see Fig. 16–7). This "sleeper effect" has been attributed to the fact that over a period of time the subject remembers a message but tends increasingly to dissociate it from its source (Hovland and Weiss, 1951).

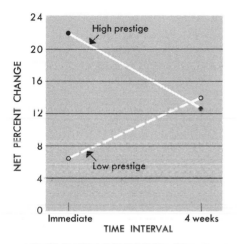

FIG. 16–7. The "sleeper effect"—the interaction between the prestige of the source to which a message is attributed and the time interval between the presentation of the message and the measurement of attitude change. (After Hovland and Weiss, 1951)

■ This interpretation is supported by a follow-up study of the sleeper effect by Kelman and Hovland (1953). They played tape-recorded messages which they attributed to high- or low-prestige sources by introductions. Attitude change was measured immediately after presentation of the message and again three weeks later. For some groups, Kelman and Hovland again presented the introductions to the speakers before assessing attitudes the second time. These groups did *not* show the sleeper effect. Thus reinstatement of cues associated with the source of a message reinstates the original effects of the source on attitude change. ■

What kind of information is most effective for producing attitude change? Peak (1955) hypothesized that the crucial beliefs that must be changed prior to attitude change are those relating to the object of the attitude to the person's goals. If the perceived relation between the object and a person's goals can be changed, then attitude change is likely to follow.

■ Carlson put Peak's hypothesis to an experimental test. He measured three things: (1) the subject's attitudes toward Negroes moving into white neighborhoods; (2) the affective value of goals which might be related to such attitudes; e.g., the subject's value for protecting property prices; (3) perceived relation between the object of the attitude and the goal; e.g., the subject's estimate of the degree to which Negroes moving into white neighborhoods would achieve or block the goal of maintaining property prices. Then Carlson set about to change the perceived relations. Under the pretext of giving the subjects a test of "reasoning and objectivity," he asked them to support the argument that Negroes moving into white neighborhoods would help the subjects to achieve their goals. Later, he also read a prepared message presenting such arguments. Then he once again measured the three items. The results showed significant changes both in the subjects' perceived relationships (3) and in the attitude toward Negroes in white neighborhoods (1). Carlson concluded that a person's attitude can be changed if the relationship between the object of the attitude and his goals are changed. (Carlson, 1956) ■

In the study just described, not all of the subjects changed their attitudes an equal amount. Figure 16–8 shows that those with extreme initial opinions tended to show less attitude change than those with intermediate initial opinions.

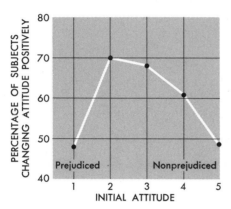

FIG. 16–8. The relationship between the original attitude and amount of attitude change in Carlson's study. Carlson tried to change attitudes by changing the subject's perceived relationship between the objects of his attitudes and his goals. (From Carlson, 1956)

Several factors may help explain this finding. First, we saw earlier that the more extreme a person's position on an attitude, the more strongly it is held. Thus, in general, we would expect extreme attitudes to change less. Other attitude studies support this hypothesis (Tannenbaum, 1956). Second, we have to take into account the "ceiling effect." People who already held very unprejudiced attitudes could not show very much attitude change because they already held the positive attitudes suggested by the message. Finally, perhaps we should take into account that not all attitudes are based on goals of which the person is aware. We have seen that prejudice may be based on ego-defensive motives. If it is, we would not expect information designed to change a person's beliefs about the attitude object in relation to conscious goals to be effective. We would predict that Carlson's technique would be most effective in changing utilitarian and value-expressive attitudes and least effective for defensive attitudes.

The Nature of the Persuader

The degree to which we accept a person's arguments depends on the person as well as the nature of his arguments. As you might expect, people are most influenced by a persuader of high prestige (Brehm, 1954), by one they consider attractive (Tannenbaum, 1956), and by one they like or expect to like, as the following study suggests.

■ Back (1951) formed two-person groups from volunteer students in general psychology classes. Before the experiment proper the volunteers answered several questions, including, "Can you describe the type of person you want to work with?"

Subjects were paired randomly, but in order to create differences in liking, members of some pairs were told, "We have found almost exactly the person you described. You'll like him a lot. What's even more, he described a person very much like you. It's quite a lucky coincidence to find two people who are so congenial."

Members of other pairs were told, "Of course we couldn't find anybody who would fit your description exactly, but we found a fellow who corresponds to the main points, and you probably will like him."

These groups were then asked to write a story based on three photographs. Each partner wrote a preliminary story, talked it over with his partner and then, still by himself, wrote a final story. In the high-liking pairs, attempts to influence the other were more equally divided between the partners, more effort was made to reach agreement, and more changes tended to occur as a result of the discussion. ■

One of the interesting facets of messages designed for attitude change is that the person listening to it or reading it is aware that someone is trying to change his attitudes. Is there a difference in the influence of a message if the listener does not feel that the speaker is trying to influence him? Allyn and Festinger (1961) put this question to an experimental test by comparing the effect of messages presented by a person whose obvious intent was to persuade and the same message "accidentally overheard" by listening in on a private conversation. The "accidentally overheard" message was considerably more effective in producing attitude change.

In the light of the findings, it is not surprising that the mass media are generally less effective as persuaders than personal contacts. This result has been reported in a number of different contexts. Lazarsfeld, Berelson, and Gaudet (1944) found this in a study of voting behavior. Katz and Lazarsfeld (1955) got this result in a study of the factors influencing such decisions as household purchases and selection of hair styles and clothing fashions. One reason often given for the result is that people are not uniformly exposed to the influence attempts of the mass media. A person *selectively* reads magazines and watches television programs that reinforce his existing attitudes and tends to ignore those which would be likely to change his attitudes. This is certainly one factor. But even if a person does expose himself to an attempt to change his attitudes, he is aware of the attempted influence and so its effectiveness is reduced.

Changing the Affective Component

Many attempts at attitude change are based not so much on changing a person's beliefs as they are on associating the object with something pleasant or unpleasant. Attractive, smiling models, drinking a particular soft drink, look down at us from billboards, and television commercials caution us against body odor. Such appeals are based on the assumption that a change in the affective component—the expectancy of pleasantness or unpleasantness—will be accompanied by changes in the other components, the cognitive and the action tendencies.

■ Rosenberg (1960) demonstrated the effects on the other components of changing the affective component alone. He began by measuring subjects' attitudes toward a number of socially significant objects: Negroes moving into white neighborhoods, national health insurance, foreign aid, etc. He found out both their positions on the attitude and their beliefs about the object. Then he hypnotized the subjects and suggested to them that in the future they would feel differently toward the object. For example, the experimenter said to one subject, "When you wake up you will be very much in favor of Negroes moving into white neighborhoods. The mere idea of Negroes moving into white neighborhoods will give you a happy, exhilarated feeling." The subjects were told they would not remember the reason for their changed feelings until a signal was given by the experimenter, at which time their former affective feelings toward the object would be restored. The subjects were then released from hypnosis, and in the following days their positions and beliefs about the objects were reexamined. Rosenberg found that the subjects not only changed their affective feelings in the direction suggested under hypnosis, but that they also expressed new beliefs—beliefs which were consistent with their new feelings. For example, a subject who favored foreign aid to underdeveloped countries prior to hypnosis now stated that in the long run foreign aid would impede the development of self-reliance! ■

Thus, a direct change in the affective component did lead to changes in other aspects of the attitude. Of course the hypnotic technique is a highly specialized and highly unusual one, and we would not expect the more common attempts to change a person's feelings toward an object to be so dramatic in its effects.

The Use of Fear

We pointed out earlier that reward and punishment do not necessarily have the same results. The primary effect of punishment is frequently arousal of anxiety rather than elimination of the undesirable behavior. Similarly, psychologists have found that trying to change an attitude by associating fear with the object may have some unexpected results:

■ Janis and Feshbach (1953) compared three forms of an illustrated talk on dental hygiene. The strong appeal emphasized the painful effects of tooth decay, diseased gums, and other consequences of poor dental hygiene. The moderate appeal presented the same dangers in a milder form, while the minimal appeal rarely alluded to the painful consequences of tooth neglect. The researchers found that although the stronger appeals aroused more concern about the teeth, students who had listened to the minimal appeal were more likely to report a week later that they were carrying out the recommended dental hygiene practice. Moreover, the "minimal" group, as compared to the other groups, was also more resistant to counterpropaganda contradicting the dental hygiene lecture. ■

One interpretation of this result is that when a person arouses anxiety in an audience, the audience becomes hostile toward him for doing this and rejects

his message. An alternate interpretation is that the people associate the fear as
much with the message as with the subject of the message. Thus remembering
the message itself is anxiety-arousing, and the subject avoids this anxiety by forgetting the content of the message. Whatever the explanation, we see that attempting to change attitudes by associating the object with strong negative
motives leads to complex and often undesired results.

Changing the Action Component

We normally think of attitude change as preceding changes in behavior toward
the object. But if changes in the other two components affect all the rest, we
might expect that changes in action would also change beliefs and motives.
Several lines of research indicate that this may be so.

■ During World War II it became advisable, for military reasons, to integrate infantry units
previously segregated on the basis of race. Before taking this step the Army surveyed the attitudes
of officers and men on the proposed procedure. Two-thirds of the white officers and more than
half of the white soldiers were opposed. Nevertheless, the units were integrated. Two months
later, the attitudes of the white soldiers were measured once again. There were striking attitude
changes in the soldiers who were members of integrated units. Now over four-fifths of the men
questioned felt that integration was a good idea. Furthermore, the attitudes toward Negroes were
most favorable in those units who shared the heaviest combat. (U.S. War Dept., 1945) ■

INITIAL ATTITUDE	INTEGRATED HOUSING PROJECTS PERCENT OF NET GAIN		SEGREGATED HOUSING PROJECTS PERCENT OF NET GAIN	
	Koaltown	Socktown	Bakerville	Frankville
Highly unfavorable	71	78	26	19
Moderately unfavorable	46	61	18	2
Favorable	13	28	15	−18

FIG. 16–9.   Changes in the attitudes of residents after living for a period in segregated or integrated units of housing projects. The figures indicate the net gain in
percent of favorable attitudes toward Negroes expressed by the residents. The residents from the integrated units showed a much greater gain in favorable attitudes
than those who lived in segreated units. (From Deutsch and Collins, 1951)

This study suggests that being in a new situation which requires contact with
a member of a minority group may change a person's attitude toward that group.
Deutsch and Collins' (1951) study of segregated and integrated housing projects
yielded a similar result. Those who lived in integrated projects showed changes,
not only in their act tendencies toward Negroes, but in their stated attitudes
about them as well (see Fig. 16–9).

Can we conclude from these studies that contact with a minority group *per se*
will lead to attitude change? There is ample evidence that the answer to this

question is no. The contacts between a landlord and his Puerto Rican tenants, between a family and its Negro cook, between a consumer and a Jewish shop-keeper do not necessarily reduce prejudice. The situations which lead to attitude change have several important characteristics:

(1) The members of the majority group are subject to some constraints which keep them in the situation that requires rather close contact with the minority group members.

(2) The members of the majority and minority groups meet on an equal status basis.

(3) The two groups have common rather than conflicting goals.

(4) The contacts with members of the minority groups are pleasant and pre-sent evidence contradictory to the initial attitudes of the majority group members.

You can see that integrated army units and housing projects are more likely to satisfy these conditions than the other kinds of interracial interactions men-tioned. Only if these conditions are satisfied has the stage been set for the changes in action toward minority group members, which, in turn, lead to changes in beliefs and feelings.

The studies on the effects of contact on attitude change are interesting, pro-vocative, and certainly socially significant. However, in observations of such complex situations, it is often difficult to isolate the variables which, in general, affect the relationship between the action component of an attitude and attitude change. To do so let us return to some laboratory studies.

■ A common act associated with an attitude is its verbal expression as an opinion. Janis and King (1954) asked subjects to give informal talks advocating positions *contrary* to their own at-titudes. On two out of three issues, those who gave the talks showed more attitude change than control subjects who listened to the talks. There were two differences between the presentations of the two issues that gave significant differences, and the third one that did not. The subjects were least satisfied with their presentations on the third issue and they had adhered more closely to a suggested outline in presenting the third issue. ■

Two later experiments support the idea that both improvisation on the part of the subject and feelings of satisfaction facilitate attitude change.

King and Janis (1956) compared the amount of attitude change in speakers who had read prepared scripts to an audience with that in speakers who gave improvised talks based on the same scripts. In both cases the speakers were expressing opinions contrary to their own attitudes. However, the speakers who improvised their own material showed significantly more change toward the position they publicly advocated than did those who read the prepared script. The experimenters interpreted their result as suggesting that in re-thinking and re-phrasing the arguments presented to him, the subject felt as though he was expressing his own ideas.

Scott (1957) tested the effects of reward on forced expression of contrary opinions. College students participated in debates concerning universal military training, night hours for women, and the de-emphasis of football. Each student was asked to debate the issue on the side contrary to his own position. After the debates, half the students were told that their classmates had voted them the winners of the debate; the other half were told that they had lost. The attitudes of the participants were then measured again. Those who had been winners showed a significant change in position toward the attitude they expressed; the losers tended to become even stronger in their original attitudes (this last result was not statistically significant, however). Furthermore, in a follow-up study, Scott (1959) showed that the attitude changes of the winners in the direction of their publicly expressed attitudes were still present ten days later.

In Scott's experiment, subjects were simply asked to take part in the debates; the reward of "winning" which followed the public presentation was unrelated to their agreement to participate. What would be the result of paying subjects money for stating opinions contrary to their attiudes? Will reward in his case facilitate attitude change?

■ College students serving as subjects were asked to perform a series of boring, repetitive tasks. When they were finished, they were placed in one of three groups. Those in the "twenty-dollar" group were asked by the experimenter to tell the next subject waiting outside that the tasks in the experiment were enjoyable and interesting. For doing this, the subjects were paid twenty dollars. The subjects in the "one dollar" group were also asked to tell the next subject of the exciting and enjoyable tasks in store for him, but they were paid one dollar for saying it. The third group of subjects served as controls; they were not asked to do anything following the monotonous session and, of course, they were not paid for performing the extra service. After this procedure, an interviewer questioned subjects in all three groups about their attitudes toward the tasks they performed in the experiment itself. There were significant differences among the groups. Both the "twenty dollar" group and the control group expressed the opinion that the tasks were boring and monotonous. However, the subjects in the "one dollar" group stated that they felt the experimental tasks really were interesting and enjoyable. (Festinger and Carlsmith, 1959) ■

How can we account for these results? Why would the subjects who received the smaller reward show more attitude change after expressing an opinion contrary to their original attitude than the subjects who received a large reward? Festinger, one of the investigators who performed this experiment, explains this result and others like it with his theory of *cognitive dissonance* (Festinger, 1957). The theory is based on the widely accepted assumption that one basic motive in attitude formation is to seek and maintain consistency among various elements of cognitive structure. If something disturbs this harmony, the organism experiences what Festinger calls *dissonance*. Dissonance is uncomfortable, a state which the organism seeks to avoid and to reduce, even though doing so may involve distortion of reality. In the experiment on monotonous tasks, Festinger intentionally created dissonance in the subjects by setting up a situation in which their actions (saying it was an interesting experiment) were contradictory to their beliefs. He reasoned that subjects who were highly paid for acting in contradiction to their true attitudes would experience less dissonance, since they could rationalize their actions by thinking, "anyone would have done the same thing for such high pay." Those subjects who received only a dollar for their "services" would have more difficulty convincing themselves that they acted only for the money, and would have to use other means to reduce dissonance. Festinger predicted that they would change their attitudes to restore harmony between their beliefs and actions. As we saw, this rather unlikely prediction proved accurate. Thus it appears that an expected external reward for acting in a manner contrary to one's beliefs does not necessarily contribute to attitude change.

To summarize: Research indicates that the expression of an opinion contrary to one's initial attitude will indeed lead to attitude change under any of three conditions: (1) if there is no other simple means for the subject to reduce the dissonance created by contradictory beliefs and acts; (2) if the expression of the new attitude is unexpectedly rewarding; and (3) if, in the process of formulating arguments for the expression of the new attitude, the subject feels that he is using his own ideas.

Participation in a Group

We form many of our attitudes in the course of our interactions with other people. Some of our attitudes we adopt from groups and individuals we admire. Thus we might expect that observing and participating in groups would have special effects on attitude change.

One of the pioneer studies on different kinds of group participation and attitude change was carried out by Lewin and his associates (1947) as part of an attempt to solve an important practical problem. During World War II, there was a shortage of the meats conventionally eaten in American households. At the same time there was a surplus of the very nutritious but little known meats such as kidneys, sweetbreads, and beef hearts. Lewin's problem was to discover the kind of one-hour program which would produce the greatest attitude change toward the unconventional meats in the groups to which it was presented. He compared two methods: Three women's groups heard a lecturer speak of the nutritional value of these meats, the importance of serving them for the war effort, and the delicious dishes that she (the lecturer) had made from the meats. In three similar women's groups a leader led a discussion about these foods, beginning with the question of why housewives like themselves did not serve beef hearts, sweetbreads, and kidneys. As a participant in the discussion, the leader stated the same facts and made the same suggestions as the lecturer. At the end of the discussion, the women were asked to indicate by raising their hands whether they would be willing to try one of these meats during the following week. Almost all the women so indicated. A week later, the women from both groups were questioned on whether they had served one of the meats. Only three percent of the women who had listened to the lecturer had served one of the meats she had not served before, whereas 32 percent of the women who participated in the discussion had served at least one of them.

Why was the discussion method so effective? If we look at the two procedures closely, we find a number of differences, each one of which may have facilitated attitude change. First, in the course of the discussion, the women were asked to think about reasons for not serving the meats, and then to think of arguments that would answer these objections. Thus they were encouraged to think about and express opinions contrary to their original attitudes. Based on the experiments by King and Janis which we described earlier, we would expect this procedure to produce more change than passive listening. Second, the women in the discussion groups were asked to make a decision on the subject, and they made public their decisions by raising their hands. A later study by Bennett (1955) showed that attitude change is increased when people are asked to decide on a position right after it has been presented. Further investigation by Hovland, Campbell, and Brock (1957) suggests that the fact that the women indicated their decision publicly may have made an additional difference.*

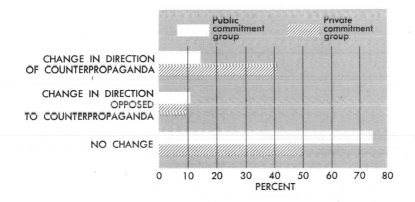

FIG. 16–10. The effect of public commitment versus private commitment on a person's resistance to counterpropaganda. (After Hovland, Campbell, and Brock, 1957)

■ High school students listened to a message taking one position on an issue (reduction of voting age). Then they wrote informal essays on their attitudes on the issue. The students in one group—the public commitment group—were asked to sign their names so that their opinions could be printed in the school newspaper. Members of the other group—the private commitment group—did not sign their names and their opinions were to remain anonymous. Next, the students in both groups listened to a message that took the opposite position from the original message on the issue. A second measure of the students' opinions showed that the students who had publicly committed themselves to a position were influenced in the direction of counter-propaganda considerably less than the students who stated their original positions anonymously (see Fig. 16–10). ■

* Not all the evidence is positive on this point; in the Bennett (1955) study the factor of public versus private commitment did not make a difference.

Another difference between the lecture and the discussion groups was that each woman in the discussion group had an opportunity to see how the other group members felt about the issue. Furthermore, they perceived consensus among the women; almost every woman in the group indicated that she would try one of the new meats. Other investigations suggest that perceived consensus among one's peers helps to change attitudes in the direction of consensus. (Kelley and Wood-ruff, 1956; Bennett, 1955). The degree to which this factor affects thinking and behavior was demonstrated in the following experiment:

■ College students were brought together in groups of eight as subjects in a perception experiment. Each group was given a series of trials in which the members were to judge which of three lines was equal to a given line. The subjects in the group were seated at a table, and each subject, in turn, stated his answer to the problem. At least this is how the experimental situation appeared to the critical subject. Actually, seven out of eight of the members of each group were confederates of the experimenter, who had instructed them to make the same incorrect judgments on each trial. If subjects make such judgments without a group setting, they make almost no errors. With the experimental group setting, however, when the critical subjects heard their peers unanimously agree that a longer or shorter line was equal to the standard line, then 37 percent of the judgments of the critical subjects were errors, the same "errors" that the confederates made. Among 50 critical subjects, 37 agreed with the incorrect answers of the majority in their groups at least once in 12 trials. (Asch, 1951) ■

Now, you may argue that the subject's judgments in this experiment do not reflect true attitude change; rather, the subjects were merely behaving as if they agreed with the other group members. Interviews with the subjects at the conclusion of the experiment clarified the relation of the behavior—making many errors—to the subject's cognitive processes, his perception. Most of the subjects' perceptions did not change as a result of the group interaction. They stated their answers in spite of, not because of, what they saw. Some of the subjects felt that their perceptions must be inaccurate and so adopted the group consensus for their answers; others felt their own perceptions were accurate but gave the group answer so as not to appear different °from their peers. A very small number of subjects reported that they actually did come to perceive the majority answer as correct. Only in the last case would we say that actual attitude change had occurred. The behavior of the other subjects is one example of what has been called *compliance*—behaving in accordance with another person or group regardless of one's own attitudes (Kelman, 1961). The fact that under social influence a person will behave in ways contrary to his own thinking is one which has special significance, and we shall look at this process more closely in the next section. For the present our point is that our behavior and attitudes tend to fit with those of other people. From early childhood we find that our own experience tends to be confirmed by the statements of others. In many cases it saves time and trial and error to accept other people's judgments. We are disturbed when our own judgments are out of line with those of people we like and trust, and we tend to bring the situation into balance by rechecking, by trying to persuade the others, by changing our attitudes, or by changing our feeling toward the other person (e.g., see Newcomb, 1961).

Attitude Change: a Summary

An attitude consists of many components, and we have seen that change in any one component may produce changes throughout the attitude. In order to change the cognitive component, persuaders construct arguments to change the beliefs of their audiences. Studies suggest that presenting both sides of an issue is more effective in changing a person's position and in "inoculating" him against counter-propaganda. Citing a prestigious source facilitates immediate attitude change, but the effect disappears over the period of a month if the cues referring to the source are not reinstated. An effective form of argument is one aimed at changing the beliefs which relate the object of the attitude to a person's goals—at least if the attitude was not formed on an ego-defensive basis. The nature of the persuader influences the degree to which a person will accept the statements presented. In general, people are more influenced by personal contacts than by mass media, by persuaders they like and admire, and by people who do not seem to be trying to influence others intentionally.

There is evidence that changing the affective component, by associating a disliked object with pleasurable feelings, will also produce changes in beliefs and actions. However, association of an object with intense fear does not have parallel effects.

A person's beliefs and feelings about an object can be changed by changes in his behavior toward it. Expressing opinions contrary to one's attitudes can lead to attitude change, especially if the behavior is unexpectedly rewarded, if the expression is in part a product of the subject, or if there is no other way for the subject to reduce the dissonance between behavior and thinking. Similarly, contact with minority groups may lead to more positive attitudes if the contacts are on an equal status basis, if they are rewarded, or if the goals of the minority group are the same as those of the majority of the people.

In producing attitude change, group participation is more effective than passive listening, given some of these conditions: (1) The participants are encouraged to think about positions opposite to their own. (2) The participants are asked to make a public commitment. (3) The participants perceive consensus among their peers.

What Factors Contribute to Compliance?

Conformity: Compliance to a Majority

When a person changes his behavior in order to comply with the norms of a group, we say he is *conforming* to the group. Since Asch's pioneering study, a number of experiments have been carried out which permit us to see which variables influence conformity. We can classify the variables into four groups: (1) the nature of the group; (2) the nature of the stimuli presented; (3) the consequences of conformity; and (4) individual differences in the crucial subject.

The Nature of the Group

As you might expect, the size and the unanimity of the prearranged "peer" group affect the amount of conformity. In a two-person group, the subject's opinion may have little effect; a group of three produces more conformity, and groups of four and five produce as much conformity as groups that are con- siderably larger.

In the original experiment, the crucial subject was faced with unanimous consensus. What would happen if the majority of group members made in- correct judgments but if one person other than the crucial subject gave the correct answer? Asch (1951) tried such a condition and found that the amount of conformity dropped sharply. Now only 5.5 percent of the subject's opinions were incorrect. With one other person to support his judgments, the critical subject was able to oppose the opinions expressed by the majority of the group.

The Nature of the Stimuli

Using an experimental situation similar to Asch's, Crutchfield (1955) found that group unanimity produced conformity to a number of different kinds of items: perceptual judgments, agreement with factual statements, attitudes on issues, and personal evaluations of self. This last type of item is particularly interesting since presumably each group member is evaluating only himself. When subjects were asked individually to agree or disagree with the statement "I doubt whether I would make a good leader," not one subject agreed. In the experimental group situation in which a prearranged number of the group agreed with the statement, so also did 37 percent of the subjects.

In our analysis of perception, we saw that the degree to which factors other than stimulus factors determine perception depends in part on the ambiguity of the stimuli. Thus we might expect that ambiguous stimuli would result in more conformity than unambiguous ones. Crutchfield (1955) found that there was considerable conformity with both kinds of material, but that ambiguous stimuli accentuated the conformity effect.

The Consequences of Conformity

We can look at conformity as a learned general habit in which a person learns to model his behavior on that of other group members. This implies that a person learns to conform or not to conform in a situation depending on the rewards and punishment in the situation. In most of the conformity studies, the subject hears the opinions of his peers and states his own opinion, but there is no further feedback. It has been suggested that an implicit motive in such a situation is desire for group approval, which tends to produce conformity. This interpretation is supported by a study reported by Walker and Heyns (1962). In this study, conformity increased when the subjects were told that people tend to like one another more when they are in agreement about common problems.

There is evidence that informational as well as affective feedback influences conformity behavior.

■ Crutchfield (1955) investigated the effects of this variable. He used two conditions: one in which on each trial the experimenter confirmed the judgments of the group, and one in which the experimenter confirmed the judgments of the individual. Confirmation of the group opinion increased the percentage of conforming judgments by the subjects from 45 percent to 70 percent. Confirmation of the individual subject's lone opinion greatly increased resistance to conformity. ■

If conformity varies as a function of the amount of reinforcement for such behavior, we might expect to find cross-cultural differences. Milgram (1961) found that Norwegians showed significantly more conformity than Frenchmen in the Asch-type of experiment. These results, Milgram felt, seemed to be in accordance with the cultural tradition of the two countries: The people of Norway are highly cohesive, with a strong sense of social responsibility and a heritage of political stability. The people of France on the other hand have a tradition of dissent. It may be that these traditions are continued in each culture through a pattern of reinforcements for conformity and/or dissent.

Individual Differences

The habit of conformity is not all-pervasive in the sense that one person conforms either in every situation or in no situation. The behavior depends, as we have seen, on a number of conditions. Nevertheless, we can look at the differences, in a given situation, between those who conform and those who do not, and ask the question "Is the tendency toward greater conformity coupled with other tendencies which form more general traits?" Personality inventories suggest that subjects who tend to conform are less intelligent, more anxious, more prone to feelings of inferiority, less realistic in self-perception and more dependent than independent subjects. Furthermore, the high conformity subjects also tend to be high in authoritarianism. (The correlation between conformity score and F-scale score is 0.48.) If skilled observers are asked to rate subjects on various personality traits, they tend to rate the independent subjects as more original, more self-reliant, more emotionally expressive, and insightful. (Crutchfield, 1955)

Obedience: Compliance to Legitimate Authority

In the conformity experiments, an individual is faced with the presence of a number of people who disagree with his private judgments. In our society, there are many situations in which we feel social pressure, even though it is transmitted to us by a single person. For example, the laws enacted by our representatives may be enforced by a single police officer. As part of the process of socialization, we learn to obey our parents, our teachers, our judges, our policemen, and other agents of society who appear to have legitimate authority.

To what extent will people obey the commands of a person in authority when the behavior demanded is contrary to the beliefs, motives, and habits of the individual? Milgram (1963) sought an answer to this very serious question with the following study:

As each subject came into the experiment, an experimenter asked him to serve as a "teacher" for a study on the effects of punishment on learning. The job of this "teacher"-subject was to give electrical shocks to another subject in another room, increasing the shock level with each error. The victim was in reality a collaborator of the experimenter, and no shocks were actually administered. The shock apparatus looked authentic however; voltage levels were clearly marked and verbal descriptions ranging from "Slight Shock," to "Danger: Severe Shock," to "XXX," appeared below the numerical designations as the number of "errors" made by the person in the next room increased, the subject serving as "teacher" increased the shock level.

DISTRIBUTION OF BREAKOFF POINT	
VERBAL DESIGNATION AND VOLTAGE INDICATION	NUMBER OF SUBJECTS FOR WHOM THIS WAS MAXIMUM SHOCK
Slight shock	
15	0
30	0
45	0
60	0
Moderate shock	
75	0
90	0
105	0
120	0
Strong shock	
135	0
150	0
165	0
180	0
Very strong shock	
195	0
210	0
225	0
240	0
Intense shock	
255	0
270	0
285	0
300	5
Extreme intensity shock	
315	4
330	2
345	1
360	1
Danger: Severe shock	
375	1
390	0
405	0
420	0
XXX	
435	0
450	26

FIG. 16–11.   The numbers of people who refused to continue after each shock level in Milgram's study. Twenty-six subjects were obedient throughout the experiment. (From Milgram, 1963)

If he hesitated in administering the required shock, the experimenter who was was sitting behind the "teacher" asked him to go on. As the shock level got higher and higher the "teacher"-subject began to hear more and more protest from the "victim" in the adjoining room. But still the order to give more shock was repeated. What did the "teacher"-subject do? How high a shock level would he be willing to administer on the orders of an authority?

The results appear in Fig. 16–11. As you can see, 26 out of 40 subjects were totally obedient; that is, they administered every shock they were ordered to administer. Only 14 of the subjects were defiant at some point in the experiment and refused to give further shocks. But you should not conclude from this experiment that the obedient subjects were aggressive, sadistic people. They showed great hesitancy in administering the high shock levels. As the shock got stronger and stronger, they showed signs of extreme tension and emotional strain: sweating, trembling, groaning, lip-biting, stuttering. Many subjects had fits of nervous smiling and bizarre laughter. One observer gave this report of a subject's behavior:

■ "I observed a mature and initially poised businessman enter the laboratory, smiling and confident. Within 20 minutes he was reduced to a twitching, stuttering wreck, who was rapidly approaching a point of nervous collapse. He constantly pulled on his ear lobe, and twisted his hands. At one point, he pushed his fist into his forehead and muttered: 'Oh, God, let's stop it.' And yet he continued to respond to every word of the experimenter and obeyed to the end." ■ [*]

In a control study, subjects were permitted to select whatever shock levels they desired to "punish" the errors. In this case almost all subjects selected shock levels in the mild ranges. Thus motives for aggressive behavior cannot account for the results. In another study, the orders for shock levels were delivered by telephone. Under these conditions subjects agreed to follow the orders, but did not actually deliver shocks as intense as the orders demanded. In still another variation, the subjects believed that the man giving the orders was not a scientist, but another subject who happened to "take over" when the experimenter was called away. In this case most of the subjects were defiant. In fact, when the "subject" giving the orders responded to the defiance by saying he would deliver the shock himself, the subjects sometimes physically prevented him from doing so. A subject who happens to give orders is not a sufficient authority.

All these results suggest that the obedient subjects were faced with extreme conflict. Their behavior was contrary to what they would ordinarily do. But the habits and motives for obedience to legitimate authority were so strong that they overrode other attitudes.

---

* From Milgram, S., "Behavioral study of obedience," *J. abnorm. soc. Psychol.*, **67**, 4, 371–378 (1963). Reprinted by permission.

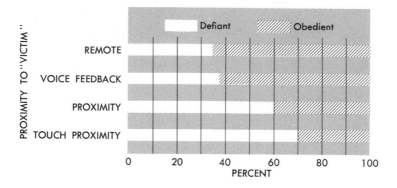

FIG. 16–12. The effect of proximity on the percentage of subjects who were defiant at any point in the experiment. (After Milgram, 1965)

Experiments in the proximity of the victim illustrated the extremes to which a few subjects would go to obey orders. Milgram hypothesized that the more the subject was aware of the presence of his victim, the less willing he would be to administer severe shocks. Therefore Milgram used four conditions: (1) remote feedback in which the subject heard his victim pounding on the wall at some shock levels up to 300 volts and thereafter heard nothing; (2) voice feedback in which the subject heard protests, moaning, and finally cries that the victim could not stand the pain; (3) proximity, in which the victim was seated a foot-and-a-half from the subject and reacted in the same way as in the voice feedback condition; and (4) touch-proximity, which involved the same conditions as proximity except that the victim received the shock only if he touched a shockplate. At the 150-volt level, the victim refused to put his hand on the plate and the experimenter commanded the subject to physically hold the victim's hand on the shockplate. (Insulation was provided so that the subject would not feel the shock.) The results supported Milgram's prediction. The more aware the subject was of his victim's presence, the lower the mean maximum shock level, and the more subjects defied the experimenter (see Fig. 16–12). But even with the subjects only a foot-and-a-half from the victim, hearing him cry out that he could not stand the pain, 30 percent of the subjects held their victim's hand on the shockplate to receive a shock level marked "Danger: Severe Shock"!

A Final Comment

We have seen that the social environment has tremendous effects on the thinking and behavior of individuals. This is not surprising when we realize how strongly and consistently habits such as conformity and obedience are rewarded. As we have grown up, we have learned to depend on the people around us to confirm our judgments, to suggest opinions, to provide models for our actions. If a person did not learn this, he would be unable to become a civilized member of society.

Compliance and attitude change are, on many occasions, necessary and appropriate. If individuals did not comply with traffic laws, the results would be chaotic and dangerous. If people did not change their attitudes when confronted with new information, then their rigidity could preclude the possibility of progress.

We saw earlier that habits that are strongly rewarded may themselves become motives. The research on obedience and conformity suggests that these habits become powerful motives indeed. But both habits and motives are aroused by situations. In the studies we described, some people discriminated one situation from another, obeying, complying, and agreeing in some cases and not doing so in others. But many people generalized obedience and conformity to such an extent that they failed to act on their own thinking. Herein lies a very serious problem: To distinguish between situations in which compliance is appropriate and those in which it is not.

Recent history has a striking example to remind us of the importance of the resolution of this problem. In Germany from 1933 to 1945, millions of people died partly because of blind obedience to Nazi authority. Milgram's studies were originally undertaken in an attempt to understand the behavior of the German people before and during World War II. Milgram's research suggests that the German people were not unique in their willingness to harm others on command.

Is it inevitable, then, that people become creatures determined by their social environments? The answer to this question has to be "No!" In the experiments in obedience and conformity, some individuals remained independent. However, this independence was possible only if the individual trusted his own ability to perceive, to interpret, and to evaluate independently of his peers and his superiors.

In discussing the person in society, we should never lose sight of the fact that society is not an impersonal abstraction, but a living, changing entity, itself made up of individuals. In a democratic society, each individual must share in deciding the direction in which the society shall move. It is extremely important that each person add his independent evaluation of issues and actions, if the society is to be truly democratic. He must decide when to conform and when to defy, when to agree and when to dissent, when to trust and when to be skeptical. In order to make appropriate decisions, he needs access to objective, accurate information.

We hope that an understanding of psychological processes can make a contribution.

Summary

Concepts

Attitude. An organization of concepts, beliefs, motives, habits, and acts associated with a particular object; the concepts and beliefs constitute the *cognitive* component; the motives constitute the *affective* component; the habits and acts are the *action* component

Opinion. The verbal expressions of an attitude

Centrality of an attitude. The degree to which an attitude affects a person's thinking and behavior

Attitude system. A cluster of attitudes which share common or similar concepts, beliefs, motives, and habits

The theory of cognitive dissonance. The theory which states that people seek consistency among their beliefs and actions and will sometimes distort reality in order to avoid this inconsistency or *dissonance*

Compliance. Behaving in accordance with the standards of another person or group, regardless of one's own attitudes

Conformity. Compliance with a group majority

Principles

1. Attitudes are frequently measured by asking a person to agree or disagree with a series of statements dealing with an object. The statements used in the test have been selected in accordance with one of several possible criteria (following the methods of Guttman, Likert, or Thurstone).

2. A person's behavior in a situation related to an attitude depends both on the attitude and the situation.

3. We can distinguish four motivational bases for attitudes: (i) utilitarian, (ii) value expressive, (iii) ego defensive, (iv) knowledge.

4. Attitudes may change as a result of changes in the cognitive component, the affective component, or the action component.

5. Attitudes may change as a function of group participation, immediate decision, public commitment, and perceived consensus.

6. Conformity depends on the nature of the group, the nature of the judgment or behavior involved, the consequences of previous conforming, and individual differences.

7. Obedience to legitimate authority has become the basis of an extremely powerful motive—so much so that some people, despite their own thoughts and feelings, will knowingly inflict pain on another person on command.

Suggested Readings

Brown, R., *Social Psychology*. Glencoe: Free Press, 1965. Not only is this book well written but it also presents a thoughtful discussion of attitude change.

Festinger, L., *A Theory of Cognitive Dissonance*. New York: Harper & Row, 1957; and Brehm, J. and A. Cohen, *Explorations in Cognitive Dissonance*. New York: Wiley, 1962. Both books presents theory and research on one approach to attitude change.

Proshansky, H. and B. Seidenburg (eds.), *Basic Studies in Social Psychology*. New York: Holt, 1965.

Newcomb, T., R. Turner, and P. Converse. *Social Psychology* (second edition). New York: Holt, 1965. A good standard text.

Krech, D., R. S. Crutchfield, and E. L. Ballachey, *Individual in Society*. New York: McGraw-Hill, 1962. Another good standard text.

Some studies on conformity in college students may be found in Walker, E. L. and R. Heyns, *An Anatomy of Conformity*. Englewood Cliffs, N.J.: Prentice-Hall, 1962.

a short guide to statistics

WHY DO WE NEED STATISTICS?

appendix I   WHICH DESCRIPTIVE STATISTICS ACCOMPLISH
WHAT OBJECTIVES?

HOW STATISTICS ARE USED TO HELP MAKE
INFERENCES AND DECISIONS

As we have discussed research in the various areas of psychology, it has probably become apparent that even an elementary understanding of psychology requires some familiarity with statistics. We have tried to introduce the student to the basic statistical concepts as we went along, whenever they were needed in our discussion of a particular problem. This appendix will present these concepts in a unified and accessible form. The material here is based partly on materials prepared by Dr. Carol Slater for her classes at the University of Michigan.

Why Do We Need Statistics?

In general, statistics are used for two purposes.

1. To present a number of scores briefly.
2. To help make decisions. For example, a psychologist who carries out an experiment must decide whether to accept or reject his hypothesis. Statistics help the psychologist make this decision. They aid him in deciding what inferences or conclusions he may draw from his data.

Which Descriptive Statistics Accomplish What Objectives?

The Frequency Distribution

A psychologist often has to obtain scores of a group of subjects on some measure of behavior. Suppose that he gives an intelligence test to a number of children. After scoring the test, he has a list of scores such as: John Q., 90, Mary J., 102, Ethel I., 111, and so on. He now has the information he wants about the probable present ability of the children to deal with intellectual problems, but the information obviously is not in a very convenient form. A list of this sort is hard to interpret. Therefore the psychologist puts the scores into an order, indicating how many students got each score. This is called constructing a *frequency distribution*.

Definition: *A representation of a set of classes or categories and the frequencies associated with each is called a frequency distribution.*

A frequency distribution looks like this:

X (score)	F (frequency: number of people getting that score)
90	1
95	2
100	7
105	4

If the group is at all large, however, a frequency distribution is still rather unwieldy. Another way of describing a group of scores gives one all this information at a glance. This is done by making a "picture" of the frequency distribution.

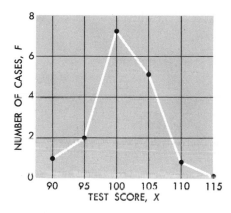

FIG. 1–1. The plot of a frequency distribution.

Making a visual representation (or picture) of a frequency distribution is called *plotting* (or graphing) the distribution. Such a plot may look like that shown in Fig. I 1.

Measures of Central Tendency

Definition: *A score which stands for (is typical of) the scores of an entire group of scores is called a measure of central tendency.*

There are three commonly used methods of measuring central tendency. The first is the *arithmetic mean.*

Definition: *The arithmetic mean is the sum of all the scores divided by the number of scores.*

Another way of saying this is to write it in mathematical symbols:

$$\text{The mean} \longrightarrow M = \frac{\sum X}{N}$$

Add or sum up the X's or the scores;
divide by the number of scores.

The second measure of central tendency is the *median.*

Definition: *The median is the score at which half the people received higher scores and half the people received lower scores.*

Question: When would the median be a better "typical" score than the mean?

Answer: When there is one or more atypical extreme score, because extreme scores affect means much more than they affect medians.

The third measure of central tendency is *the mode.*

Definition: *The mode is that score which occurs most often; the most common or "popular" score.*

If there are two modes, we say that the distribution is *bimodal.*

Measures of Variability

Methods of measuring central tendency are all ways of condensing a whole list of scores into one "typical" score. But when we represent a distribution by a measure of central tendency, we leave out one important aspect. When a psychologist is planning course work for a group of children, for example, he needs to know how much difference there is among members of the group. Are they all fairly much alike in intelligence test scores, so that only one class will be necessary, or will he have to make provisions for two or three different classes of varying levels of aptitude? We need some convenient way of talking about the degree of *variability* among the test scores.

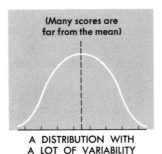
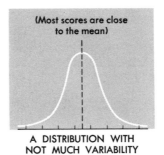

(Many scores are far from the mean)

(Most scores are close to the mean)

A DISTRIBUTION WITH A LOT OF VARIABILITY

A DISTRIBUTION WITH NOT MUCH VARIABILITY

FIG. I-2. Two distributions with the same mean but different variability.

A statistic which gives us information about variability among a group of scores is called a *measure of dispersion.* We shall talk about two kinds of measures of dispersion. The first way of talking about the variability or "spread-outness" of a distribution of scores is to find the difference between the highest and lowest scores.

Definition: *The difference between the highest and lowest scores in a group is called the range.*

This measure of dispersion is not always useful because one extremely high score or one extremely low score will lead to an inaccurate picture of the variability of the group as a whole. What we really want to know is how far, *on the average*, scores in this distribution are spread out from the middle score (see Fig. I–2).

The second kind of measure of dispersion involves talking about the typical or average distance of scores from the mean, disregarding sign. One such measure is called *the average deviation*. We compute it by finding out how far each score is from the mean, adding, without regard to sign, all these distances (which we call "deviations"), and then dividing by the number of scores. Note how similar this is to the way we find the mean, or "typical" score. This is easier to see if we write it out in symbols:

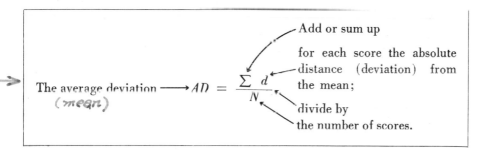

The average deviation (*mean*) → $AD = \dfrac{\Sigma\, d}{N}$

Add or sum up

for each score the absolute distance (deviation) from the mean;

divide by the number of scores.

THE STANDARD DEVIATION. Most of our mathematical training teaches us to think of $7 - 5$ as different from $3 - 5$. We would thus prefer a measure of variability which would allow us to follow our normal habits of algebraic addition and subtraction. Because we must pay attention to plus and minus signs (calculations which permit the opposite will be discussed later), we generally use a first cousin of the average deviation: the *variance*, or its square root, *the standard deviation*, which is quite similar. Here is the way to find it.

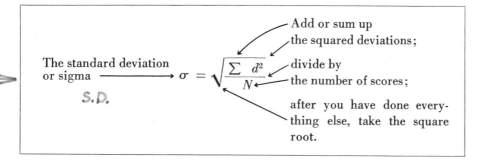

The standard deviation or sigma → $\sigma = \sqrt{\dfrac{\Sigma\, d^2}{N}}$

S.D.

Add or sum up the squared deviations;

divide by the number of scores;

after you have done everything else, take the square root.

For example, suppose that we have the following distribution of scores.

X	$\bar{X}$ d	$\bar{X}^2$ d^2
110	+10	100
105	+ 5	25
105	+ 5	25
105	+ 5	25
105	+ 5	25
100	0	0
100	0	0
100	0	0
100	0	0
100	0	0
100	0	0
95	− 5	25
95	− 5	25
90	−10	100
90	−10	100

X = 1500
N =   15
X̄ M =   100

$$\overset{S.D.}{\sigma} = \frac{450}{15} = \sqrt{30} = 5.48.$$

We add the scores and find that the total is 1500, then we divide by 15 (the number of scores) and find that the mean is 100. Next we subtract 100 from each score to get the numbers listed under d. We multiply each d by itself (i.e., square it) to get the numbers under d^2. When we add these we get 450. We then divide 450 by 15 to get 30, the variance. If we take the square root of 30, we arrive at a standard deviation of 5.48.

The more variability there is in the group of scores, the larger the σ will be. It is easier to plan class work for a group with a σ of four or five points than for one with a σ of twenty or thirty points on the same I.Q. test. Similarly, when variabilities are small, a researcher feels confident that he would get a similar mean if he repeated his experiment; if the σ is large, he cannot feel so confident. One reason for the importance of the standard deviation is that it is used, in connection with the normal distribution, in many of the inferences which constitute the second major use of statistics. (We shall discuss normal distribution in the following section.)

TYPES OF DISTRIBUTION. Now we may say that the psychologist has reduced what he knows about the score of this group of children on the intelligence test into vest-pocket size, by using a measure of central tendency to stand for all the scores in the group, and a measure of dispersion to indicate how much difference there was, on the average, among the scores. One thing that is often added to complete the description is some word to describe the *shape* of the distribution. Were there more scores at one end of the scale than the other? Was there one "popular" (modal) score or many?

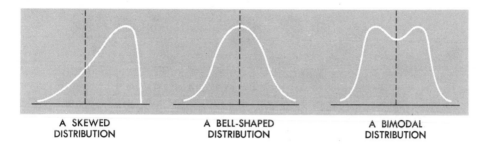

A SKEWED DISTRIBUTION   A BELL-SHAPED DISTRIBUTION   A BIMODAL DISTRIBUTION

FIG. I–3. Types of distributions.

The bell-shaped curve shown in Fig. I–3 is particularly important. Many kinds of events and scores tend to cluster about the center of their distribution, with random variations on either side of the center. When a large number of such scores are graphed, they often tend to form a distribution which looks like a curve that mathematicians call a *normal curve*. They also say that it "assumes a normal distribution." There is nothing about the normal curve that makes it more "natural" or "standard" than any of the other curves mathematicians use. "Normal" is just the name they give it. It might be better if we called it a *Gaussian* curve, after the mathematician who first wrote about it. The important thing for the beginning psychology student to realize is that, because many psychological measures fall into a distribution that is roughly bell-shaped, we can, in our work, use statistics devised for use with normal curves.

Measures of central tendency (mean, median, and mode), measures of dispersion (range and standard deviation) and labels for the shape of distributions are descriptive statistics which enable the psychologist to say a great deal about a group of scores in a very few words.

Measures of Relationship

There is one other important descriptive statistic, which is used when we want to talk about the relationship between two sets of scores. For example, suppose we have two sets of scores.

Set 1		Set II	
Scores of high-school students on a test of numerical ability		Scores of the same students on a test of verbal ability	
Mary	170	Mary	71
John	160	John	59
Joe	100	Joe	60
Edna	100	Edna	59
Larry	100	Larry	58
Mae	70	Mae	35
Harry	30	Harry	50
Mabel	30	Mabel	20
Noel	0	Noel	36

Sometimes we want to know whether there is a relationship between these two sets of scores; that is, whether certain scores on one test tend to "go with" certain scores on the other. One could say, "Mary got 170 on the NA and 71 on the VA. John got 160 on the NA and 59 on the VA. Mae got 70 on the NA and 35 on the VA. However, Noel got 0 on the NA and 36 on the VA, . . ." and so on. Using this procedure, one would hardly be likely to get any overall notion of the relationship, if any, between the two sets of scores.

A handier way of conveying this information would be to draw a picture, such as that in Fig. I–4. Here we see which scores on the NA go with which scores on the VA. In this case, we see that there is indeed a relationship. High scores on the NA tend to go with high scores on the VA, while people with low scores on the NA are most likely to have low scores on the VA. These scores are said to be *positively correlated*. We can plot this picture even more conveniently in what is called a scatter plot, as shown in Fig. I–5.

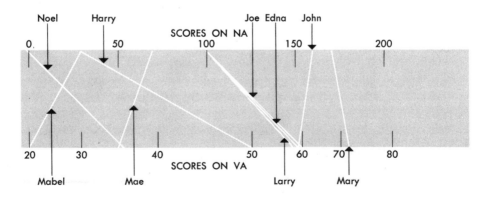

FIG. I–4. The relationship between the score each student received on number ability (NA) and the score he received on verbal ability (VA).

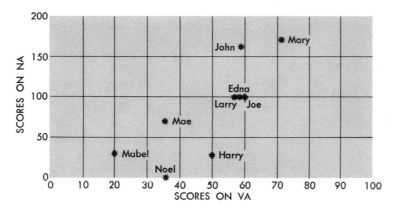

FIG. I-5. A scatter plot of positively correlated scores.

Figure I–6 is another such picture These might be the scores of a group of Navy pilots on two tests. Again we can see that there is a definite relationship between the two sets of scores; certain scores on the Q-factor test seem to go with certain scores on the Z-factor test. If we know that a man scored *low* on Q-factor, we can be pretty sure that he scored *high* on Z-factor; if he scored *high* on Q-factor, it is likely that he scored *low* on Z-factor. Again we find that the two sets of scores are related. These scores are said to be *negatively correlated*.

Ordinarily we use dots, since names take too much space. Figure I–7 is a plot of two tests that are not simply related. A high score on Alpha goes with both high and low scores on Beta; similarly, a low score on Alpha can be found with both high and low scores on Beta. If we want to predict a person's score on Beta, it does not help us much to know his score on Alpha. Making scatter plots like this, then, tells us roughly whether there is any relationship between two sets of scores.

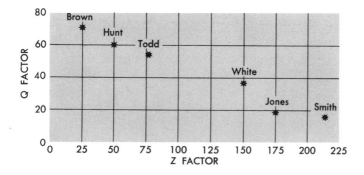

FIG. I–6. A scatter plot of negatively correlated scores.

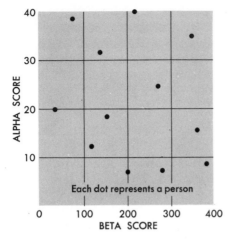

FIG. I–7.   A scatter plot of uncorrelated scores.

However, scatter plots are still not the best way to present correlation information because this method fails to give us a precise idea of how *strong* the relationship is. We would like to know more exactly how *sure* we can be that a high score on one test goes with a high score on another test, or that a low score goes with a high score. Fortunately, there is a way of expressing this in one statistic.

Definition: *The coefficient of correlation (r) indicates to what degree two sets of scores are linearly related;* that is, to what extent we can predict with a linear equation a person's score on one test if we know his score on the other.*

Mathematicians choose a formula for correlation coefficients which yields a number between -1.00 and $+1.00$. Thus correlation coefficients are numbers like 0.57 or -0.32 or 0.92.

The plus or minus sign before the number tells us which scores go with which. If there is a plus sign (or no sign) in front of the correlation coefficient, it means that high scores on one test go with high scores on the other, and low scores go with low scores. For example, height and weight are positively correlated, since tall people tend to weigh more than short people.

If there is a minus sign in front of the correlation coefficient, it means that *high* scores on one test go with *low* scores on the other, and vice versa. For example, there would be a negative correlation between the number of people at a picnic and the length of time a case of ginger ale would last; the *more* people, the *less* time the supply will last.

The number following the plus or minus sign tells us how strong the relationship is, or how accurately we can predict one score if we know the other.

---

* A linear relation is one that can be plotted graphically by a straight line.

If high scores on one test *always* go with high scores on the other test, and low scores on one go with low scores on the other, we say that there is a *perfect positive correlation*. This is written $r = 1.00$. Similarly, if high scores on one always go with low scores on the other, we have a perfect negative correlation, or $r = -1.00$.

If the score a person made on one test tells us absolutely nothing about what score he is likely to get on the other test, we say that there is *no correlation*. This is written $r = 0$. It may also happen that $r = 0$ when the relationships between two sets of scores do not fall into a straight line. For example, if as scores on one test get larger, scores on the other tend to increase and then to decrease, r may equal 0 even though we can still predict one score from another. Such a relationship is called *curvilinear*. Most relationships lie somewhere between 0 and ± 1. If there is some *tendency* for certain scores on one test to go with certain scores on the other, but they do not *always* go together, we may get $r = 0.30$ or 0.45, or 0.67 or 0.89, or some similar figure, depending on how much they do correlate.

Remember, *the nearer r is to 1, the stronger the relationship is:* that is, the better we can predict scores on one test from scores on the other test.

Beware: A plus sign does *not* mean "good," strong, desirable. A minus sign does *not* mean "bad," weak, undesirable.

Like all the other descriptive statistics, the coefficient of correlation serves as a convenient way to condense information into a usable form.

There are several kinds of correlation coefficients; when one is dealing with a small number of cases, the simplest to compute is *rho*, the coefficient of rank-order correlation. The following is an example of the computation of rho, the symbol for which is the Greek letter ρ. The mathematical formula for rho is:

$$\rho = 1 - \frac{6 \sum D^2}{N(N^2 - 1)}.$$

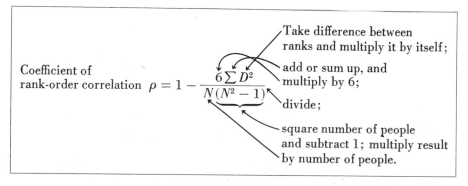

Suppose that a home-room teacher ranks seven children in the order of their intelligence, and their history teacher gives us their rank in history class.

	Rank in intelligence	Rank in history
Bobby	1	4
Betsy	2	3
Dorothy	3	2
Margaret	4	1
Billy	5	6
Sam	6	7
Alice	7	5

To compute rho, we subtract the second rank from the first and square it. Thus we have the following:

	Rank	Rank	Differences	D^2
Bobby	1	4	−3	9
Betsy	2	3	−1	1
Dorothy	3	2	1	1
Margaret	4	1	3	9
Billy	5	6	−1	1
Sam	6	7	−1	1
Alice	7	5	2	4
				26

Now we total the D^2 column. In this case the sum is 26. N is the number of people, 7; N^2 is thus 49. Substituting in the formula, we have

$$\rho = 1 - \frac{6 \times 26}{7\,(49-1)} = 1 - \frac{156}{336} = 1 - 0.46.$$

Therefore $\rho = 0.54.$

We thus find a moderate positive relationship between the ranks of our seven students on the two tests and know that the home-room teacher's ranking of intelligence is of some help in predicting which students will do well and which poorly in history.

The most commonly used correlation coefficient is the Pearson product moment correlation coefficient, which is abbreviated r. It is ordinarily used when we have *scores* for each person, rather than ranks. (We mentioned earlier that the standard deviation was preferred over the average deviation because it was used in computing other statistics, and r is one such statistic.)

Factor Analysis

When we are dealing with large numbers of tests, even correlation coefficients become very confusing. For example, if we have 20 tests, we need 190 correlation coefficients to describe their relationships. While this is simpler than remembering every person's scores on all 20 tests, it is still too much to comprehend. What we need is some way of comparing all these correlation coefficients with one another, to see if we can describe people in terms of a few fundamental traits.

Factor analysis is a statistical technique for identifying the traits underlying a group of tests. Suppose that several different tests are really measuring the *same* underlying ability in people. One would expect each of these tests to correlate with the others. But a test which measures some completely different ability would not correlate at all with these tests. Factor analysis uses this idea to find which tests tend to go together. When we have a large number of tests, factor analysis enables us to group some of the tests and infer how many underlying abilities or traits are measured by them.

The psychologist, in carrying out a factor analysis, administers a group of tests to a large number of individuals. He then correlates the individuals' scores on all of the tests, thus arriving at a table (or matrix), containing the correlation of each test with every other test. If tests are measuring the same ability they will correlate with each other and will tend to correlate with other tests in similar ways. Most tests measure several abilities, some of which are also measured by other tests in the battery. Factor analysis is a statistical technique for comparing these intercorrelations and determining how many abilities are common to the ones in the battery. Thus when we correlate a large number of tests of intelligence we find that those tests requiring use of words tend to correlate with each other more than they do with the tests requiring arithmetic. When we factor-analyze the correlations of these tests, we find one or more verbal factors and a separate numerical factor.

Using Descriptive Statistics to Evaluate a Single Score

In addition to using descriptive statistics to summarize groups of scores, the psychologist uses descriptive statistics to make sense out of the scores made by a single individual. For example, a college student comes to a counselor to talk over plans for a career. Among other things, the counselor has him take a number of aptitude tests. Two weeks later the results arrive.

Mechanical aptitude	74
Musical aptitude	50
Language skills	200
Art	69

In what areas do the student's greatest abilities lie? A single score, that is, a record of items passed or failed, cannot be interpreted by itself. Is 69 a high or low score in art? Is 200 a high or low score in language skills? There is no way of knowing just by looking at the score. In the Graduate Record Examination, for example, 200 is a very low score; the scores have been so arranged that half the people who take it get over 500.

In order to make sense out of a single score on a test, we must compare it with other scores made on the same test. We must ask how this score stands in comparison with scores made by people of the same age, by people of the same sex, or by people who have been successful in this field. Where does it fall in each of these distributions?

Definition: *A score which indicates what percentage of some group received lower scores than the one in which we are interested is called a percentile score.*

A score at the 75th percentile means that 75% of some comparison group received lower scores. Thus if only one-fourth of the people who have taken the test in the past received scores above 53, we say that a score of 53 is "at the 75th percentile."

The second major way of making sense out of a single score involves using the standard deviation. *Given the mean and the standard deviation, we can estimate where an individual falls on a distribution by assigning him a score based on standard deviations.* The more standard deviations he is below the mean, the fewer cases we would expect to find below him. The more standard deviations he is above the mean, the fewer cases we would expect to find above him. Look at the diagram of a normal distribution in Fig. I–8. You see that by the time we have gone out two standard deviations above the mean, there are only 2½% of the cases left above us.

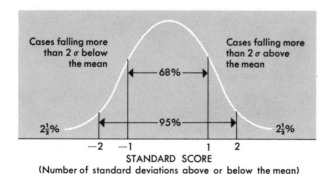

FIG. I–8.   The relation between standard scores, standard deviations, and the normal curve. A person whose score is one standard deviation above the mean receives a standard score of +1.

Definition: *The statistic which tells us how many standard deviations a score is above or below the mean is called the standard score.*

A standard score of −2 means that this score is two standard deviations *below* the mean. A standard score of +2 means that this score is two standard deviations *above* the mean.

Fortunately mathematicians can calculate the proportion of cases falling under the curve between any two points in a normal curve, and every statistics book contains printed tables showing the percentages of cases which fall under varying proportions of the normal curve. This is another reason why statisticians like to use the standard deviation.

The data useful for assessing an individual's place in a distribution of test scores are called *norms*.

Definition: *Norms are descriptive statistics—usually mean and standard deviation—computed on a large group of test scores.*

For example, the Navy General Classification Test norms tell us that for Navy recruits the mean is 50 and the σ is equal to 10. The Army General Classification Test norms tell us that for Army recruits the mean is 100 and the σ is 20.

How Statistics Are Used to Help Make Inferences and Decisions

In Chapter 1 we saw that people who are doing research are always striving for generalizations. Thus it often happens that a psychologist is not so much interested in the meaning of one score, or one group of scores, as he is in comparing two (or more) scores, or groups of scores, to decide whether they differ from each other in a way which will enable him to generalize about them. He wants to decide, for example, whether a prefrontal lobotomy affects intelligence. He wants to know whether or not a person's threshold for sound is higher when he is rested than when he is tired. He wants to know whether women are more in favor of universal military training than men. He wants to decide whether his experiment supports, or does not support, his hypothesis. To do this he must use the data resulting from his research with one sample of cases to make an *inference* about the results he would get if he tested a larger group which this sample represents.

Of course, the important word here is *infer*. How different do two sets of scores have to be before a research psychologist will dare to state that the people in Group A (who receive a certain treatment) are different from the people in Group B? The answer is: There has to be a difference big enough for the psychologist to be able to say with some confidence, "These two scores (or sets of scores) did not come from one and the same distribution. They came from different distributions, with different means."

In real life, it is possible for someone to spend days and even weeks doing the statistical work that will either allow him to make such a statement or show him that he cannot. For our purposes, it will be enough to get a fairly general idea of how it can be done. Let us therefore look at a simplified example from a neighboring discipline: anthropology.

■ While workmen are excavating on Packard Street, they stumble across a skull. Professor Gulch, of the anthropology department of the nearby university, happens to be passing by at the moment and takes possession of the skull. It would be a feather in Gulch's cap if he could say that it is *not* a skull belonging to a modern man. But, being an honest scholar, Gulch has to decide whether or not it really is different from modern-type skulls. Therefore he measures it, and finds that it is just 40 centimeters around the brow.

"Let us find out what the chances are that it might be a small skull, which differs from other skulls only by the amount of random variation we expect in human skulls," he says. So saying, Gulch draws from his pocket a handbook of anthropometrics and turns to the page which gives the mean and standard deviations of skull diameters for modern man. It might look like this: Mean $= 43, \sigma = 1$. If we drew it, the distributions would look like the plot in Fig. I–9.

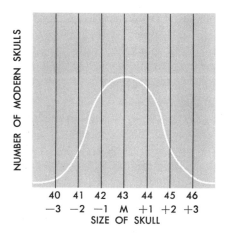

NUMBER OF MODERN SKULLS

| 40 | 41 | 42 | 43 | 44 | 45 | 46 |
| −3 | −2 | −1 | M | +1 | +2 | +3 |

SIZE OF SKULL

FIG. I–9. A hypothetical distribution of skull sizes of modern man.

Gulch can now use statistics to help him decide whether or not to accept his hypothesis that this is not the skull of modern man.

"Cheers!" exclaims Gulch. "My skull—the one I found, that is—is three sigmas below the mean!" He then asks himself how often, in such a distribution, a skull three sigmas below the mean would show up. The answer is 0.001. So Gulch is able to say, "Only one-tenth of one percent of all modern skulls are that small. I am quite willing to infer that this particular skull comes from another distribution, with a quite different mean!" ■

This example, in essence, shows what psychologists do. Statistical techniques enable them to estimate whether the differences they find between two samples are real differences, or whether the two are just two different samples from the same group. Because people vary, we expect that any time we take two samples from the same group they will not be exactly the same. The more variable the group, the more our samples are likely to differ. Consequently we use the standard deviation, a measure of variation, as the basis for our decisions about whether two samples are only as different as we would expect them to be in two samples drawn randomly from the same distribution, or whether they are so different that it is unlikely that they came from the same distribution.

Whenever we take scores or measures of a group of people and want to make a statement about *all* such people, we should realize that our sample is not a perfect representation of the group it comes from. The tendency of samples to differ from the population from which they are drawn is called *sampling error*.

A general principle of statistics is that the larger the sample, the less the sampling error. Thus Professor Gulch's case would be stronger if he had found several small skulls. For just this reason, people who are doing research ordinarily use several subjects in experiments. Other things being equal, the larger the sample the less the likelihood that the results will be in error. Nevertheless, even with large samples and a large difference, we can never say positively that there is or is not a difference. All we can say is that the probability of such a difference occurring by chance is very small.

The Binomial Expansion

Now let us consider another example. Suppose that 6 women and 2 men are elected to membership in the freshman honor society. Since the freshmen class is half men and half women, we would expect the members of the honor society to be composed of equal numbers of each sex, on the average. Of course, even if we flipped a coin 8 times we would not always get exactly 4 heads and 4 tails. Thus we cannot be sure that the number of girls elected is more than mere chance. To find out what the chances are of getting a 6-to-2 split, we can use the same technique we would use to compute the probability of getting 6 or more heads when we flip a coin 8 times.

We do this by expanding the expression $(P + Q)^n$, where P is the probability of one outcome, Q is the probability of other outcomes, and n is the number of events. On the basis of the number of women in the class, we would expect that half the honor society members would be men, that is, $P = \frac{1}{2}$. Similarly, we would expect half to be women, so that Q would also equal $\frac{1}{2}$. We have 8 events (new members of the honor society). Our expression thus becomes

$$(P + Q)^n = (\tfrac{1}{2} + \tfrac{1}{2})^8.$$

Then we expand:

$$P^8 + 8P^7Q + 28P^6Q^2 + 56P^5Q^3 + 70P^4Q^4 + 56P^3Q^5 + 28P^2Q^6 + 8PQ^7 + Q^8$$

$$= \frac{1}{256} + \frac{8}{256} + \frac{28}{256} + \frac{56}{256} + \frac{70}{256} + \frac{56}{256} + \frac{28}{256} + \frac{8}{256} + \frac{1}{256} .$$

The chances of coming out with 8 women is given by the first term, $\frac{1}{256}$. The chances of having 7 women out of 8 in the society is $\frac{8}{256}$. The chances of coming out with 6 women, as we did, is $\frac{28}{256}$. We want to know whether or not we can interpret the disproportionate number of women elected this year as just chance, or as evidence that women are really brighter than men. You say, "Well, only 28 times out of 256 would I get 6 heads in 8 tosses of a coin, so this is a pretty unlikely occurrence." But note that, to test the hypothesis that women are brighter than men, we want to know not how likely it is that exactly 6 would get elected to the society, but rather how likely it is that 6 *or more* would be elected to the honor society. To obtain this probability, we must add

$$\frac{28}{256} + \frac{8}{256} + \frac{1}{256} = \frac{37}{256}.$$

Are women more likely to be elected to the honor society than men? Since we ordinarily assume that no difference exists, unless the difference we find is quite improbable (such as a 1-in-20 or a 1-in-100 chance), we cannot say from this one year's results that women are more likely to be elected to the freshman honor society than men. If our results had been ones which occur very infrequently, by chance, we would have said that there was a *significant difference,* and we would have been willing to predict that next year more women than men would be elected. But all we can say is that even by chance we would expect at least this many women to be elected about 1 year in 7. In addition to the binomial expansion there are many other statistics we can use to determine whether two samples come from the same population. Most of these are much easier to compute for large samples than is the binomial expansion, so that these statistics are the ones commonly used in deciding what inferences may be drawn from a particular set of data.

Summary

Concepts

Frequency distribution.   A list of scores, arranged in order, telling how many people received each score or category of scores

Mean.   The average of a group of scores

Median.   The score dividing the higher half of scores from the lower half

Standard deviation.   A measure of variability of scores

Correlation coefficient.   An index of the degree of relationship between two sets of paired scores

Percentile rank (or score).   A score indicating the percentage of a group which received lower scores

Standard score.   A score expressed in terms of the number of standard deviations above or below the mean

Significant difference.   A difference likely to occur, by chance, very infrequently

Suggested Reading

Applications of mathematics to psychology are rapidly increasing, and the statistics courses of today are being broadened to bring in additional mathematical topics. This is a dynamic area of psychological work which has wide uses. If you are not able to go on to a course in statistics, you might enjoy reading a book intended to protect the average man against those who try to overwhelm him with statistics. The book is D. Huff's *How To Lie with Statistics*. New York: Norton, 1954.

psychology in today's world

appendix II

MAN–MACHINE SYSTEMS: AUTOMATION

TEACHING MACHINES AND INSTRUCTIONAL TECHNOLOGY

UTILIZATION OF HUMAN RESOURCES

THE PSYCHOLOGICAL EFFECTS OF DRUGS

MENTAL HEALTH AS A SOCIAL PROBLEM

CHANGING PATTERNS OF FAMILY ORGANIZATION

Psychology is one of the newest and most dynamic of sciences. This book has set forth some of the basic knowledge of (and "best guesses" about) psychology today. The authors hope that this presentation has stirred up curiosity, so that the reader will be interested in learning more and will continue to ask "What's new?"

This appendix will present some developments to watch in the future, developments of particular interest to the individual because they involve important current social problems.

We could point to dozens of contemporary developments involving psychology: man in space, psychological aspects of desegregation, the role of psychology in working for peaceful international relations, the problems of cultural change in the new African nations, the burgeoning research on creativity, the growing interest in relationships between psychology and religion, psychological studies of economic behavior, and many others. But we have chosen six which are representative of the range of topics for which psychological research and theory has relevance. The six we have chosen are:

1. Man–machine systems: automation
2. Teaching machines and instructional technology
3. The utilization of human resources
4. The psychological effects of drugs
5. Mental health as a social problem
6. Changing patterns of family organization

Our brief discussion in this appendix is, of course, only an introduction to each topic. Developments are so rapid that the most recent information, as this is being written, will probably be out of date by the time the reader sees these comments. For the latest developments, the student should ask his instructor for sources, and check the *Psychological Abstracts* and other bibliographic sources.

Man–Machine Systems: Automation

Modern industrial production demands that vast numbers of men and machines interact in the framework of organizations. The development of such an organization involves questions of vital importance to society and of much interest to psychologists. What tasks should be allotted to machines? How can we combine men and machines most effectively?

The trend of industry's answer to these problems is apparent. More and more work is being done by machines. Muscle power has been largely replaced by mechanical power. Machines are being integrated into systems in which automatic feedback mechanisms control some functions formerly controlled by men. But this shift from manpower to machine power is not a simple one.

In a system involving both men and machines it is not always easy to decide how to divide the labor. For example, one might expect that the greatest efficiency would be obtained if each worker's job were made as simple as possible. Yet, research shows that workers become bored and inefficient when they are given jobs that are too simple and repetitive.

At the other extreme, engineers have somtimes developed such complicated control systems for machinery that only very highly trained individuals are able to operate them. Here the psychologist's job is to determine how to adapt the task to human capabilities. For example, we saw in Chapter 6 that there is a limit to the number of separate items of information with which the human being can deal; but when these items are combined into patterns, efficiency increases. Thus a group of airplane dials can be monitored effectively if they are designed so that the needles form a pattern (such as a straight line) when they are functioning normally. Similarly, to scientists who are designing radar displays which can be operated by humans with little error, knowledge about brightness thresholds is valuable.

Knowledge about figure–ground relationships is also helpful in devising instruments. For example, to a man who is flying an airplane, it is obviously necessary to know at all times which direction is up. In most aircraft this information is provided by an indicator made up of light and dark hemispheres, with the boundary between them representing the horizon. As long as the pilot can see the ground, he sees the line as stationary and the plane as moving around it. When he is flying by instruments, however, the cockpit becomes the background, and as the plane's position changes, it seems to the pilot that the line is moving rather than that the plane has shifted. Such differences in perception are likely to result in failure to make the proper corrections promptly. Knowledge such as this is obviously important to the aircraft designer.

Knowledge of the response capabilities of human beings is also vital to the designer of a man–machine system. For example, if a human being is to communicate information, it is important that the communication code assign the most efficient response to the most common units of messages. The Morse code does this by assigning a single dot to *e*. However, the typewriter is inefficiently designed, so that the little finger of the left hand is greatly overworked and awkward sequences of fingers occur frequently.

But even more interesting than the problems of adapting individual machines to human capabilities is the problem of devising the most effective system of men and machines to accomplish a given purpose. Which jobs should men do? How many men will be required? How should information be passed from one unit in the system to another? How can efficiency be maintained once the system is established? These are complex problems, with which a great deal of contemporary research is concerned. Studies of man as an information-processing system are providing data and models about the time necessary to perform different classes of mental operations. Other psychological studies reveal characteristics of men which are particularly difficult to duplicate efficiently. For example, one of the assets of the human in a man-machine system is his flexibility. When the system requires adjustments to varying conditions based on previous experience, a learning, living organism is preferable to a machine. A system which is rigid, either because of rigid automation or because of rigid prescription of procedures, may be inefficient when the task varies beyond relatively narrow limits. Studies of simulated air-defense centers in which the task conditions vary (e.g., with the numbers of attacking and interceptor planes) suggest that effective operation of the system requires encouragement and training for flexible adaptation of actions to deal with tasks of increasing difficulty (Chapman, Kennedy, Newell, and Biel, 1959).

One characteristic of the switch to automated systems is the increase in the proportion of workers responsible for maintenance as opposed to operational jobs, which bears out our principle that human beings are more useful than machines are for tasks which require learning and problem-solving. In completely automatic factories in the future, it is likely that the majority of the workers will be involved in maintenance. This means that quite different skills will be required of the industrial worker of the future, because although operational jobs usually involve motor skills, the maintenance of complex machinery depends not on skill in replacing a part but on problem-solving ability. Like a medical doctor, the industrial maintenance man will have to diagnose a condition and determine which part is likely to cause trouble, so that it may be replaced before there is a serious loss of production. Research on "troubleshooting" as it involves machinery indicates that there are general problem-solving principles which can be applied.

What type of person can use these principles? How can we teach people to become industrial maintenance workers? Immediately we are carried back into aspects of our problem of man–machine utilization: selection and training.

A twofold training problem exists. One task of training is an old one: training a man to do the job he is assigned to do. Thus if a system requires a radar operator, someone must be trained to operate the radar. But the second task of training is to train the system as a whole; i.e., to train the men to work in harmony with their equipment. Just as we measure learning in an individual in terms of how efficiently he performs a task, so we can assess learning in a system by evaluating the degree of effectiveness with which it achieves the objectives for which it was designed. Many of the principles we discussed in Chapter 5 and later are also applicable to systems training. Thus in training air-defense systems, the System Development Corporation has used varied problems and feedback of results, just like those devices which have been found effective in promoting learning and concept formation in individuals. One of the key parts of the training program is the "debriefing" session, in which the system members discuss the results of their performance on the preceding problem. Here group problem-solving is used to arrive at improved procedures for use in future problems.

Another psychological problem becomes apparent when new systems are put into operation: the attitudes of workers toward the new system. Because of the role which one's work plays in adjustment (Chapter 13) and the resistance of work groups to changes in their work (Chapter 15), adoption of a new system is likely to arouse anxiety and unhappiness. One clue to reducing frustration and anxiety and gaining acceptance of the new system can be derived from our study of group participation in decision-making. Another clue lies in the fact that workers are more likely to be satisfied with their jobs when they feel that the job makes full use of their abilities. Automation makes it possible to reorganize the work load. When a new automated electric power plant was opened, Mann and Hoffman (1960) studied the attitudes of workers in the new plant as compared with those in the older plants. They found that one of the key factors in the high morale at the new plant was that the men felt that their new jobs were making greater use of their abilities than did their old jobs. The electric company had systematically attempted to enlarge the new jobs so that each man now had to learn more about the total sequence of production than he previously knew. By reducing the number of job classifications, the company was also able to eliminate one level of supervision, so that the workers were now closer to the top management and felt more closely involved in management decisions. By using psychological knowledge, the company was thus able to increase efficiency as well as improve worker interest and satisfaction.

Man-Machine Systems: a Summary

Development of an effective man–machine system involves the following psychological problems.

1. Determining the optimal combination of man and machines
2. Designing machines in terms of human capabilities
3. Selecting men best able to fill the required roles in the system
4. Training the men selected and the system as a whole
5. Gaining group acceptance (or developing morale) among the work group

Although some psychological principles can guide solutions to each of these problems, the present state of psychological knowledge requires that many of the problems be solved by applied research with the proposed system or its components. Both to carry out the applied work and the more basic research we need individuals with interdisciplinary training in engineering, biological science, and psychology. Unfortunately, to date there are no published accounts of research on a system embracing all these aspects, but by the time this book is published the current research should be nearing publication.

Teaching Machines and Instructional Technology

One of the most intriguing aspects of the spread of automation is that it has entered into education. Faced with a shortage of able teachers, educators are exploring the possibilities inherent in television, films, and teaching machines.

In the early 1920's S. L. Pressey developed devices by which students could take tests and immediately learn whether their answers were right or wrong. He demonstrated that such tests resulted in better learning and memory than did conventional tests scored as a whole and returned at the next class period.

In the past decade B. F. Skinner and his staff have developed similar devices which do not simply test what a student has learned from a textbook or class, but which can be used to teach students, in place of textbooks or instructors. These "teaching machines" present statements and questions in a careful step-by-step sequence. The learner answers each question and immediately learns whether he was right or wrong. Such a device naturally makes use of the principles of feedback, contiguity, and active learning.

Some of the "programs" of statements and questions placed in the machine use Skinner's method of successive approximations. (Remember the pigeons playing table tennis.) The first question is very easy; the next only a tiny bit closer to the goal; the next a shade different; and so on for hundreds of questions. If the student does not learn, it is assumed that someone has failed: not the learner, but the writer of the program.

Successive revisions of a program are carried out on the basis of tryouts aimed at pinpointing and connecting the specific places in an instructional sequence that are stumbling blocks to students in initial versions of a program. Currently, the skill and resources devoted to this crucial process vary widely from program to program. Unfortunately many so-called "programs" have been marketed which may *look* like programs, but are very poor because they have not been through such a process of development.

Skinner and some of his followers further believe that with proper programming there should be virtually no mistakes. The conventional teacher, they believe, jumps too rapidly from one point to the next, and expects students to see relationships that are obvious to experts but not apparent to students. The method used is somewhat similar to that of Socrates, since it draws students out through a series of carefully devised questions. With the teaching machine the student can go at his own pace, and after each step he receives reinforcement, for the correct answer not only provides informational feedback but also gives the student the satisfaction of knowing he was right.

The teaching machine is, of course, only as good as the program used in it. If the program explores all the facets of the material, the learner will become familiar with them; if it is restricted to certain areas, learning will be similarly restricted. Because the student writing answers to questions must obviously go more slowly than if he were simply reading a text, there is a tendency for programs to be more restricted than textbooks.

Various types of machines have been used, some utilizing films, tape, or complex machinery. But, in fact machines may not be necessary for many purposes, since sequenced programs of material and questions can be presented in workbooks or textbooks. In one such book, the student chooses one answer to a multiple-choice question; each answer directs him to a different page, where he finds more material and a new question. Thus students who make an incorrect response can be directed to pages which will show them what they did not know, while students who choose the correct answer can be directed to other pages that present new material.

Going still further toward adaptive automated tutoring are computerized systems in which various forms of responses of the student (typed answers, pointing to a spot or a two-dimensional display, etc.) are automatically evaluated by an electronic computer, to which a number of student stations are connected. With such systems, a student can not only proceed at his own pace, but also— since the computer can process data for many students simultaneously in a fraction of a second—he can follow an individually tailored sequence based on cumulative analysis of his particular needs. Large amounts of money are currently being spent on research and development of such automated tutorial systems.

Reports on the use of teaching machines indicate that many students enjoy learning with them. In a sense, a teaching machine enables each student to have his own tutor, and students using teaching machines do learn. To date, however, experimental studies comparing the effectiveness of teaching machines with that of textbooks or teachers are not conclusive, nor are there many studies indicating what type of educational objectives can be most efficiently achieved by teaching machines.

Teaching machines also raise research questions for the psychologist interested in human learning. What effect does the type of response have on learning? Does it make any difference whether a student writes out the answer, or presses a button below the correct answer, or simply reads the correct answer? What effects do differing sizes of steps from one question to the next have on the learning of different types of students? What is the effect of restricting the student's attention to one item at a time as opposed to letting him refer to various items before answering a question? Does the high proportion of correct answers encourage students who fear failure? Does the high proportion of correct answers bore the student who likes the challenge of a difficult task? Recent research indicates that it does (Moore, Smith, and Teevan, 1965).

As more and more school systems and colleges try out programmed learning, teaching machines, and related systems, it will be interesting to watch for the answers to such research questions.

Utilization of Human Resources

Related to the problem of the relative use of machines and men in education and in other systems is the problem of securing the proper distribution of roles in society. In a primitive society, for example, the society probably would not have lasted long if everyone had wanted to give up hunting, fishing, or agriculture to become a witch doctor. In a society as complex as ours, the problem is less obvious but more difficult.

How does society allocate its human resources? Individuals differ in many ways; some are talented mechanics, others talented musicians. In time of war the nation must use each individual's potentialities in such a way that he makes the maximum contribution to the war effort. Even in time of peace, however, much of a country's wealth and productivity depends on its use of human resources. Suppose that, by some arbitrary selection process, everyone who had mechanical aptitude were forced to go to law school; our mechanized society would soon grind to a stop. How does it happen that society has a workable distribution of mechanics, doctors, and bus drivers?

When one stops to think, it is amazing that we get as adequate a match as we do between the vocational choices people make when they are young and the needs of society years later. The problem of matching people and jobs becomes more and more difficult as more and more vocations call for long periods of specialized training, and as vocations develop more and more specialization. It is estimated that there are 100,000 different categories of vocations in the United States, but the boy choosing a vocation is largely unaware of the many specialties available. A national survey of high school youth (Project Talent, 1965) revealed that the great majority of young people had quite unrealistic career plans. Although young people do become more realistic during high school, about half make radical switches during the first year after high school. Fortunately there is a good deal of mobility between vocations, and, as we saw earlier, with proper training an individual can be successful in a variety of occupations. Unfortunately people who start to work immediately after high school tend to have less information about the world of work than their classmates in college preparatory courses, and most of them have not discussed career plans with a counselor.

It is not only important to the individual to consider the relationship of his intelligence, special abilities, and interests to the demands of various vocations, but it is equally as important to our society that its human resources be used in the most effective way. As we said earlier, a person may have too much intelligence to be happy and successful in some jobs. From the standpoint of society, in such a case there is waste not only in the fact that the worker is inefficient in the job he is doing, but also in his loss to the more highly skilled job which he might have done.

While we have made good beginnings in developing measures of abilities and interests, as well as in assessing the demand of various vocations for personnel, we still lack comprehensive data on the human resources of our nation and the ways in which they are developed or dissipated in the years before the individual settles into a vocation. "Project Talent" is a nationwide inventory of aptitudes and abilities of young people in the United States. In 1960, 500,000 high school students were given a two-day, 2000-item examination measuring abilities, knowledge, interests, and other personality characteristics. Follow-up studies will determine what these youths do in college or vocations, and will thus reveal what patterns of aptitudes and interests are associated both with selection of, and also with success in, various college courses and careers. In addition, associated studies will determine what the effects of various educational experiences are. Reports of some of these studies will undoubtedly appear in newspapers and magazines.

The problem of efficient utilization of human resources leads to the question, "Who should go to college?" This is particularly pressing today as colleges try to cope with the population explosion. As we give colleges more and broader functions, as money becomes available, as aspirations rise, and as occupational demands change, the percentage of youth going to college rises. While this decision as to the numbers of students to be given a college education is much beyond the scope of psychology, psychology can help improve the correctness of prediction of success in college. For example, we know that one of the factors which determines success in college and in professions is intellectual performance and that this can be measured. Intelligence tests, which are widely used as an aid to the selection of college students, have demonstrated a good deal of usefulness. In fact, as we saw earlier, the correlation between intelligence tests and college grades is about 0.4 to 0.5, a reasonably high correlation, considering the many other variables involved.

Knowing that ability is not perfectly correlated with performance, we would expect our prediction to be improved if we could measure motivation and habits of study. Unfortunately we have few good measures of these factors. We saw in Chapter 13, for example, that success in college may satisfy many motives. Consequently, a measure of any one single motive is hardly likely to improve our predictions of college success. For example, we find inconsistent and generally discouraging results when we attempt to predict grades by measuring only the need for achievement. However, one readily available measure, which combines ability, motivation, and habits, is the student's performance in high school. While high school is, of course, different from college, high school standing is usually the best available predictor of grades in college. A student's high school percentile rank correlates with his college grades by a factor of about 0.5 to 0.6. Even this correlation is not as accurate as we should like it to be.

Recent research indicates that colleges differ in what they expect of students, and also in the type of personalities their typical students have. Students seem to choose colleges matched to their own motives for attending college. As we learn more we may be able to help students do a better job of matching themselves to colleges. Research also shows that some students profit from one teaching method, while others are more likely to profit from another. Additional research may help us find the best way to help each type of student more nearly achieve his potential.

The Psychological Effects of Drugs

Psychopharmacology is the new and rapidly expanding field concerned with the psychological effects of drugs. Almost everyone is aware that tranquilizing drugs are used extensively both in mental hospitals and in general medical practice to relieve anxiety and tension. In fact these drugs are among the most widely used drugs sold by prescription. The layman, however, may be unaware of the extent to which psychopharmacologic drugs have also been used as tools in investigating the functioning of the CNS. Studies of their effects both in man and low animals have yielded new information about the manner in which CNS activity is related to behavior.

Tranquilizing drugs have had a significant impact on attitudes of psychiatrists and mental hospital personnel toward the mentally ill. The whole atmosphere of mental hospitals has changed. Since patients are less destructive, hospitals can be furnished and decorated in a more pleasing manner. Moreover, with the advent of these drugs, mental hospitals have been much more willing to permit patients to return to their home environments, so that for the first time in recent history there is hope that there may be enough space in mental hospitals for those who require hospitalization.

The psychopharmacologic drugs include both tranquilizers (or ataraxic drugs) and psychic energizers or activators.

Tranquilizers

While some of the other medical treatments for mental illness, such as electroshock, psychosurgery, or insulin shock are comparatively severe procedures causing momentary unconsciousness or stupefaction, therapy with tranquilizing drugs produces improvement in the patient's feelings and ability to communicate with others without his losing consciousness. In schizophrenic patients, for example, tranquilizing drugs reduce restless overactivity, enable patients characterized by "word salad" speech to converse intelligibly, and reduce their fears of "Communist spies" or other objects of delusions and hallucinations. These are some of the effects of tranquilizers. These effects may occur independently of one another; for example, change in feeling may occur independently of change in activity, and vice versa. So dramatic is the change in patients' symptoms with the administration of tranquilizing drugs that the use of electroshock therapy has been reduced by 80%. (Part of this reduction, of course, reflects the difference in attitudes of those in charge of treatment.)

The use of tranquilizing drugs is not restricted to those who are mentally ill. Within a few months after their introduction, tranquilizers became one of the most commonly prescribed drugs. Miltown (one of the first brand names) became a household word. The eagerness with which people sought tranquility and happiness through the drugs is not surprising, but their use does raise profound religious and philosophical questions. Traditionally men have sought inner peace through religion. What are the consequences of taking this short cut to peace of mind? The use of peyote in religious ceremonies by tribes of Indians in the Southwest has been opposed by both religious and political groups. Similarly the use of marijuana and similar drugs is forbidden by most societies. Judeo-Christian religions have stressed the importance of choice. Insofar as drugs are habit-forming or distort the individual's ability to exercise choice, religion is likely to oppose their use.

Activators

The tranquilizing drugs seem to be most effective for the agitated, tense, anxious person. For patients suffering from severe depression, another group of drugs seem to hold more promise. Benzedrine, amphetamine, and iproniazid are now names almost as well-known as the tranquilizers Miltown, chlorpromazine, and reserpine. One of these drugs, iproniazid, was first used in the treatment of tuberculosis. When physicians observed that patients taking the drug became more alert and cheerful, they tried it on mental patients. Many depressed patients, who viewed their future as hopeless and who had no ambition, became active, talkative, cheerful, and alert after beginning administration of dexedrine, iproniazid, or other energizers. In fact, patients treated with these drugs sometimes became so active that they had difficulty sleeping.

The energizing drugs apparently block the action of certain enzymes in the brain, and produce effects on the nervous system similar to those produced by secretions of the adrenal gland. The psychiatrist, with tranquilizers to quiet his patients and activators to energize them, now has increasing power to control his patients' state of mind. Will the use of these drugs eliminate the need for psychotherapy and counseling? Can we now rely on chemicals to dissolve our problems?

The answer to these questions is still in the future and the outcome will be interesting to observe. At present, psychiatrists often use combinations of drugs to break down patients' isolation so that psychotherapy may begin. It does not seem likely that drugs alone can resolve all the problems of adjustment which people face; counseling and psychotherapy will undoubtedly still be helpful for many people. But we do not know the degree to which mental illness and psychological disturbances result from psychological problems as opposed to the degree to which they result from chemical disturbances. Perhaps one individual's psychological problems arise because chemical imbalance in his nervous system prevents him from dealing with his environment normally. Perhaps another's biochemical imbalance results from the stress of problems too great to be solved. In still another case, perhaps both types of factors interact. Fortunately chemicals now exist whose effects duplicate some of the symptoms of mental illness, and by studying the way in which these chemicals (called psychotomimetic drugs) affect the nervous system, we may gain a clearer understanding of the biochemical aspects of mental illness.

Hallucinogens or Psychotomimetic Drugs

One of the drugs in this group, mescaline, has been known in crude form for centuries. When the Spanish explorers arrived in Mexico they found that there were certain cactus plants whose tops were used in religious ceremonies; they supposedly enabled the worshippers to behold the world of the gods. Despite the disapproval of the church, the *peyote* cult has persisted (although translated into a Christian communion). Chemists took the curious plant into the laboratories and isolated the substance called *mescaline*, which caused the extraordinary visions experienced by the peyote eater.

Another drug producing schizophrenia-like symptoms was discovered by accident when a chemist, Hofmann, was forced to leave work one afternoon because of a state of restlessness and dizziness. When he closed his eyes, fantastically colored images appeared. Hofmann concluded that he must somehow have absorbed some of the chemical with which he had been working, and to test this hypothesis, swallowed a small amount of it. Again he experienced the symptoms, and other investigators then began extensive studies not only of how the drug affected the healthy mind but of which drugs would counteract its effects. We now know that this drug, LSD-25, is extremely potent. A dose of one-700,000,000th of the weight of an average person is enough to cause mental symptoms. With such drugs, the person doing research on mental illness can now manipulate mental states to test hypotheses about the nature and treatment of mental illness, and even before these lines are published new discoveries will probably be made.

Mental Health as a Social Problem

We have devoted portions of several chapters in this text to problems of adjustment and mental health. In those chapters, however, we were concerned primarily with individual adjustment. We saw the important role the psychologist plays in administering diagnostic tests and in counseling the person with a problem.

In those chapters we also noted some of the psychological research which is being directed toward gaining an understanding of personality and personality change. In this section, however, we propose to look at mental health as a major social problem, and tell you of one aspect of the research that psychologists are undertaking in order to understand the feelings of normal people.

In Chapter 14 we noted the prevalence of mental illness; we saw that half the hospital beds in the country are required for the treatment of the mentally ill; we pointed out the financial and psychological cost to the society and to individual families resulting from neurosis and psychosis. Because mental illness is such an important social problem, foundations and the federal government have recently supported large-scale studies of mental health problems in America. One new direction of research has been to study the attitudes toward mental illness and the problems and satisfactions of ordinary individuals.

First let us look at attitudes toward mental illness. Surveys (Nunnally and Osgood, 1961) indicate that the general public feels an aversion toward mental illness. People distrust and fear the psychotic or neurotic person. However, only the most serious forms of disturbances are recognized as mental illness by the average person, so that the average person tends to underestimate the seriousness of neurosis and to exaggerate the seriousness of psychosis. Fewer than half the people questioned feel that they could act normally toward a person who has been mentally ill. While the better-educated people tended to have somewhat broader and less negative views of mental illness, even physicians share the public's attitudes to a surprising degree (Peterson, 1956).

But now let us turn to Americans' views of their own mental health. What things do Americans see as contributing to their happiness and unhappiness? What factors determine where and when people seek help for psychological problems? How is mental health related to other aspects of a person's position in society?

Questions such as these were the focus of a nationwide survey conducted by Gurin, Veroff, and Feld (1960). The results of the survey provided some fascinating information about Americans, their worries and their satisfactions.

As we saw in our earlier discussion of adjustment, one criterion is the individual's happiness or freedom from anxiety. One question on the national survey was: "Taking all things together, how would you say things are these days?" Thirty-five percent of the people interviewed said "very happy," 54% said "pretty happy," and only 11% answered "not too happy." When asked what things they felt happy about, over half mentioned children, marriage, or family relationships, 29% responded with answers categorized as "economic and material" sources of happiness, and 14% mentioned their jobs as a source of satisfaction. Sources of unhappiness were more scattered, although 27% of the people mentioned "economic and material" things. About a sixth of the respondents mentioned some aspect of national or world affairs. The prominence of material satisfactions in happiness or unhappiness does not refer to wealth and luxury but rather to freedom from debts and a comfortable home on the happiness side, and to unpaid bills and inadequate housing on the unhappiness side. In analyzing the sources of unhappiness, the investigators found that most people see their troubles in terms of external problems rather than in terms of their own characteristics.

Three questions concerned past emotional crises, one about "the most unhappy period of your life," one asking "have you ever felt that you were going to have a nervous breakdown?" and the third asking whether or not the interviewee had ever sought professional help in overcoming a personal problem. The most frequently mentioned source of past unhappiness was the death of a loved one. Economic and material things were again mentioned frequently (one person in eight) although these were not given as reasons for past unhappiness as often as for present unhappiness. Again the responses tended to be in terms of external stress, even for those who had at some time felt that they were going to have a nervous breakdown. Only 45% of these people saw their problem as one with which they might have been helped.

Whether or not a person sought help depended on what he saw as his problem. Those who saw problems as external were less likely to seek help than those who saw their problems as interpersonal or personal. As we might expect, those who felt inadequate as marriage partners or as parents were more willing to consider help than those who felt adequate. In general, however, readiness to seek help was less associated with unhappiness than with a self-questioning attitude toward major life roles such as parental, marital, or vocational roles. Women, young people, and more highly educated people were more ready to seek professional help than were men, older people, and those with less education. People with higher educations and those who lived in the city were more likely to define their problems in terms of mental health and were also more likely to seek psychological or psychiatric help for their problems. People with high incomes were not especially likely to see their problems in terms of mental health, but a high income does seem to make it easier for the person to seek professional guidance, once he sees the problem as one that can be alleviated by such means. Similarly, the survey showed that a person's religion was related to his willingness to seek professional guidance. Almost all Catholics who saw a problem as one that could be treated in this way had actually gone to their priest or another professional for help, while only about half the Protestants had. Protestants, however, were much more likely to use prayer as a source of help than were Catholics.

Clergymen were the most frequently consulted sources of help, but mental health agencies or professional psychologists or psychiatrists were consulted by about one-third of those who had used help. Almost as many had consulted a medical doctor (other than a psychiatrist).

These findings have important social implications. For example, it appears that disinclination to seek guidance is not solely a function of lack of resources.

Rather it seems to depend on the way a person sees his problems, and the extent to which he sees professional help as capable of helping him overcome them. Education seems to be an important determiner of these attitudes. Further, the extent to which clergymen and physicians are sought for emotional support and guidance indicates the importance of gaining more understanding of their role as a mental health resource.

Looking at the responses in terms of current views of our society, it appears that Americans are not as materialistic or as luxury-oriented as some writers suggest, but neither are they greatly worried about broader social problems, such as international affairs. Rather their concerns are centered on the immediate environment of themselves and their families. Conflict between family obligations and achievement in work seems to be reflected in many concerns.

Emphasis on the prevention of mental illness is likely to increase in the coming years. Within the next decade we should begin to see many reports on research in mental health or personality during the college years, about adjustment problems in industry, and about the role of other major institutions in mental health. As these reports appear, the reader, remembering our discussion of the value implications of mental health and the criteria of adjustment, will want to be able to discriminate empirical findings from value judgments.

Changing Patterns of Family Organization

Our last major section deals with a situation for which we cannot make confident predictions and in which psychologists are not directly involved. No one knows how it will come out, so that in this section we are simply pointing out a social development which should be interesting to all.

One of the most radical attempts at rapid cultural change ever made was begun under the Chinese Communist government. According to reports appearing in American newspapers and magazines, the Chinese commune attempted to break up completely the traditional Chinese family. When the commune was introduced in China, the government forced grandmothers and grandfathers to live in separate barracks and do such work as they were physically able to do. In the more extreme communes, husband and wife were housed in separate barracks and allowed to be alone together only for a brief period on alternate Saturday nights. Children were cared for in a communal nursery and parents were allowed to visit them only twice a month. According to a Chinese Communist magazine, "All the ties that bind the peasants are broken. . . The frames of individual families, which had existed for thousands of years, have been completely smashed." (*New Republic*, **140**, January 5, 1959, 12–15)

Our first reaction to such a description is likely to be one of incredulity and horror. The commune system seems to us to be working against the fundamental characteristics of human nature. In discussing personality development, we emphasized the importance of close emotional ties with the mother in developing one's need for approval and in developing the superego. If the commune system of child rearing were to be maintained, would such needs disappear among the next generation of Chinese? Reports indicate that the system was not continued, so that we shall never know.

Although we cannot make confident predictions about the success of the commune system in China, we do have observations of cooperative settlements in Israel which can help us to understand the problems faced by the Chinese Communists.

The *kibbutzim** of Israel are cooperative settlements, many of which were founded over a generation ago by immigrants from Eastern Europe. The founders of the kibbutzim were convinced that communal ownership of property fostered brotherhood and freedom. Holding the ideals of freedom and equality, the founders of the kibbutzim were resolved to free women from the domination of the husband and the burdens of domestic work. As a result, women in present-day kibbutzim are not economically dependent on their husbands because the kibbutz supports all its members. Each woman, like each man, works a nine-hour day. Domestic services—meals, laundry, etc.—are provided by the kibbutz. Included in the services provided by the kibbutz is the care and education of children.

When the baby and his mother leave the hospital their paths separate. The mother returns to her home; the baby enters a nursery. The mother comes every day to nurse and play with her baby, but she is not responsible for his care. As the child grows older, he may spend one or two hours with his parents in the evening, but most of his time is spent with the children in the nursery; or, after he is a year old, in the toddlers' house. As the child moves from nursery to toddlers' house to kindergarten, other women take responsibility for his care and education. But he and his kindergarten group of children will remain together until they reach high school.

There is a real difference, however, between the kibbutz system and the Chinese commune system. This is the value placed on child rearing. The kibbutz values children, and real sacrifices are made to be sure that children are well cared for. Kibbutz parents regard their children as the center of the universe. The parent who fails to spend his free time with his children is violating the norms of the kibbutz. Each evening the children become the focus of adult attention, and parents may also visit their children in free moments during the day. In contrast, accounts of the Chinese communes suggest that interaction between parents and children was discouraged or forbidden. Kibbutz parents adopted their system of child rearing as a result of their own belief in it. Chinese parents, on the other hand, apparently had to be forced to adopt the communal system of child rearing. Since we have seen in our study of personality development that parental attitudes may be more important than specific

---

* Based on Spiro, M., *Children of the Kibbutz* (Cambridge, Mass.: Harvard University Press, 1958).

child-rearing practices, we probably cannot generalize directly from the kibbutz to the commune. Nevertheless the two systems do have the following elements in common.

1. Parents are not responsible for discipline and training of their child.
2. The adults who are responsible for care and training of a child are different at different ages.
3. A child spends most of his time with groups of children his own age.

What are the results of kibbutz training?

Some social scientists who have studied the kibbutzim report that adults who have grown up in the kibbutz are characterized by insecurity, introversion, insolence, and hostility toward strangers. However, more carefully controlled comparisons of children reared in kibbutzim with those reared in ordinary Israeli villages show no consistent inferiorities, although there are the expected differences in intensity of the oedipus conflict and in sibling rivalry (Rabin, 1958). Kibbutz-reared adults seem to have thoroughly internalized the values of the kibbutz. They work hard and are able to give and receive love. In short, kibbutz training seems to work.

Could the Chinese commune systems work as well? A significant difference between it and the kibbutz system is that the commune system was established and maintained by coercion. Already there are reports that it has been modified or abandoned. Human nature is so marvelously adaptive that, if the Chinese could have maintained their system for a generation, and if it had proved successful, perhaps parents as well as governments would support the new norms. Students of human behavior would be interested in the results!

Suggested Readings

This appendix was intended to alert you to some interesting problems which are relevant to the background you have acquired in your study of psychology. Because journal articles are current, they are likely to be your best sources of further information; thus you may wish to check *Psychological Abstracts* to find them. Certain topics are of sufficient general interest to be covered also in current magazines and newspapers, and you may find additional references in the *Readers' Guide to Periodical Literature*.

Among the best current books are the following, listed under subject headings.

1. Man–Machine Systems: Automation

MANN, F., and L. R. HOFFMAN, *Automation and the Worker*. New York: Holt, 1960.

CHAPANIS, A., *Man–Machine Engineering*. Belmont, Calif.: Wadsworth, 1965.

2. Teaching Machines

LUMSDAINE, A., A., and R. GLASER (eds.), *Teaching Machines and Programmed Learning.* Washington, D.C.: NEA, 1960.

GLASER, R. (ed.), *Teaching Machines and Programmed Learning II: Data and Directions.* Washington, D.C.: NEA, 1965.

These two books above contain chapters on programming techniques, teaching machines and computerized instructional systems, and program evaluation and programmed instruction developments in mathematics, English, reading, science, and foreign languages.

Contemporary Psychology, a journal of the American Psychological Association, reviews programs and books on programmed learning in its Instructional Media Department.

3. Utilization of Human Resources

WOLFLE, D., *America's Resources of Specialized Talent.* New York: Harper, 1954.

4. Drugs

DE ROPP, R. S., *Drugs and the Mind.* New York: St. Martin's Press, 1957.

LEWIN, L., *Phantasia,* translated by P. H. A. Wirth (second edition). New York: Dutton, 1964. This is a greatly revised classic; a historical and cross-cultural survey of drugs used for psychological effects.

JARVICK, M. E., "Drugs used in the treatment of psychiatric disorders," in L. S. GOODMAN and A. GELTMAN (eds.), *The Pharmacological Basis of Therapeutics,* third edition. New York: Macmillan, 1965.

5. Mental Health

JOINT COMMISSION ON MENTAL ILLNESS AND HEALTH, *Action for Mental Health.* New York: Basic Books, 1961.

6. Family Organization

SPIRO, M., *Children of the Kibbutz.* Cambridge, Mass.: Harvard University Press, 1958.

RABIN, A. I., *Growing up in the Kibbutz.* New York: Springer, 1965.

bibliography and index

bibliography

NOTE: The boldface number in brackets at the end of each reference indicates the chapter to which the cited reference is applicable.

ADOLF, E. F. (1941), "The internal environment and behavior: III. Water content," *Amer. J. Psychiat.*, **97**, 1365–1373. **[7]**

ADOLF, E. F. (1939), "Measurements of water drinking in dogs," *Amer. J. Physiol.*, **125**, 75–86. **[7]**

ADORNO, T. W., E. FRENKEL-BRUNSWIK, D. J. LEVINSON, and R. N. SANFORD (1950), *The Authoritarian Personality.* New York: Harper. **[16]**

AICHORN, A. (1935), *Wayward Youth.* New York: Viking Press. **[14]**

ALEXANDER, F. (1937), *The Medical Value of Psychoanalysis.* New York: Norton. **[14]**

ALLISON, J. (1964), "Preference for food, magnitude of food reward, and performance in instrumental conditioning," *J. comp. physiol Psychol.* **57**, 217–223. **[7]**

ALLPORT, G. W. (1961), *Pattern and Growth in Personality.* New York: Holt, Rinehart, and Winston. **[12]**

ALLPORT, G. W. (1937), *Personality: a Psychological Interpretation.* New York: Holt. **[7]**

ALLPORT, G. W., and H. CANTRIL (1934), "Judging personality from voice." *J. soc. Psychol.*, **5**, 37–55. **[15]**

ALLPORT, G. W., and H. S. ODBERT (1936), "Trait-names: a psycho-lexical study," *Psychol. Monogr.*, **47**, Whole No. 211. **[12]**

ALLPORT, G. W., P. E. VERNON, and G. LINDZEY (1960), *A Study of Values,* third edition. Boston: Houghton Mifflin. **[7]**

ALLYN, J., and L. FESTINGER (1961), "The effectiveness of unanticipated persuasive communications," *J. abnorm. soc. Psychol.*, **65**, 35–40. **[16]**

AMERICAN PSYCHIATRIC ASSOCIATION, COMMITTEE ON NOMENCLATURE AND STATISTICS (1952), *Diagnostic and Statistical Manual: Mental Disorders.* Washington: American Psychiatric Association. **[14]**

AMSEL, A. (1958), "The role of frustrative nonreward in noncontinuous reward situations," *Psychol. Bull.*, **55**, 102–119. **[5]**

ANDERSON, J. E. (1939), "The development of social behavior," *Amer. J. Sociol.*, **44**, 839–857. **[13]**

ANDERSSON, B. (1953), "The effect of injections of hypertonic NaCl solutions into different parts of the hypothalamus of goats," *Acta Physiol. Scand.*, **28**, 188–201. **[7]**

ANREP, G. V. (1920), "Pitch discrimination in the dog," *J. Physiol.*, **53**, 367–385. **[5]**

ARING, C. D. (1957), "Senility," *AMA Archives of Internal Medicine*, **100**, 519–528. **[10]**

ARONFREED, J. (1961), "The nature, variety, and social patterning of moral responses to transgression," *J. abnorm. soc. Psychol.*, **63**, 223–240. **[13]**

Asch, S. E. (1951), "Effects of group pressure upon modification and distortion of judgment," in H. Guetzkow (ed.) *Groups, Leadership, and Men.* Pittsburgh: Carnegie Press. [16]

Asch, S. E. (1946), "Forming impressions of personality," *J. abnorm. soc. Psychol.,* **41,** 258–290. [15]

Atkinson, J. W. (1957), "The motivational determinants of risk-taking behavior," *Psychol. Rev.,* **64,** 359–372. [7]

Atkinson, J. W., and G. H. Litwin (1960), "Achievement motive and test anxiety conceived as motive to approach success and motive to avoid failure," *J. abnorm. soc. Psychol.,* **60,** 52–63. [13]

Axelrod, H. S., E. L. Cowen, and F. Heilizer (1956), "The correlates of manifest anxiety in stylus maze learning," *J. exp. Psychol.,* **51,** 131–138. [1]

Axelrod, M. (1956), "Urban structure and social participation," *Amer. Sociol. Rev.,* **21,** 13–18. [15]

Azrin, N. H. (1960), "Effects of punishment intensity during variable-interval reinforcement," *J. exp. Anal. Behav.,* **3,** 123–142. [5]

Azrin, N. H. (1959), "Punishment and recovery during fixed-ratio performance," *J. exp. Anal. Behav.,* **2,** 301–305. [5]

Back, K. W. (1951), "Influence through social communication," *J. abnorm. soc. Psychol.,* **46,** 9–23. [16]

Bakan, D. (1949), "The relationship between alcoholism and birth rank," *Quart. J. Stud. Alc.,* **10,** 434–440. [7]

Baldwin, A. L. (1945), "The effect of home environment on nursery school behavior," *Psychol. Monogr.,* **58,** Whole No. 268. [6]

Bales, R. F. (1958), "Task roles and social roles in problem-solving groups," in E. E. Maccoby, J. M. Newcomb, and E. L. Hartley (eds.), *Readings in Social Psychology,* third edition. New York: Holt. [15]

Bales, R. F. (1952), "Some uniformities of behavior in small social systems," in G. E. Swanson, T. M. Newcomb, and E. L. Hartley (eds.) *Readings in Social Psychology,* second edition. New York: Holt. [15]

Bales, R. F. (1950), *Interaction Process Analysis: A Method for the Study of Small Groups.* Reading, Mass.: Addison-Wesley. [15]

Bandura, A. (1962), "Social learning through imitation," in M. R. Jones, (ed.), *Nebraska Symposium on Motivation, 1962.* Lincoln: University of Nebraska Press, 211–269. [13]

Bandura, A. (1960), "Relationship of family patterns to child behavior disorders," *Progress Report, USPHS Project No. M-1734.* Palo Alto: Stanford University. [13]

Bandura, A., D. Ross, and S. A. Ross (1963a), "Imitation of film-mediated aggressive models," *J. abnorm. soc. Psychol.,* **66,** 3–11. [13]

BANDURA, A., D. Ross, and S. A. Ross (1963b). "A comparative test of the status envy, social power, and secondary reinforcement theories of identificatory learning," *J. abnorm. soc. Psychol.*, **67**, 527–534.   **[13]**

BANDURA, A., and R. H. WALTERS (1963), *Social Learning and Personality Development.* New York: Holt, Rinehart, and Winston.   **[14]**

BANDURA, A., and R. H. WALTERS (1959), *Adolescent Agression.* New York: Ronald.   **[14]**

BARBER, T. X. (1961), "Death by suggestion," *Psychosomatic Medicine*, **23**, 153–154.   **[2]**

BARKER, R. G., T. DEMBO, and K. LEWIN (1941), "Frustration and regression: an experiment with young children," *Univ. Iowa Studies in Child Welfare*, **18**, No. 386.   **[11]**

BARRON, F. (1958), "The psychology of imagination," *Sci. Amer.*, **199**, 151–166.   **[10]**

BARRON, F. (1957), "Originality in relation to personality and intellect," *J. Pers.*, **25**, 730–742.   **[9]**

BARTLETT, F. C. (1932), *Remembering: A Study in Experimental and Social Psychology.* London: Cambridge University Press.   **[9]**

BAYLEY, N. (1955), "On the growth of intelligence," *Amer. Psychologist*, **10**, 805–818.   **[10]**

BEACH, F. A., and J. JAYNES (1954), "Effects of early experience upon the behavior of animals," *Psychol. Bull.*, **51**, 239–263.   **[13]**

BECK, E. C., and R. W. DOTY (1957), "Conditioned flexion reflexes acquired during combined catalepsy and de efferentation," *J. comp. physiol. Psychol.*, **50**, 211–216.   **[5]**

BECKER, W. C. (1964), "Consequences of different kinds of parental discipline," in M. L. HOFFMAN and L. W. HOFFMAN (eds.), *Review of Child Development Research, Vol. 1.* New York: Russell Sage Foundation, 169–208.   **[13]**

BECKER, W. C., D. R. Peterson, Z. Luria, D. S. SHOEMAKER and L. A. HELMER (1962), "Relations of factors derived from parent interview ratings to behavior problems of five-year-olds," *Child Develpm.*, **33**, 509–535.   **[13]**

BELOFF, H. (1958), "Two forms of social conformity: acquiescence and conventionality," *J. abnorm. soc. Psychol.*, **56**, 99–104.   **[12]**

BENNETT, C. H. (1960), "Drugs and I," in L. UHR and J. G. MILLER (eds.) *Drugs and Behavior.* New York: Wiley.   **[14]**

BENNETT, E. B. (1955), "Discussion, decision, and consensus in 'group decision,'" *Hum. Relat.*, **8**, 251–273.   **[16]**

BERKO, J. (1958), "The child's learning of English morphology," *Word*, **14**, 150–177.   **[9]**

BERKOWITZ, L. (1956), "Personality and group position," *Sociometry*, **19**, 210–222.   **[15]**

BERLYNE, D. E. (1960), *Conflict, Arousal, and Curiosity.* New York: McGraw-Hill,   **[7]**

BERYLNE, D. E. (1958), "The influence of the albedo and complexity of stimuli on visual fixation in the human infant," *Brit. J. Psychol.*, 49, 315–318.   [6]

BETTELHEIM, B. (1947), "Individual and mass behavior in extreme situations," in J. M. NEWCOMB, E. L. HARTLEY (1943), *et al.* (eds.), *Readings in Social Psychology.* New York: Holt, 628–638. (Prepared from material fully reported in *J. abnorm. soc. Psychol.*, 1943, 38, 417–452.)   [11]

BIRCH, H. G., and H. S. RABINOWITZ (1951), "The negative effect of previous experience on productive thinking," *J. exp. Psychol.*, 41, 121–125.   [10]

BLADE, M. F., and W. S. WATSON (1955), "Increase in spatial visualization test scores during engineering study," *Psychol. Monogr.*, 69, Whole No. 397.   [6]

BLODGETT, H. C. (1929), "The effect of the introduction of reward upon the maze performance of rats," *University of California Publications in Psychology*, 4, No. 8, 113–134.   [5]

BLOOD, R. O., and D. M. WOLFE (1960), *Husbands and Wives: The Dynamics of Married Living.* Glencoe, Ill.: The Free Press.   [13]

BLUM, G. S. (1966), *Psychodynamics: The Science of Unconscious Mental Forces.* Belmont, Calif.: Wadsworth.   [11]

BLUM, G. S. (1954), "An experimental reunion of psychoanalytic theory with perceptual vigilance and defense," *J. abnorm. soc. Psychol.*, 49, 94–98.   [6]

BOAS, F. (ed.) (1938), *General Anthropology.* Boston: Heath.   [5, 8]

BORING, E. G., L. S. LANGFELD, and H. P. WELD (1948), *Foundations of Psychology.* New York: Wiley.   [6]

BOUSFIELD, W. A. (1953), "The occurrence of clustering in the recall of randomly arranged associates," *J. gen. Psychol.*, 49, 229–234.   [9]

BOVARD, E. W., JR. (1951), "The experimental production of interpersonal affect," *J. abnorm. soc. Psychol.*, 46, 521–528.   [15]

BRADY, J. V. (1958), "Ulcers in 'executive' monkeys," *Sci. Amer.*, 199, 4, 95–100.   [14]

BRAY, C. W. (1948), *Psychology and Military Proficiency.* Princeton: Princeton University Press.   [8]

BRAYFIELD, A. H., and W. H. CROCKETT (1955), "Employee attitudes and employee performance," *Psychol. Bull.*, 52, 396–424.   [13]

BRIDGES, K. M. B. (1932), "Emotional development in early infancy," *Child Develpm.*, 3, 324–341.   [7]

BROADHURST, P. L. (1957), "Emotionality and the Yerkes-Dodson law," *J. exp. Psychol.*, 54, 345–352.   [7]

BROGDEN, W. J. (1939), "Sensory preconditioning," *J. exp. Psychol.*, 25, 323–332.   [5]

BROGDEN, W. J., A. E. LIPMAN, and E. CULLER (1938), "The role of incentive in conditioning and extinction," *Amer. J. Psychol.*, 51, 109–117.   [5]

BRONFENBRENNER, U. (in press), "Early deprivation in mammals and man," in G. NEWTON (ed.), *Early Experience and Behavior.* Springfield, Ill.: C. C. Thomas.   [13]

BRONFENBRENNER, U., J. HARDING, and M. GALLWEY (1958), "The measurement of skill in social perception," in D. C. McCLELLAND *et al.* (eds.), *Talent and Society*. Princeton, N. J.: Van Nostrand. **[15]**

BROWN, J. S. (1948), "Gradients of approach and avoidance responses and their relation to motivation," *J. comp. physiol. Psychol.*, **41**, 450–465. **[7]**

BROWN, R. W. (1965), *Social Psychology*. New York: Free Press. **[10]**

BROWN, R. W. (1958), *Words and Things*. Glencoe, Ill.: Free Press. **[8]**

BRUNER, J. S., L. POSTMAN, and J. RODRIGUES (1951), "Expectation and the perception of color," *Amer. J. Psychol.*, **64**, 216–227. **[6]**

BUGELSKI, R. (1938), "Extinction with and without subgoal reinforcement," *J. comp. Psychol.*, **26**, 121–134. **[5]**

BURGESS, E. W., and P. WALLEN (1953), *Engagement and Marriage*. New York: Lippincott. **[13]**

BURGESS, E. W., and P. WALLEN (1944), "Homogamy in personality characteristics," *J. abnorm. soc. Psychol.*, **39**, 475–481. **[13]**

BURKS, B. S., and A. ROE (1949), "Studies of identical twins reared apart," *Psychol. Monogr.*, **63**, 5, Whole No. 300. **[14]**

BURTON, R. V. (1963), "Generality of honesty reconsidered," *Psychol. Rev.*, **70**, 448–499. **[12]**

BURTON, R. V., E. E. MACCOBY, and W. ALLINSMITH (1961), "Antecedents of resistance to temptation in four-year-old children," *Child Develpm.*, **32**, 689–710. **[13]**

BURTT, H. E. (1941), "An experimental study of early childhood memory: final report," *J. genet. Psychol.*, **58**, 435–439. **[9]**

BUTLER, R. A. (1953), "Discrimination learning by rhesus monkeys to visual exploration motivation," *J. comp. physiol. Psychol.*, **46**, 45–98. **[7]**

CAHILL, H. E., and C. I. HOVLAND (1960), "The role of memory in the acquisition of concepts," *J. exp. Psychol.*, **59**, 137–144. **[9]**

CALDWELL, B. M. (1964), "The effects of infant care," in M. L. HOFFMAN and L. W. HOFFMAN (eds.), *Review of Child Development Research*, Vol. 1. New York: Russell Sage Foundation, 9–87. **[13]**

CAMERON, N. (1963), *Personality Development and Psychopathology*. Boston: Houghton Mifflin. **[14]**

CAMPBELL, A., P. E. CONVERSE, W. E. MILLER, and D. E. STOKES (1961), "Stability and change in 1960: a reinstating election," *Amer. Polit. Sci. Rev.*, **55**, 269–280. **[1]**

CAMPBELL, A., P. E. CONVERSE, W. E. MILLER, and D. E. STOKES (1960), *The American Voter*. New York: Wiley. **[1]**

CAMPBELL, A., G. GURIN, and W. E. MILLER (1954), *The Voter Decides*. Evanston, Ill.: Row Peterson. **[1]**

CAMPBELL, D. T. (1963), "Acquired behavioral dispositions," in S. KOCH (ed.), *Psychology, the Study of a Science.* New York: McGraw-Hill. **[16]**

CAMPBELL, D. T. (1947), "The generality of a social attitude," unpublished doctoral dissertation, University of California, Berkeley. **[16]**

CANNON, W. B. (1942), "Voodoo death," *Amer. Anthrop.,* **44,** 2. **[2]**

CAREY, G. L. (1958), "Sex differences in problem-solving performance as a function of attitude differences," *J. abnorm. soc. Psychol.,* **56,** 256–260. **[10]**

CARLSON, E. R. (1956), "Attitude change through modification of attitude structure," *J. abnorm. soc. Psychol.,* **52,** 256–261. **[16]**

CARRIGAN, P. M. (1960), "Extroversion-introversion as a dimension of personality: a reappraisal," *Psychol. Bull.,* **57,** 329–360. **[12]**

CARTER, L. F. (1953), "Leadership and small group behavior," in M. SHERIF and M. O. WILSON, *Group Relations at the Crossroads.* New York: Harpers. **[15]**

CARTWRIGHT, D. and A. ZANDER (1960), "Group cohesiveness: introduction," in D. CARTWRIGHT and A. ZANDER (eds.), *Group Dynamics Research and Theory.* Evanston, Ill.: Row Peterson. **[15]**

CASLER, L. (1965), "The effects of extra-tactile stimulation on a group of institutionalized infants," *Genet. Psychol. Monogr.,* **71,** 137–175. **[13]**

CATTELL, R. B. (1965), *The Scientific Analysis of Personality.* Baltimore: Penquin. **[12]**

CATTELL, R. B. (1957), *Personality and Motivation Structure and Measurement.* Yonkers-on-Hudson, New York: World Book Co. **[1, 4, 12]**

CATTELL, R. B. (1955), "The principal replicated factors discovered in objective personality tests," *J. abnorm. soc. Psychol.,* **50,** 291–314. **[12]**

CATTELL, R. B., D. R. SAUNDERS, and G. STICE (1950), *The Sixteen Personality Factor Test.* Champaign, Ill.: Institute for Personality and Ability Testing. **[12]**

CATTELL, R. B., D. B. BLEWETT, and J. R. BELOFF (1955), "The inheritance of personality: a multiple variance analysis determination of approximate nature-nurture ratios for primary personality factors in Q-data," *Amer. J. hum. Genet.,* **7,** 122–146. **[14]**

CAVAN, R. S. (1962), *Juvenile Delinquency.* Philadelphia: Lippincott. **[14]**

CHAPMAN, R. L., J. L. KENNEDY, A. NEWELL, and W. C. BIEL (1959), "The systems research laboratory's air defense experiments," *Management Science,* **5,** 3. **[11]**

CHILD, I. L. (1943), *Italian or American.* New Haven: Yale University Press. **[2]**

CLARK, R. A., and M. R. SENSIBAR (1956), "The relationships between symbolic and manifest projections with some incidental correlates," *J. abnorm. soc. Psychol.,* **50,** 327–334. **[11]**

CLARKE, R. S., W. HERON, M. G. FETHERSTONHAUGH, D. G. FORGAYS, and D. O. HEBB (1951), "Individual differences in dogs: preliminary report on the effects of early experience," *Canad. J. Psychol.,* **5,** 150–156. **[13]**

COCH, L., and J. R. P. FRENCH (1958), "Overcoming resistance to change," in E. E. MACCOBY, T. M. NEWCOMB, and E. L. HARTLEY (eds.), *Readings in Social Psychology.* New York: Holt, Rinehart and Winston, 233–250. **[15]**

COFFMAN, W. E. (1961), "Sex differences in responses to items in an aptitude test," *Research Memo, Educational Testing Service*, No. 4. **[9]**

COHEN, J., and C. E. M. HANSEL (1958), "The nature of decisions in gambling," *Acta psychol.*, **13**, 357–370. **[10]**

COLEMAN, J. C. (1963), *Abnormal Psychology and Modern Life*, third edition. Chicago: Scott, Foresman. **[14]**

COLEMAN, J. C. (1956), *Abnormal Psychology and Modern Life*. Chicago: Scott, Foresman. [14]

CONRAD, H. S. (1932), "The validity of personality ratings of preschool children," *J. educ. Psychol.*, **23**, 671–680. **[12]**

COOMBS, C. H. (1941), "A factorial study of number ability," *Psychometrica*, **6**, 161–189. **[10]**

COOMBS, C., and D. G. PRUITT (1960), "Components of risk in decision making: probability and variance preferences," *J. exp. Psychol.*, **60**, 265–277. **[10]**

COOVER, J. E. (1917), *Experiments in Psychical Research at Leland Stanford Junior University*. Stanford: Stanford University Press. **[6]**

CRONBACH, L. J. (1960), *Essentials of Psychological Testing*, second edition. New York: Harper and Row. **[12]**

CRONBACH, L. J., and N. L. GAGE (1955), "Conceptual and methodological problems in interpersonal perception," *Psychol. Rev.*, **62**, 411–422. **[15]**

CROSSMAN, E. R. F. W. (1959), "A theory of the acquisition of speed-skill," *Ergonomics*, **2**, 153–166. **[8]**

CROW, W. J. (1957), "The effect of training upon accuracy and variability in interpersonal perception," *J. abnorm. soc. Psychol.*, **55**, 355–359. **[15]**

CRUTCHFIELD, R. S. (1955), "Conformity and character," *Amer. Psychologist*, **10**, 191–198. **[16]**

CRUZ, W. W. (1935), "Maturation and learning in chicks," *J. comp. Psychol.*, **19**, 371–401. **[8]**

DAILEY, C. A. (1951), "Some factors influencing the accuracy of understanding personality," unpublished doctoral dissertation, University of Michigan. **[15]**

D'AMATO, M. R., and W. E. GUMENIK (1960), "Some effects of immediate versus randomly delayed shock on instrumental responses and cognitive processes," *J. abnorm. soc. Psychol.*, **60**, 64–67. **[7]**

DARLEY, J., N. GROSS, and W. MARTIN (1952), "Studies of group behavioral factors associated with the productivity of groups," *J. appl. Psychol.*, **36**, 396–403. **[15]**

DAWES, R. (1963), "Illogical reasoning and related thinking distortion," unpublished doctoral dissertation, University of Michigan. **[10]**

DEESE, J., (1964), "Behavioral effects of the instruction to learn," in A. MELTON (ed.), *Categories of Human Learning*. New York: Academic Press. **[9]**

DELGADO, J. M. R., W. W. ROBERTS, and N. E. MILLER (1954), "Learning motivated by electrical stimulation of the brain," *Amer. J. Physiol.*, **179**, 587–593. **[7]**

DEMBER, W. N., R. W. EARL, and N. PARADISE (1957), "Response by rats to differential stimulus complexity," *J. comp. physiol. Psychol.*, **50**, 514–518. **[7]**

DENNIS, W. (1940), "The effect of cradling practices upon the onset of walking in Hopi children," *J. genet. Psychol.*, **56**, 77–86. **[4]**

DEUTSCH, M., and M. E. COLLINS (1951), *Interracial Housing: A Psychological Evaluation of a Social Experiment.* Minneapolis: University of Minnesota Press. **[16]**

DEVALOIS, R. L., C. J. SMITH, and S. T. KITAI (1959), "Electrical responses of primate visual system: II. Recordings from single on-cells of Macaque lateral geniculate nucleus," *J. comp. physiol. Psychol.*, **52**, 635–641. **[6]**

DIMOCK, H. S. (1937), *Rediscovering the Adolescent.* New York: Association Press. **[15]**

DOLLARD, J., L. W. DOOB, N. E. MILLER, O. H. MOWRER, and R. R. SEARS (1939), *Frustration and Aggression.* New Haven: Yale University Press. **[7, 13]**

DVORAK, A., N. MERRICK, W. DEALEY, and G. FORD (1936), *Typewriting Behavior.* New York: American Book. **[8]**

DYMOND, R. F. (1950), "Personality and empathy," *J. consult. Psychol.*, **14**, 343–350. **[15]**

EBBINGHAUS, H. (1913), *Memory: A Contribution to Experimental Psychology*, Trans. by H. A. RUGER, and C. E. BUSSINIUS. New York: Teachers College, Columbia University Press. **[8]**

EDWARDS, A. L., *Edwards Personal Preference Schedule.* New York: Psychological Corporation, 1953–59. **[12]**

EFRON, D. (1941), *Gesture and Environment.* New York: King's Crown Press. **[2]**

ELLSON, D. G. (1941), "Hallucinations produced by sensory conditioning," *J. exp. Psychol.*, **28**, 1–20. **[6]**

EPSTEIN, A. N., and P. TEITELBAUM (1962), "Regulation of food intake in the absence of taste, smell, and other oropharyngeal sensations," *J. comp. physiol. Psychol.*, **55**, 155. **[7]**

ERIKSON, E. H. (1963), *Childhood and Society.* New York: Norton. **[13]**

ERON, L. D., T. J. BANTA, L. O. WALDER, and J. H. LAULICHT (1961), "Comparison of data from mothers and fathers on child-rearing practices and their relation to child aggression," *Child Develpm.*, **32**, 457–572. **[13]**

ESCALONA, S. K. (1945), "Feeding disturbances in very young children," *Amer. J. Orthopsychiat.*, **15**, 76–80. **[3]**

ESTES, W. K. (1944), "An experimental study of punishment." *Psychol. Monogr.*, **57**, Whole No. 263. **[5]**

EYSENCK, H. J. (1961), *Handbook of Abnormal Psychology.* New York: Basic Books **[14]**

EYSENCK, H. J. (1952), *The Scientific Study of Personality.* London: Routledge and Kegan Paul. **[4, 12]**

EYSENCK, H. J., and D. B. PRELL (1951), "The inheritance of neuroticism: an experimental study," *J. Ment. Sci.,* **97,** 441–465. **[14]**

FANTZ, R. L. (1961), "The origin of form perception," *Sci. Amer.,* May. **[7]**

FANTZ, R. L. (1958a), "Pattern vision in young infants," *Psychol. Rec.,* **8,** 43–48. **[6]**

FANTZ, R. L. (1958b), "Visual discrimination in a neonate chimpanzee," *Percept. mot. skills,* **8,** 59–66. **[6]**

FELEKY, A. (1922), *Feelings and Emotions.* New York: Pioneer Press. **[7]**

FENICHEL, O. (1945), *The Psychoanalytic Theory of Neurosis.* New York: Norton. **[14]**

FERRIER, D. (1886), *The Functions of the Brain.* New York: Putnam's Sons. **[3]**

FESHBACH, S., and R. D. SINGER (1957), "The effects of fear arousal and suppression of fear upon social perception," *J. abnorm. soc. Psychol.,* **55,** 283–288. **[15]**

FESTINGER, L. (1957), *A Theory of Cognitive Dissonance.* Evanston, Ill.: Row Peterson. **[7, 16]**

FESTINGER, L., K. BACK, S. SCHACTER, H. H. KELLEY, and J. THIBAUT (1950), *Theory and Experiment in Social Communication.* Ann Arbor: Institute for Social Research. **[15]**

FESTINGER, L., and J. M. CARLSMITH (1959), "Cognitive consequences of forced compliance," *J. abnorm. soc. Psychol.,* **58,** 203–210. **[16]**

FESTINGER, L., S. SCHACTER, and K. BACK (1950), *Social Pressures in Informal Groups.* New York: Harper. **[15]**

FIEDLER, F. E. (1954), *The Influence of Leader-Keyman Relations on Combat Crew Effectiveness.* Urbana, Ill.: Group Effectiveness Research Laboratory, University of Illinois. **[15]**

FITTS, P. M. (1964), "Skill learning," in A. W. MELTON (ed.), *Categories of Human Learning.* New York: Academic Press. **[8]**

FITTS, P. M., and J. R. PETERSON (1964), "Information capacity of a discrete motor response," *J. exp. Psychol.,* **67,** 103–126. **[8]**

FITTS, P. M., and C. M. SEEGER (1953), "S-R compatibility: spatial characteristics of stimulus and response codes," *J. exp. Psychol.,* **46,** 199–210. **[8]**

FLAVELL, J. H. (1963), *The Developmental Psychology of Jean Piaget.* Princeton, N.J.: Van Nostrand. **[9, 10]**

FREEDMAN, R. (1952), "Who belongs to what in a great metropolis?" *Adult Leadership,* November. **[15]**

FREEMAN, F. S. (1962), *Theory and Practice of Psychological Testing,* third edition. New York: Holt, Rinehart, and Winston. **[10]**

FRENCH, E. G. (1956), "Motivation as a variable in work-partner selection," *J. abnorm. soc. Psychol.* **52**, 296–300; **53**, 96–99. **[15]**

FRENCH, R. L. (1951), "Sociometric status and individual adjustment among naval recruits," *J. abnorm. soc. Psychol.*, **46**, 64–71. **[15]**

FRENKEL-BRUNSWICK, E. (1949), "Intolerance of ambiguity as an emotional and perceptual personality variable," *J. Pers.*, **18**, 108–143. **[6]**

FRENKEL-BRUNSWICK, E., and R. N. SANFORD (1945), "Some personality factors in anti-Semitism," *J. Psychol.* **20**, 271–291. **[16]**

FREUD, A. (1937), *The Ego and Mechanisms of Defense.* London: Hogarth. **[11]**

FREUD, S. (1953–7), *The Standard Edition of the Complete Psychological Works*, translated by J. STRACHEY. London: Hogarth. **[1, 9, 11, 12, 13, 14]**

FUNKENSTEIN, D. H. (1955), "The physiology of fear and anger," *Sci. Amer.*, **192**, 5, 74–80. **[5]**

GAGNÉ, R. M. (1964), "Problem solving," in A. W. MELTON (ed.), *Categories of Human Learning.* New York: Academic Press. **[10]**

GAGNÉ, R. M., and E. FLEISHMAN (1959), *Psychology and Human Performance.* New York: Holt, Rinehart, and Winston. **[15]**

GATES, A. I., and G. A. TAYLOR (1925), "An experimental study of the nature of improvement resulting from practice in a mental function," *J. educ. Psychol.*, **16**, 583–592. **[9]**

GELLERMAN, L. W. (1933), "Form discrimination in chimpanzees and two-year-old children," *J. Genet. Psychol.*, **42**, 3–27. **[5]**

GERARD, H. B. (1954), "The anchorage of opinions in face-to-face groups," *Hum. Relat.*, **7**, 313–325. **[15]**

GESELL, A. (1940), *The First Five Years of Life.* New York: Harper. **[6]**

GESELL, A., and H. THOMPSON (1929), "Learning and growth in identical infant twins: an experimental study by the method of co-twin control," *Genet. Psychol. Monogr.*, **6**, 1–24. **[3, 4]**

GIBB, C. A. (1949), "The emergence of leadership in small temporary groups of men," unpublished doctoral dissertation, University of Illinois. **[15]**

GIBSON, E. J., and R. D. WALK (1960), "The 'visual cliff,'" *Sci. Amer.*, April. **[6]**

GIBSON, J. J. (1950), *The Perception of the Visual World.* Boston: Houghton Mifflin. **[6]**

GIBSON, J. J. (1929), "The reproduction of visually perceived forms," *J. exp. Psychol.*, **12**, 1–39. **[9]**

GILBERT, G. M. (1951), "Stereotype persistence and change among college students," *J. abnorm. soc. Psychol.*, **46**, 245–254. **[15]**

GIRDEN, E. (1962), "A review of psychokinesis," *Psychol. Bull.*, **59**, 353–388. **[6]**

GOLDSCHMIDT, W., *The Ways of Mankind.* On records, available from the Center for the Liberal Education of Adults, Chicago, Illinois. **[9]**

GOLDSTEIN, K. (1939), *The Organism.* New York: American Book. **[10]**

GOODENOUGH, F. L. (1932), "Expression of emotions in a blind-deaf child," *J. abnorm. soc. Psychol.*, **27**, 328–333. **[7]**

GOODENOUGH, F. L. (1931), *Anger in Young Children. Univ. Minn. Inst. Child Welf. Ser.*, No. 9. **[11]**

GOODNOW, J. J. (1963), "A test of some milieu effects with some of Piaget's tasks," *Air Force Contract AF 49(638)682*, 1963; cited by R. G. BROWN, *Social Psychology*, New York: Fress Press, 1965. **[10]**

GOODWIN, W. R. (1957), *Psychology in Action: the System Development Corporation and System Training.* Santa Monica, Calif.: System Development Corporation. **[II]**

GOTTESMAN, I. I. (1963), "Hereditability of personality, a demonstration," *Psychol. Monogr.*, **77**, 9, Whole no. 572. **[4]**

GRANIT, R. (1955), *Receptors and Sensory Perception.* New Haven: Yale University Press. **[6]**

GREENSPOON, J. (1955), "The reinforcing effect of two spoken sounds on the frequency of two responses," *Amer. J. Psychol.*, **68**, 409–416. **[8]**

GRINKER, R. R., and J. P. SPIEGEL (1945a), *Men Under Stress.* Philadelphia: Blakiston. **[14]**

GRINKER, R. R., and J. P. SPIEGEL (1945b), *War Neurosis.* Philadelphia: Blakiston. **[11]**

GUETZKOW, H. S., and P. H. BOWMAN (1946), *Men and Hunger.* Elgin, Ill.: Brethren. **[11]**

GUETZKOW, H., and W. R. DILL (1957), "Factors in the organizational development of task-oriented groups," *Sociometry*, **20**, 175–204. **[15]**

GUETZKOW, H., and H. A. SIMON (1955), "The impact of certain communication nets upon organization and performance in task-oriented groups," *Mgmt. Sci.*, **1**, 233–250. **[15]**

GUILFORD, J. P. (1959a), *Personality.* New York: McGraw-Hill. **[12]**

GUILFORD, J. P. (1959b), "Three faces of intellect," *Amer. Psychologist*, **14**, 469–479. **[10]**

GUILFORD, J. P., and R. B. GUILFORD (1934), "An analysis of the factors in a typical test of introversion-extroversion," *J. abnorm. soc. Psychol.*, **28**, 377–399. **[12]**

GUILFORD, J., R. WILSON, P. CHRISTIANSEN, and D. LEWIS (1951), "A factor-analysis study of creative thinking," *Rep. Psychol. Lab. Univ. Southern Calif.*, No. 3. **[9]**

GURIN, G., J. VEROFF, and S. FELD (1960), *Americans View Their Mental Health.* New York: Basic Books. **[2, II]**

GUTHRIE, E. R. (1952), *The Psychology of Learning*, revised edition. New York: Harper. **[5]**

GUTHRIE, E. R. (1935), *The Psychology of Learning.* New York: Harper. **[5]**

GUTHRIE, E. R., and A. L. EDWARDS (1949), *Psychology: A First Course in Human Behavior.* New York: Harper. **[7]**

GUTTMAN, L. (1950), "The basis for scalogram analysis," in S. A. STOUFFER *et al., Measurement and Prediction.* Princeton: Princeton University Press. **[16]**

GUTTMAN, N. (1954), "Equal reinforcement values for sucrose and glucose solutions compared with equal-sweetness values," *J. comp. Psychol.,* **47,** 358–361. **[7]**

GUTTMAN, N., and H. KALISH (1956), "Discriminability and stimulus generalization," *J. exp. Psychol.,* **51,** 79–88. **[5]**

HAIRE, M., and W. F. GRUNES (1950), "Perceptual defenses: processes protecting an original perception of another personality," *Hum. Relat.,* **3,** 403–412. **[15]**

HALPIN, A. W., and B. J. WINER (1957), "A factorial study of leader behavior descriptions," in B. M. STOGDILL and A. E. COONS (eds.), *Leader Behavior: Its Description and Measurement.* Columbus, Ohio: *Bur. Bus. Res. Monogr.,* Ohio State University. **[15]**

HALSTEAD, W. C. (1947), *Brain and Intelligence.* Chicago: University of Chicago Press. **[10]**

HALVERSON, H. M. (1931), "An experimental study of prehension in infants by means of systematic cinema records," *Genet. Psychol. Monogr.,* **10,** 107–285. **[4]**

HARLOW, H. F. (1962), "The heterosexual affectional system in monkeys," *Amer. Psychologist,* **16,** 1–9. **[7, 13]**

HARLOW, H. F. (1958), "The nature of love," *Amer. Psychologist,* **13,** 673–685. **[6]**

HARLOW, H. F., M. K. HARLOW, and D. R. MEYER (1950), "Learning motivated by a manipulation drive," *J. exp. Psychol.,* **40,** 228–234. **[7]**

HARLOW, H. F., and R. R. ZIMMERMAN (1959), "Affectional responses in the infant monkey," *Science,* **130,** 421–32. **[7]**

HARTSHORNE, H., M. A. MAY, J. B. MALLER, and F. K. SHUTTLEWORTH (1928–1930), *Studies in the Nature of Character,* 3 vols. New York: Macmillan. **[12]**

HATHAWAY, S. R., and E. D. MONCHESI (1951), "The prediction of juvenile delinquency using the MMPI," *Amer. J. Psychiat.,* **108,** 469–473. **[12]**

HAYES, CATHY (1951), *The Ape in Our House.* New York: Harper. **[4]**

HEBB, D. O. (1961), "Distinctive features of learning in the higher animal," in J. F. DELAFRESNAYE (ed.), *Brain Mechanisms and Learning.* Oxford: Blackwell. **[9]**

HEBB, D. O. (1955), "Drives and the CNS (conceptual nervous system)," *Psychol. Rev.,* **62,** 243–254. **[7]**

HEBB, D. O. (1949), *The Organization of Behavior.* New York: Wiley. **[3, 6, 7]**

HEIDBREDER, E. (1947), "The attainment of concepts: III. The process," *J. genet. Psychol.,* **24,** 93–138. **[9]**

HEIDBREDER, E. (1946), "The attainment of concepts: II. The problem," *J. genet. Psychol.,* **35,** 191–223. **[9]**

HEINSTEIN, J. I. (1963), "Behavioral correlates of breast-bottle regimes under varying parent-infant relationships," *Monogr. Soc. Res. Child Develpm.*, **28**, 4, 1–61. [13]

HERON, W. T. (1957), "The pathology of boredom," *Sci. Amer.*, **196**, 1, 52–56. [7]

HERON, W. T. (1942), "Complex learning process," in F. A. Moss (ed.), *Comparative Psychology*. New York: Prentice-Hall. [5]

HESS, E. H. (1959), "Imprinting," *Science*, **130**, 133–141. [4]

HESS, W. R. (1957), *The Functional Organization of the Diencephalon*, translation of J. R. HUGHES, *Das Zwischenhirn*. New York: Gruen and Stratton. [3]

HEWITT, L. E., and R. L. JENKINS (1946), *Fundamental Patterns of Maladjustment: the Dynamics of Their Origin*. Springfield, Ill.: State Printer. [14]

HICK, W. E. (1952), "On the rate of gain of information," *Quart. J. Psychol.*, **4**, 11–26. [8]

HIPPOCRATES (1886), "On the sacred disease," in F. ADAMS (trans.), *The Genuine Works of Hippocrates*. New York: Wood. Cited by S. S. KETY, "A biologist examines the mind and behavior," *Science*, 1960, **132**, 1861–1870. [3]

HNATIOW, M., and P. LANG (1965), "Learned stabilization of cardiac rate," *Psychophysiology*, **1**, 330–336. [8]

HOLLANDER, E. P. (1956), "Intepersonal exposure time as a determinant of the predictive validity of peer ratings," *Psychol. Rep.*, **2**, 445–448. [15]

HOLLANDER, E. P., and W. B. WEBB (1955), "Leadership, fellowship, and friendship; an analysis of peer nominations," *J. abnorm. soc. Psychol.*, **50**, 163–167. [15]

HOLLINGSHEAD, A. B. (1958), *Social Class and Mental Illness, a Community Study*. New York: Wiley. [14]

HOLLINGSHEAD, A. B. (1949), *Elmtown's youth: The Impact of Social Classes on Adolescents*. New York: Wiley. [2]

HOLLINGSWORTH, H. L. (1922), *Judging Human Character*. New York: Appleton. [15]

HOLTZMAN, W. H. (1961), *Ink-Blot Perception and Personality*. Austin, Texas: University of Texas Press. [12]

HOVLAND, C. I. (1937), "The generalization of conditioned responses. II. The sensory generalization of conditioned responses with varying intensities of tone," *J. gen. Psychol.*, **17**, 125–148. [5]

HOVLAND, C. I., E. H. CAMPBELL, and T. BROCK (1957), "The effects of 'commitment' on opinion change following communication," in C. I. HOVLAND *et al.*, *The Order of Presentation in Persuasion*. New Haven, Conn.: Yale University Press. [16]

HOVLAND, C. I., I. L. JANIS, and H. H. KELLEY (1953), *Communication and Persuasion*. New Haven: Yale University Press. [16]

HOVLAND, C. I., A. A. LUMSDAINE, and F. D. SHEFFIELD (1949), *Experiments on Mass Communication, Studies in Social Psychology in World War II, Vol. III*. Princeton: Princeton University Press. [16]

HOVLAND, C. I., and M. SHERIF (1952), "Judgmental phenomena and scales of attitude measurement: item displacement in Thurstone scales," *J. abnorm. soc. Psychol.*, 47, 822–832. [15]

HOVLAND, C. I., and W. WEISS (1953), "Transmission of information concerning concepts through positive and negative instances," *J. exp. Psychol.*, 45, 175–182. [9]

HOVLAND, C. I., and W. WEISS (1951), "The influence of source credibility on communication effectiveness." *Public Opinion Quarterly*, 15, 635–650. [16]

HUBEL, D. H. (1963), "The visual cortex of the brain," *Sci. Amer.*, 209, 54–62. [6]

HUBEL, D. H. and T. WIESEL (1963), "Receptive fields of cells in striate cortex of visually inexperienced kittens," *J. Neurophysiol.*, 26, 994–1002. [6]

HULL, C. L. (1952), *A Behavior System.* New Haven: Yale University Press. [7]

HULL, C. L. (1943), *Principles of Behavior.* New York: Appleton-Century-Crofts. [5, 7, 8]

HURLOCK, E. B. (1925), "The evaluation of certain incentives used in school work," *J. Educ. Psychol.*, 16, 145–159. [1]

HUTT, M., and D. MILLER (1949), "Social values and personality development," *J. Soc. Issues*, 5, 4. [1]

HUTTENLOCHER, J. (in press), "The growth of conceptual strategies," in J. S. BRUNER, *Studies in Cognitive Growth.* New York: Wiley. [10]

HUTTENLOCHER, J. (1962), "Some effects of negative instances on correct formation." *Psychol. Rep.*, 11, 35–42. [9]

HYDEN, H. (1961), "Satellite cells in the nervous system," *Sci. Amer.*, 205, 62–83. [3]

HYMAN, H. H., and P. B. SHEATSLEY (1954), "The authoritarian personality: a methodological critique," in R. CHRISTIE and M. JAHODA (eds.), *Studies in the Scope and Method of "The Authoritarian Personality."* Glencoe, Ill.: Free Press. [16]

INHELDER, B., and J. PIAGET (1958), *The Growth of Logical Thinking from Childhood to Adolescence.* New York: Basic Books. [13]

JACK, L. M. (1934), "An experimental study of ascendant behavior in preschool children," *University of Iowa Studies in Child Welfare*, 9, No. 3. [15]

JAHODA, M. (1958), *Current Concepts of Positive Mental Health.* New York: Basic Books. [12]

JANIS, I. L., and S. FESHBACH (1953), "Effects of fear-arousing communications," *J. abnorm. soc. Psychol.*, 48, 78–92. [16]

JANIS, I. L., and B. T. KING (1954), "The influence of role playing on attitude change, *J. abnorm. soc. Psychol.*, 99, 211–218. [16]

JASTAK, J. (1947), "Senile Psychosis," in A. BURTON and R. E. HARRIS (eds.), *Case Studies in Clinical and Abnormal Psychology.* New York: Harper and Bros. [14]

JENKINS, J. G., and K. M. DALLENBACH (1924), "Oblivescence during sleep and waking," *Amer. J. Psychol.*, **35**, 605–612. **[9]**

JOHN, E. R., and K. F. KILLAM (1959), "Electrophysiological correlates of avoidance conditioning in the cat," *J. Pharmacol. exp. Therapeut.*, **125**, 252–274. **[5]**

JONES, H. E. (1949), "Adolescence in Our Society," in *The Family in a Democratic Society* (Anniversary Papers of Community Service Society of New York). New York: Columbia University Press. **[13]**

JONES, M. C. (1924), "A laboratory study of fear: the case of Peter," *J. genet. Psychol.*, **31**, 308–315. **[7]**

JONES, M. (1962), "Society and the sociopath," *Amer. J. Psychiat.*, **119**, 410–414. **[14]**

JONES, M. (1953), *The Therapeutic Community*. New York: Basic Books. **[14]**

JUNG, C. G. (1923), *Psychological Types*, translated by H. G. BRYNES. New York: Harcourt Brace. **[4]**

KAGAN, J., L. W. SONTOG, C. T. BAKER, and V. L. NELSON (1958), "Personality and IQ Change," *J. abnorm. soc. Psychol.* **58**, 261–266. **[10]**

KAHN, R. L., and C. F. CANNELL (1957), *The Dynamics of Interviewing*. New York: Wiley. **[12]**

KAHN, R. L., and D. KATZ (1953), "Leadership practices in relation to productivity and morale," in D. CARTWRIGHT and A. ZANDER (eds.), *Group Dynamics*. Evanston, Ill.: Row, Peterson. **[15]**

KALLMANN, F. J. (1953), *Heredity in Health and Mental Disorder*. New York: Norton. **[14]**

KAMIN, L. J. (1959), "The delay-of-punishment gradient," *J. comp. physiol. Psychol.*, **52**, 434–437. **[5]**

KARPMAN, B. (ed.) (1951), "Psychopathic behavior in infants and children," *Amer. J. Orthopsychiat.*, **21**, 223–272. **[14]**

KARSH, E. (1962), "The effects of number of rewarded trials and intensity of punishment on running speed," *J. comp. physiol. Psychol.*, **55**, 44–51. **[5]**

KATZ, D. (1960), "The functional approach to the study of attitudes," *Publ. Opin. Quart.*, **24**, 163–204. **[16]**

KATZ, D., and K. W. BRALY (1933), "Racial stereotypes of 100 college students," *J. abnorm. soc. Psychol.*, **28**, 280–290. **[15]**

KATZ, D., N. MACCOBY, G. GURIN, and L. G. FLOOR (1951). *Productivity, Supervision, and Morale among Railroad Workers*. Ann Arbor: Survey Research Center, Institute for Social Research, University of Michigan. **[15]**

KATZ, E., and P. F. LAZARSFELD (1955), *Personal Influence: The Part Played by People in the Flow of Mass Communication*. Glencoe, Ill: Fress Press. **[16]**

KELLER, F. S. and W. K. ESTES (1945), "The relative effectiveness of four and seven hours of daily code practice," *OSRD Publ. Bull. 12161.* **[8]**

KELLEY, H. H. (1950), "The warm-cold variable in first impressions of people," *J. Pers.*, **18**, 431–439. **[15]**

KELLEY, H. H., and C. L. WOODRUFF (1956), "Members' reactions to apparent group approval of a counternorm communication," *J. abnorm. soc. Psychol.*, **52**, 67–74. **[16]**

KELLOGG, W. N., and L. A. KELLOGG (1933), *The Ape and the Child.* New York: McGraw-Hill. **[3]**

KELLY, E. L. (1964), personal communication. **[13]**

KELLY, E. L. (1955), "Consistency of the adult personality," *Amer. Psychologist*, **10**, 581–659. **[12]**

KELLY, E. L. (1941), "Marital compatibility as related to personality traits of husbands and wives as rated by self and spouse," *J. soc. Psychol.*, **13**, 193–198. **[12]**

KELLY, E. L., and D. W. FISKE (1951), *The Prediction of Performance in Clinical Psychology.* Ann Arbor: University of Michigan Press. **[12]**

KELLY, E. L., H. L. HOLLINGSWORTH, and L. M. TERMAN (1939), "Psychological factors in marital happiness," *Psychol. Bull.*, **36**, 191–203. **[12]**

KELMAN, H. C. (1961), "Processes of opinion change," *Publ. Opin. Quart.*, **25**, 57–78. **[16]**

KELMAN, H. C., and C. I. HOVLAND (1953), " 'Reinstatement' of the communicator in delayed measurement of opinion change," *J. abnorm. soc. Psychol.*, **48**, 327–335. **[16]**

KENDLER, T. S., and H. H. KENDLER (1959), "Reversal and nonreversal shifts in kindergarten children," *J. exp. Psychol.*, **58**, 56–60. **[11]**

KENNEDY, J. L. (1939), "A methodological review of extrasensory perception," *Psychol. Bull.*, **36**, 60–61. **[5]**

KEPPEL, G., and B. J. UNDERWOOD (1962), "Proactive inhibition in short-term retention of single items," *J. verb. Learn. verb. Beh.*, **1**, 153–161. **[9]**

KETY, S. S. (1959), "Biochemical theories of schizophrenia," *Science*, 129, June 1959. 1528–32, 1590–96. **[14]**

KIMBLE, G. A. (1956), *Introduction to Psychology.* New York: Ronald Press. **[5]**

KIMBLE, G. A., and N. GARMEZY (1963), *Principles of General Psychology*, second edition. New York: Ronald Press. **[5]**

KING, B. T., and I. L. JANIS (1956), "Comparison of the effectiveness of improvised versus nonimprovised role playing in producing opinion changes," *Hum. Relat.*, **9**, 177–186. **[16]**

KLEIN, G. S. (1951), "The personal world through perception," in R. R. BLAKE and G. V. RAMSEY, *Perception: an Approach to Personality.* New York: Ronald Press. **[6]**

KLINEBERG, O. (1935), *Negro Intelligence and Selective Migration.* New York: Columbia University Press. **[4]**

KLUCKHOHN, C., and D. LEIGHTON (1946), *The Navaho.* Cambridge: Harvard University Press. [2]

KOGAN, N., and M. A. WALLACH (1964), *Risk-taking: A Study in Cognition and Personality.* New York: Holt, Rinehart, and Winston. [12]

KOHLBERG, L. (1963), "The development of children's orientation toward the moral order: I. The sequence of development of moral thought," *Vita Humana*, 6, 11–33. [13]

KÖHLER, I. (1962), "Experiments with goggles," *Sci. Amer.*, 206, 62–72. [6]

KÖHLER, W., and H. WALLACH (1944), "Figural after-effects, an investigation of visual processes," *Proc. Amer. Phil. Soc.*, 88, 269–357. [6]

KRECH, D., R. S. CRUTCHFIELD, and E. L. BALLECHEY (1962), *Individual in Society.* New York: McGraw-Hill. [15]

KRECH, D., M. R. ROSENZWEIG, E. C. BENNETT, and B. KRUECKEL (1954), "Enzyme concentrations in the brain and adjustive behavior patterns," *Science*, 120, 994–996. [3]

KUTNER, B., C. WILKINS, and P. R. YARROW (1952), "Verbal attitudes and overt behavior involving racial prejudice," *J. abnorm. soc. Psychol.*, 47, 647–652. [16]

LACEY, J. I., DOROTHY E. BATEMAN, and R. VAN LEHN (1953), "Autonomic response specificity," *Psychosomatic Medicine*, 15, 8–21. [7]

LACEY, J. I., DOROTHY E. BATEMAN, and R. VAN LEHN (1952), "Autonomic response specificity and Rorschach color responses," *Psychosomatic Medicine*, 14, 256–260. [7]

LACEY, J. I., and R. L. SMITH (1954), "Conditioning and generalization of unconscious anxiety," *Science*, 120, 1045–1052. [5]

LACEY, J. I., R. L. SMITH, and A. GREY (1955), "Use of conditioned autonomic responses in the study of anxiety," *Psychosomatic Medicine*, 17, 208–217. [4]

LACEY, J. I., and R. VAN LEHN (1952), "Differential emphasis in somatic response to stress," *Psychosomatic Medicine*, 14, 71–81. [7]

LAMBERT, W. W., and R. L. SOLOMON (1952), "Extinction of a running response as a function of distance of block point from the goal," *J. comp. physiol. Psychol.*, 45, 269–279. [5]

LAND, E. H. (1959), "Experiments in color vision," *Sci. Amer.*, 200 (5), 84–99. [6]

LAPIERE, R. T. (1934), "Attitudes versus actions," *Social Forces*, 13, 230–237. [16]

LASHLEY, K. S. (1955), "The problem of serial order in behavior," in L. A. JEFFRESS (ed.), *Cerebral Mechanisms in Behavior.* New York: Wiley, 1955. [8]

LASHLEY, K. S. (1926), "Studies of cerebral function in learning. VII. The relation between cerebral mass learning and retention," *J. comp. Neurol.*, 41, 1–58. [5]

LASHLEY, K. S. (1916), "The color vision of birds. I. The spectrum of the domestic fowl," *J. Animal Behavior*, 6, 1–26. [5]

LAUBACH, F. C. (1960), "Symbology vs. illiteracy," in E. WHITNEY, *Symbology*. New York: Hastings House. **[9]**

LAZARSFELD, P. F., B. BERELSON, and H. GAUDET (1944), *The People's Choice*. New York: Duell, Sloan, and Pearce. **[16]**

LEAVITT, H. J. (1951), "Some effects of certain communication patterns on group performance," *J. abnorm. soc. Psychol.*, **46**, 38–50. **[15]**

LE BON, G. (1895), *The Crowd: A Study of the Popular Mind*. London: E. Benn (1952). Translation of *Psychologie des Foules*. Paris: F. Alcan. **[15]**

LEE, B. S. (1950), "A report of the effect of delayed auditory feedback," *J. Acoust. Soc. Amer.*, **22**, 639. **[8]**

LEEPER, R. (1935), "A study of a neglected portion of the field of learning—the development of sensory organization," *J. genet. Psychol.*, **46**, 41–75. **[6]**

LEFFORD, A. (1946), "The influence of emotional subject matter on logical reasoning," *J. gen. Psychol.*, **34**, 127–151. **[10]**

LEHMAN, H. C. (1953), *Age and Achievement*. Princeton: Princeton University Press. **[10]**

LeVINE, B. B. (1961), *Punishment Techniques and the Development of Conscience*. Unpublished doctoral dissertation, Northwestern University. **[13]**

LEVINE, J., and G. MURPHY (1943), "The learning and forgetting of controversial material," *J. abnorm. soc. Psychol.*, **38**, 507–517. **[9]**

LEVINE, S. (1960), "Stimulation in infancy," *Sci. Amer.*, **202** (May), 80–86. **[13]**

LEWIN, K. (1947), "Group decisions and social change," in T. NEWCOMB and E. HARLEY (eds.), *Readings in Social Psychology*. New York: Holt. **[16]**

LEWIN, K., C. F. MEYERS, J. KALHORN, M. L. FARBER, and J. R. P. FRENCH (1944), "Authority and frustration; studies in topological and vector psychology, III," *Univer. Ia. Stud. Child Welf.*, **20**, No. 409. **[11]**

LIBERMAN, A. M., K. S. HARRIS, H. S. HOFFMAN, and B. D. GRIFFITH (1957), "The discrimination of speech sounds within and across phoneme boundaries," *J. exp. Psychol.*, **54**, 358–368. **[6]**

LIKERT, R. (1958), "Measuring organizational performance," *Harv. Bus. Rev.*, **36**, 41–50. **[15]**

LIKERT, R. A. (1932), "A technique for the measurement of attitudes," *Arch. Psychol.*, No. 4. **[16]**

LINTON, R. (1942), "Age and sex categories," *Amer. Sociol. Rev.*, **7**, 589–603. **[13]**

LIPPMANN, W. (1922), *Public Opinion*. New York: Macmillan. **[16]**

LIVSON, N., and W. C. BRONSON (1961), "An exploration of patterns of impulse control in early adolescence," *Child Develpm.*, **32**, 75–88. **[12]**

LLOYD, K. E. (1960), "Retention of responses to stimulus classes and to specific stimuli," *J. exp. Psychol.*, **59**, 54–59. **[9]**

LOEWENSTEIN, W. R. (1956), "Excitation and change on adaptation by stretch of mechanoreceptors," *J. Physiol.*, **133**, 508–602. **[6]**

Lorenz, K. Z. (1937), "Imprinting," *The Auk*, 54, 245–273. [4]

Lorge, I., and R. L. Thorndike (1954), *Lorge-Thorndike Intelligence Tests*. Boston: Houghton Mifflin. [10]

Lowell, E. L. (1950), "A methodological study of projectively measured achievement motivation." Unpublished master's thesis. Wesleyan Univ. [7]

Luchins, A. S. (1957), "Primacy-recency in impression formation," in C. I. Hovland (ed.), *The Order of Presentation in Persuasion*, Volume I. New Haven, Conn.: Yale University Press. [15]

Luchins, A. S. (1942), "Mechanization in problem solving," *Psychol. Monogr.*, 54, Whole No. 248. [10]

Luchins, A. S., and E. H. Luchins (1959), *Rigidity of Behavior*. Eugene, Oregon: University of Oregon Press. [10]

Lumsdaine, A. A., and R. Glaser (eds.) (1960), *Teaching Machines and Programmed Learning*. Washington D.C.: NEA. [11]

Lumsdaine, A. A., and I. L. Janis (1953), "Resistance to counter-propaganda produced by one-sided and two-sided propaganda presentations," *Public Opinion Quarterly*, 17, 311–318. [16]

McArthur, C. C. (1954), "Long-term validity of the Strong Interest Test in two subcultures," *J. appl. Psychol.*, 38, 346–353. [12]

McArthur, C. C., and L. B. Stevens (1955), "The validation of expressed interests as compared with inventoried interests: a 14-year follow-up," *J. appl. Psychol.*, 39, 184–189. [12]

McCall, R. B. (1965), "Stimulus change in light-contingent bar-pressing," *J. comp. physiol. Psychol.*, 59, 258–262. [7]

McCleary, R. A. (1960), "Type of response as a factor in interocular transfer in fish," *J. comp. physiol. Psychol.*, 53, 311–321. [5]

McClelland, D. C. (1958), "Risk taking in children with high and low need for achievement," in J. W. Atkinson (ed.), *Motives in Fantasy, Action and Society*. Princeton: Van Nostrand. [7, 10]

McClelland, D. C. (1951), *Personality*. New York: Holt. [5, 7]

McClelland, D. C., and J. W. Atkinson (1948), "The projective expression of needs. I. The effect of different intensities of the hunger drive on perception," *J. Psychol.*, 25, 205–232. [6]

McCluskey, H. V. (1934), "An experimental comparison of two methods of correcting the outcomes of examinations," *School and Society*, 40, 566–568. [9]

McCord, W., J. McCord, and I. K. Zola (1959), *Origins of Crime*. New York: Columbia University Press. [14]

McFarland, R. A., and A. L. Barach (1936), "The relationship between alcoholic intoxication and anoxemia," *Amer. J. Med. Sci.*, 192, 186–198. [3, 9

McGraw, M. B. (1935), *Growth, a Study of Johnny and Jimmy*. New York: Appleton-Century Crofts. [8]

656 *Bibliography*

McKeachie, W. J. (1961), "Motivation, teaching methods, and college learning," in M. R. Jones (ed.), *Nebraska Symposium on Motivation*. Lincoln, Nebraska: University of Nebraska Press. [12]

McKeachie, W. J. (1952), "Lipstick as a determiner of first impressions of personality: an experiment for the general psychology course," *J. soc. Psychol.*, **36**, 241–244. [15]

McMurray, G. A. (1950), "Experimental study of a case of insensitivity to pain," *Arch. Neurol. Psychiat.*, **64**, 650–667. [6]

McNeil, D. (1966), "Developmental psycholinguistics," in F. Smith and G. A. Miller (eds.), *The Genesis of Language in Children and Animals*. Cambridge, Mass.: MIT Press. [9]

McNemar, O. W. (1955), "An attempt to differentiate between individuals with high and low reasoning ability," *Amer. J. Psychol.*, **68**, 20–36. [10]

McNemar, Q. (1942), *The Revision of the Stanford-Binet Scale*. Boston: Houghton Mifflin. [10]

McNemar, Q. (1933), "Twin resemblances in motor skills and the effect of practice thereon," *J. genet. Psychol.*, **42**, 70–99. [8]

Maccoby, E. E. (1964), "Effects of the Mass Media," in M. L. Hoffman and L. W. Hoffman (eds.), *Review of Child Development Research*, Vol. 1. New York: Russell Sage Foundation, 323-348. [13]

Maccoby, E. E., and W. C. Wilson (1957), "Identification and observational learning from films," *J. abnorm. soc. Psychol.*, **55**, 76–87. [13]

Mahone, C. H. (1960), "Fear of failure and unrealistic vocational aspiration," *J. abnorm. soc. Psychol.*, **60**, 253–261. [7, 13]

Maier, N. R. F. (1961), *Frustration: the Study of Behavior Without a Goal*. Ann Arbor: University of Michigan Press (reissue; originally published by McGraw-Hill in 1949). [14]

Maier, N. R. F. (1931), "Reasoning in humans, II. The solution of a problem and its appearance in consciousness," *J. comp. Psychol.*, **12**, 181–194. [9]

Maier, N. R. F., and R. S. Feldman (1948), "Studies of abnormal behavior in the rat," *J. comp. physiol. Psychol.*, **41**, 348–363. [11]

Maier, N. R. F., and A. R. Salem (1952), "The contribution of a discussion leader to the quality of group thinking: the effective use of minority opinions," *Hum. Rel.*, **5**, 277–288. [15]

Malinowsky, B. (1927), *Sex and Repression in Savage Society*. London: Kegan Paul. [11]

Mandler, G., J. M. Mandler, I. Kremen, and R. D. Sholiton (1961), "The response to threat," *Psychol. Monogr.*, **75**, No. 9, Whole No. 513. [7]

Mann, F., and H. Baumgartel (1952), *Absences and Employee Attitudes in an Electric Power Company*. Ann Arbor: Michigan Institute for Social Research. [15]

Mann, F. C., and L. R. Hoffman (1960), *Automation and the Worker*. New York: Holt. [11]

Mann, R. D. (1959), "A review of the relationships between personality and performance in small groups," *Psychol. Bull.*, **56**, 241–270. [12, 15]

Marks, W. B., W. H. Dobelle, and E. L. MacNichol, Jr. (1964), "Visual pigments of single primate cones," *Science*, **143**, 1181–1182. [6]

Marquis, D. P. (1941), "Learning in the neonate: the modification of behavior under three feeding schedules," *J. exp. Psychol.*, **29**, 263–282. [8]

Maslow, A. (1954), *Motivation and Personality.* New York: Harper. [7]

Mason, W. A. (1960), "The effects of social restriction on the behavior of rhesus monkeys. I. Free social behavior," *J. comp. physiol. Psychol.*, **53**, 582–589. [13]

Masserman, J. H. (1961), *Principles of Dynamic Psychiatry.* Philadelphia: Saunders. [11]

Mayer, J. (1955), "Regulation of energy intake and the body weight: The glucostatic theory and the lipostatic hypothesis," *Ann. N. Y. Acad. Sci.*, **63**, 15–43. [7]

Mead, M. (1935), *Sex and Temperament in Three Primitive Societies.* New York: William Morrow, 1935. [2]

Mead, M. (1928), *Coming of Age in Samoa.* New York: William Morrow, 1928. [2]

Meehl, P. E. (1954), *Clinical Versus Statistical Prediction.* Minneapolis: University of Minnesota Press, 1954. [12, 15]

Mellinger, G. D. (1955), *Communication, Consensus, and Interpersonal Attraction,* unpublished doctoral dissertation, University of Michigan. [14]

Melton, A. W. (1957), "Military psychology in the United States of America," *Amer. Psychologist,* **12**, 740–746. [11]

Meltzer, H. (1930), "Individual differences in forgetting pleasant and unpleasant experiences," *J. educ. Psychol.*, **21**, 399–409. [1]

Menzies, R. (1937), "Conditioned vasomotor responses in human subjects," *J. Psychol.*, **4**, 75–120. [8]

Messick, S., and D. N. Jackson (1961), "Acquiescence and the factorial interpretation of the MMPI," *Psychol. Bull.*, **57**, 514–532. [12]

Michigan, University of, Detroit Area Study (1956), *A Social Profile of Detroit: 1956.* Ann Arbor, Mich. [16]

Michigan, University of, Institute for Social Research, *A Study of Adolescent Boys.* Ann Arbor, Mich.: undated. [12]

Milgram, S. (1965), "Some conditions of obedience and disobedience to authority," *Hum. Relat.*, **18**, 57–76. [16]

Milgram, S. (1963), "Behavioral study of obedience," *J. abnorm. soc. Psychol.*, **67**, 4, 371–378. [16]

Miles, W. R. (1931a), "Studies in physical exertion. II. Individual and group reaction time in football charging," *Res. Quart. Amer. Assoc. Hlth.*, **2**, No. 3, 5–13. [7]

Miles, W. R. (1931b), "Studies in physical exertion. III. Effect of signal variation on football charging," *Res. Quart. Amer. Assoc. Hlth.*, **2**, No. 3, 14–31. [7]

MILLER, D. R., and M. L. HUTT (1949), "Value interiorization and personality development," *J. soc. Issues*, 5, 2–30. [13]

MILLER, D. R., and G. E. SWANSON (1960), *Inner Conflict and Defense.* New York: Holt.. [11]

MILLER, D. R., and G. E. SWANSON (1958), *The Changing American Parent.* New York: Wiley. [2]

MILLER, G. A. (1951), *Language and Communication.* New York: McGraw-Hill. [5]

MILLER, G. A., E. GALANTER, and K. H. PRIBRAM (1964), *Plan and the Structure of Behavior.* New York: Holt, Rinehart, and Winston. [8]

MILLER, G. A., and D. McNEIL (in press), "Psycholinguistics," in G. LINDZEY (ed.), *Handbook of Social Psychology.* Reading, Mass.: Addison-Wesley (new edition to be published in 1967). [9]

MILLER, J. G. (1942), *Unconsciousness.* New York: Wiley. [6]

MILLER, N. E. (1959), "Liberalization of basic S-R concepts: extensions to conflict behavior, motivation, and social learning," in S. KOCH, *Psychology: a Study of a Science.* New York: McGraw-Hill. [7]

MILLER, N. E. (1958), "Central stimulation and other new approaches to motivation and reward," *Amer. Psychologist*, 13, 100–108. [7]

MILLER, N. E. (1948a), "Displacement," *J. abnorm. soc. Psychol.*, 43, 155–178. [11]

MILLER, N. E. (1948b), "Theory and experiment relating psychoanalytic displacement to stimulus-response generalization," *J. abnorm. soc. Psychol.*, 43, 155–178. [11]

MILLER, N. E. (1948c), "Studies of fear as an acquirable drive. I: Fear as motivation and fear reduction as reinforcement in the learning of new responses," *J. exp. Psychol.*, 38, 89–101. [7]

MILLER, N. E., and J. DOLLARD (1941), *Social Learning and Imitation.* New Haven: Yale University Press. [5, 8]

M. M. P. I., S. R. HATHAWAY, and J. C. McKINLEY. New York: Psychological Corporation, 1943. [12]

MILTON, G. A. (1957), "The effects of sex-role identification upon problem-solving skill," *J. abnorm. soc. Psychol.*, 55, 208–212. [9]

MINAMI, H., and K. DALLENBACH (1946), "The effect of activity upon learning and retention in the cockroach," *Amer. J. Psychol.*, 59, 1–58. [9]

MINARD, R. D. (1952), "Race relations in the Pocahontas coal field," *J. Soc. Issues*, 8, 29–44. [16]

MONTAGUE, E. K. (1953), "The role of anxiety in serial role learning," *J. exp. Psychol.*, 45, 91–96. [1]

MOORE, J. W., W. I. SMITH, and R. TEEVAN (1965), "Motivational variables in programmed learning: the role of need achievement, fear of failure, and student estimate of achievement as a function of program difficulty," *Final Report U.S.O.E., Title 7, Grant No. 7–48–0070–149.1.* Lewisberg, Pa.: Bucknell University Press. [11]

MORGAN, C. T. (1965), *Physiological Psychology.* New York: McGraw-Hill. [3]

MORGAN, C. T., J. S. COOK, A. CHAPANIS, and M. W. LUND (1963), *Human Engineering Guide to Equipment Design*. New York: McGraw-Hill. [8]

MORGAN, J. J. B. (1941), *Psychology*. New York: Farrar and Rinehart. [9]

MORGAN, J. J. B., and J. T. MORTON (1944), "The distortion of syllogistic reasoning produced by personal convictions," *J. soc. Psychol.*, 20, 39–59. [10]

MORRISSETTE, J. O. (1958), "An experimental study of the theory of structural balance," *Hum. Relat.*, 11, 239–254. [16]

MOWRER, O. H. (1950), *Learning Theory and Personality Dynamics*. New York: Ronald Press, 1950. [8]

MUNN, N. L. (1955), *The Evolutiona nd Growth of Human Behavior*. Boston: Houghton Mifflin. [4]

MÜNSTERBERG, H. (1949), "The perception of visual movement," in W. DENNIS (ed.), *Readings in General Psychology*. New York: Prentice-Hall. [9]

MURDOCK, B. B., JR. (1961), "The retention of individual items," *J. exp. Psychol.*, 62, 618–625. [9]

MURPHY, G., and R. LIKERT (1938), *Public Opinion and the Individual: A Psychological Study of Student Attitudes on Public Questions with a Retest Five Years Later*. New York: Harper. [16]

MURRAY, H. A. (1938), *Explorations in Personality*. New York: Oxford University Press. [12]

NACHMANN, B. (1957), *Childhood Experiences and Vocational Choice: a Study of Lawyers, Dentists, and Social Workers*, unpublished doctoral dissertation. University of Michigan. [13]

NEUGARTEN, B. L., and D. L. GUTMAN (1958), "Age-sex roles and personality in middle age: a thematic apperception study," *Psychol. Monogr.*, 72, No. 17. [13]

NETTER, F. H. (1953), *The CIBA Collection of Medical Illustrations, Vol. I. Nervous System*. Summit, N. J.: CIBA Pharmaceutical Products, Inc. [3]

NEWCOMB, T. M. (1961), *The Acquaintance Process*. New York: Holt, 1961. [16]

NEWCOMB, T. M., R. H. TURNER, and P. E. CONVERSE (1965), *Social Psychology: The Study of Human Interaction*. New York: Holt. [16]

NEWMAN, H. H., F. N. FREEMAN, and K. J. HOLZINGER (1937), *Twins*. Chicago: University of Chicago Press. [4]

NUNNALLY, J. C., and C. E. OSGOOD (1960), *The Development and Change of Popular Conceptions of Mental Health Phenomena*, Final Report, Mental Health Project, Urbana: Institute of Communications Research, University of Illinois. [II]

OGBURN, W. F., and M. F. NIMKOFF (1955), *Technology and the Changing Family*. Boston: Houghton Mifflin. [2]

OLDS, J. (1958a), "Effects of hunger and male sex hormone on self-stimulation of the brain," *J. comp. physiol. Psychol.*, 51, 320–324. [3, 7]

OLDS, J. (1958b), "Self-stimulation of the brain," *Science*, **127**, 315–324. **[3, 7]**

OLDS, J., and P. MILNER (1954), "Positive reinforcement produced by electrical stimulation of septal area and other regions of rat brain," *J. comp. physiol. Psychol.*, **47**, 419–427. **[3]**

ORLANSKY, H. (1949), "Infant care and personality," *Psychol. Bull.*, **46**, 1–48. **[13]**

OSGOOD, C. E. (1952), "The nature and measurement of meaning," *Psychol. Bull.*, **49**, 197–237. **[9]**

OSS ASSESSMENT STAFF, THE (1948), *Selection of Personnel for the Office of Strategic Services*. New York: Rinehart. **[12]**

PACE, C. R., and G. G. STERN (1958), *A Criterion Study of College Environment*. Syracuse, N. Y.: Syracuse University, Psychological Research Center. **[13]**

PADILLA, S. G. (1935), "Further studies on the delayed pecking of chicks," *J. comp. Psychol.*, **20**, 413–443. **[8]**

PAGE, H. A., and J. F. HALL (1953), "Experimental extinction as a function of the prevention of a response," *J. comp. physiol. Psychol.*, **46**, 33–34. **[7]**

PAVLOV, I. P. (1927), *Conditioned Reflexes* (G. V. Anrep, tr.). London: Oxford University Press. **[5, 7, 11]**

PEAK, H. (1955), "Attitude and motivation," in M. R. JONES (ed.), *Nebraska Symposium on Motivation, 1955*. Lincoln, Neb.: University of Nebraska Press. **[16]**

PENFIELD, W., and H. JASPER (1954), *Epilepsy and the Functional Anatomy of the Human Brain*. Boston: Little, Brown. **[3]**

PENFIELD, W., and T. RASMUSSEN (1950), *The Cerebral Cortex of Man*. New York: Macmillan. **[3]**

PENFIELD, W., and L. ROBERTS (1959), *Speech and Brain Mechanisms*. Princeton, N. J.: Princeton University Press. **[3]**

PERIN, C. T. (1943), "A quantitative investigation of the delay-of-reinforcement gradient," *J. exp. Psychol.*, **32**, 37–51. **[5]**

PERKINS, C. C. (1947), "The relation of secondary reward to gradients of reinforcement," *J. exp. Psychol.*, **37**, 377–392. **[5]**

PETERSON, L. R., and M. J. PETERSON (1959), "Short-term retention of individual verbal items," *J. exp. Psychol.*, **58**, 193–198. **[9]**

PETERSON, O. L., R. S. SPAIN, L. P. ANDREWS, and B. G. GREENBERG (1956), "An analytic study of North Carolina general practice 1953–54," *J. Med. Educ.*, **31**, Part II, 1–165. **[II]**

PETTIGREW, T. F. (1958), "Personality and sociocultural factors in intergroup attitudes, a cross-national comparison," *J. Conflict Resolution*, **2**, 29–42. **[16]**

PFAFFMAN, C. (1941), "Gustatory afferent impulses," *J. cell. comp. Physiol.*, **17**, 243–258. **[6]**

PIAGET, J. (1959), *The Language and Thought of the Child* (third edition). London: Routledge and Kegan Paul. [15]

PIAGET, J. (1952), *The Origins of Intelligence in Children.* New York: International University Press. [9, 10]

PIAGET, J. (1950), *The Psychology of Intelligence.* New York: Harcourt, Brace. [9]

PIAGET, J. (1928), *Judgment and Reasoning in the Child.* New York: Harcourt, Brace. [9]

PIAGET, J., and B. INHELDER (1962), *Le développement des quantités physiques chez l'enfant.* Neuchâtel, Switzerland: Delachaux and Niestlé, 1962.

POLLIO, H. R. (1963a), "Word association as a function of conditioned meaning," *J. exp. Psychol.*, **66**, 454–460. [9]

POLLIO, H. R. (1963b), "A simple matrix analysis of associative structure," *J. verb. Learn. verb. Behav.*, **2**, 166–169. [9]

POLYAK, S. L. (1941), *The Retina.* Chicago: University of Chicago Press. [6]

POSTMAN, L. (1964), "Short-term memory and incidental learning," in A. MELTON (ed.), *Categories of Human Learning.* New York: Academic Press. [9]

POSTMAN, L., and B. H. SCHNEIDER (1951), "Personal values, visual recognition, and recall," *Psychol. Rev.*, **58**, 271–284. [9]

POWERS, E., and H. WITMER (1951), *Prevention of Delinquency.* New York: Columbia University Press. [14]

PRENTICE, W. C. H. (1954), "Visual recognition of verbally labeled figures," *Amer. J. Psychol.*, **67**, 315–320. [9]

PREYER, W. (1882), *Die Seele des Kindes.* Leipzig: Fernau. Translated by H. W. BROWN (1893), *The Mind of the Child.* New York: D. Appleton. [8]

PRIBRAM, K. H. (1955), "Toward a science of neuropsychology (method and data)," in PATTON, R. A. (ed.), *Current Trends in Psychology and the Behavioral Sciences.* Pittsburgh, Pa.: University of Pittsburgh Press. [9]

PRINGLE, M. L., and V. BOSSIO (1958), "A study of deprived children," *Vita Humana*, **1**, 65–91, 142–169. [13]

PRITCHARD, R. M. (1961), "Stabilized images on the retina," *Sci. Amer.*, **204** (June), 72–77. [6]

RABIN, A. I. (1958), "Some psychosexual differences between kibbutz and non-kibbutz Israeli boys," *J. Proj. Tech.*, **22**, 328–332. [II]

RABIN, A. I., and G. J. MOHR (1958), "Behavior research in collective settlements in Israel: VI. Infants and children under conditions of 'intermittent' mothering in the kibbutz," *Amer. J. Orthopsychiat.*, **28**, 577–586. [II]

RADKE, M. J. (1946), *The Relation of Parental Authority to Children's Behavior and Attitudes.* Minneapolis, Minn.: University of Minnesota. [13]

RAUSH, H. L. (1952), "Perceptual constancy in schizophrenia," *J. Pers.*, **21**, 176–187. [5]

RAVEN, B. H., and J. RIETSMA (1957), "The effects of varied clarity of group goal and group path upon the individual and his relation to his groups," *Hum. Relat.*, **10**, 29–45. **[15]**

RAY, W. S. (1957), "Verbal compared with manipulative solution of an apparatus problem," *Amer. J. Psychol.*, **70**, 289–290. **[10]**

REDL, F., and D. WINEMAN (1952), *Controls from Within: Techniques for the Treatment of the Aggressive Child.* New York: Free Press. **[14]**

REISS, B. F. (1946), "Genetic changes in semantic conditioning," *J. exp. Psychol.*, **36**, 143–152. **[9]**

REMMERS, H. H., and D. H. RADLER (1957), *The American Teenager.* Indianapolis, Ind.: Bobbs-Merrill. **[13]**

RICE, K. K., and C. P. RICHTER (1943), "Increased sodium chloride and water intake of normal rats treated with desoxycortisone steroneacetate," *Endocrinology*, **33**, 106–115. **[7]**

RICH, S. (1959), "Mao's big family," *New Republic*, **140**, 12–15. **[II]**

RICHTER, C. P. (1957), "On the phenomenon of sudden death in animals and man," *Psychosom. Med.*, **19**, 191–198. **[2]**

RICHTER, C. P. (1942–43), "Total self-regulatory functions in animals and human beings," *Harvey Lectures*, **38**, 63–103. **[7]**

RIESEN, A. H. (1961), "Stimulation as a requirement for growth and function in behavioral development," in D. W. FISKE and S. R. MADDI (eds.), *Functions of Varied Experiences.* Homewood, Ill.: Dorsey Press. **[13]**

RIESS, D. S. (1946), "Genetic changes in semantic conditioning," *J. exp. Psychol.*, **36**, 143–152. **[9]**

RIGGS, L. A., F. RATLIFF, J. C. CORNSWEET, and T. N. CORNSWEET (1953), "The disappearance of steadily fixated visual test objects," *J. Opt. Soc. Amer.*, **43**, 495–501. **[6]**

RILEY, M. W., and J. W. RILEY, JR. (1954), "A sociological approach to communications research," in W. SCHRAMM (ed.), *The Process and Effects of Mass Communication.* Urbana, Ill.: University of Illinois Press. **[13]**

ROE, A. (1953a), "A psychological study of eminent psychologists and anthropologists and a comparison with biological and physical scientists," *Psychol. Monogr.*, **67**, No. 2 (Whole No. 352). **[10]**

ROE, A. (1953b), *The Making of a Scientist.* New York: Dodd, Mead. **[10, 13]**

ROETHLISBERGER, F. J., and W. F. DICKSON (1939), *Management and the Worker.* Cambridge, Mass.: Harvard University Press. **[8, 15]**

ROGERS, C. R. (1961), *On Becoming a Person.* Boston: Houghton Mifflin. **[7, 14]**

ROKEACH, M. (1960), *The Open and Closed Mind.* New York: Basic Books. **[10]**

ROSEN, B. C. (1956), "The achievement syndrome: a psychocultural dimension of social stratification," *Amer. sociol. Rev.*, **21**, 203–211. **[12]**

Rosenberg, M. S. (1960), "Cognitive reorganization in response to the hypnotic reversal of affect," *J. Pers.*, **28**, 39–63. [16]

Rosenfeld, E. (1957), "Institutional change in the kibbutz," *Soc. Probl.*, **5**, 110–136. [11]

Rosenzweig, M. R., D. Krech, and E. L. Bennett (1960), "A search for relations between brain chemistry and behavior," *Psychol. Bull.*, **57**, 476–492. [4]

Ross, I., and A. Zander (1957), "Need satisfaction and employee turnover," *Personnel Psychol.*, **10**, 325–338. [15]

Ross, T. A. (1937), *The Common Neuroses*. Baltimore, Md.: William Wood. [14]

Rutherford, W. (1886), "The sense of hearing," *J. Anat. Physiol.*, **21**, 166–168. [6]

Sanford, F. H. (1965), *Psychology, the Scientific Study of Man*, second edition. Belmont, Calif.: Wadsworth. [14]

Sanford, R. N. (ed.) (1956), "Personality development during the college years," *J. soc. Issues*, **12**, No. 4. [13]

Sanford, R. N. (1943), "Personality patterns in school children," in R. G. Barker, J. S. Kounin, and H. F. Wright (eds.), *Child Behavior and Development*. New York: McGraw-Hill. [12]

Sarason, I. (1956), "Effect of anxiety, motivational instructions, and failure on serial learning," *J. exp. Psychol.*, **51**, 253–260. [1]

Schachter, S. (1959), *The Psychology of Affiliation*. Stanford: Stanford University Press. [7, 13]

Schachter, S. (1951), "Deviation, rejection, and communication," *J. abnorm. soc. Psychol.*, **46**, 190–207. [15]

Schachter, S., and J. Singer (1962), "Cognitive, social and physiological determinants of emotional state," *Psychol. Rev.*, **69**, 379–399. [7]

Schachter, S., N. Ellerston, D. McBride, and D. Gregory (1957), "An experimental study of cohesiveness and proactivity," *Hum. Relat.*, **4**, 229–238. [15]

Schafer, R., and G. Murphy (1943), "The role of autism in a visual figure-ground relationship," *J. exp. Psychol.*, **32**, 335–343. [6]

Schaie, K. W. (1958), "Rigidity-flexibility and intelligence: a cross-sectional study of the adult life span from 20 to 70 years," *Psychol. Monogr.*, **72** (9, Whole No. 462). [10]

Schlosberg, H. (1952), "The description of facial expressions in terms of two dimensions," *J. exp. Psychol.*, **44**, 229–237. [6]

Schlosberg, H. (1941), "A scale for judgment of facial expressions," *J. exp. Psychol.*, **29**, 497–510. [7]

Schramm, W., J. Lyle, and E. B. Parker (1961), *Television in the Lives of our Children*. Stanford, California: Stanford University Press. [13]

Scott, J. P. (1958), *Animal Behavior*. Chicago: The University of Chicago Press. [4]

Scott, W. A. (1957), "Attitude change through reward of verbal behavior," *J. abnorm. soc. Psychol.*, **55**, 72–75. [16]

Scottish Council for Research on Education (1949), *The Trend of Scottish Intelligence*. London: London University Press. [10]

Sears, P. S. (1941), "Level of aspiration in relation to some variables of personality: clinical studies," *J. soc. Psychol.*, **14**, 311–336. [13]

Sears, P. S. (1940), "Level of aspiration in academically successful and unsuccessful children," *J. abnorm. soc. Psychol.*, **35**, 498–536. [13]

Sears, R. R. (1961), "The relation of early socialization experiences to aggression in middle childhood," *J. abnorm. soc. Psychol.*, **63**, 466–492. [13]

Sears, R. R. (1936), "Experimental studies of projection: I. Attribution of traits," *J. soc. Psychol.*, **7**, 151–163. [11]

Sears, R. R., E. E. Maccoby, and H. Levin (1957), *Patterns of Child Rearing*. New York: Harper and Row. [13]

Sears, R. R., L. Rau, and R. Alpert (1960), "Identification and child training: the development of conscience," paper read in Chicago, American Psychol. Assoc. [13]

Sears, R. R., J. W. M. Whiting, V. Nowlis, and P. S. Sears (1953), "Some child-rearing antecedents of aggression and dependency in young children," *Genet. Psychol. Monogr.*, **47**, 135–236. [13]

Selye, H. (1956), *The Stress of Life*. New York: McGraw-Hill. [14]

Selye, H. (1950), *The Physiology and Pathology of Exposure to Stress*. Montreal: ACTA Press, Inc. [11, 14]

Senden, M. V. (1960), *Space and Sight; the Perception of Space and Shape in the Congenitally Blind Before and After Operation*. Translated by Peter Heath. London: Methuen. [6]

Sewell, W. H. (1952), "Infant training and the personality of the child," *Amer. J. Sociol.*, **58**, 150–159. [13]

Seward, J. P., and G. H. Seward (1940), "Studies on the reproductive activities of the guinea pig. I. Factors in maternal behavior," *J. comp. physiol. Psychol.*, **29**, 1–24. [7]

Shaffer, L. F., and E. J. Shoben (1956), *The Psychology of Adjustment*. Boston: Houghton Mifflin. [11]

Shaw, M. E. (1954), "Some effects of problem complexity upon problem solution efficiency in different communication nets," *J. exp. Psychol.*, **48**, 211–217. [15]

Shaw, M. E. (1932), "A comparison of individuals and small groups in the rational solution of complex problems," *Amer. J. Psychol.*, **44**, 491–504. [15]

Sheffield, F. D., and T. B. Roby (1950), "Reward value of a non-nutritive sweet taste," *J. comp. physiol. Psychol.*, **43**, 471–481. [5]

Sheldon, W. H., and S. S. Stevens (1942), *The Varieties of Temperament*. New York: Harper and Row. [12]

SHELDON, W. H., S. S. STEVENS, and W. B. TUCKER (1940), *The Varieties of Human Physique*. New York: Harper and Row. [12]

SHERIF, M. O., and C. SHERIF (1956), *An Outline of Social Psychology*. New York: Harper. [15]

SHERIF, M. O., and C. SHERIF (1953), *Groups in Harmony and Tension*. New York: Harper. [15]

SHIRE, A. (1954), *Personality Correlates of Defense Preferences*. Unpublished doctoral dissertation, University of Michigan. [11]

SINES, J. O. (1961), "Behavioral correlates of genetically enhanced susceptibility to stomach lesion development," *J. psychosom. Res.*, 5, 120–126. [14]

SINGH, J. A. L., and R. M. ZINGG (1942), *Wolf-Children and Feral Man*. New York: Harper. [8]

SKEELS, H. M. (1938), "Mental development of children in foster homes," *J. consult. Psychol.*, 2, 33–43. [10]

SKINNER, B. F. (1961), *Cumulative Record*. New York: Appleton-Century-Crofts. [5]

SKINNER, B. F. (1953), *Science and Human Behavior*. New York: Macmillan. [5, 8]

SKINNER, B. F. (1938), *The Behavior of Organisms*. New York: Appleton-Century-Crofts. [5, 8]

SKODAK, M. (1950), "Mental growth of adopted children in the same family," *J. genet. Psychol.*, 77, 3–9. [10]

SKODAK, M. (1938), "The mental development of adopted children whose true mothers are feeble-minded," *Child Develpm.*, 9, 303–308. [10]

SLACK, C. W., and R. SCHWITZGEBEL (1960), *A Handbook: Reducing Adolescent Crime in Your Community*. Privately printed. Cited in A. BANDURA and R. H. WALTERS, *Social Learning and Personality Development*. New York: Holt, 1963. [14]

SMEDSLUND, J. (1961), "The acquisition of conservation of substance and weight in children: III. Extinction of conservation of weight acquired normally and by means of empirical controls on a balance scale," *Scand. J. Psychol.*, 2, 85–87. [10]

SMITH, A. J., and A. M. FIELD (1926), "A study of the effect of nutrition on mental growth," *J. Home Econ.*, 18, 686–690. [10]

SMITH, K. U., *Delayed Sensory Feedback and Behavior*. Philadelphia: Saunders, 1962. [8]

SMITH, M. E. (1926), "An investigation of the development of the sentence and the extent of vocabulary in young children," *Univ. Ia. Stud. Child. Welf.*, 3, No. 5. [9]

SOLOMON, J. C. (1938), "Active play therapy," *Amer. J. Orthopsychiat.*, 8, 479. [14]

SOLOMON, R. L. (1964), "Punishment," *Amer. Psychologist*, 19, 239–253. [5]

SOLOMON, R. L., and D. H. HOWES (1951), "Word frequency, personal values and visual duration thresholds," *Psychol. Rev.*, 58, 256–270. [6]

SOLOMON, R. L., and L. POSTMAN (1952), "Frequency of usage as a determinant of recognition thresholds for words," *J. exp. Psychol.*, 43, 195–201. [6]

SOLOMON, R. L., and L. C. WYNNE (1954), "Traumatic avoidance learning; the principles of anxiety conservation and partial irreversibility," *Psychol. Rev.*, **61**, 353–385. **[7]**

SOLOMON, R. L., and L. C. WYNNE (1953), "Traumatic avoidance learning: Acquisition in normal dogs," *Psychol. Monogr.*, **67**, No. 354. **[7]**

SONTAG, L., and C. T. BAKER (1958), "Personality, familial, and physical correlates of change in mental ability," *Soc. for Res. in Child Develpm. Monogr.*, **23**, 87–143. **[10]**

SONTAG, L. W., C. T. BAKER, and V. L. NELSON (1958), "Mental growth and personality development: a longitudinal study," *Monogr. Soc. Res. Child Develpm.*, **23**, 1–85. **[10]**

SPIRO, M. E. (1958), *Children of the Kibbutz.* Cambridge: Harvard University Press. **[11]**

SPITZ, R. A. (1946), "Hospitalism: a follow-up report," *Psychoanalytic Study of the Child*, **2**, 113–118. **[13]**

SPITZ, R. A. (1945), "Hospitalism: an inquiry into the genesis of psychiatric conditions in early childhood," *Psychoanalytic Study of the Child*, **1**, 53–74. **[13]**

SPITZ, R. A., and K. M. WOLFF (1946), "Anaclitic depression," *Psychoanalytic Study of the Child*, **2**, 313–342. **[13]**

SPRANGER, E. (1928), *Types of Men* (P. Pigors, tr.). Halle: Niemeyer. **[7]**

STAATS, A. W., and C. K. STAATS (1959), "Meaning and *m:* correlated but separate," *Psychol. Rev.*, **66**, 136–144. **[8]**

STALNAKER, J. (1932), "Riddles: the effect of hypnosis on long-delayed recall," *J. gen. Psychol.*, **6**, 429–440. **[9]**

STAR, S. (1961), *The Dilemmas of Mental Illness.* Unpublished manuscript cited by Joint Commission on Mental Health. *Action for Mental Health.* New York: Basic Books. **[11]**

STEVENS, S. S. (1961), "To honor Fechner and repeal his law," *Science*, **133**, 80–86. **[6]**

STONE, C. P., and R. G. BARKER (1939), "The attitudes and interests of premenarcheal and postmenarcheal girls," *J. genet. Psychol.*, **54**, 27–71. **[13]**

STONE, C. P., C. W. DARROW, C. LANDIS, and L. L. HEATH (1932), *Studies in the Dynamics of Behavior.* Chicago: University of Chicago Press. **[4]**

STOUFFER, S. A. (1955), *Communism, Conformity, and Civil Liberties.* New York: Doubleday. **[16]**

STOUFFER, S. A., A. A. LUMSDAINE, M. H. LUMSDAINE, R. M. WILLIAMS, M. B. SMITH, I. L. JANIS, S. A. STAR, and L. S. COTTRELL (1949), *The American Soldier: Combat and Its Aftermath*, Vol. II. Princeton: Princeton University Press, 1949. **[7]**

STOUFFER, S. A., E. A. SUCHMAN, L. C. DEVINNEY, S. A. STAR, and R. M. WILLIAMS, JR., *The American Soldier: Adjustment During Army Life*, Vol. I. Princeton, N. J.: Princeton University Press, 1949. **[7, 12]**

STRAUS, R., and S. D. BACON (1953), *Drinking in College.* New Haven: Yale University Press. **[13]**

STREET, R. F. (1931), "A gestalt completion test; a study of a cross section of intellect," in *Teachers College Contributions to Education No. 481.* New York: Teachers College, Columbia University. **[6]**

STRICKER, G. (1963), "Scapegoating: an empirical investigation," *J. abnorm. soc. Psychol.,* **67,** 127–131. **[16]**

STRODTBECK, F. L. (1951), "Husband-wife interaction over revealed differences," *Amer. sociol Rev.,* **16,** 468–473. **[14]**

STRONG, E. K. (1955), *Vocational Interest Eighteen Years after College.* Minneapolis: University of Minnesota Press. **[7]**

STRONG, E. K. (1943), *Vocational Interests of Men and Women.* Stanford: Stanford University Press. **[7, 13]**

SUCHMAN, E. A. (1950), "The intensity component in attitude and opinion research," in S. A. STOUFFER *et al., Measurement and Prediction.* Princeton. N. J.: Princeton University Press. **[16]**

SUPA, M., M. COTZIN, and K. M. DALLENBACH (1944), "Facial vision; the perception of obstacles by the blind," *Amer. J. Psychol.,* **57,** 133–183. **[6]**

SWEENEY, E. J. (1953), "Sex differences in problem solving," *Stanford Univer. Dept. Psychol. Tech. Rep.,* No. 1. **[10]**

TAGUIRI, R., N. KOGAN, and J. S. BRUNER (1955), "The transparency of interpersonal choice," *Sociometry,* **18,** 624–635. **[15]**

TANNENBAUM, P. H. (1956), "Initial attitude toward source and concept as factors in attitude change through communication," *Publ. Opin. Quart.,* **20,** 413–425. **[16]**

TANNER, W. P., JR., and R. Z. NORMAN (1954), "The human use of information. II. Signal detection for the case of an unknown signal parameter," *Trans. of the I.R.E., Professional Group on Information Theory,* Sept. 1954, PGIT–4. **[6]**

TANNER, W. P., and J. A. SWETS (1953), *A New Theory of Visual Detection.* Engineer. Res. Institute Tech. Rep. No. 18. Ann Arbor: University of Michigan Engineering Research Institute. **[6]**

TAYLOR, D. W., P. C. BERRY, and C. H. BLOCK (1958), "Does group participation when using brain storming facilitate or inhibit creative thinking?" *Admin. sci. Quart.,* **3,** 23–47. **[15]**

TAYLOR, J. A. (1951), "The relationship of anxiety to the conditioned eyelid response," *J. exp. Psychol.,* **41,** 81–92. **[1]**

TERMAN, L. M., and M. A. MERRILL (1960), *Stanford-Binet Intelligence Scale.* Boston: Houghton Mifflin. **[10]**

TERMAN, L. M., and M. A. MERRILL (1937), *Measuring Intelligence.* Boston: Houghton Mifflin. **[10]**

TERMAN, L., and C. MILES (1936), *Sex and Personality.* New York: McGraw-Hill. [6]

THIBAULT, J., and B. WILLERMAN, "Group cohesiveness: an introduction," unpublished manuscript cited in D. CARTWRIGHT and A. ZANDER (eds.), *Group Dynamics.* Evanston, Ill.: Row Peterson, 1960. [15]

THISTLEWAITE, D. (1950), "Attitude and structure as factors in the distortion of reasoning." *J. abnorm. soc. Psychol.*, 45, 442–458. [10]

THOMAS, A., H. G. BIRCH, S. CHESS, M. HERTZIG, and S. KORN (1963), *Behavioral Individuality in Childhood.* New York: New York University Press. [13]

THOMAS, W. I. (1937), *Primitive Behavior.* New York: McGraw-Hill. [2]

THOMPSON, C. W., F. J. NAGLE, and R. DOBIAS (1958), "Football starting signals and movement times of high school and college football players," *Res. Quart. Amer. Assoc. Hlth. Phys. Educ.*, 29, 222–230. [7]

THOMPSON, L., and A. JOSEPH (1944), *The Hopi Way.* Chicago: University of Chicago Press. [2]

THOMPSON, R., and J. V. McCONNELL (1955), "Classical conditioning in the planarian, *dugesia dorotocephala*," *J. comp physiol. Psychol.*, 48, 65–68. [5]

THOMPSON, W. E., and G. F. STREIB (1961), "Meaningful activity in a family context," in R. W. KLEEMEIER (ed.), *Aging and Leisure.* New York: Oxford University Press, 177–211. [13]

THORNDIKE, E. L. (1911), *Animal Intelligence.* New York: Macmillan. [5]

THORNDIKE, E. L. (1898), "Animal intelligence: an experimental study of the associative processes in animals," *Psychol. Rev. Monogr.*, 7, 4 (Whole No. 8). [8]

THORNDIKE, R. L. (1938), "The effect of discussion upon the correctness of group decisions when the factor of majority influence is allowed for," *J. soc. Psychol.*, 9, 343–362. [15]

THOULESS, R. H. (1932), "Individual differences in phenomenal regression," *Brit. J. Psychol.*, 22, 216–241. [6]

THURSTONE, L. L. (1938), "Primary mental abilities," *Psychomet. Monogr.*, No. 1. Chicago: University of Chicago Press. [9]

THURSTONE, L. L., and E. J. CHAVE (1929), *The Measurement of Attitudes.* Chicago: University of Chicago Press. [16]

TINBERGEN, N. (1952), "The curious behavior of the stickleback," *Sci. Amer.*, 187 (6), 22–26. [4]

TOLMAN, E. C. (1951), *Collected Papers in Psychology.* Berkeley, Calif.: University of Calif. Press. [7, 8]

TRYON, R. C. (1940), "Genetic differences in maze-learning ability in rats," *Thirty-ninth Yrbk. Nat. Soc. Stud. Educ.*, Part 1, 111–119. [4]

TWINER, A. N. (1956), "A researcher views human adjustment to automation," *Advanc. Mgmt.*, 21 (5), 21–25. [II]

TYLER, L. E. (1965), *The Psychology of Human Differences*. New York: Appleton-Century-Crofts. [12]

UHR, L., and J. G. MILLER (1960), *Drugs and Behavior*. New York: John Wiley. [14]

UNDERWOOD, B. J. (1957), "Interference and forgetting," *Psychol. Rev.*, **64**, 49–60. [8]

UNDERWOOD, B. J., and R. W. SCHULZ (1961), "Studies of distributed practice: XX. Sources of interference associated with differences in learning and retention," *J. exp. Psychol.*, **61**, 228–235. [8]

UNITED STATES WAR DEPARTMENT, INFORMATION AND EDUCATIONAL DIVISION (1952), "Opinions about Negro infantry platoons in white companies of seven divisions," in G. E. SWANSON, T. M. NEWCOMB, and E. L. HARLEY, *Readings in Social Psychology*. New York: Holt. [16]

USEEM, J., P. TANGENT, and R. USEEM (1942), "Stratification in a prairie town," *Amer. sociol. Rev.*, **7**, 331–342. [2]

VANDENBURG, S. G. (1962), "The hereditary abilities study: hereditary components in a psychological test battery," *Amer. J. Hum. Genet.*, **14**, 220–237. [4]

VERNON, P. E., and G. W. ALLPORT (1931), "A test for personal values," *J. abnorm. soc. Psychol.*, **26**, 231–248. [6]

VON BÉKÉSY, G. (1960), *Experiments in Hearing*, translated and edited by E. G. WEVER). New York: McGraw-Hill, 1960. [6]

VON BÉKÉSY, G. (1953), "Description of some of the properties of the Organ of Corti," *J. Acoust. Soc. Amer.*, **25**, 786–790. [6]

VON NEUMANN, J. (1958), *The Computer and the Brain*. New Haven: Yale University Press. [3]

WALD, G. (1950), "Eye and camera," *Sci. Amer.*, **183** (Aug.), 32–41. [6]

WALKER, E. L. (1956), "The duration and course of the reaction decrement and the influence of reward," *J. comp. physiol. Psychol.*, **49**, 173. [8]

WALKER, E. L., and R. W. HEYNS (1962), *An Anatomy for Conformity*. Englewood Cliffs, N. J.: Prentice-Hall. [16]

WATSON, J. B. (1917), "The effect of delayed feeding upon learning," *Psychobiology*, **1**, 51–60. [5]

WATSON, J. B. (1925), *Behaviorism*. New York: Norton. [1]

WATSON, J. B., and R. RAYNER (1920), "Conditioned emotional responses," *J. exp. Psychol.*, **39**, 1–14. [5, 7]

WEBB, W. B. (1947), "Occupational indecision among college students," *Occupations*, **27**, 331–332. [13]

WEINSTOCK, S. (1954), "Resistance to extinction following partial reinforcement under widely spaced trials," *J. exp. Psychol.*, **47**, 318–323. [5]

WEISSBERG, N. C., and H. PROSHANSKY (1963), "The Jewish anti-Semite's perception of fellow Jews," *J. Soc. Psychol.*, **63**, 139–151. **[15]**

WELLS, W. D., and B. SIEGEL (1961), "Stereotyped somatotypes," *Psychol. Rep.*, **8**, 77–78. **[12]**

WEVER, E. G. (1949), *Theory of Hearing.* New York: Wiley. **[6]**

WEVER, E. G., and C. W. BRAY (1930), "Present possibilities for auditory theory," *Psychol. Rev.*, **37**, 365–380. **[6]**

WHITE, R. K., and R. LIPPITT (1960), *Autocracy and Democracy.* New York: Harper. **[15]**

WHITE, R. W. (1963), *The Abnormal Personality* (third ed.). New York: Ronald. **[11, 14]**

WHITING, J. W. M., and I. L. CHILD (1953), *Child Training and Personality.* New Haven: Yale University Press. **[2]**

WHITING, J. W. M., and O. H. MOWRER (1943), "Habit progression and regression— a laboratory study relevant to human socialization," *J. comp. Psychol.*, **36**, 229– 253. **[5]**

WHORF, B. L. (1956), *Language, Thought and Reality.* New York: Wiley. **[9]**

WHORF, B. L. (1947), "Science and linguistics," in T. L. NEWCOMB and E. L. HARTLEY, *Readings in Social Psychology.* New York: Holt. **[2]**

WICKERT, F. R. (1951), "Turnover, and employees' feelings of ego-involvement in the day-to-day operations of a company," *Personnel Psychol.*, **4**, 185–197. **[13]**

WIENER, D. N., and D. R. STIEPER, "Psychometric prediction of length and outcome of outpatient therapy," manuscript cited by S. SCHACHTER in *The Psychology of Affiliation.* Stanford: Stanford University Press, 1959. **[7]**

WILKINS, M. C. (1928), "The effect of changed material on the ability to do syllogistic reasoning," *Arch. Psychol. N. Y.*, No. 102. **[10]**

WINCH, R. F. (1958), *Mate Selection: A Study of Complementary Needs.* New York: Harper. **[13]**

WITTENBORN, J. R., *et al.* (1956), "A study of adoptive children. I. Interviews as a source of scores for children and their homes. II. The predictive validity of the 'Yale Developmental Examination of Infant Behavior.' III. Relationships between some aspects of development and some aspects of environment for adoptive children," *Psychol. Monogr.*, **70** (1, 2, 3) (Nos. 408, 409, 410), 1–115. **[8, 10]**

WITTMAN, M. P. (1944), "A scale for measuring prognosis in schizophrenic patients," *Elgin Papers*, **4**, 20–33. **[12]**

WOLF, S., and H. G. WOLFF (1942), "Evidence on the genesis of peptic ulcer in man," *J. Amer. med. Assoc.*, **120**, 670–675. **[14]**

WOLFE, J. B. (1936), "Effectiveness of token reward for chimps," *Comp. Psychol. Monogr.*, **12**, No. 60. **[5]**

WOLFE, J. B. (1934), "The effect of delayed reward upon learning in the white rat," *J. comp. Psychol.*, **17**, 1–21. **[5]**

WOLFLE, D. L. (1954), *America's Resources of Specialized Talent.* New York: Harper. **[II]**

WOLFLE, D. L. (1935), "The relative efficiency of constant and varied stimulation during learning," *J. comp. Psychol.,* **19,** 5–27. **[10]**

WOLFLE, H. (1932), "Conditioning as a function of the interval between the conditioned and original stimulus," *J. gen. Psychol.,* **7,** 80–103. **[5]**

WOLPE, J. (1958), *Psychotherapy by Reciprocal Inhibition.* Stanford, Calif.: Stanford University Press. **[14]**

WOODWORTH, R. S. (1958), *Dynamics of Behavior.* New York: Holt. **[7]**

WOODWORTH, R. S. (1938), *Experimental Psychology.* New York: Holt. **[9]**

WOODWORTH, R. S., and H. SCHLOSBERG (1954), *Experimental Psychology* (revised edition). New York: Holt. **[7]**

WRIGHT, H. F. (1956), "Psychological development in the Midwest," *Child Develpm.,* **27,** 265–286. **[13]**

YANG, C. K. (1959), *A Chinese Village in Early Communist Transition.* Cambridge: Harvard University Press. **[II]**

YERKES, R. M. (1921), *Psychological Examining in the U.S. Army.* Washington, D.C.: U.S. Government Printing Office. **[4]**

YOUNG, P. T. (1961), *Motivation and Emotions.* New York: Wiley. **[7]**

ZEAMAN, D. (1949), "Response latency as a function of the amount of reinforcement," *J. exp. Psychol.,* **39,** 466–483. **[8]**

ZILLIG, M. (1928), "Einstellung und Aussage." *Z. Psychol.,* **106,** 58–106. Cited by D. KRECH, R. S. CRUTCHFIELD, and E. L. BALLACHEY in *Individual in Society.* New York: McGraw-Hill, 1962. **[15]**

index

A

Absolute threshold, 165–167, **200**
and set, 184–185
Abstract thinking and brain injury, 363–364
Abstraction, 128–129
species differences in, 85–86
Academic success, prediction of, 442
Accommodation, 151
Acetylcholine, 49
Achievement motivation, 219–221
in childhood, 468–469
and college adjustment, 174
and group membership, 533
individual differences in, 253
Acquiescence, in answering questionnaire items, 433
Act, definition of, 101–102, **134**
Act selection, 133–134, 266–272
habit strength and, 269–271
motivation and, 269, 270
perception and, 266–269
Act tendencies, 117–119, 131–132, 270, 271
Action, 260–300
and attitudes, 567–569
development of, 285–293
individual differences in, 293–295
physiological basis of, 260–262
practical application of principles of, 295–298
Action component of an attitude;
see Attitude, action component of
Action decrement, 271–272, 281, **298**
Activator drugs, 627–628
Activity, 92
individual differences in, 293–294
Acts, dimensions of, 262–266
precision of, 263
strength of, 262–263
time measures for, 263–265
Adaptation level, 162–163, **199**
Adaptation, 162–164, **199**
in the perception of temperature, 160
in vision, 148
Additive mixture, 145
Adjustment (as a continuum), 486
Adler, A., 496
Adolescence, 470–472
conformity, 471
intelligence in, 472
physical development in, 470, 472
thinking in, 366–367
Adolescents, advisors to, 471
problems of, 470–471
Adolf, E. F., 210
Adorno, T. W., 573
Adrenal gland, 62, 63
Adulthood, 477–480
thinking in, 368
Affect, 118
inconsistent, 130–131
operationalizing, 206
physiological basis of, 231–233
Affective component of an attitude;
see Attitude, affective component of
Affective feedback, 118–120, **135**, 271
Affiliation motive, 214–215
and group membership, 533
and liking for college courses, 440
Afterimage, 148, 149
Age and personality characteristics, 423–424
Aggression, 227, 380, 381, 396–397
and imitation, 463–464
norms concerning, 28
in primitive cultures, 24–27
and reinforcement, 463
and sibling rivalry, 462

sociological differences in, 402
theories relating to physical
punishment and, 463
Aichorn, A., 514, 516
Alarm reaction, 380
Alcohol, and the brain, 64, 65
effects of intoxication from, 61
and memory, 320–321
and performance efficiency, 65
Alcoholism (and affiliation), 215
Alexander, F., 504
All-or-none law, 49, **66**
versus graded conduction, 50
Allison, J. K., 250, 251
Allport, G. W., 251, 252, 410, 443,
481, 527
Allport-Vernon Scale, 251–252
Allyn, J., 579
Ambiguity, 187, **200**
effect of reward on, 192
situational, 376
Ambiguous stimuli and conformity, 588
Ambivalence, 131, 243
American Psychiatric Association, 488
Amnesia, 320, 490
Amphetamine, 627
Amsel, A., 125
Anal stage, 396
Anderson, J. E., 469
Andersson, B., 210
Anger, 227, 234–235, 380, 381, 396–7
and adrenal hormones, 62, 63
Animal communication, 325
Anrep, G. V., 104
Anti-Semitism, 571, 573
Anxiety, 224
and affiliation, 214–215
and learning, 14–16
and memory, 314
operational definition of, 14
as a reaction to frustrating situations,
380, 381–382

Anxiety reaction, 489, 491
Anxiety theory of neurosis, 491–492
Aphasia, 338, **340**
Approach-approach conflict, 242, 243–245
displacement as, 385–386
sublimation as, 389
Approach gradients, 241, 244–245
Aptitude tests, 298
Arapesh, 24, 25, 33, 84
Aring, C. D., 369
Army General Classification Test, 357
Aronfreed, J., 468
Arousal, 233–235, 239–240, 501
Asch, S., 523, 586, 588
Assessment, as an empirical approach,
13–15
of personality, 410–446
Astrology, 2
Athletic ability, 294
Atkinson, J. W., 185, 221, 474
Atmosphere effect, 352
Attention, 171–172
determiners of, 172–173
development of perceptual categories
and, 191
motivation and, 186
Attention span, 172, **200**
Attitude, 560, **594**
action component of, 560–561
affective component of, 560–561
centrality of, 572, **594**
cognitive component of, 561
components of, 560–562
consistency of components of, 566–569
differentiation of, 561
dimensions of, 560–562
ego-defensive, 571
intensity of, 560–561
knowledge function for, 571–572
position on, 560–561
specificity of, 561
utilitarian, 570
value expressive, 570–571

Attitude change, 575–587
  beliefs and, 577–578
  change in action component and,
    581–584
  change in affective component and,
    579–581
  change in cognitive component and,
    574–579
  fear and, 580–581
  group participation and, 584–587
  intentional persuasion and, 579
  mass media versus personal contact,
    579
  nature of the persuader and, 578–579
  and one-sided versus two-sided
    messages, 575–576
  perceived consensus and, 586
  prestige of the source and, 576–577
  public commitment and, 585
  reward and, 582–583
  sleeper effect in, 576–577
  stating opinions contrary to one's
    attitude and, 582–583
Attitude formation, 569–572
Attitude scales, 562–566
Attitude systems, 573–574, **594**
Attitudes, and action, 567–569
  measurement of, 562–566
  organization of, 572–574
Audition 142, 154–157
  dimensions of, 154–155
  theories of, 156–157
Auditory nerve, coding in, 157
Authoritarian attitude system, 573–574
Authoritarian leadership, 546–549
Authoritarianism, conformity and, 589
  prejudice and, 573–574
Authoritarianism study, criticisms
    of, 574
Automation, 620–621
Autonomic nervous system, 63, 64, **67**
Autonomy (in the second year), 465
Average deviation, 601

Avoidance-avoidance conflict, 243
Avoidance gradients, 241, 244, 245
Avoidance training, extinction of, 226
Axelrod, H. S., 17
Axelrod, M., 531
Axon, 47–51
Azrin, N. H., 119

B

Back, K. W., 579
Bacon, S. D., 474
Bakan, D., 215
Baker, C. T., 365
Baldwin, A. L., 247
Bales, R. F., 540, 541, 542, 550
Ballachey, E. L., 549
Bandura, A., 463–464, 467, 514, 516
Barach, A. L., 65, 321
Barber, T. X., 27
Barbiturates, 65
Barker, R. G., 389–391, 472
Barron, F., 363
Bartlett, F. C., 315–317
Basilar membrane, 156
  in theories of pitch perception, 156–157
Bateman, D. E., 234
Baumgartel, H., 534
Bayley, N., 368
Beach, F., 80, 453
Beck, E. C., 117
Becker, W. C., 463
Behavior, levels of description of, 101–102
Behavior therapy, 499–500
  juvenile delinquency and, 516
Behavioral level (of studying the
    organism), 46
Behaviorism, 5, 6
Békésy, G. von, 157
Beliefs, 27
  attitude change and, 577–578
  culture and, 27

Beloff, H., 445
Beloff, J. R., 494
Bennett, C. H., 511
Bennett, E., 585, 586
Bennett, E. C., 88–89
Bentham, J., 3
Benzedrine, 65, 627
Berelson, B. R., 579
Berko, J., 335
Berkowitz, L., 552–563
Berlyne, D. E., 217, 218
Bettelheim, B., 383, 387–388, 393
Betting, studies of, 349
Biel, W. C., 620
Bimodal distribution, 600
Binet, A., 354–357
Binomial expansion, 613–614
Birch, H. G., 350
Birth order and affiliation, 215
Birth trauma, 401
Blade, M. F., 195
Blewett, D. B., 494
Blind spot, 145, 147
Blodgett, H. C., 117–118
Blood, R. O., 479
Blum, G. S., 185, 383
Bogardus Social Distance Scale, 566
Boredom, as a construct, 7, 8
Bossio, V., 455
Bousfield, W. A., 314–315
Bowman, P. H., 389
Brady, J. V., 501–503
Brain, 52–57
    alcohol and, 64, 65
    autonomous activity in, 60, 185
    drugs and, 64, 65
    electrical activity of, 53
    learning and, 60, 100
    neuronal arrangement in, 58
    parts of, 52
    self-stimulation of, 231–233

sensory nerve activity interaction
    with on-going activity in, 58–59
species differences in, 85–86
Brain injury, 61, 65, 66
    memory and, 319–320
    problem solving and, 363–364
Brain stem, 52, 55, 56, 85
    injury to, 66
Braly, K. W., 524
Bray, C. W., 157, 282
Brayfield, A. H., 477
Bridges, K. M., 246
Brightness constancy, 177–178
Broadhurst, P. L., 239–240
Brock, T., 585
Brogden, W. J., 108, 115–117
Bronfenbrenner, U., 455, 458, 530
Bronson, W. C., 445
Brown, J. S., 241, 242
Brown, R., 284, 367
Bruner, J., 180, 529
Bulbocapnine, 117
Bugelski, B. R., 112
Burgess, E. W., 478, 479
Burks, B. S., 510
Burton, R. V., 438, 468
Burtt, H. E., 310
Butler, R. A., 216

C

Caffeine, 65
Cahill, H. E., 328
Caldwell, B. M., 456
Cameron, N., 505
Campbell, A., 13
Campbell, D., 566–567, 568–569, 571
Campbell, E. H., 585
Cannell, R. L., 425
Cannon, W. B., 27
Cantril, H., 527

Cardiac muscle, 261–262

Carey, G. L., 358

Carlsmith, J. M., 583

Carlson, E. R., 577–578

Carrigan, P. M., 417

Carter, L. R., 552

Casler, L., 455

Castration, effects of, 212–213

Catatonic schizophrenia, 507

Categorization, **200**
  cultural differences in, 26–27
  development of, 190–192
  memory and, 314–317
  perception and, 180–188
  social perception and, 524

Category analysis of communication, 540–542

Cattell, R. B., 92, 412, 415, 416, 418, 421, 431, 438, 445, 494

Cattell 16 Personality Factor Test, 431

Causes versus factors or predictors, 4

Cavan, R. S., 513, 514

Cell-body, 48–51

Centile, 422

Central nervous system (CNS), 47, 52, 57–67, **66**
  endocrine glands and, 61–64
  heredity and, 88–89
  injury and, 65, 66
  learning and, 60, 100
  metabolic activity and, 59
  species differences in, 85–88
  stimuli and, 57–59
  substances ingested and, 64, 65

Central tendency, measures of, 599–600

Cerebral cortex, 52, 53
  functions of, 54–55
  injury to, 65
  maze-learning ability and, 88–89
  neuronal arrangement in, 58
  perception and, 142

species differences in, 85
stimulation of, 54

Chapman, R. L., 620

Chave, E. J., 562

Chemical senses, 157–159

Child, I. L., 31, 41

Child-training practices, culture and, 31–33
  frustration tolerance and, 403
  problem solving and, 370
  religion and, 37

Childhood, development in, early, 465–468
  late, 468–470

Chimpanzees, raised in human environments, 82, 87

Chinese communes, 631–632

Chloropromazine, 65, 627

Choice decisions, 134

Cholinesterase, 89

Chromosomes, 72–74, 94
  assortment in sex cells, 72–73
  relation of those in parents and children, 72–73

Clairvoyance, 168

Clark, R. A., 394

Clarke, R. S., 453

Classical conditioning; *see* Conditioning, classical

Cleanliness training; *see* Toilet training

Clergymen, as counselors, 630

Client-centered therapy, 496–497

Clinical versus statistical prediction, 440

Coch, L., 548

Cochlea, 142, 156

Coding of stimuli by the nervous system, 140–143

Coffman, W. E., 337

Cognition, 304–371

Cognitive component of an attitude; *see* Attitude, cognitive component of

Cognitive dissonance, theory of, 219,
    583–584, **594**
Cognitive harmony, attitude formation
    and, 571–572
  fear and, 223
  motives for, 218–219
  perception and, 191–192
Cohesiveness (group), 533–536, **554**
Cohen, J., 353
Cohesiveness, factors influencing,
    535–536
  and group consensus, 545
  and group productivity, 544–545
  operationalizing, 534–535
Coleman, L., 505, 508, 510, 512
College adjustment, 472–575
College success, 475–476
  predictions of, 4, 625–626
  student goals and, 473
Collins, M. E., 581
Color blindness, 148, 193
Color constancy, 177, 178
Color mixture, 145
Color vision, 143, 145, 148
  theories of, 149–150
Communes, Chinese, 631–632
Communication, 537
  among children, 538
  category analysis in, 540–542
  intentional, 538
  productivity and, 545–546
  social, 537
Communication channels, 539–540, **554**
Communication net, conductivity of, 540
Communication nets (in small
    groups), 539–540, **555**
  and group productivity, 546
  and leadership, 553–554
Comparative psychology, 88
Competence motives, 215–221, 222
  and attitudes, 571–572
Complementarity, in mate selection, 478

Complementary hues, 145
Compliance, 586, 587–592, **594**
  to legitimate authority, 590–592
Compulsion, 490
Computer, analogy to study of
    behavior, 46–47
Concentration, improvement of, 198
Concept formation, 329–330
Concept strength, 181–182
Concepts, **200**
  culture and, 26, 27
  development of, 190–192
  language and, 324–325
  learning of, 128–130
  memory and, 314–317, 321
  perception, 180–188
  time, 27
Concrete operations period, 365–366
Concurrent validity, 420–421
Conditioned responses, in infancy,
    188–189
Conditioning, backward, 113
Conditioning, classical, 102–104, **134**
  anxiety and, 14–15
  emotional responses and, 105
  frequency and, 104–105
  instrumental conditioning and,
    105, 108
  involuntary muscles and, 261–262
  species and, 105
  time relations in, 113
Conditioning, expectancies and, 121
Conditioning, instrumental, 105–108, **134**
  classical conditioning and, 105, 108
  involuntary muscles and, 261–262
  time relations in, 113–114
Conditioning, second order, 111
Conduct disorders, 512–516, **517**
Conductivity in a communication net, 540
Cones, 142, 145–146
Conflict, between culture and home
    training, 33–41

in college adjustment, 473–474
cultural, 40–41
Freudian theory of, 378–380
in marriage, 479
of motives, 377–378
opposing muscles and, 262
resolution of, 244–245
role, 36
Conflict, types of, 243–244
and selection of defense mechanisms, 395
Conformity, 587–589, **594**
adolescence and, 471
among the people within a culture, 29–31
and authoritarianism, 589
cross-cultural differences in, 589
feedback and, 588–589
individual differences in, 589
nature of the group and, 588
nature of the stimuli and, 588
Connotation, 326–328, **340**
Conrad, H. S., 445
Conscience, 379
Conservation, concept of, 366, 367–368
Consistency (in child training), 458
Constancy (in perception), 177–178, **200**
individual differences in, 194
Constructs, 7 10, **18**
conditioning and, 115–119, 121
culture and, 26–29
predictions and, 8
Contact comfort, 212, **254**
Contiguity (temporal), 113–114, 119
distant goals and, 248–250
Control group, 12
Convergence, 151
Converse, P. E., 13
Conversion reaction, 490–491, 492
Coombs, C. H., 337, 349
Coover, J. E., 168, 169
Copernicus, N., 3

Cornsweet, T., 153
Correlation, negative, 605–608
Pearson product-moment, 608
positive, 604–608
rank-order, 607–608
Correlation coefficient, 92–93, **94,** 605–608, **614**
Cortex; *see* Cerebral cortex
Cortin, 63
Cotzin, M., 191
Cowen, E. L., 17
Creative people, study of, 363
Creativity and intelligence tests, 361–363
Cretinism, 88
Critical periods, 289–290
in the development of thinking, 367–368
in learning skills, 83–84
Crockett, W. H., 477
Cronbach, L. J., 529
Crossman, E. R. F. W., 263
Crow, W. J., 530
Crutchfield, R., 549, 588, 589
Cruz, W. W., 288, 289
Cues, 180, **200**
activation of motives and, 237–238
drives and, 209–211
selection of defense mechanisms and, 393
Culler, E., 108
Cultural change, 39–41
Cultural conflict, 40–41
Cultural differences in conformity, 589
Cultural lag, 39–40, 42
Culturally deprived children, intelligence test scores and, 359–360
Culture, 24–26, **41**
ability of humans to profit from, 87
child training and, 31–33
children growing up without, 28–29
conformity within, 29–31

continuity of, 29–31
  maturation and, 84, 288
  mental processes and, 26–29
  sex roles and, 24–26
  sources of variability in, 33–38
Cumulative response curves, 122–123
Cunningham, B., 152
Customs, habits and, 28

D

D'Amato, M. R., 224
Dallenbach, K. M., 191, 308, 311
Darley, J., 528, 544
Darwinian theory, 5
Data, 6, **18**
  inferences and, 6–10
Dawes, R., 352
Day dreams (of college students), 389, 390
Decision making, 347, **371**
  barriers to, 369–370
Decisions, choice, 134
Deduction, 350–353
Deese, J., 318
Defense mechanisms, 381, **403**
  appropriateness of, 391–392
  attitudes and, 571
  functions of, 382
  persistence of, 398–400
  prejudice and, 571
  primary, 383–384
  secondary, 384–391
  selection of, 392–396
  sociological differences in, 402
  types of, 383
Déjà vu, 305
Delayed sensory feedback, 268
Delgado, J. M., 233
Delinquency, juvenile, 512–515
  geographic distribution in a city, 512–513

  prevention of, 516
  treatment of, 515–516
Delinquent, antisocial, 514
  dissocial, 512–514
  juvenile 512–516
Delinquents, families of, 514, 515
  MMPI profiles of, 430
Delusion, 507
Dember, W. N., 216
Dembo, T., 389–391
Democratic leadership, 546–549
Dendrite, 47–51
Denial, 383, 396
Dennis, W., 83
Denotation, 326, **340**
Dependence, 418
Dependency, species differences in, 87
Dependency and frustration in nursing and weaning, 457
Dependent variable, 12, 16, **18**
Depression, psychotic, 506, 509
Depressive reactions, neurotic, 489–490, 492
Depth perception, 150–151, 152
  in infancy, 189–190
Descriptive statistics, 598–611
Desoxyribonucleic acid (DNA), 72, 74, **94**
Detection, of obstacles by blind people, 190
  practical applications and, 196
  threshold measures of, 165–166, 186
Deutsch, M., 581
DeValois, R., 150
Development, 75
  of action, 285–293
  of internal standards, 466–468
  of language, 328–335
  of memory, 318–319
  of motives, 245–254
  of perception, 188–192
  of the person, 450–482

of reactions to frustrating situations, 396–400

Developmental stage hypothesis, selection of neurotic symptoms, 493

Developmental stages and selection of defense mechanisms, 395

Dickson, W. F., 275, 545

Difference threshold, 164–165, **199**

Dill, W. R., 546

Dimock, H. S., 534

Disarranged sentences, 336

Discipline, physical, 462–463
    verbal, 466

Discrimination, 127
    boundaries of concepts and, 181
    cultural differences in, 26

Discrimination learning, 127, **135**

Disparity, retinal, 151

Displacement, 384–386
    in phobic reactions, 489

Dissociative reactions, 490

Dissonance, cognitive; *see* Cognitive dissonance

Distributions, types of, 602–603

Disuse, atrophy of muscles and, 260
    memory and, 310–311

d-lysergic acid diethylamide (LSD 25), 65, 168, 510–511, 628

Dobelle, W. H., 150

Dollard, J., 132, 227, 284, 463

Dominance, cultural differences in sex roles and, 24–26
    leadership and, 552–553

Doty, R. W., 117

Douglas, V., 396

Drive, 208

Drive reduction as a theory of reenforcement, 110–111, 270

Drives, physiological, 208–211, 245

Drug therapy in treatment of psychosis, 512

Drugs, 64, 65, 168, 626–628; *see also* specific drug names

Dvorak, A., 298

Dymond, R., 529

E

Ear, 156

Eardrum, 156

Earl, R. W., 217

Ebbinghaus, H., 3, 306–307

Ectomorph, 423

Education, principles of problem solving and, 371

Edwards, A. L., 297, 431, 433

Edwards Personal Preference Schedule, 431–432, 433

Effectors, 47, **66**, 260–262

Efron, D., 28

Ego, 378–380

Ego-defensive attitude, 571

Ego ideal, 379
    value-expressive attitudes and, 570

Eidetic imagery, 305

Election campaigns, 12–13

Electric shock, as a negative reinforcer, 107–108
    as a UCS, 105, 108

Electrical recording, 53, 54
    from the auditory nerve, 157
    from the visual system, 148–149

Electrical stimulation, 53, 54, 231–233

Electroencephalogram (EEG), 53, 101
    and psychopaths, 515

Electroshock therapy, 511, 512, 627–628

Ellson, D. G., 168

Emotion, 223–235, **255**

Emotional bias, 352

Emotional maturity, nature of, 482

Emotional responses, classical conditioning and, 105, 108
    in infancy, 190

Emotional stability, neuroticism, 415–416

Emotions, differentiation of, 246
judgment of from facial expressions, 526–52

Empirical method, for establishing validity, 420
of identifying personality traits, 412

Empirical study, 11–17, **18**

Endocrine glands, 61–64, **67**

Endomorph, 423

Energizers, 627

Engineering psychologist, 298

Environment, cultural, 24
description of, 102
heredity and, 91–93
impact of, in infancy, 452–456
interuterine, 75
physical, 5

Epinephrin, 49, 62, 63, 233, 234–235

Epstein, A. N., 209

Equal-appearing intervals, 563, 564

Equilibrium, perception of, 142, 162

Equipment design, 297–298

Erikson, E. H., 457, 465, 468, 470, 479, 480, 481, 482

Eron, L. D., 463

Escalona, S. K., 455

Eskimos, 24, 25

Estes, W. K., 119

Estrogen, 63

Ethnocentrism, study of, 573–574

Ethnocentrism scale, 573

Euphoria, 234–235

Expectancies, act, 117–119, 131–132
conditioning and, 121
discrimination and, 127
generalization and, 127
motivational, 117–119, 131–132
perceptual, 115–117, 131–132

Experimental designs, 16

Experimental neurosis, 219

Exploratory behavior, 217–218

Extinction, 109, 110, **135**
learned fears and, 226–227
partial reinforcement and, 122–125

Extrasensory perception, 168–170

Extroversion, 417–418
in identical twins, 92
objective behavior tests and, 438

Eye, 145–148
compared to a camera, 145–146
movements of, 151, 153
neuron connections of, 147–148

Eyelid conditioning, 105

Eysenck, H., 92, 414, 415, 416, 438, 494, 501

F

Facial expressions, judgment of, 228–229, 526–527
learned and unlearned components, 245–246

Facilitation, 50, 59, 60

Factor analysis, 608–609
in Cattell 16 Personality Factor Test, 431
of connotative meaning, 326–328
honesty test data and, 438
in identifying personality traits, 412–413
of intelligence test items, 361

Factorial validity, 420–421

Factors versus causes, 4

Failure, fear of, 220
college success and, 474
in later childhood, 468–469

Family organizations, patterns of, 631–633

Fantasy, 389
development of, 396, 397

Fantz, R. L., 217

Fatigue, muscular, 273

Fear, 223
  adrenal hormones and, 62, 63
  attitude change and, 580–581
  conditioning of, 105, 108
  elimination of, 226–227
  learned, 223–224
  responses to, 225–226
  symptoms of, 225–227
Fear of failure; *see* Failure, fear of
Fechner, G., 165
Feeble-mindedness, and glutamic acid
    deficiency, 64
  and heredity, 88
Feedback, affective, 118–120, **135**, 271
  auditory, 268
  delayed visual, 268
  immediate, 295
  informational, 118–119, 128, **135**, 271
  kinesthetic, 263
  visual, 263
Feeding practices, 456–457
  child learning to feed self, 461
Feelings, 5, 6, 222–235
  dimensions of, 228–231
  homeostatic processes and, 59
  physiological bases of, 231–235
Feld, S., 37, 629
Felcky, A., 228
Fenichel, O., 415
Ferrier, D., 53
Feshbach, S., 525, 580
Festinger, L., 219, 579, 583
Field, A. M., 64
Figural after-effect, 163
Figure-ground organization, 173–174
First impressions, social perception
    and, 527–529
Fiske, D. W., 425
Fitts, P. M., 263, 265
Fixation, 398–400, **404**
Flat worm, classical conditioning in, 105
Flavors, 158

Flexibility, in perception, 195–196
  in problem solving, 362–363
Floor, L. G., 550
Followership, leadership, friendship
    and, 553–554
Forgetting; *see* Memory
Forgetting curve, 307
Form constancy, 177
Formal operations period, 366–367
Fovea, 147
Free association, 495–496
Freedman, R., 531
Freeman, F., 91
French, E. G., 533
French, J. R., 548
French, J. W., 418
French, R. L., 544
Frenkel-Brunswick, E., 195, 571
Frequency, law of, 104–105, 119
Frequency distribution, 598–599, **614**
Frequency theory of hearing, 157
Freud, Anna, 392
Freud, S., 3, 5, 6, 8, 10, 314, 378–380,
    383, 395, 396, 397, 398, 420, 493,
    495–496
Freudian theory, 9, 10, 456; *see also*
    Psychoanalytic theory
  conflict and, 378–380
  developmental stages in, 396, 397, 398
  identification and, 467–468
  obsessive compulsive neurosis and, 493
  punishment and, 462
Friendship, leadership, followership
    and, 553–554
Fritsch, G., 53
Frustration, 367–404
  anger and, 227
  individual differences in, 400
  nursing, weaning, dependency and, 457
  partial reinforcement and, 125
  practical implications of, 402–403

problem solving and, 380
sources of, 376–378
Frustration-aggression hypothesis, 463
Frustration tolerance, 400–402, **404**
and neurosis, 494
Frustrating situations, development
of reactions to, 396–400
reactions to, 380–396
F-scale, 573–574
Fugue state, 490
Functional psychosis; *see* Psychosis,
functional
Fundamental (in music), 155
Funnel technique, 572
Funkenstein, D. H., 63

G

Gage, N. L., 529
Galanter, E., 283
Gallwey, M., 530
Gambler's fallacy, 272
Garmezy, N., 124
Gates, A. I., 321
Gaudet, H., 579
Gaussian curve, 603
Gellerman, L. W., 130
General adaptation syndrome, 380
Generalization, concepts and, 129–130
science and, 10–11
semantic, 330–331
stimulus, 125–127, **135**
Generativity, 479–480
Genes, 72, 85, **94**
Genetic hypotheses on neurotic symptom
selection, 492
Gerard, H. B., 545
Gesell, A., 83, 190
Gestalt psychology, 174, 348
Gibb, C. A., 552
Gibson, E. J., 189–190

Gibson, J. G., 317
Gilbert, G. M., 524
Glove anesthesia, 490–491
Glutamic acid, 64
Goal gradient, 238, **255**
Goals, 7, 206, **254**
clarity of and group cohesiveness, 536
weighing of in decision making, 346
Goldstein, K., 363–364
Gonads, 63
Gonial cells, 74
Goodenough, F. L., 396
Goodnow, J. J., 367
Gottesman, I. I., 92
Grammar, culture and, 27
development of, 333–335
Granit, R., 149–150
Greenspoon, J., 292
Grinker, R. R., 384, 495
Gross, N., 544
Group consensus and cohesiveness, 545
Group membership, 530–532
individual differences in, 532
motivation for, 532–533
Group participation, and attitude
change, 584–586
in decision making, 621
Group procedure and group
productivity, 546–549
Group productivity, cohesiveness and,
544–545
communication and, 545–546
group procedure and, 546–549
versus individual productivity,
543–544
Group structure, emergence of, 551
Group therapy, 498–499, 516
Groups, satisfied and dissatisfied, 542
small, communication in, 539–542
task-oriented versus interaction-
oriented, 536–537

Growth, 75
Grunes, W. F., 524
Guetzkow, H. S., 358, 389, 546
Guilford, J. P., 363, 411, 417, 418, 530
Guilt, 250, 466–468
  depressive reactions and, 490
Gumenik, W. E., 224
Gurin, G., 37, 550, 629
Gustation; *see* Taste
Guthrie, E. R., 297, 417
Gutman, D. L., 480
Guttman, L., 565
Guttman, N., 125, 126, 237
Guttman scale, 565–566

H

Habit family, 283, **299**
Habit strength, 270–271
Habits, 117–119, 270, 271
  breaking of, 297
  culture and, 28, 31
  customs and, 28
  general, 131–132, 284, **299**
  norms and, 28
  values and, 28
Haire, M., 524
Hall, J. F., 226
Hallucinations, 168, 188, **200,** 628
Halo effect, 427, **446,** 528
Halpin, A. W., 550
Halstead, W. C., 364
Halverson, H. M., 81
Hansel, C. E., 353
Happiness, rural-urban differences in, 37
Harding, J., 530
Harlow, H., 129, 211, 212, 218, 454
Hartshorne, H., 437, 438
Hathaway, S. R., 430
Hawthorne effect, 275
Hayes, C., 82, 325

Hayes, K., 82, 131, 132, 325
Hearing; *see* Audition
Heart muscle, 261–262
Heat, perception of, 160–161
Hebb, D. O., 60, 178, 206, 218, 312–313
Hebephrenic schizophrenia, 508
Heidbreder, E., 329, 330
Heilizer, F., 17
Heinstein, J. I., 457
Helmholtz, H., 149, 150, 156
Heredity, 72–93
  acquired characteristics and, 73 74
  environment and, 91–93
  individual differences and, 88–93
  intelligence and, 89–92
  maturation and, 74–85
  maze learning and, 88–89
  personality and, 92–93
  species differences and, 85–88
Hering, E., 149, 150
Heron, W. T., 132, 216
Hess, E., 79
Hess, W. R., 56
Hewitt, L. E., 514
Heyns, R., 589
Hick, E. W., 264, 265
Hippocrates, 47
Hitzig, E., 53
Hnatiow, M., 261
Hobbes, T., 3
Hofmann, A., 628
Hoffman, L. R., 621
Hollander, E. P., 553–554, 528
Hollingshead, A. B., 38
Hollingsworth, H. L., 529
Holtzman, W., 436
Holzinger, K. J., 91
Homeostasis, **66,** 209–210
Homeostatic processes, automatic, 59
  behavior and, 59
  motives and, 208–211

Honesty tests, 437–438
Hopi, child training practices, 32
  cradle boards, 83
  language, 339
Hormones, 61, 63
  adrenal, 62, 63
  pituitary, 63
  sex, 63
Horney, K., 496
Hovland, C. I., 125, 328, 329, 564, 575, 576, 577, 585
Howes, D. H., 182
Hubel, D. H., 178
Hull, C., 111, 215, 270
Human nature, philosophic speculations on, 3
Human resources, utilization of, 624–626
Hunger, 209–210
  and perception, 185
Hurlock, E. B., 10, 11, 13, 16
Hutt, M., 458
Huttenlocher, J., 330, 366
Hyden, H., 60
Hyman, H. H., 574
Hypothalamus, 55–56, 59, 210, 211
  motivation and, 56
  pituitary gland and, 63, 64
Hypothesis, 9, **18**
Hysteria, 490–491

I

Id, 378–380
Identical twins, chromosome inheritance, 73
  and personality characteristics, 92
  reared apart and intelligence, 91–92
  in the study of maturation and practice, 83
Identification, 387–388
  with the aggressor, 387–388
  childhood and, 466–468
Oedipus complex and, 398
  theories of, 466–468
  in threshold measurement, 166–167
  value-expressive attitudes and, 570–571
Idiographic approach, 445, **446**
Illusions, optical, 175
Imitation, 283–284
  aggression and, 463–464
  identification and, 466–468
  speech development and, 293
Immigrants, 33, 41
Imprinting, 78–80, **94**
Incentive, 206, **254**
  electrical brain stimulation as, 231–233
  perceptual, 215–216
Incidental learning, 317–318, **340**
Independence, 418
Independent variable, 12, 16, **18**
Individual differences, in action, 293–295
  in group membership, 532
  in language, 335–338
  in maturation, 81–84
  in memory, 319–321
  in motives, 250–254
  in perception, 176, 193–196
  in problem solving, 353–364
  in reactions to frustrating situations, 400–402
  in social perception, 529–530
  as a source of variability, 35
Infancy, development in, 450–458
  impact of the environment in, 452–456
  individuality in, 451–452
  learning in, 287–288
  maturation in, 81
  perception in, 188–189
  perceptual preferences in, 217
Infant preferences and preference of attending adult, 455
Infant–mother motives, 211–212
Inferences, 6–10, **18**

Inferential statistics, 611–614
Informational feedback, 118–119, 128, **135,** 271
  and conformity, 589
Inhelder, B., 366, 470
Inhibition, 50, 59
Instinct theories, criticism of, 9–10
Instinctive behavior (instinct), 58, 75–80, **94**
  criteria for, 75–76
  human beings and, 80
  learning and, 78 80
Institutionalized children, development of, 452–456
Instrumental conditioning; *see* Conditioning, instrumental
Integrity versus despair, 481
Intelligence, 353–361
  in adolescence, 472
  biochemical differences and, 88–89
  and creativity, 361–363
  definitions of, 354
  environment and, 91–93
  heredity and, 88–89, 91–93
  identical twins and, 91–92
  measurement of, 354–358
  nutrition and, 64
  periods of development in, 365–368
  race and, 89–90
Intelligence quotient (I.Q.), 356–357, **371**
  stability of, 360–361
Intelligence test items, factor analysis of, 361
Intelligence test scores, group differences in, 358–360
  adopted children and, 364–365
Intelligence tests, 353–358
  components of, 194
  education and, 90
  identical twins and, 90–91
  intelligence and, 357–358
  memory factor in, 319

numerical ability in, 337
  prediction of college success and, 370
  race and, 89–90
  verbal ability in, 336
Intentional learning, 317–318, **340**
Interaction-oriented group, 536–537, **555**
Interaction, social; *see* Social interaction
Interest, 249, **255**
Interest tests, 252
Interference processes in memory, 308–310
Internal environment, 59
Internal standards, development of, 466–468
Interpersonal relations, 522–554
Interpersonal barriers to motive satisfaction, 376–377
Interviews, 425, 427
Intrapersonal barriers to motive satisfaction, 377–378
Introspection, 5, 6, 7
  in the study of perception, 140
Introversion, 417–418
  and objective behavior tests, 438
Involuntary muscle, 261–262
Iproniazid, 627
Isolation, 384

J

Jack, L. M., 552
Jackson, D. N., 433
Jahoda, M., 478
Janis, I. L., 576, 580, 582
Jasper, H. H., 53
Jastak, J., 506
Jaynes, J., 80, 453
Jenkins, J. G., 308
Jenkins, R. L., 514
Job satisfaction, motives and, 477
John, E. R., 100

Jones, H. E., 472
Jones, M., 515
Jones, M. C., 226
Joseph, A., 32
Judgments, of emotion, 228–229, 526–527
    of the validity of an argument,
        351–352
Jung, C. J., 338
Just-noticeable difference, 164–165, **199**
Juvenile delinquency; *see* Delinquency,
    juvenile

K

Kagan, J. L., 365
Kahn, R. L., 425, 548
Kalish, H., 125, 126
Kallman, F. J., 509
Kamin, L. G., 120
Karpman, B., 515
Karsh, E., 119
Katz, D., 524, 548, 550, 560, 570, 571
Katz, E., 579
Kelley, H. H., 523, 528, 586
Kellogg, L. A., 82, 87
Kellogg, W. N., 82, 87
Kelly, E. L., 425, 443, 479
Kelman, H., 577, 586
Kendler, H., 397
Kendler, T., 397
Kennedy, J. L., 169, 620
Kenyans, 493
Keppel, G., 312
Kety, S. S., 511
Kibbutzin, 630–631
Killam, K. F., 100
Kinesthesis, 142, 162
Kimble, G., 113, 124
King, B. T., 582
Kitai, S., 150
Klein, G. S., 195

Klineberg, O., 90
Kluckhohn, C., 27
Kogan, N., 445, 529
Kohlberg, L., 467
Köhler, I., 178
Köhler, W., 163
Krech, D., 88–89, 549
Kruechel, B., 88–89
Kutner, B., 567
Kwakuitl society, 487
Kwoma tribe, sibling rivalry in, 462

L

Laboratory versus natural settings,
    16, 17
Lacey, J. I., 130, 234
Laissez-faire leadership, 546–547
Lambert, W. W., 380
Land, E. H., 149
Lang, P., 261
Language, 86, 324–339
    animal communication and, 325
    concepts and, 191, 324–325
    development of, 328–335
    individual differences in, 335–338
    learning, 461; *see also* Speech,
        development of
    thinking and, 27
La Piere, R. T., 567
Lashley, K. S., 100, 127
Latent learning, 117–118, 270
Laubach, F. C., 360
Lazarsfeld, P. F., 579
Lazarus, R. S., 190
Leader, definition of, 549, **555**
Leaders, democratic versus authoritarian
    versus *laissez faire*, 546–549
Leadership, 549–554
    dimensions of, 550
    dominance and, 552–553

emergence of, in an unstructured group, 551–553
followership, friendship and, 553–554
functions of, 549
personality and, 551–553
special knowledge and, 552–553
Learned fears, 223–224
Learning, act tendencies and, 117–119, 131–132
anxiety, 14, 15
brain and, 60, 88–89, 100–102
concept, 128–130
conditioning and, 102–134
childhood of culture, 30–33
discrimination, 127
heredity and, 60–69
infancy and, 287–288
instinctive behavior and, 78–80
latent, 117–118, 270–271
methods of study of, 100–102
motivational, 117–119, 130–132
partial reinforcement and, 121–125
perceptual, 115–117, 128–130
species differences in, 85–88
Speech; *see* Language learning, *and* Speech, development of
stimulus-response, interpretation of, 115
Learning hypothesis, of neurotic symptom selection, 492–493
in psychosomatic disorders, 504
Learning principles, teaching machines and, 522–523
use of, in behavior therapy, 499–500
Learning theory, identification and, 466–468
Least effort, law of, 272, **298**
Leavitt, H. J., 540
LeBon, G., 3
Lee, B. S., 268
Leeper, R. W., 183–184
Lefford, A., 352

Lehman, H. C., 368
Leighton, D., 27
Leveling, 317
Levin, H., 462
Levine, S., 453, 454
Lewin, K., 389–391, 546–547, 584
"Lie" scale in MMPI, 433–434
Likert, R., 548, 564
Likert scale, 564–565
Lindzey, G., 252
Linton, R., 469
Lipman, E. A., 108
Lippitt, R., 546–547
Lippmann, W., 571
Litivin, G. H., 474
Livson, N., 445
Lloyd, K. E., 314
Locomotion, development of, 458–460
Locomotor ataxia, 162
Logic, 350–353, 371
Logic, decisions on probabilities and, 352–353
Long-term memory, 305, 313, **339**
Lorenz, K., 78, 79
Lorge, I., 357
Lorge-Thorndike test, 357
Lowell, E. L., 220
Lowenstein, W. R., 165
Luchins, A. S., 362, 527
Luchins' water-jar problems, 362
Lumsdaine, A. A., 575, 576
Lyle, J., 469

M

Maccoby, E. E., 462, 469
Maccoby, N., 550
MacNichol, E. L., 150
Mahone, C. H., 221, 476
Maier, N. R. F., 348, 399–400, 548

Maladjustment, 486–516
  categories of, 487–488
  causes of, 487
Malinowski, B., 398
Mandler, G., 234
Manic-depressive psychosis, 509
Manipulation motives, 217–218
Man-machine systems, 518–521
Mann, F., 534, 621
Mann, R. D., 413, 551
Manual dexterity, 294–295
Marital adjustment, prediction of, 443
Marks, W. B., 150
Marquis, Dorothy, 287
Marriage, 478–479
  conflict in, 479
  expectations of, 478–479
Martin, W., 544
Maslow, A. H., 221, 222
Mason, W. A., 454
Mass media, attitude change and, 579
  effects of, in childhood, 469
Massed versus spaced practice, 281–282
Masserman, J. H., 376, 380
Mate selection, in birds, 78–80
  in people, 478
Maternal care, importance of, in
    infancy, 454–456
Maternal motives, 211
Mating rituals in the stickleback, 76–78
Maturation, 75, **94**
  behavior dependent on, 75–85
  behavioral, 81
  critical periods in, 83, 289–290
  culture and, 84, 288
  individual differences in rate of, 81–84
  interuterine environment and, 75
  neural, 81
  practice and, 83, 288–290
  species differences in, 81–82
Maturational limits and learning,
    287–288

Maturity, nature of, 481–482
May, M. A., 437, 438
Mayer, J., 210
Maze learning, heredity and, 88–89
  species differences in, 85
Mazes, 106–107
McArthur, C. C., 476
McCall, R. B., 215
McCleary, R. A., 105, 190
McClelland, D. C., 185, 206, 220, 349
McClusky, H. V., 306
McConnell, J. V., 105
McCord, J., 515, 516
McCord, W., 515, 516
McFarland, R. A., 65, 320
McGraw, M. B., 288
McKeachie, W. J., 440
McMurray, G. A., 161
McNeil, D., 333, 334
McNemar, Q., 362
Mead, M., 24–26, 32
Mean, 33–34, 42, 599, **614**
Meaning, analysis of, 325–328
  individual differences in, 335
  measurement of, 326–328
Meaningful memory, 319
Median, 599–600, **614**
Meehl, P. E., 440–441, 529
Mellenger, G. D., 528
Membership (in groups); *see* Group
    membership
Memory, 304–324, **339**
  affect and, 9, 314
  alcohol and, 320–321
  applications and principles of, 321–324
  arousal of, 318
  brain injury and, 319–320
  categorization and, 314–317
  comparison of long-term and
    short-term, 313
  development of, 318–319
  individual differences in, 319–321

interference processes in, 308–310
measurement of, 306
motivation and, 314
set and, 317–318
testimony and, 322–324
time and 308–314
types of, 305–306
for visual forms, 317
Memory span, 315
Mental age (M.A.), 356
Mental health, American view of
their, 629–631
as a social problem, 628–63
Mental illness; *see also* Maladjustment,
Psychosis, Neurosis, Psychosomatic
disorders, Conduct disorders
attitudes toward, 629
hypothesis of biochemical factors in, 65
Mental processes, 6–10, 19
culture and, 26 29
Menzies, R., 261
Merrill, M. A., 355
Mescaline, 65, 168, 628
Mesomorph, 423
Messick, S., 433
Metabolic activity, 59
Meyers, C. E., 395
Miles, C., 176
Milgram, S., 589, 590–592, 593
Miller, D. R., 37, 402, 458
Miller, G. A., 166, 283, 333
Miller, J. G., 166
Miller, N. E., 132, 223–224, 231,
244–245, 384, 385–386
Miller, W. E., 13
Milner, P., 231
Milton, G. A., 358
Miltown, 627
Minami, H., 311
Minard, R. D., 568–569
Minnesota Multiphasic Personality
Inventory, 429–430, 433

Mnemonic devices, 321
Mode, 600
Modesty training, 465–466
Monchesi, E. D., 430
Montague, E. K., 15
Moore, J. W., 623
Moral concepts, learning of, 250
Morale, industrial, 621
Morgan, C. T., 262
Morgan, J. J. B., 323, 352
Morrissette, J. O., 572
Morton, J. T., 352
Mother surrogates, 211
Motivated forgetting, 9, 314
Motivation, 206–256
act selection and, 269–270
attention and, 186
attitude formation and, 570–572
efficiency of performance and, 239–240
group membership and, 532–533
memory and, 9, 314
perception and, 185–187, 190–192
risk taking and, 349
social perception and, 524
thresholds and, 186
Motivational principles, practical
applications of, 254
Motive satisfaction, barriers to, 376–378,
300
Motive strength, aroused and selection
of defense mechanisms, 394
efficiency of performance and, 239–240
stored, 236–237
Motives, activation of, 236–238
classification, 208–222
competence, 215–221
culture and, 27
definition of, 206, **254**
development of, 245–254
general, 131, 249–250, **255**
individual differences in, 250–254
job satisfaction and, 477
learning of, 117–119, 130–132

learning of culture and, 31
operationalization of, 207–208
physiological, 208–211
physiological basis of, 231–235
positive and negative, 240–242
problem solving and, 349
self-esteem, 221
social, 211–215
values and, 27–28, 251–252
Motor nerves, 47, **66**
Mowrer, O. H., 120, 291
Mueller-Lyer illusion, 175
Mundugumor, 25, 33
Munn, N. L., 80
Münsterberg, H., 323–324
Murdock, B. B., 312
Murphy, G., 192, 564
Murray, H. A., 220, 431, 432, 436
Muscle tone, 262
Muscles, 260–262
Musical ability, 194

N

Nachmann, B., 477
Negative affect, 206
    physiological basis of, 233
Negative transfer, 279–280
Negativism (in the second year), 465
Negroes, and intelligence test scores,
    89–90
    service to, 567
Nelson, V. L., 365
Nerve impulse, 49–51, **66**
Nerves, 52
    motor (efferent), 47, **66**
    sensory (afferent), 47, **66**
Nervous system, 47–67
    autonomic, 63, 64, **67**
    central, 47, 52, 57–67, **66**
    endocrine system and, 63–64
    heredity and, 88–89

methods of studying, 52–56
parasympathetic, 63, **67**
pathways in, 57–59
species differences in, 85–86
sympathetic, 63, **67**
Neugarten, B. L., 480
Neurons, 47–51, 60, **66**
    activity of, 101
    arrangement of, 58
    connection of rods and cones to,
        147–148
    threshold of, 51, 58, 59, **66**
Neurosis, 414, 488–501, **517**
    anxiety theory of, 491–492
    causes of, 491–492
    cross-cultural studies of, 493
    frustration tolerance and, 494
    incidence of and amount of stress, 494
    onset of symptoms in, 493–495
    symptom selection in, 493
    traumatic, 494–495
    treatment of, 495–501
    types of, 488–491
Neurotic depressive reactions, 489–490
Neurotic paradox, 493
Neuroticism, 415–416
    and objective behavior tests, 438
New Republic, The, 631
Newcomb, T. M., 572, 587
Newell, A., 620
Newman, H. H., 91
Niacin, 64
Night vision, 148
Nimkoff, M. F., 40
Nondirective therapy, 496–497
Nonsense syllables, use of, 306–307
Norepinephrin, 62, 63, 234–235
Normal curve, 603
Norman, R. Z., 184
Norms, 28, 41
    statistical, 421–422, 611
    values and, 28

Numerical ability, 336
Nunnally, J. C., 629
Nutrition, and central nervous
    system, 64

O

Obedience to legitimate authority;
    see Compliance
Objective behavior measures and
    personality assessment, 437–438
Objects, 102, **134**
    learning of, 128
Observation, as a prerequisite for
    science, 3
Obsession, 490
Obsessive-compulsive symptoms, 490
Obstruction method, 207
Occupation and personality
    characteristics, 424
Odbert, H. S., 410
Oddity problem, 128–129
Oedipus complex, 397–398
    and identification, 467
Office of Strategic Services, assessment
    procedures of, 428–429
Officer candidate school, prediction
    of success in, 443
Ogburn, W. F., 40
Old age, dependency in, 480
    integrity versus despair in, 481
    problems of, 480–481
    social relationships in, 481
    thinking in, 368–369
Olds, J., 231–233
Olfaction; *see* Smell
Operational definition, 5, **18**
    of affect, 206
    of boredom, 8
    of group cohesiveness, 534–535
    motive, 207
    pleasantness, 9

Opinion, 561, **594**
Oral stage, 396
Organic psychosis, 505–506
    treatment of, 506
Organization, perceptual, individual
    differences in, 195
Orientals, service to, 567
Originality, 362–363
Orlansky, H., 456
Osgood, C. E., 326, 629
Overtones (in music), 155

P

Pace, C. R., 473
Padilla, S. G., 289
Page, H. A., 226
Pain, sense of, 142, 161
Pain blindness, 161
Paradise, N., 217
Paranoid schizophrenia, 507–508
    size constancy and, 194
Parasympathetic nervous system, 63, **67**
Paresis, general, 506
Parker, E. B., 469
Parsimony, law of, 9–10
Partial reinforcement, 121–125
    extinction and, 124
    overlearning and, 124–125
    schedules of, 122–124
Pavlov, I. P., 104–105, 109, 111, 219, 376
Peak, H., 577
Pearson product moment correlation, 608
Pellagra, 61, 64, 506
Penfield, W., 53, 54, 338
Percentile rank, 422
Percentile score, 610, **614**
Perception, 140–202
    absence of stimulation and, 167–168
    act selection and, 266–269
    depth, 150–151, 152
    development of, 188–193

early experience and, 83–84
extrasensory, 168–170
improvement of, 196–197
individual differences in, 176, 193–196
motivation and, 185–187
personality and, 187
practical application of principles
    of, 196–199
problem solving and, 347–348
social; *see* Social perception
stimulus change and, 162–166
subliminal, 166
Perception, of body position, 162
of flavor, 158
of heat, 160–161
of objects, compared to person
    perception, 522–530
of pitch, theories of, 156–157
Percepts, 180–188
culture and, 26, 27
learning of, 115–117, 128–130
Perceptual categories, 180–188
development of, 190–192
Perceptual defense, 185–186
Perceptual incentives, 215–216
Perceptual speed, 194
Perceptual stimulation, importance of,
    in infancy, 452–455
Perceptual vigilance, 185–186
Performance, 260–298
effects of praise and reproof on, 11, 12
efficiency of, 272–273
Perin, C. T., 113
Perkins, C. C., 114
Person perception; *see* Social perception
Personality, 410, **446**
development of, 450–482
dimensions of, 414–419
heredity and environment in, 92–93
judgments of, 527–530
leadership and, 551–553
physical characteristics and, 422–423

sociological variables and, 423–425
Personality assessment, 410–446
interviews in, 425, 427
objective behavior tests in, 437–438
projective tests in, 434–437
questionnaires in, 429–434
rating scales in, 427–429
Personality measures, pure versus
    mixed, 440
Personality profiles, 445–446
Personality questionnaires, 429–434
limitations of, 433
Personality traits, 411, **446**
assessment of, 419–439
identification of, 411–413
organization of, 445–446
prediction of behavior and, 439–443
unique, 443
Personality types, 410–411
Personnel psychologist, 298
Peterson, J. R., 265
Peterson, L. R., 311
Peterson, M. L., 311
Peterson, O. L., 629
Pettigrew, T. F., 574
Peyote, 628
Philosophers' speculations on human
    nature, 3
Phobic reaction, 489, 492
Physical characteristics and personality,
    422–423
Physical energy, 5
in audition, 155–156
sense modalities and, 142
vision and, 143
Physical self-awareness, development
    of, 456
Physiognomy, 2
Physiological level (of studying the
    organism), 46–47
Physiological needs, motives related
    to, 208–211

Piaget, J. P., 332, 365–368, 470, 538
Pigments, absorbing, in the retina, 150
  mixture of, 145
Pitch, 154–155
  theories of, 155–156
Pituitary gland, 63
  nervous system, control over, 63, 64
Place theory of hearing, 156
Play therapy, 497–499
Pleasantness, and recall, 9
  as a dimension of feeling, 228–231
Pleasantness-unpleasantness, as an
    interpretation of reinforcement, 111
Pleasure principle, 378
Pollio, H. R., 328, 330
Polyak, S. L., 147
Positive affect, 206
  physiological bases of, 231–233
Positive transfer, 279–280
Postman, L., 180, 314, 318
Postsynaptic membrane, 50
Potlatch, 487
Powers, E., 516
Practical applications, 17, 18
  of action principles, 295–298
  of memory principles, 321–324
  of motivational principles, 254
  of perception principles, 196–199
  of problem-solving principles, 369–371
  of understanding frustration, 402–403
Practice, massed versus spaced,
    281–282, 297
  whole versus part, 279, 296
Praise versus reproof, effect on
    performance, 11–12
Precognition, 168
Prediction, of college success, 4, 625–626
  as a goal for science, 10
  from hypotheses, 9
  and theoretical explanation, 12–13
  of voting behavior, 12–13
Predictive validity, 420

Prejudice, and authoritarianism, 573–574
  and defense mechanisms, 571
  and enforced contact, 581–582
  and frustration, 403
Prell, D. B., 494
Prentice, W. C. H., 317
Preoperational period, 365
Pressey, S. L., 622
Pressure, 142, 159
Preyer, W., 287
Pribram, K. H., 283, 320
Pringle, M. L., 455
Pritchard, R. M., 153
Proactive inhibition, 308–310, 340
  and short-term memory, 312, 313
Probability matching, 353, 371
Problem solving, 344–371
  application to education, 371
  central nervous system and, 363–364
  discovery of an alternative in, 347–353
  elements of, 344–347
  frustration and, 380
  individual differences in, 353–364
  motives and, 349
  past experience and, 349–350
  perception and, 347–348
  set and, 362–363
Problem solving principles, practical
    applications of, 369–371
Productivity, group; *see* Group
    productivity
Professionals, background of
    successful, 476–477
Progestin, 63
Project Head Start, 359–360
Project Talent, 624
Projection, 386–387, 396
Projective tests, 207, 434–437
Proshansky, H., 525
Pruitt, D. G., 349
Psychoanalysis, 378, 495–496

Psychoanalytic theory, 415, 416, 418;
  see also Freudian theory
  psychosis and, 510
  psychosomatic disorders and, 504
  schools of, 496
Psychology, comparative, 88
  history of, 4–6
  social; *see* Social psychology
  study of behavior in, 5, 6
  study of consciousness in, 5
Psychoneurotic reaction, 491
Psychopath, 515
Psychopharmacology, 626–628
Psychosis, 414, 505–512, **517**
  causes of functional, 509–511
  drug studies and, 510–511
  functional, 506–511
  organic, 505–506
  psychoanalytic theory of, 510
  treatment of functional, 511–512
  treatment of organic, 506
Psychosomatic disorders, 501–505, **517**
  symptom selection in, 504
  treatment of, 504–505
Psychotherapy, 495–501, **517**
  client-centered, 496–497
  effectiveness of, 501
  group, 498–499
  varieties of, 497–501
Psychotic patients, case histories of,
  509–510
  family histories of, 509
Psychoticism, 416–417
Psychotomimetic drugs, 65, 628
Punishment, 119–120, **135**, 247–248,
  462–464

Q

Questionnaires, personality, 429–434;
  see Personality questionnaires

R

r, 608
Rabin, A. I., 633
Rabinowitz, H. S., 350
Race, intelligence and, 89–90
  personality characteristics and, 424
  psychological differences and, 89
Radler, D. H., 470–471, 571
Range, 600–601
Rank, O., 401
Rank-order correlation, 607–608
Rasmussan, T., 54
Rating scales, 426, 427–429
  use of standard situations in, 428–429
Rationalization, 388
Ratliff, F., 153
Rausch, H. L., 194
Raven, B. H., 536
Raynor, R., 105
Reaction formation, 388
  learning of, 397
Reaction time, 264–265, **298**
Reactive inhibition, 271–272
Reading, critical periods in, 83
Realism-psychoticism, 416–417
Reality principle, 378
Reasoning, 347, **371**
Recall, 306
  effects of pleasantness and
    unpleasantness on, 13
Receptors, 47, **66**, 142
  auditory, 156
  cold, 160
  equilibrium, 162
  kinesthetic, 162
  pain, 161
  smell, 158
  taste, 158
  vision, 145–148
  warm, 160

Recognition (in memory), 306
Recognition of patterns, training methods for, 196–197
Redintegration, 179, **339**
and memory, 305
Redl, F., 516
Reflex, 58, **66,** 75, 133, 285
classical conditioning and, 102–105
instinctive behavior and, 76
Refractory period, 51
Regression, 389–391
Reinforcement, 110–111
partial, 121–125, **135**
secondary, 111–112, 114
theories of, 111–112
Reinforcer, definition of, 110, **135**
negative, 110
positive, 110
primary, 111
secondary, 112, **135**
Reiss, B. F., 331
Relationship, measures of, 603–608
Reliability, 419–420, 421, **446**
Religion, child training practices and, 37
voting and, 13
Reminiscence, 282
Remmers, H. H., 470–471, 571
Repression, 314, **340, 383**–384
Reserpine, 65, 627
Responses, 5, **18,** 101, 134
conditioned, 102–105, 115
species differences in, 88
Reticular formation, 56, 59
and arousal, 233
and thyroid secretion, 62
and tranquilizers, 65
Retina, 142, 143, 144, 145–146
constant image on, 153
Retinal disparity, 151
Retroactive inhibition, 308–310, **340**
Reversal learning, 397

Reward, 119–120, 247–248
and attitude change, 582–583
and learning of culture, 31
and perception of ambiguous figures, 192
Rho, 607–608
Rhodopsin, 148, 150
Ribonucleic acid (RNA), 60
Richter, C. P., 210
Riesen, A. H., 453
Riess, A. J., 514
Rietsma, J., 536
Riggs, L., 153
Riley, J. W., 469
Riley, M. W., 169
Roberts, L., 338
Roberts, W. W., 233
Roby, T. B., 111
Rodrigues, J., 180
Rods, 142, 145
Roe, A., 371, 476 477, 510
Roethlisberger, F. J., 275, 545
Rogers, C. R., 481, 496–497
Rokeach, M., 362
Role, 26, 35–37, 41; *see also* Sex role conflict, 36
Rorschach, H., 436
Rorschach ink-blot test, 435–436
Rosen, B. C., 424
Rosenberg, M. J., 580
Rosenzweig, M. R., 88–89
Ross, D., 463, 467
Ross, I., 533
Ross, S. A., 463, 467
Ross, T. A., 489
Rote memory, 306, 319
Rousseau, J. J., 3
Rural-urban differences in intelligence test scores, 359
Rutherford, W., 157

S

Salivation as a conditioned response in dogs, 104–105, 108

Samoans, child training practices of, 31–32

Sampling, construction of intelligence tests and, 360–361
  error, 612–613
  random, 38
  voting surveys and, 13

Sanford, F. H., 491

Sanford, R. N., 371, 423, 475, 571

Sarason, I., 15

Savings measure of memory, 306

Scatter plot, 604, 605

Schachter, S., 214–215, 234–235, 461, 541, 544–545

Schafer, R., 192

Schedules of reinforcement, 122–125

Schizophrenia, 506–509
  types of, 509–510

Schlosberg, H., 228–231

Schneider, B. H., 314

Schramm, W. J., 469

Schultz, R. W., 281

Schwitzgebel, R., 516

Scientific explanation, 3
  and psychology, 4

Scientists, successful, backgrounds of, 476–477

Scott, J. P., 92

Scott, W. A., 582–583

Sears, P. S., 469

Sears, R. R., 387, 457, 460, 462, 463, 465, 467, 468

Seashore Measures of Musical Talent, 194

Second year, development in, 458–465

Secondary reinforcement, 111–112, 114, 247, 248

Secondary reinforcer, 112, **135**

Second-order conditioning, 111

Seeger, C. M., 265

Self-esteem, motive for, 221, 379
  and value-expressive attitudes, 570

Self-stimulation (of the brain), 231–233

Selye, H., 380, 381, 488, 501

Semantic differential, 326–328

Semantic generalization, 330–331

Semicircular canals, 142, 162

Semi-starvation studies, 389

Senden, M. V., 188

Senile deterioration, 505–506

Sensations, distinguished from perception, 140
  and introspective psychology, 5

Sense modalities, 143, **199**
  nervous system coding and, 140–143
  species differences in, 86, 88

Sense organs, 52

Sensibar, M. R., 394

Sensitivity (of a test), 421

Sensory acuity, individual differences in, 193

Sensory deprivation, 216

Sensory interactions, 167

Sensory-motor period, 365

Sensory nerves, **66**
  firing in and Weber's Law, 165

Separation from mother in infancy, 457–458

Serial acts, 267, **298**

Set, **200**
  and memory, 317–318
  and perception, 182–184
  and performance efficiency, 272–273
  and problem solving, 362–363
  and social perception, 523
  and thresholds, 184–185

Sewall, W. H., 462

Seward, G. H., 207

Seward, J. P., 207

Sex, cultural norms for, 28
  personality characteristics and, 424
Sex cells, chance assortment of
    chromosomes in, 72–73
  effects of radiation on, 74
Sex characteristics, secondary, 63
Sex differences, 90
  and cultural norms, 24–26
  in perception, 176
  in problem solving, 358
Sex hormones, 63
Sex motives, 212–214
Sex roles, adolescent attitudes
    toward, 472
  in old age, 480
  in primitive societies, 24 26
Sexual interest, in children, 465–466
Sharpening, 317
Shaw, M. E., 543, 546
Sheatsley, P. B., 574
Sheffield, F. D., 111, 575
Sheldon, W. H., 423
Sherif, C., 535, 551
Sherif, M., 535, 551, 564
Shire, A., 392
Short-term memory, 305, 313, **339**
  and proactive inhibition, 312, 313
  and time decay, 311–314
Shuford, E. H., 209
Shuttle box, 107–108
Sibling rivalry, 461–462
Siegel, B., 423
Sign stimulus, 78, **94**
Significant difference, 91–92, **94**, 614, **614**
Simon, H. A., 546
Simon, T., 354
Simple schizophrenia, 507
Simultaneous contrast, 148, 149
Sines, J. O., 501
Singer, J. E., 234–235
Singer, R. D., 525

Singh, J. A. L., 289
Situation, psychological meaning of
    439–440
"Situation-hurdle" interpretation of
    attitudes and action, 568–569
Size constancy, 177–178
Skeels, H. M., 364
Skills, acquisition of, 275–283, 295–297
Skin senses, 159–161
Skinner, B. F., 113, 122, 124. 278,
    622, 623
Skinner box, 106, 112
  cumulative records from, 122–123
Skodak, M., 364
Slack, C. W., 516
"Sleeper effect" in attitude change,
    576–577
Smedslund, J., 367
Smell, 142, 157–158
Smith, A. J., 64
Smith, C. J., 150
Smith, K. U., 268
Smith, M. E., 331
Smith, R. L., 130
Smith, W., 623
Smooth muscle, 261–262
Social class, 37–39, **42**
Social communication, 537
Social interaction, 537, **554**
  analysis of, 539–542
  group cohesiveness and, 536
  nonverbal, 538
Social motives, 211–215
Social perception, 522–530
  accuracy of, 526–530
  categorization and, 524
  first impressions and, 527–529
  individual differences in, 529–530
  motivation and, 524
  set and, 523
  unique features of, 526–527

Social psychology, description of, 522, **554**

Social relationships in old age, 480

Socialization, 29–32
cultural differences in, 31–32

Society, 24, **41**

Socioeconomic status, and intelligence test scores, 358–360
and personality characteristics, 424
and vocational choice, 476

Sociogram, 534

Sociological differences in defense mechanisms, 402

Sociological variables and personality, 423–425

Sociology and social psychology, 522

Solem, A. R., 548

Solomon, R. L., 119, 182, 226, 380

Sontag, L. W., 365

Spatial abilities, 194–195

Species differences, in abstraction, 85–86
in dependency, 87
in maturation, 81–82
in nervous systems, 85–88
in sense modalities, 86

Species-specific behavior, 75–80

Speech, development of, 132, 290–293;
see also Language

Spiegel, J. P., 384, 495

Spinal cord, 52

Spitz, R. A., 452, 457

Spontaneous alternation, 217–218, 271

Spontaneous recovery, 109, 110, **135**

Spranger, E., 251, 252

Staats, A. W., 330

Staats, C. K., 330

Stabilized retinal image, 153

Stage, of exhaustion, 380
of resistance, 380

Stalnaker, J., 310

Standard deviation, 33–34, 42, 601–602, **614**

Standard score, 610, **614**

Standard situations and rating scales, 428–429

Stanford-Binet Intelligence Test, 357

Statistical concepts, 598–614

Statistical method, for establishing validity, 420–421
of identifying personality traits, 412–413

Statistical versus clinical prediction, 440

Statistics, descriptive, 598–611
inferential, 611–614
purposes of, 598

Stevens, L. B., 476

Stereotypes, 524, 571

Stern, C. R., 473

Stevens, S. S., 423

Stickleback, courtship ritual of, 76–78

Stieper, D., 215

Stimulants, 65, 512

Stimuli, 5, **18**, 102, **134**

Stimulus change, in perception, 162–166
as a reward, 216–217

Stimulus generalization, 125–127, **135**
concepts and, 129–130
primary, 190
transfer and, 279

Stimulus predifferentiation, 297

Stimulus-response compatibility, 264–265, **298**

Stone, C. P., 92, 472

Stouffer, S. A., 224, 225, 226, 400, 510, 572

Strauss, R., 474

Street, R. F., 195

Street Gestalt Completion Test, 195

Streib, G. F., 481

Stress, psychological, and ulcers, 501–504

Stressor, 380

Striated muscle, 262

Stricker, G., 571

Striped muscle, 262

Strong, E. K., 252, 253

Strong Vocational Interest Inventory, 252–253, 425, 476

Study habits, 321

Study methods, 198

Subculture, 37–39

Sublimation, 389

Substitution, 388–389

Subtractive mixture, 145

Successive approximations, 277–278, 296, **299**

Successive contrast, 148, 149

Suchman, E. A., 561

Sullivan, H. S., 496

Supa, M., 191

Superego, 378–380

Survey Research Center, 12, 13, 14, 476

Swanson, G. E., 37, 402

Sweeney, E. J., 358

Swets, J., 186

Syllogisms, 350–352

Sympathetic nervous system, 63, **67**, 233

Symptom selection in neurosis, theories of, 492–493

Synapse, 49, 50, **66**

Synaptic growth, theory of, 60

Synaptic vesicles, 49

T

Taboo, 27

Tachistoscope, 183

Tagiuri, R., 529

Tannenbaum, P. H., 578

Tanner, W. P., 184, 186

Task-oriented groups, 536–537, 542, **555** types of, 542

Taste, 142, 158–159

Taste blindness, 159

Taste buds, 142, 158

Taylor, D. W., 544

Taylor, G. A., 321

Taylor, J. A., 14, 15, 16

Tchambuli culture, 25–26

Teaching machines, 622–623

Teevan, R., 623

Telepathy, 168–169

Television, effects of, in childhood, 469

Temperature, perception of, 142, 160–161

Terman, L., 176, 355

Teitelbaum, P., 209

Test norms, 421–422

Testimony and memory, 322–324

Testosterone, 63, **227**

Thalidomide, 75

Thematic Apperception Test, 220, 436–437

Theoretical method, for establishing validity, 420 of identifying personality traits, 413

Theory, 8–11, **18**

Thibault, J. W., 535

Thinking, 347, 371 cultural differences in, 27 development of, 364–369 subvocal movement and, 5

Thirst, 210

Thistlewaite, D., 352

Thomas, A., 451

Thomas, W. I., 27

Thompson, H., 83

Thompson, L., 32

Thompson, R., 105

Thompson, W. E., 481

Thorndike, E. L., 3, 270, 276–277

Thorndike, R. L., 357, 543

Thouless, R. H., 194

Threshold, absolute, 165–167, **200** difference, 164–165, **199** motivation and, 186 neuron, 51, **66** perceptual, 143 rods and cones, 148

set and, 184–185
two-point, 160
Thurstone, L. L., 336, 337, 413, 563
Thyroid gland, 61, 62, 88, 294
Timbre, 155
Time, concept of, 27
decay hypothesis, 310–314
effects on memory, 310–314
Time relations, in conditioning, 113–114
in punishment, 120
Tinbergen, N., 78
Titchener, E. B., 5
Toilet training, 248–249, 460
Tolman, E. C., 206, 270
Tongue, regions of, and taste, 158–159
Traits, personality; *see* Personality traits
Tranquilizers, 65, 512, 626–627
Transfer of training, 279–280, 296, **299**
Transference, 496
Transmitter substance, 49, 50, 60
and maze learning, 88–89
Transposition, 179, **200**
Traumatic neurosis, 494–495
Trial and error learning, 275–276, **299**
Trust, development of, 457
Tryon, R. C., 88
Two-phase movement, 269, **298**
Two-point threshold, 160
Two-string reasoning problem, 348
Tyler, L., 442
Type descriptions of personality, 410–411

U

Ulcers, peptic, 501–504
Unconscious processes, 8, 9, 222
Underwood, B. J., 281, 309, 312
Unique personality traits, 443
Unpleasantness, effect on recall, 9
Useem, J. P., 39
Useem, R., 39
Utilitarian attitude, 570

V

Validity, 420, **446**
types of, 420–421
Value-expressive attitude, 570–571
Values, 27, 28, **255**
college students', 475
scale of, 250–251
Vandenberg, S. G., 92
Van Lehn, R., 234
Van Lennep, D. J., 434, 435
Van Lennep Room Test, 434–435
Variability, measures of, 33–34, 600–602
sources of, 33–39
Verbal ability, 336
Verbal analogies, 336
Verbal discipline, 466
Verbal reinforcement, 292
Verbal report, 6, 8
and absolute threshold measurement, 166
Verbalization, in learning skills, 296
Vernon, P. E., 251, 252
Veroff, J., 37, 629
Vestibular sacs, 142, 162
Visceral muscle, 261–262
Vision, 142, 143–153
Visual cliff, 189–190
Vocabulary, development of, 331–332
Vocational choice, 475–477, 624
Volley principle, 157
Voting behavior, 12–13
rural-urban differences in, 37

W

Wald, G., 146
Walk, R., 189
Walker, E. L., 271, 589
Walking, maturation and practice in, 83
Wallach, H., 163

Wallach, M. A., 445
Wallen, P., 478, 479
Walters, R. H., 514, 516
War of the Ghosts, 315–316
Water jar problems, 362
Watson, J. B., 5, 6, 7, 105
Watson, W. S., 195
Weak-link hypotheses in psychosomatic
    disorders, 504
Weaning, 31, 456
Webb, W. B., 475, 553–554
Weber, E. H., 164–165
Weber-Fechner Law, 164–165
Wechsler Adult Intelligence Scale, 357
Weinstock, S., 124
Weiss, W., 329, 576–577
Weissberg, N., 525
Wells, W. D., 423
Wever, E. G., 157
White, R. K., 534, 546–547
White, R. W., 221, 383, 481, 491, 508, 515
Whiting, J. W. M., 31, 120
Whitney, E., 322
Whole versus part learning, 279, 296
Whorf, B. L., 27, 339
Wickert, F. R., 477
Wiener, D. N., 215
Wiesel, T., 178
Wilkins, C., 567
Wilkins, M. C., 352
Willerman, B., 535
Williams, A. C., 296
Wilson, W. C., 469
Winch, R. F., 478
Wineman, D., 516
Winer, B. J., 550

Withdrawal, as a reaction to
    frustrating situations, 380–381
Witmer, H., 516
Wittenborn, J. R., 365
Wittman, M. P., 440–441
Wolf, S., 504
"Wolf" children, 290
Wolfe, D. M., 479
Wolfe, J. B., 112, 114
Wolff, H. G., 504
Wolfle, D. L., 350
Wolpe, J., 500
Woodworth, R. S., 269, 327
Woodruff, C. L., 586
Word association, method, 327, 328
    individual differences in, 338
Word concept formation, 328–331
Wright, H. F., 469
Wundt, W., 5
Wynne, L. C., 226

Y

Yarrow, P. R., 567
Yerkes, R. M., 89, 90
Young, P. T., 111
Young, T., 149
Young-Helmholtz theory (of color
    vision), 149–150

Z

Zander, A., 533
Zeaman, D., 274, 275
Zillig, M., 528
Zingg, R. M., 289
Zola, I. K., 514